The Mormon Image in the
American Mind

The Mormon Image in the American Mind

FIFTY YEARS OF PUBLIC PERCEPTION

J. B. HAWS

OXFORD
UNIVERSITY PRESS

Oxford University Press is a department of the University of Oxford.
It furthers the University's objective of excellence in research, scholarship,
and education by publishing worldwide.

Oxford   New York
Auckland   Cape Town   Dar es Salaam   Hong Kong   Karachi
Kuala Lumpur   Madrid   Melbourne   Mexico City   Nairobi
New Delhi   Shanghai   Taipei   Toronto

With offices in
Argentina   Austria   Brazil   Chile   Czech Republic   France   Greece
Guatemala   Hungary   Italy   Japan   Poland   Portugal   Singapore
South Korea   Switzerland   Thailand   Turkey   Ukraine   Vietnam

Oxford is a registered trademark of Oxford University Press
in the UK and certain other countries.

Published in the United States of America by
Oxford University Press
198 Madison Avenue, New York, NY 10016

Library of Congress Cataloging-in-Publication Data
Haws, J. B. (John Ben), 1974–author.
The Mormon image in the American mind : fifty years of public perception / J. B. Haws.
pages cm
Includes bibliographical references and index.
ISBN 978-0-19-989764-3 (hardcover : alk. paper) — ISBN 978-0-19-989765-0 (ebook)
1. Mormons—Public opinion.   2. Church of Jesus Christ of Latter-day Saints—
History.   3. Mormons—History.   4. Mormon Church—History.   I. Title.
BX8611.H39 2013
289.3'73—dc23
2013009459

9 8 7 6 5 4 3 2 1
Printed in the United States of America
on acid-free paper

For Laura,
and for Parley, Marshall, Truman, and Ashley

Contents

Acknowledgments

It seems appropriate, considering the recent worldwide financial crisis, that I join the ranks of investment banks, insurance companies, and even national treasuries to acknowledge that everywhere I look, all I see are mounting debts! Only in this case, I am happy to count those debts. To Professor Robert Goldberg I owe a double measure of gratitude for his help in first suggesting both the title of this project and its "Romney to Romney" framing and the title of this project, and then in carefully guiding the project to completion. The end result is better because it bears evidence of his influence at every turn. I appreciate Professors Goldberg, Eric Hinderaker, Rebecca Horn, David Knowlton, and Paul Reeve not only for their assistance and suggestions on this project, but also for being the type of teachers who inspire students. I am lucky to have been their student.

I have learned as much about family loyalty and love as just about anything else in this process. My parents and my seven sisters and their husbands have been trusted readers and sounding boards, with keen eyes for source material, too. Immense thanks to that crew: Greg and Debi Haws, Sunee and Kyle Eardley, Katie and Dan Dannehl, Rindi and Greg Jacobsen, Stalee and Clint Weston, Joni and Jaron Allred, Judi and Mike Coburn, and Millie and Robert Lewis. My in-laws have also met the gold standard on that same account: Richard and Andrea Favero, Diane and Jon Calvert, Michael and Andrea Favero, Lane and Kristen Favero, and Katie and Mike Toone. My mother, Debi Haws, and sister Judi Coburn also deserve repayment plus an exorbitant interest rate for transcribing hours of interviews.

I appreciate those who graciously sat for interviews and offered their candid appraisals of these Mormon moments. I also appreciate officials at the LDS Church's Public Affairs Department for allowing me to access many of the documents that detail their recent activities. The professional and capable staffs of the LDS Church History Library, the Harold B. Lee Library at Brigham Young University, and the Marriott Library at the University of Utah also deserve special mention.

I feel fortunate to work with a remarkable group of colleagues, and so many have offered their talents of analysis and inquiry and expression—not only at BYU, but also in LDS Seminaries and Institutes, at gatherings of the American Academy of Religion, the Conference on Faith and History, the Mormon History Association, and the Mormon Media Studies Symposium. This project has also benefited from research grants from BYU's Religious Studies Center. Thanks to Alex Baugh and others at the RSC. Also at BYU, Susan Bettis, Jeanine Ehat, Linda Godfrey, Patty Smith, Cheryl Snelgrove, and Lori Soza merit special appreciation. They are allies of the first rate. I am grateful to student assistants Michael Cope, Kindal McGill, Jeff Stevenson, David Wall, Theodore Davis, Natalie Larson, Emily Matthews, Sarah Porter, and Lindsay Quick, for their attention to numerous details. I am sure, unfortunately, I have missed others on Patty Smith's team at the Religious Education Faculty Support Center who also assisted—they deserve better than this generic statement of gratitude.

Cynthia Read and Charlotte Steinhardt at Oxford have been simply wonderful, from start to finish. I am grateful, too, for the insights offered by Oxford's readers.

I also need to give a nod to so many unnamed individuals who devote time and talent to making Internet resources the boon that they have been for this project. I appreciate those who have digitized periodicals, who blog and embed links, who write and edit for Wikipedia, and so on. Not only is this "new media" age an important facet of the story that follows, but new media also made telling this story easier.

A note about my perspective seems in order. So much of writing history is representation, and that representation, inevitably, is influenced by the choices and position of the author. My interest in this story derives from my experience as a Latter-day Saint who has lived through many of the events described here. I currently teach at Brigham Young University, so my interest in Mormon history also has a professional component. Still, I have tried to be true to the voices of the various parties that have been involved in this decades-long, image-shaping dialogue.

While they bear no responsibility for my conclusions, what follows would not have been possible without the assistance and cooperation of all of the aforementioned individuals—who can freely redeem my "IOUs" at any time.

Finally, my extraordinary wife, Laura, and my children—Parley, Marshall, Truman, and Ashley—come up last for thanks because in reality, they are my bottom line. I am happy to defer to them as the majority stockholders on my time futures!

The Mormon Image in the
American Mind

1

Framing a Collage

George Romney was born in Mexico in 1907. Sixty years later, he was running for president of the United States.

Romney was not the son of a diplomat stationed abroad, nor the child of some businessman overseeing the foreign arm of an American company. George Romney was born in Mexico because his grandparents had settled in Chihuahua with other expatriate American Mormons in hope of escaping the climate of persecution that dogged their church and those of its members who practiced polygamy. He was born the year after an investigative committee of the U.S. Senate had recommended the revocation of the seat of newly elected Utah senator and Mormon apostle Reed Smoot. Smoot, though not a polygamist himself, had been forced to wait in political limbo while Senate hearings dragged on for three years and weighed claims that his church had continued to endorse plural marriage, even after the church's official—if ambiguous—disavowal of the practice in 1890. (George Romney's parents married in 1895. He was the grandson of polygamists, but the son of monogamists.) Finally in 1907, the full Senate rejected the committee's recommendation to expel Senator Smoot, and Smoot retained his seat against the wishes of literally millions of American citizens who had signed petitions decrying his election. Considering all of this, George Romney's story becomes one more dramatic reminder in American history that much can (and did) change over the course of just a few decades. In 1968, Romney was both a committed Mormon and a leading contender for the Republican presidential nomination—a combination that would have seemed all but impossible in the world into which he was born.[1]

By the 1960s, to many of his contemporaries, George Romney's credentials seemed White House–worthy. His innovative leadership as chief of the American Motors automobile corporation had famously reenergized the sagging company while giving rise to the compact car. His prominent role in the company's television commercials gave him "household name" status. He had been elected governor of Michigan for three consecutive terms after leading the convention that crafted that state's new constitution. Romney had also achieved wide recognition for his progressive position on race when he withheld support from his party's 1964 presidential nominee, Barry Goldwater, because Romney felt that Goldwater was too conservative on civil rights. George Romney approached politics like he did his Latter-day Saint faith—"missionary zeal" almost became the media's catchphrase for Romney.

It was that faith, however, that would have made his candidacy so unlikely only two generations earlier. After all, it would have seemed almost incredible to his progenitors that *The Nation* would one day suggest, as it did in 1962, that Romney's Mormonism was one of the "assets" to his political fortunes, a significant component of his "attractive public image."[2] *The New Republic* even called him "a kind of political Billy Graham."[3]

Fast forward forty years to 2007, to one of those coincidences of history that seems to almost cry out for comparisons: George Romney's son Mitt threw his hat into the ring of presidential politics. Mitt Romney's presidential credentials seemed equally promising. He had inherited both his father's smile and capacity for big business success. After leading Bain Capital through years of impressive growth, the younger Romney saved the floundering and scandal-riddled Salt Lake City Olympics in 2002. On the heels of that Olympic turnaround, Mitt Romney celebrated victory in the race for the governorship of Massachusetts— as a Republican—and thus drew the immediate attention of national observers. As with his father, and as might be expected, people repeatedly took note of Mitt Romney's religion, but somehow the assessments this time were different. After Mitt Romney had withdrawn from the 2008 presidential campaign, Karl Rove, longtime chief strategist for President George W. Bush, told Fox News that he would pick Romney as his running mate if he were John McCain, but added that "Romney is not without flaws." Rove continued, "There's...the Mormon problem, which was really sort of astonishing to me."[4] One Christian ministry's website had even declared, months earlier, that "if you vote for Mitt Romney you are voting for Satan."[5]

Anyone with an eye for headlines might be tempted to latch onto this "asset" to "problem" and "Billy Graham" to "Satan" public opinion trajectory as a way of summing up forty years of the changing public image of Mormonism. Of course, history is rarely this linear and never this neat (the attractive tidiness of the "Romney to Romney" bookends notwithstanding). Still, these selected appraisals of the two erstwhile candidates do suggest something: being a Mormon in the public eye meant something different in 2008 than it did in 1968.

On the surface, it seemed in the 2008 campaign season that public opinion numbers had not changed all that much since the late 1960s. Gallup found in 1967, for example, that 75% of voters would not hesitate to vote for a Mormon for president, all other qualifications being equal. In that poll, only 17% of voters said definitively that they would *not* vote for a Mormon.[6] Forty years later, the results of a December 2006 *Los Angeles Times*/Bloomberg poll did not seem all that different: voters were asked if they could vote for a Mormon if "your party nominated" the candidate and he or she was "in general agreement with you on most issues." Only 14% said that they could *not* vote for a Mormon in that scenario.[7]

But when the question was asked in a different way, the numbers told a different story. A December 2006 ABC News/*Washington Times* poll left out the qualifiers about a party's nomination, or the issue-based agreement, and simply asked if certain "attributes [that] might be found in a candidate...would make you more [or less] likely to vote for that candidate for president"; 35% of respondents said that they would be "less likely" to vote for a Mormon candidate. An NBC News/*Wall Street Journal* survey that same month was even bleaker from the Mormon standpoint. More than half of the respondents—53%—said "they were very uncomfortable or have some reservations about voting for a presidential candidate who is Mormon."[8]

These numbers hint at something that *does* seem to have changed: tone. In 1968, it was as if the newsworthy result was that, remarkably, three-quarters of the nation's population would have no problem voting for a Mormon—a sign of just how far Mormons had come, considering a past relationship with the American public that had been, to say the least, troubled. By the 2008 campaign, however, it was as if the newsworthy fact was that, remarkably, one-quarter to one-third of Americans would be less likely to vote for a Mormon—and this in a day ("our post-denominational age," as Harvard law professor Noah Feldman tagged it) when the calls for, and celebration of, tolerance and pluralism had never been louder. Perhaps starkest of all, in contrast to the 17% in 1967 who said they would *not* vote for a Mormon, a 2007 Harris poll reported that 29% "of Republicans...probably or definitely would *not* vote for a Mormon for president."[9]

Indeed, much can change over the course of just a few decades.

And then Mitt Romney ran for president again, in 2012. Much, it seemed, had changed in only a few years.

With an eye on these three presidential campaigns, this study seeks to understand *what* had changed, and *why*, in the four decades between the campaigns of Romney father and Romney son—and then to understand as well what made the national conversation about Mormonism in 2012 feel so different from the way it felt in 2008.

Why, for example, was attention to George Romney's Mormon faith relatively muted when compared to the recent media coverage of Mitt Romney? Why were the theology of the Latter-day Saints and their status as "Christians" mostly nonissues in 1968 but such hotly contested matters in 2008 and in the 2011–2012 presidential primary season—and then, at the very least, ubiquitous talking points after those primaries? What do these shifts in public perception say about changes in The Church of Jesus Christ of Latter-day Saints, its membership, and the various segments of American society with which Mormons interact?

These seasons of intense publicity for the father and son candidates—and, more importantly, for their church—become the opening and closing benchmarks in a study that seeks to measure and interpret changes in public perception of Latter-day Saints by focusing on a series of similar news-making "Mormon moments" in the four decades between the Romney campaigns. These moments include the 1978 revelation that opened priesthood ordination to black males, the church's campaign against the Equal Rights Amendment, the nationwide screening of a movie called *The God Makers*, Brigham Young University's 1984 national championship in football, the mid-1980s trial of forger and bomber Mark Hofmann, the 2002 Salt Lake City Winter Olympics, and the 2005 bicentennial of Joseph Smith's birth, among others. They represent episodes in which Mormons registered significant national attention, and as such, these moments lend themselves to interrogation regarding not only the evolution of Mormonism's public *image* but also the public *dialogue*, with all of its various interlocutors, that has produced and continues to produce that image.

There is an institutional voice in this dialogue, as The Church of Jesus Christ of Latter-day Saints and its affiliated entities have increasingly committed to energetic outreach efforts. Mormon individuals have also participated in unofficial capacities as activists or filmmakers or celebrities or even vocal dissenters, each shaping the image of their church through independent and collaborative projects. National and local media outlets have not only reported news but also molded impressions. Finally, groups that have coalesced around religion or race or politics have also vied for power, sometimes supporting and sometimes challenging Mormon claims. Historian Spencer Fluhman's important book on nineteenth-century anti-Mormonism, *A Peculiar People*, opens with this observation: "It will become clear to readers of this volume that LDS identity has been crafted in dynamic tension with its critical appraisals."[10] That same framing, that sense of dynamism and discourse and discord, also fits well with the twentieth- and twenty-first-century story of Mormon identity considered here. This is a story of action and reaction, give and take, a process through which the meaning of "Mormon" has taken shape in the American mind.

The shape of that image has been tugged at, pushed back, and tweaked by many hands, almost continuously, since surprise and outrage—as well as sympathy and curiosity—over Joseph Smith's gold plates and visions first smoldered in upstate New York, even before he officially organized what would become the LDS Church. From the days of its genesis forward, Mormonism has attracted attention for reasons spiritual and historical. The Church of Jesus Christ of Latter-day Saints believes itself to be distinct from all churches, Christian and otherwise, because it holds that pristine Christianity, and the Christian church's sacramental authority, were lost shortly after the New Testament era but then providentially restored to the earth through new prophets, beginning with Joseph Smith in 1820, in order to lift the world from denominational confusion. Because of the singular importance, as Mormons see it, of this restoration for the salvation of humanity, the LDS Church declares that its divinely appointed mission is to spread this message in all the earth, literally. Understandably, these aggressive truth claims can antagonize, and the large proselytizing force of Mormon missionaries, an almost omnipresent reminder of conflicting worldviews, threatens established religious groups as it pursues potential converts.

At the same time, every portrait of contemporary Mormonism is framed by the movement's past. The church's faithful officially practiced plural marriage during the second half of the nineteenth century. So-called "fundamentalist Mormon" splinter groups continue polygamy today, and sensational headlines reinforce the popularly perceived connection between polygamy and modern Latter-day Saints, much to the consternation of contemporary Mormons. Charges of political authoritarianism and official racism in the past also shadow the church's image. In matters sacred and profane, then, the church must contend with a theology and a history that arouse suspicion and discontent. Church leaders have not dismissed such concerns. The challenge before them has been to navigate the American mainstream as a "peculiar" but not "pariah" people.

The currents within this mainstream can be unpredictable, however. The line separating "unique" or "distinctive" from "odd" or "aberrant" can be precarious. Newer, positive impressions do not always displace the persistently influential collective memory of past antipathy. Nationwide surveys during Mitt Romney's candidacy repeatedly implied that a combination of factors had brought public opinion about Mormons (as *individuals*) to new levels of favorability on the one hand, but had yet to dispel deep-seated suspicion and serious scrutiny of the church—the *institution*—in the minds of a surprisingly sizable segment of the U.S. population on the other hand. While there is in this a risk of oversimplifying a complex story, this growing image bifurcation nevertheless consistently seems to get at the heart of the matter, such that these mixed results become compelling for what they can reveal about a church's relationship with the larger cultural and religious context in which it partly acts and is partly acted upon.

A Note on Sources and Terms

It almost goes without saying that something as varied and diverse as the spectrum of American opinion is not easily or simply measured. Since this is a study of competing claims, it is important to distinguish between assessing perceptions—which *is* the focus here—and judging a group's truth claims—which is decidedly *not* the focus. With that in mind, various sources serve herein as vehicles for exploring the American public opinion landscape, but many of these vehicles are hybrids with acknowledged limited ranges, especially when the aim is to reach a constantly moving target like public perception.

From a quantitative standpoint, the results of opinion polls provide important data—but relevant polls in this case have been infrequent. The furor over Mitt Romney has meant that there are ample poll data—from many angles of inquiry—regarding Mormonism and U.S. opinion as related to the 2007/2008 and 2011/2012 campaigns. Unfortunately though, for most of the periods considered in this study, Mormons only rarely registered on the radar of national pollsters, and even then the questions about Mormons in those surveys were mostly brief and superficial. Still, they do provide points of reference for later comparisons. The LDS Church has also commissioned some outside survey work and has conducted much of its own. However, consistent church polling efforts only began in earnest later in the periods to be considered here (which in itself says a great deal about the changing nature of church initiatives), and most of these survey results are proprietary and off-limits to researchers. Although some polls from the late 1970s and early 1980s have been made available, more often than not this study mines other resources for evidence regarding outside perceptions of Latter-day Saints and their church.

Where polls are not available, other sources of information have their own inherent strengths and weaknesses. In evaluating and using these sources, this project has benefited from the model offered by other studies of public opinion. Several books that have traced changes in public perception of various minority groups or social movements have effectively tapped into venues that give voice to what historian George Frederickson called the "spokesmen" who "most readily communicated to a fairly large public." This study attempts to follow the path that others have blazed.[11]

Traditionally, most prominent among these platforms for the opinion-leading "spokesmen" have been national periodicals, and much can be inferred from the significant number of articles on Mormons and Mormonism in a wide variety of these outlets. Magazines and newspapers both reflect and impact public opinion, but it is admittedly difficult to gauge how much of what is projected is absorbed by readers. Still, some conclusions can be reasonably made. Reviews of nationwide periodicals over time can indicate upticks in coverage of—and interest in—certain topics. There were a number of such dramatic increases in press attention to Mormons over the past half century. Analysis of these reports can reveal not only moments when Mormons had greater exposure, but also what types of information readers were exposed to as that information passed through media filters—data that become especially important at times when these news outlets were, for many Americans, the primary source of information about a minority group like Mormons.[12]

When this study uses the terms "Mormons," "Mormonism," "Latter-day Saints," or "the LDS Church," it uses those terms as basically equivalent labels for the membership of The Church of Jesus Christ of Latter-day Saints (head-quartered in Salt Lake City, Utah)—or, in the important case of dissident or disaffected Mormons, for individuals who once belonged or once actively partici-pated in that church and still are publicly identified by those labels. Not included in the scope of these terms are members of other churches or organizations that trace back to the original church movement initiated by Joseph Smith—in other words, these labels do not refer to members of the Reorganized Church of Jesus Christ of Latter Day Saints (now the Community of Christ) or smaller churches that in a similar way have broken with the Utah church. Although some observ-ers disagree with the exclusivity of this approach, it nevertheless seems to fit best the current self-understanding of both Salt Lake–based Mormons and that of other churches that see Joseph Smith as their founder yet do not self-identify as "Mormons" precisely in order to distinguish themselves from the Salt Lake church. Plus this almost always corresponds with the way that media outlets have used the terms "Mormon" and "Latter-day Saint," although, as shall be seen, exceptions and confusion related to this terminology would play a role in late-twentieth-century Mormon image controversies.

Mormonism Unvailed, the first anti-Mormon book, came off of Eber D. Howe's Painesville, Ohio, press in 1834. The church at which Howe took aim was barely four years old and claimed just over four thousand members. The church's founder, Joseph Smith, Jr., was, at twenty-eight years old, still a young man but well accustomed to heated contests over his reputation and that of his fledgling flock. In many ways, E. D. Howe was only compiling and codifying arguments that, by 1834, had already been circulating for almost a decade and would yet rage for decades to come.

For his part, Howe drew on the research and creativity of Doctor Philastus Hurlbut, a one-time Mormon whose disaffection grew into bitter disdain for the church he once claimed as his own. Hurlbut collected and sold affidavits from Joseph Smith's early associates, and, with remarkable consistency, the witnesses he selected emphasized the untrustworthiness, laziness, and craftiness of the entire Smith family. Howe and Hurlbut also suggested that Joseph Smith's pur-ported translation of the ancient records that became the Book of Mormon was nothing more than the rough plagiarizing of a contemporary romantic novel by Solomon Spaulding. The arguments and testimonials presented in *Mormonism Unvailed* would be rehearsed and rehashed in a litany of similarly themed future publications. Howe's book became a prototype, the opening (book-length, at least) volley in a protracted struggle over religious ideas that would surround the church, its prophet, and its people.[13]

The subsequent barrage, flying back and forth, has not let up almost 180 years later. A 2013 search of the holdings of LDS Church–owned Brigham Young University's Harold B. Lee Library filed under the subject heading "Mormon Church—Controversial Literature" (a euphemism for what Latter-day Saints see as anti-Mormon literature) yielded 1,300 results. Another search for "Book of Mormon—Controversial Literature" returned over 200 results. At the same time, a search for Mormon apologetic works brought up 280 items—280 reminders that this has certainly never been a one-sided debate, and that the Latter-day Saint response to perceived attacks over the years has often been spirited.[14] The stark opposition of these categories can tend to obscure the reality that not everything—and not even *most* things—written about Mormonism fits into either the "anti-" or "apologetic" pigeonholes. On the other hand, the stark opposition of these categories brings into focus the polarizing quality of Joseph Smith's claims to modern revelation. True, *Mormonism Unvailed* and its successors represent an extreme form of inquiry into the reputation of the Latter-day Saints, yet even more objective and recent portrayals of the Saints almost invariably treat, however briefly, the same historical origins that E. D. Howe and Philastus Hurlbut derided. Clearly, the history of Mormonism's contested image is a long one.

A substantial number of commentators have documented that long history of competing media depictions of Mormonism. Jan Shipps, for example, has been at the forefront of Mormon studies for years. Her influential observations about the media's treatment of the LDS Church, together with her inventive approach to measuring and then graphing the relative positive/negative tone of hundreds of articles about Mormonism, have laid important groundwork for subsequent research. Richard Cowan is another scholar who has kept a finger to the pulse of national periodical coverage of Latter-day Saints, beginning with his doctoral dissertation at Stanford University in 1961. Over time, five of Cowan's graduate students at Brigham Young University extended his initial study, writing theses on Mormonism's image in national periodicals that cover, when combined, the period from 1950 to 2004. These foundational projects have proven to be an invaluable resource.[15]

The media timeline that Jan Shipps and Richard Cowan and others have traced becomes a supportive scaffolding here. This study seeks to build on that framework by extending the media timeline through Mitt Romney's two campaigns. But the periodical literature framework is just a starting point. This study also seeks to cover that scaffolding by weaving together the stories of various actors in this drama of perception creation. More will be said, for example, about several underexplored church-sponsored organizations and affiliates, especially the church department that has been known variously over the years as the Church Information Service, Public Communications, Special Affairs, and, for the past twenty years, Public Affairs. A detectable and determined departmental shift in the mid-1990s toward proactive bridge-building has had far-reaching effects on church outreach and consequently on Mormonism's national exposure.

Also, since the late 1970s, the story of the Mormon image has increasingly become the story of Mormonism's interaction with evangelical Protestantism, and these interfaith encounters merit serious attention. Not only do important indicators signal that the role of religion in this country has changed over the past forty years, but also that simultaneously something changed in the stance taken by many of the country's conservative Christians toward Mormons. The emergence of the Christian Right as a political force, beginning in the late 1970s, and a concurrent resurgence of faith-based anti-Mormon activities raise questions about correspondence—about cause and effect—that must be explored.

Changes in the nature of readily accessible mass media channels over the past several decades have also made the story more complex, but at the same time more interesting. When George Romney ran for president, the number of news outlets with a national reach was limited to a handful of well-known venues. By Mitt Romney's run, however, the rise of "new media"—online magazines, Internet blogs, social networking, video-sharing sites—has meant that the number of "media" voices now has the potential to proliferate almost infinitely. Yet that proliferation also provides opportunities to measure public interest and impressions of Mormonism based on the number and variety of "new media" voices.

Likewise, there has been a veritable explosion in Mormon studies, and several of the specific "Mormon moments" to be considered here have generated a number of fine articles and even some book-length treatments.[16] This work draws on many of these publications as they contribute to the narrative of the church's engagement with public opinion. Oral histories and interviews with key figures from all sides of this perception-shaping dialogue become vital, too, in fleshing out the meaning of the substantive changes in the church's approach and in understanding the perspectives of observers outside of Mormonism. In many cases, these interviews provide a sense of the conversations and counsel that have resulted in the church policies pertinent here, as well as the impressions these policies and initiatives have generated outside the church. Readers recognize that human memory can be fallible or colored by individual bias or intervening experience. Because of that, documentary resources—church statements, internal memos and departmental histories, diaries, anti-Mormon literature, and apologetic responses—make the processes of action and reaction more readily apparent and offer important contemporary corroborations of, or correctives to, these reflective interviews.

"A New Era"

Therefore, while public opinion may not always be measured with precision, what emerges from these sources is a composite picture of modern Mormonism, a collage of sorts that has been years in the making. This study seeks throughout to zero in on various elements of that composite picture—to pull out various "snapshots" that make up the collage—and ask how those elements, when combined, give the composite its overall effect. As with all pictures, that overall effect can appear differently from different angles.

Parts of that composite were drawn over the course of the church's first century, when questions about the Mormon image were almost always hopelessly polarizing. By George Romney's time, though, those less-flattering portraits had been overshadowed by new pictures of Mormons that appeared in the 1930s and 1940s. Thomas Alexander, for example, persuasively closed his important study about the LDS Church during the first decades of the twentieth century with a description of 1930s-era markers of Mormon identity. These markers—such as adherence to the teetotaling Word of Wisdom or enthusiasm for genealogy—had virtually displaced polygamy.[17] Subsequent attention to Mormon ingenuity and resourcefulness during the Great Depression (the church launched an extensive welfare system in 1936) and to Mormon patriotism during World War II further rehabilitated the Mormon image by blending it with the shared American experience. These new, positive patterns in the Mormon mosaic became even more prominent in the two decades following World War II, when several organizational and philosophical shifts in the LDS Church during this period of unprecedented growth proved to be instrumental in setting contemporary Mormonism on its current course and giving it greater visibility in communities across the nation.

This backdrop increases appreciation for the textures and colors that make up the image of Mormonism in the four-plus decades bounded by the Romney campaigns. In general, observers agree that Mormons received unprecedented positive press well into the 1960s. In fact, there is a consensus among social scientists and historians alike that as the 1960s opened, Mormons had so successfully shed the "pariah" label that, instead of painting them as a threat or a menace, national reporters characterized Latter-day Saints as upstanding, moral, and patriotic people—and, if anything, a little quaint.[18] Thus to some, Mormonism registered so little disapproval because it had become as noncontroversial as it was anachronistic, a pioneer-based movement destined to fade away as outmoded and obsolete.[19] At the hands of other media outlets, the LDS Church, while still portrayed largely as a western U.S. church, was "simply another denomination" in the landscape of American religions, a stand-out product of the Second Great Awakening with a remarkably energetic membership.[20]

One portentous challenge to that positive (or at least benign) *institutional* image was on the horizon, however. By the mid-1960s, some periodicals began to draw attention to the church's policy prohibiting black men from being ordained to the church's priesthood. But even that charged issue only registered occasionally on the media radar earlier than 1965. Considering the national ambivalence about the civil rights movement, perhaps it should not be surprising that the priesthood issue was so apparently unremarkable in the public's opinion of Latter-day Saints that it was not even mentioned in sociologist Thomas O'Dea's landmark study of the Mormons in 1957.[21] That would all change during the lead-up to the presidential campaign season of 1968, for while Romney himself was noted for his progressive position on civil rights, his church was not. The church's position prohibiting men of Black African descent from holding the priesthood became increasingly notorious in a nation that was itself in the throes of a civil rights revolution—and thus became an early indication that public opinion about the *church* might diverge from public esteem for the church's *members*.

Still, in George Romney's day, one repeated catchphrase seemed representative of the spirit of the times. Mormon mission presidents, the church's governing "general authorities," and contemporary scholars sensed that the decades after World War II opened for Latter-day Saints a "new era."[22] In this new era for Mormonism, one of her native sons—of pioneer stock, no less—strode onto the stage of American politics and, for a time, captured the nation's imagination with talk of a Mormon president. A new era, indeed.

2

"George W. Romney Is Ready and Has the Faith": Mormonism in the 1968 Presidential Campaign Season

"I have decided to fight for and win the Republican nomination and election to the Presidency of the United States."[1,2] With these words at a November 1967 press conference, Governor George Romney of Michigan made official what had long been obvious: he was a candidate in the presidential race of 1968. His announcement brimmed with the hope and optimism befitting a potential frontrunner—and for much of the previous year, repeated polls confirmed that George Romney did, for a time, enjoy frontrunner status. Yet by November 1967, Governor Romney was suffering through that singular sort of public capriciousness reserved for presidential contenders. Support for his candidacy had peaked three months before he had even declared that he was running, so that by the time of his announcement, ironically, he was slipping fast in the polls (Figure 2.1).

For one American community, though, George Romney was not simply a charismatic also-ran who would find his way into the footnotes of history. George Romney was a Mormon, and for fellow Latter-day Saints, he was the first of their co-religionists to make a serious entrée into presidential politics. Romney had garnered widespread backing as no previous Mormon had.[3] This unprecedented level of attention made him, in the eyes of his fellow church members, a test case of sorts, a gauge of the state of national opinion and awareness of their faith. Thus it seemed only natural that the precipitous downturn in George Romney's presidential fortunes prompted contemporaries to ask if his aspirations fell victim to his politics or to his Mormonism.

At first glance, and for readers familiar with Mitt Romney's recent fortunes, the answer to that question might seem patently clear, especially after considering that George Romney and his church were essentially only one generation removed from heavy and concerted opposition to Mormon participation in

Figure 2.1. George Romney campaigning in 1970 for Utah Republican Congressional candidate Richard Richards with Utah state legislator (and the author's grandfather) Ben Fowler. At the time, Romney was Secretary of Housing and Urban Development in the cabinet of Richard Nixon, his one-time rival in the race for the Republican presidential nomination. Photograph courtesy of Ben Fowler.

national government. However, the realities of the 1968 campaign were more complex and surprising. In retrospect, George Romney's religion was mostly a nonfactor in his fall from popular grace. A clumsy (yet honest) comment about the Vietnam War proved devastatingly more consequential than his well-known religious affiliation. This is not to say, though, that the relative insignificance of Mormonism in the demise of Romney's run for the White House also meant that George Romney's run was insignificant for Mormonism. Quite the opposite was true, for a number of reasons.

A decade in the public's eye—first as president of American Motors and then as a popular three-term governor of Michigan—gave George Romney as recognizable a national profile as perhaps any Mormon since Brigham Young. Americans knew he was a Mormon; it's just that this did not seem to affect their voting preferences. In 1967, 75% of voters polled by Gallup stated that they would not hesitate to vote for a Mormon for president, all other qualifications being equal—and only 17% of voters at the time said definitively that they would *not* vote for a Mormon. Contrast that with 2007 or 2011, when opinion surveys repeatedly showed that up to twice as many Americans in those years were hesitant about voting for a Mormon presidential candidate.[4]

This book is not about presidential politics per se, but presidents and would-be presidents repeatedly pop up in the narrative. At least part of that is a function of attention—nothing draws the interest of the American press or the American people like presidential politics. The United States presidency is, as Theodore Roosevelt memorably put it, the ultimate "bully pulpit," which often means that those vying for that pulpit speak from only slightly less-visible rostrums. This level of national interest makes George Romney's campaign a good base point from which to measure the subsequent developments in American politics *and* religion *and* Mormondom that made the treatment of Mormonism during Mitt Romney's campaign so markedly different from that of his father's—which in turn makes a current question so symbolic, in all its implications: "Is America ready for a Mormon President?"[5]

In 1844, that question was answered, in a sense, by an angry mob who made Joseph Smith, founder of Mormonism, the first U.S. presidential candidate to be assassinated mid-campaign.[6] But in 1968, the answer to that question seemed to be an almost dispassionate "why not?" Considering that Martin E. Marty, one of the deans of American religious history, could say that Mormons were "safely describable as the most despised large group" in America at the end of the nineteenth century, this new sense of voter objectivity toward a Mormon candidate was, to say the least, noteworthy.[7] It said something about the confluence of currents in the U.S. political mainstream, as well as the culmination of decades' worth of LDS Church efforts to merge into that mainstream.

George Romney's prime time on the American stage was post–John F. Kennedy, yet pre–Religious Right. The denominational mood of the day was one of ecumenism; the Republican Party's mood was one of flux. And the image of The Church of Jesus Christ of Latter-day Saints in the 1960s was perhaps best characterized as one of benign wholesomeness—this was, as one observer has memorably put it, the "golden era of Mormonism."[8]

"I Believe in an America where the Separation of Church and State Is Absolute"

Any discussion about the place of religion in the presidential campaign of 1968 must begin with a speech given in September 1960.[9] Then-Senator John F. Kennedy set the tone for a political era with an address at the Rice Hotel in

Houston, Texas. This young Massachusetts Democrat and Roman Catholic stood before a crowd of Protestant ministers and forcefully declared that if elected president, his loyalty would be to the Constitution of the United States.[10] He spoke to still-rampant nativist fears that a Catholic chief executive might defer to the wishes of a foreign power (the Pope in Rome), or give preference to parochial schools over public education (through tax breaks for Catholic parents), or bring to pass any of the other dire predictions found in colorful anti-Catholic campaign literature.[11]

There appeared pamphlets with titles such as "Can a Man be a Loyal Roman Catholic and a Good President of the United States?" (The pamphleteer, Dallas pastor W. A. Criswell, did not think so.) Paul Blanshard and Carl McIntire linked (if only by comparison) Catholic power with Communist power. Prominent ministers like Norman Vincent Peale expressed doubts about the sincerity of Catholic assent to first amendment separation of church and state.[12] In spite of all of this, John F. Kennedy did in 1960 what Alfred E. Smith, the first Catholic Democratic nominee, could not do in 1928: win the White House. The election of a Roman Catholic president, albeit by a very narrow margin, seemed to signal that a growing tolerance, one that bucked long-held prejudices, had chipped away at what had been a tacit religious test for presidential office: Protestant faith.[13] Kennedy's memorable lines in Houston ("It is apparently necessary for me to state once again—not what kind of church I believe in, for that should be important only to me—but what kind of America I believe in") were so persuasive that they flavored the political discourse for a decade and a half's worth of election cycles. His speech (and victory) made any hint of religious divisiveness in the public square come off as distasteful. (Figure 2.2).

George Romney, importantly, also played a supporting role in setting that tone. Two years before he even ran for governor of Michigan and six months before candidate Kennedy's Houston speech, Romney participated in the Fair Campaign Practices Committee. The make-up of the committee reflected the strong post–World War II push toward interreligious dialogue and cooperation. The highly ecumenical group counted as members "prominent rabbis, Catholics, various Orthodox and Protestant leaders, and Carl F. H. Henry, editor of *Christianity Today*, the flagship magazine of evangelicalism."[14] It is not surprising that Romney would be a natural choice to represent his faith on this national stage. He had served as CEO of American Motors since 1954, and he had a background in politics from his earliest job as a Washington lobbyist for the aluminum industry. By 1960, the year of his service on this Fair Campaign Practices Committee, his name was being mentioned as a Republican candidate for the U.S. Senate; at the same time, he was the presiding officer over a number of widespread Latter-day Saint congregations that made up the church's Detroit Stake (diocese).[15] Romney's work on the committee would soon take on a special relevance to his own political career.

Figure 2.2. Presidential candidate John F. Kennedy meeting with LDS Church President David O. McKay (center) during a stop in Salt Lake City. As president, Kennedy would later say of the Mormons: "As the Mormons succeeded, so America can succeed, if we will not give up or turn back." Photo courtesy of The Church of Jesus Christ of Latter-day Saints.

After its March 1960 meetings, this Fair Practices committee issued a "Special Statement on Religion in the 1960 Campaign." Its five recommended guiding "principles" centered on the premise that "no candidate for public office should be opposed or supported because of his particular religious affiliation"—therefore, "a campaign for a public office is not an opportunity to vote for one religion against another."[16]

The spirit of this statement, and especially John F. Kennedy's Houston speech, reverberated widely. When the issue of religion first came up in the 1962 Michigan governor's race, George Romney's opponent swiftly called the topic out of bounds. Incumbent John Swainson, according to *Time* magazine, "rebuked" one such critic (the president of Michigan's AFL-CIO), and emphatically requested that "the discussion of religion [be] eliminated as a campaign matter." That kind of dismissal or distancing was not then, nor would be now, unexpected from a savvy candidate, but Governor Swainson's rebuke seemed to represent something larger in terms of prevailing attitudes. *Time* went on to complain about a week when "discussion raged irrelevantly around the tenets of the Mormon Church."[17] *Time's* tagging of such "discussion" as "irrelevant" says much about politics and religion in this post-Kennedy, Vatican II decade.

In fact—and as unexpected as that "irrelevance" seems in today's political climate—historian Randall Balmer used George Romney's presidential campaign as his "exhibit A" in making the case for pre-1976 "disregard for candidates' religion."[18] When presidential candidate Romney appeared on *Meet the Press* in October 1967, for example, the topic of Mormonism was not even broached.[19]

Of course, this point can be overstated and it could be construed to mean that George Romney's religion was somehow anonymous during his campaigns.[20] Quite the opposite was true. George Romney's name and his faith were often in the same sentence. As *Christianity Today* put it in 1969, "his name and Mormonism have become fused in the popular mind."[21] People knew Romney was a Mormon, but, as Balmer has asserted, it was as if "religion simply did not"—or because of the Kennedy precedent, *should* not—"enter into the political calculus."[22]

From its earliest days, Mormonism had repeatedly sparked widespread curiosity—and that continued to be true, as shall be seen, during George Romney's run. Still, curiosity and criticism are different matters, and, as shall also be seen, public perception is as much a product of tone as it is of topic.

In line with Randall Balmer's assessment, then, by 1967 it appeared that a majority of America's voters shared Governor Swainson's sentiments.[23] The Gallup numbers mentioned earlier—that less than 17% of voters in 1967 definitively declared they would *not* vote for a Mormon candidate—had to be heartening for the Romney camp. But the same numbers raise questions for later investigators. What did those voters envision when they thought of a Mormon candidate in 1967? That is, what did Americans believe about Mormons in the late 1960s, and what were the sources of their impressions? Finally, how were those impressions expressed when the generic idea of a Mormon candidate took on concrete form in the person of George Romney?

Buildings and Baptisms: The Mormon Diaspora

Talk of a Romney presidency, or of a "golden era of Mormonism," was a far cry from the nineteenth century, when Mormons were best known for their practice of one the "twin relics of barbarism" (polygamy), or when they appeared more often than not on the public stage as harem-building mesmerizers whose exploits were exposed in popular novels.[24]

How far had Mormonism come in terms of public respectability by the 1960s?

Consider this: In the fall of 1839, Mormonism's founder, Joseph Smith, Jr., traveled to Washington, D.C., to seek redress for his people's recent property losses in Missouri. A year earlier, Missouri Governor Lilburn Boggs had ordered that all Mormons leave the state or be exterminated. After the governor issued his order, Joseph Smith himself spent the winter of 1838–1839 in a dungeon cell in Liberty, Missouri—he was eventually allowed to escape, perhaps since the case for treason was deemed too weak—while thousands of his followers trudged overland to Illinois in desperate conditions. The following autumn, with extensive documentation in hand, Joseph Smith's party went from office to office in the nation's capital looking for a sympathetic ear. Though politely rebuffed by one official after another, President Martin Van Buren's dismissal, as Joseph Smith biographer Richard Bushman noted, "stung" most of all: "Your cause is just, but I can do nothing for you." Apart from states' rights complications, the possibility of angering Missouri voters in the year before an election, and this over the cause of a tiny minority sect, seemed an imprudent risk.[25]

But in the 1960s, U.S. President Lyndon Johnson visited Salt Lake City on multiple occasions to see David O. McKay, the latest in the line of Joseph Smith's successors—once even unannounced.[26] President Johnson said of that unscheduled Utah stopover, en route to Sacramento, "I could not fly over Utah without stopping to see President McKay.... I always feel better after I have been in his presence."[27] President McKay was apparently the first religious leader that newly sworn-in President Johnson invited to the White House for counsel, and President Johnson's admiration for the Mormon leader was one of his stated reasons for urging the Defense Department to modify their chaplaincy requirements in order to allow Mormon elders to continue to serve in that capacity (Figure 2.3).[28]

In the 1960s, the Mormon star seemed to be on the rise. What had changed?

First, there were simply more Mormons by the 1960s. What had been true in the 1830s—that the LDS Church was small and localized—was dramatically less true of the LDS Church in the mid-twentieth century. The importance of that growth on the Mormon image can hardly be overstated. Church membership in the two decades following World War II more than doubled, and this rapid expansion touched nearly every aspect of institutional and societal Mormonism. The church's growth also profoundly affected the way Mormons presented themselves to others and, in turn, the way that others perceived the Mormons.

Some telling indicators put that growth (and accompanying growing pains) into perspective. By a convenient historical coincidence, in the same year that Mormons celebrated the centennial of Brigham Young's arrival in the Salt Lake Valley, their membership rolls swelled to one million Saints for the first time. Essentially, then, it had taken the church 117 years from its founding in 1830 until the pioneer centennial of 1947 to reach the million-member mark. Remarkably, church members numbered over two million only sixteen years later (1963); the three-million-member mark came eight years after that (1971).

Figure 2.3. President Lyndon B. Johnson said of LDS Church President David O. McKay, "I could not fly over Utah without stopping to see President McKay. I always feel better after I have been in his presence." Photo courtesy of The Church of Jesus Christ of Latter-day Saints.

Because of the way Latter-day Saint congregations are organized, statistics related to wards (analogous to parishes) and stakes (analogous to dioceses) often provide a more accurate barometer of real church growth. Since a sizable number of local members is required to lead and staff congregations at the ward and stake levels—and that on a strictly unpaid and voluntary basis in Mormonism's lay-leadership model—the proliferation of these self-sustaining church units reflects the presence of a sufficiently large and committed group of Mormons in a given region. By year end 1947, there were 169 church stakes, which were further subdivided into 1,425 wards and branches. In 1965, there were 412 stakes, and 3,897 wards and branches, meaning that church unit growth more than kept pace, proportionally, with church membership growth during the period.[29]

These numbers have more to say. For example, between 1950 and 1960, the total number of Latter-day Saints increased by 52%. In that same decade, though, the number of Latter-day Saints living outside of North America doubled, meaning that 10% of Mormons lived outside of North America in 1960, up from 7.7% in 1950. This internationalizing trend did not slow from there. (Less than four decades later, in 1996, the church announced that Latter-day Saints living outside of the United States outnumbered those living in the United States for the first time.)[30]

An ever-larger corps of proselytizing missionaries stoked the engine driving this expansion. In 1947, 2,132 missionaries were called to serve for (mostly) two-year, full-time terms. In 1965, more than three times that number—7,139—embarked on missionary service. This increase in the number of missionaries was not simply a proportionate result of total membership growth, since the ratio of missionary-to-member in 1965 was 42% higher than its 1947 counterpart.[31] The enthusiasm generated by the church's numeric successes, when coupled with the mantra of then-church President David O. McKay—"every member a missionary"—seemed to focus Mormon attention and energy on expansion like never before.

In fact, whenever observers have looked to account for this growth—especially this international growth—the personal leadership of David O. McKay looms large. The length of his presidency (1951–1970) made it only natural that his imprint would be on many important church decisions, but his influence had more to do with temperament than with tenure.

McKay was forty-seven years old and a member of the church's Quorum of the Twelve Apostles (the second tier in the church's hierarchy) when LDS President Heber J. Grant asked him and a traveling companion to circumnavigate the globe to visit Mormon branches worldwide. Elder McKay's year-long tour of international LDS missions in 1921 gave him a firsthand perspective that was unique among his colleagues in the church's administration. He visited Japan, China, Polynesia, Australia, New Zealand, Egypt, Palestine, and Europe; his travels suggested to church members living in the Great Basin a new way of thinking about the potential scope and scale of Mormonism.[32]

Much of the institutional evolution in the post–World War II church can be traced to President McKay's approach to a proselytizing paradox of sorts that involved emigration to Utah. For decades—since the church's inception—conversion to Mormonism most often also meant "gathering" with the Saints to a geographical center place. Jackson County, Missouri; Kirtland, Ohio; Nauvoo, Illinois; the Rocky Mountain corridor—all had been designated church gathering locations and imbued with the sacred significance of "Zion." Zion is a complex term in Latter-day Saint thinking. One conception of Zion is that of a promised land, a place of safety and security with millennial connotations. During at least the nineteenth century, when Mormons spoke of Zion, they had this conception almost exclusively in mind. They were headed for a specific place, a specific community—or, later, a specific region of proximate communities—where they could practice their religion together with Latter-day Saint neighbors. Most important, these communities also had temples (which are distinct from the

"chapels" used for Sunday meetings) nearby. Mormons believe that temple rituals make possible family unions that transcend death. These rites comprise the
highest form of worship for Latter-day Saints, such that committed converts
would anxiously seek to participate in temple worship. In thousands of cases,
that meant converts would move their families to the Intermountain West,
where Mormons and their temples could be found. During Brigham Young's
presidency, these immigrants provided the manpower needed to carry out his
ambitious colonizing plan. Hundreds of new towns sprung up throughout what
is now Utah, Idaho, Arizona, and even into California, Mexico, and Canada, an
area that later geographers would identify as the Mormon cultural region.[33]

During the first decades of the twentieth century, several converging realities caused leaders to reconsider the church's emphasis on gathering to a central Zion. Economics played a role, since opportunities for employment in the
agricultural-based economy of the Intermountain West could not meet the needs
of all new arrivals. A nascent Mormon out-migration from the Utah-Idaho cultural region would grow steadily larger through the years of the Great Depression
and the displacement caused by World War II military and industrial needs.

There were simultaneous indications that church leaders were promoting the
personal and spiritual significance of Zion over its (yet future) geographic significance.[34] Symbolism from the biblical book of Isaiah took on renewed importance, as LDS general authorities began to emphasize the need for "stakes" in
various locations so that Zion's "tent" could be enlarged to cover the earth.[35]
Such stakes began to appear outside of the Rocky Mountain Mormon cultural
region—in Los Angeles in 1923, in San Francisco in 1927, in New York in 1934.[36]

These important shifts in mind-set solidified into official church positions
under President McKay. What had been trends during the presidencies of his
predecessors now became trademarks of his presidency. He removed any ambivalence about the need for converts to gather to an American Zion, first in his
statements about building the church "locally" wherever members found themselves, and even more effectively in his announcements in the early 1950s of
new temples to be built in England, Switzerland, and New Zealand. In the words
of his son Lawrence: "[He] preached that Zion was not so much a matter of geog-
raphy as it was a matter of principle and feeling, that the Spirit of God is within
you. He preached that people should stay where they are. The gathering place
was no longer Missouri or Utah."[37]

President McKay's statements gave momentum to a shift in Mormon
demographics. Internationally, Latter-day Saints increasingly stayed put.
Domestically, Latter-day Saints increasingly spread out. Historian Jan Shipps
tallied up the number of church stakes that were created in the United States
from 1945 to 1965, and of the 241 new U.S. stakes in the post–World War II
era (which in itself is an impressive indication of growth), more than half of the
stakes (130) were organized outside of the Mormon culture region. "By 1960,"

Shipps wrote, "only Kentucky, Tennessee, and the Dakotas could not claim at least a thousand members of the LDS Church."[38]

Mormons also now sensed the importance of becoming a permanent presence in their respective communities. As President McKay's presidency began, Mormon leaders were often painfully aware, however, that the physical symbols of that permanent Mormon presence—church buildings—left much to be desired. David O. McKay's First Presidency made it a priority to change that deficiency. The church embarked on a building program with almost staggering ambitions. The general prosperity of postwar America as well as generous donations from members who responded to church teachings about the importance of tithing made possible the expenditures required for what the *Deseret New*'s "Church News" section would call "the largest building program in the history of the Church."[39] One telling example of this increase in revenue gives a sense of the new resources available to church planners: In a year when church membership increased by less than 4% (1951–1952), President McKay announced "that tithing receipts were up 217% from the previous year."[40] Those monies were soon put to constructive use.

Henry D. Moyle was President McKay's counselor in the First Presidency, and in that capacity he was assigned as the supervisor of the churchwide building program. Unlike some of his more fiscally conservative predecessors, he felt that the church's postwar surplus funds should be dedicated to improving the circumstances under which church units met and operated. Indications of the scope and scale of the work that President Moyle supervised came in his 1963 accounting of construction activity: "In the past twelve years," he reported, "we have built 56% of the 3,500 meetinghouses we now have in the world, 1,941 in number—more than were built in the preceding 120 years of Church history."[41]

While some of his colleagues among the general authorities felt that President Moyle's style, described as "aggressive" or "energetic" or "driving," emptied church coffers too quickly (and indeed a mid-1960s budget freeze was instituted by Henry Moyle's successor because of depleted cash reserves), it was difficult to argue with the positive effects of the building boom on the church's image.[42]

Latter-day Saints saw a cyclical pattern connecting church growth and new facilities with new local prominence in various locales. David McKay's biographers summarized the pattern this way: "In addition to strengthening existing church members, the building program catalyzed proselytizing efforts." As a case in point, they quoted the comments of William Bates, who was a member of the first stake presidency in England: "It absolutely multiplied the number of baptisms, and it raised the status of the Church tremendously." Henry D. Moyle, Jr., saw the building emphasis as "[differentiating] us from being a cult to being a substantial religious organization, one that people would respect and listen to." This correlation was not lost on observers who noted that "although other factors also contributed to the proselytizing successes, 1961–1965 saw the five highest annual numbers of convert baptisms in Church history, triple those of the previous five years."[43] For these and so many other reasons, it is not difficult to understand why a recent biography of David O. McKay carried the subtitle "The Rise of Modern Mormonism."[44]

All of this meant that by the 1960s, Americans saw new Mormon buildings in communities across the nation and new Mormon faces in all aspects of national life. In politics they saw Ezra Taft Benson, Mormon apostle and Dwight Eisenhower's Secretary of Agriculture. In sports they saw world champion boxer Gene Fullmer, a lifelong Mormon, and professional golfer Billy Casper, a recent convert to Mormonism. And in industry, they saw George Romney, a prime example and product of the growing Mormon diaspora.

But it was more than increasing numbers that also seemed to raise the church's public profile. An important part of that change was also the concerted (and newly professionalized) institutional effort to harness the visibility of several recognizably Mormon icons.

Identifying Icons: Mormon Public Relations

For many Americans in the late 1960s, the word "Mormon" most naturally preceded the words "Tabernacle Choir." The choir sang at Lyndon Johnson's 1965 inauguration; President Johnson phoned LDS Church President David O. McKay on that same day to say "that the singing of the Tabernacle Choir was the best thing in connection with the inaugural."[45] In 1959 the choir won a Grammy for "Battle Hymn of the Republic," the song that would become its trademark anthem, an anthem that combined, significantly, faith and patriotism.[46] Gold record-level sales confirmed what one observer remembered about this era: the "ubiquitous presence" of the Tabernacle Choir extended to "almost every American home equipped at that time with a sound system and roundtable for playing the 'new' LP records."[47] The sheer breadth of coverage provided by weekly nationwide broadcasts (which already by 1963 *Time* could call "the longest sustained network program in history") made the Tabernacle Choir, in *Time* magazine's view, "the most powerful unofficial missionary that The Church of Jesus Christ of Latter-day Saints ever had."[48] Public esteem for the choir marked its inclusion in memorial services for presidents Franklin D. Roosevelt and John F. Kennedy, as well as its participation in the "first worldwide television satellite broadcast, transmitted from Mt. Rushmore" in 1962 (Figure 2.4).[49]

The choir had been an instrumental ambassador—perhaps *the* instrumental ambassador—during the period when Mormons went from being the nation's most despised large group to "super-American" (Martin Marty's words).[50] The choir had sung at the 1893 Chicago World's Fair, only three years after LDS prophet Wilford Woodruff announced the official discontinuance of polygamy,

Figure 2.4. The Mormon Tabernacle Choir at Mt. Rushmore, July 1962, as part of
the first worldwide television satellite broadcast. Copyright Intellectual Property, Inc.
Reprinted with the permission of The Church of Jesus Christ of Latter-day Saints.

and (certainly not unrelated) only three years before Utah achieved statehood.
In 1911, the choir embarked on a well-publicized tour of several eastern states
and garnered favorable reviews. In particular, that 1911 tour (including ten concerts at New York City's Madison Square Garden and a performance at the White
House) helped to offset the waves of negative press about Mormons that had
not abated since the protracted Reed Smoot hearings four years earlier. The tour
coincided with Theodore Roosevelt's letter to *Collier's* magazine in defense of
Mormons—another indication that Latter-day Saints were moving beyond the
public opinion nadir of that just-past decade.[51]

The choir's popularity also meant that by the 1960s, many listeners would
have known the voice of the choir program's narrator, church apostle Richard
L. Evans. Not only was he the host of the weekly "Music and the Spoken Word,"
but he also served as president of Rotary International in 1966–1967. He traveled across the United States and to dozens of different countries in that presidential capacity, but his voice and image traveled even more extensively on radio
and television. The short sermons that Elder Evans inserted between songs
from 1930 (the year he began with the choir) to 1971 (the year of his death)
were mostly nondenominational in content. His inspirational but generically
Christian themes endeared him to many listeners.[52] Ironically, when Richard
Evans died, *Time* magazine noted that "many of the show's faithful listeners

did not realize Evans was a Mormon; they considered themselves followers of 'Richard Evans' church,"!53 Because of the broad appeal of those messages, even those listeners who did recognize that the program's host was a Latter-day Saint found common ground in the Christian tenets he espoused, such that the choir's broadcast could not help but "[produce] admiration for the performers and the people they epitomize[d]."54

Of course, the choir's drawing power did not go unnoticed among Latter-day Saint leaders eager to cultivate increased exposure for their faith. In fact, the expansion of official church public relations–type efforts connected directly to the choir's success. By the middle of the twentieth century, apostle Mark E. Petersen, a former newspaperman, was urging his colleagues to create a church department to handle press inquiries and press releases, apart from efforts designed primarily for proselytizing.55 Church leaders did not act on his proposal for almost a decade. It would take the successful publicity surrounding a 1955 Tabernacle Choir tour to convince his colleagues that such a division of labor would be in the church's best interest. That 1955 tour was the choir's first to Europe. Church leaders felt that the scope of this tour, where audiences were generally unfamiliar with both the church and its choir, required the assistance of a seasoned public relations firm. The church therefore turned to the Robert R. Mullen firm in Washington, D.C., for help.

LDS officials were pleased with the results of the Robert Mullen agency's marketing and publicity strategy surrounding the choir's European tour, so much so that they continued their contract with Mullen for another decade and a half. Mullen and David Evans, a Salt Lake City advertising executive, suggested to church leaders the advantages of having employees in-house, working in the same direction as Mullen's group.56

Thus, by the mid-1950s, the time seemed right to return to Apostle Petersen's recommendation about a church press agency. In 1957, the Church Publicity Department (soon to be renamed the Church Information Service) came into being. Theodore Cannon, initially "on loan" from the church-owned *Deseret News*, led the department, which in the beginning consisted of one assistant, Lorry Rytting, and one secretary.57 Expansion came quickly, however; by 1964, the office had tripled its staff.

In effect, the new department absorbed the "publicity" functions of its predecessor (the Radio, Publicity, and Mission Literature Committee), while leaving the proselytizing functions to the church's missionary department. This arrangement meant that the focus of the Church Information Service was essentially journalistic: Cannon's staff issued press releases and news bulletins regarding Mormon pageants or temple construction groundbreakings or regional conferences; they wrote scripts for tour guides at historical sites; and, significantly, they served as points of contact for inquisitive reporters.

Up to this point, many Mormon leaders (including some who personally remembered the turn-of-the-century turmoil) had been perpetually wary of a national press corps that they had perceived as incorrigibly antagonistic.[58] While there had been recent and encouraging signs of improved media treatment of Mormons, many of the church's senior officials had been soured by earlier and extensive abuses, leaving them with a well-developed bunker mentality. As Rytting remembered it, "the prevailing view at Church headquarters was probably that the press would never give us a fair shake."[59] Several cooperative ventures worked together to soften those views. Earl Minderman from the Mullen agency, for example, put in motion a project that eventually resulted in a 1958 *Saturday Evening Post* piece on the church's welfare program that a Church Information Service employee characterized as "very positive."[60] Earlier that same year, church staff offered assistance to Hartzell Spence in preparing his story on the Mormons for the January 1958 edition of *Look* magazine.[61] The growing number of "favorable and accurate articles" gradually won over church leaders to the publicity department's position that "it [was] far better for the church to provide solid factual information than for the church to force reporters to find outside sources, which were usually inaccurate and often critical." At the same time, the Church Information Service staff felt they "earned a reputation as news-oriented people who wouldn't give reporters the run-around, who would be as honest and forthright as they could, and who would try to implement their requests for interviews and facts and information." This new public relations philosophy began to "change attitudes, both inside and outside the church."[62]

Here again President McKay provided a visible lead. His disposition made him especially well-suited for encouraging the church into new interpersonal and institutional connections.[63] He advocated friendships across faith lines through personal example, even accepting a blessing at the hands of Episcopal Bishop Arthur W. Moulton, and then blessing Reverend Moulton in return.[64] Under President McKay's leadership the LDS Church donated money toward the remodeling of a Presbyterian church in Ogden, Utah, and toward "Israel bonds," as evidence, he said, of "sympathy with the effort being made to establish the Jews in their homeland."[65] The American Jewish Congress paid public honor to the LDS Church in the April 25, 1955, edition of its national publication, *Congress Weekly*, for "the aid and comfort which it has steadfastly given the Jewish community."[66] Seven years later, hundreds of Utah's outstanding citizens—"the majority of them not members of The Church of Jesus Christ of Latter-day Saints"—feted David O. McKay in a 1962 gala banquet.[67] The evening's invocation was offered by the Right Reverend Monsignor Patrick A. Maguire, and Rabbi Sidney Strome offered the benediction. A Catholic friend, J. P. O'Keefe, conducted the program, and Joseph Rosenblatt, a Salt Lake Jew, offered this tribute: "We pay honor to David O. McKay, not that his theology is akin to ours, but really rather that it is not, for I think that we know him best as the ideal of what we look for in the great American.... We see every day his talent for harmonizing diversities...."[68] In a 1970 obituary tribute that says as much about Mormonism's new national visibility as it does about the changing climate of interfaith relations, *Time* magazine suggested that President McKay "was perhaps the first Mormon president to treat non-Mormons as generously as members of his own faith."[69]

President McKay provided Mormonism a recognizable and respected face.[70] He registered on several late-1960s Gallup polls of America's most admired men. He counted as friends prominent minister and author Norman Vincent Peale and motion picture giant Cecil B. DeMille.[71] It seems fitting that President McKay supported the development, within the Church Information Service, of a "formal hosting operation" in the early 1960s, with its stated purpose of accommodating important guests at the church's Salt Lake City headquarters campus.[72] It also seems fitting that he personally approved the church's most ambitious and costly foray into hosting visitors in a location far from that campus—the Mormon Pavilion at the New York World's Fair of 1964–1965 (Figure 2.5).[73]

Figure 2.5. Designers opted for a recognizable façade when they recreated the spires of the Salt Lake Temple for the Mormon Pavilion at the New York 1964–1965 World's Fair. Some six million visitors toured the pavilion. Copyright Intellectual Property, Inc. Reprinted with the permission of The Church of Jesus Christ of Latter-day Saints.

Even though church leaders decided relatively late to commit to the idea of a full pavilion (at the urging of the still-fledgling Church Information Service department), fortuitously two prime and adjoining lots on the fair's campus came open unexpectedly.[74] The church secured a site next to the fairgrounds' main gate—a gate serviced directly by a subway stop—for its pavilion. Originally, the next lot was designated as a food service station, but a company bankruptcy forced the contracted food provider to withdraw from the fair. LDS leaders took advantage of the opportunity to turn this neighboring parcel into a garden area, complete with benches and a reflecting pond. Drawn in undoubtedly by its convenient and prominent location, as well as by what had to be a welcome opportunity for quiet in the garden area, six million visitors passed through the Mormon Pavilion. It is telling that nearly one in six visitors requested that Latter-day Saint missionaries make follow-up calls at their homes to explain more about the Mormon beliefs and practices mentioned in the pavilion's exhibits, requests that totaled almost one million.[75]

The designers of the pavilion took full advantage of distinctly Mormon symbols—both with a façade that replicated the easternmost three spires of the iconic Salt Lake Temple and with signature appearances by the Tabernacle Choir. Once inside the pavilion, visitors viewed a film centered on the core Mormon belief in the eternality of marriage and family bonds. The film, entitled "Man's Search for Happiness," and corresponding exhibits grew out of collaborations between Salt Lake City advertiser (and contracted public relations consultant for the church) David Evans and BYU film producer Wetzel Whitaker, under the close direction of church advisers like Harold B. Lee (an apostle) and Bernard P. Brockbank (an assistant to the twelve apostles). Murals of Old Testament prophets and scenes from the life of Christ stood next to paintings representing episodes in LDS Church history. An Italian sculptor created a "marble duplicate" of Berthel Thorvaldsen's "The Christus," a statue that became the pavilion's centerpiece.[76]

Based on thousands of comments left in the pavilion's guest registry, visitor after visitor confirmed that the carefully planned exhibits largely succeeded in clarifying Latter-day Saint beliefs about the divinity of Jesus Christ, the importance of the Bible, and the need for a restored church of Jesus Christ. Perhaps more than anything else, the primacy and potential perpetuity of family relationships, even beyond death, made lasting impressions on visitors to the pavilion.[77]

The New York World's Fair was a crowning triumph for the nascent Mormon public relations effort, a signal of just how far that effort had come since the days of a tiny "Bureau of Information" booth built for tourists on Salt Lake City's Temple Square in 1902.[78] The planning, execution, and especially the success of the Mormon Pavilion confirmed for Mormon leaders the wisdom of this institutional move and proved to have a significant effect on Latter-day Saint outreach efforts. Not only did the church continue to participate in subsequent World's Fairs, but many of the innovations church planners first attempted in New York—missionaries as guides, the use of filmstrips—came to characterize the growing number of LDS visitors' centers across the nation. In fact, most of the very components of the Mormon Pavilion, from the artwork to the building materials, found their way into new chapels and projects. Finally, the substantial allocation of financial and human resources to the World's Fair project left no doubt that public relations had assumed a new importance in the church's overall agenda.[79]

While initially some LDS general authorities balked at the cost of participating in the World's Fair (church public relations promoters estimated that the pavilion would cost $3 million), no one was disappointed with the return on investment. A Church Information Service employee remembered that the Mormon Pavilion was "one of the top ten [exhibits] in total attendance at the entire fair."[80] The opportunity to inform was unprecedented; hosts at the pavilion handed out 500,000 pamphlets and sold 100,000 copies of the Book of Mormon over the course of the year.[81] LDS congregations in the eastern United States, especially in New Jersey and New York, welcomed thousands of new converts in the years immediately following the fair, and those investigators came almost invariably through pavilion contacts.[82] In fact, of all the church's missions worldwide, those covering New York and New Jersey led the way in the number of newly baptized members in 1965.[83] From a Mormon perspective, even more noteworthy than the sizeable boost to the church's proselytizing efforts was the surge in public goodwill toward Mormonism. Workers who sorted through "nearly a million . . . comments in the guest register books" felt that "less than 1% of the comments were negative."[84] The fact that thousands of Americans—especially on the East Coast, where the LDS Church was still small—spent time engaging the doctrines and practices of Latter-day Saints led one of the church's mission presidents in the area to conclude that the World's Fair "has done more to change public opinion in this area and give the Church status than any other event in our lifetime."[85]

"Real-Life Leave-It-to-Beaver Families"

Both the visibility of the Tabernacle Choir and the exhibits of the Mormon Pavilion reinforced what media outlets were commonly reporting about the Latter-day Saint lifestyle.[86] The Mormon emphasis on family was highlighted in profiles of boxing champion Gene Fullmer, this "broken nosed Mormon Elder" who was a "doting father and a regular church-goer."[87] When Fullmer won the middleweight belt, the *Saturday Evening Post* dubbed him "boxing's pious battler." The magazine reported that he celebrated his championship with a couple of bottles of "pop," since he did not drink or smoke, "in keeping with the tenets of his Mormon upbringing." The *Post* observed that Fullmer did not use profanity and that he tithed fully on his winnings.[88]

The Word of Wisdom, Mormonism's code of clean living, also figured prominently in repeated articles of golfing great and recent Latter-day Saint convert Billy Casper. Casper joined the LDS Church in the middle of his highly successful professional career, and the change was apparent to reporters. *Time* summed up what was inescapably obvious: "William Earl Casper, 35, used to be a fat, sickly Congregationalist, who won a lot of money playing golf. He is now a slim, healthy Mormon. Nothing else has changed."[89] Because others saw Casper as "an enthusiastic missionary" for his newfound faith, his "fasting and praying," "not cussing, or using booze, coffee, [or] tea" inspired several extensive media features exploring his recently adopted Mormon lifestyle.[90] It is easy to see why historian Jan Shipps argued that the contrast between patriotic, family-centered, "clean-cut" Latter-day Saints and "counterculture," war-protesting "hippies" solidified in American consciousness the Mormon image of wholesomeness.[91] And no one came to personify that image of Mormon religiosity in the 1960s in the national media more than George Romney.

Romney's face became familiar to the nation a decade before his presidential run. He took the reins of American Motors in 1954, only months after a merger between Nash-Kelvinator and Hudson Motors had created that company. Almost immediately Romney began to shake up Detroit. He testified before Congress about the anti-trust threat of the "Big Three" automakers, as well as the excessive might of labor unions.[92] (The leaders of the United Auto Workers and the AFL-CIO never forgave him for that and doggedly opposed his subsequent political campaigns.) *Time* magazine featured Romney on the cover of its April 6, 1959, issue as the "dinosaur hunter," because of his strategy of promoting compact cars over the behemoths coming out of Detroit's factories.[93] Romney became his company's very visible spokesman, touting the virtues of American Motors' Rambler model wherever he went.

The company's dramatic loss-to-profit turnaround from 1957 to 1958 garnered him the Associated Press's accolade "Man of the Year" in the category of industry leaders.[94] Plus the well-documented success of American Motors under Romney's leadership drew the attention of Republican Party officials. Romney's skill in communicating the need for grassroots reform propelled both the growth of his Citizens for Michigan statewide committee and his ascension to the vice-presidency of the Michigan constitutional convention. Midway through the rewriting of the state's constitution, George Romney entered the race for governor.[95] As noted, from the outset of that race, Romney's Mormonism figured into most media profiles.

In many ways, because media reporting on the markers of Latter-day Saint life in the 1950s and 1960s seemed so consistent, "Mormon" as a descriptor was rich in connotation and implication. Thus, while John F. Kennedy's presidential run had undoubtedly served to mute *judgments* about a candidate's religion, it did not change the reality that Mormonism was a defining *characteristic* of George Romney's public image. "Mormon" often served as a kind of descriptive shorthand.[96] Jacqueline Kennedy quipped in 1960 that the hubbub over her husband's Catholicism was "so unfair" since "he's such a poor Catholic."[97] The same, however, could not be said about George Romney and his religious devotion.

During the very years that he was gaining national attention for his successes at American Motors, George Romney served his church as a prominent lay leader. As president of the Detroit Stake, he presided over congregations covering much of Michigan and parts of Ohio and Canada. He was one of only 200 such LDS stake presidents worldwide at the time he was placed in that office in 1952.[98]

His earliest ecclesiastical service had been in Great Britain, where he had labored as a full-time missionary for the church from 1926 to 1928. His missionary years received repeated mention by reporters who followed his campaign. They saw in him the style of an evangelist working to inspire his audience. As a car salesman, *Newsweek* described Romney as possessing "hot missionary zeal and vast physical stamina," and then reminded readers of his proselytizing work in England; such a connection was impossible to miss in the title of the *Newsweek* article "Detroit 'Missionary' at Large."[99] *Time* characterized George Romney as a "Bible-quoting broth of a man who burns brightly with the fire of missionary zeal."[100] The *Nation* commented favorably that his soap-box style derived from his literal soap-box encounters in his missionary days.[101]

Just as with Gene Fullmer and Billy Casper, reporters repeatedly fastened on Romney's abstinence from alcohol, tobacco, tea, and coffee—abstinence that had become a ubiquitous mid-twentieth-century marker of Mormonism. There was related attention to Romney's physical fitness and youthful appearance. The *Saturday Evening Post* had a memorable photo of then-Governor Romney running in full stride with a golf bag in tow. The magazine reported that to get maximum results he played three golf balls at a time over a six-hole course, running between strokes.[102]

His commitment to Sabbath observance received consistent mention, too, as did his practice of monthly fasts and faithful payment of a 10% tithe.[103] He was portrayed as a family man, through and through. His wife, Lenore, was constantly by his side. At the time of his presidential campaign his youngest son, Mitt, served as a church missionary in France. National news organizations noted the marriage of his older son, Scott, in a ceremony at the church's Salt Lake Temple. The faith, reporters noted, had been passed in full measure to the next generation of Romneys.

George Romney, like other Mormons in the news, seemed the very picture of *Coronet* magazine's celebratory headline "Those Amazing Mormons."[104] Pioneer work ethic, stable families, old-fashioned values, aversion to vice—these were the featured qualities that made the *Nation* concede that Romney's "personal life is impeccable," and at the same time predict that his Mormonism would be one of the "assets" in his political journey.[105]

But if the outlook for Mormons seemed this rosy in the 1960s, why the conclusion of a contemporary writer (and fellow Mormon) that religion sank Romney's hopes?[106] Why the conflicting evaluations from interested observers of the church's public image during the period? In essence, was it the height of the church's public perception "golden era," or the return of the "severe criticism" of an earlier generation?[107] The best answer, it seems, is a layered one.

Evaluating the Criticisms: Religious Zeal, Real Autonomy, and Racial Attitudes

Those historians who have focused on national periodicals of the 1960s seem right in their claims that *print* media appraisals of Mormons took a somewhat negative turn in the second half of the decade. This negativity followed several tacks, all of which did, to an extent, touch the Romney campaign.

Some writers turned George Romney's apparent strength—his morality—into a liability. It was not uncommon for articles to play on a variation of the "too good to be true" theme.[108] Historian Dennis Lythgoe's most intriguing—and compelling—suggestion in his retrospective evaluation of the campaign is that George Romney suffered in the polls because he was portrayed as *too* religious.[109] There is a basis to this conclusion, considering the tone of a number of articles on Romney. Opponents joked that it was like "running against God" to face him.[110] More damaging were implications that he took a messianic approach to his political destiny, that he saw things in moral black and white, that he was unyielding and uncooperative when he made a decision.[111] Reporters and opponents took exception to the fact that he fasted and prayed before making the decision to enter the governor's race—this seemed to imply a "pipeline to God."[112] This kind of intrusion of personal piety into politics seemed so unusual at the time that some saw it as manipulative.

Next, and considering the hierarchical structure of Mormonism, it is not surprising that budding concerns over Mormon power also made their way into media appraisals of the candidate and his church. Several lengthy articles in the 1960s explored the church's unabated growth, in terms of both membership and building projects. This era saw early speculation about the church's financial holdings—the details of which the church did not readily disclose—and brought new attention to the diversified investments, enterprises, and income managed from Latter-day Saint headquarters. While some reporters did raise concerns about the LDS Church's supposedly unquestioned hegemony in Utah politics, as well as the hefty influence the church wielded in several other western states, there did not appear in 1967–1968 anything like the anti-Catholic fears surrounding John F. Kennedy's potential subservience to the Vatican.[113]

Thus even if some commentators harbored skepticism about the extent to which a committed Mormon like Governor Romney could maintain true independence in his political decision-making if church leaders decided to intervene, there seem to be some compelling reasons to doubt that these reports were as damaging as has been suggested to either Romney's or Mormonism's public image.

For example, the neutralizing effect of the at least as many nationally circulated articles that expressed admiration for Romney's adherence to his principles must be taken into consideration. Every print offering in these magazines would, of course, be filtered through the disparate viewpoints of their far-flung readership. That media representatives who influence public opinion do not always accurately reflect public opinion seemed the message in Stewart Alsop's admission that "[Gus] Scholle [president of Michigan's AFL-CIO] and the scoffers in the Michigan press corps are in the minority. Almost everybody else who knows Romney likes and admires him."[114]

Point of view also becomes an important, but elusive, variable in evaluating the tone of a media piece. Reactions to *Fortune* magazine's 1964 presentation of the church's wealth provide a case in point. While some observers lumped this article with those that negatively portrayed Latter-day Saint economic and political might, two Church Information Service employees raved about it.[115] Even though *Fortune* "got into some sensitive areas as well," the "full, factual, detailed information" included in the article prompted a church public relations officer to call it "the best I have seen on the church."[116] Even Neil Morgan in *Esquire*— whose article was the source of the oft-repeated guess by former Utah Governor J. Bracken Lee that the LDS Church had a daily income in excess of $1 million— wrote that "there are other churches which withhold financial statements. There is nothing scandalous about a prosperous church."[117] The potential for any such "scandal" seemed additionally mitigated by consistent descriptions in these same articles of the considerable Mormon expenditures in welfare relief efforts.[118]

In response to fears about the church's potential for flexing its political muscle, there also appeared articles that offered countering evidence. The *Los Angeles Times* reported in 1966 that "if Michigan Gov. George Romney, a Mormon, wins the Republican nomination for President, he will have the full backing of his church but will be his own man, David O. McKay, President of the Church of Jesus Christ of Latter-day Saints, told the *Times*. 'I hope he gets it!' boomed Dr. McKay, 93. 'He would make a good President. Very good! He is an independent thinker. He will go his own way—and that usually is a very good way.'"[119] A simultaneous exchange that occurred between Mormon Congressmen and the church's leadership must have reinforced to readers that, on political matters, independence indeed was acceptable, and that Latter-day Saint politicians were not punished for disagreeing politically with church elders. In 1965, the church's First Presidency urged Mormon legislators to oppose President Lyndon Johnson's plan to repeal the so-called "right to work" section of the Taft-Hartley Act. President McKay opposed the repeal for what he saw as an intrusion upon freedom of choice, since he saw the repeal as making union membership obligatory for workers. A letter sent to the eleven Mormon U.S. representatives and senators prompted a publicized response from several of those legislators, who expressed their disagreement with the presidency's position. *Time* magazine made an inquiry about this apparent rift, asking if the church leadership's position was a binding policy, to which President McKay responded that "it [was] only an opinion."[120]

In an earlier generation, the peculiarities of Mormon history and theology had given countless reporters and commentators ammunition for their exposés. But by the late 1960s, these were aspects of Mormonism that received relatively little attention and criticism.[121] There were occasional references to the unique doctrines of the church, but most came in politely worded assessments, like the *Christian Century*'s 1962 view that "the Mormon past includes a number of historical and dogmatic positions not generally accepted by the middle-class American mainstream."[122] What seems striking about this editorial is the opinion that Mormonism's aberrant positions were in the *past*. Even that perennial bugaboo of polygamy seemed to be passed over most often as a legacy of frontier experimentation; Neil Morgan in *Esquire* stated flatly, "Polygamy has ceased to be an issue in Mormon country."[123] Historian Dale Pelo's statistical analysis offered the same conclusion: in comparing his study of Mormonism in national periodicals in the 1960s with Richard Cowan's similar study (which used an identical scoring system) for periodicals before 1960, Pelo found that polygamy appeared as a theme in only eight articles in the 1960s, as compared with polygamy's 177 appearances in magazines during the century between 1851 and 1960.[124]

There were exceptions, like the 1967 article in *Fact* magazine that openly ridiculed Joseph Smith and assailed George Romney's judgment for following such a "psychopath."[125] But the rarity of encountering such claims in the media coverage of Mormonism and George Romney, in hindsight, seems to speak louder than the occasional critic.

Another article that struck out at Mormonism's theological foundations offered clues, perhaps unintentionally, as to why there did not appear more religiously based objections to a Latter-day Saint candidate. In early 1968, Anthony Hoekema, professor of theology at Calvin College (Grand Rapids, Michigan) worried, in the pages of *Christianity Today*: "Many people have the impression that the Mormon teachings are not basically different from those of historic Christianity." That line is very telling. As he put it, the "Christ of Mormonism is not the Christ of scripture," such that "we cannot classify Mormon teachings with those of historic Christianity."[126] Hoekema's pointed criticisms demonstrate clearly that there was, in George Romney's day, religious opposition to Mormons; but Hoekema's words reinforce perhaps a more salient point—that the rationale behind such opposition was not well known or appreciated. The *National Observer* claimed that polls showed "thousands of voters consider[ed] the Mormon Church as something of a theological outcast."[127] Yet because of the Latter-day Saints' "tremendous welfare program," their "willingness to sacrifice," and their belief in the Bible, it is difficult to know what would have prevailed in the minds of the American public: the "suspect...theological grounds," which were rarely delineated clearly, or the so-called "surface characteristics" of Mormonism that were "similar to those of many conservative denominations," characteristics admitted even by theologians like Hoekema who opposed Latter-day Saint tenets.[128]

To be sure, uncertainty about where Mormonism fit in the family of world faiths cropped up in the 1960s. Mormon Missionary guides at the New York World's Fair recorded that one of the five most commonly asked questions by the visitors to their pavilion was, "Why have we been led to believe that the Mormons are not Christians?"[129] But that question did not seem to have the political potency that it would carry decades later.

This was certainly due in part to the spirit of the Second Vatican Council. From 1962 to 1965, Catholic bishops (and observers from other churches) had convened in Rome for a series of conferences that reshaped Catholicism's stance toward other Christian confessions along the lines of openness, tolerance, and cooperation. This feeling was reciprocated by other denominations, signaling, as two prominent historians put it, "the beginning of a new era in relation of the Churches to one another."[130] A number of American Protestant denominations put aside differences and joined together in interfaith organizations in the 1960s. Vatican II was in the air, contributing to a public reluctance to split theological hairs.

Yet another dynamic was also at work here. Those religionists in the 1960s who were most likely to oppose Mormonism on theological grounds—that is, fundamentalist, evangelical Christians—were also very likely, in these middle decades of the twentieth century, to be conscientiously avoiding politics. The rise of the Religious Right was still a decade in the future when George Romney ran for president, so the burgeoning counter-cult movement and its anti-Mormon thrust were still largely confined to an evangelical subculture, far from national headlines.[131]

What readers *did* find at the time was the generic assessment of the more liberal and ecumenical publication *Christian Century*, which specifically referred to Mormons as Christians. It would have been difficult for the *Christian Century*'s audience to conclude anything otherwise when they read that the "fundamentals" of Mormonism include "the centrality of Jesus Christ in [the] revelatory experience" of Joseph Smith, and that "vital to the whole Mormon movement is a concept of the role of the ever-living Christ in the process of salvation."[132] Importantly, the *National Observer* magazine asserted that the LDS Church was a *Christian* church, but not a *Protestant* denomination.[133]

In any case, like *Time* stated in 1967, "for many Republicans,...George Romney's political creed [was] more important than his religious doctrine."[134] In covering Mormonism, media outlets tended to focus most on church members and their *lifestyle*-related beliefs and practices rather than the Latter-day Saints' core articles of faith.[135] Because of that focus, it would have been understandable if other readers came away with the same conclusion as that voiced by *The New York Times Magazine*'s Carl Carmer: "No other religious group in America 'lives' its religion with such emphasis."[136]

Another factor in this image equation deserves mention. An exclusive emphasis on the print portrayals of *national* magazines discounts the other media outlets that had a hand in shaping the Mormon image in the 1960s—and thus can skew assessments about the state of Mormonism's public image. Newspapers, for example, reached millions of readers and operated under different constraints of space, interest, and time than did magazines. These variables affected the type of reporting on Latter-day Saints that arrived on doorsteps across the nation. An employee in the Church Information Service reported that, by 1966, his agency received from around the nation some 4,000 newspaper clippings *per month* dealing with some aspect of Mormons and Mormonism. His evaluation was that "most of these [were] routine and favorable."[137]

Perhaps even more influential than descriptions of Mormons in *print* were depictions of Mormons in *pictures*.[138] Jan Shipps has argued persuasively that, as television became increasingly important in the 1960s, so too did the images of Mormonism on television (especially since, as Shipps noted, the majority of electronic media portrayals of Mormons did not mention issues surrounding race as often as did national magazines). Her recollections and observations about "the contrast" between the "radical Left" and the Latter-day Saints "made the image of the Saints even more appealing than it had been in the fifties, making this a time when at least middle America's perceptions of the Saints would be overwhelmingly positive." From her position as an outside observer of Mormonism, she asserted it was not "at all uncommon to hear" in that era "that Mormons are 'more American than the Americans,'" since "radio and television broadcasts,...almost as a reminder that the entire nation had not gone the way of the much-maligned, pot-smoking, flag-burning counterculture, featured all sorts of images of Mormons as neat, modest, virtuous, family-loving, conservative, and patriotic people."[139]

If positive portrayals of the admirable aspects of Mormonism at least served to offset the purported downsides of the faith—Mormon zeal, authoritarian leadership, disproportionate regional political influence—one crucial issue from the 1960s still must be reckoned with: what about Mormons and race relations?

Observers agree that no aspect of Mormonism was portrayed so controversially and negatively in the 1960s as the church's policy of prohibiting the priesthood ordination of blacks. This issue received far more attention at the time than did any question about the appropriateness of labeling Mormonism "Christian." Essentially, the reporting connected to George Romney's campaign introduced this facet of Mormonism to the nation, and (as will be discussed in the next chapter) this issue ignited a firestorm of protests in the years immediately following that campaign.[140]

In The Church of Jesus Christ of Latter-day Saints, "priesthood" does not signify a special class or clerical office. Instead, because the church is led by its lay members, priesthood ordination is open to all Mormon males older than twelve. This nearly universal ordination to the priesthood for Mormon men allows them to officiate in church rites and ceremonies, particularly the most important sacraments that take place in the church's temples—like temple marriages and family "sealings" that extend family ties beyond the grave. Before 1978, the only men excluded from the priesthood—and the only men and women excluded from temple rites—were those of Black African descent.

In 1969, in the midst of growing controversy, members of the church's First Presidency reiterated this long-standing position in a letter to all local church leaders that was later released to the press. From the church's earliest days, they wrote, Latter-day Saint prophets had "taught that Negroes [*sic*], while spirit children of a common father, and the progeny of our earthly parents Adam and Eve, were not yet to receive the priesthood." Historians raised questions as to whether or not Joseph Smith instituted the prohibition, but there was no question that it was in force at least by the time of his successor, Brigham Young. Various church commentators had offered their opinions about the reasons for the restriction. In some cases, these explanations paralleled traditional Christian interpretations of the Bible, which designated blacks as the seed of Cain or Ham. In others cases, Mormons drew on doctrines that were unique to their faith, such as the proposal that decisions and actions in humanity's pre-earth existence had predisposed some spirits to be born into a race that could not hold the priesthood. Officially, however, the church's First Presidency reminded readers that the policy was in place "for reasons which we believe are known to God, but which He has not made fully known to man."[141]

Blacks could (and did, in small numbers) join the LDS church and participate in its Sunday services and auxiliaries. The First Presidency wrote in its 1969 letter, "We have no racially segregated congregations." Likewise, Mormon leaders had repeatedly stated that the restriction would one day be lifted—and, by extension, black families subject to the restriction could one day be sealed

posthumously by proxy rites, the Mormon practice of performing temple ordinances for deceased ancestors.[142] For that reason, the phrase "not *yet* to receive
the priesthood" in the First Presidency's statement was crucial. The letter
included an earlier pronouncement from church President McKay, who anticipated a change in the future: "Sometime in God's eternal plan, the Negro will be
given the right to hold the priesthood." Yet that change could not come "until
God reveals His will in this matter, to him whom we sustain as a prophet." The
First Presidency thus concluded, "Were we the leaders of an enterprise created
by ourselves and operated only according to our own earthly wisdom, it would
be a simple thing to act according to popular will. But we believe that this work is
directed by God and that the conferring of the priesthood must await His revelation. To do otherwise would be to deny the very premise on which the Church is
established."[143]

Church leaders recognized that outsiders "who do not accept the principle
of modern revelation may oppose our point of view," and they understood that
such opponents must have deemed Mormon support for civil rights legislation
(reiterated in the 1969 letter) disingenuous or insincere. Yet for Mormons, "the
seeming discrimination by the Church toward the Negro is not something which
originated with man; but goes back into the beginning with God."[144]

Such sentiments grated, understandably, on numerous ears. Those historians
who have detected a downturn in the church's public image in the 1960s, at least
in the pages of the nation's periodicals, have focused primarily on the reporting
that surrounded the race issue. Without question, this policy met with consistent disapproval by writers everywhere; this was the one *Mormon*-related issue
that always raised uneasiness about George Romney's political views.[145] But
despite the consistency of those media censures of the church, there does not
seem to be a simple answer about the effect that even this issue had on Romney
or, by extension, the church. Instead, paradoxes abound.

Because the issue of civil rights legislation was nationally divisive, so too reaction to the Latter-day Saint position, in a divided public mind, must have been
mixed. Martin Luther King's famous description of the country's most segregated hour—the hour of Sunday worship—was undisputed. Racial integration
of church services and membership was problematic for a number of denominations. While it could be argued that the "separate but equal" philosophy behind
segregationist policies did not restrict black religious participation and leadership in the same way that the Mormon priesthood policy did, the persistence of
segregated churches at least spoke to an entrenched prejudice that touched many
faith groups. Though Jerry Falwell, for example, later stated that his heart began
to change in the mid-1960s about racial integration, his Thomas Road Baptist
Church did not admit black members until "sometime around 1970."[146] *Christian
Century* issued several sharp editorials calling on Mormon leaders to reverse their
policy concerning the ordination of blacks. It is telling that in two cases, those

editorials that focused on Mormonism appeared on the same pages as other editorials that rebuked the University of Mississippi, in one case, and several Baptist colleges, in another, for their refusals to comply with civil rights statutes.[147]

Polls from the era confirm the widespread divergence of opinion about race relations, including those in a religious context. One survey found that 67% of Southern Baptists, 34% of Missouri Synod Lutherans, and 28% of Presbyterians agreed, in 1966, that "it would probably be better for Negroes and whites to attend separate churches." Yet in a concurrent survey among Latter-day Saints in Utah and San Francisco, only 12% of Mormons agreed with the statement.[148]

This same collection of surveys demonstrated that Mormons "could not be considered outside the national consensus in their external attitudes toward African Americans."[149] This conclusion is certainly not meant to suggest that Latter-day Saints harbored no racial prejudices. However, considering the proliferation of media reports that listed "inferiority of the Negro" as a tenet of Mormonism, it is very likely that many contemporaries would have been surprised to learn that Latter-day Saints were no more racist in their views than the average American. When the LDS Church's First Presidency asked "members of the church everywhere to do their part as citizens to see that [civil] rights are held inviolate" for "the Negro, as well as those of other races," such a request must have seemed contradictory, to say the least.[150] Yet in their own minds, many Latter-day Saints did see the priesthood prohibition as different from civil rights equality. While those general Mormon sentiments could not have been as well known or as well publicized as the negative press coverage, George Romney's support of the civil rights movement *was* well known and well publicized.[151]

That is precisely what makes the public image impact of the priesthood prohibition so difficult to assess, at least in connection with Governor Romney's presidential run. Almost without exception, every reporter who commented about the church's position toward blacks followed that discussion with an admission that Romney's record of aggressively lobbying for civil rights legislation was undeniably commendable. In fact, Romney's oft-repeated recourse when challenged about his church's stance was, in essence, "Look at my record." He often effectively parried such challenges by pointing out that it was his faith's teachings about charity and the brotherhood of humanity that motivated him in his pursuit of racial equality before the law.[152]

In the spring of 1967, Romney visited Salt Lake City, conferred with church president McKay, and met an interfaith ministers' meeting "at his forthright best." He answered "the inevitable questions" about the status of blacks by saying, "I was raised in the conviction that the Declaration of Independence and the Constitution are divinely inspired documents of the Creator, and all mankind is the child of God with basic rights." He said, "I have fought to eliminate racial discrimination. I want to be judged on the basis of my actions rather than someone's idea of what the precepts of my faith are." The reporter enthused: "It was a confrontation reminiscent of John Kennedy's with the Greater Houston Ministerial Association in 1960, where Kennedy convinced many skeptical Protestants that a Roman Catholic could be a fair President."[153] When Romney appeared on *Meet the Press* in 1964, the panelists did not mention the priest-hood policy, but one asked: "What is your attitude, as a Mormon and as a public official, toward Negroes?" Romney replied, "My attitude is that a Negro is a child of God just like I am... I believe our most urgent domestic problem is to wipe out human injustice and discrimination against the Negroes."[154]

George Romney's consistency on this civil rights front came across, too, as a mark of personal integrity. In a telling piece, a *New York Times* reporter quoted a Republican Party official in Virginia who made it clear that Romney would have played it safer *not* to have taken such a strong stand for civil rights. The reporter then concluded, "If his Virginia debut provides any evidence, Mr. Romney will face the civil rights issue directly in his Southern campaigning rather than soften his stand to make friends among Republicans with strong feelings against equal opportunity legislation in housing and employment. In his first Southern political speech last night, the Governor deliberately chose to include a clear, forceful endorsement of civil rights that could have been *easily avoided*."[155]

National readers must have had various reactions. Some undoubtedly read into these reports that Romney could stand independently from what they judged to be the dictums of a regressive church. Others might have felt sympa-thy about the difficulty in resolving here, as in so many other cases, this aspect of apparent racial disparity, especially considering the articles which highlighted the diversity of opinion among Latter-day Saints—general authorities and gen-eral membership alike—over their degree of support for civil rights legislation, and over the potential timing of a revelation which could change the priesthood policy.[156] There is evidence that still others felt concern that Romney was too lib-eral and that his church's prohibition was an appropriate internal safeguard.[157] All in all, there seems to be no straightforward barometer by which to judge just how reports of the Mormon position on priesthood would have registered in the unsettled national climate of the 1960s.

The Insiders' View: Surprises from the Romney Campaign Interviews

One intriguing documentary collection, preserved in the papers of George Romney's good friend and fellow Mormon, J. Willard Marriott, brings all of this into focus and offers perhaps the clearest view of what it meant for a Latter-day

Saint to run for president in 1968. The Romney team conducted dozens of exploratory interviews nationwide, state by state, with county and state party chairs, congressmen, business leaders, and press representatives, to assess local and regional feelings about a possible presidential campaign. Staffers then prepared summaries of those interviews (including numerous direct quotations) to give George Romney and his advisers a feel for the political pulse of the country in November and December 1966. The collection contains reports for twenty-six states. Significantly—unexpectedly—reports on only *five* of these interviews, out of more than a hundred (even from the traditional geographic strongholds of conservative Christianity), mention Romney's religion.[158]

Mormonism was seen as a political bonus in at least two states. As might be expected, the interviewers found ready support for Romney among his co-religionists in Utah. But the suggestion that the Mormon vote would be a significant factor in Oregon led one observer there to foresee a Romney victory in that state, too.[159]

The governor of Arkansas's press representative said, "Romney's religion could give him some trouble in the Bible Belt. They figure he belongs to some abnormal religion." That same representative still declared, "I think Republicans can win with Romney and not with Nixon."[160] A former governor of New Hampshire who was an avowed Nixon supporter complained that Romney was "sanctimonious," that he "[wore] his religion on his sleeve," and that he had "to be more than an itinerant preacher."[161] Another prominent Republican in that state (and Romney booster) worried that several well-known Mormons there who thought they "own[ed] Romney" could "embarrass him."[162] The Republican Party chairman for a county in New Jersey expressed that "some folks don't like the Mormon bit," even as his counterpart in another county "predict[ed] that Romney will get the New Jersey delegates."[163]

That was the extent of Mormon-related comments in these interview reports.

It is readily apparent that not all of those interviewed—not even most of those interviewed—were decided Romney supporters; many planned to back Richard Nixon or Ronald Reagan or "favorite son" candidates like Charles Percy of Illinois. Still, positive appraisals of Romney's image were far more common than negative comments. Nationwide, party leaders judged Romney's morality, his optimism, his family values as working for his benefit. The most dominant favorable opinion was that George Romney was a winner, and the Republican Party wanted a winner. Over and over these GOP representatives worried that Richard Nixon, though well qualified to serve the nation, would be unable to escape the "loser" label.

While Mormonism apparently came up almost never in these interviews, Barry Goldwater came up almost always. By far the most prevalent concern about George Romney shared by these local Republican leaders was Governor Romney's very public refusal to endorse Goldwater's nomination in 1964.

Senator Goldwater still enjoyed strong support in the party, and many felt that Romney's earlier stance was a stinging betrayal. The Republican Party was, in these years, in the midst of a transformation. The Goldwater camp had been motivated by a conservative ideology that favored a strict interpretation of the Constitution, one that limited federal powers to those granted explicitly in that document. This platform resonated widely and energized a conservative groundswell that would reap future election-day successes, even though Senator Goldwater himself suffered a defeat in 1964 of historic proportions.[164]

Romney, on the other hand, was becoming the flag bearer for the moderate wing of the GOP. (Romney reportedly waffled, initially, about whether to run for governor as a Republican or a Democrat in 1962.[165]) As a senator, Barry Goldwater, true to his libertarian leanings, had voted against the 1964 Civil Rights Act on the grounds of its questionable constitutionality. George Romney took exception to that stand and had argued for stronger civil rights-related planks in the 1964 party platform, amendments that were defeated at the convention. Far more disconcerting than Mormonism to many of those whom the Romney team interviewed was George Romney's so-called "liberal" positions, especially on civil rights. The irony that a Mormon candidate was the party's highest-profile pro–civil rights candidate complicates any simple appraisal of the media's treatment in the 1960s of the LDS Church and race relationships (Figure 2.6).

As might be expected, the exploratory interviews conducted in the South were the least promising for the Romney team. This apparently was not because of a Bible Belt reaction to perceived Mormon eccentricities; local Republicans worried that a Romney-led national ticket would sink state and county GOP candidates. The Romney representative who conducted interviews in Mississippi found that local party officials soured on Romney on two accounts: he "acted like a spoiled brat in 1964," and "everybody remembers the picture of the governor of Michigan marching down the street in a civil rights demonstration. Not even Lyndon Johnson has done that."[166] Georgians who sat for interviews saw Romney's rift with Goldwater as "the kiss of death," concluding that he "couldn't carry a state in the South" because "he's such a liberal," so much so that "from a racial standpoint, he's never been given much credit in Georgia for being strongly conservative on the race issue."[167] Similar complaints about Romney's liberal race-related politics surfaced in interviews conducted in Alabama, Arkansas, Louisiana, South Carolina, and Ohio as well. In Kansas and North Carolina, some Republicans were enthusiastic that a Romney nomination would actually improve the GOP's chances among black voters. After all, even as media outlets described the LDS Church's priesthood policy, they also noted that George Romney's popularity with Michigan's black voters increased measurably in each of his three campaigns for governor.[168]

Outside of the South, there emerged in these interviews considerable optimism that the nomination in 1968 would go to George Romney. Several opinion

Figure 2.6. An indelible image: As governor of Michigan, George Romney joined a June 1963 march demonstrating against race-based discrimination in housing. A Republican leader in Mississippi noted in dismay that "not even Lyndon Johnson has done that." Reprinted with the permission of the Walter P. Reuther Library, Wayne State University.

leaders in the party expressed the view that their respective state delegates would eventually fall into Romney's column.[169] These interviews, coming as they did in the closing months of 1966, coincided with the general feeling captured by a *New Republic* columnist in December 1966: "Some Washington writers have all but given him the nomination already."[170]

This prediction of Romney's success, made in 1966, seemed to be borne out by public opinion surveys throughout 1967.[171] Importantly, even as articles which highlighted the candidate and his religion appeared with increasing frequency, Romney did not drop in preelection polls.[172] The steadiness of his popularity throughout 1967 should not be ignored for what it can say about public acceptance of a Mormon candidate, and this popularity did not seem affected by criticism over his religious zeal or his church's policy toward black members.[173] It stands to reason that just as many American voters found themselves attracted to Romney's high principles as troubled by them.

Brainwashing, Backtracking, and Backing Out

But his poll numbers did drop precipitously, almost overnight, after a comment George Romney made about the Vietnam War gained traction in the national media. In an August 31, 1967, interview with a Detroit television station, Romney explained his changing position on Vietnam by saying that he had been, essentially, "brainwashed" by military leaders on an earlier trip to that country.[174] He announced that he now favored ending the conflict and leaving Vietnam. Not only was brainwashing an emotionally charged term in this era of Cold War espionage and POW torture, but it also implied a lack of mental toughness or at least perceptiveness.[175] Pundits, even sympathetic ones, had long been concerned about Romney's lack of experience in foreign affairs. This concern surfaced almost as regularly in the exploratory interviews as did his rift with Barry Goldwater. A survey of national newspapers show that throughout the spring and summer of 1967, reporters focused first on George Romney's reluctance to state his position on Vietnam and then his decision to support the White House's escalation of the conflict. Even throughout those months, though, as media outlets tried to pin the Michigan governor down on the Vietnam issue, Romney's position in the polls held steady. It was only after the notorious brainwashing comment that misgivings about Romney's deficiencies in foreign policy translated into a measurable fall from presidential contention.[176]

Not only did newspaper after newspaper reinforce the impression that Vietnam had done Romney in, but his friends and advisers privately conceded the same. In a strongly worded letter in October 1967, a frustrated J. Willard Marriott asked Romney to stop trying to explain his Vietnam statement, since the "news men" only wanted to "rehash Viet Nam and brainwash," and that had negatively affected Romney's "image and popularity" in just a matter of "a few weeks."[177]

Of course, single-cause explanations by definition ignore the complex interplay of historical factors that contribute to an event or trend and thus should always be a little suspect. Still, it is difficult to escape the conclusion that George Romney's Vietnam statement (and overall approach to the Vietnam issue) proved to be, by far, the single most damaging blow to his presidential campaign.[178] He had successfully weathered jabs over his religion and his views on race, but he could not recover from the spectacular knockout punch that came, seemingly, out of nowhere, just as the fight was getting interesting.

In the end, George Romney's presidential aspirations were never put to a ballot test. While he officially announced his candidacy in November 1967 (less than three months after the "brainwashing" misstep), he withdrew from the race on the eve of the New Hampshire primary, in February 1968. Even with his rapid descent in the polls, his withdrawal came as a surprise to many who knew

Governor Romney and the tenacity and energy with which he had approached every previous endeavor, from the oft-repeated story of his seven-year courtship of his future bride to his aggressive advocacy of compact cars. In that same spirit, the *New York Times* noted that "Mr. Romney's decision to withdraw confounded those who had thought his Mormon religious background would not permit him to 'quit' so soon. A dogged determination had been his trademark since he entered Michigan politics in 1962."[179] It seems that the writing on the wall for Romney was his inability in early 1968 to persuade the Republican governors to give him their public endorsements—although earlier, privately, many had expressed support. In fact, one governor proved to be pointedly prophetic. His message to the Romney camp in 1966 was that he planned to openly back Romney "when the time is right," provided that Mr. Romney did not "foul up somewhere along the road."[180]

Perhaps if George Romney's campaign had extended well into the primary season, or even if he had secured the Republican nomination, the increased scrutiny that would have come with such a position might have invited more serious debates about the acceptability of a Mormon president. As history stands, however, and considering the intensity of the media spotlight that *did* shine on George Romney and his church, it is difficult to speculate whether more attention would have been detrimental or not. That is because in hindsight, and as far as can be determined from available evidence, George Romney's active membership in The Church of Jesus Christ of Latter-day Saints did not seem to torpedo his presidential chances. If anything, as portrayed in the media and as judged by political advisers, his principled life was his most attractive feature.[181] Even in the midst of the Vietnam troubles, one such adviser suggested that Romney should speak *more* of his religious views and appeal to Americans' faith in the guiding hand of providence at that troubled time.[182] Such a suggestion only underscores again that there was apparently little worry that Romney's Mormonism made American voters uncomfortable in the 1960s.[183]

Surely the precedent of John F. Kennedy still influenced the political climate of 1968, as did the spirit of religious ecumenism in the United States. The success of Kennedy's campaign, and the memory of his legacy, strengthened the increasing consensus view that a candidate's record must mean more than a candidate's religion. Suggestions that a candidate's private religious life disqualified him from office came to appear inappropriate in politics, almost taboo.[184] At the same time, there could be no question that Mormonism was not as well known, especially outside of the West, as JFK's Roman Catholicism. In this case, though, the ignorance factor did not seem to translate into a fear factor. Exposure to the church either through the media or through the church's publicity-generating organs (the Tabernacle Choir, World's Fairs, proselytizing missionaries) seemed to leave the public with shared positive impressions: Mormons were hard-working, patriotic, family-centered, clean-living, and Christian—though with some anomalous beliefs and practices that were mostly vestiges of the past. In this regard, George Romney only deepened those positive impressions.

George Romney's political life, inasmuch as it coincided with the height of the civil rights movement, in effect opened a national discussion about the Mormon policy of prohibiting priesthood ordination to black members. At the very least, however, Romney's vigorous support of civil rights must have carried the message that racial issues raised a multiplicity of opinions within the LDS Church, just as those issues did within so many other American institutions.[185]

Yet in the months immediately following the 1968 campaign, disapproval for the Latter-day Saints' priesthood policy became more vocal and more fiery (literally). Here was an early indication that Americans could hold one opinion of model Mormons who did not have skeletons in their closets, and another of a church that seemingly did.

3

Church Rites versus Civil Rights

College basketball games can get heated, but rarely this heated. Paul James, who was for decades the broadcast voice of the Brigham Young University Cougars, remembered the night he dodged a flaming Molotov cocktail during halftime of a BYU–Colorado State basketball game.[1] It was early February 1970 when Colorado State students staged the latest in a string of anti-BYU protests at athletic events. After a relatively uneventful first half of basketball in Fort Collins, Colorado, a group of about one hundred students occupied the floor to demonstrate their strong opposition to the LDS Church's policy of restricting black men from priesthood ordination. BYU, the church's university, was an easily accessible target for their rancor.

The hundred or so protesters refused to leave the floor at the request of university administrators. Upset at the delay, some fans in the stands called out for the protesters to leave. These calls were met with defiance from those on the court. Fists flew, as did various objects and obscenities, and police in riot gear eventually arrived. In the midst of the escalating tensions, James saw the improvised bomb just in time. He ducked beneath his broadcast table and watched as the bottle filled with gasoline landed on the court, unbroken. A CSU student custodian used his broom to extinguish the burning rag before the bottle's contents could ignite and explode. The halftime chaos ended with multiple arrests but fortunately only one hospitalization: a local reporter had been hit on the head by a piece of metal thrown from the stands (Figure 3.1).

In the face of so much controversy, the win/loss column became almost an afterthought during BYU's troubled 1969–1970 season. The Cougars' struggles on the court mirrored their parent institution's simultaneous struggles in the court of public opinion. The LDS Church's priesthood policy became national news during George Romney's campaign; by 1970, it had become an activist's cause. Week after week the on-field performances of BYU sports teams were overshadowed by pregame or postgame demonstrations and denunciations.

Conflicts related to civil rights were inescapable as the 1960s drew to a close. These were the years of the Detroit riots, the assassination of Martin Luther

Figure 3.1. A Brigham Young University cheerleader looks on as demonstrators take over the basketball court at Colorado State University, February 1970. Photograph by Barry Staver; reprinted with the permission of *The Denver Post.*

King, Jr., the violence at the 1968 Democratic Convention in Chicago. It was also in 1968 that two young black sprinters, Tommie Smith and John Carlos, raised gloved fists and bowed their heads as the "Star-Spangled Banner" played over loudspeakers at the Mexico City Olympics. Photos of their "black power" salute became almost instantly world famous. If the medal stand had become a pulpit from which to preach the message of equality, Dr. Harry Edwards had become the evangelist.[2]

Dr. Edwards taught at San Jose State College, the school that Smith and Carlos attended. In his writings and lectures, Edwards urged African American athletes to become activists, to use their visibility to advance the crusade to end persistent racism. Accordingly, Edwards leveled his sights at Brigham Young University, a school that appeared on San Jose State's schedule in several sports. He warned James, the BYU broadcaster, "If Mormon dogma regarding the blacks is not changed..., anybody who goes with the BYU football or basketball team had better wear a hard hat and an asbestos suit. Whatever conference BYU is in, we will destroy!" His call to arms eventually rallied a sizable corps of recruits. Protests ranged from signs of silent solidarity—black armbands worn by players and coaches—to outright refusals to compete.[3]

The strategy to target the LDS Church through BYU was a smart one from a publicity standpoint. By the late 1960s, BYU had become the nation's largest church-owned university and one of the nation's largest private universities. Much of that growth was due to the energetic lobbying of BYU President Ernest

L. Wilkinson and the foresight of LDS Church President David O. McKay.[4] President McKay's background in higher education made him a ready ally for the church school, and BYU President Wilkinson took full advantage of that predisposition. Wilkinson was described as having a "tempestuous nature" and being "strong willed" (and this in a public tribute offered by church apostle Harold B. Lee after Wilkinson's announced resignation!).[5] Even those sympathetic to him admitted that "because of [his] single-mindedness he sometimes seemed gruff, inconsiderate," but his undisputed effectiveness in fulfilling President McKay's vision of an expanded and reputable Brigham Young University forever changed the face of the school.[6]

During Wilkinson's two-decade tenure (1951–1971), "the student body increased six-fold to more than 25,000, the size of the faculty quadrupled, the number of faculty holding Ph.D.s rose 18%, the number of departments doubled, the first of some twenty doctoral programs were authorized, library holdings rose nearly 500%, and the number of permanent buildings jumped more than twenty-fold."[7] All told, this dizzying pace of construction meant that the "five or six academic structures on [BYU's] upper campus" in 1951 were only the first of "254 permanent and 85 temporary academic building" that would occupy the same campus just "twenty years later."[8]

Because of logistical and economic complications, Wilkinson was forced to drop his larger plan for establishing a number of church junior colleges that would feed into the Provo school, a plan that would have made BYU "the flagship of an entire system of church-sponsored higher education."[9] But in building the Provo campus as he did, Wilkinson was in essence christening a new flagship for Mormonism. BYU's faculty and athletics and arts programs became highly visible ambassadors of church outreach efforts, and the expanded school came to play a correspondingly expanded role in shaping the public perception of its parent institution—BYU often became a stand-in for the church. Plus BYU's athletic success at the time (for example, Western Athletic Conference titles in basketball in 1965, 1967, 1969, 1971, and 1972 and NCAA basketball tournament appearances in four of those years; also six top-five finishes in NCAA track and field championships from 1965 to 1971, and the national title in 1970) meant that protests at BYU sporting events were bound to draw media attention—and they did.

Yet like the Colorado State Molotov cocktail, the fiery rhetoric and activism seemed to fizzle out relatively quickly instead of igniting. The initial explosiveness of the protests soon died down, so that by the mid-1970s, the priesthood policy no longer attracted the level of attention that it had drawn only five years earlier. Part of that change was due to growing public distaste for the protest movement, as well as growing public ambivalence about the need for continued emphasis on racial issues after the seeming success of the civil rights legislation of the 1960s. In almost every case of protest, and in almost every community,

the actions and reactions that surrounded the demonstrations served to underscore just how polarizing this issue could be. Part cause and part effect, too,
were the Mormon responses to these protests, as LDS Church and BYU officials
launched new institutional outreach initiatives when earlier they might have
simply hunkered down to wait out the barrage. The pointed press inquiries and
the sometimes-violent protests surrounding Brigham Young University sports
teams early in the decade had, ironically, largely waned by 1978, when the most
significant announcement to come out of Salt Lake City in the twentieth century set news wires abuzz across the globe. That announcement, the revelation
that lifted the church's restriction on priesthood ordination for black men, profoundly affected both the self-image and the public image of Mormonism.

The 1960s witnessed a progression in the Latter-day Saint response to critics
of its priesthood policy. In 1964, church President David O. McKay counseled
the acting president of BYU against approving articles for the school's newspaper that dealt with the priesthood issue, since, he reasoned, outsiders did not
accept the revelatory basis behind the policy and any discussion of the issue
would only bring embarrassment to the church.[10]

Then George Romney's presidential campaign brought national attention to
the restrictions placed on black Mormons, and protests mounted against BYU
athletics to the point that they could not be ignored by the church. At first, BYU
officials did little more than restate its nondiscrimination position. The ineffec-
tiveness of those statements in satisfying angry activists meant that protesters
began to achieve institutional support from the faculties and administrations of
other universities at the same time BYU felt that support slipping away. The difficulty for Mormons was that their disavowals of racism were not, as sociologist
Armand Mauss aptly put it, "terribly convincing to most political commentators
and image makers in the country, so Mormons increasingly came to be suspected
of harboring racism in their hearts as well as in their churches and thereby of
lending at least passive resistance to the goals of the civil rights movement."[11]
These very public condemnations prompted equally public church rebuttals.

From Protests . . .

The 1969–1970 protests over the church's racial policies were not the first tied
to this issue. As early as 1963, members of the National Association for the
Advancement of Colored People (NAACP) informed Mormon leaders of their
intention to picket the church's semiannual General Conference if those leaders did not make clear their stand regarding civil rights legislation. President
David O. McKay authorized his counselor Hugh B. Brown to speak officially in
favor of civil rights. His statement ended with this charge: "We call upon all men
everywhere, both within and outside the Church, to commit themselves to the

establishment of full civil equality for all of God's children. Anything less than this defeats our high ideal of the brotherhood of man." The church's leadership maintained, however, that the religious issue of priesthood ordination stood separate from that of legal equality.[12]

The leader of the Salt Lake City office of the NAACP responded favorably to this statement by "asking all NAACP branches throughout the nation not to demonstrate or picket any LDS missions or churches."[13] As the decade progressed, however, George Romney's campaign created intensified interest in, and dissatisfaction with, church explanations of the priesthood policy. Romney's campaign also revealed the spectrum of Latter-day Saint thought on the issue.[14] Reports on the Mormon policy in the 1960s consistently mentioned the oft-expressed belief that black men would one day be eligible for priesthood ordination. Media outlets, as well as some outspoken Latter-day Saints, characterized various church leaders as more or less likely to embrace such a change in policy. The priesthood question invariably drew comparisons with the church's decision to discontinue the practice of plural marriage in the late nineteenth century. With varying degrees of cynicism, observers discussed the possibility—and proximity—of a revelation that would effect a change in the priesthood prohibition.[15]

The volume of such speculation rose, for example, when the media learned about Africans who had encountered Latter-day Saint literature and petitioned the church to send missionaries. The church made some investigative forays there, and even announced by press release its plans to open an official Nigerian mission in January 1963. Such plans were delayed and eventually aborted, however, because of a combination of factors. Nigerian students studying in the United States voiced their strenuous objections to the church's priesthood policy in letters to their government and hometown newspapers. The Nigerian authorities balked at approving visas for Mormon missionaries after receiving information about the priesthood restrictions. Just when it appeared that visas would be made available in late 1965, the logistical challenges of running church units without local lay holders of the priesthood prompted the church's hierarchy to reconsider its plans. The projected mission to Nigeria was tabled, and that postponement was extended by the outbreak of the Nigerian civil war just over a year later. The church would not restart those efforts again until 1978, but the publicity surrounding these earliest attempts kept the complexities of the church's priesthood policy in the forefront of Mormon minds.[16] The subsequent sports-related protests would squarely set the issue in the public's mind, too.

The first few demonstrations against BYU seemed to be the isolated actions of a handful of players and their supporters. University officials at places like the University of Texas–El Paso and San Jose State College denounced those early scuffles and withdrew the offending athletes' scholarships. However, as the protests grew in numbers and frequency, by late 1969 university administrations began to make institutional concessions to the protesters, and some even severed their ties with Brigham Young University. It did not take that level of official censure to capture the attention of LDS Church authorities, however. They closely monitored even the earliest protests, rightly sensing that this current could eventually swell the tide of dissatisfaction against the priesthood prohibition into a national torrent.

It began in the spring of 1968, when eight members of the University of Texas–El Paso track team emphatically withdrew from a meet held at BYU in April. The track coach promptly dismissed the eight athletes, all black, from the team. One of those UTEP athletes was Robert Beamon, who only a few months later would set a world record in the long jump at the Mexico City Olympics. His abilities and those of his teammates notwithstanding, the reprisals against them were swift and decisive—and divisive.

Early reports of the athletes' withdrawal had them declaring that "Mormons teach that Negroes are descended from the devil."[17] President Ernest L. Wilkinson of BYU quickly released a statement to refute such a notion, and this early response outlined the points Wilkinson would repeatedly make in the months to come: "We are sorry to learn Negro athletes at the University of Texas at El Paso have threatened not to participate in our track meet. Their statement as to the belief of BYU as respects the Negro is based on erroneous information and is untrue. We do not discriminate because of race, and we have Negro students in our student body"—which was technically true, even though those students numbered only in the handfuls.[18]

Despite the provocative "descendants from the devil" misinformation, the focus of the UTEP incident, at least in the press, stayed mostly on UTEP officials. *Sports Illustrated* used the incident as part of a feature to highlight "the racist atmosphere at UTEP."[19] When asked about rescinding the athletes' scholarships, the school's president told *Sports Illustrated*, "I regret this very much. These are good boys. But they either collectively or individually hoodwinked themselves into the conviction that we wouldn't let them all go. A whole lot of pushing has been done by Negroes, and that pushing is going to hasten the day when your Negro comes close to equality. But I think in this case they paid a . . . price to win their point. . . . This is a price that no college athletes in this country have ever yet paid for a point on this issue. They were laying down their collegiate athletic lives, and they surely knew it." The track coach said, "I didn't kick them off; they quit." Perhaps the most controversial point in *Sports Illustrated*'s investigation into the UTEP situation was the purported use of a racial epithet by that school's athletic director as part of his assertion that the black athlete "is a little hungrier, and we have been blessed with some real outstanding ones."[20]

Behind the scenes, though, the dynamics that drove the UTEP protest created additional difficulties for BYU officials. Two weeks after the track meet, Ernest Wilkinson recorded in his diary that his monthly meeting with church apostles (who functioned as BYU's board of trustees) lasted two and a half hours, and it was "a very rough meeting."[21] He shared with the board two letters he had received. One came from UTEP's President Joseph M. Ray: "Without any suggestion at all of trying to run your business, I think your institution will be a thorn in the side of the Conference until such time as you recruit...a...Negro athlete. Until you do, all explanations that the charges are not true will not carry the ring of conviction."[22]

The recruiting situation was a complicated one. Before 1969, black students at BYU could try out for athletic teams—if they made the team, they were then given an athletic scholarship. A limited number of black athletes had joined BYU squads on that basis.[23] Coaches did not, however, actively pursue black athletes with scholarship offers.[24] Several factors played into this decision. Part of it, BYU officials explained, was sheer demographics: there were, they said, relatively few blacks in the Intermountain West, the region from which BYU drew most of its athletes, and even fewer in Provo. BYU officials worried about the morale of black students who might feel uncomfortably isolated in a racially homogeneous community like Provo—not an unreasonable concern, they asserted, considering that officials at other universities had expressed that this was indeed a challenge for their black athletes, and that without even the complicating awkwardness that would surely be part of these prospective athletes' campus lives at BYU because of the Mormon priesthood issue.[25] Apart from population makeup, though, concerns over the increased prospect of interracial marriage also made some Latter-day Saint general authorities hesitant about a change in BYU's recruiting practices.[26] Interracial marriage divided the American public in general in the late 1960s. In 1965, 48% of American adults surveyed by Gallup said that they "approved" of "state...laws making it *a crime* for a white person and a Negro to marry"; only 46% disapproved.[27] Mel Hamilton, a Wyoming player who would later join his teammates in a protest against BYU, originally lost his football scholarship two years earlier when his coach found out about Hamilton's plans to marry his white girlfriend. The coach later reinstated Hamilton's scholarship, but the episode was fraught with the tension created by cultural norms against interracial marriages.[28] Yet for believing Latter-day Saints at the time, there was an additional religious dynamic involved, since the priesthood prohibition also meant that marriages between blacks and whites could not be solemnized in the temple, and children from such marriages would not be eligible for priesthood ordination or temple attendance.

This recruiting issue figured into what Wilkinson reported was "the main controversy" discussed in the board meeting, one that "arose out of [another] letter I had received from the Denver Office of the Department of Health, Education, and Welfare, informing us that a team of five persons would be on our campus for three days to determine whether we are complying with the Civil Rights Act. This, in and of itself, did not disturb us, but we learned, unofficially, that we were the only university in this area to be visited in such a manner, and that the committee was 'out to get us.'" Even though Wilkinson told the board that "a complete [internal] survey of our institution...found that we are comply-ing in every respect with the Civil Rights Act," he was wary of the investiga-tors' visit, because "a committee which has made up its mind in advance without knowing the facts, will often not listen to the facts."[29] Officially, a representative from the Department of Health, Education, and Welfare told BYU legal repre-sentatives that "BYU...received one of the initial visits from HEW representa-tives...because of the low number of Negroes on the campus." However, one of these BYU representatives reported to President Wilkinson, "I personally feel...the special attention to BYU is being given because of the notoriety given to the Church doctrine related to the Negro holding the Priesthood. Therefore, this matter is one which requires most careful consideration with a broad per-spective not only of the BYU as an institution but of the possible steps being taken to embarrass the Church."[30]

Wilkinson came to that May 1 board meeting armed with recommendations, even in advance of the government committee's visit. The board gave unani-mous approval for a reiteration of the policy of nondiscrimination in the school's admissions process, a move that "[ratified] its prior decision that there shall be no discrimination at the University." The trustees also approved a statement dated April 30, 1968, to be distributed to local employers and "all recruitment sources" from the "BYU Placement Center": "This is to inform you that Brigham Young University is an Equal Employment Opportunity employer...without discrimination as to race, color or national origin. In view of the fact that BYU is maintained by the Church of Jesus Christ of Latter-day Saints, all employees are required to adhere to the standards of the said Church."[31]

With these measures, the school had, in fact, anticipated many of the requests that would come from the compliance officers of the Department of Health, Education, and Welfare. The investigative team asked the school to publicize its nondiscrimination policy in its next university catalog, as well as remind employers and landlords who advertised on campus that they too must comply with "equal opportunity" standards.[32] In a follow-up evaluation several months later, the investigators gave the school high marks for its "compliance with Title VI of the Civil Rights Act of 1964."[33]

This praise for BYU's increased emphasis on its nondiscrimination policies, did not, however, mute the critics of the school's athletic teams. UTEP President Ray's "thorn in the side of the conference" prediction was all too prescient. At the time, President Wilkinson wrote in his diary that "the implications of [Ray's] let-ter of course are that an effort would be made to get us out of the Conference."[34] Wilkinson guessed right.

The next serious flare-up came in the fall of 1968, in the days leading up to BYU's football game at San Jose State College. The situation there was compli-cated by a struggle within the San Jose State team over the BYU issue. When

San Jose's black players said they would not play BYU, reportedly "the white members of the [San Jose State] team urged the President to cancel the colored [*sic*] members' grants-in-aid, stating that if the President did not they would not go this week to play Arizona State."[35] This internal split showed again just how charged—and clouded—the national atmosphere surrounding racial issues was at the time. San Jose's coach did keep his team together, even though the team's "blacks were not talking to the whites" when they played Arizona State. The following week, when BYU came to San Jose State, only 2,800 fans (half of them BYU supporters) were in the stands. Black students and players boycotted the game and picketed the stadium, carrying signs that condemned alleged Mormon doctrines. Rumors about planned violence drew a large police force to the game, but the threats did not materialize into actual disturbances.[36]

LDS Church authorities saw these developments as troubling omens. And, though it would have dumbfounded their opponents, some church authorities saw the protests as unjustified because of BYU's stated non-discrimination policies, the realities of the student body's makeup notwithstanding. Church apostle Richard L. Evans met with President Wilkinson in September 1968 and expressed that he "was greatly concerned because of unjust criticism against our not having Negro players on our teams." BYU was about to announce the construction of a huge, 20,000-seat sports arena, but Evans "feared that the announcement...might intensify this criticism and that we might sometime find ourselves with[out] any Conference in which to play."[37] Wilkinson delayed signing a contract for the construction of the arena for over a year.[38] Then Hugh B. Brown, a member of the church's First Presidency, telephoned President Wilkinson on Thanksgiving Day, 1968, about "a call he had from San Jose concerning the game." A week earlier President Wilkinson had "spent a good deal of time" trying to "influence...San Jose [to] not [cancel] our game"; after the call from his church leader, Wilkinson spent the holiday afternoon making telephone calls to confirm that the game would go on as planned.[39]

Before the fall of 1969, and despite these student-led boycotts, most of BYU's Western Athletic Conference (WAC) institutional colleagues maintained a hard line against protesters. In March 1969, just a month after a hundred students "filed onto the playing floor" and "[asked] the crowd to boycott" the BYU–New Mexico basketball game, the University of New Mexico Athletic Council "warned athletes they would be subject to suspension for refusing to participate against BYU." A week later, "Dr. Milton Leech, acting president of University of Texas at El Paso, refused to call off a track meet with BYU." The conference commissioner, Wiles Hallock, "released a statement in which he said he supported the actions taken by member institutions to deal with disruptive tactics of protesting groups." At the same time, the conference "refused a request by University of Texas at El Paso students to investigate charges of racism at Brigham Young University."[40]

Beneath this surface of apparent institutional support, however, the ground was beginning to crumble. California State College at Hayward canceled a spring 1969 nonconference baseball game with BYU and Stanford University did the same with a scheduled tennis match, "because of alleged discrimination at BYU against minority groups." Stanford also "asked [BYU] to cancel" a basketball game scheduled for December 1970, but BYU officials "called attention to the contract and refused." The Riverside Baseball Tournament sent word in June 1969 to the BYU team that it "would not be invited" to return to the tournament in 1970 "because of racial unrest the visit might produce."[41]

By October 1969, WAC institutions began to hint at a change in their relationship with BYU. When student officers of the WAC schools met in October 1969, the contingent of students representing the University of Utah introduced a resolution that "all member schools ... are to take action to sever all relations" with BYU. The delegations of only two schools voted for the resolution, but it was symbolic of the growing pressure university presidents faced.[42] That pressure intensified dramatically after the most publicized BYU-related controversy so far took place in Laramie, Wyoming, in mid-October 1969.

Fourteen football players at the University of Wyoming asked Coach Lloyd Eaton if they could follow the lead of the San Jose State team and wear black armbands when they played BYU. While students at San Jose considered their school "heads and shoulders above other schools in the nation" for its progressive approach to student activism, Wyoming was an altogether different environment.[43] Coach Eaton was by all accounts a no-nonsense disciplinarian, and he had previously warned his team not to engage in any protest activities (over racial issues or the Vietnam War).[44] Thus when the fourteen black players approached the coach on the day before the game, each sporting the armband he hoped to wear the following day, Eaton dropped them from the team on the spot for even making such a request. Student and faculty groups expressed outrage at Coach Eaton's decision, but community groups vocally backed the coach— Wyoming fans even booed the expelled athletes (who watched the game from the bleachers) at the stadium the next day.[45] A firestorm had been kindled.

Only a week after the Wyoming game, BYU's President Wilkinson called the "hundreds of television and radio broadcasts and newspaper articles" about the players' expulsion "the worst publicity campaign against the BYU we have ever experienced."[46] Several aggravating factors seemed to figure into his assessment. BYU officials sensed a subtle but critical change in tactics surrounding the Wyoming protest, of which the players' black armband display was only a small part. The student organizers in Laramie had made explicit in a statement carried nationally on the UPI wire that they opposed the "'inhuman and racist' policies" of The Church of Jesus Christ of Latter-day Saints. Paul James, BYU broadcaster, expressed to the Executive Committee of BYU's Board of Trustees his observation that "until the Wyoming game most of the protests and demonstrations had been leveled against BYU, and only indirectly against the Church, although that was their ultimate target. [President Wilkinson's] statements as to non-discrimination at BYU...had largely answered their criticism. At the Wyoming game, however, the criticism was directed pointedly at the Church with BYU being only incidental." James presented to the committee "twenty-seven stories which appeared on the national wire services (AP and UPI)" over the course of just three days (October 20–22)—"all referred in one way or another to the 'racist policies' of BYU and/or the LDS Church."[47] Because of this, Wilkinson felt that the Wyoming protest was "the specific incident which...brought" the anti-BYU movement "into *national* attention," and linked that movement in a much more publicized way with something broader than merely the absence of black athletes at the Provo school.[48] The church's priesthood policy now began to dominate the conversation.

In addition, something about the reprisals against the Wyoming players in this case appeared especially harsh and excessive. The fourteen athletes had asked to wear armbands, not sit out the game. The coach's discipline and the community's disdain drew criticism nationwide to Wyoming and BYU officials alike. BYU observers rightly worried that as protesters and the press focused as much on the institutions that hosted BYU as they did on the Cougars themselves, conference unity could be dealt a fatal blow.[49]

Already the BYU administration noticed some disquieting signs of dissent among its sister schools. UTEP President Joseph Smiley "unofficially" passed word to one of BYU's deans that "BYU should resign from the conference," even though he added that he "had not made up his mind as to his official attitude."[50] The president of the University of Utah hinted to a BYU vice president that he, too, might "vote to oust BYU from the Conference" if others took that position.[51] Conference Commissioner Wiles Hallock told the *Denver Post* in late October 1969 that "the situation might lead to a split in the conference." While he "[rejected] absolutely these charges of racism" as "false," and publicly expressed optimism about surmounting the protests, in a private memorandum distributed to conference athletic directors, he warned that the "existence of the Conference, as presently constituted, may be threatened" if "Brigham Young University...by word or action" could not "relieve the pressure, if this be possible, on its fellow Conference members."[52] This was, as the commissioner told the Associated Press, "the whole problem of membership of BYU in the Conference."[53] In another newspaper interview, he stated simply, "I fear it is going to get worse before it gets better."[54]

Commissioner Hallock proved to be prophetic. The 1969 football season drew to a close, but BYU and its WAC competitors had still not weathered the worst of it. As the conference basketball season opened, BYU learned to expect picket lines and handmade signs at every stop. At the University of New Mexico, protesters threw eggs at the ROTC color guard during the National Anthem and then threw balloons filled with chemicals onto the court. An anti-BYU rally at the University of Arizona arena turned just as ugly when a furious crowd stormed the gym's chained doors but were rebuffed by a heavy police force. Even the school's student body president was arrested for his role in the fracas.[55]

This season of riots owned President Wilkinson's time and attention, but it is less clear how coverage of the protests affected public perception of BYU and Mormonism. The sheer complexity and variety of national attitudes about race, integration, student protests, and violence make precise answers elusive. In November 1969, one month after the "black 14" incident at Wyoming, the *New York Times* featured a front-page article that explored the surge in protests by black athletes. The article mentioned BYU in several paragraphs, but the thrust of the piece was a statement made by an athletic representative from Indiana University: "The whole country is going through something it has never gone through before." The *Times* documented "reports from 24 universities and colleges across the country [that] show that black militancy is stirring in such widely dispersed schools as" the University of Florida, Notre Dame University, the University of Texas, and the University of Wisconsin. None of the turmoil at those schools dealt with BYU. For example, "black basketball players [at Notre Dame] demanded—and received—a public apology" because the crowd "[booed] when there were five black players in the game against Michigan State." Resolution came after "all sides agreed that the booing was aimed at the quality of play, not the color of the players." Indiana's football coach, John Pont, "dismissed 10 of 14 black players from his team . . . when they boycotted practice two days in a row. They were dissatisfied with the way some black players were being treated." Several black football players at Wisconsin "boycotted the annual football banquet" because of the "attitudes of a varsity end coach, who was promptly dismissed." With this in mind, did anti-BYU activity simply blend into the larger national scene of widespread campus protests—and was the impact of the negative publicity against BYU thus blunted? In an ironic twist, some university officials saw black militancy as backfiring against the athletes. The same *New York Times* article quoted a *Detroit News* columnist who asserted that even though "nobody says publicly they are not recruiting as many blacks as they were," the fact was that "[coaches were] just not recruiting" black athletes as before, for fear of increased strain on their programs.[56]

Outside of the locker room, when it came to larger issues related to integration, poll results in 1970 also showed a persistent public opinion split: while 46% of respondents told surveyors that they favored an integrated society, still 44% of men and 41% of women answered that they would "rather [blacks] establish their own separate black society."[57] A majority of men and women nationwide felt "blacks in America are trying to move too fast."[58] Would an American public thus divided would also taken similarly divergent conclusions from media reports about the disputed degree of racism in BYU policies and practices?

Public opinion studies from the era also reveal that a large majority of Americans strongly disapproved of the protest mentality that swept so many college campuses, whether those protests took aim at the Vietnam War, racial inequality, or the authoritarian structures of society—66% of women and 63% of men told pollsters that they opposed the protesters' aims and goals; more than 80% of respondents opposed their tactics.[59] During the one-hour clean-up delay because of the pregame vandalism at the BYU–New Mexico basketball game mentioned earlier, for example, police scoured the crowd for culprits. Less-than-sympathetic fans, angry at the disturbance, readily pointed out the perpetrators. In an era in which President Nixon won the White House on a "law and order" campaign, many citizens saw these athletic protests as one more example of the excesses of the counterculture movement.[60]

Even media coverage of disproportionately violent police retaliation against demonstrators did not seem to sway public sympathy to their causes or means. In 1968, students opposed to the Vietnam War occupied campus buildings at Columbia. The number of journalists who reported on the police's harsh treatment of the protesters was, in one observer's opinion, just "enough to convince many Americans that universities were being taken over by revolutionaries."[61] Similarly, the notorious police brutality swirling around the 1968 Democratic Convention in Chicago—publicized everywhere in graphic TV footage—deeply troubled viewers nationwide, yet the majority "overwhelmingly, if inaccurately, blamed [the violence] on the protesters."[62] The prevalence of these anti-protest sentiments at least raises doubts about the breadth of support that student demonstrators might have won in their actions against BYU, especially if those who disapproved of student activism in general focused more on disruptive and violent students and less on the causes those students supported.[63] One Latter-day Saint educator who worked on the University of Washington campus in the late 1960s and early 1970s observed that even most students there had little concept of the reasons for the opposition toward BYU.[64]

Still, the thing that occupied the minds of BYU officials and their ecclesiastical superiors in late 1969 was the growing number of voices that tagged Mormons as racists. Latter-day Saint leaders worried that the potential for a reputation-related disaster was high. National opinion favored civil equality, and as the Mormon priesthood position came to be portrayed more frequently as an affront to that ideal, Latter-day Saint leaders sensed that this charge could quickly derail Mormonism's image, which up through the 1960s had been steadily improving.[65] President Wilkinson, in a report prepared for the LDS Church's leading elders, argued that "in the past two or three decades the people of the world have come to recognize that the LDS Church is an organization which promotes a highly respected way of life," but "if a 'racist' image gets planted effectively into the minds of people they will be far less inclined to wel-come us than they have been in the past."[66]

Wilkinson worried that the ripples that extended from the BYU epicenter could rock other Latter-day Saint organizations and programs as well. In his 1969 report, he explicitly recognized the collateral damage that the LDS Church's Institutes of Religion might suffer. These educational facilities for Mormon young adults stood adjacent to colleges nationwide, including colleges like San Jose State, Stanford, and the University of Washington—the very institutions at the eye of the protest maelstrom. Mormon students at these schools felt the tug of divided loyalties and the sting of criticisms from their classmates.[67] A group of Black Panthers even stormed the LDS Institute at the University of Washington. A confrontation was averted at the last moment when the group's leader ordered his companions back to their vehicles, since they were looking for "the Mormon Church," not "The Church of Jesus Christ of Latter-day Saints," as the sign on the front of the building read.[68] While this incident said something about persistent misunderstandings about Mormon identity and the actual name of the church, it also sent a grave warning that the anti-BYU demonstrations were bound to become a larger and persistent *church* concern, one that could affect missionar-ies and members across the country.

Mormons had good reason to be worried about the "racist" label. They also felt they had good reason to assert that such a label was unfair. Sociologist Armand Mauss concluded from several late-1960s opinion studies that "Mormons could not be considered outside the national consensus in their external civic atti-tudes toward African Americans."[69] It may have surprised outsiders to learn that far more Latter-day Saints favored whites and blacks worshipping in the same church than did respondents from other denominations.[70] In a compara-tive study of social and racial attitudes at Brigham Young University and Biola College ("a Protestant church-related university"), researchers determined that "Mormon ethnic attitudes" were *not* "at variance with ethnic attitudes in the 'general culture.'" In fact, their study suggested that "the Mormon subjects were more accepting of Negroes, American Indians, and Caucasians as compared to the Protestant sample" in terms of "formal social acceptance." The overwhelm-ing majority of Mormons surveyed stated that they would readily accept a change in the priesthood prohibition if the church's prophet were to announce such a change. The study implied that religious belief, not racism, drove most Mormons' opinions about the prospects of blacks being admitted to the priest-hood.[71] Still, it is not difficult to see why any suggestion about racial tolerance among Mormons would be overshadowed by the priesthood policy and the discomfort it caused, even if most Mormons genuinely felt what their leaders repeatedly expressed, that the priesthood policy was separate from civil rights matters and should not be construed as justification for racial discrimination.[72]

Mormon coaches working at other universities had no problem coaching black players. To *Sports Illustrated*'s William Reed, this meant that the Mormons-as-racists and even the BYU-as-racist protest rationales were "getting fuzzier all the time." His case in point: the basketball coach at the University of Arizona, the same coach who waited with his team as police kept rioters from breaking into the gym prior to that infamous BYU game in 1970, was a Mormon—a Mormon *bishop*, no less. Three of his five starting players were black, and all five wore black wristbands during the game. *Sports Illustrated* quoted several BYU players (some who were not LDS) who wanted their pro–civil rights sentiments made very clear. This same article also reviewed Utah State University's recent victory over BYU. Like Arizona, Utah State's squad was coached by a Latter-day Saint (LaDell Anderson), and his best players were black athletes Marv Roberts and Nate Williams.[73] Even the *Sports Illustrated* article's subtitle spoke to this: "Mormon policy is one thing, the views of BYU's team are another, and the differences are quite surprising."[74]

One implication in that subtitle, though, was troubling. As with stories about George Romney the candidate, many of the news pieces related to BYU athletics—and to the LDS position on the priesthood—consistently reinforced the impression that there was an *individual* versus *institutional* disconnect over race-related issues.[75] While the suggestion of such a disconnect might have reflected well on prominent Mormons who seemed more progressive than their church, it did not bode well for the institution's reputation. It was that worry that prompted President Wilkinson's lengthy memorandum to his church supervisors in late 1969, since "nationwide negative publicity which would brand us as a racist *institution*, could do irreparable damage to the Church's missionary effort."[76] He warned that "attacks on the Church relative to 'racial policies' will continue, and expand beyond the black community."[77]

Indeed, the severest publicity blows came not from student protesters but from university administrators and faculty. Stanford University President Kenneth Pitzer announced in November 1969 that his school was discontinuing future intercollegiate activities with BYU. The faculty senate at the University of Washington likewise voted to cancel its athletic contests with BYU, even though it meant forfeiting a bond worth several thousand dollars signed as part of the contractual agreement for a scheduled basketball game with the Cougars.[78]

These actions against BYU (and simultaneously against the LDS Church) gave the protests a new level of legitimacy. Accordingly, they also prompted a new level of aggressive response, especially from the BYU administration, with the support of its board of church apostles. President Wilkinson was not content to simply react to criticism. "We never win a publicity contest," he wrote, "by being on the defensive."[79]

. . . To Proactivity

As Ernest Wilkinson saw it, there were only a few options for the LDS Church and its university in late 1969. BYU could withdraw from the Western Athletic Conference, but that might be interpreted as an admission of guilt and intransigence over racial issues. If the school gave up athletics altogether, the church would lose the publicity and goodwill that a successful collegiate sports program generated. If BYU maintained the status quo, Wilkinson predicted that the other conference schools would themselves withdraw, one by one, from the conference and isolate BYU. To him, the best option was to "develop a statement of policy that our administration, faculty, athletic personnel and press relations staff may use in countering the charges of racism." He worried that "our story is being told—by our detractors, by those who are uninformed, by almost everyone except us. . . . In the past our lips have been largely sealed. We ask that our tongue be loosed," because "refusal" to "adequately answer negative charges . . . is usually interpreted, fairly or unfairly, as an admission of guilt."[80]

So urgent did President Wilkinson see this course of action that he did not wait for board approval before launching his first counteroffensive. Stanford's announcement about dropping BYU came in November 1969. Wilkinson wanted to issue a statement in response, and he wanted to "clear [the statement] with the Executive Committee" before he released it. However, "the Executive Committee could not meet" before the December holidays, but N. Eldon Tanner of the church's First Presidency "advised [Wilkinson] that under the circumstances [he] should use [his] best judgment as to the news release."[81] Wilkinson's "best judgment" prompted him to have Heber Wolsey, head of public relations for the school, hand deliver a strongly worded statement to "major newspapers and radio and TV stations in the San Francisco Bay area."[82] Other school representatives delivered the statement to broadcasters and editors in Los Angeles, New York City, and Philadelphia.

BYU's response to Stanford was anything but apologetic. Instead, it took President Pitzer to task for dropping BYU for alleged discriminatory practices when in fact BYU's "compliance with the Civil Rights Act [had] been certified by the Department of Health, Education, and Welfare." Stanford officials had stated that they would only schedule activities with institutions that agreed to "pledge that no person shall, on the basis of race, color, or national origin, be excluded from participation in, be denied the benefits of, or be subjected to discrimination in any activity officially sponsored by the institution." BYU countered that it fully agreed with the Stanford standard. If, therefore, Stanford could not reasonably have severed ties with BYU over discriminatory *practices*, the break must have been because of the religious *beliefs* of the LDS Church. BYU challenged this move, wondering if Stanford would eventually drop Notre Dame because of the Pope's teachings on "priesthood, or celibacy, or divorce, or birth control." Would Jewish schools be dropped because of Orthodox beliefs about Jews' "chosen people" status?[83]

The statement was received well both inside and outside LDS Church circles. "A number of the members of the [church's] Twelve [Apostles]... called [Wilkinson and his team] to congratulate" them.[84] BYU administrators received a "flurry of letters" that "deplored the action of Stanford's president" in severing ties with BYU—and "many of the letters were from non-Mormon Stanford alumni."[85] One such alumnus (and former Stanford athlete) sent a check for $5000 to BYU to show his disapproval of President Pitzer's decision.[86] Another Stanford graduate arranged a meeting with Stanford's Secretary of the Board of Trustees, and told President Wilkinson that several trustees were "indignant" and "all stirred up about Pitzer's manifesto."[87] Even the "superintendent of public instruction in California... came to BYU's defense" in the wake of the Stanford announcement and openly praised the stability and patriotism of BYU.[88]

The logic of BYU's complaint against the Stanford decision resonated on other campuses, and officials at a number of universities used similar arguments to defend BYU's autonomy and character when pressed to drop the school from their schedules. They challenged protesters with questions about freedom of religion and the appropriateness of politicizing athletics. When Nathaniel Russell, president of the Tucson branch of the NAACP, requested that President Richard A. Harvill of the University of Arizona cancel the upcoming Arizona-BYU basketball game, Harvill responded tersely that a public university should not evaluate religious beliefs.[89] Kenneth Baker, president of Seattle University, told his faculty in August 1970 that disassociating from BYU "because of the priesthood doctrine of the Mormon Church is itself discriminatory and contrary to the whole American tradition of freedom of religion."[90] The managing editor of *The Creightonian* (Creighton University) commended his university's decision to keep BYU on its basketball schedule, since "BYU itself does not discriminate against blacks."[91] William Reed of *Sports Illustrated* let his personal sentiments be known as he closed his report of the protest season. After quoting BYU athletic director Stan Watts—"I've always felt the field of competition is the wrong place to settle racial or religious issues"—Reed offered his own, "Amen, coach, amen."[92]

After the Stanford-inspired press release, BYU public relations officials launched a tour of other protest hot spots. University spokesman Heber Wolsey acknowledged that "it has never been our policy at BYU to retaliate against unfair accusations." However, the decision to reverse that general practice was made because "we believe that the public is entitled to know our policy as it actually is, and not as it is interpreted by those who may not have taken the time to study it."[93] This admitted course change in public outreach spoke to the seriousness of the perceived impact of these widespread censures.

Wolsey appeared on a call-in radio show in El Paso, Texas, during the height of the athletic protests controversy, even when local Mormons counseled him against tangling with the show's host, who had been notoriously hard on the church. Instead of attacking Wolsey, the host expressed appreciation for the spokesman's frank, head-on approach to the issues and invited him back for a follow-up interview so that more air time could be devoted to the positive aspects of the Mormon belief system.[94]

At a meeting in Wyoming after the "black 14" football incident, student organizers pressed Wolsey to bring a black Latter-day Saint for a planned question-and-answer session. He called Darius Gray, a black Mormon convert who worked for KSL television in Salt Lake City. The two shared the stage with three individuals representing the disgruntled students and faculty at the University of Wyoming and faced questions from an audience that numbered in the hundreds. Gray disarmed the crowd almost immediately when he noted, "Over there, where those other men are sitting, there's a pitcher of ice water and three glasses and over here, where Heber and I are sitting, there's nothing, nothing at all. That looks like a case of rank discrimination to me." He evoked even more laughter in an exchange with Willie Black, the PhD candidate who had initiated the Wyoming protests. When Black tried to ask a question of Wolsey and Gray, his microphone went dead. He tried a second time, but the microphone still would not work. Gray quipped, "Looks like the good Lord's not with you tonight, Willie"; Black's good-natured laughter at the jab "relaxed the whole audience," such that the local Mormon stake president, after the meeting, told Wolsey and Gray, "I wish the church would send you two to every stake in the church."[95]

Despite the initial skepticism of local LDS officials about receiving fair treatment from media and community leaders, Wolsey made them believers through his philosophy "to be as helpful and open and candid as we can be."[96] When the University of Washington stated its intention to drop BYU from its schedule, Wolsey met with "fifteen of the top black leaders of Seattle" to discuss the church's priesthood policy. He pushed for the meeting after an interview with the editor and publisher of a black newspaper in Seattle. Wolsey called the interview and the subsequent newspaper piece "probably the best interview I've ever had." However, the lunch meeting with the community leaders in Seattle left him feeling, as he described it, "totally whipped, beat to a pulp." "It was a vicious, mean, tough, rough meeting," he said, one defined by pointed questions about Mormon beliefs on racial equality. After it was over, one of the participants told Wolsey that "all [we] wanted to know was if this representative of the Mormon Church was a racist or not . . . [and we] found out you're not a racist." The editor in Seattle who had arranged for the luncheon likewise told Wolsey that the reason he had published negative articles about the LDS Church was "that's all I've ever heard about Mormons."[97]

When Wolsey returned from Seattle, he recommended that BYU "buy a full-page newspaper ad in all the newspapers up in the Northwest and just let people know who we are."[98] The school's board approved Wolsey's recommendation. The result was "Minorities, Civil Rights, and BYU," a "full-page statement in the leading papers in Washington and Oregon citing the official policy of BYU ... that students of any race, creed, color, or national origin were accepted for admission to Brigham Young University."[99] The ad was actually more of a "position paper," one that the school's public relations team crafted by combining a number of observations about BYU and Latter-day Saints in general.[100] The ad included the report from the investigative team of the Department of Health, Education, and Welfare that affirmed Brigham Young University's compliance with the Civil Rights Act of 1964, as well as the LDS First Presidency's 1963 pro–civil rights statement. It also quoted "a black minister in California," who said, "after several congregations of Mormons helped him build a church, ... 'I can't say enough good or praise for these Mormon people. They are the greatest people I have ever met in my travels.'"[101]

BYU administrators received a number of "telegrams and letters concerning" the ad. One writer said, "I am a Roman Catholic Mexican American. I want to take this opportunity to voice my approval of your full-page ad in the *Oregonian* of April 1. It has changed my thinking of the entire Mormon philosophy."[102] This was precisely the type of mind-set shift that BYU campaigners sought to cultivate.

What also quickly became obvious was that a visit to the school's campus was often the most effective remedy for misconceptions about the prevalence of racism among Latter-day Saints. BYU in this way became its own best advertisement, and the school welcomed visitors. The contrast between the apparent tranquility in Provo and the chaos at other campuses made an impression on reporters and readers alike, so many of whom held the opinion that colleges were descending into anarchy.[103] It is difficult to quantify the effect that these positive impressions about BYU students had on the public mind in countering vocal criticism about the priesthood ban, yet contemporary observers nevertheless asserted that this mollifying effect was real.[104]

For example, Hollis Bach, regional director of the federal Office for Civil Rights, concluded his 1969 report to BYU President Wilkinson with this tribute: "Since our visit to your campus last spring, we have visited a number of institutions of higher education. We think you might like to know that we still consider Brigham Young as being one of the very finest schools we have visited."[105] John Dart in the *Los Angeles Times* wrote an extensive piece about "a campus of peace and patriotism." He noted that "many non-Mormon conservatives in the country feel BYU ... has a fine reputation." It was "the campus' lack of protest demonstrations, beards, miniskirts, cigarettes or stimulants of any kind plus evidence of patriotism and reverence" that "brought glowing praise" for the school and its standards.[106]

Observers from the Association of College Unions International left Provo "convinced that the Church and BYU are sincere about their commitment to 'the Fatherhood of God and the Brotherhood of Man.'. . . The Team's visit to BYU and to Salt Lake City uncovered no evidence of racist practices."[107] University of Arizona administrators, who did not want a repeat of the January 1970 pre-game riot when the BYU football squad returned to Tucson in the fall, sent a fact-finding team to Provo in October 1970. The six-person committee included three student leaders (two of whom were black), two student athletes (both black), and a black faculty member. After they "visited with several university officials and, literally, hundreds of BYU students" over the course of three days, they reported that they "could find nothing to indicate that Brigham Young University is a racist institution or that there may be any more or less racism present than at any other school."[108] The impact of their published findings was almost immediate. Only nine months removed from the violent demonstration prior to the January basketball game, the *Tucson Daily Citizen* carried the head-line "Mood Changes Toward BYU." The contrast in the days leading up to the Arizona-BYU football game was noticeable, and in the newspaper's opinion, "the change in mood is a direct result of a fact-finding committee's visit to BYU cam-pus last week."[109]

The Tucson team reported to BYU officials that "many students of sister WAC schools perceive BYU students as being bigoted toward blacks," but that "mis-conception of image" could "be rectified," and should be, "as soon as possible." Perhaps unexpectedly, the group proposed that BYU actively recruit *more* black students and student-athletes. It seems telling that the black athletes on this investigative committee felt that BYU had an unwarranted "defeatist" attitude about recruiting African Americans. They did not feel that the priesthood restric-tion presented an insurmountable obstacle; their opinion was that BYU, with its facilities and programs, could "sell" itself by "[showing] it's got more to offer" than other Utah universities that had succeeded in attracting black recruits.[110]

President Wilkinson had been pressing for a similar change in recruiting phi-losophy. He reasoned that such a modification in policy would go a long way in demonstrating the sincerity of BYU's anti-discrimination guidelines, and that the benefits would outweigh any potential difficulties.[111] This was also the posi-tion taken by BYU's student newspaper as early as December 1968, when the *Daily Universe* reported that most BYU students wanted the school to recruit more black athletes.[112] The school did make such a change, a move that was as significant as any other in the early 1970s. By Wilkinson's own admission, the school's previous recruiting philosophy was not widely known. Yet by early 1970, BYU officials made it a point to tell reporters that the school's staff was actively recruiting black athletes, and the *Los Angeles Times* reported that the first such recruit, football player Ron Knight, had transferred to BYU from Northeastern Oklahoma A&M.[113]

The very presence of black athletes in BYU football, basketball, and track uniforms softened criticisms, and corresponded with other initiatives at the school.[114] University administrators invited prominent black Americans to address university assemblies. Leon H. Sullivan, pastor, author, and "founder of the Black Self-help Opportunity Centers, received a standing ovation from the student body" when he appealed for "brotherhood" among "Americans, white Americans, Asiatic Americans, Afro-Americans, all of us who are here."[115] Alex Haley, author of *Roots*, spoke at a university forum in 1972 (and was awarded an honorary degree by the school in 1977). Wynetta Martin, a black faculty member, joined the nursing school in 1970, and a graduate student from Nigeria, Oscar Udo, filled a teaching assistant role in the sociology department.[116]

As modest as they were, these visible changes to the racial makeup of the BYU campus signaled something important. Instead of dismissing the outspoken activism against the school's purported discriminatory practices, university officials took steps to offset those charges. In its larger context, LDS Church officials also showed a growing responsiveness to complaints about the church's racial policies.[117] Still, one conclusion in the Association of College Unions' committee report on its BYU visit seemed inescapable, and went beyond the recruiting of athletes or the hiring of university faculty: "the mere existence of the [LDS priesthood] doctrine must inevitably diminish the sense of worth and dignity of every black person whether or not he is or wishes to be a member of the Church of Jesus Christ of Latter-day Saints."[118] In the midst of the protest years and after, there were indications that, absent a change in the offending church policy itself, Mormon leaders made an increased effort to lessen that sting of offense, if possible. As new evidence of these developing Mormon attitudes and approaches garnered attention, protests and press coverage of the priesthood issue seemed to fade accordingly.[119]

One such initiative involved LDS Church periodicals. An important 1971 editorial in the church's monthly magazine, the *Ensign*, warned church members of the incompatibility of racial prejudice and Christian practice: "unity must be the goal of nationality and ethnic groups in the Church who consider themselves superior to some other group."[120] Other Mormon publications featured stories on church-sponsored outreach to neighbors in the black community. This coverage, intended primarily for a Latter-day Saint audience, seemed designed to heighten Latter-day Saints' social consciousness, to remind Mormon readers that the priesthood policy did not justify racial isolationism. For example, two *Church News* articles meant for dissemination to Latter-day Saints focused on church cooperation with black congregations of other faiths. The first article from June 1970 was titled, instructively, "Bonds of Brotherhood." It told the story of Reverend M. A. Givens Jr., of Deliverance Temple, Church of God in

Christ, and his request for assistance in raising funds to complete construction of his congregation's building in Salt Lake City. The article recounted how "the [general authority–level] Presiding Bishopric accepted the opportunity as a challenge to the Mormon youth to raise at least $30,000 for the building." All told, "28,000 [Mormon] young men and women participated in the project" and raised funds well over the initial goal. The article quoted "Rev. J. R. Jennings, Fresno, Calif., one of the founders of the Church of God in Christ," who called "the project '. . . the thrill of my life. This is such an outstanding and unique demonstration of Christianity.' He told the group, 'You are some of the most wonderful and outstanding people I know of in the world.'"[121]

The second article, "Toward Understanding," detailed the experiences of Mormon leaders in Merced, California, who "rallied . . . members to match contributions and hours to rebuild New Hope Baptist Church, a small Negro congregation." The leader of the Baptist church, "Rev. Blackman, in expressing his feelings for the time, money, and work contributed by the 'Mormons,' said, 'I can't say enough good or praise for these Mormon people. . . . My own father couldn't have been better to me than these people have been in helping us complete our building. I believe the Lord sent them here,' he said."[122]

Some observers must have seen these reports as self-congratulatory or patronizing or promotional. Yet church leaders also focused more privately on the situation of black Mormons, a group facing special hardships in all of this. A lesser known but important development took place in 1971. Three young black men, including Darius Gray, met and decided to petition the church hierarchy for an official program specifically designed to address the needs and concerns of the estimated two hundred or so black Mormons in the Salt Lake area.[123] The "Genesis Group" was the result. Three apostles organized the group, and Genesis received frequent visits from church general authorities—unmistakable indications of the importance that authorities accorded the new association.[124] The group met weekly for fellowship and activities; group members continued to attend their respective regular congregational meetings (wards) for church sacraments. Reminiscences by the group's earliest members suggest that church leaders did not want Genesis to be construed as a publicity stunt; in fact, church leaders counseled group members to "avoid media attention," since "this is not a tourist attraction."[125] Still, national media noted the church's move favorably as a "[sign] of responding to criticism of its anti-Negro theology."[126] This seemed only another instance where public concerns generated new awareness among the Latter-day Saint leadership.

Mormon leaders also took steps to explain the priesthood prohibition to outsiders. In 1972, the leadership of the Disciples of Christ canceled plans to hold its 1975 national meeting in Salt Lake City. The denomination had changed its convention plans to show opposition to the LDS Church's priesthood policy. Heber Wolsey (now an employee with the LDS Public Communications

Department) and Darius Gray reprised the roles they played in Wyoming three years earlier. LDS officials dispatched the two to Indianapolis, where for two days the Mormon emissaries met with the Disciples' leading officials and fielded questions about Latter-day Saints' beliefs and practices. Darius Gray must have surprised not a few of the assembled leaders when he told them, "There is no conflict between the color of my skin and my religion."[127] When asked directly about the oft-noted success of LDS missionary efforts, Gray answered, "From a personal standpoint....I...sought the Lord in prayer and I did indeed receive a firm answer and I've been a Latter-day Saint for seven years."[128]

A follow-up letter from the Disciples' president spoke to the effect of the visit: "[The] visit was a spiritual blessing to all of us who shared in the conversations....We certainly have a better understanding of the position of the Church of Jesus Christ of Latter-day Saints....We understand that the doctrine of your church with respect to the exclusion of blacks, women, and children from the priesthood rests not upon any human judgment of inferiority but upon a divine purpose as communicated to your First President, Joseph Smith. We were heartened by your statement that this doctrine might be changed by divine revelation if the purpose for which God first revealed it has been fulfilled."[129]

As the meeting between the two delegations concluded, the Disciples were "apologetic" about misunderstanding Mormon doctrine; Wolsey's sense was that they would not have canceled the Salt Lake City convention if they would have had accurate information before making a decision.[130] This seemed to him to be another endorsement for proactive public relations.

Darl Andersen, a Mormon in Arizona, took that same tack when he organized the Mesa Interfaith Communications' monthly breakfasts.[131] In 1972, Andersen arranged for the group to tour church facilities in Salt Lake and BYU campus facilities in Provo. Larry Norris, a pastor at Velda Rose United Methodist Church in Mesa, later admitted in a letter to Andersen that he "had grown up with a set of myths concerning the Mormon Church," since he had "lived in the eastern part of the country most of [his] life" and had "little exposure to LDS beliefs." One such "misconception...was that the LDS Church was prejudiced and racist against black people." However, "after interacting with LDS people from Brigham Young University and...in Mesa, Arizona," Pastor Norris wrote that he "[detected] absolutely no personal feelings from LDS people of prejudice or racism against the black people. In fact," he observed, "they seem to ascribe to the black brethren, as well as all people, a profound human dignity and worth, capable of unlimited human growth." Norris admitted that he still did "not understand why the black man cannot hold the Priesthood in the Mormon Church," but he also gathered that "the Mormons do not really know why, either." The explanation Norris took away from his Utah trip was expressed through his analogy of a wise father asking his young children to do something that the children did not yet understand. The Arizona pastor "did not accept the LDS Church philosophy at this point—but not because I think it is racist or prejudiced. It is because I operate by another set of beliefs that I believe are more in according with my background and personality. After associating with LDS people, I think it is a miscarriage of justice to label them as racist or prejudiced." He recommended "a serious re-examination of Mormon theology and social action" to those who "[believed] the LDS Church beliefs and doctrines are prejudiced and racist."[132]

These Mormon efforts were not the only factor at work in tempering the antagonism aimed at BYU and the LDS Church over racial inequities.[133] Public opinion polls suggest that student protests on the whole were falling out of favor, even among activists, in the early seventies.[134] The Harris Survey in 1970 found that less than half of the nation's college students felt "there should continue to be demonstrations and protests"; just as many (47%) felt that the "usefulness" of demonstrations was "over and other means of bringing about change can be more effective."[135] Also in 1970, when nationwide blacks were polled about the best ways to "make real progress," there was decided ambivalence about "taking to the streets in protest" and "supporting militant leaders": 40% supported those actions, 40% opposed those actions, and 20% were "not sure."[136]

Other attitudinal indicators suggest that racial issues in general occupied a place of diminishing importance in the public mind as the decade progressed, as what looked like national "success" in achieving civil rights benchmarks appeared increasingly self-evident. By 1973, only 7% of nationwide respondents mentioned "race" and "discrimination" when asked about the "biggest problems facing the country."[137]

This is not to say that media references to the church's priesthood position disappeared after the rash of anti-BYU protests subsided early in the 1970s, but only that they diminished noticeably in frequency and volume.[138] In 1974, for example, the NAACP brought a lawsuit against the Boy Scouts of America for alleged discriminatory practices in the way youth leadership positions were filled by LDS-affiliated scout troops. The practice among Mormons had been to appoint the congregation's deacons quorum president (a priesthood leadership position for twelve- and thirteen-year-old boys) as the troop's senior patrol leader. The controversy arose when black Mormon young men were passed over for senior patrol leader spots because they could not hold priesthood leadership appointments.[139] Latter-day Saint leaders quickly issued instructions to discontinue that practice and make all scouts eligible for patrol leadership. The concession did not appease the NAACP, and the association made plans to continue the suit—even issuing subpoenas to the church's current prophet Spencer W. Kimball.

Yet the end of this episode again seems indicative of the receding interest that the issue held for reporters and readers—a three-paragraph blurb tucked inside the *New York Times* announced that the Boy Scouts' lawyer had asked that the suit be dismissed, and little more came of it.[140] In that same year (1974), *Time*'s coverage of the opening of the church's Washington, D.C., Temple relegated the priesthood issue to a footnote, and *Newsweek*'s announcement of the selection of new church President Spencer W. Kimball did not mention the issue at all.[141]

"Without Regard for Race or Color": 1978

Ironically, it would be President Kimball who would issue the revelation that ended the priesthood prohibition, four years into his tenure as the church's prophet.[142] Several things about the timing of the announced revelation seemed surprising. Sociologist Armand Mauss observed that "when the church finally dropped its traditional racial restrictions in 1978, there had been no significant outside pressure to do so for several years."[143] Darius Gray remembered that the announcement "was something totally unexpected. It did not come as a result of political pressure, because there was none in 1978."[144]

Also, when Spencer Kimball took the church's helm shortly after President Harold B. Lee's death, he was beloved throughout Mormondom for his compassionate service, yet few expected many innovations from the administration of an aging, conservative Mormon descended from church pioneers. His predecessor had died unexpectedly in December 1973. Lee was younger than Kimball, the apostle who was in line to succeed him, and Lee's rapid decline in health surprised everyone. President Lee had been a principal force behind the church's welfare plan in the 1930s and the centralized administrative program of "priesthood correlation" in the 1960s. His influence on Mormonism was not lost on a wider public; *Time* called him the "longtime guiding administrative genius of the church."[145] Everyone expected Lee to be the one to introduce revolutionary changes, not the seventy-eight-year-old Kimball. This sentiment came from both without *and* within the Mormon community. *Time* mused that "the new president is not likely to change Mormon views on the family or race."[146] The editor of the *Deseret News*, William Smart, surmised that Kimball's "presidency seemed likely to be pretty much a caretaker administration." Even Boyd K. Packer, another apostle, "assumed that the era of innovation instituted by President Lee had ended and that a new era of consolidation and refinement had arrived. He later admitted wryly, 'I've never been so wrong.'"[147] The 1978 revelation that changed the priesthood policy was an emphatic indication that the prognosticators were mistaken.[148]

Although attention and outrage over the prohibition had long since waned, the announcement of the policy change instantly drew the public eye back to Salt Lake City.[149] Not only did June 9, 1978, become an "I remember where I was when I heard the news" moment for Mormons worldwide, but "*Time* and *Newsweek* magazines stopped the presses on their weekend editions to get stories in, and the news made the front page of the *New York Times*." [150] Even President Jimmy Carter publicly hailed the decision.[151]

As dramatic as the news was, the vehicle of its transmission from the church was not. The change was announced via a simple one-page statement that mentioned nothing about racism or protests or even blacks themselves. The church's new position was that "by revelation [the Lord] has confirmed that the long-promised day has come when every faithful, worthy man in the church may receive the holy priesthood...without regard for race or color."[152] When pressed, church spokesmen were instructed to reply that the announcement spoke for itself.

Professor Sterling McMurrin of the University of Utah called it "the most important day for the church in this century," and the ramifications of the change were felt almost immediately.[153] Two days after the announcement, Joseph Freeman was reported to be the first black man ordained an "elder" in the church. He and his wife were "sealed"—ceremonially married for eternity— in the Salt Lake Temple only days later.[154] Within five months, LDS missionaries arrived in Nigeria to organize officially the congregations of believers who had waited more than a decade for that day, and new missionary horizons opened in places like the Dominican Republic, Puerto Rico, and Brazil, as well as in many neighborhoods in the United States (Figure 3.2).

Figure 3.2. When LDS missionaries arrived in Nigeria in the months following the 1978 revelation that extended priesthood ordination to men of African descent, they found hundreds of would-be converts anxiously waiting, as this line of baptismal candidates attests. Photograph by Janath Cannon. Copyright Intellectual Property, Inc. Reprinted with the permission of The Church of Jesus Christ of Latter-day Saints.

Yet as important as this change would prove to be for worldwide Mormonism, and as intense as the criticism of the church's policy had been earlier in the decade, when the long-awaited revelation was announced, the media spotlight that shone on Salt Lake proved to be bright, but brief. Essentially, by the end of the summer of 1978, its shine was directed to other Mormon-related actors and dramas. The announcement was for all intents and purposes the extent of the story. The revelation did not spawn renewed and widespread scrutiny of Mormonism's race-related issues. Instead, most of the reports took a congratulatory if reproving, "it's-about-time" tone.[155] The general sense in related news articles was that the Mormon hierarchy had finally come to grips with the modern ideal of racial equality, an ideal that most rank-and-file Latter-day Saints were already prepared to embrace.[156]

What the 1978 revelation *did* spawn was speculation. There was speculation that the church's rapid growth would only increase exponentially now that the final barrier to "respectability" had been removed.[157] More pertinent at the time, coming as the revelation did in the middle of the national debate over the Equal Rights Amendment, there was also speculation that perhaps a similar sea change might affect the status of women in the church.[158] Therefore, as historic as the 1978 revelation was, hindsight offers perspective as to why it was overshadowed in contemporary coverage of Mormonism: by 1978, national conversations were less about race and more about gender—and those conversations raised the issue of Mormon influence in larger debates about the role of women and families in society. Already by the mid-1970s—before the momentous priesthood change—Wendell Ashton, from his position at the head of the church's Public Communications Department, felt that the issue of equality for women was overshadowing the church's priesthood policy when it came to reporters' interests.[159]

Yet earlier in the decade, when the protests against BYU sports *had* repeatedly thrust accusations of discrimination into the limelight, Mormon public relations officials showed that they were not satisfied with damage control alone, even as the harshest condemnations dwindled away. What Latter-day Saint publicists began to look for was a campaign that could divert the public's focus from the negative publicity of protests to the positive aspects of Mormon theology. An emphasis on "eternal families" seemed just such a campaign.

4

The Politics of Family Values: 1972–1981

The outside pressure of student protests and official censures by universities and civic and religious bodies in the early 1970s did not force a change in the LDS Church's priesthood policy. What that outside pressure did prompt, though, was an intensification of the church's public relations efforts. There was a sense that to rehabilitate the Mormon image, so pocked by the anti-BYU demonstrations, public attention needed to be refocused on core Mormon tenets other than the priesthood ordination policy. Preeminent among those tenets was the centrality of the family and the Latter-day Saint belief in family relationships that would endure even in the afterlife. This new proactive posture resulted in an expanded and vigorous publicity campaign in the 1970s, with "family" as that campaign's touchstone message.

Just as the LDS Church became an outspoken champion for traditional families, however, political trends in the 1970s seemed to threaten the very family model that Latter-day Saints preached. From the church's perspective, the decade's most serious threat came from the Equal Rights Amendment. Church leaders decided to oppose ratification of the amendment and encouraged church members to do the same. The level of their political involvement was unprecedented and surprisingly effective, and this drew sharp criticism from the amendment's supporters, some of whom were Mormons distressed at their church's intrusion in the nation's political life. Yet for Latter-day Saint officials, the decision to speak out against the ERA was part and parcel with their pro-family agenda. It was an identity they sought to cultivate.

Obscurity, Not Opposition, Is the Problem

By 1972, Latter-day Saints had faced a half-dozen years of unprecedented media attention. In rapid succession, reporters had zeroed in on George Romney, the death of President David McKay, and the protests directed at BYU—yet a church survey showed that many Americans still did not know enough about the LDS Church to have an opinion about Mormons. Church officials conscientiously went about trying to change that. [1]

Fifteen years had passed since the Church Information Service opened shop in a small office with employees essentially on loan from a Salt Lake advertising agency. The Information Service was initially charged with answering press inquiries and publicizing Mormon Tabernacle Choir tours. Throughout the 1960s, forward-thinking employees had pushed for more responsibilities and opportunities to spread information about Mormonism through media contacts and public expositions. The New York World's Fair convinced church leaders of the potential of localized outreach, of visitors' centers, and of multimedia operations on a grander scale of production. [2] These potentialities came to organizational fruition in 1972 when the Church Information Service was replaced by the Public Communications Department. [3]

This structural change was more than merely a departmental renaming. Lorry Rytting worked for the Church Information Service in the 1960s, and then returned to the Public Communications Department in 1974, after a few years away to complete graduate work. What he found in the new department was "a very progressive, supportive attitude on the part of the Church" that resulted in "a solid professional staff at headquarters." Rytting agreed with another church employee who saw this "significant shift in emphasis" as "[going] from the idea that we don't, in effect, want media publicity to the idea that we'll hire the best people we can possibly hire to help us with the public relations program." [4] While the restructured department certainly built on what had happened before, there was a palpable sense of "newness" in 1972. This was a top-down impulse that began literally at the top of Mormondom. New LDS Church President Harold B. Lee (installed in July of 1972) had, as an apostle, been the driving force behind the administrative changes in the "correlation" program of the 1960s, and "professionalization" had been one of that movement's themes. [5]

While "correlation" quickly and permanently secured its spot in Mormon vocabulary, the movement, as gradual and internal as it was, did not generate headline news. Still, it would be difficult to overstate the significance of this administrative reconfiguration's effect on the shape and look of modern Mormonism. [6] The new demographics of the post–World War II church meant that the inefficiency and duplicate efforts of the various arms of church administration could no longer be ignored. In 1960, President McKay authorized then-church apostle Lee to head a committee charged with reducing and combining the quickly multiplying curriculum manuals. In the end, however, Elder Lee's committee recommended sweeping changes at church headquarters that extended well beyond curriculum and amounted to an administrative overhaul. Over the course of the 1960s, church auxiliaries were placed under the direction of the Quorum of the

Twelve Apostles (with the apostles reporting to the governing First Presidency). The decision to bring all church activities and entities under one hierarchical umbrella proved to have far-reaching consequences. It would eventually mean that on any given Sunday, in any given location, Mormons would all be learning from the same church-produced materials. They would read the same articles and see the same graphics in their magazines.[7] Church architecture would eventually reflect this correlation trend as well, as uniform construction plans gave all new Mormon buildings a recognizably similar appearance.[8] These changes together afforded leaders a high degree of control in terms of the official messages and images disseminated among church members. This movement in turn worked to reinforce impressions of a Mormon cultural homogeneity that, as shall be seen, often recurred in media coverage of Mormons.[9]

Increased centralization of policy making and publications also required an increased number of professional employees to conduct the church's day-to-day business.[10] This burgeoning bureaucracy of accountants and editors and distribution coordinators outgrew church administrative facilities so rapidly in the late 1960s that a new Salt Lake City high-rise headquarters was announced. This twenty–eight–story office building eventually opened in 1972, designed to accommodate over two thousand church workers. The main tower was flanked by two shorter annexes that carried on their façades giant reliefs of the globe, symbolic of the worldwide oversight centered in that headquarters complex.[11]

In that same administrative vein, President Lee gave two clear signals that showed he took a keen interest in the "professionalism" of the new Public Communications Department.[12] First, he "initiated a search for someone to head up" the revamped public relations department, a department that he "envisioned" as a "kind of marketing program."[13] His search led him to former newspaperman and advertising executive Wendell Ashton. Next, Lee instructed Ashton that his department was to report directly to the First Presidency of the church, bypassing any intermediary level of hierarchical supervision. Ashton jumped into his managing director role with gusto—and he drafted BYU public relations officer Heber Wolsey to serve as his chief assistant. The two proved to be a potent combination in responding to the vision of their president.

Lee told Ashton that he "wanted to broaden the program worldwide." Ashton took this directive to heart and created a network of local volunteers who trained as public communications specialists. This network numbered over 1,200 by 1978. President Lee also asked Ashton to be involved in "the creation of exhibits for visitors centers." One of the new department's first major initiatives involved a massive public open house that preceded the dedication of the church's Washington, D.C., Temple in 1974 (Figure 4.1). Finally, President Lee challenged Ashton's department to "get creatively into television and even perhaps into motion pictures." Because Heber Wolsey's graduate training and professional experience had been in radio and television broadcasting, Ashton's

Figure 4.1. LDS Church President Spencer W. Kimball and his wife Camilla greet First Lady Betty Ford at the open house of the church's newly constructed Washington, D.C., temple in 1974. Over 750,000 visitors toured the temple before it was dedicated for religious rites. The temple tour spoke to visitors about the LDS Church's belief in eternal family ties, as well as its growing presence in the eastern United States. Photo courtesy of The Church of Jesus Christ of Latter-day Saints.

lieutenant was ideally suited to take up that charge. "The whole thrust of our department," Ashton remembered, "was to take the initiative and not wait to respond to people seeking information."[14]

One of Ashton and Wolsey's first decisions was to invite a frank evaluation of the current state of Mormonism's public image. They commissioned an outside research firm to conduct a study of religious attitudes and opinions in six urban areas: Seattle, Los Angeles, Kansas City, Dallas, Chicago, and New York City. The results of this August 1973 survey quantified and confirmed what Mormon leaders had already suspected: in the words of church apostle Boyd K. Packer, "obscurity" rather than "opposition" was the problem.[15]

If coverage of George Romney's campaign had taught interested Latter-day Saint observers anything, it was that membership in the Mormon Church inspired very little public consternation, apart from questions from some quarters about outdated racial attitudes. When the press painted a portrait of a Mormon subject, what resulted most often was a depiction of traditional values—patriotism, frugality, honesty, and moral rectitude. Admirable though these qualities were, they made Mormons out to be, as historians Chiung Hwang Chen and Ethan Yorgason put it, "a model minority," respected but still alien.[16]

That model minority status was reflected in the 1973 survey. Respondents were asked what descriptors came to mind when Mormonism was mentioned. Three of the top five free responses were "closely united," "help one another/welfare program," and "good people, hard workers, industrious." At the same time, only 3% of those surveyed mentioned Mormonism when asked "which one religion, not counting your own, do you think you would feel most comfortable with?" That compared with 21% who answered "Presbyterian," 15% "Southern Baptist," 12% "Lutheran," 9% "Roman Catholic" and "Episcopalian," 8% "Unitarian," and 4% "Jewish." Survey analysts took particular note of the fact that, in the 18- to 35-year-old age group, three times as many respondents stated that they would feel more comfortable "being a Jew than a Mormon." It seemed apparent in this study that many Americans did not see Mormonism as belonging to the family of Judeo-Christian faiths.

By far the most common response to the question about general impressions of Mormons was "I don't know." Even with recent media attention of the late 1960s and early 1970s, 36% of those surveyed evidently were not familiar enough with the LDS Church and its members to venture any opinion. Even with the increasing notoriety and publicity surrounding Mormon missionary enthusiasm, 60% of respondents could remember a visit from Jehovah's Witnesses, but only 16% recalled visits from Mormons. Two out of five people remembered reading literature from the Jehovah's Witnesses, but only half as many could remember reading LDS literature.

In digesting these results, researchers concluded that the survey reflected a general ignorance of LDS beliefs. And when people *did* think of Mormonism, they thought of a strict religion that expected much from its members. Public attention and opinion focused on Mormon *lifestyle*, on what Mormonism expected of its adherents, rather than what it gave them.

Sociologist Thomas O'Dea wrote in 1971 that Mormonism's modern relevance hinged on several key questions: Is Mormonism a defense mechanism for converts who want to resort to anachronistic values in a modernizing world? Or does it offer humanity a deeper understanding of the divine-human relationship?[17] If this 1973 survey suggested to LDS public relations officials that Americans generally perceived Mormonism as a bulwark of conservative values, church leaders wanted to emphasize instead what Mormonism offered along the lines of O'Dea's second proposition. In their view, what Mormonism preached was a gospel that centered on the salvation of families. The church's Public Communications Department staff consciously went about broadcasting that gospel, quite literally. In the 1970s, Mormons keyed on new media techniques to reshape public perception and cement the link between "families" and "Mormons."[18] As Wendell Ashton put it, "When [LDS] missionaries knock on doors, we want people to immediately think, 'Oh yes, the Mormons. They're the ones who have family unity."[19]

Family: Isn't It About Air Time?

LDS Church leaders were no strangers to the power of electronic media; in fact, the church had already been, for years, a significant proprietor of television and radio stations.[20] Now they latched onto a new possibility in the 1970s. Mormon public relations officials realized that because the Federal Communications Commission urged broadcasters to donate time for free public service announcements (and tracked that donated time as well), there was an opening for quality commercials that met such a need. Public Communications employees therefore devised a new series of thirty- or sixty-second spots they called *Homefront* [21]

The first few of these commercials were, even in church broadcasters' opinions, "rank amateur."[22] However, by the second year (1973), the decision was made to spend more on production. Writers in Utah created the spots, which were then produced by industry professionals in Southern California. While this was a more expensive process, the investment in favor of quality paid off for the church. The short commercials were distributed by church-owned Bonneville International and they quickly became favorites of TV and radio station operators seeking to fill their government-mandated community service air time.[23]

The simplicity and humor of the commercials made them memorable. A father would be sitting in an easy chair reading a newspaper when an off-air narrator asked the man, "Remember last week when you said next week you were going to spend more time with your children? It's next week."[24] Or a businessman at a boardroom table would be closing a meeting when the speakerphone on the table came alive with his daughter's voice, who insistently told her father that she loved him, and then waited for his response, much to the enjoyment of his coworkers. A narrator then concluded, "If you love them, tell them."[25]

By 1976, four years after the *Homefront* debut, church public relations officials estimated that these commercials had received "31 million dollars' worth of free radio and television time."[26] They played on 95% of the nation's television stations and 50% of radio stations. The spots won national awards in their second year of airtime.[27] They dealt with themes such as parent-teenager communication, genealogy, conflict resolution, avoiding divorce—always with the closing tag line: "a message from The Church of Jesus Christ of Latter-day Saints—the Mormons" (Figure 4.2). Perhaps no other media initiative did more to link Mormonism with family values. Historian Richard Bushman called the commercials "a work of genius," a good-will campaign that "got [Mormons] farther than any other campaign." Stephen Allen, who began his church employment in the Public Communications Department and later became director of

A public service message produced for

THE CHURCH of
JESUS CHRIST
of LATTER-DAY
SAINTS

by Bonneville Productions
130 Social Hall Avenue—Salt Lake City, Utah

© 1979 The Church of Jesus Christ of Latter-day Saints
50 East North Temple—Salt Lake City, Utah 84150

Getting the bugs
out of your
MARRIAGE

(A list of known symptoms and secret
cures from the Divorce Bug himself)

Figure 4.2. "The Divorce Bug" was one of the LDS Church's family-first public service messages as part of the hugely successful *Homefront* media campaign. The radio and television spots began airing in the 1970s. Photo courtesy of The Church of Jesus Christ of Latter-day Saints.

the church's Missionary Department, noted that when "surveys were conducted in those early years, asking people 'When you hear the word 'Mormon' what comes to mind?' people would say: 'Well, I think of polygamy; I think of racist; the Osmonds; the Mormon Tabernacle choir.' Those were probably the four top answers. After *Homefront* had been on the air for some number of years, as we'd ask that question again, the number one answer was: family. 'You're the Church that believes in families.'"[28]

The public response to *Homefront* prompted Ashton and Wolsey's team to expand its family focus into a longer, paid-programming endeavor. The result was an hour-long production that the church aired in December 1976 in the "54 top markets of the country."[29] The show featured recognizable television personalities from the era, some Mormon, like the wildly popular Osmonds, and some not, like Ruth Buzzi (famous for her run on *Laugh In*), Bill Bixby (*The Incredible Hulk*), Melissa Sue Anderson ("Mary" on *Little House on the Prairie*), and Gary Burghoff ("Radar" on *MASH*). Interspersed throughout the program were "commercials inviting people to phone in for a free booklet describing [the church's] family home evening program and giving hints on how to communicate with children."[30] This offer of a direct order telephone line for free literature was an innovation that quickly came to characterize LDS media outreach. This first attempt at such outreach generated a substantial reaction. Over 90,000 viewers contacted church volunteers in response to the offered materials. Significantly, some "ministers of other faiths" requested "hundreds of copies" to "distribute the booklets to their congregations." [31]

The Public Communications office organized another kind of direct contact in connection with *The Family...and Other Living Things* broadcast. Church members living in the regional markets where the program would be aired were encouraged to invite friends and neighbors into their homes to view the program and then talk about the church's Monday-night "Family Home Evening" program. In the 1950s, church President McKay had inspired an initial grass-roots mentality with his "every member a missionary" slogan; Wendell Ashton's group likewise encouraged every member to join in this publicity effort and distributed "referral cards" to advertise and promote the televised special.[32]

This involvement of local members was in keeping with Ashton's expansion of volunteer church public communications specialists. As early as 1967, the Church Information Service had published a handbook entitled, "How to organize a public relations program in stakes and missions: The Church of Jesus Christ of Latter-day Saints." The idea was that each stake-level (diocese) ecclesiastical unit of the church would designate a public communications representative. During Ashton's watch, by 1976, the number of those stake and mission regional public communications workers surpassed one thousand.[33] Based on the handbooks distributed to these volunteers (a revised edition was published in 1973, after the transition from the Church Information Service to the Public Communications Department), these local specialists were to be publicity agents first. The handbook suggested multiple strategies in seeking out local opinion makers, supplying them with press kits, and submitting ideas for news stories to regional media outlets. Clearly, and in line with the 1973 religious attitudes survey commissioned by the church, this approach was one more piece of evidence that LDS leaders felt obscurity was the principal obstacle to favorable impressions about the church. The local public relations volunteers were charged with proactively combating *mis*information about the church by focusing first on the lack of information generally about Mormonism.[34]

Church leaders also saw in the nation's bicentennial celebrations in 1976 an opportunity to highlight Mormon patriotism. More than two years before, a churchwide committee was appointed to spearhead Latter-day Saint participation. The emphasis again was local. Church members were encouraged to enter floats in community parades, offer musical groups and speakers for community presentation, and, most important, provide volunteers for community service projects. These efforts generated the hoped-for attention.

By the fall of 1976, church headquarters had collected over one thousand newspaper articles that documented Mormon bicentennial activities. Particular recognition went to church service groups. Initially, the church's bicentennial committee had asked that each member contribute one full day (twenty-four hours) of community service sometime during the 1976 calendar year. That proposed benchmark set the churchwide goal at three million donated service hours during the year. However, already by the fall of 1976, the total donated labor throughout the nation was more than double that.[35]

The 1976 celebrations also gave the singers of the Mormon Tabernacle Choir, those most recognizable Latter-day Saint ambassadors, another chance to perform on a national stage. The choir sang for President Gerald Ford at a July 3 event at the John F. Kennedy Center for the Performing Arts. Seated next to the U.S. President was church president Spencer W. Kimball. The choir shared that evening's "Honor America" stage with Bob Hope, Art Linkletter, and the Reverend Billy Graham. The following evening, the choir sang at the "Pageant for Freedom," an outdoor event broadcasted nationally that culminated in the fireworks display at the Washington Monument. [36]

The *Homefront* commercials, *The Family...and Other Living Things* broadcast, and the bicentennial coverage attracted precisely the type of attention Mormon publicists wanted. These initiatives presented Latter-day Saints as community-minded, patriotic, and family-centered (Figure 4.3). At the same

Figure 4.3. Almost as a visual representation of his church's family-centered theology, LDS Church President Spencer W. Kimball presents U.S. President Jimmy Carter with a statue of a mother and father helping their child learn to walk. President Carter was in Salt Lake City to commemorate National Family Week. Photo courtesy of The Church of Jesus Christ of Latter-day Saints.

time, human-interest media profiles of celebrity Mormons repeatedly reinforced these themes.

Jack Anderson, for example, was a Pulitzer Prize–winning investigative journalist. *Newsweek* called him the "most widely syndicated columnist in America and perhaps the most controversial."[37] Apart from his column, Anderson gained notoriety as a Mormon biographical feature story in nearly a dozen periodicals. A *New York Times Magazine* writer suggested that "few reporters ever go from writing news to being news ... and no reporter has made the passage more conspicuously than Jack Anderson in 1972."[38] This "active and loyal Mormon" was "a devoted family man who prefers to spend Sunday in church and at home with his wife and nine children."[39]

Mormon golfer Johnny Miller's devotion to his family likewise came through in articles that detailed his life on the pro golf tour. In contrast to most of his high-living fellow athletes, Miller and his family, a reporter noted, could "usually be found in the motel coffee shop, amid high chairs, hot dogs and spilled glasses of milk." Miller remarked to a *Newsweek* interviewer that "spending time with the family is really my favorite activity. In the end, how good a parent you are has got to be more important than whether you shoot a 68 or a 71." That same *Newsweek* reporter called Miller's "swing ... as graceful and consistent as any on the professional-golf tour," and then added this commentary about the nonsmoking, nondrinking Miller: "his clean-living image is as flawless as his game."[40]

Hotel magnate J. Willard Marriott told *Forbes*, "There are two reasons for my success ... the first is my church, the other is my wife." That magazine's six-page feature on the Marriott chain's soaring profits and loyal employees concluded that "the unity and success of the Marriott family also is a testimonial to the unity and thriving success of Mormonism, the Church of Jesus Christ of Latter-day Saints." The same article noted that Marriott was "an influential Republican" who "put on President Nixon's inaugural"—there was even a photo of the two men side by side, smiling. The photo's caption told readers that "Bill Marriott Sr. ... sponsored last year's Honor America Day, co-chaired by Bob Hope and Billy Graham."[41] (Fourteen years later, former President Nixon and Reverend Graham would speak at J. Willard Marriott's funeral.)[42] Portrayed as patriotic, generous, and optimistic, Marriott's family was also described by a writer in *Potomac* magazine as "one of those families a great many people in the United States still hope to have."[43]

Church communications officials often drafted famous Saints to help with institutional publicity efforts. They sought advice from Jack Anderson on dealing with the media; they called on Johnny Miller to be a headliner at a 1976 "Meet the Mormons" event held in the Cleveland Coliseum; and they invited Bill Marriott to join George and Lenore Romney and other prominent Mormons on a "Public Communications Advisory Council."[44]

As reputable as the likes of the Marriotts and Romneys were, though, no family came to epitomize Mormonism in the 1970s more than the Osmonds. This group of singing siblings got their first big break in the early 1960s when Andy Williams's father heard them perform at Disneyland. They became regulars on Williams's television variety show throughout that decade. As the brothers matured and began writing and selling their own music, their rise to recording success was nothing short of meteoric. *Newsweek* put it into perspective: "In 1972 the Osmonds broke the mark, held by Elvis and the Beatles, for selling the most gold records in a year—eleven."[45] This so-called "Osmondmania" was uncontrollably contagious, it seemed. Greyhound Bus Lines decided that it would "no longer charter buses for Osmond travel since fans spray-paint[ed] love notes on the buses."[46]

Superficial though show business can be, the Osmond family's earnestness impressed even initially cynical observers. In a piece for *Atlantic Monthly*, Sara Davidson detailed the ups and downs of other contemporary artists who had eventually lost the favor of their fickle teenage fan base, especially when those artists' carefully cultivated images of innocence wilted under the weight of intense scrutiny. That same reporter, however, contrasted this with the Osmond family's stability in a turbulent industry. After spending two weeks with the group, she concluded that "their religious conviction seems to be the cement holding the entire structure together."[47] She described their weekly "family night" gatherings, where they would read scriptures and pray together. They all paid tithing on their substantial earnings. They did not smoke or drink tea or coffee or alcohol—and perhaps most ironic to the reporter, fifteen-year-old Donny, the most adored teen idol of the group, could not even date until he turned sixteen, based on the church's standard. While Davidson conceded that some media personnel felt like they had experienced "an overdose of saccharine" when they met the family, she was "fascinated with the Osmonds, because they seem the most ambitious, energetic, and congenitally happy group of people I have ever seen living together."[48] Likewise, pop music icon Dick Clark said, "You simply cannot deal with better people.... Their word is as good as gold. What they promise they deliver. I only wish that some of the acid rock groups I've handled had one-tenth the professional and personal integrity of the Osmonds."[49]

The potential boost for the church's image that the Osmonds' star power represented was not lost on the Public Communications Department. The Osmonds responded enthusiastically to invitations to take part in the *Homefront* commercials and *the Family—and Other Living Things* prime-time special. Church publicists reaped the benefit of having such famous spokespersons. The Osmonds' involvement in the project opened some broadcasting doors that might otherwise have remained closed to the church's offerings.[50]

This spotlight on Mormon families seemed to come from many angles in the 1970s. Judy Klemesrud of the *New York Times* offered the Mormons as counter-evidence for those who despaired that American families in the 1970s were "headed down the drain in a swirl of divorce, drugs, venereal disease, alcohol, [and] adultery." She wrote in 1973 that "for at least [this] one sizable group in American Society, the family is still the thing." As opposed to those who felt "marriage...children...family" were "passé," the East Coast Latter-day Saints depicted in Klemesrud's full-page feature—business leaders, Harvard graduates, sports stars—devoted Monday nights to "family home evening." Klemesrud highlighted the low divorce rate among Mormons, a rate dramatically below the national average. Apart from the emphasis on family inherent in the home evening program, many of the Latter-day Saints she interviewed also attributed the low incidence of family disintegration to the church-prescribed "abstinence from alcohol, tobacco, coffee and tea."[51]

In this era of drug experimentation and abuse, the Mormon "Word of Wisdom" lifestyle generated new attention thanks to a study by UCLA researcher Dr. James Enstrom, reported in the September 1975 edition of the journal *Cancer*. Dr. Enstrom determined that the "1970–72 cancer mortality rate among California Mormon adults [was] about one-half to three-fourths that of the general California population," and Utah Mormons had "the lowest rate in the entire country." A University of Utah team published similar findings in January 1976 in the *New England Journal of Medicine*. References to these articles found their way to other periodicals, including *Reader's Digest*, *Family Circle*, and the *Washington Star*.[52]

Positive press for the Mormon health code prompted Latter-day Saint leaders to organize the aforementioned "Meet the Mormons" event in Cleveland to commemorate Joseph Smith's receipt of the revelation that outlined the Word of Wisdom. The Mormon prophet was living in Kirtland, Ohio (just outside of Cleveland), when he recorded the revelation in 1833. The January 1976 celebration saw the efforts of the institutional church and those of individual celebrities converge in a large-scale way. Two church general authorities acting as hosts led the conversation about Latter-day Saint lifestyle with a panel of some of Mormonism's most famous Americans. Latter-day Saint convert Harmon Killebrew, who at the time sat in fourth place on major-league baseball's all-time home run list, was one of the luminaries, as was Cy Young Award–winning pitcher Vernon Law. George and Lenore Romney and astronaut Don Lind were also featured guests. Golfer Johnny Miller, unable to attend because of scheduling conflicts, sent prerecorded comments about his family and faith. The event's concluding speaker was church president Spencer W. Kimball.

A winter storm in Cleveland that day did not keep away the 17,000 people who filled the Cleveland Coliseum. An estimated 12,000 of those guests were not Latter-day Saints. Church leaders had again emphasized a grassroots campaign to invite neighbors and friends to hear some of Mormonism's most recognizable and well-respected spokesmen.[53]

Public interest in events like this one and in the broadcast spots disseminated from Salt Lake City created a palpable sense of optimism among the church's media watchers. Wendell Ashton told an interviewer in 1976, "We feel our image IS improving." That interviewer, Dennis Lythgoe, a contemporary observer of Mormon media trends—specifically print media—added his opinion that indeed the "image of Mormonism seems to have changed from unfavorable in the 1960s to favorable in the 1970s."[54]

Compared to the agitation of the late 1960s and the early 1970s, by the middle of that latter decade media coverage of Mormonism was mostly noncontroversial.[55] This provided an opening for church public relations officials to focus on proactive publicity efforts rather than reactive damage control. Looking back, however, as hopeful as things seemed for Mormon publicists in 1976, this period was actually the calm before a storm. It was in 1976 that the church issued its first official statement about the Equal Rights Amendment.

"It's Now Do or Die for the ERA: Mormon Power Is the Key"—Opposition over Obscurity

The LDS Church's family-centered public relations campaign took on greater urgency in the 1970s because the ERA (and, in a related way, *Roe v. Wade*) changed the national context of that campaign. The decade saw many of the premises central to Mormonism's pro-family theology take on new political overtones. From the Mormon standpoint, the church's media messages thus became critical to winning hearts and minds not only about Mormonism, but also in support of the traditional family ideal that seemed to be under constitutional siege. To the church's leadership, the seriousness of that threat warranted initiatives that were as much about influencing public policy as they were about public perception. Promotion of the church's family focus thus merged with— and reinforced—its resistance to the ERA. [56]

In the years before the ERA, Latter-day Saint general authorities had spoken out, on occasion, regarding community issues that they deemed morally significant. Mormon influence on Utah's liquor laws, for example, was undisputed, and numerous news features in the 1960s characterized the church's dominance in that state as simply an accepted fact of life. This reality raised little concern because it seemed so provincial.[57]

Yet in the case of the ERA, Mormon beliefs became politicized in a way that seemed altogether different, both in degree and scope. Church leaders at many levels encouraged Mormon mobilization against the amendment, and that mobilization proved effective in a number of states other than Utah. The church's expanded reach and its explicit activism inspired new criticisms from without *and* within. Moreover, as the battle over ERA ratification dragged on, and as every state took on "make-or-break" significance, Utah, Idaho, and Nevada claimed center stage.

By 1976, thirty-three states had ratified the Equal Rights Amendment, passed by Congress in 1972: "Equality of rights under the law shall not be denied or abridged by the United States or any state on account of sex." The approval of only five more states would give the brief statement constitutional authority. The ERA campaign in the 1970s built on fifty years of abortive attempts to adopt the amendment. Congress first considered it in 1923; the Senate, more than once, had even approved a similar amendment in the years after World War II. Yet never had its passage seemed as assured as it did in the mid-1970s.[58]

In retrospect, though, the years 1973–1974 marked a pivotal shift nationally for the inertia of the ERA. Twenty-two states (including Idaho) ratified the ERA in 1972, and eight more joined that group in 1973. But after 1973, during the congressionally extended nine-year window for ratification, only five more states approved the amendment. At the same time, five states rescinded their earlier support. What reversed the amendment's initial momentum so drastically?

First, the flurry of ratifications in 1972 ignited a counteroffensive led by conservative activist Phyllis Schlafly. She organized STOP-ERA ("Stop Taking Our Privileges") and quickly became the amendment's most visible antagonist. For Schlafly's group, the amendment had the potential to undermine traditional protections for women, such as child support in the case of divorce or exclusion from the military draft.[59]

Then *Roe v. Wade* was added to the mix in 1973. The significance of this court case on the fortunes of the ERA cannot be discounted, since advocacy for the amendment was subsequently linked (by both the amendment's opponents *and* proponents, with obviously differing degrees of approval) with the divisive issues of abortion-on-demand and federal funding for abortion. In response, Phyllis Schlafly, a Roman Catholic and a staunch foe of abortion, only expanded her organizational opposition to the amendment with a new political coalition, Eagle Forum, in 1975.[60]

This same national pattern seemed to be repeated regionally in the Rocky Mountain states. At first, the ERA did not evoke much reaction from the Latter-day Saint leadership. Although the Mormons were strong advocates of the traditional nuclear family, they also had a long history of advocating rights for women. Joseph Smith had organized the church's auxiliary for women in 1842, and this "Relief Society" numbered over a million members by the 1970s. The territorial legislature had given Utah women the vote in 1870 and again in the state constitution of 1895. Brigham Young promoted equal educational opportunities for women, such that just under half of the University of Deseret's 223 students in 1869 were women. Several LDS women of the nineteenth century even attended medical school at the urging of church authorities.[61]

When the ERA campaign came to the Mormon cultural region, therefore, few were alarmed. The brief amendment seemed innocuous and almost self-evident to a nation focused on civil equality. In terms of states with high Mormon populations, Idaho considered the amendment first. The ERA passed smoothly through the Idaho legislature, where a number of Mormon representatives voted in favor of it. However, here again, timing played a major role—and as the Utah legislature prepared to consider the amendment in early 1975, concerns about the ERA had intensified across the country—and crystallized at LDS Church headquarters. One active ERA supporter, Jane Mansbridge, later argued that instead of assuaging the public's worries about the ERA's potentially revolutionary effects (like the loss of alimony or unisex bathrooms, for example), the most radical element of the pro-ERA camp acknowledged that a societal shake-up *was* possible and even desirable. Mansbridge concluded that this brash response frightened average voters: "Many state legislators were unwilling to give the [Supreme] Court 'new words to play with,' rightly fearing that this could eventually have all sorts of unforeseeable consequences they might not like and would not be able to reverse."[62] Confronted with the prospects of this type of radical feminism and the emerging abortion wars, LDS Church leaders took a determined stand to protect the traditional family. It was, they felt, at the core of their faith.[63]

The church's position coalesced first in discussions between the women's Relief Society presidency and several apostles who served as advisors. In fact, Belle Spafford and Barbara Smith, successive presidents of the women's auxiliary, were the first general church officers to speak against the ERA. Spafford, the church's Relief Society president since 1945 and past president of the National Council of Women (1968–1970), explained her opposition to the amendment in a July 1974 speech in New York City. Barbara Smith replaced Spafford as general president of the Relief Society in October 1974, and two months later spoke against the ERA in an address to LDS students at the University of Utah. Both women reacted against the ERA because it was "vague" and "broad," meaning perhaps that it could become so "inflexible" legally that it would "[nullify] all laws...which now provide favorable treatment for women."[64] Barbara Smith later discussed her speech with President Kimball, who endorsed her comments. The "Church News" section of the church-owned *Deseret News* then published an anti-ERA editorial in January 1975, a month before the Utah legislature voted on the amendment. (Not surprisingly, considering the Mormon majority, the legislature voted down the amendment.)

Finally, in October 1976, President Kimball and his counselors in the First Presidency issued an official statement. "There have been injustices to women before the law and in society generally," the statement read. "These we deplore. There are additional rights to which women are entitled. However, we firmly believe that the Equal Rights Amendment is not the answer. While the motives of its supporters may be praiseworthy, ERA as a blanket attempt to help women could indeed bring them far more restraints and repressions. We fear it will even stifle many God-given feminine instincts. It would strike at the family, humankind's basic institution. ERA would bring ambiguity and possibly invite extensive litigation. Passage of ERA, some legal authorities contend, could nullify many accumulated benefits to women in present statutes. We recognize men and women as equally important before the Lord, but with differences biologically, emotionally, and in other ways. ERA, we believe, does not recognize these differences. There are better means for giving women, and men, the rights they deserve."[65]

The timing of these statements caused perhaps as much consternation among pro-ERA Mormons as did their contents. Because the first hint of an official church position against the amendment did not come until midway through the initial seven-year ratification period, some questioned the ideological integrity of the Latter-day Saint campaign to defeat the ERA. They asked why the amendment did not spark Mormon resistance three years earlier, and suggested that opposition to the ERA ran counter to the church's long tradition of supporting women's rights. Some even wondered if an outspoken minority of conservative church leaders pressured a new First Presidency (installed in December 1973 after Harold B. Lee's death) to end its silence on the issue.[66]

The church's position, however, was that the timing of the statements reflected a growing appreciation of the ERA's implications, implications that were not fully apparent in 1972 or 1973. Those potentialities challenged church tenets related to the critical role of women in the traditional family structure, tenets that, by all accounts, had been consistently conservative for decades. As the church's supporters saw it, while it may have been the relatively new church president Spencer W. Kimball who announced the church's opposition to the amendment, church publications and general authorities had sounded warnings about feminism long before the ERA.[67]

President Harold B. Lee, President Kimball's predecessor, was, for example, an outspoken opponent of abortion and a vocal proponent of traditional marriage. For years he had expressed concerns about social trends that threatened family structures and roles, particularly the role of mothers. Not only did he decry abortion as a "heinous crime" because it destroyed a human life, he deplored the connection between abortion and sexual promiscuity.[68] "Some say that with an abortion during the first few months of pregnancy there is nothing wrong. That is one of the most hellish things that has ever been said to try to destroy the fountains of life."[69] He saw that type of permissiveness as a tool "Satan uses...to destroy the family."[70] Only one month after being named president of the church, Lee warned in August 1972 that "Satan's greatest threat today is to destroy the family, and to make a mockery of the law of chastity and the sanctity of the marriage covenant."[71] He also worried that external, societal forces—"the speed of modern living"—threatened to unravel marriages and families. In the face of such challenges, he urged the women of the church to "make a career of motherhood. They must let nothing supersede that career."[72] "A mother's influence is far-reaching," he told BYU students. "Someone said when you train a boy you're just training another individual, but when you train a girl you're training a whole family. So important is the work of a mother. Children are the product of her life or hands, her teaching, her training."[73]

President Lee died in late December 1973. His successor wasted no time in sounding the same themes about the importance of women's roles in the family. In his first news conference as church president, Spencer Kimball reaffirmed the church's position "that under normal circumstances, 'the place of women is in the home,'" since "the most sacred privileges that a woman could have are in the home" as "a partner with God" in nurturing children.[74] Like President Lee, President Kimball was careful to emphasize that this did not imply male superiority. Marriage was a "full partnership" of "equals," partners who were meant to be different but "complementary."[75]

To the church's opponents in this debate, including dismayed pro-ERA Mormons, these statements represented the reactionary fears of an entrenched patriarchy guided by a Victorian model of domesticity rather than revealed Mormon doctrine. Some made the argument that the LDS emphasis on stay-at-home motherhood was comparatively recent and contrasted unfavorably with Mormon views of feminine capabilities in the nineteenth century. These commentators located the shift in Mormon mind-set at the turn of the twentieth century, a byproduct of Mormonism's post-polygamy Americanization, which at that time meant adopting the prevailing middle-class morality. Accordingly, detractors read official praise for homemaking and full-time motherhood as a diversionary tactic to confine women to domestic prisons disguised as pedestals of honor. [76]

To believers, though, these statements emphasizing traditional roles for women went far beyond backward-looking retrenchment. They derived from a fundamental belief in the divinely ordained, complementary natures of men and women, a belief that framed for Mormons their model of the family. In this view, the church's anti-ERA stance was a response to those who sought to destabilize this family model and blur crucial distinctions between men and women, rather than a reversal on women's issues. Women had been given the supremely important task of bearing and caring for children, church leaders stressed. No other effort or endeavor could match the significance of that divine trust, a significance underscored by Mormon beliefs about the eternal nature of family relationships. The decision to take a public stand against the ERA and come out in support of already circulating anti-ERA arguments also corresponded to the church's push for a more proactive publicizing of its family-centered theology in the 1970s. As historian Jan Shipps put it, the church wanted to be "on record" as an advocate for the protection of families. [77]

Both sides were as passionate about their positions as they were critical of the shortsightedness of their opponents. What no one disagreed about was that the effect of the LDS Church's statement was immediate. The weight of Mormon opinion clearly pivoted on the fulcrum of these church pronouncements.[78] Utah legislators soundly defeated the motion to ratify the amendment one month after the "Church News" editorial. Then Idaho's citizens voted to rescind their state's ratification in January 1977, just as the "International Women's Year" (IWY) opened. It was then at an "International Women's Year" convention in Utah that the Mormon position on the ERA first conspicuously translated into concerted public action against the ERA.

In every state, women met at IWY gatherings to elect delegates for a national convention. These representatives also voted on a platform-type inventory of issues to determine the policy priorities of the nation's women. Most Utah Mormons initially disregarded the gathering because of its presumed feminist agenda. However, church leaders recognized the statement that Mormons could make if they could influence the Utah IWY convention's delegation and its policy positions. Church general authorities thus asked each stake and ward in Utah to supply a handful of women to attend the Utah IWY convention and vote for positions that favored traditional family roles. What followed from those requests surprised nearly everyone.[79]

The Utah convention's organizers had planned for no more than four thousand attendees. Instead, over thirteen thousand women packed the meeting hall.[80] The women who supported more conservative positions easily overwhelmed those who favored abortion rights, family planning, or, importantly, the ERA. In fact, many Mormon participants remembered that they were simply instructed by local church leaders to vote "no" on every proposal. This confused some critics of the Mormon intervention, because they felt that several of the proposals were friendly to traditional families and motherhood. In their recollections of Utah's IWY meeting, ERA supporters denounced what they remembered as men with walkie-talkies directing throngs of obedient women voters. To critics, this became almost the prototypical case of female subservience to male priesthood authority. To supporters of the church's cause, though, this convention represented a stirring example of the influence that like-minded citizens could have on family-related political decisions. Outraged and confused feminists (including some Latter-day Saint attendees) were convinced that their convention had been stolen from them. However, the majority of Mormon women at the conference sensed that they had scored a victory for their values.

Mormon women had a similar impact on other state IWY conventions. Cleo Fellers Kocol, a pro-ERA delegate at the Washington convention, described her displeasure at seeing "Mormon women, wearing long gowns and Stepford-wife

expressions, clustered around their men and [waiting] for signals on how to vote."
This group, "two thousand strong, ... swelled the ranks of participants twofold"
and swayed the convention to vote for "an anti-abortion recommendation." [81]
Regardless of how groups on both sides of the debate interpreted the implications of that IWY convention season, no one could deny that Mormons effectively replicated these organizational successes in their subsequent anti-ERA
ventures. Latter-day Saints were just as active in massive letter-writing campaigns to state legislators, in distributing literature to neighbors, and especially
in donating funds to political action committees in various states.

At the same time, some individual Mormons seemed particularly well placed
to exert significant influence (critics saw it as unfair influence) on the ERA
vote. The Idaho attorney general considered (but later dropped) legal action
against church apostle Boyd Packer "for allegedly violating the state's lobbyist
registration law" when he gave a speech in Pocatello and encouraged Idahoans
to vote to rescind ratification.[82] Ms. magazine charged Nevada State Senator
and Latter-day Saint James Gibson with backroom political wrangling to defeat
the amendment.[83] The loudest outcry surrounded federal judge and Latter-day
Saint Marion Callister. In a strange twist of the district court lottery system, the case that considered the constitutionality of Idaho's ERA rescission
landed in Judge Callister's courtroom. Women's rights activists demanded that
Judge Callister recuse himself because of his religious affiliation. The National
Organization for Women (NOW) even took its complaints to the 9th Circuit
Court in San Francisco, but the petition for Judge Callister's removal was
denied.[84]

Complaints like these began to appear in more and more media venues, especially after a church member named Sonia Johnson took the lead in criticizing
the purportedly questionable ethics behind LDS efforts to defeat the ERA. No
other modern Mormon dissident had generated the level of attention that would
come to her and the "Mormons for ERA" crusade that she launched.

Johnson came to the ERA debate even later than her church.[85] She and her
husband and their children had lived overseas during the first years of the ERA
ratification process. They moved to Virginia in 1976, the same year that the LDS
First Presidency stated its opposition to the amendment. But it was not until
1978, when Johnson and her husband attended a meeting at their local church
ward, that she became uneasy. The meeting had been billed as an information
session, but the presentation struck Johnson as overt propaganda against the
amendment. Not only that, she felt that the male church leader who spoke
against the ERA cared little about the actual issues in the debate and instead
condescendingly reminded the assembled women that the leaders of the church
would look after their welfare. Unconvinced by the church's arguments against
ratification and furious at the leader's patronizing tone, she decided to oppose
actively the position articulated by Latter-day Saint leadership.

It was Johnson's participation in a July 1978 Washington march that cata-pulted her into the national spotlight. The demonstration in favor of the con-gressional extension of the ratification period saw Johnson and twenty others march with a banner read "Mormons for ERA." The banner seemed such a strik-ing oxymoron that it drew press attention as well as an invitation for Sonia Johnson to testify before a Senate committee conducting hearings about reli-gious groups' opinions on the ERA. Johnson and her husband both held doctoral degrees and had taught at universities in Korea and Malawi. Her education and experience made her an articulate presenter and she impressed many of those at the hearing. It was, however, an exchange during the question-and-answer portion of the hearing that captured the most attention. Senator Orrin Hatch of Utah, a Mormon, accused Johnson of insulting the majority of Mormon women generally and his wife specifically with her insinuation that the pro-ERA point of view was the stance of intelligent Mormons. The heated confrontation drew reporters to Sonia Johnson by the dozens.[86]

In the ensuing whirlwind of media interviews, Johnson denounced more forcefully the LDS Church's posture and participation in the ERA ratification process. Johnson famously accused the Mormon hierarchy of "savage misog-yny."[87] Perhaps her most provocative tactic was to suggest that ERA support-ers refuse to listen to the gospel message of Mormon missionaries until the church changed its position on the ERA: "If a missionary comes to your door, tell him you are not interested in a church that is fighting equal rights."[88] While Latter-day Saint leaders had repeatedly stated that members could vote their conscience on this issue, the public nature of Johnson's accusations seemed to force the church's hand.[89] Her local lay pastor ("bishop" in Mormon parlance) convened a disciplinary council in late 1979 to consider charges of apostasy against Johnson. The attention she had garnered before only assured that the atmosphere of her church hearing would be, to say the least, charged.

Jan Shipps's essay in the *Christian Century* called the event "the most cel-ebrated excommunication since Savonarola's day," and a Mormon observer described the Sonia Johnson episode as "perhaps the most conspicuous media event in [LDS] church history" to date.[90] Over two hundred cameramen, report-ers, and sign-waving supporters waited for Johnson to emerge from the Virginia meetinghouse where the council was held. Several days later, she met report-ers on the driveway of her home to read the letter that her bishop had sent to announce the excommunication. The bishop, Jeffrey Willis, decided to take a step rare in Mormon disciplinary procedures, which are typically transacted confidentially. He opted to release a statement announcing Sonia Johnson's excommunication. He was careful to explain that Sonia Johnson's excommu-nication did not stem from her opinions about the ERA but from her public disparagement of the church's leadership and vocal opposition to its missionary efforts.[91]

Excommunication is, for Mormons, the severest form of church discipline, stripping those under its stricture of the standing and privileges of membership. The explicit aim of this extreme measure is to encourage the disciplined Saint to repent and apply for readmission through rebaptism. Instead of pursuing that course, though, Sonia Johnson appealed the decision of the bishop's council, taking her case to the members of the church's First Presidency. They upheld the bishop's verdict.[92]

While pre–Sonia Johnson coverage of Mormon anti-ERA activities had made its way occasionally into the pages and programs of national media outlets, her excommunication easily multiplied that coverage tenfold. Memorialized as a martyr, her ouster from the church gave her a platform from which to publicize her crusade. [93]"Mormons for ERA" never claimed more than several hundred members, yet the group for its size had a wildly disproportionate impact on the Mormon image, at least in terms of media momentum. There was something forlorn in the way Sonia Johnson was portrayed—alone, vulnerable, staring down the all-male hierarchy of the LDS Church. The fact that reports on Johnson's excommunication almost without fail mentioned that her local bishop was a personnel director for the CIA only added to the overall feeling of conspiratorial intrigue.[94]

Something was changing in nationwide reporting on Mormonism. It was the introduction of "fear" as a theme. Now national newspapers reported that Mormon feminists feared for their membership and, by extension, for the eternal salvation of their families, should excommunication render their temple "sealings" (the Mormon sacrament of eternal marriage) void.[95] Non-Mormon ERA activists feared the impact of Mormon money and mobilization in swing-state ratification battles. Iris Mittgang, chairwoman of the National Women's Political Caucus, called the LDS Church "the single most significant enemy of women's equality in this country." NOW president Eleanor Smeal said, "Phyllis Schlafly is not our key opponent. It is the array of the right and their financial backers, of which the Mormon church is a key part."[96] Observers everywhere began to express concern about the influence any centralized church could exert in national politics, and it was clear that these observers had the LDS Church in mind when they voiced these fears.[97]

Mormons found themselves in the most unflattering light when their anti-ERA tactics came up for questioning. Sonia Johnson charged that the church's use of its facilities and resources for politicking and organizing violated its tax-exempt status. Latter-day Saints consistently maintained that while the church's top leadership opposed the amendment, the efforts to organize actual campaigns were local. Johnson complained that church general and regional authorities acted as consultants. Because of the respect and deference most Mormons accorded these leaders, she denounced what she saw as their use of standing and position to unduly coerce Mormons into action.[98]

What especially angered Sonia Johnson was that this Mormon involvement seemed to her to be intentionally covert. She denounced the organization of "community" groups that did not mention explicitly their Latter-day Saint backing. She criticized letter writers who consciously left out their Mormon ties. Her most stinging accusations challenged the ethics, if not the legality, of this Latter-day Saint strategy—and she had a knack for getting her message heard.[99] The frequency of her group's demonstrations kept her supporters on the media radar. Protest tactics ranged from banners pulled by airplanes over LDS General Conference gatherings to vocal interruptions of church meetings.[100] Every Sunday for nearly a year in 1980, a handful of women picketed the construction site of the LDS Church's Seattle-area temple in Bellevue, Washington. The weekly demonstrations turned into daily ones during the temple's public open house, until finally, twenty women and one man were arrested for chaining themselves to the complex's three gates and blocking entrance to the now-completed temple. Protesters claimed to have photo evidence of Mormon security guards "[knocking] two" of these women onto the "wet sidewalk" during the scuffle to remove them from temple property (Figure 4.4).[101]

Figure 4.4. "Mormons for ERA" leader Sonia Johnson was arrested after chaining herself to the gates of the LDS Church's new Seattle, Washington, temple in November 1980. For nearly a year, ERA advocates had protested weekly at the temple site. Associated Press photo. Reprinted with permission.

Persistent Themes and Turning Points

Yet after all of this, and as damaging as these reports had the potential to be, opposition to the ERA did not prove to be the death knell for Mormonism's improving image. For one thing, ERA ratification failed. Even ERA supporters have admitted that, by the early 1980s, the amendment had lost its momentum. Most lawmakers thus appeared to accept the doubts expressed by ERA opponents over the public's interest in changing the Constitution.[102] Perhaps this growing indifference about the amendment's passage tempered backlash against its strongest opponents. Also, Sonia Johnson's protests about the covert nature of the church's opposition to the amendment seemed at least partly borne out by other critics' complaints that the church's impact on the ratification process was not widely recognized outside of the West.[103] While newspapers and magazines paid substantial attention to Latter-day Saint actors and actions *at the time*, in the long run other ERA opponents received the lion's share of the credit (or blame) for the amendment's demise. Phyllis Schlafly and her "STOP ERA" dominate most histories of the ERA, and Latter-day Saints often figure into those histories only in the list of the amendment's denominational opponents.[104]

Writer Chris Rigby Arrington had predicted in 1980 that "for years to come when Americans think of Mormonism, they will think of Sonia Johnson before they think of polygamy or the Tabernacle Choir." Based on the inflammatory coverage Johnson generated in 1979 and 1980, Arrington's speculation at the time would not have seemed outlandish. Yet her prognostication did not match what actually transpired. By 1982, a close watcher of Mormon media trends recognized that already "Sonia has passed somewhat from the spotlight."[105] Three decades later, even many Mormons do not know Johnson's story. Ultimately, other themes from the Equal Rights Amendment era would outlast the story of Sonia Johnson.

The first such theme was Mormonism's family focus. Some outside observers asserted that Mormon political activism in the 1970s actually strengthened the church's image by highlighting the consistency of its family-centered gospel.[106] In this sense, the aggressive publicity campaign in the 1970s that integrated temple open houses, paid advertising time, and public service announcements had produced results. These proactive initiatives made significant headway in terms of linking in the public mind "concern for families" with "Mormons."

Political opposition did not slow that campaign. In the midst of the most heated years in the ERA debate, from 1978 to 1981, the church's Public Communications department launched a massive magazine advertising blitz through inserts in *Reader's Digest*. That monthly periodical, with its circulation of twenty million-plus subscribers, carried eight-page pull-outs dedicated to various aspects of Latter-day Saint beliefs. Heber Wolsey told an interviewer in 1979 that "we started our inserts in the *Reader's Digest* with very general family themes, so we could get people to feel the universality of our concern about family."[107] Accordingly, the first insert carried the title, "Can You Have a Happier Family Life?"[108] Reader response (in terms of requests for follow-up information) was larger than any previous media contacting endeavor and convinced the Latter-day Saint decision-makers that the campaign validated its significant expense. The church commissioned the Starch Readership Study to monitor the distribution of the inserts. Church employee Lorry Rytting reported that the Starch Company concluded that, "of the estimated twenty-nine and a half million primary adult readers of *Reader's Digest,* we've had approximately 50-plus percent of a sample say, when surveyed later, 'Yes, I remember seeing [the church's ad].' We've had 40-some percent who remember seeing the page on which the Church logo appeared. We have something like 20%, roughly, who say they read all or most of a section of the ad. Those figures translate into millions of readers."[109]

The *Homefront* public service commercials also continued to receive extensive airtime in the late 1970s and into the 1980s. More than that, they garnered numerous industry accolades. A 1979 television ad about "marriage solidarity" entitled "Try Again" won three CLIO awards—the so-called "Academy Award of Broadcast Advertising." These first television CLIOs for the *Homefront* project came after the series had already won six radio CLIOs.[110] The frequency of these "family first" radio and TV spots dwarfed even the rate of stories related to Mormon opposition to the ERA, and the effect these commercials had on Mormons' wider reputation was measurable in public opinion polls.[111]

In hindsight, then, Mormonism's pro-family public relations campaign simply seemed to play louder than did objections to the church's political position on the ERA. Yet even if specific attention to Mormon influence in the anti-ERA campaign did not last long, the LDS Church's involvement in the ERA struggle seemed to have created an almost subconscious wariness of Mormons, such that the *idea* of the Mormons taking a political stand became more troubling than Mormons' stand on any specific *issue.* And that theme seemed to subsume more than eclipse the story of Sonia Johnson. Thus the church's opposition to the ERA did mark a critical moment in the development of Mormonism's modern image, even if Sonia Johnson and her support of the ERA no longer took center stage. The larger story may have been the way that the tenor of Mormon-related media features changed. The coverage began to be colored by a vague anxiety about Mormonism's hidden might and agenda, as if there was something to be feared in Mormonism after all.[112]

In connection with the ERA, this apprehension about Mormon influence seemed largely confined to a few media observers and disgruntled activists (including some outspoken Mormons) who complained that the LDS agenda was underreported and underrecognized. That would soon change.[113]

If the stage was set in the 1970s, the real drama would be enacted in the 1980s, so much so that the mid-1980s can be seen as an important turning point—and perhaps *the* important turning point, at least in the last half-century—in the trajectory of American public opinion of Mormonism. In 1977, 54% of respondents to a Gallup poll rated Mormons on the "favorable" side of a numeric scale—a favorability high points for years to come. Fourteen years later, in a 1991 study by the Barna Group, half that many (27 percent) saw Mormons favorably.[114] Overlapping controversies in the 1980s would become the one-two punches that would leave the Mormon image measurably bruised.

Some of Mormonism's oldest foes, evangelical Christians, were about to rejoin the fray with surprising vigor. The LDS Church had raised its profile in the 1970s, and its opposition to abortion and the ERA had made it a political force to be reckoned with in the nation's policy debates. The LDS position on these issues seemed to align Mormons with the powerful new "Christian Right" coalition that was emerging in the late 1970s.[115] To the uninformed, such an alignment might have aided Mormonism's bid for recognition as an authentic Christian body. But Mormonism's higher profile and its family focus also made it a *proselytizing* force to be reckoned with in the nation's *religious* contests. To conservative Christians, this only meant that they needed to redouble their efforts to counteract the family-friendly image that the LDS Church was projecting. Competition for souls worked against any political partnership.

5

Familiar Spirits, Part One:
The Early 1980s

"Mormons are winning over Baptist souls at a rate of '231 every single day.'" This lament came from Dr. Edmond Poole, "associate pastor of First Baptist Church in Dallas," in an interview with *Newsweek* magazine in March of 1985. Arthur Criscoe of the Southern Baptist Sunday School Board in Nashville was likewise distraught that LDS missionaries were "moving across the Southland...knocking on doors, penetrating." New Latter-day Saint temples in Atlanta (1983) and Dallas (1984) stood as monuments to that Mormon penetration into evangelical Christianity's traditional stronghold. In *Newsweek*'s view, a "turf war" was in full swing (Figure 5.1).[1]

The relationship between conservative, evangelical Protestants and Latter-day Saints had long been adversarial. Ministerial associations spearheaded the anti-polygamy campaigns of the nineteenth century, and Protestant leaders then (and since) most often described Mormonism as something other than a Christian religion. Yet what happened in the 1980s seemed different, in tone and tactics. Because of that, what had largely been a sectarian conflict bubbled to the surface of national consciousness, and Christian warnings about the Mormon "cult" swayed opinions among new audiences *outside* of the religious community. This begs a question: Why did familiar anti-Mormon charges gain wider traction in the 1980s? In other words, why did more Americans begin paying attention to anti-Mormon claims?

Political influence is part of the answer. In the 1973 opinion survey commissioned by Latter-day Saint public relations officials, Mormons ranked rather low compared to other religions when it came to perceived public influence and clout.[2] But a decade later, the LDS Church's efforts to defeat the ERA had evoked a flurry of complaints across the nation about Mormonism's previously unrecognized access to the levers of power. Those who opposed the political and ideological positions of Latter-day Saint leaders drew new attention to Mormonism's reported wealth and organizational might. Suddenly, Christian churches that

The Emergence of Mormonism on the American Landscape, 1950–1965

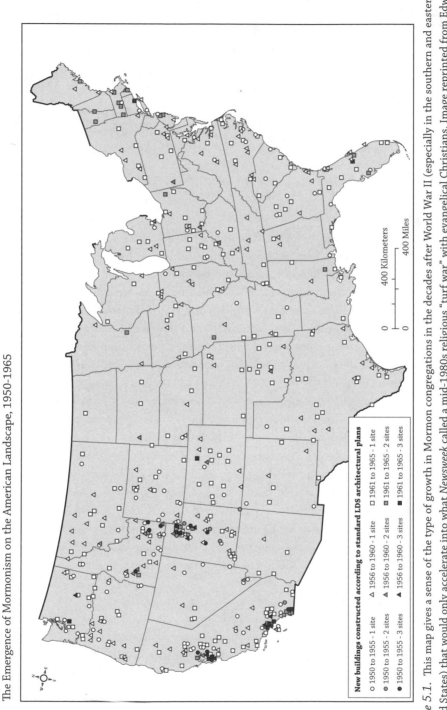

Figure 5.1. This map gives a sense of the type of growth in Mormon congregations in the decades after World War II (especially in the southern and eastern United States) that would only accelerate into what *Newsweek* called a mid-1980s religious "turf war" with evangelical Christians. Image reprinted from Edwin Scott Gaustad and Philip L. Barlow, *New Historical Atlas of Religion in America*, New York: Oxford University Press, 2000, p. 304. By permission of Oxford University Press.

worried about losing congregants to Mormon missionaries were not alone in sounding alarms about Mormon growth.

At the same time, many of these same Christian churches had also taken a new interest in politics in the late 1970s. The buildup to the presidential election of 1980 had given rise to the "New Right," the "Christian Voice," the "Moral Majority." With surprising force and speed, an evangelical Christian political movement was born. Fundamentalist preachers, concerned about the impending end of the world, sought to reclaim America as a Christian nation and thus save souls drowning in the tide of secularism.

The irony of this political situation was that evangelical Protestants and Latter-day Saints favored very similar pro-family agendas. Their social priorities aligned closely. Yet this did not make them easy allies, nor did it mean that theological hatchets would be buried for the greater good. Instead, what seemed to worry many Protestants was that Mormons' social morality would grant Mormonism legitimacy in the eyes of religious Americans. Such legitimacy would only increase the threat of Mormon proselytizing, since it would simultaneously decrease perceptions of Mormon peculiarity and thus open more doors for Mormon missionaries. If anything, parallel political positions meant that concerned Christians would have to work that much harder to distinguish themselves from the heterodox Mormons. For those who saw Latter-day Saints as a classic "wolf-in-sheep's-clothing" group, raising their voices in warning took on a new urgency.[3]

They received help from some energetic allies. Several groups of ex-Mormons took the campaign against their former faith to new levels. Exposés by disgruntled Latter-day Saints had been a staple of anti-Mormon literature since the days of E. D. Howe and his 1834 *Mormonism Unvailed*.[4] Yet again, something about the intensity of these efforts in the 1980s made them almost a new breed. Never before had these publications achieved the "bestseller" exposure that they did in the 1980s, when millions of viewers watched *The God Makers* series of movies, or hundreds of thousands of readers bought the companion book. Significantly, these anti-Mormon productions focused much of their attention on the religious rites that took place behind closed doors in Latter-day Saint temples. This new emphasis on Mormon secrecy only reinforced accusations of cultlike behaviors.

The word "cult" carried with it new dread after the 1978 tragedy at Jonestown, Guyana. Jim Jones and his People's Temple followers killed a U.S. congressman and the journalists who accompanied him. These atrocities became only more shocking with the subsequent mass suicide of more than nine hundred that church's members. Thus critics who labeled the LDS Church a "cult" threw long shadows onto the Mormon image. Was the LDS Church too clandestine, too rich, too powerful, too centralized to be trusted? The sheer repetition of these themes made them difficult for Mormon public relations officers to combat—and made them difficult for Americans to ignore. To many Latter-day Saints, history seemed to be repeating itself, as if the most strident critics of Mormonism from a century earlier reappeared in 1980s-era counterparts. The vocal resurgence of evangelical Christianity was only the first such reincarnation.

"America Can Be Saved": The Rising Religious Right and Its Mormon Dilemma

1976 was, *Newsweek* declared, the "year of the Evangelical."[5,6] What is remarkable about that designation is that the label "evangelical" itself was just coming into the national vocabulary. Yet before the year was out, an evangelical was preparing to move into the White House. Jimmy Carter was a self-described "born-again" Christian, as were an estimated 50 million other Americans, to the surprise of many secular pundits and commentators.[7] This large segment of the nation's population had flown under the radar because many evangelicals had intentionally kept out of the public sphere for half a century. However, a societal shake-up was changing all of that.

At the outset, it is important to note that in that group of 50 million, there were as many shades and denominational degrees of evangelicalism as there were books in the New Testament.[8] This diversity makes any discussion of the history of evangelicalism a little slippery, since the meaning of some terms is difficult to pinpoint. Still, the commonalities that bind those who count themselves part of this conservative Christian movement, especially in its twentieth-century American context, do make some definitions possible.[9]

The beliefs that demarcate evangelical Christianity from other brands of American Protestantism—so-called "mainline" Christianity, or "liberal" Christianity—center on biblical inerrancy and experiential religion. In other words, evangelicals hold that the Bible is historically and doctrinally reliable *and* sufficient. The creedal hallmarks of American evangelicalism were set down in a series of books published between 1910 and 1915 entitled *The Fundamentals: A Testimony to the Truth*. These twelve volumes, sent free of charge to "every pastor, evangelist, missionary, theological professor, [and] theological student...in the English speaking world," were the culminating rejection of a nineteenth- and early-twentieth-century liberalizing trend in Christian theology.[10] Several prominent Christian thinkers, especially Germans in the Tubingen school—Ferdinand Christian Baur, Ludwig Andreas Feuerbach, David Strauss—had won support for their interpretations of the Bible as allegorical rather than historical, and for their efforts to demystify the "historical Jesus." Proponents of this so-called "higher criticism" maintained that the Bible's value was in its moral messages rather than its dubious accounts of actual miracles or human development. This approach to scripture swept through divinity schools and captured the intellectual allegiance of a number of key American Christian thinkers.[11] In practical terms, this liberalizing thrust also drove the so-called "social gospel" in the decades preceding World War I. Social gospel proponents like Washington Gladden and Walter Rauschenbusch preached that society as a whole could refashion itself along the lines of Christian ethics and thus usher in an era of millennial peace. In this view, churches were primarily vehicles for charity and progressive reform.[12]

In response to what they saw as an erosion of the pillars of Christianity, conservative Christian writers reacted with the *Fundamentals* series. Essentially, these statements of the Christian faith encapsulated the doctrines that continue to define evangelicalism: "the inerrancy of the Bible, the deity and virgin birth of Jesus, the substitutionary atonement, the bodily resurrection of Jesus, and the second coming."[13]

The booklets also lent their name to a new movement in American Christianity. As most writers have used the term, "fundamentalism" is a particular wavelength on the spectrum of evangelical Christianity, yet the two movements—especially in their twentieth-century American context—are often treated interchangeably. Fundamentalists, as George Marsden memorably characterized them, are evangelicals who are "angry about something."[14] In this sense, the term "fundamentalist" has most often designated those evangelicals who set themselves apart through stricter behavioral guidelines. Fundamentalists' fear of worldly encroachment motivated their withdrawal to the private sanctuaries of church organizations and communities of like-minded individuals. Dismay over changing mores in the twentieth century prompted some fundamentalists to shun dancing, makeup and modern clothing styles, and popular music and movies. Importantly, their withdrawal from public life often included a conscious retirement from political involvement. Instead, they focused on the impulse that has always been at the very heart of conservative Christianity—the drive to *evangelize*, to win souls for Christ. [15]

This also reflected a pervasive pessimism that legislation could stop the world's march toward degeneration. The influential theology of premillennialism convinced many Christians that only the Second Coming of Christ and the concomitant destruction of wickedness could refashion society for the promised millennium of peace. *Individual* spiritual readiness, not social activism, was the only hope.[16] A young Reverend Jerry Falwell, in a well-known sermon in 1965 entitled "Ministers and Marchers," chastised colleagues who seemed too entrenched in politics. "We have a message of redeeming grace through a crucified and risen Lord. This message is designed to go right to the heart of man and there meet his deep spiritual need. Nowhere are we commissioned to reform the externals. We are not told to wage wars against bootleggers, liquor stores, gamblers, murderers, prostitutes, racketeers, prejudiced persons or institutions, or any other existing evil as such. I feel that we need to get off the streets and back into the pulpits and into our prayer rooms."[17]

For this reason, Reverend Falwell said he "would find it impossible to stop preaching the pure saving gospel of Jesus Christ, and begin doing anything else—including fighting Communism, or participating in civil-rights reforms." Many of his co-religionists did not even vote in presidential elections before the 1970s.[18]

Why, then, did so many fundamentalists do a political about-face in the late 1970s and involve themselves so passionately in national politics? Ironically, those who advocated such a change based much of their reasoning on the very premillennial theology that earlier had made them pessimistic about society's future. End-time prophecies played a decisive role in driving conservative Christian political action in the 1970s and 1980s.

New Testament authors focus considerable attention on Jesus Christ's promised return to the earth. However, many of the passages that deal with this return are cryptic, the apostle John's Revelation being the prime example. In the second half of the 1800s British evangelical writer John Nelson Darby offered a definitive framework to decipher the Bible writers' predictions: dispensationalism. Darby fit all of the symbolic references scattered throughout the apocalyptic sections of the New (and Old) Testament into a plausible time line of both earth's *history* (each biblical epoch of that history was called a "dispensation") and earth's *future*. To believers, Darby provided the key for understanding the premillennial world. Darby's ideas found their way to an extremely able distributor, Cyrus Scofield. Scofield, an American pastor, published a study Bible in 1909. Scofield's Bible incorporated Darby's writings in the commentary and notes that accompanied the biblical text. In reprint after reprint, Scofield's Bible sold over 20 million copies and solidified Darby's dispensationalism as the standard approach to fundamentalist eschatology.[19]

Everywhere they looked in the twentieth century, dispensationalists could see evidence that the end was near. The dispensationalist timeline included a prophesied return of the Jews to their homeland in Palestine. The creation of the Jewish state in 1948, and then Israel's occupation of Jerusalem in 1967, seemed the undeniable fulfillment of that prophecy. Dispensationalists also predicted the rise of a powerful "anti-Christ" who would unite the world under a deceptive, satanic government. The United Nations seemed a likely vehicle for such a takeover. Finally, the Bible's description of a massive battle-to-end-all-battles at Armageddon had Israel's enemies descending in hordes from the north and east. The Soviet Union and China seemed to be perched geographically to launch just such an attack.[20] All of this, plus the widening reach of religious skepticism, corresponded in fundamentalist minds with the last satanic offensive before the return of Jesus Christ. Society was on an irreversible course toward corruption; Christians' only hope was to pull souls from the sinking ship Babylon. "I view this world as a wretched vessel," revivalist preacher Dwight L. Moody had said in 1899. "The Lord has given me a lifeboat and said, 'Moody, save all you can.'"[21] Six decades later, the situation seemed more desperate than ever.

Even in America the forces against them were mounting. The Supreme Court, for example, unwittingly pricked the political consciousness of fundamentalist Christians with a series of decisions in the 1960s. *Engel v. Vitale* (1962) and several related cases proved to be watershed events in the development of what would become the Christian Right.[22] These cases dealt with religious practice on public school property. To the dismay of evangelical Christians, as the Court was striking down school prayer and Bible reading in schools on one hand, it seemed to be protecting purveyors of pornography and convicted criminals on the other. The threat of secularism, it appeared, now extended into the very communities that fundamentalists had for so long sought to protect. Many fundamentalist leaders began to call for an end to their self-imposed exile from public life.

Some evangelicals had long been public figures. Billy Graham, most notably, had advised U.S. presidents beginning with Dwight Eisenhower, and Graham and "other evangelical preachers had worked unflaggingly since the 1940s to win new converts." As such, and as one historian put it, "there was nothing new to the 1970s about emotional, born-again Christians."[23] Something about what began taking place in the mid-1970s was new, however. Prominent fundamentalists called for a Christian *movement*, the active politicking of a new lobbying coalition. They aimed to stanch the bleeding from America's religious soul. The gravity of the perceived official attacks on religious practice meant that spiritual readiness for Jesus' return became inextricably tied to social activism.[24] Evangelicals wanted government policies that protected religious liberty and proscribed the proliferation of vice, so that their message of salvation could reach a ready audience. Jerry Falwell told a *Christianity Today* interviewer in 1981 that "in order for the churches in America to evangelize the world, we need the environment of freedom in America that will permit us to do it," and that as long as the principles related to the sanctity of the traditional family "have been honored in this country,...God has honored the United States."[25] Plus many evangelicals saw the importance of putting a degenerate America back in God's favor as a matter of (literally) biblical proportions, since the United States was destined to play a guardian role in defense of Israel. A strong national defense network and militant anti-communism therefore became political priorities.[26]

In the 1970s, the time to mobilize such a movement seemed right. Evangelist Jack Van Impe called events in the Middle East "God's 'timepieces.'"[27] The pulse of that clock counting down to doomsday only accelerated after the Six-Day War in 1967 and Israel's war with Egypt and Syria in 1973. At the same time, several stars in the constellation of ministerial heavyweights aligned. The so-called "electronic church" was reaching its zenith. Radio ministries had abounded throughout the twentieth century, but the potential represented by television audiences drew dozens of preachers to create new programming. These broadcasts gave individual pastors regional and, in some cases, national appeal, and thus a wide-spread pool of financial contributors. Many of these same well-known preachers were among those who were most convinced that the moment for a Christian reentry into national politics and a reclaiming of national morality had arrived.[28]

After all, in 1976 one of their own was running for president. Governor Jimmy Carter of Georgia seemed to be the very antidote to the post–Richard-Nixon, post-Vietnam, post-1960s malaise plaguing the nation. Just as various Supreme Court decisions threatened to eliminate all vestiges of religion from public life, and just as Americans appeared to have given up hope in the trustworthiness of their leaders, along came a candidate who pledged total honesty with the American people. He professed his lifelong fidelity to his wife and family, and even taught Sunday School classes at his local Baptist church. Jimmy Carter attracted evangelical voters by the millions.

The irony is that President Carter betrayed these evangelical supporters— at least in their eyes.[29] He did not push the school prayer legislation that they proposed. He did not support tax exemptions for parents who sent their children to religiously based private schools. Even his promised advisory council on the state of the family backfired with his fundamentalist constituents—they decried efforts by his appointees to drop traditional definitions of the family in favor of alternative models.[30] Many voters who had rallied to President Carter readily jumped into his opponent's camp four years later. By that time, the evangelical Christian political machine was beginning to hum.[31]

Such was the backdrop for the election of 1980, when a new strategic vision emerged from groups like the Christian Voice and the Moral Majority, whose battle cry became "traditional family values."[32] Focus turned to voter registration and voter turnout. Jerry Falwell's Moral Majority rallied ten million voters (four million of whom were newly registered) to the polls in 1980.[33] Those voters came equipped with candidate "report cards" of sorts. The Christian-based organizations interviewed candidates or mined their voting records to establish their respective positions on key issues such as abortion or the ERA. These report cards were distributed in churches and neighborhoods across the country. [34] By June of 1980, still five months before the election, many liberal Democrats, even formerly powerful incumbents, could feel the ground giving way beneath their feet. All indications pointed to an approaching landslide, and come it did.

Everywhere, media pundits emphasized the role of the new Religious Right.[35] Headlines proclaimed things like "Congress Democrats Running Scared," or "Religious Right Goes for Bigger Game," or "The Religious Right: How Much Credit Can It Take for Electoral Landslide?"[36] The fact that Vice President-elect George Bush felt the need to downplay publicly the impact of the Moral Majority in the election's outcome only speaks to the prominence that the conservative Christian bloc had achieved. President Ronald Reagan's aides confirmed that he planned to make these Christian coalitions and their leaders an integral part

Figure 5.2. President Ronald Reagan touring the LDS Church's cannery in Utah, with Gordon B. Hinckley of the church's First Presidency in September 1982. At a rally later that day in nearby Hooper, Utah, President Reagan said of the LDS welfare plan, "If more people had had this idea when the Great Depression hit, there wouldn't be any government welfare today or any need for it." Photo courtesy of The Church of Jesus Christ of Latter-day Saints.

of his advisory team. Reverend Falwell was openly jubilant. To evangelicals, it seemed that Ronald Reagan personified the type of president that they had hoped for in Jimmy Carter.[37]

Yet Ronald Reagan also apparently esteemed Mormons, and to evangelicals this was a troubling sign of Mormon prominence. Early evidence of that came in the form of Mormon cabinet and staff appointments and the president's 1982 visit to Utah (Figure 5.2). On that trip he called the Mormon Welfare Plan "one of the great examples in America today of what people can do for themselves if they hadn't been dragooned into the government's doing it for them." He reasoned that "if more people had had this idea back when the Great Depression hit, there wouldn't be any government welfare today or any need for it."[38]

These overtures toward Latter-day Saints only made for a new twist in a developing paradox. With conservative Christians looking for political allies, Mormons seemed a natural choice. Mormons had long spoken out against abortion, for example, even before that cause was adopted widely by conservative evangelicals. Surprisingly, *Roe v. Wade* did not generate immediate, wholesale opposition from the evangelical community. Some evangelical publications classed the verdict as upholding the cherished right to choose and preserving freedom from an imposed morality. The separation of church and state was, after all, a historic tenet in Baptist thinking. Reverend W. A. Criswell, former president of the Southern Baptist Convention, said after the *Roe v. Wade* decision, "I have always felt that it was only after a child was born and had a life separate from its mother that it became an individual person and it has always, therefore, seemed to me that what is best for the mother and for the future should be allowed." [39] Recognizing in the mid-1970s that many Protestants were not yet up in arms over the decision, editorials in *Christianity Today*, the flagship magazine for American evangelicalism, chastised readers who dismissed abortion as a Catholic or Mormon concern and then called for a religious rethinking on the issue.[40]

Within five years, organizers of the emerging Christian political coalition decided that the implications of open access to abortions seemed representative of all that was wrong with a libertine society—and they were "surprised, even horrified, at the rising number of abortions following the *Roe v. Wade* decision."[41] As with threats to school prayer or religiously motivated private education, abortion seemed to be a severe attack on the moral values that protected the integrity of the traditional family.

Here, then, was obvious common ground on which evangelicals and Mormons could presumably form a united front, especially in the face of the Equal Rights Amendment, legislation that seemed yet another offensive in this same anti-family campaign. It quickly became apparent, as both Mormons and Christian leaders like Jerry Falwell made national headlines for their strenuous opposition to the ERA, that Mormons and evangelicals felt impelled by similar concerns.[42] And, since the two groups had largely operated along parallel paths, it seemed only strategically sensible that Christian activists would push to involve Mormons in the Moral Majority or the Christian Voice.[43]

Yet this gave many conservative Christians serious pause. Passing a political litmus test did not validate Mormons' *religious* credentials. Shared social values were not as critical as shared Christian creeds to most evangelicals. On that point, Mormon-evangelical relationships had always fractured. After all, the very series of books (*The Fundamentals*) that had spawned the fundamentalist movement had also denounced Mormonism as "thoroughly anti-Christian" for "the shameful way in which it dishonors the Bible and the Christian religion." An entire chapter was devoted to "[protecting] . . . communities from the curse" of this "most erroneous and harmful system."[44] In the search for souls Latter-day Saints and evangelicals had long been competitors; an added complication in 1980 was that those religionists most opposed to Latter-day Saint theology were often also those most interested in securing positions of national political influence. Joining with Mormons seemed unacceptable, as if such an association somehow tainted the legitimacy of the rising Christian crusade and gave too much credibility to the Mormon cause. If the aim was to preserve America as a nation founded upon and guided by the precepts of Christianity, an alliance with a heterodox sect seemed to undermine and weaken that very goal.

To be sure, Mormons were not the only religionists to fall suspect in the eyes of evangelicals. Some evangelicals even called to repentance those in mainline, traditional Protestant denominations (Episcopalians, Presbyterians, the United Church of Christ), accusing them of accepting a form of Christianity diluted by modernism. Mainline Protestants countered that evangelicals were intolerant and close-minded. Some bemoaned the rise of the politicized Religious Right and protested that they were being squeezed out of the fold of "authentic" Christianity.[45] Yet they could only watch as their mainline churches dwindled and evangelical churches boomed—"from the mainline to the sideline," in the words of historian Bruce Shelley.[46] Evangelicals' growing numbers, their broadcast networks, and their effective use of political organizing tactics maximized their impact.[47] Because of that, some observers argued that the Christian Right gave the false impression that it spoke for all Christians, let alone all born-again Christians.[48] Clearly, there was neither political nor religious uniformity even among evangelical Christians—the sheer diversity of the Protestant movement virtually assured that.

Evangelical opposition to Mormonism, though, was different, and it found wide support among conservative Christians everywhere. Mormons, in their eyes, were not like Episcopalians or Lutherans who had allowed liberalism to influence their interpretation of scripture. Mormon theology was, in fact, heresy. Considering this, historian Jan Shipps has made a compelling argument that Mormons played a primary role in conservative Christians' search for self-definition. Shipps built on the work of the Fundamentalism Project at the University of Chicago and suggested that Mormons became in the 1980s the sociological "other" against whom Christian fundamentalists defined themselves. Because the fundamentalist/evangelical political movement was based on a number of loose coalitions, it was easier to maintain the group's boundaries by defining what it was *not*, rather than what it *was*. Mormonism's similar social and moral positions made it an ideal candidate, since fundamentalist Christians could define their orthodoxy by contrasting it with Mormonism's heterodoxy. Mormonism became therefore a theological foil, the marginalized "other" that personified the danger of religious deception—and evangelicals were not shy in saying so.[49] Richard Lindsay, who took over as managing director of the LDS Church's public communications department in 1983, recalled what he felt was a pleasant encounter with several evangelical Protestant leaders on a trip to Washington, D.C., to meet with President Reagan. After returning home, Lindsay wrote to one of the pastors: "Hey, when you come out this way I would really love to have you meet the Presidency of the Church." Lindsay received what he called a "very quick returned note that said, 'Dear Richard, I love you, but I hate your theology.'"[50]

Sentiments like these made many of Jerry Falwell's evangelical constituents balk when he repeatedly included Mormons (albeit, in reality, in small numbers) on his list of Moral Majority partners, along with Catholics and Jews. Reverend

Falwell had reason to give his movement the appearance of being broad-based, especially considering the negative backlash in the media against the Moral Majority's fundamentalist core.[51] In his efforts at inclusiveness, however, Falwell found himself in the minority among his conservative Christian colleagues.

Perhaps the most blatant expression of these early misgivings came in a *Christianity Today* interview with Falwell. The *Christianity Today* interviewer asked him if he would ever preach on his television program against "the deceptive advertising in the *Readers Digest* by the Mormons." Judiciously, Falwell said that he would not attack Mormon members of his political coalition. The interviewer countered with what evangelicals certainly knew was the critical issue: "Say that in Salt Lake City they took the Moral Majority position right down the line, but because of false doctrine, they would not ultimately go to heaven....I'm concerned that we could get the country morally straight and people would still go to hell." Reverend Falwell answered that "if a nation or a society lives by divine principles, even though the people personally don't know the One who taught and lived those principles, that society will be blessed. An unsaved person will be blessed by tithing to the work of God. He'll still go to hell a tither, but God blesses the principle."[52] Indeed, the rumblings of an impending storm were growing louder.

Then in 1980 and 1981, the LDS Church announced that it would build temples in Atlanta, Georgia, and Dallas, Texas, making them the sixth and thirteenth temples, respectively, that were started during LDS President Spencer Kimball's six-year-old administration. The number of these ongoing construction projects was in itself remarkable, since only sixteen temples had been completed in the century before President Kimball. But there was something additionally significant about temples in Atlanta (Figure 5.3) and Dallas (Figure 5.4). The planned establishment of this type of Mormon presence in two symbolic strongholds of American evangelicalism grabbed the attention of religionists across the Bible belt. As in American politics in the late 1970s, it was as if Mormons had intruded onto a homeland that needed to be defended. The Mormon incursion could not be ignored.[53]

Anxious evangelicals were well aware that an increasing number of Americans accepted that Mormons *were* Christians in their overall outlook and belief system, even if they were still an anomalous bunch of Christians. The more liberal and ecumenical publication *Christian Century* referred to Mormons as Christians.[54] Profiles on the Mormon Tabernacle Choir highlighted the group's repertoire of traditional Christian music.[55] Most painful, the Mormons were winning Christian converts in droves.[56] This was at the heart of the dilemma for evangelicals. To them, Mormons were not simply Christians with a few odd practices; they were a people who worshiped the wrong Jesus, a non-Trinitarian Jesus. Mormon growth was thus actually at odds with evangelical goals to reclaim America for Christianity.[57]

Figures 5.3. LDS temple in Atlanta. The announcement of plans to build LDS temples in Atlanta and Dallas in 1980 and 1981, respectively, signaled the growing Mormon presence in the "Bible Belt" heartland, a presence that alarmed many evangelical Christians who opposed Mormon theology. Copyright Intellectual Reserve, Inc. Reprinted with the permission of The Church of Jesus Christ of Latter-day Saints.

Figure 5.4. LDS Temple in. Dallas. Copyright Intellectual Reserve, Inc. Reprinted with the permission of The Church of Jesus Christ of Latter-day Saints.

That is what made the statement from the *Christianity Today* piece about "the deceptive advertising in the *Readers Digest* by the Mormons" so telling. Evangelicals had long felt that the LDS Church was essentially a non-Christian cult. Mormonism was one of the "four major cults" described in Calvin College professor Anthony Hoekema's 1963 book by the same name.[58] The father of "countercult" apologetics, Walter Martin, dealt with LDS history and theology in his widely read textbook, *Kingdom of the Cults* (1965).[59] But by the late 1970s, concerned Christians feared that the LDS Church's successful advertising campaign had obscured the religion's true identity. A case in point: in 1979, a Gallup poll found that only 11% of respondents classified Mormonism as a cult.[60] While the number of people who held this opinion about Mormons was double or triple the number of people who regarded other American denominations (Catholics, Baptists, Methodists) as "cults," the survey nevertheless indicated that only a decided minority of Americans felt that Mormons deserved this pejorative label. Yet as in American politics, that decided minority knew how to get its voice heard.

With renewed urgency, Walter Martin published in 1978 *The Maze of Mormonism*, a three hundred-page-plus treatise on what he called the "fastest growing cult in the world." Martin warned Christians about the "occultic side of Mormonism," the "alien force that pulsates through the Mormon Church." He saw the imprint of those that the Bible calls the "spiritual rulers of darkness." That same year, John L. Smith, a longtime Protestant missionary in Utah, provocatively published an article in his anti-Mormon newsletter invoking similarities in the "cult patterns" of "the Jim Jones ruse." He concluded that Mormonism "contains all the bizarre possibilities of the Jones Cult"—the "secrecy," the requirement of "total allegiance," the "henchmen who were as ruthless as" the leader. His piece was reprinted by the Florida-based *Bible Believers Bulletin* and ended with this line: "Cultism—by whatever name—is fraught with sinister results. Avoid it like a plague." Other ministries sold audiocassette lectures with titles like "The Mormon Dilemma: Christian or Cult?" or "The Marks of a Cult." Yet even with this proliferation of anti-Mormon material, nothing exploded onto the scene like former Mormon Ed Decker's late-1982 film called *The God Makers*. Christians who saw this as a public perception battle, with casualties measured in souls, found in the film their most potent ammunition.[61]

The God Makers: "No Family in America Is Immune to This Cult's Deception"

The God Makers represented something new in anti-Mormon polemics.[62,63] It went further than simply repeating that Mormons were not Christians—a charge that Mormons were well accustomed to by the 1980s. After all, some form of "Are Mormons Christians?" was one of the five questions most commonly asked of guides at the church's 1964 World's Fair exhibit.[64] The persistence of that question had even prompted Latter-day Saint leaders to add "Another Testament of Jesus Christ" as a subtitle to the Book of Mormon in 1982, in hope of dispelling misunderstandings about the message and intent of that scripture.[65]

But instead of depicting Mormonism as a religion that had strayed from the Christian fold, *The God Makers* (and the "wave" of anti-Mormonism that the movie inaugurated) suggested something more sinister, something based less on Mormon confusion and more on Mormon cunning.[66] Ed Decker's film aimed to expose Mormonism's supposed occult—and even demonic—ties. Decker and the members of his "Saints Alive" group (also known as "Ex-Mormons for Jesus") were former Mormons who, after their respective conversions to evangelical Christianity, felt compelled to reveal the LDS Church for what to them it really represented—a dangerously alluring counterfeit of Christianity. Based on that guiding philosophy, their film pulled no punches.[67]

The God Makers opens with an aerial shot of the LDS Church's Hawaii Temple. From the beginning, the tone is ominous: "It looks beautiful from the outside," a narrator says, "but when you peel off the mask and talk to the victims, you uncover another part of the story. The documented evidence you are about to see may seem unbelievable, but it is all true." This opening scene then cuts away to a man who asserts, "When they took my family, there wasn't anything else to live for. I tried to kill myself." Another man says quietly, "They've turned my beautiful children against me." A young woman describes "the brainwashing techniques of this organization" as "really incredibly effective." The next shot is of Ed Decker sitting with two lawyers. Decker proposes a "class-action lawsuit" for the "victims" of "one of the most deceptive and most dangerous groups in the entire world." Decker tells the attorneys, "I have documentation that ties it into the occult and to Satanism." The younger of the two lawyers listens skeptically and then responds, "I have a hard time believing you. . . . These people pride themselves in a sense of family togetherness . . . and a very conspicuous form of moral rectitude." Decker shoots back, "That's part of the incredible deception, and . . . we need to expose it." Only then do viewers discover that this unnamed organization is, in fact, The Church of Jesus Christ of Latter-day Saints, "one of the wealthiest and fastest-growing religions" in the world, thanks to its "carefully groomed, Osmond-family image."[68]

"To most of us," the narrator warns, "Mormons appear to be real Christians who live their faith." Two ex-Mormons agree: "These people seem to be Christian . . . they had the same attributes." Naïve converts are lured in, according to one former member, by the church's "social program, which was fabulous" or "the family atmosphere." An anxiety over Mormon growth pervades the movie. Repeated references to the church's army of young missionaries, or to the chapels that were being built at a rate of two every day around the world, or to estimates that the LDS Church membership could number 70 million within only a few decades, mark the film's narrative.

Yet *The God Makers* leaves little doubt that what is to be most feared about the Mormons is their bizarre doctrine, taught secretly inside cloistered temples but not disclosed to potential converts. The bulk of the film proceeds with almost no musical accompaniment; however, the scenes that discuss Joseph Smith's epiphanies or Mormon temple rituals play against a soundtrack that even Sandra Tanner, an avowed opponent of the church who appeared in the film, later called "spooky."[69]

A choppy cartoon segment gives a brief overview of Latter-day Saint beliefs, which apparently center on the precept that "billions of...highly-evolved humanoids" rule the universe. Two of these "extra-terrestrial humanoids from a distant star called Kolob visited a 14-year-old boy"—a "treasure-seeker...known for his tall tales"—"named Joseph Smith." This event launched Mormonism, a religion with the ultimate purpose of helping men and women become part of the exalted "humanoid" ruling class. When the cartoon ends, the same lawyer who protested earlier shakes his head and says, "This sounds like science fiction or Greek mythology." Ed Decker explains, "That's why it's such a secret. That's why even the Mormons don't talk about it. They're embarrassed by it, too."

At a number of screenings of *The God Makers*, as soon as the lights came up at the movie's end, Mormon viewers were anxious to dispute statements such as this one. To Latter-day Saints, *The God Makers* presented a caricature of Mormonism that left them dumbfounded more than embarrassed. The film seemed based on distortions that made their church unrecognizable. For example, according to the movie, the "secret ceremonies" in the temple "are reserved for an elite few," such that "even most Mormons have never seen" them. While this assertion was technically true if "most" meant a simple majority (since only actively participating *adults* worship in the temple), it also belied the reality that hundreds of thousands of Mormons had participated in these rites over the years, a number not readily suggested by the phrase "an elite few." Likewise, the film's insinuation that Joseph Smith's death somehow superseded that of Jesus Christ would likely have been as offensive to a Mormon viewer as it would have been to an evangelical. Yet because the film warned viewers that Mormons had been instructed to use Christian terminology when talking with others, *God Makers* effectively rendered any Mormon claim to Christian faith suspect. In fact, those who discussed Latter-day Saint theology in the movie pointedly used the qualifier "the *Mormon* Jesus" to separate LDS beliefs from those of traditional Christianity.

In this way, the movie grated on Mormon sensibilities as it portrayed a church and a culture that seemed foreign to most Latter-day Saints. There were testimonials in the film from a half-dozen women who said their Mormon bishops encouraged them to divorce their evangelical Christian husbands—and those women saw this as the ultimate hypocrisy for a church with a family-friendly façade. Another woman related that a psychiatric-nurse friend asked her, "Why is it that there are so many [Mormon] women in my [hospital] ward?" There was a father in the film who said that his teenage son had recently committed suicide because of church pressure to conform—symptomatic, the movie implied, of a suicide rate in Utah that "one of the world's foremost experts on Mormonism" called "much higher" than the national average. Yet perhaps nothing in the film jarred Latter-day Saints as much as the depiction of temple rites and theology, especially in a cartoon-animated segment that seemed designed to be intentionally crude and ridiculous in its presentation format.

While the film was unapologetic in its dismissal of Mormonism's sacred tenets and ordinances, several interviewees did strike a tone of sympathy for the unknowing Mormon believer. A college professor who scoffed at the authenticity of the Book of Mormon sadly admitted that it "never ceases to amaze how many intelligent people are Mormons but are locked in and won't even take another look" because of a culture that emphasized "[accepting] what their church leaders" say rather than a "sit down and study" for yourself approach. Sandra Tanner suggested that LDS missionaries should not necessarily be blamed for perpetuating Mormon falsehoods, since "Mormon leaders are deliberately keeping from [them] the true history of their religion because they know [Mormons] will have a hard time believing it's from God if [they] saw how it really was all put together." Nor did most Mormons know, as Ed Decker revealed near the end of the movie, that in Anton Szandor LaVey's *The Satanic Bible* under "infernal names," "Mormo" was the god of the living dead, king of the ghouls—and Mormons, not surprisingly to Decker, are obsessed with converting the dead. For Decker's group, all of the evidence pointed to the same conclusion: Joseph Smith borrowed more from the occult than he did from authentic Christianity. This message, they felt, demanded an audience, and they certainly found one.

No previous anti-Mormon campaign had carried as far and as wide as *The God Makers*. By late 1983, the movie was being shown to "about 1,000 audiences a month," often to "standing-room only crowds."[70] Part of its appeal was its documentary approach. Commentary by expert witnesses and even some Latter-day Saints gave it credibility and a sense of fairness, since the Mormons who appeared on the film only seemed to corroborate (at least in the final edit) the sensational claims made by outsiders. Yet the film also succeeded because it came at a time when there was a heightened awareness of Mormon gains, in converts, prestige, and acceptance. Utah pastor Bill Heersink, who watched as *God Makers* screenings spread from church to church, concluded that "a lot of religious people" need "something they can really be against—that's where they get their identity," especially in settings like Utah, where evangelicals' minority status created "insecurity and fear." Similar apprehension over Mormonism's growing nationwide presence fueled newspaper advertisements for the movie in Mississippi, Ohio, and California, all of which carried the same message: the "film unmasks the myth of Mormonism—from Family Home Evening to the Actual Secret Temple Rituals."[71]

Apart from the sheer sensational nature of the material, the number of prominent evangelicals who endorsed the film also gave it added exposure and authority. Promotional materials quoted Hal Lindsey, who wrote the 1970s dispensationalist best-seller *Late Great Planet Earth*: "This incredible motion picture is a must for everyone." Cult expert Walter Martin called the movie "a factual, accurate analysis...devastating!" A prominent author and pastor of an influential California mega-church said the movie was "dynamite! The most powerful thing I've seen. Get your Mormon friends to view it!"[72]

The plea to "get your Mormon friends to view it" highlighted one of the significant aims of the movie campaign. Part of this new thrust of anti-Mormon activity was to reclaim Mormon converts who had left traditional Christian denominations to become Latter-day Saints. In interviews and speeches, Decker and his associates did not mince words about their objectives.[73] They consistently raised the point that the majority of those who joined the LDS Church—"75% of their converts"—came from Christian backgrounds.[74] They proposed that this threat to orthodox Christianity could be thwarted by "[looking] behind the 'Osmond image'" that attracted Mormon converts in the first place.[75]

Decker's Saints Alive representatives often attended screenings of the film for question-and-answer sessions following the movie. Salt Lake City pastor Greg Johnson, an ex-Mormon teenager in 1983, described himself as something of a "trophy" for evangelicals, since he had left the LDS Church and was willing to attend screenings of *The God Makers* "every Sunday night in Southern California" to share his conversion story. Johnson later reflected that it was not until he had left Mormonism that he realized "the great angst" evangelicals felt toward Latter-day Saints. He described that angst as a feeling that "the Mormon Church is a burning building," such that a "sense of urgency" and a "desire to...rescue" led Saints Alive to characterize the church as a "cult" and Joseph Smith as a "charlatan."[76]

This overt counter-evangelizing strategy was only one of several factors that made the impact of the *God Makers* phenomenon unique. The extent of the *God Makers*' reach—in the neighborhood of a quarter of a million viewers a month in 1984—made it virtually impossible for concerned Mormons to neutralize, and the movie's broad appeal both revealed and reinvigorated deep-seated feelings about the Mormon menace to "true" Christianity.[77]

The rift showed up in unlikely places. In the spring of 1983, the team from a Mormon congregation in Morehead City, North Carolina, was voted out of a Christian softball league by its denominational competitors. The Baptist,

Methodist, and Pentecostal teams reportedly did not feel animosity toward individual Mormons; however, they did not feel it appropriate to include them in a "Christian" league. Newspapers in the state decried this exclusion as hypocritical and praised the local recreation department for rescinding the league's county park privileges. In response to being dropped from public parks, the Christian league representatives "responded that allowing the Mormon team to join could set a precedent that eventually would require the Christian league to accept Satan worshippers and other religious cults. One league member cited a passage from the Bible's Book of John—it tells Christians not to accept every doctrine—as proof that the Mormon team should be excluded from the league."[78] Their stance was that "we cannot extend the hand of Christian fellowship to those who do not believe in the same Jesus Christ."[79]

This was not merely a fringe view championed by a few Christian extremists. Dean Merrill, senior editor for *Leadership* magazine, wrote an article in Dr. James Dobson's January 1984 *Focus on the Family* publication. He described how he and his wife learned about weekly family nights from the parents of their son's friend. These friends, Merrill revealed, "belonged to a non-Christian religious sect." They were Mormons. When Merrill found out about his neighbors' dedicated family time, he decided he "was not going to be outtaught by people I felt were seriously mistaken in their faith. It was time for me to put my actions where my convictions were as a Christian father."[80]

Tom Minnery, senior editor of *Christianity Today*, wrote a telling letter to a Mormon who protested that magazine's decision to publish ads for *God Makers* and other blatantly anti-Mormon materials. Minnery's response was brief but pointed: "Dear Mr. McHarry: Thank you for your thoughts in response to the Ed Decker advertisement in *Christianity Today*. We Christians must always be charitable with one another. Yet, I must point out to you that we do not consider the Mormon Church to be Christian. Its doctrinal views carry it a far distance from orthodox Christianity. Mormonism is not, as you say in your letter, a large denomination. It is a movement unto itself, completely separate from Christian denominations."[81]

Not every Christian group that opposed the spread of Mormonism also countenanced *The God Makers'* approach, though. Pat Robertson's Christian Broadcasting Network, for example, canceled one of its programs because of that program's intended use of the *God Makers'* cartoon segment. Robertson wrote that he made the decision after "several high ranking Mormons said that ridicule of this nature would enrage them and would not be considered in the interest of fairness.... They just asked that we not participate in a show which ridicules their sacred rituals. I agreed to that, and will continue to do so." Yet Robertson made it clear that he nevertheless found Mormon doctrine heretical, even though "the Mormons are very wonderful people in their family life and their diligence to support patriotic concepts of our country. I totally disagree with their religious points of view and find them unbiblical. Nevertheless, we do not gain by hatred and ridicule. We gain by love and demonstration of the truth." [82]

Other Protestant ministers agreed that relying on *The God Makers'* "offensive...negative criticism" and "terrible distortions" was not the best way to counteract Mormonism.[83] Still, the sheer level of nationwide interest in, and responsiveness to, Ed Decker's movie spoke to the underlying fear of Mormon intrusion in the competitive religious marketplace.[84] Many Christians in the mid-1980s were all too aware that "in the U.S., Mormons [had] swelled their ranks by 41% since 1970. By comparison, during this period, Southern Baptists expanded by 22%, Roman Catholics grew 8% and Episcopalians declined by 15%."[85]

Very often, evangelical detractors of "non-Christian" Mormonism used growth figures such as these to give their criticisms relevance. They left little doubt that the battleground was the field of church proselytizing. The same *Newsweek* article, mentioned earlier, that had a Dallas-area pastor worrying about the number of Baptists-turned-Mormons, reported that in Texas alone "Mormons claim...5,000 convert baptisms...over the last two years—a rate of 60 [sic] a day."[86] During a TV talk show in Seattle, a young woman representing Saints Alive told viewers, "As a Christian, I became interested in [Saints Alive] just because of how many people are being deceived. If you look at how many people have become Mormons, 40,000 people are estimated to [have] become Mormons just because of Donny and Marie [Osmond]." A pastor in Washington told a reporter there, "We could have just as easily singled out any other (religion)...[but] with the growth of Mormonism and the facts of what is going on behind the scenes in Mormonism, (we felt) that people need to know what was taking place and what it was really all about....I would say they are a perversion in what they have done to their people."[87]

The official LDS response to these assaults was muted. Below the surface, however, the wheels of the church's public relations mechanism churned. The long-standing official LDS position was that the church would not respond point-by-point to its detractors, but instead try to reflect its true identity by moving forward with its work.[88] Thus the church filed no lawsuits (a point that, ironically, Saints Alive used to its advantage to bolster the purported accuracy of its claims) and published no direct rebuttals of *The God Makers* in the form of books or tracts for dissemination by missionaries.[89] The LDS Church's First Presidency reasoned in a December 1983 letter to local church leaders that "this opposition may be in itself an opportunity. Among the continuing challenges faced by our missionaries is a lack of interest in religious matters and in our message. These criticisms create such an interest in the Church...We have evidence to indicate that in areas where opposition has been particularly intense, the growth of the Church has actually been hastened rather than retarded."[90]

The intensity of that "opposition" meant, though, that the movie and its traveling advocates reached millions of Americans. Still, *The God Makers* did not attract much *national* news coverage. In many ways, the context of the debate seemed limited to the evangelical/fundamentalist Christian subculture. Thus national media outlets did little more than note that the fast-growing LDS Church had always generated opponents, and evangelical Christians were flocking to a new movie that portrayed some of their traditional charges against the Mormons.[91] In contrast, *local* papers, especially those in the Pacific Northwest and California (Saints Alive was headquartered in Issaquah, Washington), did generate heat over the movie, primarily because advertisements for screenings prompted numerous letters to the editor.

The community-level nature of *The God Makers* controversy matched a guiding philosophy of the LDS Church's Public Communications staff: "the public perception of the Church is a local phenomenon."[92] In keeping with that philosophy, church officials decided that the best way to combat *The God Makers* campaign would be a decentralized, regional or community-specific counteroffensive to match the local church distribution model that Ed Decker's group employed.

Decentralized did not in this case mean detached or disinterested. Yet some of the church's public relations strategists worried that a strenuous, headquarters-level rebuttal campaign might "perpetuate a sense of persecution and alarm because it would deal only with the negative portion of publicity that the Church is getting as opposed to a more balanced approach." Such a campaign, they reasoned, could easily backfire, since it "could be used against the Church and could reinforce a 'siege' mentality."[93]

Therefore, even though internal LDS Public Communications Department memos from late 1983 and 1984 reveal that anti-Mormon activities were a constant subject of discussion between Mormon headquarters-based strategists and local volunteers across the country, it was those volunteers who were assigned the lead in their respective locales.[94] The vast majority of newspaper accounts that dealt with Saints Alive–type activity quoted a local or regional director of LDS Church public relations, rather than a Salt Lake-based spokesman, evidence that the volunteer network envisioned by Wendell Ashton in the 1970s had succeeded, at least, in its stated aim of establishing contacts with the media. These public relations representatives were encouraged by their superiors in Salt Lake City to promote positive stories about local Mormons to offset negative publicity surrounding *The God Makers*. The volunteer representatives were then advised to parry future attacks with an appeal to anti-defamation sensibility, rather than a direct confrontation of Saints Alive's claims. In this vein Mormon officials petitioned school districts to ban screenings of *The God Makers* in high schools and urged newspapers to be more selective in their publication of abusive advertisements and readers' letters. [95]

These efforts yielded some results. The *Mesa (Arizona) Tribune* and the *Atlanta Constitution* refused ads for screenings of *The God Makers*. A Hillsboro, Oregon, paper gave the local LDS stake (diocese) president the "last word" in a series of letter-to-the-editor debates over Mormonism's Christian status. A California LDS public communications team advertised a film featuring LDS members' statements about their belief in Jesus Christ. Several radio stations and newspapers in Sacramento announced the screening of this Mormon movie. The film was shown at a series of simultaneous meetings at LDS Church buildings in the area, and it succeeded in softening at least the antagonism of Saints Alive's Sacramento representative. A Eugene, Oregon, newspaper even ran an extensive feature that disputed some of the most derogatory claims in *The God Makers*. Ed Decker had asserted that teen suicide in Utah was several times higher than the national average, and that the murder of children in Utah also dramatically exceeded national averages. Decker's movie insinuated that child abuse and neglect were epidemic in Mormon families. All of these claims were demonstrably and statistically false, according to the story in the *Eugene Register-Guard*, and the newspaper had some of those who were interviewed for the film, including Decker himself, backtracking about the reliability of their sources. [96]

Importantly, some community religious groups also rallied around the LDS Church in their denunciation of *The God Makers* and the tactics of Ex-Mormons for Jesus. Roger Keller, a Presbyterian minister in Arizona, led an interfaith push to oppose the distribution of what he called "religious pornography." He used that phrase in a letter to the editor that he wrote the day after he saw the movie. That descriptive condemnation of the film found its way into more and more media reports in local newspapers, and a number of churches publicly disassociated from sister congregations who opted to show the movie. Reverend Keller also pushed the Arizona chapter of the National Conference of Christians and Jews (NCCJ) to issue a statement opposing the film. Initially, some of his colleagues thought a public statement would be "overkill," but he pressed them to action. His reasoning was that "if this were about Catholicism or Judaism, you wouldn't bat an eye" over issuing such a statement, but "everyone's religious freedom is also my religious freedom." In an ironic twist, Ed Decker's group sued the NCCJ for $25 million for impeding the sale of the film, although a California judge quickly dismissed the suit.[97]

Despite these inroads made by Latter-day Saints and their sympathetic supporters, *The God Makers*, it seemed, would simply not go away. Ed Decker made news with allegations about death threats, drive-by shootings, and attempted assaults against him and other members of Saints Alive by Latter-day Saint vigilantes.[98] He garnered attention with his claim that 10,000 Mormons had left the LDS Church and subsequently found Jesus as a result of *The God Makers* movie and the pair-by-pair missionary work that Saints Alive initiated in the 1980s. Decker's organization also estimated that it had prevented 15,000 potential converts from joining the Mormons, based on declines in the annual rate of growth reported by the LDS Church.[99]

Mormon leaders downplayed Decker's group's role in the supposed numerical losses in church membership, citing instead a reduced missionary force that still made remarkable gains for the church—some 200,000 converts in 1985.[100] Yet they did not deny the increase in anti Mormon fervor. Church leaders conceded that this marked opposition was the most vigorous since the days of persecution over polygamy.[101]

The God Makers even fueled a backlash against an LDS Church building project as far away as Jerusalem. In the mid-1980s, the LDS Church was in the process of constructing an extension center for its Brigham Young University study-abroad program in Jerusalem. The center's location on the Mount of Olives drew the attention of local Israelis, as did the center's connection to a church with a reputation for aggressive proselytizing. Despite Mormon promises to refrain from missionary work in Israel, and despite support for the BYU center from Jerusalem Mayor Teddy Kollek, intense opposition against the Latter-day Saints' plans flared up in 1985—protest marches, inflammatory local headlines, even a bomb threat.[102] In the summer of 1985, Mormon leaders charged "Decker and his group, Saints Alive" with "fomenting protests by orthodox Jews in Israel." That summer, "Saints Alive showed the 'God Makers'...to a committee of the Israeli Knesset" and "[helped] organize a letter-writing protest campaign" directed at Mayor Kollek.[103]

The impact and durability of the Saints Alive campaign took even Mormon public relations officials by surprise. One of the church's employees remembered that "early on...the thought was that it was a small group of people, they're extremists, and no one is going to pay attention to them. They are not going to bother the church....Let's just ignore them and continue on doing our work. We quickly learned that wasn't the case."[104] It was not that the lack of national media coverage of the film lulled Mormon leaders into indifference about *The God Makers*; the vigorous activity of the church's volunteer network showed that was not the case. Yet for church leaders accustomed to a long history of public opposition, the threat posed by *The God Makers* and its purveyors did not at first seem a cause for undue alarm. "'This happens in cycles,' [Lewiston, Idaho, LDS Stake President Richard N.] Young said of the film. 'Every 10 years or so we have very heated anti-Mormon feelings. Then it subsides."[105] Somehow, though, the effect of the grass-roots *God Makers* campaign on outside perception of Mormonism seemed different. Instead of subsiding, it snowballed.

Considering the long history of evangelical/Mormon polemics, what made *The God Makers* so singularly successful, in that it gained so much traction in evangelical circles?

Its explosiveness seemed both a product of timing and topic. Roger Keller observed that the film flared up at "a natural flashpoint between evangelicals and Latter-day Saints." He borrowed an analogy from physics: "two bodies can't occupy the same space at the same time." In the late 1970s and early 1980s, evangelicals and Latter-day Saints clearly vied for the same space. Both groups, Keller noted, "[claimed] to restore New Testament Christianity"—or, in the case of evangelicals vis-à-vis mainline Protestants and a liberalizing American society, *preserve* New Testament Christianity—and they therefore competed for converts to their respective restorations.[106] To attract newcomers, both groups had also prominently raised the banner of family values, even to the point of overt political activism. If anything, though, these similar objectives compelled evangelicals to highlight their disagreements with Mormons.

In the late 1970s, evangelicals were on the march. Their numbers swelled, thanks to a host of energetic outreach ministries and charismatic television preachers. Well-publicized interpretations of biblical end-time prophecies pulled in throngs of converts convinced that world events portended the imminent return of Jesus Christ. All around them they saw evidence of moral deterioration and court-mandated hostility toward religious practice in the public square. These conservative Christians worried that if America became an inhospitable host for Christianity, such a turn would threaten all prospects for worldwide evangelizing before the end came. Several of evangelical Christianity's most prominent leaders therefore sought to shape their movement's growing ranks into a political constituency to combat initiatives that threatened traditional values—the ERA, abortion, pornography. For many in the movement, political involvement represented a significant change after a half-century of public withdrawal. The elections of 1976 and especially 1980 were moments of political reawakening.

Importantly, whether in terms of religion or politics, coalitions and associations characterized the evangelical movement. The denominational diversity of Protestantism meant that a large number of churches qualified, in evangelical eyes, as acceptable venues for dispensing the true Christian faith. It was adherence to common creeds rather than a central ecclesiastical structure that gave a church evangelical legitimacy. In such a diffuse movement, it seemed simpler and more economical to designate which churches were *not* acceptable or Christian. The Church of Jesus Christ of Latter-day Saints thus became a chief target in the 1980s precisely because of the success of its recent efforts to gain acceptability and promote its Christianity. The Mormons seemed to defend the same traditional values that evangelicals prized, yet to evangelicals, this only obscured the reality that Mormon proselytizing worked *against* their evangelizing aims. The dramatic growth of The Church of Jesus Christ of Latter-day Saints offered sufficient reason for urgency.

In 1984, sociologist Rodney Stark predicted that the world's nearly six million Mormons could easily grow their ranks to 260 million by the year 2080, if their rate of growth held steady. As he put it, Mormonism "[stood] on the threshold of becoming the first major faith to appear on earth since the prophet Muhammed rode out of the desert." Though Stark initially regarded this research and its publication "as minor," he was surprised that his "projections...attracted considerable media attention." Some of that "attention [was] prompted by Mormon-bashers seeking to alarm the world about the impending LDS take-over."[107] Not everyone shared Professor Stark's tongue-in-cheek attitude about the Mormon takeover. Some political activists saw Mormon power as a legitimate threat to liberal democracy. Yet an even greater number of Americans saw Mormon growth trends as foreshadowing religious disaster for the authentic Christian faith.

Historian Jan Shipps drew widespread notice when she wrote in 1985 that Mormonism was a new religious movement. She suggested that Mormonism was to Christianity what Christianity was to Judaism.[108] For those who saw Mormonism as a Christian heresy, though, her description was unsatisfactory and incomplete, since it suggested that the religion incorporated authentic Christianity. In *The God Makers*, these evangelical critics found confirmation that Mormonism was something far removed from Christianity—and deceptively so. *The God Makers* resonated with them because it was presented as a convincing counterattack that unmasked the LDS Church's misleading façade.[109] The film thus became the weapon of choice in this battle for souls and legitimacy.

What made this 1980s brand of opposition especially potent, too, was that the same effective use of broadcast media that had facilitated conservative Christianity's political rise also drove the wide dissemination of *The God Makers'* case against Mormonism. In 1984, a year after the film's premiere, LDS public communications officials recognized that while anti-Mormonism was "certainly not a new phenomenon...there has been, however, an increase in the usage of 'public' channels of communications for these messages, particularly in newspapers and over radio and TV."[110]

For many of its viewers, the imprint made on the Mormon image by a *God Makers* screening was deeper and longer lasting than the effect of even a nationally circulated, controversial magazine essay about covert Mormon ERA opposition or Mormon wealth. *The God Makers* reached a specific consumer. Because of the film's distribution model, the movie was shown most frequently to those who attended church, and in the early 1980s, attendance at evangelical churches was sharply on the rise. These church attendees were often the very people that Mormon missionaries sought to find and enlist as investigators, since spiritual matters were, ostensibly, already a priority for regular worshippers. Seeing the movie at a local church gave the presentation added credence, since a trusted pastor often endorsed and arranged for the showing.[111] In the Mormon view, therefore, the challenge that *The God Makers* represented was that it reached a crucial target audience—local churchgoers—and perpetuated falsehoods in an environment of trust.

The premise of the movie, and the premise of Saints Alive, was that good people with honest intentions could be duped by a skillfully masked occult organization.[112] This explanation of how seemingly good people could belong to a non-Christian cult allowed for a psychological disconnect of sorts for viewers who could thus differentiate between well-liked Mormon neighbors and the counterfeit organization that had blinded them.[113] Millions of evangelical Christians saw *The God Makers* as a definitive representation of the Mormon deception.[114] The Mormon image, at their hands, came out battered and bruised.

Some Latter-day Saints saw this coming, but for others it was jolting. In the early 1980s, Lorry Rytting, an analyst at LDS headquarters, had developed "News Map," a computer database that tracked Mormon-related news items. He issued what a colleague called a "thoughtful and urgent appeal to be aware" of the uptick in anti-Mormon media, but "it just wasn't in the consciousness of the [church hierarchy] until the [*The God Makers*] movie really created some problems."[115]

There is no question that the movie did create significant public perception problems for the LDS Church. At the same time, though, and outside of its admittedly large niche audience, *The God Makers* struggled for credibility. By 1992, Ed Decker claimed that he had sold 400,000 copies of his *The God Makers* book, yet the release of the sequel film *The God Makers II* in that same year drew mostly censure.[116] The NCCJ had "condemned the [first] video for purveying 'half-truths' and 'faulty generalizations.'"[117] That group criticized the second film even more strongly for "[carrying] the odious scent of unreasoning prejudice." The NCCJ denounced *The God Makers II* for its reliance on "unsubstantiated stories" to represent the church as an "evil empire founded upon sexual exploitation, predatory greed and Satanism."[118] The claims in the sequel seemed too outlandish even for those outside the church; a cable television operator thus denied a request to show the film on its "community-access channel" after learning that the film "slanders a Mormon leader by calling him a bisexual."[119]

Even before the sequel was released, a Houston-area library made news when it refused to accept Ed Decker's *God Makers* book from an Assemblies of God minister who tried to donate it. The minister charged the library and the city council with censorship, but the chief librarian and mayor responded that the book was not accepted because of problems with "bias and balance."[120] And as prolific and renowned as Sandra Tanner was as a publisher of anti-Mormon tracts in Utah, she still admitted to some "reservations about the [first *God Makers*] film" because of "exaggeration" and "overstatement."[121] Utah pastor Bill Heersink noted that by the time of *The God Makers II*, it had become increasingly clear that Tanner mistrusted Ed Decker. This "rift" hurt both the second film and the Saints Alive cause even in anti-Mormon circles.[122]

Therefore, as widely viewed and inflammatory as it was, the impact of *The God Makers* on the Mormon image, by itself, most likely would have been limited to an important but specific demographic group (evangelical Christians) if it had not been that the movie's themes and allegations seemed simultaneously corroborated by other more mainstream sources. National periodicals, broadcast news organizations, and secular publishers turned their attention to Mormonism when a series of scandals rocked Salt Lake City in the 1980s and early 1990s. These additional voices suggested that perhaps evangelical shots at the LDS Church's dark "underside" had hit their mark.[123] The producer of *The God Makers* had claimed, "If the truth be known about the Mormon Church, the average American citizen would live in fear"; echoes of her warning began to reach new ears.[124]

6

Familiar Spirits, Part Two:
The 1980s and Early 1990s

A century before the ERA or *The God Makers*, in the thick of congressional sanctions against Mormon plural marriage, a Massachusetts newspaper suggested that "not polygamy but the power of the Priesthood is the real danger... The essential principle of Mormonism is not polygamy at all but the ambition of an ecclesiastical hierarchy to wield sovereignty: to rule the souls and lives of its subjects with absolute authority, unrestrained by any civil power."[1] If old suspicions about Mormons' despotic dreams were given new life in the 1980s, it was concern over the church's "ambition" to "wield... absolute authority" more than doctrinal disputes with evangelicals that drove those suspicions and turned Mormon-related controversies into national news. Broadly speaking, theocracy was more worrisome than theology.

In the 1960s and 1970s, the large number of Mormon state legislators in Utah must have seemed largely irrelevant to most Americans. Regional politics were one thing; amendments to the U.S. Constitution, however, quite another. The effectiveness of Mormon mobilization against the ERA awakened new awareness of—and anxiety over—the church's size and power. Intrigued journalists began publishing articles and books that used the word "empire" to describe what they saw as the still-underestimated financial and political clout of the LDS Church.

If that clout *was* underestimated by the general public, these writers intimated, the church was succeeding in its aims, since the Mormon hierarchy intended that some things remain concealed. In fact, a shade of institutional secrecy colored much of the reporting on Mormonism in the 1980s, and this carried far beyond revenue disclosure. Journalists sensed that new currents in Mormon history were churning up evidence that called into question official accounts of the church's origins. While early on only a few media outlets chronicled what seemed like church efforts to suppress such evidence, virtually every news organization in the country flocked to Salt Lake City when a series of three bombs turned historical controversy into homicide. To the church's dismay, even the eventual discovery that the bomber, Mark Hofmann, was also a master forger of historical documents did little to quiet rumors about church cover-up and conspiracy.

These rumors owed their persistence, in part, to other troubling incidents of violence that seemed to spring from Mormonism's past. Several so-called "Mormon fundamentalists" who continued to operate in a sort of polygamous underground took their religious beliefs to murderous ends. Despite the LDS Church's efforts to distance itself from these offshoot groups, new attention to twentieth-century polygamy reinvigorated nineteenth-century fears about the Mormon belief system.

As the church sought publicly to define boundaries between the mainstream and the extreme, some writers and scholars on Mormonism's liberal periphery complained that these recent scandals had made the church's leadership increasingly intolerant of dissenting or alternative voices. As if to confirm their fears, six of the most outspoken of these Mormon intellectuals were excommunicated from the church in September 1993. Church leaders insisted that they had a responsibility to protect members from apostasy. Critics saw it as the latest in a string of disconcerting events that demonstrated that the Mormon hierarchy sought to control, repress, and even silence those who would mar its public face.

No longer was the conflict solely about religious proselytizing. Evangelicals' sectarian misgivings about Mormonism seemed to find secular and sometimes salacious counterparts in the headlines that came out of Salt Lake City in the decade after *The God Makers*. The Mormon image was taking hits on all sides. From different places and for different reasons, conservative Christians, investigative journalists, and Mormon intellectuals all seemed to harbor similar suspicions about the LDS Church: Mormons did not want their true story getting out, and the church used its power and wealth to preserve its standing and protect its secrets.

"Big Brother"

In Gallup's 1979 survey about the differences between a "cult" and a "religion," pollsters asked, "How [do] you...decide that a religious organization is a 'cult' instead of a church or religion," or how do you "distinguish between a cult and a religion?" (This was the same survey in which 11% of respondents classified Mormonism as a cult.) The number one answer given was that the group's "head is a person playing God." Few made that charge against Mormonism. The number two answer to the pollsters' question, however, was that a cult "[controlled] the lives of [its] members."[2]

Unfortunately, Gallup did not ask a corresponding follow-up question a decade later, so there is no comparative poll by which to gauge changes in opinion over the course of the 1980s regarding Mormonism's "cult" status. What can be traced, however, is the increasing number of groups and individuals in the 1980s and early 1990s that depicted the LDS Church as an organization that indeed "controlled the lives of its members."

On that score, *The God Makers* and Saints Alive had made brazen accusations against the Mormons. *Christianity Today*, too, reported in 1982 on Jim Rogers, a Mormon-turned-evangelical Christian whose wife left him "on the advice of a Mormon bishop"—and then disappeared. The magazine informed readers that "Rogers does not, in fact, know where his children and former wife are."[3] Yet other accusations about Mormon authoritarianism, though not as dramatic perhaps as this one, were not limited to the evangelical community.

Kenneth Danforth wrote a seven-page feature for *Harper's* in 1980 titled "The Cult of Mormonism," yet there was no discussion of theological disagreements with other Christians. Instead, Danforth's essay took exception to the church's more mundane interests. He argued that "of all the cities in the Western World, none is so firmly in the moral, economic, and political grip of a prudish cult" than was Salt Lake City. One of the church members he interviewed worried that Utah "was run virtually as a dictatorship" by the church. What especially troubled Danforth was that there was no public accountability for the church's income and expenditures, since the church did not make that information available even to its members. He was skeptical when spokesman Wendell Ashton said that he trusted the church's First Presidency. Danforth countered, if "everything is on the up and up, . . . why do they object so strenuously to opening the books?" He also suggested that "the church has a reputation for fighting tax assessments and never paying an uncontested penny." He noted that Associated Press reporters Bill Beecham and David Briscoe had recently interviewed "more than fifty sometime fearful persons" to put together "the most comprehensive picture we have of the Mormon financial empire." Ironically, though (critics would say) not unexpectedly, "not a single newspaper in Utah published their story."[4]

James Mann in *U.S. News and World Report* painted the same portrait of purported church control over Utah media outlets. Not only did the "secretive council of 12 elders" choose the church's president, the group "[refused] to disclose financial details." In a similarly clandestine way, "most church influence is exerted behind the scenes. . . . through devoted members who hold virtually all the top political posts and do most of the private hiring. When a recent television documentary was prepared on the emotional strains of Mormonism upon women, editors blocked its broadcast until the program's length was doubled to include more footage on the church's point of view."[5]

A two-part, front-page series in the *Wall Street Journal* in 1983 noted that "civil libertarians" worried about Mormon hegemony over "every aspect of life" in Utah, especially at the level of state legislation. University of Utah professor J. D. Williams, a Mormon who was "critical of the church's political involvement," told the newspaper that "non-Mormons can only look toward the Mormon Church and wonder, 'What is Big Brother doing to me today?'" In that same vein, the *Journal* observed that "leaders of Mormonism double as overseers of a financial empire."[6]

While the focus of these articles was the church's dominance in Utah, the inescapable implication was that Mormons had also quietly extended their financial influence well beyond Utah. Danforth reported that Mormons were in top management positions at "Phillips Petroleum, Safeway, Nabisco, Anaconda, Del Monte, and Western Electric." Gordon B. Hinckley of the church's First Presidency told the *Wall Street Journal* that "the business involvement which we have is a very, very minor part of our activity," yet his disclaimer was overshadowed by the reality reported in these articles that the church owned television and radio stations across the country, plus department stores and office buildings. "All told," Danforth figured, "this monolithic enterprise brings in more than $3 million dollars a day—more than a billion dollars a year—into one central apostolic kitty." More than that, "the church ... has sent out its tentacles into the boardrooms of America."[7]

Such was the basic thesis behind two book-length treatments on Mormonism that came from respectable, national, secular presses in the mid-1980s. These books put apprehension about the growing Mormon influence on a new, highly documented footing. In 1984, Robert Gottlieb and Peter Wiley published *America's Saints: The Rise of Mormon Power*, and in 1985, John Heinerman and Anson Shupe published *The Mormon Corporate Empire*. Not only did the credibility of their books' publishing houses distinguish them from *The God Makers*–type fare, their focus on politics and economics over theology appealed to a more general reader. Therefore, even though these new publications may not have shared in the same sensationalism of evangelical anti-Mormon tracts, they nevertheless reached new audiences and raised serious questions about the public reputation of the LDS Church. Gottlieb and Wiley called theirs the story of "an increasingly potent political force, flexing its muscle nationally in Congress and in the White House." Their book also aimed to profile "the little-known men at the top who control" this "economic empire." The dust jacket of Heinerman and Shupe's book told readers that they held in their hands "a thorough examination of Mormonism as a corporate entity that influences the lives of *all Americans*."[8]

To those who felt that such claims about the breadth of Mormon influence were simply overstatements meant to sell books, the authors pointed to a recent example. As the 1980s opened, the U.S. Defense Department proposed building, in the vast desert straddling Utah and Nevada, a network of over 4,000 shelters located along 9,000 miles of roadway on which constantly moving MX missile carriers would travel. The scheme was designed to make the missile launch sites into moving targets, so that the Soviet enemies could not destroy the American warheads in one quick strike. While the plan promised Utahans thousands of related jobs and billions in construction dollars, the LDS Church took exception to the increased burden of risk that Utah and the West would bear. In a May 1981 statement, the First Presidency opposed this threat of attack specifically, as well as the idea of nuclear proliferation generally: "We repeat our warnings against the terrifying arms race in which the nations of the earth are presently engaged. We deplore in particular the building of vast arsenals of nuclear weaponry. We are advised that there is already enough such weaponry to destroy in large measure our civilization, with consequent suffering and misery of incalculable extent.... We are most gravely concerned over the proposed concentration in a relatively restricted area of the West. Our feelings would be the same about concentration in any part of the nation. . . . With such concentrations, one segment of the population would bear a highly disproportionate share of the burden, in lives lost and property destroyed, in case of an attack, particularly if such were to be a saturation attack."[9]

Ironically, though many media writers took the same antiproliferation stand taken by the LDS hierarchy, they nevertheless criticized the church's statement for its seemingly blatant self-interest. These critics interpreted the Mormon statement as supporting a good cause, only for the wrong reason. Some wished that Mormons had opposed the arms race more vocally before it had arrived in their backyard, and they saw hypocrisy in the church's use of its political influence for strictly "parochial interest."[10] This anxiety over the church's decision to impose its will on the nation came across in a piece written by historian William Appleman Williams. He observed that the "Mormons display a very shrewd understanding of the kind of national power that can grow out of organizing a relatively small number of people in a specific region."[11] When the Reagan administration soon dropped the MX plan, Mormon lobbying received much of the credit—or blame.[12]

Gottlieb and Wiley agreed that President "Reagan's decision to move the MX...was a measure of his respect for the views of the church." In fact, "with the election of Ronald Reagan...the Saints emerged from a shadowy existence to become...an integral part of the ruling coalition," thanks to the number of Mormons on Reagan's advisory team. Heinerman and Shupe went further in suggesting that high-ranking Mormon military officers carried out the wishes of church superiors and advocated for a location other than Utah or Nevada for the MX missile site—just one example of the "potential" for well-placed Mormons to "significantly [affect] policymaking."[13]

In arguing that Mormons did exert power nationally, Heinerman and Shupe warned that "most people do not know the real Church of Jesus Christ of Latter-day Saints," the church that believed it was "God's providence" that their "movement and...crusade" eventually "assume political and economic control of the United States." *The Mormon Corporate Empire* argued that openly proclaiming such a belief would be "abrasive," to say the least; therefore, Mormons downplayed their wealth and their political involvement in a show of "public-relations conscious[ness]."[14]

With statements such as these, *The Mormon Corporate Empire* certainly took on the style of an exposé more than *America's Saints* did. Heinerman and Shupe likewise came under more fire for underhanded and "unethical" reporting tactics; some sources accused Heinerman, a "disillusioned Mormon," of deliberate "misrepresentation" and misinterpretation in his research. Anson Shupe later told historian Jan Shipps that such deception was necessary to get accurate information, and that he had also used similar techniques in his investigations of the Unification Church (the "Moonies").[15]

Yet even though *America's Saints* was more measured in tone, the LDS Church spoke out against it, issuing "an unprecedented" rebuttal "of a book written by non-Mormons." In the preface to the paperback edition of their book, Gottlieb and Wiley reprinted LDS spokesman Richard Lindsay's statement (which had come out two weeks before America's Saints initial release): "*America's Saints* . . . is so preoccupied with politics, power, 'dirty linen,' and 'closet skeletons' that the book captures little of the real essence of its subject . . . This focus seems not to result from ignorance, but by design." Gottlieb and Wiley noted that this warning only heightened interest in their upcoming book and probably propelled it "to the top of the Utah best-seller list, where it stayed for six months."[16] Still, the authors conceded that by "[flexing] its muscle," the church persuaded the majority of its members to avoid the book—and even persuaded a local television station to leave Gottlieb and Wiley off of a scheduled panel discussion of Mormonism. The authors saw the church's reaction to their book as "symbolic of the state of Mormonism today," where the church "seeks to protect its members" and its public image "from what it perceives as hostile outside forces."[17]

Worse for the church, a rash of articles in 1984 and early 1985 called Utah the "stock-fraud capital of the nation." *Newsweek* asked, "What makes the folks in Utah so gullible" that they fall for outrageous scams? The answer that *Newsweek*, Businessweek, and *Forbes* gave: Mormonism naturally promotes blind trust in other church members, especially if the name of a prominent Mormon is "bandied about." Businessweek reported that "the SEC estimates that some 10,000 state residents lost up to $200 million through . . . fraud and flagrant mismanagement" of investments "over the past three or four years." To outsiders, these types of losses seemed symptomatic of a people who either submitted too readily to voices of authority or who became too easily enamored of quick prosperity. Both charges fit the characterizations of Mormonism that bubbled to the surface in the early 1980s.[18]

If power and wealth were the motifs in these books and articles, the church's purported grip on the flow of information was the subplot. For church representatives during the first half of the 1980s, the sheer repetition of these themes by Mormonism's evangelical detractors and journalistic chroniclers made damage control increasingly difficult. When three homemade bombs brought Mormon controversies to the level of national consciousness, however, mitigating the "hostile outside" reports became nearly impossible.

History as Theology

On the morning of October 15, 1985, a bomb disguised as a package killed Utah businessman Steven Christensen. A second bomb that same day killed Kathleen Sheets, the wife of Christensen's business partner. Initial reports centered on the financial trouble of their investment firm. Police surmised that disgruntled investors were exacting revenge. That speculation quickly dissipated, however, when a third bomb blew up the next day, severely injuring a young Mormon man named Mark Hofmann.

Reporters from across the country sped to Salt Lake City. The threat of a bomber on the loose alone made for headlines, but when police unexpectedly named Hofmann the bombing *suspect*, the story took on a dimension of intrigue that captured everyone's attention—and that did not bode well for Mormon officials.

Like wildfire, word spread that the link between the victims was the buying and selling of Mormon historical papers. Crime reporters hurriedly gathering background information learned from Mormon insiders that over the past five years, Hofmann had "discovered" dozens of manuscript documents that called into question the official narrative of Mormon origins. There were whispers about a church cover-up, since this new "evidence" of chinks in Joseph Smith's traditional story threatened to rock the foundations of Mormonism and raised specters from the Mormon past. As in politics and finance, critics had a field day with what they saw at the heart of this crisis: institutional censorship and individual gullibility.

Perhaps the best way to understand the relationship between the Mark Hofmann saga and its effect on the public perception of Latter-day Saints is to start at the end, when Hofmann sat as a convicted murderer and forger and gave prison interviews to police investigators seeking to sort out the intricacies of his complex plot. In one of those interviews, Hofmann revealed that he lost faith in Mormonism when he was fourteen years old, though he continued to profess an active belief and participate in church worship accordingly. He even served two years as a full-time missionary for the church in England. However, his true feelings motivated him with a desire "to change Mormon history," to "[rewrite]...Mormon history" and show it a "fairytale."[19] In effect, the church's public image was at the very heart of Hofmann's plans.

For a time, he succeeded in dramatic fashion. Database searches of national media electronic archives reveal that *The God Makers* movie only generated a half-dozen stories in widely circulating national and regional periodicals. A similar database search for stories on Mark Hofmann yields two hundred thirty results.[20] To get a sense of why Hofmann captured the imagination of so many historians and reporters, it is necessary to understand not only what had been happening at the church's Historical Department, but also why Latter-day Saints cared so much about history in the first place.

History for Mormons, it has been observed, often plays the role that theology plays for other religionists.[21] That is, it offers the girders, the framework, on which to build their belief system. That foundation for Latter-day Saints was laid by a series of historical events, and the church's truth claims stand or fall on the reality of those events. Did Joseph Smith really see and converse with God the Father and Jesus Christ? Did an angel named Moroni really lead Joseph Smith to an ancient record written on golden metallic plates that, when translated providentially, became the Book of Mormon? Did John the Baptist and Peter, James, and John from the New Testament really bestow on Joseph Smith and his associate Oliver Cowdery the authority to reconstitute *the* Church of Jesus Christ? These, and a litany of similar questions, constitute the critical test of Mormonism. Millions of Latter-day Saints have found the evidence for these claims compelling. Church critics have deemed the claims outrageous, and even dangerous. What no one disputes, though, is that in this drama, history takes center stage.

In the early 1980s, several parties had obvious stakes in this contest over the historicity of Mormonism's origins. Christians who saw the LDS Church's explosive growth as the rising threat of a counterfeit faith welcomed any evidence that discredited the testimony of the church's founder. For them, historical controversy made good counterevangelizing fodder.[22] Investigative journalists, always interested in uncovering that which has been hidden or suppressed, were drawn to Latter-day Saints for different reasons—and among those reasons was Mormons' demonstrated ability to organize nationally in a political cause. Such devotion and obedience to a leader's call raised curiosity about Mormonism's hold on its followers. With a skeptical eye, many in the media also began to ask if the Latter-day Saint leadership intentionally repressed damaging historical data to keep unity in the ranks. Could the appearance of contrary evidence, therefore, undo the growing might of Mormonism?[23]

On the other side stood Latter-day Saints, who cared very much about the reputation of their church's founder and his followers. Mormon sermons and missionary tracts have always stressed that confirmation of the truthfulness of Mormonism could never come through a study of church history alone; instead, the most important evidence is a spiritual confirmation, a witness from Heaven that speaks to an individual's soul. However, Mormon leaders have also recognized that there must be a "climate" of believability in which investigators could pursue a spiritual witness. As Latter-day Saints see it, aspersions cast upon Mormonism's historical claims raise shadows of doubt that might make honest inquiry and evaluation impossible. Hence their long-standing interest in the public's perception of their faith—it is directly connected to the prospects for proselytizing new adherents. For that reason, and for most of the twentieth century, Mormons had been seen as very protective, even defensive, of their history.[24]

Beginning in the 1970s, several restructurings at the LDS Church Historical Department signaled a relaxation of that protective posture. Apostle Howard W. Hunter was appointed Church Historian in 1970 when his predecessor, Joseph Fielding Smith, became president of the LDS Church. Elder Hunter led a push to reorganize the department and open access to the archives in an attempt to replace defensiveness with scholarly outreach. Within a decade, however, these efforts were receiving mixed reviews at church headquarters, since openness came with a cost. Increased access allowed for increased scrutiny, and some historians interpreted the historical record in ways that challenged traditional understanding. What the Mark Hofmann investigation exposed to the outside world was a long-running internal debate that pitted some Mormon intellectuals against their ecclesiastical superiors. The intelligentsia-versus-hierarchy nature of this conflict only made the church look guilty as charged when critics from without and within labeled it repressive.[25]

There was no hint of that future conflict in 1972, though, when young Mormon historians were riding a wave of optimism. In that year, church leaders gave the work of the so-called "New Mormon Historians" a strong endorsement when they named one of them, Leonard Arrington, Church Historian.[26] To many, Arrington's appointment seemed as symbolic as it was structural. The history department, like so many other church divisions in the 1960s and 1970s, took a decided turn toward professionalization in 1972.

Even three decades later, historians remember Leonard Arrington's tenure affectionately as "Camelot" or the "Arrington spring." Because of the way researchers were welcomed at the archives, historian D. Michael Quinn felt that "every day was Christmas morning." A flowering of Mormon history marked the 1970s. Arrington tapped two other university professors as his assistants, James Allen and Davis Bitton. They invited a rotating cadre of young Mormon scholars to work on diverse projects at the archives. The output under Arrington's ten-year supervision was noteworthy. By one tally, Historical Department employees produced "twenty-eight books and monographs, approximately two hundred chapters in books and articles in professional journals, and more than one hundred articles in semiprofessional outlets." [27]

The opening of the Church History Division and the appointment of Leonard Arrington seemed another sign that church authorities saw the Mormon image in the 1970s as relatively secure. For that reason, this was an important moment.

This lowering of the guard over archival access corresponded with the proactive approach taken by Wendell Ashton and Heber Wolsey in public communications. Significantly, Arrington and his associates initiated serious Latter-day Saint outreach to the nation's academic community. They placed on the shelves of university libraries across the country new works like the widely praised *The Mormon Experience*, Arrington and Bitton's history of the Latter-day Saint movement designed as an introduction for non-Mormon readers. Never had Mormon historical sources, and the experts on those sources, been more accessible.

But not everyone in Camelot was pleased. Arrington's guiding philosophy, as he stated it in 1966, was that historians could "[investigate] the Mormon past in human or naturalistic terms without rejecting its divinity."[28] Though, as Davis Bitton put it, "the historians saw themselves as loyal members," some LDS leaders felt that this naturalistic approach made these professional histories spiritually sterile.[29]

The publication of one book in particular illustrates well the tensions that surrounded the church's history department. That book was *The Story of the Latter-day Saints* by James Allen and Glen Leonard. One of Leonard Arrington's principal objectives was the publication of a reliable one-volume history of Mormonism. This thrust eventually went in two complementary directions: Arrington and Davis Bitton wrote *Mormon Experience* (published nationally by Alfred A. Knopf in 1979) primarily with outside readers in mind. Their departmental colleagues, Allen and Leonard, took on the task of writing a one-volume history for Latter-day Saint readers. *The Story of the Latter-day Saints* (1976) was the result.

Although the book was published by Deseret Book, a church-owned press, some church general authorities expressed discomfort with the text. They worried that there was not enough emphasis on the miraculous events that marked the church's foundational years, and too much emphasis on the wider historical context in which Mormonism originated. Plus, the book did not shy away from Mormonism's most controversial moments or its most controversial chroniclers. Glen Leonard said that he and Allen wanted to be "open and trustworthy," to "raise difficult questions and answer them in a helpful way." The authors discussed the Mountain Meadows massacre, polygamy, and blacks and the priesthood, and their extensive bibliography included sources that were critical of the church. Leonard felt that their "internal audience"—Mormon readers—"liked the more human approach" of the book, but Arrington's interpretation of the complaints of a handful of concerned general authorities was "that [the book] was too 'secular'—that the history was not flavored or balanced sufficiently with spiritual experiences and faith-promoting stories."[30]

There is anecdotal evidence that most of the church's apostles approved of the book, and it proved very popular among Mormon readers.[31] Over 10,000 copies sold in just four months, and the Public Communications Department ordered 5,000 copies to distribute to libraries.[32] To public relations officers, the book seemed a positive reference source for researchers and newsmakers. But the book's opponents in the church hierarchy proved sufficiently insistent, and there was no second printing for sixteen years. Curt Bench, a Deseret Book employee at the time, called the decision "puzzling," and noted that opposition to *The Story of the Latter-day Saints* "threw a lot of cold water" on the enthusiasm that had been building around the history division.[33] In Michael Quinn's view, this book's publication was a "watershed" event, since "it created...concern" for some in the church's highest leadership circles "about what Leonard Arrington and his staff were doing." From "that point on, things became tense."[34]

Similar controversies did indeed mark an increasing number of the department's projects in the second half of the 1970s. Biographies of church leaders that seemed too humanistic in their treatment of personal foibles raised red flags for some apostles. They worried that such an approach might weaken church members' faith in a leader's teachings. Others countered, however, that such realistic portraits offered hope to church members who were equally human and imperfect.[35]

Some apostles made public their concerns about these new trends in Mormon historical writing. Ezra Taft Benson in two 1976 speeches warned students at BYU and then employees in the church's educational system to be wary of these humanizing histories. "There have been and continue to be attempts to bring [a humanistic] philosophy into our own Church history," he said. "The emphasis is to underplay revelation and God's intervention in significant events and to inordinately humanize the prophets of God so that their human frailties become more apparent than their spiritual qualities."[36] Benson, president of the Quorum of the Twelve Apostles at the time, even counseled against purchasing these types of publications.[37]

Apostle Boyd K. Packer repeated a similar message at a similar venue in 1981. He told Church Educational System teachers that "there is no such thing as an accurate or objective history of the Church which ignores the Spirit. You might as well try to write the biography of Mendelssohn without hearing or mentioning his music, or write the life of Rembrandt without mentioning light or canvas or color." He was emphatic about the serious ramifications he saw in such a historical philosophy: "Historians seem to take great pride in publishing something new, particularly if it illustrates a weakness or mistake of a prominent historical figure. For some reason, historians and novelists seem to savor such things. If it related to a living person, it would come under the heading of gossip. History can be as misleading as gossip and much more difficult—often impossible—to verify.... The historian or scholar who delights in pointing out the weakness and frailties of present or past leaders destroys faith. A destroyer of faith—particularly one within the Church, and more particularly one who is employed specifically to build faith—places himself in great spiritual jeopardy."[38]

Internally, these warnings translated into more restrictive oversight of the Church Historical Department. In a move that church leaders attributed to the technicality of titles more than a change in job description, Leonard Arrington became the director of the history division rather than Church Historian in 1977. To Arrington's colleagues, however, the implication was clear. As the 1970s closed, it became increasingly apparent that the "Arrington spring" was a fleeting season. [39]

Divided opinions about the nature and value of the department's work in the church's highest circles essentially doomed the history division's most ambitious project. Over a dozen authors had been contracted to prepare books to be included in a planned sixteen-volume church history collection. The original idea was that the volumes would be released in 1980, to commemorate the church's sesquicentennial. It was obvious well before 1980, however, that church leaders generally agreed there were too many complications in giving an imprimatur to so many individualized histories, especially considering the problematic nature of some periods in the LDS past. Several of the prepared volumes did find their way to other publishing houses, and several appeared as stand-alone histories. However, the official disavowal of the project seemed to mark the end of an era.[40]

Opponents of the history division's work argued that having church *employees* write and publish church history gave the impression of official endorsement. The First Presidency decided that the best option would be to disband the history division. Beginning in 1980 and continuing through 1982, several long-time employees (including Leonard Arrington) transferred to the new Joseph Fielding Smith Institute for LDS History at Brigham Young University. Some obtained appointments at other universities. The guiding rationale expressed by church leaders was that the university setting provided a more conducive atmosphere for independent research and writing.[41]

As pivotal as this decade was for Mormon historiography, though, most of the turbulence between historians and church elders remained localized. Few outside the community of LDS historians were aware of the internal struggles at the church archives. However, as a growing number in the academic community cried foul, the rumblings coming out of Salt Lake City made their way onto the pages of various periodicals. The independent Mormon journal *Dialogue* published an article by Davis Bitton in 1983 in which he expressed "personal disappointment" at the "lack of mutual respect" of "our critics" who were "never . . . willing to sit down and talk over matters with us." Non-Mormon historian Lawrence Foster was more pointed in an essay published that same year. He had been invited to study at the LDS archives in 1974. From his vantage point, he saw changes at church headquarters as representing "a growing fear, a loss of true confidence in the Mormon message, and an unwillingness or inability to accept the richness and complexity of the Latter-day Saint faith." Foster complained that "at times Mormonism appears to be a public relations shell without substance."[42]

As church leaders questioned the motives and methods of some historians, some historians in turn replied that church authorities did not want to face the historical truth—and this was why those authorities tightened access to documents accordingly. The *Salt Lake Tribune* quoted University of Utah professor James Clayton, who described these changes as "intellectually and morally irresponsible from the historians' point of view."[43] *Newsweek*'s Ken Woodward told *Sunstone*'s Peggy Fletcher in 1980 that he sensed "that the Mormon hierarchy is not particularly interested in reaching, maintaining, and sustaining their more thoughtful members...You can't do this by hammering home authority, authority, authority."[44] Two years later, Woodward's article in *Newsweek* cited an LDS Institute teacher in New York City who worried that instead of being "intellectually honest...we are being asked to indoctrinate and overlook uncomfortable facts."[45] A Utah writer predicted in a *Humanist* essay that the "preponderance of official prosecution in the future is likely to continue to be directed at scholars," since in "the Mormon faith freedom of speech is often stifled as it approaches those borders where heresy begins: questioning the verities may lead to a loss of faith." His observation of the growing conflict was telling: "external barbs are more easily deflected than internal ones."[46]

"Rewriting ... Mormon History"

It was into this already-delicate situation that Mark Hofmann dropped his "discoveries." [47] His first move was strategically brilliant. In the spring of 1980, Hofmann was a pre-med student at Utah State University and an avid collector of historical documents. He arrived at the office of a church employee (an instructor at the LDS Institute of Religion adjacent to the Utah State campus) with a folded and apparently aged piece of paper that he had already examined with a library curator. Both the curator, Jeff Simmonds, and the religion instructor, Danel Bachman, immediately recognized that the document bore the identifying marks of a famed page in Mormon history, the "Anthon transcript"—several lines of hieroglyphic-type characters that Joseph Smith copied from the metallic plates he had discovered. Martin Harris, Joseph Smith's scribe at the time, showed the characters to a New York City antiquities scholar named Charles Anthon. Anthon's reported opinion that the characters showed resemblance to Egyptian and other Near Eastern writing styles left Martin Harris so sufficiently convinced of the book's ancient provenance that he later mortgaged his farm to finance publication of the Book of Mormon. While the church had long held in its possession manuscript copies of Book of Mormon characters, what Hofmann brought to Danel Bachman that day in 1980 seemed even more promising as the original transcription of those characters.[48]

After an intense authentication process involving various experts, church leaders announced the discovery in a news release. Mormon historians celebrated the transcript as the earliest known sample of Joseph Smith's handwriting. In the summer of 1980, the *Ensign* (the church's official magazine) and *BYU Studies* (the university's quarterly journal) both published articles describing the find.[49] Hofmann wanted the church to own the transcript and the Smith family Bible in which he said he had found the folded document; in exchange, he accepted some rare Mormon money from pioneer times, and a first edition copy of the Book of Mormon that lacked a title page.[50] His first forgery had succeeded famously, and the exchange process provided Hofmann a brief acquaintance with several church apostles, as well as instant notoriety among Mormon history aficionados.[51] He would soon cement his reputation with a rapid series of monumental document acquisitions.

Though Bachman described the Anthon transcript as "perhaps . . . one of the most important and significant documents of church history to be discovered in this century," it was Hofmann's next "find" that would draw outside attention to the trade of Mormon historical papers. Only four months after finalizing the exchange of the Anthon transcript, Hofmann returned to LDS Church headquarters with another sheet of aging paper. This one contained the words of a blessing that Joseph Smith pronounced on the head of his eleven-year-old son in 1844. The blessing was in the handwriting of Thomas Bullock, a church secretary whose script was well-known to Mormon archivists. Not only that, but the blessing bore the signature of Joseph Smith, just as the Anthon transcript did. In this case, however, the particulars of what the document said garnered more attention than did the discovery of another sample of Joseph Smith's handwriting. The blessing, written in the first person, had Joseph Smith declaring that his son was to be his successor as the church's prophet. Six months after the date on the blessing, Joseph Smith was killed at the Carthage, Illinois, jail.[52]

Latter-day Saints today assert that Brigham Young and the Quorum of the Twelve Apostles were the divinely designated successors to Joseph Smith. However, hundreds of Mormons had stayed in Illinois and other Midwestern states when Brigham Young led the majority of the Saints west to the Rocky Mountains three years after Joseph Smith's death. Eventually, many of those who did not follow the apostles coalesced into a new organization around Joseph Smith III. The group called itself the Reorganized Church of Jesus Christ of Latter Day Saints (RLDS), and when Joseph Smith III came of age, he was designated the church's prophet.[53]

In time, the Reorganized Church moved its headquarters to Independence, Missouri, and pursued a theological path that rejected polygamy but did include

lineal, father-to-son succession in the presidency. By 1981, the group was much
smaller than that of its Salt Lake City religious cousins, numbering just over
220,000. But the RLDS had always steadfastly maintained that Joseph Smith
had ordained his son to be the prophet.[54] Now Mark Hofmann offered documentary proof of that blessing.

Time and *Newsweek* both devoted stories to the find, which Hofmann said
he discovered in a collection of Thomas Bullock papers that he had purchased
from a Bullock descendant.[55] Mormon leaders in Salt Lake City downplayed the
impact of this latest discovery. Instead of attempting to bury the document, LDS
Church officials made it public, even trading the blessing, which they acquired
from Hofmann, to the RLDS Church in exchange for a copy of an early Mormon
book. Despite this display of detached interest, Mormons readily recognized
that this second forgery struck at a pillar of their faith. Prophetic succession
was a key tenet for Latter-day Saints, a tenet manifested in their confidence
that they followed a divinely chosen leader. This was not lost on media outlets
that reported that the transcribed blessing "lends strong historical support to
the Reorganized Saints," and "fortifies a major tenet of faith" of the "Missouri
group."[56] *Time* quoted "historian D. Michael Quinn, of the Mormons' own
Brigham Young University, [putting] it even more bluntly: the terms of the
blessing 'mean only one thing in the Mormon Church, that Joseph Smith III
would be president of the church.'"[57]

The story made the *Los Angeles Times* and *New York Times*.[58] Many Mormon
historians accepted the blessing as authentic. They explained it away, however,
by noting that Joseph Smith III did not meet the conditions that would qualify
him for church leadership—that is, he did not remain a faithful member of the
church, which would have required that he continue with Brigham Young and
the other apostles until he came of age. Michael Quinn said it this way: in the
blessing "we have...a wonderful, beautiful blessing of a prophet-father to his
son, which the son ultimately rejected. There is a great tragedy in that."[59]

A Mormon media watcher, writing in 1982, felt that "within a month, the
discovery was old news."[60] *Christianity Today* quoted RLDS historian Richard
Howard: "The Mormon Church has settled the issue of descent to their satisfaction, and we have settled it to ours." Looking back, what might have been
most significant about the episode was that it brought attention to the existence of the RLDS Church ("an unaccustomed standing" for that church[61]), and
this offered a chance for national writers to consider the contrasts between
these two branches of Joseph Smith's followers. Importantly, it prompted this
analysis from *Christianity Today*: "The Missouri church is far closer to orthodox
Christianity in its views of Scripture and the Trinity than the *decidedly unchristian* brethren in Utah."[62] For those LDS officials concerned with the Mormon
public image, this type of assessment made the attention to Mormon history
all the more troubling. Hofmann's most spectacular discoveries were yet to

come, and they would provide ample fodder for those determined to prove that Latter-day Saints were "decidedly unchristian."

Over the next three years, Hofmann's activities dominated conversations about Mormon document. Mark Hofmann seemed to have an uncanny knack for unearthing precious Mormon memorabilia.[63] For a church so intensely interested in documenting its past, his finds were treasures. Yet Mormon historians often spoke about them with a sense of uneasiness as they sought to work them into the traditional narrative, since deviations from that narrative could sow seeds of doubt for believers. Because of that, Curt Bench, who ran Deseret Book's rare book trade and became a close friend of Mark Hofmann, described these years as "an exciting time, but a disturbing time."[64] If these discoveries chipped away at the reliability of the faith's foundational events, what could be said about the stability of the church that was built on those pilings?

That is why none of Hofmann's previous forgeries matched the eventual impact of a purported Martin Harris letter from 1830 that he brought to the church's attention in January 1984. In the letter, Harris described to a newspaper editor named W. W. Phelps (who eventually converted to Mormonism) the events that led to the publication of the Book of Mormon. As mentioned earlier, Martin Harris was one of Joseph Smith's earliest and most influential backers. But the events Hofmann's Martin Harris described in this letter differed radically from Joseph Smith's personal history, an account that the LDS Church had canonized as part of its Pearl of Great Price scriptural collection.[65]

Where Hofmann's forgery departed from this official history was in the character and nature of the guide that led Joseph Smith to the ancient record that became the Book of Mormon. Hofmann's Martin Harris recounted that a young Joseph Smith told him it was a salamander-like creature rather than an angel that met Joseph at the spot of the buried metallic plates, and that the salamander then morphed into human form. Thus the Harris letter became known simply as the "Salamander Letter."[66]

After the church declined to buy the letter from Hofmann, he sold it to Latter-day Saint businessman Steve Christensen.[67] News of the letter swept through the Mormon historical community and even prompted an inquiry from Richard Ostling of *Time*. Throughout 1984, as Christensen declined to release the letter until it had been authenticated, speculation about its contents appeared in the *Los Angeles Times* and in Jerald and Sandra Tanner's newsletter.[68] Christensen donated the letter to the church in the spring of 1985. When the church did print the text of the letter in the April 28, 1985, edition of the *Church News*, it included a statement by Gordon B. Hinckley of the First Presidency: "No one, of course, can be certain that Martin Harris wrote the document. However, at this point we accept the judgment of the examiner that there is no indication that it is a forgery. This does not preclude the possibility that it may have been forged at a time when the Church had many enemies. It is, however, an interesting document of the times." President Hinckley then sounded a reassuring note: "Actually, the letter has nothing to do with the authenticity of the Church. The real test of faith which both Martin Harris and W. W. Phelps had in Joseph Smith and his work is found in their lives, in the sacrifices they made for their membership in the Church, and in the testimonies which they bore to the end of their lives."[69]

The church's release of the letter, however, poured fuel on the flames.[70] The nearly simultaneous appearance of an 1825 letter from Joseph Smith to one of his earliest employers, Josiah Stowell, added to the controversy. The Josiah Stowell letter had Joseph Smith transmitting information about treasure seeking and divining rods, activities that seemed consonant with a belief in shape-shifting salamanders. (Mark Hofmann had also forged the Josiah Stowell letter.) These two discoveries seemed to confirm what critics had long accused: the murky origins of Joseph Smith's religion carried the deep imprint of magical and superstitious practices.[71]

What gave these reports about Mormonism's magical roots special salience in 1985 was that they seemed to corroborate strongly the serious claims made in the 1982 movie *The God Makers*. Those who had seen the movie now could hear echoes of the film's condemnation of Joseph Smith in these discovered documents. They could understand why Mormon officials would reportedly want to keep such information closely guarded from supposedly deluded church members. Joseph Smith himself had admitted that he had accepted employment in treasure-seeking ventures in his youth, but the abortive efforts he described felt far removed from his later religious activities.[72] That is what made the Salamander Letter troubling for some Mormons, so troubling in fact that one Mormon historian told *Time* magazine in May 1985, "It's an incredible crisis of faith for me.... It means our historical foundation becomes a nice story that has no connection to reality." *Time* also quoted a California couple who wrote "to friends explaining... [that] new revelations about the Mormons' founding prophet... destroyed their belief" in Mormonism.[73]

It was the tragic loss of life rather than the loss of personal faith, however, that brought this largely in-house affair to the attention of national readers. One of the first Mormon researchers granted access to the Salamander Letter by its private owner called the manuscript "a potentially explosive document"; no one in May 1985 knew just how prescient his words would be only five months later when Hofmann's bombs killed Steve Christensen and Kathleen Sheets.[74]

These brutal crimes drew scores of reporters from around the country, but the Hofmann bombings created some unique journalistic challenges. National interest in the story seemed driven by the greed and violence that pervaded the Mark Hofmann case, especially when he, a bombing victim himself, was named the principal suspect. Yet the story had a complex *religious* component, too. Journalist Peggy Fletcher Stack, then editor of *Sunstone*, noted that "the papers tended to send their crime reporters to Utah and they knew nothing about Mormons and had everything wrong." Historian Jan Shipps agreed. Media outlets soon "realized that their crime reporters did not know enough about Mormonism to cover the story properly, but they were afraid that their religion reporters would not be able to describe what was happening satisfactorily because they did not know enough about crime and about the legal maneuvering that immediately started after Hofmann was charged with murder." Because both Stack and Shipps were prominent in the field of Mormon studies, reporter after reporter turned to them for background. In their experience, it was obvious that the majority of these journalists possessed "an abysmal lack of knowledge of Mormonism."[75]

That crucial observation cannot be overlooked. It reveals much about the type of reporting—and reporting mishaps—that would surround the Mark Hofmann affair. As the investigation into the bombings progressed and as journalists began to research the connection between Mark Hofmann and his victims, they learned about Steve Christensen's involvement as a client and an underwriter of Hofmann's documentary treasure hunts, and as an early owner of the Salamander Letter. These reporters quickly latched onto the import of Hofmann's most recent and most controversial finds, since these documents seemed to shake the historical foundations of the prosperous LDS Church. It was this element of intrigue that dominated media coverage of the Hofmann bombings.

Stories about these so-called "Mormon murders" used words like "the strange labyrinth of Mormon history," "shadowy," and "notoriously secretive" to paint a picture of historical scandal and cover-up.[76] The Mormon archives, seemingly closed and impenetrable, became the backdrop for concealed controversy. In January 1986, three months after the bombings, the *New York Times* reported, "There have been no arrests, but if nothing else, the police investigation has revealed the church's hierarchy to be obsessed with stopping any tampering with the church's official account of its past."[77]

That is why, journalists assumed, there had been so much interest in the mysterious McLellin collection. Over the course of several months preceding the bombings, Mark Hofmann had contacted a network of people to assist him in the acquisition of what he said would be an extensive set of the papers of William McLellin.[78] McLellin was an early associate of Joseph Smith; in fact, McLellin had even been one of the church's original twelve apostles. However, McLellin fell out with the Mormon prophet in 1838. He turned against the church and supported the Missouri state government's efforts to expel Latter-day Saints from the state. What Hofmann told investors he had discovered was a collection of McLellin diaries and letters, and the owner of the collection was willing to sell. Confidentially, Hofmann had disclosed that the documents would prove so damaging to the character of Joseph Smith that they would only be safe in church hands.[79] In fact, reporters noted, one of the investors who was so actively seeking the McLellin collection was a church general authority who had apparently used his position on the board of directors of a Salt Lake City bank to help Hofmann secure a $185,000 loan. The implication was that this Mormon leader was undoubtedly under the direction of church superiors to suppress the whole set of documents, even though he publicly stated that he was acting on his own "as a banker," and "not as a representative of the church."[80]

As reporters pieced together the complexities of Hofmann's dealings, it soon became clear that he had been trying to sell the same collection to multiple investors. He used advance payments from various investors to keep other debtors at bay. It was apparent that the motive behind the bombings was *time*—Hofmann needed a diversion to hold off anxious buyers so that they did not discover that Hofmann was double-crossing them. Curt Bench soon realized that Hofmann was "a master manipulator" who "kept everyone separated so that they couldn't compare notes." What was not as readily apparent, even in the first months after Hofmann's arrest, was that he was also a master forger, and that the McLellin documents in question never existed.[81]

Throughout the developing saga, the church's silence seemed to some a tacit admission of complicity. In reality, the church's silence highlighted a significant public relations challenge. Legal restrictions prevented church spokesmen from making an immediate response. Because the church was a major party in the Hofmann criminal investigation, detectives and attorneys advised that church officers and employees not discuss the pending case. From the church's perspective, this allowed the national press to make unchallenged insinuations about official entanglement in the web of deceit.[82] Church leaders saw misleading ambiguity everywhere in the media. *U.S. News and World Report*, for example, never mentioned that Mark Hofmann was charged with *forging* the Salamander Letter when it declared that "whoever leads the Mormons into the 21st century will have to grapple with the disturbing effects of the bombing deaths of two Mormons who played a crucial role in authenticating the 'white salamander' letter, which contradicts church teaching on the founding of the religion." There was little LDS leaders felt they could do publicly to counter such incriminating and incomplete assessments.[83]

This situation lasted for nearly fifteen months, as investigators built their case against Mark Hofmann.[84] Instead of facing a trial, however, Hofmann entered into a plea bargain in January 1987.[85] By the time of his admission of guilt, his story had lost much of its momentum. Reporting about the verdict did not command the same level of attention as did initial speculation about the crime. From the LDS Church's perspective, this drop in coverage and exposure only exacerbated the injuries that the crimes inflicted on the church's reputation, because for many readers, the record was never set straight. After Hofmann's conviction, LDS apostle Dallin H. Oaks said that he "was saddened but not surprised that the news coverage of the truth about the forgeries and lies of Mark Hofmann was small by comparison with the earlier trumpeting of the claims that his newly discovered documents destroyed faith, compromised Church leaders, and rocked the foundations of the Church." [86]

Typical of the difficulty for rehabilitating the Mormon image was a sequence of events with the *Los Angeles Times*. The church protested vehemently against the *LA Times*'s coverage of the Mark Hofmann episode, especially because the newspaper referred to an unnamed source who accused the church of hiding a history written by the church's "second elder," Oliver Cowdery.[87] In 1986, the church stated officially that a thorough search of its archives turned up no such "Cowdery history." Then, in October 1986, the *Salt Lake Tribune* revealed that through the course of the criminal investigation, it became clear that the unnamed source was, in fact, Mark Hofmann.[88] He had planted the information about the Cowdery history and its supposed references to Joseph Smith's early occult practices to give his forgeries additional credence. Yet in late March and early April 1987, the *Los Angeles Times* still ran a two-part feature on the Hofmann murders that included references to the Cowdery history—but no mention that Hofmann had fabricated the whole story.[89] Finally, after the transcripts of Hofmann's police interviews were released, and Hofmann's role in the creating the Cowdery history rumor was undeniable, the *Los Angeles Time*'s retraction appeared in a column tucked on page twenty-nine of the paper.[90]

The juxtaposition of the prominence given the initial feature as opposed to the insignificance of the eventual retraction prompted a rare public complaint from one of the church's apostles. Dallin Oaks in an August 1987 address chastised the Los Angeles newspaper for "journalistic injustice," "[offending] with a succession of big bangs" and then "[trying] to back out with a small whimper."[91] Oaks also called the *New York Time*'s coverage of the Hofmann episode "character assassination." The *New York Times* had reported that the church "hid in a vault . . . documents that cast doubt on the church's official version of its history"; Oaks wondered why that same newspaper did "not mention in its long [February 11, 1987] article that the church had published a detailed list of its Hofmann acquisitions almost a year earlier," or that "the most prominent Hofmann documents used to attack the origins of the Church—including Martin Harris' so-called Salamander letter, Joseph Smith's treasure-hunting letter to Josiah Stowell, and the Joseph Smith III blessing—were all made public by the Church many months before the bombings triggered intense public interest in this subject."[92] The *New York Times* did devote a page-27 story to Elder Oaks's speech and his strong objections, but there were no editorial apologies. In fact, the story concluded by noting that "Leonard R. Harris, a spokesman for the *Times*, said Friday, 'The editors of the *Times* believe our reporting on the Hofmann case has been entirely factual'"; likewise, "Noel Greenwood, deputy managing editor of *The Los Angeles Times*, responded: 'We're certainly not in the business of bashing churches or any other organization. We cover them like we do any other part of the news and I think our coverage in this case has been responsible.'"[93] All signs pointed to the reality that surmounting the fallout of Mark Hofmann's frauds would be, for church image makers, an uphill climb.

The degree of difficulty of such a climb was made clear in the publication of Steven Naifeh and Gregory White Smith's 1988 book, *Mormon Murders: A True Story of Greed, Forgery, Deceit, and Death*. They approached the Mark Hofmann case with the intent to demonstrate, as a church spokesman saw it, that "the church paid huge sums to Hofmann for incriminating documents to keep them from becoming public and was, therefore, guilty of a cover-up." Rare books dealer Curt Bench was interviewed by Naifeh and Smith, and he later debated the authors publicly about their conclusions. Bench felt that the two "didn't know Mormon history," but that "they just wanted to sell books." Because of this, he and Jan Shipps both agreed that *Mormon Murders* was the "worst" of the Hofmann-related books that appeared.[94]

What informed Naifeh and Smith's approach was their assertion that, "since receiving a revelation in 1839, Joseph Smith determined that 'the punishment for dissent in his church would be death.'"[95] Director of the LDS Church's Public Affairs Department, Richard Lindsay, called that claim "preposterous." In fact, Lindsay issued a full-out assault on the book and its authors, so inaccurate and "scurrilous" did the church deem *Mormon Murders*. He condemned Naifeh and Smith, two Harvard-educated lawyers, in a point-by-point refutation for imply-ing that "the church tried to dampen the investigation into Hofmann and to suppress evidence." Lindsay responded that "the church cooperated fully with federal, state and local law enforcement officials responding to every inquiry and request. All 48 documents acquired from Hofmann were made available to law enforcement officials." Lindsay's chief complaint was that, "indefensibly, they (Naifeh and Smith) attempt to make the church culpable with Mark W. Hofmann in the ensuing tragic outcome."[96]

While the facts may have been on Lindsay's side, publicity was not. *Mormon Murders* was an "alternate Literary Guild selection," and "was published in both hardcover and paperback" editions nationwide.[97] One reviewer heaped glowing praise on the authors for their work in showing how "church officials...used their enormous power throughout Utah to clamp down on the investigation of the crimes and to obscure the church's connection to the killer." This kept the church's president from testifying in court where he would have been "revealed as a liar." In other words, this was the "Mormon Watergate—with the glaring difference that, in this case, officialdom won." The reviewer concluded with this prediction: "No matter what your opinion going in, you'll finish 'Mormon Murders' with a vastly different view of those clean-cut young men in their white shirts and ties pedaling their bikes, and peddling their beliefs, through the world's neighborhoods."[98] Another reviewer, in the *Los Angeles Times,* called the book "a rich trove of details about the deceit, lying, and covering up by top [Mormon] church leaders."[99]

So long-lasting and damaging did this and other books on the Hofmann affair seem to be that Mormon leaders gave Richard Turley, an attorney and the managing director of the church's history department, full access to minutes, vaults, and archives, to write an account of the church's interaction with Hofmann. The meticulously footnoted *Victims* (1992) was the result. Published by the University of Illinois Press, Turley's work received praise from historian Jan Shipps for "[adding] to and [correcting] the historical record," since "he had access to materials that were unavailable to any of the other authors."[100] Turley's offering was well received by the academic community, but it did not enjoy the circulation that *Mormon Murders* did four years earlier. Still, the church's aggressive response to Naifeh and Smith's attack said something about a change in the way LDS officials might respond to serious affronts, and portended a change in public relations philosophy that would come to fruition later in the decade.

Reverberations

A month after the bombings, Jan Shipps wrote in the *Christian Century* that "sufficient time has elapsed since the events of October 15 and 16 [the dates of the bombings] for that story to have turned into yesterday's news. Yet for the most part this has not occurred. Interest in these particular instances of violence is still great enough to keep the story alive, not just in Utah, but throughout the nation. It is possible that this continuing interest can be explained by the extent to which, in this instance, life imitates art—that is, if a finely constructed detective story can be called art. The elements are all there. The tragic events of last month brought destruction into the lives of three apparently ordinary people. But these apparently ordinary individuals were also Latter-day Saints—Mormons—members of a community that, despite its intense Americanness, still seems to have a somewhat exotic air about it."[101]

One unexpected fruit did grow out of these thickets. Something about Mormonism's "exotic air" struck Jerry Kaplan, CEO of Macmillan Publishing Company. "It was 1984, and the BYU Jerusalem Center and the Hofmann documents were both receiving media attention." Intrigued, Kaplan "asked Charles E. Smith, the head of Macmillan's Reference Division, 'What do you know about the Mormons?'" When Smith reported that he could find "specialized titles but no basic reference materials in the New York City Public Library, Kaplan then proposed that Macmillan add an encyclopedia about Mormonism to its library-oriented publications." Eight years later, the result was the five-volume *Encyclopedia of Mormonism*, a landmark in Mormon publishing that involved 738 contributors (mostly LDS, but with some notable exceptions) writing 1,128 articles—a million words on all aspects of Mormon history and belief and practice. The inception of an in-depth encyclopedia, coming when and how it did, was an early sign that these well-publicized controversies could translate into curiosity, into openings for conversations that would invite—perhaps demand—new responses from LDS leaders and thinkers.[102]

But in the tangle of the 1985-1987 Hofmann ordeal, it was the "exotic" picture of Mormonism that kept emerging. After the Hofmann scandal quieted, the intensity of attention to Mormons noticeably waned. Yet try as they might, over the course of the next half-dozen years, Latter-day Saints had difficulty in dispelling the lingering sense that theirs was a church involved in cover-up and deceit and murder. Troubling stories seemed to appear just often enough to reopen the case against Latter-day Saint acceptability.

Polygamy, for example, came back to haunt the Mormon image in the 1980s, as a new brand of radicalized polygamists, the so-called "fundamentalist Mormons," made national headlines. Ever since the 1890 revelation that discontinued plural marriage in the LDS Church, a small minority of church members persisted in forging new polygamous unions. While the permissibility of such new marriages during the first dozen years after that 1890 "Manifesto" was something of a gray area, in terms of church practice, the LDS hierarchy took a definite stand against polygamy in the middle of the first decade of the twentieth century (in the midst of the Reed Smoot Senate hearings). That meant that new polygamists defied their leaders' orders and thus forfeited their membership in the church, since from that point on, twentieth-century polygamists were excommunicated. Yet they continued to practice their faith quietly in rural enclaves throughout the West, mostly ignored by civil authorities and outsiders.[103]

This way of life lost its relative anonymity due to the bloody infighting of the LeBaron polygamist clan in the 1970s and 1980s. One of the clan's leaders, Ervil LeBaron, son of excommunicated Mormons, made the news and police most-wanted lists for a series of assassinations against family rivals. Most of the members of LeBaron's group lived in religious colonies in northern Mexico, and most had been recruited from the ranks of mainstream Mormonism. Because of this connection to the LDS Church, reporters inevitably mentioned the church and its polygamous past to give background to LeBaron's worldview. Most disturbing was that LeBaron claimed that his hit list was the product of divine revelation.[104]

Though Ervil LeBaron died of a heart attack in a Utah prison in 1981, his name continued to make news throughout the decade. That same year, Ben Bradlee and Dale Van Atta published *Prophet of Blood: The Untold Story of Ervil LeBaron and the Lambs of God*. The book opened with the 1977 murder of another polygamist leader, Dr. Rulon Allred. Tragically, LeBaron had ordered Allred's death to lure LeBaron's brother to the subsequent funeral, though that decoy plot failed. Almost unbelievably, LeBaron had also ordered the death of one of his daughters. A reviewer of the book noted that "LeBaron's 11th wife, Vonda, was his most willing killer.... Devoted to her husband, she shrugged off her 'sheltered, innocent, and Mormon-dominated childhood' and became a 'murder-ess in the name of God.'"[105]

Sadly, the violence did not end with the LeBarons. In 1984, two brothers, Ron and Dan Lafferty, brutally murdered the wife and infant daughter of their younger brother. The Laffertys claimed that they had received communication from heaven to carry out the killings, and that their destiny was to lead the LDS Church. They, too, had recently decided to practice polygamy. A section-one *Chicago Tribune* story on the Lafferty killings noted that "70%" of Utah's residents "share Lafferty's Mormon roots," and that Dan had been "an elder in his church." LDS Church spokesman Don LeFevre told the reporter that "Dan and Ronald Lafferty had been excommunicated from the church the year before the murders," but that information only made the killings slightly less "vexing in Utah because, as...LeFevre [acknowledged], the Mormon faith holds that God communicates with the devout through revelations. LeFevre said that based on revelations to its leaders, the church often has changed its policies.... 'We believe, for example, that a father can receive a revelation about what is best for his family, but we certainly do not believe in breaking the laws of the land,' LeFevre said. 'These people did not have a revelation.'"[106]

No one accused LDS leaders of condoning these crimes, but the repeated inference that these crimes came from an (admittedly deranged) interpretation of Mormon doctrine raised a guilt-by-association challenge for Latter-day Saint spokesmen. Understandably, the *Chicago Tribune* noted that "Mormon leaders fear that the public may mistakenly link these slayings with the mainstream church."[107]

Subsequent headlines did little to resolve that confusion. If anything, media reports muddled things further, especially for readers unfamiliar with the LDS Church's official position on polygamy. *The Oregonian* reported the 1987 arrest of Ervil LeBaron's sons under this title: "Mormon sects' feud takes new twist."[108] When later that year Ervil's former "trigger man," Daniel Ben Jordan, was killed while deer hunting, the *Chicago Tribune*'s headline proclaimed, "Polygamy, slayings link Mormon cults: Utah shooting latest in 15-year feud."[109] When yet another family of polygamists (the Singer-Swapp family) in small-town Marion, Utah, bombed an LDS chapel in 1988 and then initiated a stand-off with FBI agents, *The Economist* reported on "Mormon dissidents: Polygamy under siege."[110]

Though most of these newspaper reports did clarify that the criminal participants were *excommunicated* Mormons, the distinction often became fuzzy. The term "Mormon" readily served as an ambiguous shorthand for reporters to describe both members of the LDS Church *and* the break-off polygamist groups. For example, the same *Chicago Tribune* article that noted that "Mormons outlawed the practice [of polygamy] in 1890" also reported only one sentence later that "*Forbes* estimated there are about 10,000 Mormons who practice polygamy."[111] A UPI story stated that modern polygamists were "not mainstream Mormons." However, the same story concluded that these men who believed "the more wives the better" were only "[realizing] the Mormon principle of 'trial'—that God expects his people to be 'tried' by many marriages."[112] A memoir written by Rulon Allred's daughter left a book reviewer for the *New York Times* doubting whether "The Church of Jesus Christ of Latter-day Saints, the official Mormon Church, no longer polygamous but still dedicated to the subordination of women and the affirmation of their inferiority, is ... self-evidently a better environment for women than the fundamentalist group would be if it were not persecuted."[113] No wonder LDS spokesmen worried in the 1980s about the reemergence of polygamy as a public image albatross. Any perceived association between Mormons and the likes of the LeBarons, or the Laffertys, or the Singer-Swapps only deepened impressions of Mormon deviance.

While church leaders were trying to distance themselves from these splinter groups, one very talented writer—and former Mormon—argued that these criminals represented Mormonism carried to its logical extremes. Arizona journalist Deborah Laake published in 1993 *Secret Ceremonies: A Mormon Woman's Intimate Diary of Marriage and Beyond*. The book climbed bestseller lists and set Mormons' teeth on edge. Laake related that her book was a reaction to the Mormon-related scandals of the 1980s: "I understood that while these newsmakers [LeBaron, Singer, Hofmann] weren't typical Mormons, their shocking stories weren't coincidences, either. Around the roots of all the lunacies were packed typical Mormon teachings, and one teaching in particular: that all Mormon men are 'priesthood holders,' anointed with the literal, supernatural, nearly unlimited authority to act for God on earth, and are headed into an eternal life where they will themselves become gods who rule entire worlds. It's a theological concept that, tucked into a brain that's egotistical or unbalanced, is a match to dynamite."[114]

Laake also discussed and disparaged LDS temple worship based on her experiences, just as Ed Decker did in his *God Makers* franchise. However, several things made Laake's book even more galling for Mormons. The *God Makers* series never achieved the status of mainstream fare that *Secret Ceremonies* did. Laake "[devoted] only seventeen pages" of the memoir "to LDS temple rites," but because the book was "on the *New York Times* bestseller list for fifteen weeks" as a hardcover edition, and even longer as a paperback, her dissatisfaction and disputes with her former faith reached a broader audience.[115]

Yet for a Mormon reader, the revelation of the temple ceremonies might not have been the most damaging or disturbing aspect of this book. Far more troubling were the book's pervasive themes, as Laake saw them: Mormonism's psychic control over its members, its teetering on the edge of fanaticism, and the cruel patriarchy of its men. She felt that church doctrine forced her mother to stay in an unhappy marriage, which then became part of the cultural brainwashing that led Laake to enter into marriage with a man she didn't love, against her better judgment. Within nine months, after an attempted suicide, she filed for divorce.

After her dreams of an eternal marriage were shattered, she reported that she tried to counsel with various church leaders. At her hand, though, these leaders came across as "patronizing," "smug," "bullying," "unhearing," and bent on humiliating a young, fragile woman. She did not mince words about the role that her resentment played in driving her memoir. She wondered why, despite recent controversies, "informed people were continuing to take the church of my childhood at face value, as nothing more complex than a likable, family-oriented creed that embraces America's most wholesome and unambiguous values? For although Mormonism is benign and even steadying when viewed superficially, it has also long been providing to the world glimpses of the dark disturbances lying just beneath the surface."[116]

She therefore wanted to "bring into the light" the "unnerving, mystical core" of Mormonism that essentially centered on Joseph Smith's "spiritualism," a "doctrine that every member of his church was surrounded by fabulous ghosts." Laake reported, incredulously, that her family members told stories about encountering such ghosts. Not only did she thus cast Mormon doctrine—or at least her atypical interpretation of it—in a bizarre light, she warned that the contemporary LDS Church was policed by leaders who used "McCarthy-esque tactics" to "[silence] or [incapacitate] ... Mormons who question the pronouncements of modern authorities."[117]

Her book quickly sold more than half a million copies, and the sensational, tell-all nature of her writing made her a sought-after guest for television talk shows.[118] Even early on, reviewers of Laake's book noted that she seemed to blame excessively her Mormon upbringing for three failed marriages and other psychological problems. Yet these types of accusations only intensified public interest in Laake and her work and precipitated what Laake described as televised shouting matches with Mormon women who called her a liar.[119] So widespread was the book's impact that church authorities approved a press release that mentioned the book by name, a step not even taken a decade earlier with *The God Makers*. The statement expressed "[disappointment] that our sacred beliefs, or those of any other religious group, would be commercially exploited." After reiterating that "the Church teaches that men and women are to walk beside one another as companions, friends and partners," the brief statement concluded by asking that others "respect our sincere desire that sacred things not be trampled upon."[120]

Although Laake had admittedly left Mormonism long before writing the book, her explicit description—and mockery—of sacred temple procedures prompted church leaders to make official her break with the church in April

1993. Ironically, Laake credited her excommunication from the LDS Church and the church's explicit opposition to Secret Ceremonies with making her book a best-seller, since these sanctions against her only heightened interest in her story and appeared to confirm her complaints about the Mormon patriarchy.[121] "Just days after the book came out in April 1993," one newspaper reported, "a Mormon bishop showed up at New Time's office [where Laake worked as a reporter] to inform Laake that she was to be excommunicated. Just as the banner 'Banned in Boston' guaranteed book sales in earlier decades, the orchestrated Mormon opposition to Secret Ceremonies clinched this book's popularity. 'If they had just ignored the book, it might have gone away,' Laake says. 'Instead, they made complete jerks of themselves, and the book has just sold better and better.'" The reality that her fame—and thus her impact on the Mormon image—was partly fueled by church efforts to protect its image was emblematic of any number of public relations paradoxes in the 1980s and early 1990s.

As it would turn out, other Mormon authors experienced notoriety after excommunication in 1993. Laake was only the first. Some Latter-day Saint scholars continued to publish on the disputed aspects of Mormon history that Mark Hofmann had purportedly exposed. They contended that Hofmann's forgeries had been believable because his creations fit so well in the overall milieu of the Mormon past.[122] Also, several of these historians worried that the Hofmann crisis motivated what they saw as the church's reactionary retreat into historical defensiveness just as interest in Mormon topics was growing as never before. These writers felt compelled to continue the dialogue about challenging issues in Mormon theology and practice, even after Mormon officials explicitly warned them against broaching such topics.[123] A showdown seemed inevitable, and the most famous of the resultant skirmishes came to be known as the "September Six."[124]

In September 1993, six prominent Mormon scholars were disciplined—five excommunicated, and one disfellowshipped (a disciplinary step below excommunication). The three women in the group had written and spoken on the evidence and precedence for women's ordination to the priesthood and for the worship of a "Mother in Heaven." The men in the group had publicly parted with church leaders on their interpretation of scripture and church history.

"Purge" was the media's watchword for the September expulsions. This type of action against "self-described loyal members" raised warning flags about the church's increasing rigidity and intolerance of dissent. From the church's perspective, the excommunications were a last resort, the culmination of repeated attempts to work with individuals who blatantly denied the church's doctrines and authority. The scholars' supporters, however, saw their persistence as "[sounding] an alarm that intellectuals have about had enough of the [LDS] church's intimidation tactics on its followers."[125]

For this reason, what on the surface might have seemed like an internal matter quickly became a controversy that spilled over the borders of the Mormon community. Instead of necessarily reaching a large number of outside *readers*, though, these homegrown critics had a far-reaching impact because of what they *represented* to outside observers: cracks in the Mormon monolith, and the "McCarthy-esque tactics" that Laake warned against. One of the church's apostles told the *Deseret News* that the term "purge is loaded with meaning and a dirty piece of name-calling," and that the disciplinary decisions were made at the local level. Still, Michael Quinn felt the timing of his excommunication was delayed until September as part of "a calculated decision on the part of church headquarters" to have "the maximum effect they knew it would have." In fact, Quinn felt like church leaders anticipated "the media splash," knowing that it would send a message to the church's membership.[126]

Regardless of the underlying motivation or coordination behind the disciplinary councils, the fact that journalists Richard and Joan Ostling devoted a chapter of their book, *Mormon America* (1999), to the September Six episode and its fallout speaks to the important, enduring legacy of these excommunications. Paul Toscano even received calls from the BBC about the disciplinary action taken against him. In his view, "an emotional reaction to institutions that are controlling" drove the widespread interest in the story. He blamed the church's image problems on its leaders, since "the leaders...are ashamed of Mormonism," particularly Mormonism's past.[127] To some, the purge seemed part of a larger effort in Mormonism to rid itself of radical legacies by shearing off its left *and* right fringes, disciplining liberal intellectuals and polygamist fundamentalists, freethinking scholars and apocalyptic survivalists.[128]

The impression that the church sought to sanitize its past, and use "intimidation tactics" to do so, came not only from the spate of excommunications, but from complaints by BYU faculty members who were dismissed or denied tenure because of their positions, as they saw it, on Latter-day Saint theology and history.[129] Outcries about intellectual freedom came from other quarters besides the church's university, too. *Sunstone* magazine, an increasingly liberal exponent of Mormon viewpoints, first sponsored an annual symposium in 1979. In 1991, the church's First Presidency and Quorum of the Twelve issued a statement urging members to stay away from unnamed symposia that "[contain] some (though admittedly not all) presentations that result in ridiculing sacred things or injuring The Church of Jesus Christ, detracting from its mission, or jeopardizing the well-being of its members." Paul Toscano saw in this making of *Sunstone* "off limits" an ominous shift from the appearance of openness in the 1970s and early 1980s. Deseret Book had even allowed Curt Bench to sell books at early *Sunstone* conferences. In contrast, some church members in the early 1990s claimed that they had been threatened with discipline when they spoke out against these prohibitions.[130]

In late 1993 a grandson of the Mormon prophet added to the turbulence when he announced that he was leaving the church. Steve Benson was a Pulitzer Prize–winning cartoonist for the *Arizona Republic* who complained that the LDS Church had misrepresented the truth about his grandfather Ezra Taft Benson's "incapacitation." President Benson took the church's helm in late 1985 upon the death of Spencer W. Kimball. At the time, most commentators feared an abrupt turn toward ultraconservatism given Benson's praise of the John Birch Society and his strong statements against communism and feminism in the past.[131] Yet those fears never materialized. Instead, the sharpest controversy that surrounded Benson was his poor health in the early 1990s. By the time of Steve Benson's publicized departure from the church, "the elder Benson... [had] not spoken publicly in more than three years." Steve Benson implied that such a situation called into question the church's claim to divine and prophetic guidance.[132]

The church responded that all of its apostles were recognized by members as prophets, seers, and revelators, and thus the day-to-day administration of the church continued uninterrupted despite the president's poor health.[133] At various times in the church's history, other past presidents had suffered through periods of incapacity because of advanced age and because the prophetic call was always a lifelong position. In those cases, the president's counselors in the First Presidency acted in his stead. Yet no previous counselor had been subjected to as much scrutiny as had been Gordon B. Hinckley, counselor first to an ailing President Kimball and then President Benson. President Hinckley was essentially the only functioning member of the First Presidency during the *God Makers* controversy and the Hofmann scandal, because President Kimball's health also seriously limited his activity at the time. Then, in 1993, President Hinckley was again the face of the church's administration during the 1993 flare-ups about the church's anti-intellectualism. The public absence of the ordained prophet only gave critics additional ammunition when attacking the church's traditional hierarchal structure.[134] Steve Benson's actions and statements were the exclamation points on a decade's worth of denunciations of the Mormon leadership as a group purportedly jealous of its power and prestige—and protective at all costs of its image.

What a difference two decades made. In the 1973 opinion survey commissioned by the LDS Church's Public Communications Department, the church ranked low in terms of secrecy and suspicion, and even lower when it came to perceived public influence. Martin Marty, one of the country's most eminent historians of religion, wrote in 1981 that "by 1980, the Mormons had grown to be so much like everyone else or, perhaps, had so successfully gotten other Americans to be like them, that they no longer inspired curiosity for wayward ways." In retrospect, there is significant irony in that pronouncement. Marty could hardly have guessed the extent to which curiosity, consternation, and even contempt for the wayward ways of Mormonism would experience a rebirth *after*

1980 and spawn what apostle Dallin Oaks called "some of the most sustained and intense Latter-day Saint Church-bashing since the turn of the century." The negative effect was measurable. A 1991 study by the Barna Group suggested that just 6% of Americans viewed Mormons "very favorably." Three times as many respondents had given Mormons that rating in a poll only fourteen years earlier.[135]

The late 1980s and early 1990s had not been kind, either, to those in church public relations who seemed to find themselves repeatedly in the uncomfortable position of making careful press statements and answering thorny questions about church-related controversies.[136] Part of this difficulty was due to the fact that the simultaneous proliferation of positive human interest stories on successful Mormons in the 1980s did not seem to sway public perception of the LDS Church *as an institution.*[137] This "Mormon individual" versus "Mormon institution" image discrepancy spoke to another irony for Mormon image watchers—the decade's controversies coincided with some of Mormondom's most significant publicity triumphs. Sharlene Wells for example, the daughter of a church general authority, was named Miss America in 1984 (Figure 6.1).

Figure 6.1 1984—A University Publicist's Dream: Within the same calendar year, Brigham Young University claimed both a Miss America (Sharlene Wells, center, as Miss BYU in 1983, with her father, LDS Church general authority Robert E. Wells) and a national championship football team (see Figure 6.2). Both stories became human-feature high points for Mormons in the decade; then-BYU President Jeffrey R. Holland said, "I suppose there's nothing in the history of the university that has brought us the attention in the media that this has." Photograph by Mark A. Philbrick/BYU.

Only four months later, in January 1985, the BYU Cougar football team was crowned national champion, an achievement that brought unprecedented press attention to Provo—and unprecedented press attention to the number of BYU athletes who put sports on hold to serve two-year missions for the LDS Church around the globe (Figure 6.2). Yet even in the coverage of these and other celebrity Mormons, there lingered an inescapable sense of pervasive institutional control. At the same time that reporters expressed admiration for Mormons' moral rectitude and missionary service, they also derided them for being "clones" and an army of "do-rights." *Rolling Stone*, for example, hit hard: "Drinking, smoking, premarital sex—they're all taboo at Brigham Young University, the nation's largest private college, where obedience, *not thought*, is rewarded and snitches are big men on campus. Good Mormon, America!" As Mormon faces popped up in every arena of American life—more than ever before—their prominence did not erase public discomfort about the church that guided those smiling men and women.[138]

Indeed, the era's LDS-related scandals proved to have considerable staying power. National attention to those scandals initially caught some church officials by surprise, and their first reaction seemed to be to say as little as possible. Church spokesmen thus often had an adversarial relationship with the media corps. One church representative even challenged a reporter in the early

Figure 6.2. Coach LaVell Edwards and the Cougars' 24–17 Holiday Bowl victory over Michigan preserved a perfect 13–0 season and secured a national championship. Photograph by Mark A. Philbrick/BYU.

1990s, "Why is *that* news?" She responded, "I'll tell *you* what's news...I get to decide what's news."[139] The unpredictability of "what's news" became a reality that was driven home for Mormons again and again in the 1980s and early 1990s. It was a reality that would quietly prompt a wholesale rethinking of the church's approach to public relations and a retooling of its image, an image that had become weighed down with charges of authoritarianism, secrecy, and defensiveness.

7

Standing a Little Taller: 1995–2005

On March 13, 1995, Bruce Olsen, managing director of the LDS Church's Public Affairs Department, introduced Gordon B. Hinckley as the fifteenth president of The Church of Jesus Christ of Latter-day Saints.[1] President Hinckley stepped to the microphone in the newly renovated lobby of the Joseph Smith Memorial Building (formerly the Hotel Utah) and caught everyone by surprise by initiating a press conference. Peggy Fletcher Stack, religion reporter for the *Salt Lake Tribune*, remembered that "the press corps was kind of taken aback" when Hinckley opened the floor for questions, since "that was really unheard of . . . and we didn't really have questions" ready. The result was a room full of reporters "scrambling and writing down a bunch of questions." It was apparent to Stack and her colleagues that day that with President Hinckley's accession to the presidency, "the doors were thrown open."[2]

More evidence of that came one year later when President Hinckley hosted *60 Minute*'s Mike Wallace in a series of interviews and tours at LDS Church headquarters (Figure 7.1). After the previous decade's Mormon-related controversies and the accompanying rough treatment (as the church saw it) at the hands of the press, Hinckley understood that participating in a *60* carried some risks. Only hours before the program aired on April 7, 1996, President Hinckley told Mormons gathered for the church's semiannual General Conference, "We have no idea what the outcome will be. If it turns out to be favorable, I will be grateful. Otherwise, I pledge I'll never get my foot in that kind of trap again." Everyone laughed loudly, but a little nervously, too.[3]

The *60 Minutes* broadcast that evening left President Hinckley satisfied that "Mike Wallace had been . . . 'very decent' to him and the Church." Mike Wallace, in turn, found himself, by his own admission, "surprised by Gordon Hinckley's humor and his candor, neither of which I expected. We raised the issues that were on the minds of skeptics, he was willing to answer every question, and his answers were reasonable. . . . We have done stories on many organizations, including churches, but I can honestly say we have never had an experience quite

Figure 7.1. New LDS Church President Gordon B. Hinckley surprised CBS reporter Mike Wallace by agreeing to an interview for *60 Minutes* during the first year of his presidency. President Hinckley's openness with the media became a hallmark of his office. Photograph by Don Grayston. Reprinted with the permission of *the Deseret News*.

like that one." A new era had opened for Latter-day Saint publicity, and Gordon Hinckley was the standard-bearer.[4]

As a young college graduate with a degree in journalism, Hinckley essentially created the church's public relations department in its first incarnation, the Radio, Publicity, and Mission Literature Committee—a "department" that he staffed single-handedly for years, beginning in the 1930s. Because of that background, when he later became an apostle and then a counselor in the First Presidency, he was regularly tapped by his associates to act as the point man during controversial episodes. Hinckley represented the church before the media on such issues as the ERA and the role of black members in the church, and his colleagues' advanced age meant that he was often the only functioning member of the First Presidency during *the God Makers* and Mark Hofmann storms. Yet now, as the church's senior leader, he could speak with new authority. He himself noted, "There is a vast difference between being a counselor and a president." Even when the presidents with whom he served were ill, he had been careful to acknowledge the limits of what he might say and do without their authorization. "I had previously been in a situation of having responsibility without authority, [and] suddenly I had responsibility and authority." It quickly became obvious that he planned to use that authority to make himself and his office more accessible to outsiders.[5]

The timing, it seemed, could not have been more ideal. As the decade of the 1990s opened, the groundwork for a new Public Affairs Department had been laid. The department received a new director, one who had vast experience in public relations and steered his department that way. The First Presidency (with Gordon B. Hinckley as its day-to-day operational head) then commissioned a year-long brainstorming task force, the Communications Futures Committee, to make recommendations for new public outreach initiatives. The committee's report, issued only months before Hinckley became the prophet, would have a profound effect on the direction of the church's image-shaping efforts over the next dozen years. As these streams of influence converged—new voices at the Public Affairs Department, recommendations from the Communications Futures Committee, President Hinckley's background as a journalist and publicist for the church—the result was a subtle but steady course change, from mass-marketing, publicity-type campaigns to focused, relationship-driven interaction with the nation's media, government, and institutional "opinion leaders." "It became evident," said Mark Tuttle, a supervisor in the Public Affairs Department, "that we don't have the budget to change mass opinions. . . . If you can't get to the hundred million people, why not get to the ten people who do get to the hundred million people?"[6]

Taken together, these developments contributed to the sense that the LDS Church now sought to build bridges instead of bunkers. This shift was palpable, even to outside observers. Eight months into his presidency, Hinckley had lunch at the Harvard Club in New York City with thirty such opinion leaders— "*Newsweek* editor-in-chief Richard Smith; John Mack Carter, president of Hearst Magazine Enterprises; Andrew Heyward, vice president and executive producer of the CBS Evening News; Associated Press religion editor David Briggs;" and, of course, Mike Wallace. During a question-and-answer session after lunch, one of the attendees said, "President Hinckley, you are obviously not afraid to answer the tough questions. It has been my perception in the past that there were certain secretism to the workings of the Church. By your very presence, you indicate to me openness. Is this a new openness, and is the Church concentrating on opening up some of its formerly less known facets to the public?" President Hinckley did not hesitate: "There is only one situation that we don't talk about, and that is the sacred work that takes place in our temples. . . . We enter into covenants and ordinances there that are sacred and of a character that we don't talk about in public. . . . But the door is wide open on everything else."[7]

These proved to be more than idle words meant to pacify inquiring journalists; they represented a new philosophy. In many ways, public relations efforts during President Hinckley's administration can be understood as responses to the charges of the 1980s and early 1990s—secrecy, authoritarianism, exclusiveness. As church officials took their cues from President Hinckley, evidence of openness abounded, especially in the way Mormons interacted with the media during two of the church's biggest news-making moments—the sesquicentennial wagon train in 1997 and the 2002 Winter Olympics. Yet this era of openness also prompted new outreach initiatives to evangelical Christians, African Americans, and historians and others in the academy. Over the course of the next ten years, a new picture of The Church of Jesus Christ of Latter-day Saints developed. The church had a new confidence, a new level of ease with its identity, as if there was nothing to hide. Journalists and their audiences responded eagerly to this open-door policy, this chance to look behind the curtain of Mormonism—and to the church's satisfaction and relief, they seemed to like what they saw.

Out of "the Defensive Mode": Public Affairs and the Media

After a period of transition in the 1980s, the Public Affairs Department was ready to carve out a new identity, establish a new personality.[8] Under Wendell Ashton and Heber Wolsey in the 1970s, the department (then called "Public Communications") had been an effective advertising team. The *Homefront* radio and television commercials and inserts in *Reader's Digest* magazines characterized the department's aims and successes in creating favorable feelings about the LDS Church's family focus.

In 1984, church leaders moved the audiovisual arm of public communications, as well as oversight of church visitors' centers, to the church's missionary department. The direct contacting approach of these campaigns seemed to fit better the missionary department's aim of seeking out interested investigators. This took from Public Communications/Special Affairs (the department's new name) its most visible outreach initiatives and left the department to deal with public policy issues and the media.[9]

This was not an easy task, and not everyone in the department was sure of the direction to proceed. Initially, staffer Val Edwards saw the department's post-*Homefront* emphasis as a "broadly based program" of "community service" on issues "where there seemed to be some kind of a fit for our values." In this vein, department director Richard P. Lindsay demonstrated the potential for bridge-building initiatives during his tenure from 1983–1989. His professional background was in the public sector, as both a civil servant and an elected official. This experience in government social services served him well as he worked to involve the LDS Church in community action coalitions, most notably in the fights against alcohol and pornography.[10]

The Religious Alliance against Pornography, for example, honored Mormons for doing more than any other church to combat pornography through media messages. Lindsay was one of four religious leaders invited to testify before a senate subcommittee about the "problems of family breakdowns in the United States." The church's Washington, D.C., Public Communications bureau hosted an interfaith press conference at which representatives of "Islamic, Jewish, Protestant, Catholic, and Sikh faiths pledged long-term involvement in seeking solutions to drug abuse and drug-related crimes." These types of issue-based alliances built friendships and heralded a potential for improving outside perception of the church, especially with like-minded religious leaders. At the same time, though, Mormon participation in these coalitions often brought to the surface the discomfort that some evangelical partners endured when they associated with Mormons.[11]

The church's public relations team did enjoy some behind-the-scenes success in fostering partnerships on public morality during the 1980s. Much more visible, however, were the media grillings church spokesmen faced at seemingly every turn, as controversial episodes unfolded, ranging from the Hofmann bombings to the disciplining of prominent Mormon scholars. Since top church leaders felt occasionally mistreated in the way the press handled these incidents, it is not surprising that public affairs representatives tended toward reticence. Journalist Peggy Fletcher Stack certainly felt that chill: "When I first started [at the *Salt Lake Tribune*]..., President Benson was not well and not present much and so I think that my experience with the public affairs—good people all, I enjoyed my interactions with them—but it seems like they saw their job as withholding information, holding back." Her description fit with what Val Edwards remembered about his first ten years with the church, as the public affairs department's media relations philosophy evolved only slowly. He joined the department's staff in the 1980s, when "we [had] virtually no relationship with the media at that time. We were a response team,... [and] I think... the department was seen as just a channel by which the desires and... messages of the [general authorities] were taken to the news media." Because of that, "we really weren't on the radar screen of many journalists," who wanted more than terse official statements.[12]

The suspicion that Mormon officials were "withholding information" during this era of successive controversies hurt the church's public image bottom line. The Mormon reputation seemed to have taken a measurable hit since the high point of Ashton and Wolsey's family-focused advertising efforts in the 1970s. In its 1991 survey about American attitudes toward various churches, the Barna Research Group noted that "the only denomination in the survey"—which also included questions about Baptist, Catholic, Methodist, Presbyterian, and Lutheran churches—"for which more Americans had a negative impression than a positive impression was the Mormon church, also known as the Church of Jesus Christ of Latter-day Saints"; 37% ranked Mormons unfavorably in 1991, while only 18% gave Mormons an unfavorable rating in 1977. When those who expressed no opinion were removed from the study, the 1991 results were even more dramatic: "Nearly six out of ten people who had an opinion of the Mormon Church said their impression was a negative one."[13]

When director Lindsay was called to be a church general authority in 1989, he was replaced by Bruce Olsen, a man with an extensive public relations background. Olsen had directed public communications at Brigham Young University and had done consulting work in the corporate arena. His appointment seemed to signal that his church superiors were prepared to reshape the department's aims, as well. Olsen learned later that his hiring came after a search committee headed by apostle David B. Haight quizzed several Mormon executives nationwide about top prospects in the field of public relations. Importantly, the impulse for departmental transformation was as much bottom up as it was top down. As he was introduced to his staff, Olsen remembered the number of department employees who shook his hand and "found a way to say, 'I hope we are going to be more proactive.'"[14]

Proactivity had been the watchword during another time of transition for church outreach—the 1970s. In that era, the proactive impulse translated into an aggressive advertising blitz centered on Mormonism's family-centered theology. As the 1990s opened, though, public relations proactivity meant a different sort of campaign. There was a decided shift in attention toward cultivating meaningful contacts with local and national opinion *makers*. What Bruce Olsen wanted was to leave behind "the defensive mode . . . where the department [had] spent most of the time."[15]

The evolution of this new mind-set and its visible outcomes speaks to the push-pull nature of LDS Church administration at the point where hierarchy and bureaucracy intersect. In its corporate structure, the church and its operations are overseen by centralized ecclesiastical leaders, the general authorities. However, under their supervision, church departments are run by professional managers. The role of these managers is not only to follow the direction of their ecclesiastical superiors, but also to make recommendations to those superiors. While ultimate decision making rests with the general authorities, the professionals can wield considerable influence. Mark Tuttle described it as the junction of information and inspiration: general authorities "expect . . . the best staff work . . . to supply the information that's important for them so they can have the inspiration to make it right." What seems to have propelled the Public Affairs Department in the 1990s, therefore, was the confluence of a skilled and energetic professional staff under Bruce Olsen, and a receptive group of general authorities, most notable among them Gordon B. Hinckley. Olsen's staff pressed forward in the direction that Hinckley and several of his apostolic colleagues by disposition and experience were ready to go, and conversely, Bruce Olsen's staff responded eagerly to general authorities who encouraged openness.[16]

One early example of this came in 1994, when at the urging of Olsen's department that church general authorities "[become] the spokesmen to represent
the Church with the media," Mormon apostle M. Russell Ballard sat down with
Nightline's Ted Koppel for a fifty-minute interview. "As soon as the red light
on the camera came on," Elder Ballard remembered, he felt like he was "hanging by the ropes" because of Ted Koppel's tough questions. Yet in the end, the
apostle said, "I don't think I embarrassed the church." Ballard, a member of the
general authority–level Public Affairs Committee that oversaw Bruce Olsen's
department, concluded, "We had the choice either to accept and speak for
ourselves or to say no and let Koppel tell his mass audience that the Mormon
Church chose not to respond." The decision to "speak for ourselves," Ballard felt,
had "an impact on the [general authorities], helping us all see that we could meet
with the national press."[17]

Sentiments like these signaled a growing agreement with Olsen's push to narrow his department's activities to match its new motto: "awareness, answers,
and bridges." He called for staff to receive formal public relations training and
certification. He likewise recommended to church authorities that the name of
the department be shortened to "Public Affairs" to reflect its more specialized,
public relations outlook. The name change was made in 1991.[18]

The official stamp of approval on the newly named department came early
in the form of a retooled *Public Affairs Handbook*, sent to regional church volunteers in 1992 to replace various versions of the manual that dated back to
1967. The 1992 handbook was dramatically different than earlier editions.
A missionary-type emphasis drove the manuals that had been produced in 1967
and then slightly revised in 1973 and 1977. There was little question that the
purpose of "good public relations" then was to "[open] many doors; and . . . provoke people behind closed doors to come out, look up the missionaries, and
discover the Gospel for themselves." These earlier handbooks were filled with
instructions for generating local publicity for the church, publicity intended "to
do more than improve the image of the Church before all mankind. We aim to
help bring the gospel to all nations."[19]

A different tone characterized the 1992 handbook. This new manual spoke to
the types of image problems that had pummeled the church in the 1980s. The
pamphlet reminded volunteers that "effective public affairs work can decrease
substantially the effect of misinformation about the Church and can limit its
negative effect by creating a climate of goodwill, mutual respect, and trust
between the Church and the community." While the new handbook did include a
line recognizing that "public affairs work . . . can help people become more receptive to missionaries," the primary charge was to "provide accurate responses to
misinformation about the Church and defamation of it."[20]

The earlier handbooks had mentioned "religious leaders" in the list of prominent community figures that Mormon public relations volunteers should know,

yet that brief acknowledgement was essentially the extent of the instruction on interfaith outreach in the previous editions of the booklet. Significantly, the 1992 handbook contained an entire section on "interfaith relations," with the aim being "simply to develop friendships that will increase understanding and promote religious tolerance." The 1992 version also included new instructions about "[increasing] public understanding that members of The Church of Jesus Christ of Latter-day Saints revere Jesus Christ as the Son of God, the Savior and Redeemer of mankind." Both changes suggested that the resurgence of "cult" accusations in the 1980s was clearly on the minds of Mormon officials.[21]

So was the need for outside help. The First Presidency, under the de facto leadership of President Hinckley, commissioned the "Communications Futures Committee" in January 1993 to give recommendations. In so doing, the church's hierarchy sought input on the best ways to facilitate "awareness, answers, and bridges." The committee sifted through suggestions that came from "thirty-five of the Church's top media professionals" from "all over the country" who over the course of a year "gathered in brain-storming sessions and committees to review these issues." The report ultimately proposed fifteen action items. In retrospect, the subsequent two decades confirmed that this committee's report proved to be a defining document for Mormon public relations efforts. While several of the recommendations came to fruition years later—such as establishing a church-sponsored cable/satellite channel (like BYUtv, launched in 2000) or disseminating information by means of the incipient "Electronic Highway"— two suggestions had a more immediate impact.[22]

The committee urged leaders to "avoid the nickname 'Mormon'" and emphasize instead the full "Church of Jesus Christ of Latter-day Saints" title. To bolster that effort, the committee also suggested that the church reconsider its "cumbersome, difficult-to-read" five-line logo and give more printed prominence to the "Jesus Christ" portion of its name. Accordingly, in 1995, the church unveiled a three-line logo, with the words "Jesus Christ" occupying the center line in a noticeably larger font. Subsequently, every press release the church sent to media representatives included a note asking that journalists discontinue references to the "Mormon Church" and use either the church's full title or "Church of Jesus Christ" as a shorter alternative. It was clear that evangelical attacks had made an impact. At the center of this concerted campaign was the desire to shed the non-Christian, cultist label, since so often the descriptor "non-Christian," when applied to Mormons, also seemed to imply "aberrant" or even "deviant." Instead, LDS officials wanted to locate their faith within the fold of thoroughly Christian—though not Catholic or Protestant—denominations, and thus replace its exotic reputation with the instant familiarity that came with the "Christian" designation in American society.[23]

Next, the committee also recommended that the church retain the services of a well-known public relations firm, something that it had not done since the administration of President David O. McKay, when the Tabernacle Choir began its first European tour. Bruce Olsen noted that "consequently, David O. McKay was probably one of the best known leaders of the Church in the United States...to that point." The anticipated "advantages" of turning again to outside public relations specialists would be to "extend by a factor of five the number of media contacts the Church now enjoys" and "identify [influential individuals] friendly to the Church who would defend the Church and carry...positive messages." The recommendation proved persuasive; in the mid-1990s, the church hired New York–based Edelman Public Relations Worldwide.[24]

Edelman and Hinckley made ready partners. The public relations firm set up the November 1995 luncheon at the Harvard Club where President Hinckley met Mike Wallace. Though at the luncheon he had accepted Mike Wallace's request for a future interview, when he returned to Salt Lake City, Hinckley had "second thoughts." Bruce Olsen remembered that several church colleagues were concerned about possible embarrassment. Some non-Mormon outside consultants told Olsen "they wouldn't touch this with a twelve-foot pole." Yet President Hinckley did not back away from his initial agreement. Even Mike Wallace seemed a little surprised that the interview actually happened, so unprecedented was it. He opened his interview by asking, "Can you tell me the last President of the Mormon Church who went on nationwide television to do an interview with no questions ahead of time so that you know what is coming?" When President Hinckley admitted that he could not, Mike Wallace essentially wondered why President Hinckley would break from what seemed like a traditionally "secretive attitude" and take the risk. President Hinckley responded, "Because I felt it was an opportunity to tell the people of America something about this great cause in which I have such a keen interest."[25]

Apostle Neal A. Maxwell noted at the time, "President Hinckley respects the media, but he is not afraid of them....And he doesn't feel compelled to gloss over any of our shortcomings as a people. He doesn't put forward any gilding or veneer." Because of this demonstrated openness, after the 60 Minutes piece, there was almost an insatiable media appetite for the chance to interview a Mormon prophet, and his colleagues at church headquarters agreed "there is no General Authority...better prepared to be interviewed by the press than President Gordon B. Hinckley."[26]

Within the first three years of his presidency, President Hinckley was interviewed by reporters for the New York Times, Wall Street Journal, Time magazine, and the BBC. He appeared on a full-hour Larry King Live call-in show on CNN in September 1998 and again in December 1999 (Larry King had married a Mormon in 1997). These appearances were in addition to numerous interviews and press conferences at nearly every stop during his whirlwind tours of foreign nations. Transcripts of those interviews reveal that not many of the questions that reporters asked had changed over the course of the decades. Inevitably there was interest in polygamy, the history of blacks and the priesthood, the church's wealth, its treatment of dissidents. Yet there was something disarming about President Hinckley's unruffled candor. He readily admitted that there had been challenges in the past, but his optimism for the future permeated these interviews. He gave the clear impression that Mormons looked to the future rather than feared the past.[27]

For example, the *60 Minutes* piece included a brief sound bite from former Mormon Steve Benson, who complained that "when [the prophet] has pronounced the church's position on any issue, it is incumbent upon the members of the church to pray, pay, and obey." President Hinckley responded, "Well, that's a clever statement from Steve, whom I know." Then he said, "Our people have tremendous liberty, they're free to live their lives as they please." Mike Wallace asked, "Really?" President Hinckley assured him, "Surely. They have to make choices. It's the old eternal battle—the forces of evil against the forces of good." In the final edit of the piece, Mike Wallace's next voice-over comment seemed to minimize the controversy: "The critics acknowledge they represent a tiny minority of Mormons." Later in the broadcast, Wallace said, "There are those who say, this is a gerontocracy, this is a church run by old men." President Hinckley was quick with his rejoinder, "Isn't it wonderful? To have a man of maturity at the head, a man of judgment, who isn't blown about by every wind of doctrine?" Mike Wallace shot back, "Absolutely, as long as he's not dotty." Both laughed as President Hinckley said, "Thank you for the compliment." Significantly, the *60 Minutes* segment ended with Mike Wallace talking about one of Mormonism's most attractive doctrines, the belief that "families will be reunited, and will live together forever in heaven."[28]

Some of Mike Wallace's colleagues complained that he had not been hard-hitting enough in the interview. Bruce Olsen remembered that the show's producer, as he was editing the footage of the December 1995 interview, insisted that the exchange was "too positive." Wallace was sent back in March for more questions. Yet even then, the *Salt Lake Tribune* noted, "Veteran TV interviewer Mike Wallace looked like he was tossing softballs to Mormon Church President Gordon B. Hinckley...but it may have been a case of the media-savvy Hinckley deflecting hardballs." Wallace at the time said, "We raised the issues that were on the minds of skeptics, he was willing to answer every question, and his answers were reasonable." Wallace's esteem for Hinckley was evident. He wrote the foreword to President Hinckley's best-selling book *Standing for Something*, published by Random House in 2000. Wallace also was a special guest at Hinckley's 95th birthday celebration in 2005. He told reporters then that ever since their initial 1995 encounter, he had been "impressed" by the Mormon president's "courage and imagination." He was likewise "impressed by Mormons he meets." "When you come out here and talk to people, you look in their eyes, they're so damned happy," he said. "Everyone looks so innocent. Maybe there's something we've been missing."[29]

In its ten-page feature on the Mormons in August 1997, *Time* magazine also trumpeted the "Mormons'...Great Trek to social acceptance" and had President Hinckley "downplaying his faith's distinctiveness. The church's message, he explained, 'is a message of Christ. Our church is Christ-centered. [Christ is] our leader. He's our head.'" The Presbyterian Church (U.S.A.), *Time* noted, had "issued [in 1995] national guidelines stating that the Mormons were not 'within the historic apostolic tradition of the Christian Church'" and "must be regarded as heretical." Yet the magazine also observed that with the change to the LDS Church's logo, as well as the earlier addition of the "Another Testament of Jesus Christ" subtitle to the Book of Mormon, Mormons appeared to be "downplaying their differences with the mainstream." For Latter-day Saints, however, this was not simply a public relations ploy. It was a shift in theological emphasis, an attempt to publicize its core Christian tenets and answer the charges made against the church to the contrary. *Newsweek* asked historian Jan Shipps if the fact that "Mormon rhetoric [was] becoming more overtly evangelical" signaled that "the Mormons [were] going mainstream." "Not at all" was how she responded. "After a century of cultivating their separate identity as a religious people, Mormons now want to stress their affinities with traditional Christianity yet highlight their uniqueness."[30]

Time conceded that Latter-day Saints made a good case for their "affinities with traditional Christianity," since "no other denomination" beside the Mormons "can so consistently parade the social virtues most Americans have come around to saying that they admire." This focus on Mormon virtues overshadowed the discussion of Mormon controversies. Even though a paragraph of the article was dedicated to complaints surrounding the September Six excommunications, *Time* countered, "It is hard to argue with Mormon uniformity when a group takes care of its own so well." The article ended with President Hinckley's assessment of the church's history: "From that pioneer beginning, in this desert valley, where a plow had never before broken the soil, to what you see today...this is a story of success." *Time's* David Van Biema's concluding thoughts were telling: "Will it succeed? Will the generations of young Mormon men who have so avidly evangelized...make the church as *respected a presence* in Brazil or the Philippines *as it is in* Utah, Colorado, or, for that matter, *America as a whole*?...It would be unwise to bet against more of the same."[31]

President Hinckley seemed to be a leader who matched the 1970s *Reader's Digest–type* impressions people had of Mormons. He did not strike people as a cultist or a charlatan. Far from it, in fact—he was articulate, wise, practical, warm, and witty. Public Affairs Department staffers were ready to capitalize on the momentum that his exposure generated. Several significant "Mormon moments" in the media spotlight gave these strategists a platform from which they could reinforce the idea that Mormons were not the strange cultists that they had sometimes been painted. These were opportunities to underscore what their prophet was saying at every stop: Mormons were Christians, Americans, and neighbors.

"We're Not a Weird People": The Pioneer Sesquicentennial and the Winter Olympics

While they did not want the "weird" label,[32] church public affairs representatives were happy to receive—and generate—attention of the right sort, and that is precisely what happened when dozens of horse- and ox-drawn wagons rolled over 1,000 miles from Iowa to Salt Lake City from April to July 1997. Pioneer enthusiasts, not church leaders, put together the historical reenactment to commemorate the same trek that Mormons had first made 150 years earlier to escape the persecution they had endured in Missouri and Illinois. Officials at the LDS Public Affairs Department quickly saw the potential of tapping into an event that was both quintessentially American *and* Mormon. Not only was westward migration a defining theme in both American and Mormon history, something about the scale and authenticity of the reenactment drew reporters from around the globe (Figure 7.2). The church was ready. Earlier in the year,

Figure 7.2. Broadcast trucks and covered wagons: in 1997, media outlets worldwide covered the sesquicentennial wagon train reenactment of the original Mormon pioneer trek. Church officials were surprised by the level of interest and experimented with new technologies in disseminating information to journalists. Copyright Intellectual Property, Inc. Reprinted with the permission of The Church of Jesus Christ of Latter-day Saints.

as Public Affairs employees sensed a growing curiosity in the wagon train, they took a significant step in the direction of "creating stories," not just "responding to stories." Utilizing a new technology, a Public Affairs team produced a CD-ROM for media personnel with information about the original journey and its commemorative counterpart. The team included on the disks journal entries from Mormon pioneers, maps, photographs, and statistical information. Eleven thousand of the CD-ROMs were "distributed to... newspaper and electronic media organizations throughout the world." The response, from the church's standpoint, was remarkable.[33]

Journalists from Germany, France, England, Argentina, Austria, and Japan came to cover the trek. Latter-day Saints in Ukraine drew attention with a mini-reenactment in their homeland. All told, the trek "generated international news programs that reached more than 160 countries." The coverage in the United States was even more comprehensive. M. Russell Ballard, the apostle who oversaw this sesquicentennial celebration, noted that "requests for... interviews... multiplied and escalated almost beyond our ability to control." The wagon train prompted the *Time* feature mentioned earlier, as well as major articles in *Newsweek* and on the Associated Press and United Press International wires. CBS's *This Morning*, ABC's *Good Morning America*, and NBC's *Today Show* devoted segments to the wagon train. PBS premiered *Trail of Hope*, a documentary about the Mormon pioneers. The film garnered excellent viewer ratings in markets such as Houston, Milwaukee, Nashville, Chicago, and St. Louis, and above average ratings in Los Angeles and Cincinnati. Ballard said in August 1997, "When we can finally assess the number of newspaper articles and the extent of the television and radio coverage of the sesquicentennial, we will likely find that the Church has had more media exposure this year than in all the other years of our history combined." Public opinion analyst and recently appointed church general authority Richard Wirthlin observed in 1997 that "it was particularly gratifying to note that most of this coverage was positive," such that the wagon train commemoration provided for more "goodwill than any other single activity the Church has initiated in the last 50 years."[34]

This level of attention evoked several responses at church headquarters. One was an acceleration of President Hinckley's general "letting down our guard" type détente with the press. Public Affairs (and the Edelman Group) had been pushing to have general authorities "accessible to the news media," and the interviews with President Hinckley and the coverage of the pioneer sesquicentennial seemed to confirm the wisdom in that accessibility. There was a detectable shift away from guardedness. Apostle Ballard said in 1997, "Some people worry about why we're so successful and like to speculate about our finances," but he counseled against defensiveness. He recognized that "concentrating on Church finances might be a little offensive to us," but the 1997 *Time* story that highlighted the church's economic strength actually "perked [the] interest" of the "leaders of industry [who] want to know how we do it." Church representatives now saw silver linings where before they had seen media storm clouds. Accordingly, several of the church's apostles participated in "bridge-building meetings" with East Coast media and government power brokers arranged by the Edelman team: U.S. Senators Joseph Lieberman and John Ashcroft; General Colin Powell; Peter Jennings of *ABC News* and Bob Abernathy of *NBC News*; and the editorial board of the *New York Times*. [35]

There were promising signs that this type of outreach, especially the overtures to media personnel, produced results. During the first few years of President Hinckley's tenure, one of the church's touchstone objectives came from a phrase in the scriptural Doctrine and Covenants. That passage charged the church with coming "out of obscurity." Few doubted that the media's attention to Mormonism during 1997 had indeed diminished the church's "obscurity." In his research that examined media coverage of Mormons from 1991 to 2000, BYU graduate student Casey Olson found that the number of national periodical articles devoted to Latter-day Saints in the 1990s was nearly quadruple that of the previous four decades—and by his rating system, the more recent coverage was overwhelmingly less negative. After the controversies over race relations, the ERA, and the Hofmann bombings, Olson called the 1990s "a rebound of favorable magazine reporting on the Church after some twenty years of generally unfavorable press."[36]

Yet there was more to this concentrated attention on key opinion leaders than seeking publicity for publicity's sake. In the past, Public Affairs managers Mark Tuttle and Val Edwards remembered, their department had looked for ways simply to get feel-good stories about Mormons in the news; success was judged on the number of times Mormons were mentioned in clipped articles. Now, they aimed to do more than just highlight Mormonism's family-friendliness, but to tackle public perception problem areas as well. Public Affairs saw the potential impact that focused, packaged messages distributed in press kits or highlighted in press interviews could have in changing past prejudice toward the church. There was striking evidence that President Hinckley's media appearances and the pioneer reenactment achieved success along those lines, clearing roadblocks that repeatedly seemed to hinder the church's public image, like questions about Mormonism's "Christian" status. A Frank Magid study in the late 1970s demonstrated that "roughly 32% of the county would say that Mormons believed in Jesus Christ. . . . By 1998, . . . we were finding that 78 to 80% of people said that Mormons believed in Jesus Christ." From the church's standpoint, that was a significant improvement.[37]

Encouraged by these positive indicators, public relations analysts at church headquarters hoped to make similar headway in dispelling other long held misconceptions about Mormonism. Questions about the continued practice of polygamy and distrust over the church's "closed society" presented persistent challenges to the LDS Church's reputation. With that in mind, the Public Affairs Department targeted several specific, popular myths about the church as the next—and undoubtedly biggest—Mormon media moment loomed on the horizon: the 2002 Winter Olympics in Salt Lake City (Figure 7.3).

In July 1995, when the International Olympic Committee named Salt Lake as the 2002 host city, misgivings immediately arose about the role the church could—or should—play during the newly dubbed "Molympic Games." Reporters as well as many Utahans worried that an army of Mormon missionaries would be stationed at street corners to capitalize on the influx of unevangelized visitors. After all, the Olympic spotlight could draw unparalleled attention to the Mormon message. Ultimately, President Hinckley announced a policy that allayed outsiders' fears and paradoxically raised the church's profile: Mormons would not proselytize during the Games.[38]

That announcement brought nods of approval from virtually every quarter and almost instantly improved outsiders' preconceptions about what to expect from their Latter-day Saint hosts. Yet other preconceptions were not so easily resolved, and pre-Olympics reports from around the country (and especially from around the world) revealed that qualms about Mormonism's

Figure 7.3. When the world came to Utah: the Salt Lake City skyline transformed for the 2002 Winter Olympics. A twenty-story banner decorated the LDS Church Office Building, just left of the iconic Salt Lake Temple. Olympic organizers also asked the church for use of the property that became the medals plaza (in the foreground of the photo), and the church agreed. One Olympic official called community generosity and support for the Olympics in Salt Lake a "breath of fresh air." Photograph by Tom Smart. Reprinted with the permission of the *Deseret News.*

past prompted familiar questions about its present state. The Public Affairs Department prepared carefully to tackle these types of questions, since the decision not to proselytize did not equal a decision to avoid publicity. Latter-day Saints knew that a media onslaught would be inevitable. In fact, they invited it.

In 2002, the Public Affairs Department reported to the church's First Presidency that it was not "placing stories just to increase column inches or to receive any kind of coverage. We are looking for media stories that help...solve problems that affect the reputation of...the Church or help the public better understand issues that affect the Church." In its five-year plan preceding the Olympics, the department designed "a web site specifically oriented to journalists," as well as "press kits," and video and photography packages to "be made available to visiting journalists and posted on the Internet media site." Four months before the Olympics opened, Public Affairs reported to its church superiors that it had "47 story packages currently available on [the] Church web site," and that NBC had asked for "18 of our video news releases,...intending to use them at different times during their international broadcasting of the games." "Our strategy," department officials concluded, "is to provide a number of stories for the national and international media so that the only story about the Church is not Mountain Meadows or polygamy—substitute positive for negative."[39]

These prepackaged vignettes included a ten-minute "Myths and Reality" video hosted by star NFL quarterback (and Brigham Young descendent) Steve Young and former Miss America Sharlene Wells Hawkes. The pair tackled three prevalent misconceptions. They told viewers that no one who currently practiced polygamy was accurately called a "Mormon," since the church had disavowed the practice a century earlier. Next, in response to charges that Mormonism was a closed society that took care only of its own, the video highlighted the church's worldwide humanitarian program. That program began in earnest in 1985, when the church initiated a fund-raising fast for Ethiopia. Over the next two decades, the church's program had grown to include disaster relief efforts, widespread inoculations against measles, and a wheelchair initiative that provided aid to people regardless of religious affiliation, with total donations to date in the hundreds of millions of dollars. Finally, in response to the claims that Mormons were not Christians, Hawkes said that Mormons "are Christian to our core," but with an acknowledged difference: Mormons believe that the church of Jesus Christ needed to be restored, since important doctrines had been lost in the centuries after the New Testament era. She also explained that one of those doctrines was a belief in the eternality of family ties. The importance of this central doctrine motivated the accelerated construction of Mormon temples, since the religious ceremonies that bind families together take place only in temples.[40]

This focused counteroffensive against negative stereotypes, together with the other Olympics-timed media vignettes, yielded measurable results. Public opinion surveys conducted by the church demonstrated that "feelings toward the LDS Church have improved significantly." Survey respondents in 2002 rated the church five points higher than they did in 1998—from 40.3 to 45.3—when asked to measure their feelings on a "0 to 100 thermometer scale," with "0" representing a "very cold, negative feeling," and "100" representing a "very warm, positive feeling." The poll results were even more significant in terms of targeted misunderstandings. When asked, "As far as you know, do members of the Church of Jesus Christ of Latter-day Saints believe in Jesus Christ?" 81% of respondents answered "yes" in 2002 as opposed to 68% only one year earlier. An overwhelming majority of those surveyed in 2002 (80%) also answered that the LDS Church "discouraged" polygamy. Overall, Public Affairs officials saw these trends as indicating that "knowledge about the LDS Church has steadily increased." Surveyors asked, "How much do you feel you know about The Church of Jesus Christ of Latter-day Saints, whose members are sometimes called Mormons?" The number of people who answered "a great deal" doubled between 1998 and 2002 (from 7% to 14%), those who said "some" increased by two-thirds (from 25 to 41%), and those who answered "very little" decreased by a third (from 67% to 46%).[41]

These statistics seemed directly proportional to other indicators that pointed to the effective reach of the media initiatives that the church had put into place. The website that Public Affairs created for the media tallied over 900,000 hits between June 2001 and May 2002. During the Olympics, representatives assisted 3,300 journalists at the church's temporary News Resource Center in the Joseph Smith Memorial Building across the street from Temple Square. The sheer volume of coverage was staggering, but the results seemed to bear out the potential impact inherent in the "core purpose" vision statement adopted by the church's Public Affairs Department as it entered the twenty-first century: "build strategic relationships with opinion leaders who affect the reputation of the Church of Jesus Christ, and whose actions and influence can help or hinder the Church's mission."[42]

There were several Olympic images that the church hoped would linger, like NBC anchorman Tom Brokaw's interview of President Hinckley. Brokaw described the Mormon leader, then ninety-one years old, as "an energetic, enormously thoughtful man." A columnist for the Washington Post noted that "The Tabernacle Choir shared top billing with the celebrities; Temple Square got almost as much TV time as Bob Costas." Editorials in the Washington Times and the Chicago Sun-Times gave the Olympic hosts "gold" ratings for the quality of the games, both for the hospitality of the locals as well as the success of the church's efforts to "overcome stereotypes." The Chicago Tribune concluded that "the church's contribution turned into a plus after years of fear that these would be the Mormon Games." International Olympic Committee President Jacques Rogge even gave special commendation to the hundreds of foreign language–speaking former Mormon missionaries who joined the huge cadre of volunteers. President Hinckley told the church's April 2002 General Conference that "visitors...who came with suspicion and hesitancy...feeling they might get trapped in some unwanted situation by religious zealots...found something they never expected." Outsiders agreed. "The subtle approach, in the end, was a brilliant move by the church," one columnist wrote. "The only religious shenanigans and Bible-thumping at the Winter Games came courtesy of angry other denominations, whose members circled Temple Square with anti-Mormon signs and pamphlets and posters." The irony was that, in the end, "everyone looked nutty except the Mormons, who looked golden."[43]

To a remarkable extent, it seemed as if President Hinckley had successfully navigated his church across the troubled waters of mistrust that separated Mormons and the media. As never before, Mormons seemed to move comfortably in the American mainstream, in terms of their full participation in the larger society. They were a homegrown success story, more and more defined by recent gains than by their complex past. In the wake of that journey, the Mormon prophet's influence opened channels of communication with other groups that had long looked askance on the LDS Church—the African American community, evangelical Christians, historians and other academics. While these outreach efforts only occasionally made headlines, Mormons measured success in terms of goodwill and mutual understanding rather than only good press.

"Colorblind Faith"

Few would have guessed in the 1960s that the National Association for the Advancement of Colored People (NAACP) would ever invite the Mormon prophet to address its leadership convention.[44] Yet three decades after the NAACP threatened to picket the Mormons' General Conference and urged officials from various countries to refuse visas to Mormon missionaries, Gordon B. Hinckley was at the podium of the association's Western Region One Leadership Conference. He had just returned from a tour of several African nations. Two firsts related to that trip signaled the church's maturing presence there. Not only was Hinckley the first president of the LDS Church to visit that continent (outside of South Africa), while there he also announced plans to build the church's first temple on the continent outside of South Africa (in Ghana). Leaders of the NAACP were impressed with the message that such a trip sent. Thus, along with the invitation to speak, as remarkable as that was, the NAACP representatives gave Hinckley a Distinguished Service Award and a standing ovation after he told the gathering,

"Each of us is a child of God. It matters not the race.... We are sons and daughters of the Almighty."[45]

The year of that NAACP address, 1998, marked twenty years since President Spencer W. Kimball announced the revelation that ended the prohibition on the priesthood ordination of black Mormons. In the intervening decades, hundreds of thousands of blacks had become fully participating Latter-day Saints in Africa, in the Caribbean, in Brazil. The growth of Mormonism's U.S. black membership had been decidedly slower. The lingering bad taste of accusations about Mormon racism was harder to swallow in the American setting where it had been so pronounced.

Despite opinion surveys showing that Mormons harbored demonstrably less-racist attitudes than did the American public generally, the specter of past official discrimination continually reappeared in descriptions of the church in the 1980s and 1990s. By the late 1990s, some Mormons clamored for a church apology over the previous policy, or at least over the opinions of past Mormon leaders regarding blacks' cursed lineage. However, other church members, including several prominent black Latter-day Saints, countered that an apology for the restriction would be tantamount to a denial of the reality of the revelation, a "'detriment' to church work," and "a catalyst to further racial misunderstanding," since "there is no pleasure in old news, and this news is old." When pressed about this, President Hinckley said simply, "The revelation continues to speak for itself." One observer of racial attitudes in Mormonism, sociologist Armand Mauss, interpreted this approach—what he called "benign neglect"—as "the apparent hope that with time all such vestiges of racism would eventually die a natural death," an "assumption that the abandonment of the restrictive racial *policy* in 1978 was meant implicitly to include an abandonment of the various traditional *doctrinal folklore* that had once been used to justify that policy."[46]

There had been, in fact, high-level disavowals of that "doctrinal folklore." Two church apostles explicitly labeled these erstwhile and unofficial explanations as speculative, personal views, *not* church doctrine. Two months after the announced June 1978 revelation, Bruce R. McConkie told a large gathering of church educators, "Forget everything that I have said, or what President Brigham Young or President George Q. Cannon or whomsoever has said in days past that is contrary to the present revelation. We spoke with a limited understanding and without the light and knowledge that now has come into the world." In a newspaper interview on the ten-year anniversary of the 1978 change, Dallin H. Oaks also observed that the "reasons" some "people put to" the priesthood restriction "turned out to be spectacularly wrong," even "reasons given by general authorities." Still, long-held perceptions proved difficult to dispel. Therefore, rather than issue another statement and stir up "old news," it seemed that church public affairs representatives opted for an actions-speak-louder-than-words approach to convey what Mauss called "the sincere message" that "real changes have taken place in the ways in which the church looks upon black people." The public affairs focus became increased cooperation with African American community leaders.[47]

Some of these friendships started spontaneously at the local level. In the midst of the Los Angeles riots in 1992, for example, two Mormon stake (diocese) presidents in Southern California organized efforts to truck food to the First African Methodist Episcopal (AME) Church and Zion Missionary Baptist Church, where volunteers were distributing supplies to needy residents trapped in the aftermath of the chaos. The Mormon caravans lasted for several days, and the undertaking forged a bond with Reverend Cecil Murray, pastor at First AME. Reverend Murray used his influence to persuade Los Angeles Mayor Tom Bradley to end "a six-year delay in the issuance of a building permit for a Mormon stake center in the area." The new stake center became the host site for a joint Mormon/African American Heritage Society Black History Month conference in February 2002.[48]

The church's intense interest in genealogy and family solidarity made those themes a natural focus of its Black History Month or Martin Luther King Day commemorations. Gatherings were held in the church's regional center in Oakland, California, and at the visitors' center adjacent to the Washington, D.C., Temple Annual African American Family History Conferences began convening at the church's Salt Lake City Family History Library in 2003. Yet the church's most significant contribution to African American genealogy proved to be more far-reaching than any of these conferences. Over the course of a decade, the church used its resources and expertise to create a digital database of the Freedman's Bank records. The Freedman's Bank was established after the Civil War as a lending institution for former slaves, and records for its nearly 500,000 depositors were housed at the National Archives. A Mormon researcher, Marie Taylor, teamed up with black Latter-day Saints author Darius Gray to spearhead the project. By early 2001, volunteers had computerized the personal information of the Freedman's Bank depositors. Initially, the church sold the CD-ROM at cost; it was advertised for seven dollars. Eventually, the records were made available free of charge on the church's family history website.[49]

This boon for genealogists made it the most highly publicized of the church's cooperative initiatives with America's black community. Syndicated columnist Leonard Pitts called it a "godsend." A Florida reporter saw the CD as "an extraordinary shaft of light" for black researchers who often found their family history murky. Significantly, the database's release made the front pages of traditional African American newspapers like the *Los Angeles Sentinel* and the *Baltimore Afro-American*. What is perhaps most telling is that these papers did not mention the Mormons' former priesthood restriction. Instead, they cheered the expanded possibilities for "descendants of slaves" to "know thyself"; for that, they said, "Hats off to the Mormons."[50]

This is not to say that no one saw the Mormons' interest in this project as ironic. The *Los Angeles Times* noted that "to some, African Americans and Mormons are strange bedfellows," since "until the church's 'revelation on priesthood' in 1978, blacks could not become Mormon priests." Yet in the *Los Angeles Times* article, that brief observation was sandwiched between enthusiastic tributes offered by genealogist Charles Meigs, Jr., and historian Eric Foner—an indication, perhaps, of the diminishing relevance of a decades-old controversy. [51]

In a number of cases, this type of treatment of the priesthood issue seemed characteristic of a new media outlook on Mormon race relations. As in the *Los Angeles Times* report, the priesthood prohibition was duly noted in a number of news stories, yet the former policy commonly appeared now as a historical side note, a postscript that was less and less representative of contemporary Mormonism. More attention was given to strides that the church had made in distancing itself from charges of racism. Mormons had long come to expect that every feature on their church would raise the priesthood restriction as an almost obligatory nod to their church's history. However, what was new and unexpected during President Hinckley's tenure was the number of reports that recognized Mormon diversity. Concerted community outreach and urban proselytizing efforts did not go unnoticed. For example, while such a headline would have been difficult to predict a generation earlier, the *Chicago Reporter*—a periodical devoted to racial issues—called Mormonism a "colorblind faith" in 2006. In 2005, the *New York Times* described a Latter-day Saints congregation in Harlem as "one of the most racially integrated" in the city, "with about equal numbers of white and black worshipers." Front-page stories that same year in the *Philadelphia Inquirer* and the *Baltimore Afro-American* documented Mormon growth in the inner-city neighborhoods of New York City, Philadelphia, and Detroit; church leaders also called Oakland, Los Angeles, Houston, and Washington, D.C., "black Mormon strongholds" after a decade of significant expansion. This growth was marked by new meetinghouses and enthusiastic African American converts. The *Afro-American* quoted black Mormon leader Don Harwell, who saw these recent gains as evidence that "people are getting past stereotypes put on the church." Philadelphia resident and president of the local Relief Society (the LDS women's auxiliary) Ingrid Shepard explained to the *Inquirer* that "the church's history [was] less important to her than her experience in it." Shepard said simply, "I have never felt that [the church] is racist."[52]

Church leaders actively promoted this new face of Mormonism. There was a noticeable uptick in the number of articles and especially photographs in church periodicals that highlighted the racial diversity of the membership. Public affairs officials utilized in their press releases prominent black Mormon lay leaders, like stake presidents Ahmad Corbett in New Jersey and Tony Parker in Atlanta.

Motown star Gladys Knight, who had joined the LDS Church in 1997, headlined the gala celebration of President Hinckley's ninetieth birthday in June 2000. Her "Saints Unified Voices" choir won a Grammy in 2006 for Best Gospel Choir Album, and she lent the trophy to the church for display in its museum as part of an exhibit highlighting the accomplishments of Mormon women.[53]

In keeping with the public affairs focus on relationships with opinion leaders, Mormon officials also actively continued to foster new friendships where old suspicions had lingered. When church general authority D. Todd Christofferson traveled to Houston in 2002 for a meeting with local Mormons, a regional public affairs team also planned a luncheon for "30 top-level African-American leaders in the Houston area." Elder Christofferson's presentation centered on the Freedman's Bank project. One of the pastors in attendance, W. E. Lockett, wrote an article "for his faith group's [Christian Methodist Episcopal Church] publication"—a "publication that reaches over one million members"— "outlining what The Church of Jesus Christ of Latter-day Saints is doing for the African-American community." Pastor Lockett publicly came to the church's defense in 2008 when confusion arose over the Mormons' connection with Fundamentalist Church of Jesus Christ of Latter Day Saints (FLDS) leader Warren Jeffs, when Texas state officials raided Jeffs's ranch because of accusations of systemic child abuse. Pastor Lockett related, "Our church burned on Christmas morning in 2005. The very next week, Giff Nielsen [LDS Church leader] was over with a check that actually helped us to settle in our new office facilities. I had the keys to two of [the LDS church's] facilities for almost a year, where I could go in an office at any time. And we had a chance to, on a couple occasions, in a small way, reciprocate. We are committed to our friendship and our mutual working together. There is absolutely no reason that we see that we would not work together."

Pastor Lockett was then asked about "those who may be opposed to the [LDS] church." His advice was to "take the time to get to know members of The Church of Jesus Christ of Latter-day Saints, and/or attend any of their churches in the communities or just know some of those who are working in their community, and they would change their mind."[54]

Changing the public's mind about Mormonism's stand on racial equality was a priority for LDS officials who took their lead from Gordon B. Hinckley. He told the NAACP in 1998 that he was "deeply troubled" by any remnant of prejudice that remained in America; this was still his message eight years later when he declared at the church's General Conference that "no man who makes disparaging remarks concerning those of another race can consider himself a true disciple of Christ." Statements like these earned the praise, and deepening trust, of community leaders. Southern California AME Pastor Cecil Murray remembered a 2004 conversation with President Hinckley: "I was in Salt Lake City, a guest of the Mormon Church. I met the president and all. As we sat around the conference table, he apologized for the role the Church had played in participating in slavery. He says, 'I have learned of the background of your church and the founding of your church, and I want to apologize for whatever role the Mormon Church has played—not only there—but has played in racism in America.' [Pastor Murray's AME church was founded by Biddy Mason, who had been a slave to a Mormon convert.] I said, 'I thank you very much for making that statement. It is certainly true that the Mormon Church has been a factor in discrimination, but you've done so much good—and now to hear these words—I would certainly say that your hearts are right.'"[55]

"Dialogue Is the Christian Option"

The NAACP was not only the group to hold a convention in Salt Lake City in 1998.[56] That was also the year the Southern Baptists chose Utah as the site for their national meeting. Reporters envisioned missionary mayhem when the Baptists descended on Mormonism's capital, and they predicted a "holy war" carried out on street corners and doorsteps. After all, as one writer noted, "probably no other organization in the nation has played a bigger role in perpetuating the idea that Mormonism is a cult than the Southern Baptist Convention." The group made no secret of its plans to evangelize the Mormon heartland with its "Crossover, Salt Lake City" campaign. Thousands of volunteers—"Utah shock troops," the *New York Times* called them—were armed with pamphlets and videos created specifically for a Latter-day Saints audience. The *Los Angeles Times* reported that the Southern Baptists' North American Mission Board spent "about $600,000" to "[saturate] Salt Lake City…with billboards and radio and television spots." Yet despite the traditional hostility that existed between the two groups, especially considering the resurgence of countercult rhetoric, the anticipated religious "rumble" in Salt Lake City never happened. When the Baptists came in June, the LDS Church–owned *Deseret News* published an editorial "[welcoming] them with open arms and hearts," with the "hope their stay is pleasant and productive." Two months earlier, President Hinckley had asked Latter-day Saints to avoid confrontations with those of other faiths. "We must not become disagreeable as we talk of doctrinal differences," he told a General Conference audience. "There is no place for acrimony." Senior apostle Boyd K. Packer told BYU students, "If you meet someone who challenges our right to the title Christian, do not confront them. Teach them—peaceably." The visiting Baptists observed that Mormons opened their doors rather than slammed them shut when the Baptists came calling; many Mormons told reporters that their own church missionary service made them more amenable to treating the visitors respectfully.[57]

It was not only President Hinckley's magnanimity on this occasion that soft-ened the Baptists' landing on the state, but his repeated appeals to Mormons and non-Mormons alike for increased religious tolerance. To members of his church, in his very first General Conference (April 1995) as the LDS president, he "[pled] with our people everywhere to live with respect and appreciation for those not of our faith.... We must be willing to defend the rights of others who may become the victims of bigotry." He then "[called] attention to these striking words of Joseph Smith spoken in 1843": "If it has been demonstrated that I have been willing to die for a 'Mormon,' I am bold to declare before Heaven that I am just as ready to die in defending the rights of a Presbyterian, a Baptist, or a good man of any other denomination; for the same principle which would trample upon the rights of the Latter-day Saints would trample upon the rights of the Roman Catholics, or of any other denomination."[58]

To those not of his faith, his repeated invitation was simple: "Bring with you all the good that you can, and then let us see if we can add to it." His message resonated with Mormon scholars who were just opening an unprecedented but mostly behind-the-scenes dialogue with evangelical Christians.[59]

Participants in this dialogue have pointed to the 1991 publication of BYU religion professor Stephen E. Robinson's *Are Mormons Christians?* as the point of genesis. The premise of the book was that many of Mormonism's supposedly heretical tenets had in some form or another been espoused by a number of Christianity's luminaries, like Augustine or Clement or Martin Luther. While Robinson's book was intended primarily to inform Latter-day Saints, the title proved provocative enough to draw attention from evangelical Christians. Greg Johnson was the student body president at the Denver Theological Seminary, and he suggested to the faculty there that they prepare a formal response to the book. Johnson, himself a former Mormon and a veteran of *The God Makers* tour of a decade earlier, had experienced a change of heart about traditional anti-Mormon polemics. "None of this," he felt, "[had] been very productive," since "feelings [were] deeply cemented on both sides." Johnson felt that vigorous but respectful academic interaction would be a more productive way to define the differences between the two belief systems. In line with that approach, he invited Professor Robinson to come to Denver as the featured guest of an "Are Mormons Christians?" conference at the seminary. Despite Johnson's guaran-tees that civility would prevail, Robinson declined what he felt was an invitation to an evangelical "ambush."[60]

The conference convened as planned, and a persistent Johnson forwarded the videotaped conference to Professor Robinson. Robinson was intrigued by the comments of one of the Denver Seminary's faculty members, Craig Blomberg. The two began to correspond. As they both expressed dismay over the mutual misunderstanding that had soured relationships between their respective faith groups, they contemplated the possibility of a jointly authored book project. The result was *How Wide the Divide?: A Mormon and an Evangelical in Conversation*, published in 1997 by the evangelical press InterVarsity.[61]

As remarkable as the text of the book was, even more remarkable was the fact that they were having the conversation. Greg Johnson remembered how delicate the situation was after the book's publication—the authors visited the campuses of BYU and the Denver Seminary, though the visits were kept mostly under wraps, for fear of inciting protests from antagonists who viewed this collaborative venture with suspicion. In the book, Blomberg and Robinson dealt with four traditionally divisive theological areas: the definition of scripture, God and deification, Christ and the Trinity, and salvation. Each expounded his beliefs, expressed misgivings about the other's position, and then the two combined for a joint conclusion. Both expressed surprise at how much agreement they had found. Robinson especially took care to differentiate between official Latter-day Saints doctrine and the rumored or speculative Mormon teachings that had colored *The God Makers*. While Craig Blomberg remembered that many countercultists responded that Robinson was either lying or else an atypical—even "dissident"—Mormon, Blomberg offered genuine appreciation for the clarification. What became apparent in the book was that Robinson's background (he received his doctorate in biblical studies from Duke University) made him "theologically bilingual." Because Mormons and evangelicals did not always mean the same things even when they used the same words—words like "faith," or "works," or "saved"—Robinson could translate Mormon theology using terms familiar to evangelicals, and interpret Blomberg's concerns accordingly.[62]

The book and, more importantly, the approach were groundbreaking. Another BYU professor trained in biblical studies, Robert Millet, adopted the same posture in a speech he gave to the university's student body in advance of the Southern Baptists' Salt Lake City convention. Like President Hinckley, he counseled against confrontation or debate. Like his colleague Stephen Robinson, he called for a clear delineation of Mormon doctrine in terms that outsiders would understand. His advice was to "stay in control," "stay in order," and "stay in context."[63]

Thus, by the time the Southern Baptists arrived in Salt Lake City, the potentially explosive encounter had largely been defused by a variety of hands. The church's prophet had clearly implied that Mormons were to refrain from any effort to "out-proselytize" the visiting Baptists. And the LDS Public Affairs Department used the press attention that the Baptists' convention generated to foster better relationships with media outlets. After the department sent out "letters ahead of the conference to some ninety religion editors, more than thirty . . . called in to see [Public Affairs representatives] while in Salt Lake"—and after the convention closed, LDS representatives expressed satisfaction with the accuracy of journalists' efforts to distinguish between Mormon and Baptist beliefs. Even former President Jimmy Carter (himself a Southern Baptist Sunday school teacher) added his opinion in an interview with the *Deseret News* that Mormons were Christians.[64]

It was into this new climate of calm that BYU professors, encouraged by President Hinckley's call for tolerance and cooperation, and evangelical scholars, intrigued by what seemed like a new Mormon openness, followed Blomberg and Robinson's lead and inaugurated a decade of dialogue. These interfaith and inter-campus exchanges quickly came under the institutional auspices of the Richard L. Evans Chair of Religious Understanding at BYU. This professorship had been endowed in 1972 as a memorial for Evans, a Mormon apostle and former president of Rotary International. A non-Mormon admirer of Evans named Lowell Berry proposed the chair as a way to honor a man he called one of "the two greatest Christians he ever met" (the other was Billy Graham). Upon Elder Evans's death in 1971, Berry became the initial underwriter of the chair, and, until his death, he "continued his support over the protest of some of [the] fundamentalist directors" of his foundation. For its first twenty years, BYU professor Truman Madsen occupied Evans Chair. He was a pioneer in academic outreach, using his Harvard connections to draw heavyweights like Krister Stendahl, David Noel Freedman, and Raymond Brown to Provo. Madsen spearheaded symposia that invited serious scholarship on parallels between Mormon practice and ancient Jewish and Christian teachings, on Eastern burial rites and Mormon views of the afterlife, and on the concept of the temple in Judaism and Mormonism. He played a critical role in legitimizing Mormon studies with scholars that BYU's Hugh Nibley called "number one, top-drawer in their fields." Madsen also was a central figure in the production of the four-volume *Encyclopedia of Mormonism*, published by Macmillan in 1992—even enlisting several of his friends of other faiths to write entries.[65]

While Madsen built important bridges with top Jewish, Catholic, and mainline Protestant academics, Madsen's successors in the Evans Chair turned their attention to evangelical Christianity. Robert Millet, a Louisiana native and former dean of religious education at BYU, was named to the Evans Chair in 2000, as was former Presbyterian minister and Mormon convert Roger Keller (by then the chair had been expanded to include two professorships). Their backgrounds made their outreach to evangelicals a natural turn.

In the years before occupying the Evans Chair, Professor Millet became acquainted with Greg Johnson when the young pastor visited the BYU campus following *How Wide the Divide*'s publication. The two began meeting for lunch and informal theological discussions. Word of their friendship spread, and in November 2000, a Park Utah, congregation invited them to engage in a public dialogue about Latter-day Saints and evangelical cooperation. This initial invitation resulted in dozens of subsequent stops for a presentation they dubbed "A Mormon and an Evangelical in Conversation." Eventually, they would replicate this program over fifty times in churches and college campuses across the United States and in Canada and England.[66]

The year 2000 also saw the initial meeting in what would become a series of semiannual roundtable discussions on Mormon and evangelical theology. Each fall, the group met in conjunction with the American Academy of Religion/ Society of Biblical Literature conventions. In the spring, the group alternated between Brigham Young University and Fuller Theological Seminary in Southern California. Stephen Robinson, Robert Millet, David Paulsen (a former Evans professor), and Roger Keller, among others, represented BYU. Initial evangelical attendees included Craig Blomberg and Greg Johnson, as well as Richard Mouw (president of Fuller Seminary), David Neff (editor of Christianity Today), and professors Craig Hazen and James Bradley (from Biola University and Fuller Seminary, respectively). While these meetings went on with very little fanfare, the fruits that grew out of these relationships were more visible.

The professors engaged in campus exchanges and guest lectureships at Biola University, Westmont College, Fuller Seminary, and Wheaton College. A conference on "Salvation" at Brigham Young University in the spring of 2002 drew Christian scholars from across the nation to Provo. The church's Public Affairs office repeatedly used the Evans professors in advisory capacities. When USA Today and the Washington Post asked Public Affairs to conduct live, on-line chats, Robert Millet received the assignment. The department even cosponsored several of Millet and Johnson's public presentations. Roger Keller represented Mormonism during monthly meetings of the Interfaith Roundtable, which convened in the months leading up to the Olympics. He and his roundtable colleagues reported on the venture at a meeting of the World Parliament of Religions in Barcelona. All around seemed subtle signs that Mormons and other religionists were finding common ground.[67]

These budding friendships did not mean that there was no evangelizing in these interchanges, or that Mormon doctrine had suddenly become acceptable to evangelicals. There were significant reminders that while Mormonism was better understood, it was still suspect. In 1998, for example, two evangelical Christian graduate students wrote a memorable essay for Trinity Journal about the state of Mormon apologetics. Their thesis was that after The God Makers, Latter-day Saints scholars had crafted serious responses in defense of their faith and history, yet evangelicals had not paid attention. Thus the authors concluded that evangelicals were "losing the battle and not knowing it." They proposed an equally serious response to recent Mormon apologetics. The result was a collection of essays in 2002 entitled The New Mormon Challenge. The volume had chapters with titles like "The Absurdities of Mormon Materialism" or "Rendering Fiction: Translation, Pseudotranslation, and the Book of Mormon." It also contained this clarion call to arms by coeditor Carl Mosser: "It is clear to me that the current evangelical response to Mormonism . . . does not significantly retard the spread and growth of the LDS faith...at the expense of orthodox Christianity. We must somehow bring about...'a change in the process' if we want to prevent Mormonism from becoming one of the larger worldwide faiths at our expense."[68]

Ironically, several of the contributors were also participants in the nascent Mormon/evangelical semiannual discussions. Richard Mouw, for example, wrote the foreword. He saw this book as different from earlier evangelical treatments of Mormon doctrine. "The respectful tone of these essays," he wrote, made for "a laudable attempt to set the record straight" after evangelicals had been guilty of "bearing false witness against our LDS neighbors" in "[propagating] distorted accounts of what Mormons believe." Despite that conciliatory opening, BYU's David Paulsen in a lengthy review still classified the book as "anti-Mormon" and far less than "respectful," since it included descriptors of Mormonism like "parasite," "pagan," "cult," and "worse than scientific poppycock." Not surprisingly, Craig Blomberg remembered that *New Mormon Challenge*'s appearance "created a significant...glitch" when the Mormon/evangelical dialogue group met again. (He himself had written a chapter titled "Is Mormonism Christian?," concluding that it was "neither intolerant nor extreme nor uncharitable" to "claim that Mormonism is not Christian.") Blomberg observed that some of "the BYU people thought that our...conversations meant we would never again go in print with any criticism of LDS religion. I don't think any of us had understood it in that way." He argued that there is still "a time and a place for evangelism, for proselytizing, for critics," but "that is not all that should happen." Thus, to Blomberg and his colleagues, the dialogue group was important because improved understanding was also "something that desperately needs to happen." Yet that did not obviate evangelical scholars' sense of obligation to witness for what they still saw as authentic Christianity.[69]

Some evangelicals felt even more conflicted by these growing friendships. One prominent pastor told Robert Millet, "I speak with you, I read your books, and I feel your passion for the Lord and your commitment to him. It has touched me deeply. And that is why our association is so wonderful but so painful for me, because I believe your way of life is flawed and doctrinally incorrect." Still, if doctrinal flare-ups were nothing new, what *was* new was the two sides' willingness to continue, even in the face of these admitted conflicts. Greg Johnson was pleased that the associations survived being "significantly tested by criticisms on both sides." Professor Blomberg noted that in the first semiannual meeting after *The New Mormon Challenge*'s publication, the group took "a couple of hours [to] debrief...their reactions" to the book, and "that really cleared the air....We did lose a couple of people on each side who might have continued with us otherwise," but "the majority seemed...ready to move on with what we had been doing." [70]

The resilience of these relationships was evident at three key moments. In 2003, Greg Johnson's "Standing Together" Utah ministry organized local pastors to speak out against the vocal street preachers who witnessed to Mormons attending LDS General Conference at Temple Square. Obviously, not every conservative Christian was ready to join a dialogue group with Mormons. Instead, these street preachers favored a boisterous, confrontational style, with bright placards and megaphones—and endurance. Their no-holds-barred, top-of-their-lungs approach included the use of images that portrayed Joseph Smith as a devil and ridiculed elements of Mormonism's sacred temple ceremonies. In October 2003, Pastor Johnson asked local colleagues, "At what point do we become complicit" if nothing is done to favor civility over shouting matches? The result was "Mission Loving Kindness." For the April 2004 LDS General Conference, Johnson's group obtained street permits from city authorities, so that his credentialed representatives could occupy the sidewalks normally commandeered by the anti-Mormon street preachers. For this gesture of goodwill, President Hinckley sent Pastor Johnson and his associates a letter of appreciation.[71]

Pastor Johnson also saw "Mission Loving Kindness" as factoring into the LDS hierarchy's remarkable decision to open their historic Tabernacle in 2004 to evangelist Ravi Zacharias. Zacharias later remembered that it was "to everyone's surprise" that the First Presidency accepted Robert Millet and Greg Johnson's proposal to hold such an event on Temple Square. This invitation alone spoke volumes about how far the Mormon/evangelical dialogue had come. "Even then," Zacharias reported, "I hesitated"; this was unprecedented territory for the Christian apologist. He rightly anticipated that there would be "critics who objected to my being there." Yet he decided to take that chance when "several key evangelical leaders and professors from across the country urged me to accept the invitation." To naysayers who saw Zacharias's friendliness to Mormons as compromising orthodox Christianity (he also had "a personal meeting with the First Presidency"), the evangelist answered, "I have no doubts about the differences between the LDS faith and the historic Christian faith," but "there are numerous instances in Scripture where Jesus went to those of a contrary view and with grace, sowed one small seed at a time." Because, Zacharias related, "the courtesy and graciousness extended to me by every Mormon leader and professor with whom I came into contact cannot be gainsaid," he asked detractors, "must not our methods be in keeping with our message?"[72]

In that same vein, perhaps the most talked-about moment on that memorable night came during Richard Mouw's introductory remarks before Zacharias's address. Even more directly than he did in his foreword for *The New Mormon Challenge*, Mouw apologized for evangelicals' misrepresentation of Mormon beliefs and practices: "I know I have learned much from this continuing dialogue, and I am now convinced that we evangelicals have often seriously misrepresented the beliefs and practices of the Mormon community. Indeed, let me state the case bluntly on this important occasion especially to you LDS folks who are here this evening: we evangelicals have sinned against you. The God of the scriptures makes it clear that it is a terrible thing to bear false witness against our neighbors, and we have been guilty of that sort of transgression in things that we have said about you. We have told you what you believe without making a sincere effort first of all to ask you what you believe."[73]

Reaction to Mouw's apology was immediate and fierce. Greg Johnson was "lambasted" by Utah ministers who accused him of "[setting] back the cause of Christ twenty years" by promoting the event and thus making Mormonism appear acceptable. Colleagues accused Richard Mouw of validating Joseph Smith and Mormon scripture. Utah Pastor Bill Heersink remembered that many of his coreligionists were "so programmed to [anti-Mormon] cult literature" that Mouw's statement "[looked] like...compromise," especially since they found "most offensive" the fact that Mouw "presumed to speak for all evangelicals."[74]

Yet Mouw and other leading evangelical thinkers kept at it. In another unprecedented move, Mouw wrote an endorsing introduction *and* afterword for Robert Millet's 2005 book, *A Different Jesus?: The Christ of the Latter-day Saints.* Here was a prominent BYU (Millet) professor publishing a book on Mormon beliefs for Eerdmans, one of the nation's leading Christian presses—something that would have seemed unthinkable two decades earlier. Not only that, but the president of the Fuller Seminary (Mouw) wrote at the book's end, "I think that an open-minded Christian reader of this book will sense that Bob Millet is in fact trusting in the Jesus of the Bible for his salvation. That is certainly my sense." True, the mixed reaction to the book's release matched the divisiveness that followed Mouw's comments at the Tabernacle, and these strong responses spoke to a grass-roots reticence to embrace interfaith dialogue with Mormons (something that would soon come to dog Mitt Romney's campaign). However, the growing support for these types of projects also signaled that a new era had opened on the "opinion leader" level. This meant that Christian bookstores now carried books like David Rowe's *I Love Mormons* and videos like the Salt Lake Theological Seminary's *Bridges* series alongside older fare like *The Cult Explosion* or *Cult Proofing Your Kids.* That alone was a remarkable change, and to Mormon image watchers, a hopeful sign.[75]

"The Truth...Can't Hurt Us"

It was not only with their evangelical counterparts that Mormon scholars made inroads.[76] BYU's Institute for the Study and Preservation of Ancient Religious Texts (ISPART) embarked in the 1990s on a translation series of classic Islamic and Eastern Christian works. ISPART also responded to a 1999 invitation to digitize and restore ancient Syriac Christian writings that were housed in the

Vatican library. Harvard's Frank Moore Cross, Jr., who had become a close associate of Truman Madsen, recruited several BYU professors to join elite Dead Sea Scroll translation teams. In Madsen's estimation, "this put us on the map."[77]

In March 2003, Yale University hosted a conference on Mormonism that featured leading Mormon historians and philosophers like Richard Bushman, Kathleen Flake, and David Paulsen. Three hundred people attended sessions dealing with Joseph Smith's theological contributions. Robert Millet called the conference "a major breakthrough," showing that "Latter-day Saints were no longer being completely ignored" in the world of academia. There were other signs that Mormons were far from being ignored. Paulsen's work went to print in journals like the *Harvard Theological Review*, *Faith and Philosophy*, and *Analysis*. The *Boston Globe* noted that everywhere "colleges scramble to offer curriculum on Mormon religion." Utah Valley University's Religious Studies Program launched an annual Mormon Studies conference in 2001. Claremont Graduate University and Utah State University endowed Mormon Studies Chairs, and the University of Utah's Tanner Humanities Center inaugurated an annual Mormon Studies graduate fellowship. It is also telling that the American Academy of Religion initiated a Mormon Studies subsection for its annual meetings beginning in 2007.[78]

As a long-time, prominent student of Mormonism, British anthropologist Douglas Davies considered the differences between the LDS Church in the 1970s and the LDS Church in the new millennium. "I would say the real issue is the one of size"—and for Davies, that was reflected not just in terms of membership, but also in terms of academic output: "One of the biggest differences I think has been the growth of [a] generation of Mormon scholars in the social sciences as well as in history."[79] Mormon author and University of Richmond professor Terryl Givens noted that "Rodney Stark's 1984 prediction that Mormonism [would] become the next major world religion," even if Stark's "straight line growth predictions [do not] hold true ... [helped] shift Mormonism more toward the center of sociological interest." That growing public interest in, and exposure to, Mormons, as well as a growing body of Mormon-related scholarship, became mutually reinforcing causes *and* effects.

Nowhere in the world of Mormon scholarship was President Hinckley's "nothing to hide" mantra generating more attention, though, than in the field of history—especially the church's official sanction of several new projects in Mormon history. Much had quietly changed since historian John L. Brooke won the Bancroft Prize for his 1994 book *The Refiner's Fire: The Making of Mormon Cosmology, 1644–1844*. In his book he fully embraced, and then extended, the magical and hermetic roots theory to explain Joseph Smith's revelations. Brooke also chastised LDS Church leaders for attempting to disguise those roots by "closing its archives" and "ordering the faithful to 'follow the brethren' and grab the 'iron rod' of doctrinal authority." Brooke could not so easily have made the same claims a decade later. Not only did reviewers complain that Brooke overlooked the biblical basis of Joseph Smith's theology, but the church also answered his—and others'—criticisms by engaging in a revolutionary program to make its archival holdings accessible.[80]

First came a set of DVDs issued by the church in 2002 intended for university and research libraries. The seventy-four disks included digitized copies of the church's nineteenth-century documentary treasures, including minutes of the church leadership councils, Brigham Young's Letterpress Copybooks, the journals of several early apostles (including church presidents Lorenzo Snow and Joseph F. Smith), and the Revelations Collections, transcriptions of church revelations from 1831 to 1876. Even more significant, the Church History Department announced a sweeping project to publish every document that owed its provenance to Joseph Smith—every journal entry he wrote or dictated, every transcribed sermon, letter, and revelation. In a noteworthy reversal of the 1982 move that saw most of Leonard Arrington's staff moved out of church employ, LDS officials brought back a number of prominent Mormon historians to work in the department to prepare the volumes of Joseph Smith's papers. Newly appointed Church Historian Marlin K. Jensen (a church general authority) called it "the most significant Church history project of this generation." The church made it a point to note that "with selective editions, documents may be excluded because they are of less interest or importance or about topics not emphasized in the collection." But this was to be a *comprehensive* edition, not a *selective* one, and "comprehensive editions make no such exclusions."[81]

What seemed additionally significant about this gesture toward openness was that the church actively reentered the realm of researching, writing, and publishing, even creating a new, official Church Historian's Press for its Joseph Smith Papers project. Managing director of the Church History Department Richard Turley received permission in 2001 to write a new book on the Mountains Meadows Massacre, long seen as "the single darkest episode" in Mormonism's history. He and two other historians employed by the church, Glen Leonard and Ronald Walker, were given access even to materials in the First Presidency's Vault. [82]

Meanwhile, Richard Bushman also benefited from special archival support during the preparation of his landmark biography, *Joseph Smith: Rough Stone Rolling*, published in 2005, the bicentennial of the Mormon prophet's birth. Bushman's book was not an official church publication; it was published by Alfred A. Knopf. Yet church leaders did give Bushman "access to the materials . . . assembled" for the Joseph Smith Papers project, even before the documents went to press. Plus, church-owned Deseret Book promoted the biography. That was a conspicuous indication of the "sea change" taking place at the Church History Department. Whereas Deseret Book had quietly let *The Story of the Latter-day Saints* sell out three decades earlier because of concerns over controversial content, now the bookstore was promoting a sympathetic yet honest (sometimes painfully so) biography of Mormonism's founder. Bushman was a practicing Mormon. He had even served prominently in the church as a stake president. Yet he did not shy away from the most inflammatory of topics, including the origins of plural marriage and Mormon temple rites. Bushman's book sold over 100,000 copies and created a new standard for future studies of Joseph Smith. Historian Harry Stout said, "There is no question that this biography is the best book ever written about Mormonism's founding father, and America's greatest homegrown prophet."[83]

In the church's most concrete expression of support for what Richard Bushman called the "fluorescence of Mormon studies," Hinckley's First Presidency announced in 2005 that the church would build a new, state-of-the art Church History Library across from Temple Square. Previously the library and archive facility had occupied a wing of the Church Office Building, but that meant that access to the church's materials was limited to weekday business hours. The new stand-alone building would allow for longer operating hours during the week and on Saturdays, a clear sign that Mormon officials wanted to provide a more welcoming atmosphere for visiting researchers. All of these changes prompted a church archivist to say in 2007 that when critics publicly complained that the church had closed its archives, the department's registry showed that either they had never visited or had not visited in recent years.[84]

In fact, after the first ten years of Gordon Hinckley's administration, it seemed that the Mormonism of 2005 would surprise in almost every way those who had not "visited" in recent years. Two events can be seen as a fitting capstone for the decade; both took place less than a year apart in Washington, D.C. On June 23, 2004, coincidentally President Hinckley's ninety-fourth birthday, President George W. Bush presented the Mormon leader with the Medal of Freedom, the nation's highest civilian honor. At the ceremony, President Bush said, "Millions of Americans reserve a special respect for Gordon B. Hinckley, . . . [a] wise and patriotic man." The tribute then described "his tireless efforts to spread the word of God and to promote good will," efforts which "strengthened his faith, his community and our nation." Hinckley received special recognition for "humanitarian aid, disaster relief and education funding across the globe."[85]

The following May, the Library of Congress hosted a conference to commemorate the bicentennial of Joseph Smith's birth. This "Worlds of Joseph Smith" conference drew a remarkable roster of participants, including biographer Robert Remini and Columbia University historian Randall Balmer. The two-day conference emphatically marked the culmination of a decade of academic and religious outreach and cooperation.[86]

These two Mormon moments in the nation's capital carried a special poignancy for Latter-day Saints who noted the irony that almost two centuries earlier, Joseph Smith and his associates had likewise traveled to Washington only to be rebuffed by President Martin Van Buren, in the aforementioned "your cause is just, but I can do nothing for you" episode.[87]

In 2004 and 2005, this nineteenth-century memory seemed far removed from twenty-first-century realities. Instead of being snubbed as his predecessor had been, now the latest in the line of Joseph Smith's successors was publicly feted by an American president, recognized for what he and his church accomplished. Then, at no less a venue than the Library of Congress, Washington, D.C., gave Joseph Smith a measure of the regard that was denied him in his lifetime, as some of the nation's top scholars gathered to consider his legacy. That same year (2005), a poll conducted by the Discovery Channel listed Joseph Smith among their one hundred "greatest Americans."[88]

These tributes were also acknowledgements of what President Hinckley had accomplished through his openness and optimism. On the ten-year mark of his presidency, Jennifer Dobner of the Associated Press quoted historian Jan Shipps "[crediting] Hinckley with fostering a broader understanding of the church to mainstream Christianity." Shipps described it as an effort to "legitimize Mormonism as a form of Christianity, but not just an idiosyncratic form of Protestantism . . . it's Christianity plus."[89]

Hinckley's leadership thus gave new standing to Mormonism's public image. His was consistently a message about the church's future, and by all accounts, that future looked bright. Mormon growth was unabated, and the church appeared vibrant and energized, modern and extroverted. The reason for that growth, Hinckley told interviewers, was that the church's doctrines provided an anchor in a time of shifting values. He seemed to personify such solidity. He also seemed to redefine the relationship between Mormonism's past and its future. While Hinckley himself was well grounded in the church's history, and while he seemed unafraid to investigate even potentially thorny areas, he most often defused past controversies with his sincere "that's in the past—let's move on" mind-set. The church's Public Affairs Department, and the Mormon scholars they teamed with, followed their prophet's lead and took the initiative in reaching out to media, academic, and ethnic minority "opinion leaders." In so doing, they appeared to make real progress in their aims to "build effective relationships . . . and help solve problems." Truman Madsen's longtime hope was that outreach would induce others to "speak up for the Mormons, at least with understanding." Such indeed looked to be the case, as an array of new voices, from Mike Wallace to the NAACP to Richard Mouw, said positive things about The Church of Jesus Christ of Latter-day Saints. [90]

Importantly, it was not only those Mormons who acted in official capacities that increased the church's visibility and generated growing public interest in the religion in the first decade of the new millennium. During President Hinckley's administration the number of LDS temples more than doubled, a building boom that staked Mormonism's place on the nation's landscape—but just as visible was the new territory claimed by Mormon celebrities, authors, and independent filmmakers, as they sought to express and situate their faith in the nation's pop culture scene. And as Mormons became more visible, they also became bigger targets for shots and "shout outs" from some of America's cultural heavyweights. Mormons' new group self-confidence would thus be both validated and vexed on bigger stages than ever before.

8

Familiar Faces: Mormons and American Popular Culture in a New Millennium

Many Utah moviegoers were in for a double take in early 2000. There, in the middle of the posters that adorn all theater lobbies, was an oversized advertisement that featured two obviously Mormon missionaries and announced the upcoming release of *God's Army*. No matter that the majority of Utah's residents were Mormons, this poster still created some mild disbelief. A theatrical release about Mormon missionaries? The buzz generated by the advertisements only intensified as the movie's opening drew near. On its first weekend, Richard Dutcher's *God's Army* was the box office winner in Utah. Mormons felt the pull of this entirely new experience: watching a film *about* Mormons, written and produced *by* Mormons, but in the local megaplex rather than the church's visitors' center. Mormon independent film was born.[1]

Of course, filmmaking was nothing new to Mormonism. In fact, the church had embraced the medium decades earlier, producing award-winning public service commercials as well as full-length historical and educational features packaged for distribution by missionaries and church teachers. Lavishly produced films about the life of Jesus Christ, the Book of Mormon, and Joseph Smith and his pioneer followers became staples of the church's large theater in downtown Salt Lake City's Joseph Smith Memorial Building. Yet the advent of a Mormon film "scene" in the early 2000s, a movement that was not about officially sponsored projects or portrayals, offered one more signal that Mormons seemed to be everywhere in American culture.

By the middle of the first decade of the new millennium, there had been plenty of Mormons prominently displayed before the public eye—almost a parade of them in the 1990s and 2000s. Name almost any arena of American life, and Mormons could point to recognizable coreligionists. Mormons made their marks in business, literature, sports, journalism, government, and politics—even on reality television. On the whole, Mormons were satisfied with the treatment their fellow Saints received. They were portrayed as different, yet respected—even accepted. There were signs that a growing number of Americans saw Mormons as one more intriguing piece of the nation's pluralistic puzzle, as Mormon peculiarities seemed more interesting than threatening.

Even when they were the targets of comedians, Mormons recognized that this too was somehow a cultural status symbol. Enough people knew enough about Mormonism that the jokes were widely understandable. Likewise, even when the church strongly protested the inaccuracies in some depictions, it recognized that this attention was "inevitable once an institution or faith group reaches a size or prominence sufficient to attract notice," a tolerable side effect of the very growth the church sought. Therefore, just as Mormon officials began to let down their guards when facing questions about church government or history, Mormons also opted against defensiveness when laughter came at their expense. The church even released a statement that referred to a number of potentially offensive popular media portrayals of the religion and then stated, "There is no need to feel defensive when the church is moving forward so rapidly." Some Latter-day Saints writers went even further; they beat outsiders to the punch line. The emergence of independent Mormon films suggested that Mormons were comfortable enough in their public identity to poke fun at themselves, to risk revealing the quirks that often defined their community. In many ways, these unofficial portrayals of Mormon life reflected the institutional maturity and self-confidence that characterized President Hinckley's administration, as if Mormons were not hiding things, not even their own idiosyncrasies.[2]

Sitting in packed houses, watching *God's Army*, Mormons laughed at all-too-familiar scenes of missionary immaturity. They empathized as one of the missionaries fell prey to anti-Mormon literature and gave up his ministry. They sat almost reverently as the protagonist prayed for, and experienced, the epiphany that kept him at his ministry—and all of this was happening in a movie theater. It was a remarkable moment for Mormonism, a reminder of the growing number of voices engaged in the dialogue over the meaning of Latter-day Saints' faith and lifestyle.

That is what makes Mormonism's place in the nation's popular culture so revealing. Public and press reactions to celebrity Latter-day Saints speak to the layers of connotations that the descriptor "Mormon" carries with it. Outside artists' treatment of the Saints offers clues about the persistence—or obsolescence—of stereotypes and caricatures. The work of Mormon artists likewise reveals how Mormons see themselves, or at least want to be seen by others. Mormon reaction—official and unofficial—to all of this suggests the extent to which church members are willing to tolerate, and in some cases celebrate, Mormonism's perceived public persona.

Sociologist Thomas F. O'Dea and historian Dean May both argued persuasively that Mormons constitute an authentic American ethnic group, bound by

common customs, language, and worldview. If so, the internal and external conversations that were set against the backdrop of Mormon and American popular
culture in the first few years of this new century worked to push and pull at the
borders between assimilation and accommodation on the one side, and the preservation of a people's defining distinctiveness on the other.[3]

Modern Iconography: Famous Latter-day Saints

A telltale sign of Mormonism's undisputed arrival in the public's consciousness
was the appearance of *Mormonism for Dummies* in 2005. The popular *Dummies*
series had already dealt with topics as divergent as computer programming
and crocheting, but at the time only a comparatively few of the books focused
on religion. Mormonism joined Judaism, Islam, and Catholicism as early
"Dummies" categories. The publisher enlisted two Mormon authors, Jana Riess
and Christopher Kimball Bigelow, to write the book, and their fast-paced, con-
versational prose drew readers into a remarkably thorough exploration of all
facets of Latter-day Saints' life and history.[4]

One hallmark of the *Dummies* books is the "lists of ten." One such list in
Riess and Bigelow's book discussed "Ten Famous Mormons." The names were
not unexpected. They included the Osmonds, NFL Most Valuable Player Steve
Young, former Miss America Sharlene Wells, and singer Gladys Knight. Yet the
list also showed the diversity of accomplished Mormons. In the world of business, author Stephen R. Covey was a best-selling consultant. His book *The 7
Habits of Highly Effective People* sold more than fifteen million copies, and *Time*
magazine called him "one of America's 25 most influential people." At the highest levels of broadcast journalism, Jane Clayson co-anchored CBS's *The Early
Show* with Bryant Gumbel, beginning in 1999. In politics, Republican Senator
Orrin Hatch served prominently in leadership roles, chairing, for example, the
powerful judiciary committee on three different occasions.[5]

Mormons are cheered by lists like this. A number of commentators have
noted that Mormons seem intrigued, sometimes to the point of obsession, with
those in their ranks who achieve celebrity. Much of that interest is understandable, since such success often translates into public acceptance. Mormons view
their famous fellows as playing an important role in diminishing misconceptions. Seeing Mormons achieve very visible recognition as world-class athletes
or top-flight reporters, for example, contributes measurably in the quest to demonstrate, in President Hinckley's words, that Mormons "are not a weird people"
who are confined to rural Utah or dress in pioneer garb. In the constant struggle
to differentiate modern Mormonism from fundamentalist polygamists, LDS
Church members hope that the prominence of Mormons who are fully engaged
in public life can dispel lingering prejudices.[6]

There is another factor about Mormon celebrity that gives these individuals even greater potential for image impact. Observers have noted that Mormons in the news are almost always identified by their religious persuasion, in contrast to newsmakers who belong to other denominations. Reporters universally include this biographical detail whenever their stories deal with Mormon athletes or authors or entertainers—or criminals. That reality alone is telling. It implies the potency of "Mormon" as shorthand, as a packed adjective that instantly delivers information about a person's value system and cultural inheritance. It also implies that Mormons still comprise a recognized minority group, whose ventures into prominence are still noteworthy to the degree that they seem anomalous. Yet, with the exception of lawbreakers or deviants, Mormons seem pleased to see the press identify their coreligionists as such, especially to the extent that such designations boost positive impressions about the church's rapidly growing numbers and, more importantly, Mormon lifestyle.[7]

At the same time, Mormons appreciate it when their celebrity fellows are not embarrassed to identify their faith. Such loyalty seems to reaffirm the church's outreach-minded mantra that Mormonism is something to celebrate and share rather than to hide. This boost to group solidarity and pride energizes the Mormon community and provides an opening for conversations about how the faith is lived in its American context. The Utah-based magazine *This People* started in the 1980s (and ran through the late 1990s) with just such a focus. The church-owned *Deseret News* added a weekly special section, *Mormon Times*, in 2008 that fills the same role with its numerous features on Mormons in the public's eye.

As publications like these can attest, there seem to be a lot of Mormons in that national spotlight. The online information resource Wikipedia lists ten times as many famous Latter-day Saints as Riess and Bigelow were able to include in their book. Lists like these buttress *Sunstone* editor Stephen Carter's observation that "Mormonism is no longer a huddled group of bedraggled saints on the edge of a salt lake.... Mormonism is a fact now—that's all there is to it. We're big. We have interesting people out there who are doing interesting things."[8]

A sampling of those "interesting people" would include literary luminaries like Orson Scott Card, Richard Paul Evans, and Stephenie Meyer. Card became a star in the science fiction galaxy when his *Ender's Game* series won the two most prominent awards in that genre, the Hugo and the Nebula awards, in consecutive years (1985 and 1986). He next won Locus awards for installments in the *Alvin Maker* series, a story that loosely paralleled Joseph Smith's life and drew on Mormon theological themes in an imagined, alternate-universe American setting. Richard Paul Evans created an unexpected phenomenon when his originally self-published novel *The Christmas Box* eventually went on to sell over eight million copies for Simon & Schuster and inspire an Emmy-winning television movie.[9]

Yet no other Mormon writer (and few contemporary writers in general) took the reading public by storm like Stephenie Meyer. The BYU graduate released her novel *Twilight* in 2005. Her story of a reformed vampire and the teenage girl who fell in love with him became more than a best-seller; it became culturally ubiquitous. The original installment spawned three sequels, and each book was made into a movie (the last book into *two* movies). *USA Today* noted that "Meyer's domination" of that newspaper's "best-selling books list . . . for the past 12 months has smashed records that until now had belonged to J. K. Rowling" of *Harry Potter* fame. Remarkably, fifty-five million of Meyer's books sold in 2008 and 2009.[10]

Television gave several other Mormons a comparable reach. Glenn Beck, the talk show host who headlined first for CNN (in 2006) and then Fox News (from 2008 to 2011), joined the LDS Church in 1999. He detailed his conversion story in *An Unlikely Mormon*, a DVD distributed by church-owned Deseret Book. Beck gradually established a multimedia franchise, adding books and a speaking tour to his top-rated talk shows. Beck joined Meyer on *Time*'s annual "100 most influential people" list. Beck's style and outspoken conservatism made him a polarizing but popular figure; he himself expressed awareness of the occasional discomfort his politics cause for some fellow Mormons. He also sparked concern among Christians who worried that Beck's popularity might facilitate his "[morphing] from America's professor to America's pastor." "Glenn Beck makes it a little bit harder in that he doesn't wear his Mormonism on his sleeve," Biola University professor Craig Hazen said. "When he does give spiritual talks it's fairly generic. In fact I can imagine devout evangelical Christians watching him for years and not having a clue that he might be a Latter-day Saint. He has come out of the closet on several, carefully orchestrated situations to talk about his specific beliefs as a Mormon. Apart from that when you carefully try to pick it apart, it's very difficult to find his Mormon beliefs through his generic spirituality," and that was "a danger point" because "that would pave the way for people to more easily embrace his ideas"—more on that in chapter 10.[11]

Reality television programming also brought instant celebrity to several Mormons. Ken Jennings, a Mormon returned missionary, became the undisputed king of quiz shows in 2004 when he won a record seventy-four *Jeopardy!* contests in a row (the previous record had been eight) and an unparalleled $2.5 million purse. This winning streak led to appearances on *The Late Show with David Letterman*, as well as a variety of other game shows. Celebrity interviewer Barbara Walters "named him one of the ten most fascinating people of the year." Jennings soon found himself in good company, as Mormons triumphed on *The Biggest Loser*, *The Rebel Billionaire*, and *Survivor*. *Newsweek* observed that "Mormons have colonized reality TV as if they'd been assigned there by Brigham Young himself." Three recognizable Mormons reached the final rounds of *American Idol*, at the time the nation's top television show. Two were high schoolers when they sang their way to prominence—Carmen Rasmussen made it to the round of six contestants in 2003 (as did Brooke White in 2008), and David Archuleta was the show's runner-up in 2008.[12]

Yet it was more than achieving household-name status that made the fame of these Mormons significant. It was the way they represented Mormonism to the public through the filter of media portrayals. Ken Jennings told a writer for an online Mormon magazine, "Many press interviews I've done have brushed on tithing and the Word of Wisdom...and I've received a truly astounding amount of mail from Protestants and various other 'friends of other faiths' complimenting me on my clean-cut appearance, willingness to tithe, etc., with nary a 'but you're going to hell. Your biggest fan, Agnes.' If nothing else, in some parts of the country, I'm sure it's good to have a Mormon on TV who evidently doesn't have horns and ten wives."[13]

Stephenie Meyer, at the hands of numerous feature writers, not only came to symbolize the priority Mormons give to the family in her decision to be a stay-at-home mom, but to some commentators she also subtly stood for Mormon morality in having her characters consciously choose to abstain from premarital intimacy. Jane Clayson likewise received as much attention for her decision to walk away from the news desk in favor of raising a family as she did for her journalistic career. "My faith is what guides me and what guides my decisions," she told the *Boston Globe*. Kim Clark, dean of Harvard Business School, surprised the academic world when he gave up his top-tier position to assume the presidency of the LDS Church's four-year college BYU-Idaho in Rexburg, a school that was only a few years removed from being a junior college. He explained to colleagues that he could not turn down an invitation from President Hinckley. "Imagine getting a call from Moses," he said. Clearly, reporters noted—even if with a bit of incredulity at times—his commitment to his faith was foremost. [14]

The stories that surrounded these celebrities focused more on lifestyle than on theology, and in so doing they reinforced some of Mormonism's best-known traits—clean living and family solidarity. The stories also combined to paint a picture of strong commitment to a faith that in many ways defines its adherents. Often that dedication came across as impressive, sometimes as excessive, and sometimes oppressive. A fine line separated what some saw as moral fortitude and integrity and others saw as blind obedience and intolerance. In that vein, not every modern Mormon celebrity has personified loyalty to the faith. Julie Stoffer made waves when she appeared on MTV's *Real World* in 1999. By participating in the show, she forfeited her enrollment status at Brigham Young University. Part of the honor code to which all students at BYU submit is an agreement not to live in coed housing. Some commentators saw the expulsion as ironic, since Stoffer actually felt she was an advocate for her beliefs. Yet the church's university did not rescind its decision, and Stoffer admitted, "I wasn't wearing the Osmond smile all the time. I said things that were wrong some-times. I was human [but] I don't think I did anything against church teachings." More troubling for many Mormon observers was Todd Herzog's victory on the CBS reality competition, *Survivor*. Herzog described himself as an openly gay Mormon, and his prominence highlighted the growing controversy about the place of homosexuals in the LDS Church—and then ignited an Internet comment-board "debate...over whether someone could even be gay and still be a good Mormon." Herzog told *Newsweek* that he "[hoped] he opened peo-ple's eyes about the church" and "also [hoped] he opened some Mormons' eyes about the real world." Mormon discomfort surrounding Herzog foreshadowed the way this issue would come to the surface during the fight over California's Proposition 8 and its aftermath in 2008 and 2009.[15]

Still, famous faithful Mormons seemed to outnumber the disgruntled or the maverick. *ESPN* highlighted Larry H. Miller's devotion to Sabbath observance. The Utah car dealer did not attend games when the Utah Jazz, the NBA team he owned, played on Sundays—even if the game was a crucial play-off matchup. Danny Ainge, a college and NBA star in his own right, presided over the Boston Celtic organization that won the league's championship in 2008. He was named NBA Executive of the Year by the *Sporting News*. At the same time, he presided over his church's local ward (parish) as its bishop, a lay ministry that required ten to twenty hours of weekly volunteer labor. Neleh Dennis, the second-place finisher in the 2002 edition of *Survivor*, chose to bring her scriptures as her only allowed "luxury item" at the show's sparse outpost.[16]

Mormons also made positive headlines collectively. An extensive nationwide survey of American teenagers published in 2005 led researchers to conclude that Mormon teenagers prayed more, participated in religious services more, and understood their faith better than teens from any other religious group. The study's lead author, University of North Carolina sociologist Christian Smith, told the *Deseret News*, "I'm not saying they're all perfect. I'm not try-ing to idealize Mormon kids." But in terms of belief and "social outcomes," he said, "Mormon kids tend to be on top." The study drew talk-show attention and generated in numerous Internet postings what two authors called "Mormon envy."[17]

Many outside observers did see this level of religiosity, also symbolized by BYU's lock on the *Princeton Review*'s "stone-cold sober" designation, as com-mendable, even enviable. Yet to others, Mormon devotion became laughable—especially when entertainers and filmmakers turned their craft on the faith. Popular media productions that treated Mormonism gave voice to both of these sentiments—Mormons-as-admirable and Mormons-as-abnormal—and some-times even Mormon-as-aberrant. What was different in the first years of the new millennium was that this mixed bag came as an offering not only from non-Mormon hands but from Mormon ones as well.

Moving Pictures, Moving Targets

Sometimes Latter-day Saints played in stories as an expected trope. *The Simpsons* animated television series featured a scene in a 1998 episode that had two aliens coming to Homer and Marge's door. Homer looked out the window and said, "Not the Mormons!" Part of the humor was in the shared experience that many viewers could relate to—by 1994, church officials estimated Mormon missionaries had knocked on one-third of the nation's doors. Yet something else made the joke funny: Mormons were different enough to be, well, alien. While Mormons themselves could join appreciatively in the laughter, satisfied that their door-to-door proselytizing efforts were bringing the church recognition, the scene was still slightly unsettling, as if it begged the question, just how different is *too* different?[18]

The creators of another animated television series, *South Park*, had fun with Mormons on a number of occasions (more on that in chapter 10, too)—and used Mormons to dig at other Christians, as well. *South Park* spares no one, but being featured on the show was not necessarily a sought-after cultural badge of honor; the parodies could be piercing. In one episode, as a number of adherents of other faiths are burning in hell, the condemned souls are informed that the Mormons did have it right and are the only ones in heaven—a not-too-subtle jab, perhaps, at Christians who have snubbed Mormons. Yet in "All about the Mormons," another *South Park* episode in 2003 devoted entirely to Latter-day Saints, Mormons took plenty of punches, too. The episode reflected the complex place Mormons occupy in the American mind. The Mormon family in the episode, the Harrison family, is so likable and accomplished that a neighborhood boy and his father both initially intend to beat up the Mormons, but instead are won over by their kindness. However, the episode then turns to a spoof of LDS history that portrays Mormon faith claims as ridiculous and Mormon believers as dupes. Yet the unflappable Mormon characters in the episode maintain their composure even when they are accused of blatant stupidity. At the end of the episode, a Mormon character even takes the moral high ground, offering friendship where others only offered prejudice. In commenting on a number of misrepresentations of its history and practices, the LDS Church in 2009 referred back to the 2003 *South Park* episode, calling it "a gross portrayal of Church history" and noting that "individual Church members no doubt felt uncomfortable." Church public affairs officials also observed that the episode "inflicted no perceptible or lasting damage" to the church's growth. Still, the show was an important commentary on public perception of Mormonism, reinforcing ideas about the high personal standards of individual Mormons but also about the institutional and official strangeness of Mormon beliefs.[19]

Nowhere did Mormon characters inhabit a more complex space than they did in Tony Kushner's *Angels in America*, a play that won Tony Awards and a Pulitzer

Prize in the 1990s and then multiple Emmy Awards as an HBO mini-series in 2003. Several principal characters in the story are Mormons: a young husband who slowly admits to himself that he is gay; his wife, who is addicted to Valium; and the young gay man's mother, who becomes the caregiver to another character dying of AIDS. One historian of Mormon film noted that "those Latter-day Saints aware of *Angels* have always found it inaccurate and often sacrilegious and offensive" for its seeming caricature of Joseph Smith and its portrayal of Mormon narrow-mindedness. Yet researchers who pored over nationwide reviews of the play concluded that reviewers paid little attention to the Mormon elements of the play. The same could be said of media reports related to the mini-series. Beyond noting the subtle dramatic irony that a conservative member of the family-friendly LDS Church left his wife for a man, most writers did not comment on the Mormon connection, at least not to the extent Mormon viewers might have feared that they would, considering the play's controversial themes.[20]

Ironically, while Mormons may not have appreciated being included in the drama, some outsiders saw it as a positive thing. After all, the mini-series was hailed as "the national theatrical event of the year" and "one of the best television movies ever made." Oskar Eustis, who had directed the play's premiere, said that Kushner chose Mormonism "as part of the play's framework" because "ongoing revelation" and the "belief you can reinvent yourself...in Mormonism is something Tony [Kushner] sees as a pure expression of what is positive." One reviewer said that "the film is not disrespectful to Mormons," and that the "Mormon mother Hannah becomes one of the most enlightened characters in the story." Who could ask for more than having Meryl Streep play the part of the Mormon heroine, "the most effective agent of hope in the entire play"? Yet the same reviewer conceded that *Angels in America* "does take some shots at certain cultural aspects" of the faith. These "shots" were obviously less significant to outsiders than they were to Mormons, since those "cultural aspects" were the very types of perception issues that troubled Latter-day Saints. Mormons saw this as a "lack of empathy toward [the play's] Mormon characters. All the other characters are eventually accepted into the tapestry of hope presented in the denouement, but Latter-day Saints—and conservatives—are either cast off or must shed their provincial Mormon and conservative identities."[21]

Overall, *Angels in America* did not in the end cause a significant stir among the LDS faithful, simply because the mini-series's "R-rated language, brief nudity and sexual situations" made it the type of entertainment "not regularly patronized by most American Mormons," such that "many Latter-day Saints [were] unlikely to encounter" the show. However, Latter-day Saints became much more conscious of another of HBO's programs in 2006, *Big Love*, because of the church's vigorous reaction to its announced release. In many ways, the premise of the program was a church public affairs nightmare. The story was set in contemporary

Salt Lake City, the capital of Mormondom. Yet the main characters were not Mormons, but fundamentalist polygamists who had shed the rural compound lifestyle in favor of urban assimilation by keeping their polygamy secret. The church saw the potential for confusion as almost assured, just at the time when it was working strenuously to differentiate itself from practicing polygamists. Despite assurances from the show's creators that they "tried to draw a distinction between polygamous groups and The Church of Jesus Christ of Latter-day Saints," it was obvious to "both foes and proponents of polygamy" that the "LDS Church's fears about the show [would] be realized." Observers pointed to the producers' "repeated uses of the Salt Lake Temple as a backdrop, depiction of female [Mormon] missionaries and references to Mormon culture."[22]

Church general authorities sent to every local bishop in the United States and Canada a letter with an official response if there were "inquiries about the show." The church's Public Affairs Department also released a statement bemoaning Big Love's Utah setting as more than "enough to blur the line between the modern Church and the program's subject matter and to reinforce old and long-outdated stereotypes," especially since "this distinction is often lost on members of the public and even on some senior journalists." One sign of the church's growing clout was that it persuaded HBO to run a disclaimer statement prior to the show's opening to clarify explicitly the distinction between polygamists and Mormons. However, by March 2009, the church complained that "more and more Mormon themes [were] being woven into the show," and the Mormon characters were "often unsympathetic figures who come across as narrow and self-righteous." Most egregious from a Mormon standpoint, the Big Love producers announced that their show's polygamists would recreate a Latter-day Saints temple endowment ceremony during an episode in the 2009 season. Mormon leaders felt that HBO had betrayed its "earlier assurances" about maintaining a clear distinction between the fundamentalists and the Latter-day Saints, and they were "offended" that "their most sacred practices are misrepresented or presented without context or understanding." Though many Mormons independently called for a boycott of America Online (AOL), a Time Warner sister company to HBO, the church refrained from making the boycott call official. Instead, the church said that "it would [not] risk being distracted from the focus and mission...to preach the restored gospel of Jesus Christ throughout the world."[23]

While such pointed official responses to pop culture depictions of Mormonism were relatively rare, they nevertheless signaled several important realities. Despite its stated aloofness, the church was keenly aware of these depictions and their potential for impact, and Mormon leaders knew they had good reason to be worried, especially when polygamy reappeared. After all, Big Love was an Emmy-nominated show whose well-publicized premise reached audiences even beyond its viewership.[24] A February 2002 Saturday Night Live sketch on the eve of the Salt Lake City Winter Olympics showed just how difficult it was for the church to bring clarity to the polygamy issue. During the sketch, Will Ferrell and Dan Aykroyd played Mormon missionaries (on skis) who join an Olympic downhiller in the middle of her race. While she tries to explain to them that she needs to concentrate on her race, they disregard her polite requests and continue to talk about the Book of Mormon and aspects of Latter-day Saints history. Finally, the exasperated racer says, "Get out of here!" Will Ferrell's character calmly responds, "I know what you're thinking. Polygamy is over. No one has more than one wife anymore. We simply don't do it." After a well-timed pause, Aykroyd's missionary admits, "I do it." Ferrell then concedes, "A few of us still do it, but mainly no."[25]

Even if this *Saturday Night Live* spoof caused church public affairs representatives to wince a little, the direction of the dialogue would not have surprised them, based on research that they had recently conducted. A 1999 study showed that polygamy "consistently...emerges as the most entrenched, dominant and damaging of all stated perceptions of the Church." When respondents were asked, "What comes to mind when I mention the Mormon Church?," "polygamy" and "missionaries" "tied...for second place, exceeded only by 'Salt Lake City.'" Not only that, but it almost went without saying that "when asked whether the polygamy association makes people feel more positive or negatively toward the Church, 8% said positively, 77% said more negatively."[26]

The church public relations team made measurable strides in overcoming these stereotypes with the press kits and video offerings they prepared for the 2002 Olympics. A fear of losing that hard-won ground prompted strong reaction not only to *Big Love*, but also against a 2003 book by best-selling author Jon Krakauer, *Under the Banner of Heaven*. Krakauer's subtitle spoke volumes: "A Story of a Violent Faith." He did little to differentiate between fundamentalist polygamists and mainstream Mormons, primarily because the thesis of his book was that all sects that originated with Joseph Smith are inherently dangerous in their blind devotion to a so-called "prophet." Krakauer wondered aloud how the belief system and cosmology of so many of his seemingly upstanding friends and neighbors could also somehow spawn the fanatical, remorseless killers Ron and Dan Lafferty, ex-communicants of The Church of Jesus Christ of Latter-day Saints, or forger and bomber Mark Hofmann, or Elizabeth Smart's kidnapper Brian David Mitchell. His answer: "There is a dark side to religious devotion that is too often ignored or denied."[27]

This was not the faith most Mormons knew, and they said it. The church published three rebuttals by prominent Latter-day Saints who pointed out the numerous historical errors that clouded Krakauer's narrative of past and present Mormonism. Michael Otterson, director of media relations in the church's Public Affairs Department, soberly told the Associated Press, "One could be forgiven for concluding that every Latter-day Saint, including your friendly

Mormon neighbor, has a tendency to violence. And so Krakauer unwittingly puts himself in the same camp as those who believe every German is a Nazi, every Japanese a fanatic, and every Arab a terrorist." Otterson's final assessment of the book could also aptly describe how Latter-day Saints viewed a number of these similarly themed productions about Mormonism: "Krakauer's portrayal of The Church of Jesus Christ of Latter-day Saints is utterly at odds with what I—and millions like me—have come to know of the Church, its goodness, and the decency of its people."[28]

But the church's strong words against the book did not diminish its luster in the eyes of a reading public. Reviewers saw the book as both "illuminating" and "scrupulously reported." The book's staying power was also reflected in the fact that *New York Times* columnist Maureen Dowd turned to Krakauer for information about Mitt Romney's religion in 2007 and quoted passages about Joseph Smith's ties to "black magic." Dowd turned to Krakauer because, in her words, "Mormonism is opaque."[29] That murkiness in many minds was what made, at least in part, Krakauer's opening comments so memorable, and so haunting: "To much of the world, this [Tabernacle] choir and its impeccably rendered harmonies are emblematic of the Mormons as a people: chaste, optimistic, outgoing, dutiful. When Dan Lafferty quotes Mormon scripture to justify murder, the juxtaposition is so incongruous as to seem surreal." The lasting popularity of Krakauer's book (and thus its potential for damage, from the LDS point of view) was demonstrated by the fact that it still landed at tenth on *The New York Times Book Review*'s Paperback Non-Fiction Best Sellers List on May 18, 2008, after sixty-five weeks on that list. And in 2011, news that a movie based on the book was headed to production with the backing and input of Hollywood heavyweights promised the story even longer life.[30]

Picturing "Peoplehood"

Given the complexity of Mormonism, it is not surprising that many Mormons felt that these outside views of the faith would miss its essence.[31] The *Washington Post* quoted Mormon director Richard Dutcher in 2006: "If Mormons...let other people tell their stories, they will end up with something very far from reality." There was, he realized, a glaring lack of homegrown portrayals that captured an insider's understanding of the meaning of Mormonism. This impetus drove Dutcher to try his hand at depicting his religion for a wider audience and blaze the path for other filmmakers. Not only did his *God's Army* do well at box offices in Utah, but it received favorable reviews nationwide and played in theaters from New York to California, eventually garnering three million dollars, "a smash by indie-movie standards."[32]

In reality, many (if not most) of the films that followed Dutcher's played to the Mormon niche audience. Still, they became an important commentary on internal conversations about what *was* essentially "Mormon," and what it was that church members portrayed to the world.[33] These films included insider comedies like *Singles Ward* and *The RM [Returned Missionary]*, historical dramas like *The Work and the Glory*, and realistic portrayals of coming-of-age missionary passages, like *The Other Side of Heaven* and *The Best Two Years*. They also included films that challenged Mormon stereotypes—some in a light-hearted way, like the fish-out-of-water *Mobsters and Mormons*; and some in a heartfelt way, like the documentary *New York Doll*, which traced Arthur "Killer" Kane's journey from playing bass for the 1970s-era trend-setting band The New York Dolls, to finding Mormonism after two decades of burn-outs and disappointments. Over two dozen of these Mormon feature films appeared in less than ten years, and they played an important role in perpetuating something that Martin Marty observed: "What's interesting about the Mormons is that they are from a mixed ethnic stock not much different from the rest of the majority and yet they are a distinct people. A story makes a people."[34]

Telling that story in film gave these depictions of Mormonism new dimensions of texture and depth, a nuanced view that to Latter-day Saints felt more true to life than what they often saw as two-dimensional snapshots or caricatures of their faith.

The potential for diverse Mormon storylines—and for diverse takes on the meaning of Mormon history—was demonstrated in other documentaries that found wide play nationally on PBS stations. Lee Groberg followed his 1997 film on the Mormon pioneer trail with films on the life of Joseph Smith (*American Prophet*, 1999) and on the reconstruction of the Nauvoo Temple (*Sacred Stone*, 2002). *American Prophet* was especially noteworthy for its inclusion of non-Mormon religious scholars—Notre Dame's Nathan Hatch, Pepperdine's Richard Hughes, Cornell's R. Laurence Moore—who, in contrast to Jon Krakauer, spoke glowingly of Joseph Smith's theological and organizational contributions. Brown University historian Gordon Wood called Joseph Smith "obviously the most successful American prophet that we've ever had," and the church he established "the most powerful uniquely American religion that we've had." Robert Remini from the University of Illinois at Chicago admitted that as a historian, he personally did not believe Joseph Smith's claims about divine communication. "However," he added, "you can say, 'Look what he did.'" Then he closed with a potent rhetorical question: "Is one human being capable of doing this without divine help or intervention?"[35]

These subtle evidences of growing public acceptance of Mormons and their leaders encouraged Latter-day Saints, who have always been mindful of their "peculiar people" status. In 1994, church researchers determined that 36% of Americans had Mormon friends or relatives. A decade later, not only had the church's U.S. membership grown by a million, but the number of Mormons appearing on the public stage more than kept pace with that growth. Mormons hoped that these indicators of exposure translated into a clearer picture of what the faith was and what it was not. One observer noted the hopeful sign that "old stigmas remain, but increasingly more substantive treatments or objective critiques of Mormonism are appearing." Even when controversial depictions surfaced in scenes of *Big Love* or on the pages of Krakauer's *Under the Banner of Heaven*, Latter-day Saints reasonably hoped that Mormon celebrities and artists offered persuasive counterevidence.[36]

One final basis for that hopefulness was Mormons' presence in national politics. In 2006, the year that Mitt Romney entered the presidential race, Latter-day Saints were no strangers to the nation's capital. Former Utah Governor Michael Leavitt was President Bush's Secretary of Health and Human Services. After the 2006 election, over a dozen members of Congress were Mormons. Most importantly, because the Democrats seized the majority in the Senate in that election, Nevada's Harry Reid, an active Mormon, became their majority leader.

For these reasons, many Mormons hoped that the rumors swirling around Massachusetts Governor and former Salt Lake City Olympic Chairman Mitt Romney in early 2006 would prove to be true and that Romney would enter the 2008 presidential race. With the type of exposure that had come to the church during the 1997 wagon train reenactment or the 2002 Winter Games, Mormons anticipated that a Romney campaign would bring more of the same—in-depth explorations of their faith that gave context to its history, accurate profiles of its people, and clear refutations of conventional stereotypes.

It was not that Mormons saw the state of their church's image through blinders or rose-colored glasses; the "0–100 favorability thermometer" polling during the Olympics revealed that the church had a long way to go to overcome negative impressions, since respondents scored the church only in the mid-forties. What that polling had also suggested, though, was that there was a correlation between increased knowledge about Mormonism and improved public perception of the faith. It seemed reasonable to expect that press attention to Mitt Romney would provide for that same type of improvement.

Mormons were in for a surprise.[37]

9

Suspicions and Surprises: The 2008 Presidential Campaign Season

"It's suicide—I don't see [who] can raise it without appearing to be a bigot." This was Boston College political science professor Dennis Hale's response when the *Boston Herald* asked him about the role Mitt Romney's Mormonism might play in the upcoming campaign—for governor of Massachusetts in 2002, that is. Still, Hale suggested that Romney would be well served to "voluntarily broach the subject...[and] talk about his religious values to allay fears that this is not a weird cult living in the hills." In 1994, Romney had lost a Massachusetts election when Mormonism played a significant role. In 2002, though, just as Hale predicted, Romney's religion did not spell his downfall, and the Republican became governor. This victory for the GOP in a statewide race in Massachusetts instantly catapulted Romney into the constellation of his party's rising stars.[1]

Because of that, as his four-year term as governor drew to a close in 2006, Romney was actively considering a run for the presidency. Several Mormon scholars met with Romney's advisors and warned about the potential for Mormonism to be a political liability. Those who raised these concerns remembered later that many of Romney's advisors were skeptical, believing, like Dennis Hale, that slanders against Mormonism would constitute political "suicide" and bigotry. To these unconvinced advisors' surprise, not only did Mormonism come up, it arguably was the heavy blow that knocked Romney out of the 2008 presidential race. Many Mormons were just as stunned as Romney's unsuspecting advisors. They had reason to believe that after a decade of frequent, positive press coverage, most Americans were comfortable with Mormons in the public square. However, as Romney's run generated an unprecedented number of opinion surveys about the public's perception of Mormonism, a clearer picture about American attitudes toward the LDS Church came into focus. What Mitt Romney's campaign exposed was a latent, smoldering suspicion—a fear of the unknown—that recent bridge-building efforts and prominent Mormons had not extinguished.[2]

Most obvious was persistent animosity from the evangelical Christian camp. Despite the remarkable book collaborations and joint symposia that resulted from Mormon and evangelical dialogue, this same spirit of reconciliation and cooperation had not "trickled to all the pews." The majority of nonevangelical Americans viewed Mormons as Christians; the opposite was true, and emphatically so, for evangelical Americans. Numerous conservative Christians vocally raised doubts about the fitness of any Mormon for the presidency, and because of the clout that the Religious Right wielded in the Republican Party, these doubts reverberated widely.[3]

Yet concerns about the "Mormon question" were also voiced by other groups, particularly by representatives of the media who challenged, sometimes blatantly so, the rationality of Mormonism's truth claims, and thus impugned by implication the intelligence of any who believed those claims. Insinuations about the LDS hierarchy's authoritarian hold on its members also drove fears about Romney's intentions. In other words, the religious issue was as central to Mitt Romney's campaign as it was incidental to his father's, forty years earlier.

Nothing, not even the 2002 Olympics, drew attention to Mormonism like Mitt Romney's bid for the White House. The sheer volume of coverage devoted to the man and his faith meant that there was much that was good, from the church's standpoint, in publicized depictions of the religion. However, this coverage also meant that old stereotypes of Mormons were repeated often enough to project these images onto a larger-than-ever screen. This was evident in 2007 in a landmark, four-hour PBS documentary, *The Mormons*, and then again in 2008, during national coverage of scandals involving the reclusive—and polygamous—Fundamentalist Church of Jesus Christ of Latter Day Saints (FLDS). Mormons certainly enjoyed more name recognition than ever before, but it was clear that their brand was less positive than they had hoped.

A week before Mitt Romney would eventually withdraw from the race in early February 2008, LDS Church President Gordon B. Hinckley died at the age of ninety-seven. President Hinckley was universally esteemed as a highly successful ambassador for his church. Yet the tributes to this dynamic leader, as widespread and glowing as they were, underscored again the long-running disconnect between public respect for individual Mormons and public wariness for institutional Mormonism. Peggy Fletcher Stack of the *Salt Lake Tribune* mused, "As much [as people] might not have liked Mormonism, they couldn't help but like Gordon B. Hinckley. He was just likable and so Mormons really thought, 'Wow, the whole country loves us'—even as the undercurrent never went away." It was the continued strength of that undercurrent that both dragged on a racing Romney and abruptly reminded his coreligionists that they still had a long road to travel toward public acceptance.[4]

"Certain Religious Views Should Be Deal Breakers in and of Themselves"

It was apparent that Hugh Hewitt was a Romney fan when he opened, in 2007, a pointed discussion about the elephant (appropriately) in the Republicans' room.[5] Hewitt's book, *A Mormon in the White House?: 10 Things Every American Should Know About Mitt Romney*, opened with this bit of praise: "I have never met a more intellectually gifted, curious, good humored, broadly read, and energetic official than Mitt Romney." Hewitt even admitted that "if the California primary were held tomorrow, I would indeed vote for Mitt Romney." Yet it was apparent to Hewitt that the road ahead would not be a smooth one for Romney. In a number of conversations with prominent Republicans, Hewitt sensed that nearly everyone was reluctant to talk about the "Mormon problem," because it would dredge up the sticky reality that Romney's faith might effectively disqualify him, even in a nation without "a religious test for office." Hewitt's book was a response to those initial warning signs, a call especially to conservatives that "bigotry about Romney's faith ought not to be a legitimate part of this campaign, or any future campaign for the presidency."[6]

It had, though, already played a decisive part in a past campaign. In 1994, Romney, then the chairman of Bain Capital, challenged Massachusetts Senator Ted Kennedy. One reporter called the young Mormon business leader and family man the "perfect anti-Kennedy." Remarkably, Romney held a lead in the polls over the powerful career politician only months before Election Day. He seemed to be riding the tide of anti-Democrat, anti-incumbent sentiment that swept the nation during the 1994 election cycle. As Romney supporters saw it, that is when desperation prompted Senator Kennedy to join his nephew, Congressman Joseph Kennedy, in dragging Mormonism through the mud. The younger Kennedy intimated that Mormons relegated women and blacks to "second-class [citizen]" status because they were not eligible for the priesthood. Senator Kennedy picked up the same refrain. First he publicly objected to the Roman Catholic Church's similar stand on the ordination of women, and then he chastised Romney for not likewise objecting to the Mormon position. More damaging, however, was the elder Kennedy's assertion that Romney was tainted by his association with a racist church, since Mormons did not extend the priesthood to black members until 1978. "Where is Mr. Romney," Ted Kennedy asked reporters, "on those issues in terms of equality of race prior to 1978 and other kinds of issues in question?" Eventually Joseph Kennedy apologized for stating incorrectly that the LDS Church still banned blacks from holding church offices, but his uncle told reporters that "some questions about Romney's religion were appropriate." It was those suggestive questions that left suspicion about Mormonism hanging in the air.[7]

Both Romney and a number of pundits were surprised by what seemed like an uncharacteristic move for the senator, considering the role that the Kennedy family had played in fighting religious prejudice. Romney even referred to that Kennedy legacy when he angrily questioned the senator's tactics. "In my view," Romney said, "the victory that John Kennedy won was not for just forty million Americans who were born Catholic, it was for Americans of all faiths. And I am sad to say that Ted Kennedy is trying to take away his brother's victory." Several months earlier, Senator Kennedy had told reporters that "his opponent's religion should not be an issue," and even in September his press secretary tried to maintain that line. "This is about racial prejudice and bias against women," Kennedy spokesman Rick Gureghian. "No one is raising religion as an issue. What is being raised is his indifference and silence in the face of religious bigotry and bias." Few were persuaded by that disclaimer, however. A *Boston Globe* political correspondent said, "Of course, it's about religion.... Mormonism is an exotic concept in Massachusetts. It's part of [Kennedy's] game plan to create doubt about his opponent any way he can."[8]

The Kennedy campaign also sowed other doubts about Romney as an enemy of American labor by highlighting companies that Romney's firm had bought and then closed or consolidated. Yet it was obvious that, as one commentator observed, "The attacks [against Mormonism] had their desired effect." Romney lost the Senate race by seventeen percentage points.[9]

Kirk Jowers, director of the Hinckley Institute of Politics at the University of Utah and a Romney advisor, observed that Senator Kennedy was essentially "anti-Mormon" for only "two months" of that 1994 campaign. He "had been a friend to the church," and especially to Utah Senator Orrin Hatch, for years before, and he was a friend to the church afterward. Kennedy reaffirmed that friendship and admiration for Mormons a half-dozen years later when he toured the newly completed Boston LDS Temple. When the church originally proposed building a temple in Boston, the announcement raised the ire of its potential neighbors, so the LDS Church enlisted other religious groups in the area to back its plans on the basis of religious freedom. Catholic, Protestant, and Jewish groups publicly expressed support for the temple, as well as the much-contested appeal to place a steeple on the new building. As Senator Kennedy toured the building, he added his voice in favor of the steeple. Within the year, a steeple adorned the new temple. What was most ironic about that VIP tour was that Mitt Romney, who had been an LDS stake (diocese) president in Boston, was Senator Kennedy's guide. The reunion of the two former rivals at a Mormon temple seemed symbolic, as if to say that Kennedy had made peace with Romney and his faith.[10]

Less than two years later, when Mitt Romney became the state's governor, Massachusetts appeared willing to follow the senator's lead and let bygone misgivings about Mormonism be bygones. During that 2002 gubernatorial race,

Jowers felt like "the media wouldn't get near" the "anti-Mormon stuff" like they did in 1994. It was, to Jowers, as if they were saying, "We really feel bad about the way we covered [Romney's] last [campaign]," even "a little dirty."[11]

Romney's staff had anticipated that the coverage of the presidential race of 2008 would mirror his experience in Massachusetts. They knew that there would of course be "fascination" about Mormonism, as Jowers put it, but they hoped that this interest and attention would come in an early media "feeding frenzy," something along the lines of the 1994 campaign. Then, after this "binge," after they "got [Mormonism] out of [their] system," Jowers said that Romney's camp expected that journalists and pundits would keep the focus on substantive issues, as in the 2002 campaign for governor. Instead of coming to a quick, intense boiling point, however, the Mormon issue slowly simmered for months beginning in late 2006, so that by the time of the primary season in 2008, the question of religion was superheated and ready to bubble over in explosive fashion.[12]

Part of the surprise for Romney supporters derived from the reality that Massachusetts voters were not representative of the nation's electorate. Evangelical Christians did not constitute as powerful a political presence there as they did in other parts of the nation, where they "[wielded] a disproportionate influence in primary elections." Because of this, Mormonism became a concern for many voters nationally in a different way than it had been for Massachusetts voters during the 1994 race. It seems hard to deny that Senator Kennedy brought up Romney's religion for any other reason than tactical survival. In contrast, a dozen years later, millions of voters based their opposition to a Mormon presidential candidate on principle rather than political expediency. This type of opposition ran deeper and thus was more difficult to unseat.[13]

The first memorable blow did not come from the Religious Right, though, but from the left-leaning online magazine *Slate*. The magazine's editor, Jacob Weisberg, penned a December 2006 editorial that was prescient in the way that it predicted nearly all of the contours of the yet-future debates over Romney's faith. Weisberg noted that "various evangelical sects continue to view Mormonism as heretical, non-Christian, or even satanic," but that a "shared faith in social conservatism" would still cause "evangelical leaders" to give Romney a second look (which they did). He also surmised that those same conservatives would ask questions about Romney's apparently "moderate views on abortion and gay rights" during his Massachusetts campaigns, views which Romney said had since turned in a more conservative direction. Weisberg therefore suggested that Romney would be charged with "flip-flopping" on these issues (which he was). Still, the most negative of Weisberg's points was that "moderate and secular voters" should "rightly" make "Romney's religion...an issue," because "someone who truly believed in the founding whoppers of Mormonism" demonstrated "a basic failure to think for himself or see the world as it is." In his article, Weisberg anticipated the counterargument that "you [are] a religious bigot if you wouldn't cast a ballot for a believing Mormon"; his response was that "Joseph Smith was an obvious con man. Romney has every right to believe in con men, but I want to know if he does, and if so, I don't want him running the country."[14]

Kirk Jowers felt that this magazine piece "caught people off guard," because instead of "dancing around Mitt and Mormonism" with "more high-minded rhetoric" about the LDS Church being an "interesting...religion," Weisberg unapologetically called the church's founding "a transparent and recent fraud." Hugh Hewitt labeled Weisberg "a bigot, and an unashamed one." Hewitt and others worried that "the Left will relish the assault on Romney's religion" since that could lead more generally to the "routine dismissal...[of] any man or woman who believes in revelation as well as reason." Catholic priest and prominent author Father Richard John Neuhaus questioned the political motives of those "who would use religion to oppose a candidate for the presidency," noting that "in the game book of unbridled partisanship, any stick will do for beating up on the opposition."[15]

Still, Weisberg's piece undeniably gave voice to sentiments that would come to appear more and more pronounced in American opinions about Mormonism, especially for religious Americans—and this despite cautions by Hewitt and his co-blogger Dean Barnett that "if it becomes permissible to question the tenets of Romney's faith, all religious people will be vulnerable." The public proved to be very ambivalent when asked about the notion of a Latter-day Saint running for president, and that ambivalence was evident in numerous polls that approached the Mormon issue from a variety of angles.[16]

Some of that uncertainty came to the fore as early as December 2006, two months before Romney officially announced his candidacy in mid-February 2007. A Los Angeles Times/Bloomberg poll asked voters if they could vote for a Mormon if "your party nominated" the candidate, and he or she was "in general agreement with you on most issues." Only 14% said that they could not vote for a Mormon in that scenario. Little had seemingly changed since 1999, when Gallup asked almost an identical question in anticipation of Utah Senator Orrin Hatch's truncated bid for the presidency in 2000. In that March 1999 poll, 79% of respondents said that they would vote for their party's nominee if he or she were a Mormon; only 17% said they would not.[17]

A December 2006 ABC News/Washington Times poll told a different story, however. This survey left out the qualifiers about a party's nomination, or the issue-based agreement, and simply asked if certain "attributes [that] might be found in a candidate...would make you more [or less] likely to vote for that candidate for president." Thirty-five percent of respondents said that they would be "less likely" to vote for a Mormon candidate. Only 7% of respondents said that they would be "less likely" to vote for a black candidate; 14% said the same about a female candidate. An NBC News/Wall Street Journal survey that same month was even bleaker from the Mormon standpoint. More than half of the respondents—53%—said "they were very uncomfortable or have some reservations about voting for a presidential candidate who is Mormon."[18]

Again, this obvious wariness was not just a manifestation of traditional evangelical Protestant animosity toward the LDS Church. While by 2007 a Harris poll did reveal that "twenty-nine percent of Republicans...probably or definitely would not vote for a Mormon for president," another study showed that "among those who identify themselves as liberal, almost half say they would not support a Mormon for president." For Mormons who had seen the first decade of President Gordon B. Hinckley's tenure as a time of remarkable public outreach, these indications of outright rejection stung—and stunned. Mormon Historian Richard Bushman, whose prominence in academia made him an unofficial spokesman for the faith, felt that "Mormons had come to the conclusion that their religion was pretty much accepted. But these horrendous poll results that indicate that Mormons are not first-class citizens because of their religion were terribly shocking." What was it that made people so dismissive of a Mormon candidate? Journalists and political commentators often agreed on the answer: it was too much unfamiliarity with Mormonism on the part of most Americans, and too much familiarity with Mormonism on the part of fundamentalist Christians.[19]

"An Issue [for] Moderate and Secular Voters"

Mitt Romney essentially had to walk two tightropes.[20] Astute commentators noted that if Mitt Romney spoke too much about his religion in the hope of educating the uninformed, he was bound to draw attention to the theological sticking points—extra scripture, the nature of the Trinity, modern-day prophets—that alienated evangelicals and spawned the charges that Mormons were not Christians. But if he chose to remain tight-lipped about his faith or dodged questions about his beliefs, he would perpetuate Mormonism's reputation for secrecy.

It was precisely this reputation that contributed to a widespread but mostly nebulous uneasiness surrounding the LDS Church's public image. A nationwide majority (57%) told a CBS poll that "they know little or nothing about Mormon beliefs and practices." Yet almost that same number of Americans (56%) in an earlier survey had said that they felt as though Mormons were "mostly unlike" or "completely unlike" them, in terms of basic beliefs and values. It was apparent that even though many Americans did not feel like they were well acquainted with the LDS faith, they felt like they knew *enough*—knew enough to see Mormons as different, as "other." What seemed to drive that outlook was the feeling that there was in Mormonism a "disconcerting split between its public and private faces."[21]

Harvard University Professor of Law Noah Feldman, writing in the *New York Times Magazine*, saw the church's "public face" represented best by the "pairs of clean-cut missionaries in well-pressed white shirts." They personified "the wholesome success of an all-American denomination with an idealistic commitment to clean living." In many ways, Mitt Romney matched that public face of Mormonism. He was repeatedly characterized as "telegenic" and "the most handsome man in the room," and his strong family life and service as a church leader were well known.[22]

"Yet at the same time," Feldman observed, "secret, sacred temple rites...call to mind the church's murky past, including its embrace of polygamy." This made up the church's "private face," the visage that made "outsiders uncomfortable, wondering what Mormonism really is." Early in the campaign season, people suggested that Romney matched that private face of Mormonism, too. During his 1994 campaign for the Senate, Romney had expressed a pro-choice public policy position on the issue of abortion (even though personally he opposed abortion). However, leading up to the presidential race of 2008, he stated that he had changed his mind, and that he thought *Roe v. Wade* should be overturned. In this shift to the political right on abortion, observers questioned his sincerity. Was he "a glossy and robotic candidate who will say anything to get elected?" Like his church, which "some [saw] as overly wholesome and plastic," was he more concerned with perception than with "authenticity?"[23]

These essentially were the anxieties that drove opposition to Romney's candidacy from more liberal commentators. This blow was the "left hook," to use historian Craig Foster's apt phrase from his remarkably exhaustive book about the melee over Mitt Romney's first campaign. The barrage included *Atlantic Monthly* blogger Andrew Sullivan, who posted in November 2006 "a photograph, obtained on Wikipedia, of an anonymous man and woman wearing [temple] garments, which Mormons hold sacred because they are associated with temple ritual." Sullivan wrote that at least "Mitt Romney will never have to answer the boxers or briefs question. But will he tell us whether he wears Mormon underwear at all times, including when asleep?"[24]

"Does anyone ask Hillary Clinton to describe her underwear?" was the way that one commentator responded to these types of inquiries. Notwithstanding protests like this, it was clear that fascination surrounding Mormon temple worship was not going to let up. Two *Newsweek* writers asked Mitt Romney "if he [had] done baptisms for the dead," one of the "secret temple rituals." Mormons are baptized as proxies for individuals who died without baptism, a practice that had recently drawn national scrutiny when a number of Jewish groups reacted strongly to reports that overzealous Mormon volunteers were performing the ritual for Holocaust victims. High-ranking Mormon officials met with Jewish leaders to reassure them that they would insure the practice was discontinued, but this did not fully assuage those who took offense at what they interpreted as

Mormons' self-righteous presumptiveness. This context figured into *Newsweek's* suggestion that Romney "looked slightly startled" by the question about baptisms for the dead, a look which they intuited to mean that he was aware "of how odd" his affirmative answer "will sound to many Americans."[25]

One of the ironies in these types of interrogations was that many journalists seemed conflicted by the reporting that they nevertheless felt compelled to do. Historian Laurie Maffly-Kipp observed that *Atlantic Monthly* writer Sridhar Pappu "admitted he was uncomfortable asking [a] question" about "temple garments," even though in the end he "did ask the question." Pappu wrote that "the issue of a candidate's religion 'should have died with the election of Jack Kennedy,'" but he still had to ask Romney, "How Mormon are you?" The mystery of Mormonism seemed to have its own gravitational pull.[26]

This meant that on the one hand, there were complaints, like that of *Boston Herald* reporter Dave Wedge, that "publishing pictures of the [temple garments] in ridicule is as blasphemous to Mormons as posting pictures of Allah is to Muslims." Yet on the other hand, others, like John Dickerson writing for *Slate*, felt that these seemingly bizarre elements in Mormonism called for an explanation: "If they're talking about your bloomers, it's time to clear things up."[27]

This is what must have created a conundrum for Romney—and for Mormons watching the contest over their image from the sidelines. It became apparent that some vocal observers felt that Mormonism, by its very nature, demanded an exposé to keep one of its believing cultists out of the White House. MSNBC's Lawrence O'Donnell used a December 2007 appearance on *The McLaughlin Group* to offer his opinion that Mitt Romney belonged to a "ridiculous" church that was "based on the work of a lying, fraudulent, criminal named Joseph Smith who was a racist, who was pro-slavery, [and] whose religion was pro-slavery" (Joseph Smith actually ran for president in 1844 with an antislavery plank in his platform).[28] O'Donnell later said that "he would like to criticize Islam," but he did not do so "because of fears for his personal safety." However, since "Mormons are the nicest people in the world" he reasoned that they would "never take a shot at me."[29] Here again was this recurring theme—recognition of the unassailable morality of individual Mormons in the same breath with suspicion about the questionable motives of the church. One Mormon reviewer noted, incredulously, that instead of creating a backlash, O'Donnell's comments, especially about Mormon racism, found a supporter in Frank Rich of the *New York Times*, who saw Romney's obedience to his church as confirmation that he was a "follower and a panderer." Rich even suggested that "it's incredible that Mr. Romney's prejudices get a free pass from so many commentators."[30]

Few Mormons, though, felt like Mitt Romney got a free pass on anything related to Mormonism. Scott Pierce, writing in the *Deseret News*, mused, "Imagine for a moment that O'Donnell had said this about members of other religions. He'd never be seen on TV again." However, as both Mormons and non-Mormons noted, the same rules of civility did not seem to apply to discussions about Mormonism. Reporter Peggy Fletcher Stack remembered feeling "just appalled with my profession, frankly" because of "coverage of Mitt Romney...I thought it was terrible and appalling the kind of things that people got away with saying that they would not get away with saying about other faiths." Mike Allen of Politico called it "a sort of PC [political correctness] exemption for Mormons such that people feel free to talk about them in a way that we don't feel free to talk about...any other religious group."[31]

Part of that unfortunate (from the Mormon standpoint) LDS exceptionalism seemed to derive from the church's proximate provenance, in terms of both time and place. Jacob Weisberg complained that Mormonism lacked the "eons" of existence that had permitted "Christianity and Judaism...to splinter, moderate, and turn their myths into metaphor." E. J. Dionne of The *Washington Post* recognized that "any tradition is at a disadvantage if its scripture was written 150 years ago instead of 1,000, 2,000 or 6,000 years ago" since "it's harder to explain away inconvenient things." HBO's Bill Maher said in February 2007, "People don't know about Mormonism, and when they find out they will be amazed at how weird it really is. It's even weird by the standards of other religions, and we know that they're weird." Maher, who often spoke derisively of religion in general, reserved special objections for Mormonism since Latter-day Saints "believe in some stuff that is demonstrably—you can prove that it's not true. I mean, you can't prove about Jesus; it was 2,000 years ago. But Joseph Smith...lived less than two centuries ago. And he was, excuse me, a con-man."[32]

Understandably, as USA Today noted, by late 2007, "some Mormons feel that the Church of Jesus Christ of Latter-day Saints, as it is officially called, now faces closer scrutiny than Romney's political record." Certainly, Romney's policy views were of prime interest, too. He received extensive attention for his healthcare reforms in Massachusetts and his plans for improving the nation's economy. Yet even *Newsweek* conceded that months before the primary season, "the Mormon question loomed larger than any other over Romney's young campaign."[33]

Despite the candidate's repeated insistence that he would not be a spokesman for his church, he could not escape the role that the media seemed to thrust upon him, that of standing in for Mormonism. Thus coverage of his campaign effectively became a revelation of the qualms that a number of national opinion leaders held about the faith, qualms that Mormons had hoped had dissipated during the decade prior to Romney's campaign. Many Mormons had seen the media's treatment of their church during the first ten years of President Hinckley's tenure as ranging from balanced to remarkably positive. Historian Jan Shipps noted that the "thousands of reporters" who "flocked to Salt Lake City" during the 2002 Olympics, for example, "wrote stories about the faith that focused on" what she called "Mormon behavior": "wonderful families," "gracious hosts," "humanitarians," "friendly." Yet in so many stories about Mitt

Romney, journalists turned to "Mormon theology," and this type of reporting gave voice to apprehensions that felt reminiscent of the 1980s, when scandals over assumed Mormon cover-up and intrigue and clandestine practices marred the church's image. Mormons came to realize that in large measure, uncertainty and even fear surrounding their beliefs and rites may have gone dormant, but they had not disappeared. Thus Utah Senator Bob Bennett would say, "There have been more anti-Mormon comments made in the press than I expected."[34]

Even if they were unexpected to Mormons, these comments were representative of widely held impressions of the church, a reality confirmed in a church-sponsored qualitative study by the public relations firm APCO in the fall of 2007. After a series of "focus groups as well as in-depth interviews with" unnamed East Coast "opinion leaders," these researchers compiled a report rich in its revelations about the basis for many of the complaints against Mitt Romney.

Perhaps most striking about the study's conclusions was that "not a single person (including several theologians) could describe what happens at a Mormon service." This finding would have come as a shock to most Latter-day Saints, especially since their worship services have always been open to visitors and have always been informal and congregational in style. What the researchers discovered was that most people did not differentiate between the closed nature of LDS temples and the openness of local meetinghouses. At the center of this surprising unfamiliarity was the repeated "imagery [of being excluded from family members' Mormon weddings]." The seeming secrecy surrounding temple weddings "in particular serves as shorthand for the often-expressed view that Mormons are disinclined to provide information about the specifics of the faith and what goes on in a Mormon service." Interestingly, even though the "LDS Church [was] described as the most aggressive at outreach for proselytizing," that did not improve respondents' sense of familiarity with Mormon beliefs and practices. In fact, proselytizing "was generally associated with the hidden objectives" that outsiders saw driving Mormon efforts to "mainstream their religion in recent years" and achieve "elevated visibility." This led researchers to conclude that "real communication is lacking, and, for many, Mormons were disinclined to 'reach out to other religions,'" preferring instead to "interact with their co-religionists and their families rather than expose themselves to likely cultural criticism."[35]

What *had* come to be expected by Mormon image watchers was another thread that ran prominently throughout the church-commissioned study: once again, the same individuals who were wary of the church's institutional intentions were also "extraordinarily positive" in their "unprompted impressions of Mormons they knew." Interviewees described Mormons as "family oriented," possessing "strong moral values," "honest and trustworthy," "devout and committed," "achievement oriented," "committed to education," "charitable," "friendly," "wholesome," and "loving and caring." However, researchers found, "the Mormon Church is also associated strongly with archetypes that revolve around social observations rather than personal characteristics." This meant that the church as a whole was described as "clannish and closed off," "hierarchical," "white and socially homogenous," "intolerant of dissent, obedient," and "superficial, image conscious." Just as other observers had noted, these researchers found that "at a systemic level, then, suspicion and cynicism abounds. But at the personal or values level, Mormons are widely admired, even by those who are nominally uncomfortable with their presumed conservative views." Intriguingly, they also concluded, "This distinction was not applied to the discussion of *any other religious group*."[36]

These findings, and the apparent singularity with which they pertained to Mormonism, beg a question—why did this wide admiration for Mormons, an observable phenomenon, not translate readily into broad acceptance of the idea of a Mormon presidential candidate? Significantly, it seems that publicity surrounding the lifestyle of members of the LDS Church, undeniably an important part of the church's "brand," was not seen as "substantive," in the sense that such publicity did not necessarily produce an "awareness of key elements of Mormonism" sufficient to dispel doubts about the *real* Mormonism. In other words, as researchers put it succinctly, "For most, the LDS Church is defined by its controversies . . . by its reaction to issues that arise, or from stereotyped notions of what Mormons do." In retrospect, so much of the attention to Mormons in the late 1990s and early 2000s focused positively on notable Mormon individuals and their Mormon lifestyle. This shift in focus may have left the controversies of the 1980s and early 1990s sidelined, but it was now evident that it had not left them settled.[37]

Documentary Evidence

As all of this in 2007 swirled around Mitt Romney (who essentially became a proxy for his church), well-known filmmaker Helen Whitney premiered a landmark documentary on PBS venues *Frontline* and *American Experience* called, simply, *The Mormons*. This was an unprecedented feature—four hours over the course of two nights in prime time. The film had taken years to complete, and the church had offered remarkably full cooperation to Whitney and her crew. While it was not Mitt Romney's run that inspired the documentary (Whitney had started the project long before Romney's declared candidacy), the timing of its release could not have been more ideal in terms of capitalizing on the heightened interest in the faith. On the last night of April and the first night of May, viewers experienced what can best be described as a snapshot of American opinion of Mormons and Mormonism. All of the admiration and anxieties that Romney's run had brought to the surface seemed to find their way into Whitney's probing picture of The Church of Jesus Christ of Latter-day Saints.[38]

The first two hours of the film traced the church's history, from Joseph Smith's founding epiphanies, through his murder at Carthage, Illinois, to the Saints' establishment in the Intermountain West. The second two hours treated issues related to the contemporary church, including its role in missionary work, politics, and recent humanitarian efforts. Whitney sifted through an astounding number of interviews—she and "her crew spoke to at least 1,000 Mormon and other scholars, historians, as well as devout and dissident members" of the LDS Church—to piece together a portrayal that sought to provide a platform for multiple voices. "Helen gets us," was the opinion of former *Sunstone* editor Elbert Peck. "I've never known an outsider who has understood us so completely. She knows all sides of every controversy and is sympathetic to all of them." Ex-Mormon scholar D. Michael Quinn agreed. He spoke for many when he called Whitney's film "the finest documentary that has ever been done" on Mormonism, because she "drew on all of the constituencies."[39]

This almost universal praise for her thoroughgoing background work did not eliminate all dissatisfaction, however, as various "constituencies" debated over how much airtime their respective positions received in the finished product. Utah television reporter Chris Vanocur, for example, felt the documentary was "too positive in favor of the LDS Church and a more exposé-like approach was needed." In contrast, University of Richmond professor Terryl Givens, a prominent spokesman for the Mormon perspective on the documentary, called Whitney "an exceptionally gifted filmmaker" and concluded that her work mostly "achieved a good balance." Yet Givens, a bright star in Mormon studies with four successive books published by Oxford University Press, also reacted strongly against the seemingly inordinate time Whitney devoted to the tragic violence at Mountain Meadows and to polygamy, especially modern, fundamentalist polygamy. (Whitney herself "[acknowledged] that she had differences with PBS executives," and that while "filmmakers always want the final cut, . . . they don't get it.") Givens's objections mirrored the most commonly expressed concerns about the film from active Mormons—there was a problem with proportion. Whitney told the *Salt Lake Tribune* that she had "more than forty hours of film" to whittle down; Mormons wondered why, then, a full half-hour, one-eighth of the documentary, was devoted to polygamy in its nineteenth- and twenty-first-century incarnations, and another lengthy segment to the Mountain Meadows Massacre.[40]

Givens did not dispute that these elements needed to be included; he disputed their overemphasis. "It strikes me that one of the curiosities of media engagement with Mormonism is the assumption that there has to be two sides. Helen Whitney talked frequently about the need for balance and the need to present 'both sides.' It strikes me that if you're doing a documentary on the history of the Quakers nobody would talk about both sides. If you were studying the Presbyterians nobody would say you have to cover both sides. Why does one automatically assume or impose upon Mormonism a polarizing model of understanding? That has always struck me as anomalous and deserving of scrutiny."[41] It was this "polarizing" tendency that, in Givens's view, did "a grave disservice to the church in light of Helen's stated objective to get beyond the stereotypes. Nineteenth-century polygamy is part of Mormon history and deserves to be told. But there is no possible justification for including Warren Jeffs. It is a misrepresentation at best and defamation at worst."[42]

LDS Church Historian Marlin K. Jensen was one of a handful of Mormon general authorities who sat for interviews with Helen Whitney. While he felt that "any time you get four hours on PBS that is essentially positive material, I don't think you can hope for much more," he also acknowledged that several senior apostles were not "generally very happy with it," mostly because "some of the things were a little unbalanced." Elder Jensen said that because the church was willing "to cooperate" with Helen Whitney, she "became a great friend of the church." Still, he conceded that despite the number of books someone reads or interviews someone conducts, it is extremely difficult to "capture the essence of Mormonism" or "the strength of the church." That is why he felt non-Mormons gave the film more positive reviews than Mormons did, and why he rated the documentary an "overall...plus, especially for the non-Mormon audience."[43]

The "mixed reviews" by ambivalent Mormons that Elder Jensen described were not on the whole surprising, considering the contrasting images of the church that the documentary displayed. But it was in those contrasting images that Mormons gained insight into the current state of their public image.[44]

Some issues seemed to have diminished drastically in significance, changes, perhaps, that spoke to the effectiveness of church efforts to mitigate controversy. The documentary's discussion of blacks and the priesthood, for example, only occupied five minutes of the four-hour film, and the emphasis was on *internal* deliberations as the impetus for change rather than external or political pressures. In fact, the documentary highlighted the diversity of contemporary Mormonism as it told the story of Betty Stevenson, a black woman who was "a recovering addict recently out of prison" when she joined the LDS Church in Oakland, and then served as president of the Relief Society (the woman's auxiliary) in her congregation at the time of the film.[45]

This lack of controversy surrounding the race question (especially when compared to the time the film spent on polygamy) corresponded with what APCO researchers found in their October 2007 study of public perceptions of Mormonism. Remarkably, in all of their conversations with opinion leaders, "the race issue did not arise without prompting." Researchers thus concluded that not only "was the race issue...less well known," but it "was generally less problematic than polygamy because historical racism has been present in other faiths and organizations." In essence, in the public's mind, race-related controversies marked the history of nearly every church. This universality did not make racial inequities excusable, only more understandable, more relatable.[46]

So while racial issues were not seen as the unique legacy of Mormonism, polygamy was. Helen Whitney's film certainly reflected that, as did coverage of Mitt Romney's campaign. The history of Mormonism's priesthood prohibition did arise during the campaign, mentioned most prominently by the Reverend Al Sharpton, yet it was not the central Mormon issue in 2008 that it was in 1994 during Romney's Massachusetts Senate race. (In a 2011 nationwide survey conducted by Gary Lawrence's research firm, only 15% of respondents said "yes" when asked if "Mormons are racist"; 73% said "no.")[47]

Nor had the history of the priesthood restriction been the consistently conspicuous identity marker that polygamy had been. Researchers concluded from the APCO study that, "of course, polygamy remains a top-of-mind issue and is always mentioned as a problem." Terryl Givens's concern that the documentary was bound to perpetuate these stereotypes was therefore well reasoned. In 2006, when FLDS leader Warren Jeffs was on the FBI's "Ten Most Wanted" list, numerous stories inaccurately implied a link between Jeffs and the LDS Church. Two years later, in the midst of the 2008 presidential primaries, a child abuse scandal rocked the Texas temple compound of the Fundamentalist Church of Jesus Christ of Latter Day Saints (FLDS). Hundreds of children were taken into state custody, and the episode shot to the front pages of newspapers across the country. Mormon officials were dismayed by the results of a poll that showed that "36% of those surveyed thought the FLDS polygamous group was 'part of' The Church of Jesus Christ of Latter-day Saints and 29% said they were not sure." Because plural marriage was one of those shorthand descriptors that called to mind layers of Mormon oddity, reporters covering the Romney campaign repeatedly mentioned it. Therefore, even though, as one commentator noted, it was slightly ironic that Barack Obama's father was a polygamist, and Romney's closest polygamous progenitor was his great-grandfather, Senator Obama was not defined by (and especially not aligned with) his distant and mostly absentee father's belief system; but since Governor Romney still adhered to the faith of his fathers, he often *was* defined by that belief system. Many in the media (and Helen Whitney's documentary) focused almost exclusively on Mormon polygamy as a symbol for the religion's troubled past. Their repeated question was, in one form or another, "Could ancestors haunt Romney?"[48]

Mormon viewers were pleased to see in Helen Whitney's film positive portrayals of what Noah Feldman called the church's "public face." For example, an extensive segment on the church's relief efforts in the aftermath of Hurricane Katrina in 2005 cast an extremely favorable light on the church. "Mormon relief trucks were on their way before the hurricane had even made landfall," the documentary reported. A resident of the storm-ravaged area remembered that while U.S. troops and even the president were flying over the storm-ravaged area, "nobody was there on the ground with us except for the Mormons in their yellow T-shirts, who showed up to help us clean up.... They're part of my family now—always will be.... They got into my heart."[49]

This was welcome publicity, because even though the church had donated hundreds of millions of dollars' worth of humanitarian aid over the past two decades, and had done so in partnership with numerous other religious groups, the APCO study found that "the Church welfare program, being somewhat insular, is not well known." One Jewish leader interviewed as part of that study said, "I know [Mormons] have a relatively high standard of living. And, unlike Catholics, they do very little, if any, outreach to the poor."[50] The church's Public Affairs Department admitted that this was a difficult misperception to dispel, since seeking accolades for the good work that it tried to accomplish could come off as mercenary. However, Mormon leaders also recognized the importance of correcting the mistaken view that Mormons only took care of their own, since this notion only reinforced stereotypes about Mormon clannishness and reflected unfamiliarity with the church. (That was certainly the case after Hurricane Andrew, when "one local official thanked the many who helped in the cleanup, including members of the Mormon Church and members of The Church of Jesus Christ of Latter-day Saints"!) To walk this fine publicity line, the church had adopted a standardized "Mormon Helping Hands" logo on brightly colored T-shirts to give their volunteers a recognizable look, and then decided to "[let] media attention come as a natural byproduct of the efforts themselves" rather than "[trying] to force this awareness as some kind of missionary push or as an effort to seek public validation." Helen Whitney's spotlighting of these efforts was a "natural [publicity] byproduct" that Mormons were happy to accept.[51]

Less favorable pictures of Mormonism's "private face," though, made Mormon viewers squirm during the documentary. They heard in the film echoes of those voices that were simultaneously expressing hesitation about a Mormon presidential candidate. There was Yale University anthropologist Michael Coe, in the opening minutes of the film, characterizing Joseph Smith, like all "shamans," as a "faker" whose "sense of destiny" led him to claim the divine communication that made his creation believable. Another lasting image was classics scholar Margaret Toscano's description of the church council that resulted in her excommunication. As she recounted what she felt was the intimidating male dominance of the procedure, the cameras panned to an austere room with wooden chairs set up in an arrangement reminiscent of an inquisition. It was obvious to Mormons that this was not how such councils are conducted, but this "misimpression" (in Elder Jensen's words) had the apparently intended effect of reinforcing criticisms about Mormon intolerance and hierarchical control. Tal Bachman's commentary about his missionary service in Argentina struck an equally emotional chord. The son of Canadian rocker and Mormon convert

Randy Bachman (of The Guess Who and then Bachman Turner Overdrive), Tal explained that his immersion in, and commitment to, the missionary experience was so complete that he would have blown himself up "like a suicide bomber" if his superiors had told him to do so. Mormons cringed at this unmistakable allusion to extremism and terrorism, especially as Bachman explained that he later left the church after he came to feel that it was all a human invention, albeit an invention that inspired its followers to lead better lives.

Helen Whitney's *Mormons* was memorable for all of these reasons, but perhaps its strongest contribution was in the way that it allowed thoughtful outsiders to vocalize their thoughts on where Mormonism was situated on the nation's public opinion landscape. In the first two-hour segment, respected historian Jon Butler spoke about the early persecution that Mormons experienced in a number of locales. Yet his comments seemed as applicable to the presidential campaign of 2008 as they did to the Hawn's Mill Massacre of 1838: "The hatred of Mormonism is mysterious. It's fascinating. It's perplexing. Mormons were plain old white, largely English-descended American farmers who were God-fearing, lived in agricultural settlements, and wanted the best for their children, for their wives, for their families. Why would they be so hated? It has to do with the fear of the unknown, fear of power and hierarchy. Did the Mormons really think for themselves, or did Joseph Smith think for them? The fear of unknown personal practices, polygamy, the fear of unknown beliefs—all of these things made the Mormons feared. It made Americans worry about them. And yet underneath, there is still something else that's hard to get at. There's still something else about Mormons that seems so odd, so peculiar, and yet it's difficult to put a historian's finger on what that is."[52]

Only two weeks after the documentary's initial broadcast, the Pew Forum on Religion and Public Life invited Mormon historian and Joseph Smith biographer Richard Bushman to speak to a panel of journalists and academics on the topic "Mormonism and Democratic Politics: Are They Compatible?" During the lively question-and-answer session that followed Bushman's remarks, Sally Quinn of the *Washington Post* made some revealing comments about the challenges that have repeatedly dogged the Mormon image. She told of reading two memoirs by Martha Beck, a Harvard-educated Mormon woman who left Boston when she found out that she was expecting a baby with Down syndrome. She and her husband sought the community support for their decision to continue this pregnancy that they knew they would find in Utah but that they did not find at Harvard. However, as Sally Quinn recalled, Beck "had an absolutely horrendous experience" in Utah. Beck tried "to fit in" as a teacher at Brigham Young University, but "found that the church was very unaccepting, very dogmatic, and she couldn't teach what she wanted to teach. Because she spoke out against some of the beliefs, she was in effect banned or banished from the church," and eventually left Mormonism and moved to Arizona.[53]

Quinn's next comments were perhaps the most telling: "I think that read-ing a book like that—I have no knowledge of Mormons at all, really, but read-ing Martha's books, I was absolutely appalled at some of the things that I read about the Mormon Church and the closed-mindedness and demands on people that they adhere to their beliefs or they will get banished."[54] Before Professor Bushman could respond to Quinn's query, John Wilson of *Books and Culture* entered the conversation. He pointed out that from his experience of reading "a lot of…memoirs in the last 20 years," including Beck's books, the ones that "have gotten the most attention" often "turned out to be downright hoaxes." He raised a "red flag" of credibility with Beck's work, too, since he pointed out, "oddly enough, the author did not mention the fact that she and her husband both came out—he as gay and she as lesbian." This "context" had obvious bear-ing, in Wilson's view, since "whether you think the official Mormon teaching on that is right or wrong, it is very clear what the teaching is"; Wilson's point was that Beck's orientation—not clear in the memoir—would color her treatment of the LDS Church.[55]

Like Wilson, Professor Bushman felt "some of the factual basis of it is thrown into doubt." But Bushman went further. "In terms of shunning, this is a kind of stereotype of the way religious communities work," but "if you lived in a Mormon community, you wouldn't feel like this was happening all of the time, that peo-ple were in danger of being shunned." He admitted that "there are examples," and that this could be "a sort of mixture of her own paranoia with some actual actions," yet "it would be very hard to persuade any Mormon that anything like that goes on."[56]

Still, the reality was, Sally Quinn (and undoubtedly others like her) had their only exposure to Mormonism in books like these. (Significantly, within a few years of this exchange, LDS spokesman Michael Otterson was invited to join, as a contributor, the *Washington Post* blog *On Faith*, a blog that Sally Quinn founded and moderated.) Quinn said about Beck's book, "I think that kind of story is where a lot of these perceptions come from. I don't know whether every word she wrote was true or not. It sounded pretty true." This led Quinn to ask, "How Mormon is Mitt Romney? I mean, is he someone who would adhere to all of the beliefs of the church? In Martha Beck's case, when she went against church policy, she was banned or banished. Would that happen if Romney dis-agreed with the church, and particularly their positions on women?"[57]

"There Are Some for Whom These Commitments Are Not Enough"

There was another group of Americans who, like Sally Quinn, also wondered, "How Mormon is Mitt Romney?" This group, though, unlike Sally Quinn and many of her colleagues, possessed substantial knowledge about Mormons. For them, it was not the unknown that they feared. It was the token of legitimacy that Mitt Romney's victory could give to his faith. Millions of Americans who counted themselves in the ranks of the Religious Right were extremely troubled at the thought of casting such a vote. [58]

In contrast to those liberal commentators and journalists for whom the very idea of religious devotion seemed to signal irrationality or instability, a powerful, conservative constituency within the Republican Party valued a candidate's religiosity above almost anything else. The Pew Research Center reported in September 2007 that 44% of Republicans "completely agree that it is important for the president to have strong religious beliefs." Only 26% of Democrats and 23% of independents felt that same way. In this survey, Mitt Romney was "the candidate seen as far and away the most religious," yet here was the irony that would haunt Mitt Romney's campaign, especially among those who should have been his "natural allies." Pew researchers concluded that "the political benefit Romney receives from this perception [of his religiosity] is being offset by the concerns that some voters express about Mormonism." In a surprise to outsiders who saw Mormons and evangelicals as conservatives cut from the same cloth, 36% of "white Republican evangelical Protestants ... express reservations about voting for a Mormon." In Richard Bushman's words, Mormons' (and Romney's) "natural allies, which are all conservative Christians, refuse to accept them as allies, and that makes it very difficult."[59]

Some commentators noted that conservative opposition to Romney, especially on the basis of religion, seemed more surprising than did opposition from liberal quarters. After all, it was understandable that those on the political left would take issue with a candidate whose position on social issues appeared faith-based and uncompromising. But opposition from the right on those same counts? For observers who were acquainted with the long-running conflict between Mormons and evangelicals, however, it came as no surprise that the ugliness of this decades-long debate would smear the 2008 election cycle. Yet many evangelicals seemed just as conflicted about their opposition to Mitt Romney's candidacy for religious reasons as did journalists and liberal pundits who were embarrassed to be administering a de facto religious test for office. It was difficult for many evangelicals to justify their rejection of a candidate who seemed to match their values and aims so well. In the end, though, that rejection said much about the state of Mormon/evangelical relations.[60]

Because evangelical Christianity is neither a monolithic body of believers nor a religion centered under one organizational head, outspoken evangelicals expressed a variety of opinions about Mitt Romney and the idea of a Mormon candidate generally. Hugh Hewitt asked two prominent evangelical professors at Biola University in Southern California if they could vote for a Mormon for president. Professor John Mark Reynolds answered, "Yes, absolutely, and I think that having Mormonism be a disqualifier for office is inappropriate." Professor Craig Hazen, who had participated in academic dialogue with Mormon scholars, also answered, "I would." Emerging reports of stark evangelical repudiations of a Mormon presidential candidate even drove one evangelical writer to team with a Mormon on their new blog, "Article VI," in support of Mitt Romney. Yet on the other side, the loudest rumblings came from reports like that of Robert Novak, who wrote in April 2006 that "prominent, respectable Evangelical Christians had told [him]...that millions of their co-religionists cannot and will not vote for Romney for President solely because he is a member of The Church of Jesus Christ of Latter-day Saints."[61]

When these Christians explained their reasons for refusing to consider a Mormon candidate, it became clear that *The God Makers*–type of anti-Mormonism enjoyed continued vigor. Ted Haggard, president of the National Association of Evangelicals, said, "We evangelicals view Mormons as a Christian cult group. A cult group is a group that claims exclusive revelation. And typically, it's hard to get out of these cult groups. And so Mormonism qualifies as that." Still more extreme were the comments of Reverend Bill Keller on his website, LivePrayer.com, when he called a vote for Romney "a vote for Satan.... Romney getting elected president will ultimately lead millions of souls to the eternal flames of hell!!!" No matter that Romney looked and acted like a Christian; "Mr. Romney, like all members of his satanic cult, is a liar. A liar!"[62]

Even those Christians who were not as willing to endorse brash statements like those of Reverend Keller nevertheless admitted to worries over legitimizing Mormonism. Mormons and non-Mormons alike recognized that electing a Mormon president would open a new era for public interest and investigation into Mormonism. At the same time, having a Mormon in the nation's highest office would drastically diminish the religion's "weirdness." For many Christians, this spelled disaster, as such public acceptance was bound to open new doors for Mormon proselytizers. Already evangelicals were worried that to the undiscerning outsider, Mormonism was indistinguishable from evangelical Christianity. Ted Olsen in *Christianity Today* said in 2006, "With their strong family values, constant Jesus talk, and passion for evangelism, Mormons seem almost like evangelicals' cultural twins. In some ways, they represent our ideal." Olsen suggested that this made conservative Christians uncomfortable, since they preferred their "differences stark." After all, they saw themselves as competing with Mormons for the same converts. This meant that even though obviously "Judaism is not a Christian faith...most Southern Baptists had absolutely no problem with an observant Jew running for vice president," said Richard Land, president of the Southern Baptist Convention's Ethics and Religious Liberty Commission, in February 2007. "The difference [between Judaism and Mormonism] is that Judaism is not an actively evangelistic faith." Even though Land had earlier offered provisional support for the idea of a Mormon candidate, he lamented the following November that "there are now more Mormons that used to be Southern Baptists than any other denomination." For many, all matters of political agreement were trumped by concerns over eternal salvation.[63]

This was clear in reaction to a May 2007 *Christianity Today* piece co-written by BYU professor Robert Millet (a Mormon) and Roanoke College professor of religion Gerald McDermott (an evangelical). Their basic premise was that the nation was not electing a "theologian-in-chief," and that "Mormon beliefs are not as un-evangelical as most evangelicals think." The two reported that "doctrinal distance between Mormons and evangelicals...has not stopped important evangelical leaders—such as Richard Land, the late Jerry Falwell, Franklin Graham, Chuck Colson, and Cal Thomas—from saying that these doctrinal differences should not by themselves disqualify Romney from a presidential nomination." Yet the broadminded opinions of these national leaders and interfaith dialogue participants did not necessarily represent, or sway, opinions at the grass roots. The article quickly generated eighty-five mostly blistering online responses. One reader wrote, "What a disgrace to *Christianity Today* for posting such rhetoric and lies on their site." Another added, "This article stunned me! I could hardly believe my eyes when I saw who authored the same." The seriousness with which many evangelicals approached this issue was evident in this response: "As a 'magazine of evangelical conviction,' *Christianity Today* owes its readers a Biblical perspective, not one that paints Christians as hate mongers when they expose Mormon teachings...[This article] did not say that the Mormon belief system could cost someone their eternal soul! This is too high a price to be 'politically correct.'"[64]

Some evangelicals did attempt political correctness, or at least preferred to disguise their anti-Mormonism behind other issues (as some commentators saw it), simply because it sounded too blatantly bigoted to say that they would not even consider voting for a Mormon. Dan Bartlett, "a former White House advisor, suggested that the 'flip-flop' label may have actually been covering up the real problem—Romney's Mormonism." Bartlett reasoned, "People are not going to step out and say, 'I have a problem with Romney because he's a Mormon.' What they're going to say is he's a flip-flopper." His observations matched a study conducted by Vanderbilt and Claremont Graduate University researchers. They found that "26% of those who accused Romney of flip-flopping also indicated that Mormonism, not flip-flopping, was their real problem with Romney." Fifty-seven percent of respondents who identified themselves as evangelicals admitted "a bias against Mormons." Denver Seminary Professor Craig Blomberg was not surprised with this anti-Romney vitriol, because despite his (and others') decade of friendly collaboration with Mormon scholars, he was unconvinced that these "theological conversations" were having a "trickle-down effect" on local churchgoers. As Utah pastor Greg Johnson put it, "*God Makers* and that genre of material are still alive and well."[65]

Conservative Christian voters faced a thorny paradox as they contemplated a Mormon candidate. Many of them worried that liberal elements wanted to marginalize the political participation of openly religious individuals. This meant that evangelical opposition to Romney's candidacy might only further the aims of anti-religion activists. Hugh Hewitt's colleague Dean Barnett had warned in response to Jacob Weisberg's *Slate* piece that "if members of other religious communities support the attacks on Romney's faith because of some animus towards Mormonism, the weapon they legitimize will in short order be turned against them."[66]

Yet supporting the campaign of a man whose faith seemed heretical gave them pause, too. Even some of the Christian leaders who backed Romney reflected that tentativeness. Bob Jones III was a good example. He announced in October 2007 that he endorsed Mitt Romney. "As a Christian I am completely opposed to the doctrines of Mormonism," Dr. Jones told *USA Today*. "But I'm not voting for a preacher. I'm voting for a president. It boils down to who can best represent conservative American beliefs, not religious beliefs."[67] Professor Blomberg said of Bob Jones's endorsement, "If it would have been physiologically possible my jaw would have dropped to the ground. I didn't think I would hear that in my life time. It became very clear that political issues had trumped religious issues, which the last time I checked is what political campaigns are supposed to be about." Still, it soon became equally clear that political issues did not trump religious issues for everyone.[68]

In the same month that Jones gave his support to Romney, *Newsweek* reported that the Mormon candidate was leading in the polls in New Hampshire and Iowa. Things had never looked more promising for Mitt Romney, despite the rumors and innuendos swirling around his campaign and his church. Something Bob Jones said at the time of his endorsement, though, carried a hint of foreboding. *USA Today* asked him "whether Romney's religion was a stumbling block for him." Dr. Jones answered, "What is the alternative, Hillary's lack of religion or an erroneous religion?" In the weeks to come, especially in states like Iowa and South Carolina, what many evangelical Christians found *was* an alternative, a way to oppose Romney's Mormonism *and* still support an avowedly religious candidate. They voted for former Arkansas governor and Baptist minister Mike Huckabee.[69]

Before Huckabee's surprise emergence, many pundits saw the pool of electable conservative Republicans as rather shallow. Early frontrunner Rudy Giuliani had what many Christians saw as a checkered family background, and he was pro-choice on abortion. Senator John McCain (eventually the party's nominee) was often dismissed as too old and an untrustworthy "maverick." His campaign seemed to lack the financial backers he would need to win. Television star and former Senator Fred Thompson generated some initial excitement, but when his official entrance in the race was plagued by delays and indecision, voters quickly cooled to him. A number of insiders saw Romney as the favorite, citing his business success, his proven leadership in turning around a scandal- and debt-ridden Salt Lake Olympics, and his very visible commitment to family and faith. Throughout the ups and downs of 2007, "Romney was the only Republican candidate the media consistently treated as viable."[70]

Romney won, as expected, the pre-primary Iowa straw poll in August 2007. He had spent considerable time and money on his campaign there, and he enjoyed a large lead. Yet it still was clear that none of the candidates, Romney included, had roused the conservative Christian wing of the Republican Party. Governor Huckabee skillfully stepped into that void. As the fall of 2007 progressed, Mike Huckabee made up ground in the polls by appealing to Iowa evangelical base. Though Huckabee's campaign seemed woefully underfunded, he made good use of the resources he did have, scheduling meetings with groups of pastors and employing evangelical superstars like best-selling *Left Behind* author Tim LaHaye.[71]

As it became obvious that Romney's lead was shrinking, Huckabee spoke openly about his religious convictions. He ran commercials with this statement: "Faith doesn't just influence me. It really defines me." He stressed his affinity with conservative Christians: "Let us never sacrifice our principles for anybody's politics. Not now, not ever." Then came the blow in December 2007 that made the former Arkansas governor infamous among Mormons. Huckabee asked a reporter, "Don't Mormons believe that Jesus and the devil are brothers?" While he later tried to say to Utah radio host Doug Wright that these famous "eleven [sic] words were completely misconstrued," and that he "[had] never said anything unkind about Mormons," to Latter-day Saints it was obvious that Huckabee had dredged up one of *The God Makers'* prime charges.[72]

Governor Huckabee apologized to the Romney camp after the quote appeared in the *New York Times Magazine*, saying that "he never thought his query would appear in the story," and he was only repeating something "he had heard." His purportedly off-handed question seemed more than a little disingenuous to some observers, though, especially since he had just answered the reporter's question as to whether he considered "Mormonism a cult or a religion" with, "I think it's a religion...I really don't know much about it." That surprised some observers who remembered that Governor Huckabee delivered a keynote address to the Southern Baptist Convention in 1998 in Salt Lake City, the same convention at which reporters were given a book called *Mormonism Unmasked*.[73] While the campaign staffs of senators McCain and Brownback had also distributed materials that raised questions about Mormon beliefs, Huckabee's carefully casual comment ("asked in an innocent voice," the reporter said) seemed more strategically potent, especially considering his evangelical credentials. Huckabee, it seemed, had struck a widely resonant chord. In a telling headline, The *New York Times* proclaimed that "Huckabee Is Not Alone in Ignorance on Mormonism," and that ignorance offered an opportunity to capitalize on voter uncertainty. Kirk Jowers called Huckabee's approach "probably the most craven use of anti-Mormonism," noting that "it knocked Mitt from his pedestal and it was the beginning of the end there."[74]

Mitt Romney's response at the time was that "attacking someone's religion is really going too far. It's just not the American way, and I think people will reject that."[75] Unfortunately for the Romney camp, Iowa voters did not reject Mike Huckabee or his tactics, at least not in enough numbers to preserve Romney's lead. What did come through loud and clear in Iowa was Huckabee's appeal among those voters who recognized in him, and even in his insinuation about Mormonism, a "coded language to evangelicals."[76] Romney finished second to Huckabee in Iowa's early January 2008 caucuses, and then second to a resurgent John McCain in New Hampshire's primary election. These runner-up finishes in two states where he had recently enjoyed such a strong lead—and where he had devoted so many resources—were described by media observers as "bitter" and "humiliating" losses.[77] Romney's momentum, that all-important political commodity, slowed accordingly. Though he did win the Michigan primary and the Nevada caucus voting, he only came in fourth in South Carolina, another state where evangelical voters had long expressed reservations about choosing a Mormon candidate. Mitt Romney had one more hope—success on Super Tuesday, February 5, when a number of states held primary elections. Prospects that day quickly turned grim, however, beginning in West Virginia. Mitt Romney had led the delegate count on the first ballot of caucus voting, but then John McCain's team instructed his supporters to give their votes to Huckabee on the second ballot, who thus had enough votes to secure a majority victory. The day ended on a down note for Romney, as well, even though he had won in seven states (including a 90% majority in Utah). Delegate-rich California went to John McCain. Instead of delaying what many saw as inevitable, Romney surprised some supporters, but endeared himself to the party faithful, by quickly announcing his withdrawal from the presidential campaign two days later. No Mormon had ever come so close to the nation's highest office. Still, as Romney's campaign closed, many Mormons were surprised at how far they felt from public acceptance. Filmmaker Helen Whitney had essentially predicted that emotion nearly a year earlier. She said that "PBS officials urged her to add [Romney] to her film about Mormons" because, as she observed, "he's emblematic of how far the Mormons have come and the distance they have to go."[78]

Apparitions and Aftermath

Repeatedly during Mitt Romney's campaign, commentators used two historical figures as benchmarks against which Mormonism's public image journey was measured. Allusions to John F. Kennedy and George Romney offered a basis for evaluating the state of Mormonism's wider reputation. In both cases, the parallels seemed obvious—perhaps more important, so did the differences.

It was only natural that profiles of Mitt Romney would invite comparisons to Kennedy, another Massachusetts politician whose presidential aspirations met with religiously motivated resistance. Because both belonged to faith groups whose trustworthiness was questioned by Protestant Americans, everyone wondered if Mitt Romney would make a "Houston speech" similar to the one that candidate Kennedy made in 1960 to dispel concerns over Rome's potential control of the White House. "I do not speak for my church on public matters," Kennedy had emphasized, "and the church does not speak for me." He promised that he "would resign the office" of the presidency rather than put his personal beliefs or "outside religious pressures or dictates" ahead of the "national interest."[79]

In December 2007, a month before the first primaries, Romney finally did acquiesce to the growing number of voices calling for him to make a comparable statement about his religious beliefs. His speech was titled "Faith in America." Romney, like Kennedy, strenuously denied suggestions that a religious hierarchy would dictate his policies. "Let me assure you," he said, "that no authorities of my church, or of any other church for that matter, will ever exert influence on presidential decisions." Like Kennedy, Romney focused less on Mormon beliefs and more on the American ideal of religious liberty. However, unlike Kennedy— and this was significant—Romney felt compelled to express his belief in Jesus Christ as "the Son of God and the Savior of mankind." He realistically told his audience at the George H. W. Bush Presidential Library that "there are some for whom these commitments are not enough."[80] In that, he proved to be prophetic, for unlike JFK, Mitt Romney could not seem to rise above what he himself called the religious "comma problem"—everywhere he was referred to as "Mitt Romney, a Mormon." No less an insider than Michael Steele, chairman of the Republican National Committee, told a radio call-in show a year after the election that his party "rejected Mitt because it had issues with Mormonism."[81]

A number of other commentators proved equally prophetic in connection with Romney's speech. Peggy Fletcher Stack of the *Salt Lake Tribune*, for example, took exception to journalist Kenneth Woodward's early call for Romney to explain his religious beliefs. She reacted, "It's not up to him to explain Mormonism to the country. That is not his job, and the second he starts down that path, he is in quicksand." Historian Laurie Maffly-Kipp agreed. She wrote in August 2007, "Even if Romney were to explain his religious beliefs at length, I doubt that most people would feel more at ease. It is hard to imagine that anything Romney says on the subject would be taken at face value by the many Americans already predisposed to be suspicious of the LDS Church." In the end, those who expected that Romney's explanatory speech—any speech, for that matter—would leave many Americans unsatisfied guessed right. National Public Radio's Howard Berkes talked with Phil Roberts, president of the Midwestern Baptist Theological Seminary, who described "the basic Mormon tactic" as "stay simple,... use the same expressions,... [give]... the impression of a similar if not the same belief system." However, Roberts felt that the approach would "backfire" for Romney, since after the speech, "people will now be asking themselves the question, well, what does he really believe? He didn't articulate it fully. Let's see if we can find out."[82]

It was in this sense of uncertainty and skepticism, or in the misgivings inherent in Mike Huckabee's insinuation about Mormon heterodoxy, that one could detect what historian Jon Butler called that "something else about Mormons that seems so odd, so peculiar." In part because of this, Romney did not succeed in the same way that Kennedy did. This was also a reflection of the differences in how conservative Protestant Christians have viewed Roman Catholicism and Mormonism. While many Protestants believe that the Catholic Church may have corrupted or squandered its spiritual inheritance, they nevertheless share with Catholicism a belief in the Christianity of the early creeds, creeds that defined the Trinity and the nature of Jesus Christ. Indeed, Protestants trace their theological genealogy through the Catholic Church. They do not feel, though, any such affinity with Mormons, who claim to have restored pristine Christianity after other denominations, Catholic *and* Protestant, fell into apostasy. A wayward relative was one thing; a heretical outsider was another.[83]

Yet the limited effectiveness of Romney's speech was perhaps more a product of a momentous change in the political climate of the United States. Observers often drew comparisons with Mitt's father, George Romney, to illustrate that fundamental transformation. Two *Newsweek* reporters recreated a memorable image of the two Romneys. In the fall of 1994, when Senator Ted Kennedy had made Mitt's Mormonism an issue during the Senate race, the elder Romney stood with his son at a press conference. After the younger Romney had fielded a number of questions dealing with the religious issue, "George seized the microphone: 'I think it is absolutely wrong to keep hammering on the religious issue.'" The *Newsweek* reporters, in remembering that moment, rightly noted that George Romney had been "shredded by the press during his presidential run, but not on account of his religion." George Romney's annoyance at what he saw as unfair treatment of his son could not, however, change the reality that "in the three decades since [he] had last run for office, religious issues had moved to the center of American politics."[84]

The political ascendancy of the Religious Right during the four decades between the respective Romney runs gave that Christian constituency significant clout in the Republican Party. The problem for Mormons generally and for Romney specifically was that many, many Americans (perhaps 35–40% of adults) considered themselves evangelical Christians, more than any other religious affiliation—and only a decided minority of evangelicals saw Mormons as Christians. This numerical advantage made Mormons appear "disproportionately disliked in these polls."[85] For Jay Tolson of *USA Today*, in a conversation with Mormon apostle M. Russell Ballard in 2007, the impact of the evangelical vote was undeniable. "We probably wouldn't have had this discussion of Mormon theology 40 years ago when George Romney, Mitt's father, made a brief run for the presidency," Tolson observed. "But the evangelical upsurge and the return to orthodoxy in recent years have made people more aware of creeds and beliefs. As a result, there are many Christians who call themselves orthodox, whether Protestant or Catholic, who consider your theology heretical, even in some of the same ways that the beliefs of the ancient Gnostic Christians were thought to be heretical." Indeed, Mitt Romney's campaign felt the political potency of Christian conservatives, a group that carried remarkable weight in several key state Republican parties and resisted full political partnership with Mormons for religious reasons—something that did not figure into George Romney's campaign.[86]

The fact that religion now played a central role in the public square meant that people not only talked about Mitt Romney's Mormonism *more* than they did his father's faith, but they also talked about it *differently*. Since 1968, a number of Mormon moments in the national spotlight had given the LDS Church unprecedented visibility. One result of this increased attention was that many more Americans in 2008 had a point of reference from which to judge Mormonism than they did in 1968, even if that point of reference was a vague familiarity with a Mormon celebrity or controversy. An awareness of Mormon celebrities often centered on the Latter-day Saints lifestyle, while an awareness of Mormon controversies often centered on the church's distinctive past. This meant that many Americans could associate Mormonism with a new (usually positive) trademark, like family solidarity, along with an old (usually negative) one, like polygamy.

The prevalence of this image dichotomy came into focus most clearly when President Gordon B. Hinckley died only a week before Super Tuesday. Joel Campbell, a professor at BYU and a columnist who writes on Mormonism in the media, characterized "99% of the coverage of President Hinckley's death [as] indeed positive." In a lengthy tribute, National Public Radio suggested that Hinckley would be "remembered for changing the way Mormons and their church were presented to the world." Jan Shipps credited him with "moving [Mormonism] from the margins to the mainstream."[87]

Yet this public praise for Gordon B. Hinckley coincided with public reservations about the political and ecclesiastical aspirations of the church he had led. This was the Mormon perception paradox—widespread respect for undisputed individual morality coexisting with a surprisingly pervasive uncertainty about the group's defining mentality. Jan Shipps called it "the difference between the Olympics image and today's image."[88] In that vein, it seemed reasonable to see

President Hinckley as personifying the "Olympics image" and Mitt Romney as symbolizing "today's image." President Hinckley exuded friendliness and optimism, kindness and humanitarianism. These were the qualities that many Americans saw in their Mormon neighbors across the country. Mitt Romney, in contrast, became the lightning rod for strikes against a church that many saw as defined by its unusual past and unsettling practices. The episodes of intense interest in Mormonism in the years since George Romney's presidential run meant that the church's story received frequent retellings. Since what was odd or unexpected often proved most memorable, the repetition of this story gave certain themes—polygamy, temple secrecy—significant staying power in the public's mind. As they watched the reappearance of these issues mar that "Olympics image," Latter-day Saints learned again during Mitt Romney's campaign that some demons were difficult to exorcize.

Still, as surprising as the persistent prejudice against Mormons and Mitt Romney may have been for Latter-day Saints who had hoped that such hostility was in the past, the negative publicity did not douse all optimism that Mitt Romney's campaign could in the long run become another step forward in bridging what Latter-day Saints saw as this public perception gap. For good reason, church officials had remained mostly silent about Mitt Romney's run for the Republican nomination. They wanted to avoid any impression that they were driving his campaign or influencing his decisions. Apostle M. Russell Ballard went so far as to say to USA Today, "There's a real brick wall between the campaign and the church." After Romney had withdrawn from the race, however, Elder Ballard, chairman of the church's Public Affairs Committee, spoke more freely about "the attention, including the negative images" that came with the campaign—all of which he characterized "as an opportunity." He reasoned, "We're trying to overcome some of these biases and bigotry. The only way people are going to better understand is if they have an opportunity to talk to us." In that respect, he said, "I'd much rather have people talking about us than ignoring us." It seemed a brave face for a brave, new reality about the unvarnished state of Mormon image challenges.[89]

National reaction to the candidacy of a "thoroughgoing Mormon" revealed perhaps more clearly than it had been revealed for years that, as Jan Shipps put it, "Mormons are part of the cultural mainstream, but they have not been and are not part of the religious mainstream." If defining the problem was the first step to tackling it, the optimism expressed by Elder Ballard at the close of Romney's campaign becomes more understandable. If Mormon culture and lifestyle had achieved acceptability in American society, Mormon religious beliefs, which are not so easily depicted or explained, were still clearly suspect. This discrepancy between the gains the church had made, and the challenges it still faced, made an exchange between Richard Bushman and Newsweek's Kenneth Woodward in May 2007 especially relevant to the immediate future of Mormonism's public image. When Bushman asked Woodward if reporters who asked religion-related questions of Mitt Romney should ask equivalent questions of Senator John McCain, Woodward was quick with his response: "I don't think so. I think this is the Mormon time at bat. It will have to be done once, it seems to me, and then it won't have to be done again."[90]

Mormons, and Americans in general, would not have to wait long to test Woodward's power of prognostication. Only four years later, not one but two Mormons contended for the presidency.

10

"I Don't Think This Is Really 'a Moment'": Proposition 8, Plays on Broadway, Presidential Campaigns in 2012—and Paradoxes

For Mormons, getting a handle on the public's perception of their faith can sometimes feel like tracking the progress of a polar expedition. The complicating factor is that the expedition moves, but so does the ice, the "ground" beneath them.[1] Sometimes what appears to be movement in a seemingly desirable direction meets with the reality of reversal, thanks to unexpected currents. Many Latter-day Saints felt that the ground had moved under their feet in unexpected ways in 2008. Their sense of setback begged a question: Why did the attention on Mitt Romney in 2008 *not* fit the trend that had seemed so apparent in the recent history of the Mormon image—the trend that suggested that even while opinions of the LDS institution tended toward the negative, opinions of LDS individuals had been consistently more positive?

The simple answer is that many Americans—and these were very vocal Americans—saw a vote for Mitt Romney as a vote for institutional Mormonism. Because of the inescapable symbolism of the U.S. presidency, this vote came to represent for some a referendum on the religion itself. This was a question of trustworthiness and acceptability. When people spoke warmly of Mormons as good neighbors or hard-working humanitarians or honest businesspeople, a level of live-and-let-live detachment was still possible. For many, however, the universal connection, real or figurative, of every American and every American institution to the presidential office made such detachment impossible. A vote for Mitt Romney for president would be in some way a gesture of personal assent to place power in the hands of a man loyal to an institution whose credibility was, in many eyes, far from established or settled. What this meant is that for a large number of voters, it made no sense to talk about Mitt Romney as an *individual* separate from the institutional church. The deepest reality—and this came to the fore in 2007 and 2008—was that for a sizable segment of Americans, active, believing Mormons were inseparable from their church. When push came to shove, Mormons *were* identical to their institution, and no degree of political correctness or personal affection could be allowed to muddy those waters.

And because in Mitt Romney's particular case politics were involved, the faith question took on special urgency. Historic fears of Mormons' theocratic ambitions contributed to a latent suspicion that Mitt Romney, as a loyal Latter-day Saint, would be submissive to the goals and aims that came out of Salt Lake City. Jane Barnes, who co-wrote Helen Whitney's 2007 PBS documentary *The Mormons*, suggested in the *New York Times* that Romney's 2007 speech on religion troubled her more than reassured her: "In 1960, as a presidential candidate, John F. Kennedy declared his absolute belief in separation of church and state, but also in an America 'where no religious body seeks to impose its will directly or indirectly upon the general populace or the public.' In his 2007 speech on religion, Mitt Romney only said that no authorities of his church would 'exert influence on presidential decisions.' What if the church illegally used its money and influence to defeat Roe v. Wade or to pass the Federal Marriage Amendment while Romney was president? Would he protest from the Oval Office? Or would he be a sheep?"[2]

What this said to Mormons could be summed up in a comment made in March 2010 by LDS Church Historian Marlin K. Jensen. He highlighted just how difficult and unpredictable traveling on the floes of public opinion can be. "Over the twenty-one years that I have been [an LDS Church general authority]," he said, "I don't know if we have made much headway or not."[3]

Some context gives his statement added significance. Elder Jensen was named to the church's hierarchy in 1989, at a time when *the God Makers* and Mark Hofmann turbulence still rumbled in the distance, and a new tempest, this one triggered by the controversial excommunications of a number of Mormon fundamentalists and academics, was just about to break over Salt Lake City. Considering that background, Elder Jensen's evaluation of the church's progress—or lack thereof—speaks to a sense that the same outside wariness that swirled around Mormonism at the end of the 1980s had not dissipated two decades later. "I think the degree of suspicion and misunderstanding that was manifest [during Mitt Romney's 2008 campaign] took everyone here by surprise," Jensen continued, especially after "all of the efforts through the years of missionaries, media offerings, and President Hinckley's great efforts as probably our best public affairs person ever."[4]

Importantly, it seems apparent that the lack of headway Elder Jensen referred to was *not* about name recognition. There is little question that in recent decades, Mormons have made significant gains in that direction. In 1977, almost 29% of respondents to a Gallup poll chose the "don't know the name" option when asked an opinion about "Mormons/Latter-day Saints." Thirty years later, the story was completely different. Pollster Gary Lawrence determined in February 2008 that 98% of Americans "have heard of Mormons." Public awareness of Mormons and Mormonism had likely never been higher in the United States than it was after Mitt Romney's first presidential campaign, and some identifying markers were more indelibly imprinted on the Mormon brand than ever before.[5]

Many of these impressions resulted from successful public relations campaigns that the church had initiated over the years, and telltale hints of that success often cropped up in unexpected places. During the 2007 edition of college football's annual Georgia vs. Florida "Cocktail Party," Georgia players, in a preplanned show of solidarity, flooded the field to celebrate their team's opening touchdown. The CBS commentator told his broadcast partner that the celebration "looked like a Mormon Tabernacle Choir breakout." The off-handedness of the comparison suggested that the choir, the church's earliest ambassador, had become so iconic as to have embedded itself in the national cultural consciousness. Likewise, when Thomas L. Friedman profiled JetBlue airline founder (and Mormon) David Neeleman in his 2005 bestseller *The World Is Flat*, he called Neeleman "one of those classic American entrepreneurs and a man of enormous integrity"—a man who donated bulks of his salary to support a "catastrophe relief fund" for employees and their families. Friedman focused especially on Neeleman's innovative use of stay-at-home moms as online reservation agents. It was as if at Friedman's hand, "Mormon" became shorthand for family values, like he took for granted that he did not have to explain what his readers already knew, that the Mormon ethic was one of family-friendliness.[6]

However, what also became clear to Mormons as the first decade of the new millennium came to a close was that all too often, public familiarity with their faith was more superficial than substantive. A fall 2007 Pew study stated the case in plain terms: the Mormon religion "[has] gained increasing national visibility in recent years. Yet most Americans say they know little or nothing about [the] religion's practices." NBC's late-night host Conan O'Brien memorably put that sentiment to music. He and the cast of *The Tonight Show* in 2009 dedicated a holiday song to Latter-day Saints. The chorus said it all: "Mormons, Mormons, Mormons—we haven't got a clue." While they sang, images of Donny and Marie Osmond (as well as members of the Amish community) flashed on the screen. That sense of "[knowing] little or nothing" about Mormonism speaks directly to Elder Jensen's retrospective concerns about the church's image, since fear of the unknown contributes significantly to the persistence of "suspicion and misunderstanding" and kept alive in 2008 the same concerns about Mormon secrecy or heresy that abounded twenty years earlier.[7]

But as pollster Gary Lawrence suggested in his 2008 study, something more than ignorance was at work here. When asked how much they knew about different religious groups, the number of non-Mormon Americans who said they knew little about Mormons was relatively similar to, though slightly lower

than, the number of nonevangelicals who said they knew little about evangelical Christians (41% and 49%, respectively). Yet when expressing their opinions
about both Mormons and evangelical Christians, many more respondents gave
Mormons an unfavorable rating (49% for Mormons; 33% for evangelicals).
While this disparity can be partly accounted for in the sheer numerical strength
of evangelicals, since it is likely that many evangelicals in the non-Mormon
respondent camp would have expressed strongly unfavorable views of Mormons,
Lawrence nevertheless struck a chord when he concluded that the Mormon
"image is being driven by both an ignorance and fear factor."[8]

But that was 2008—and perhaps the ground was about to shift again.

This book began with the proposition that something significant could be
gleaned by comparing the role Mormonism played in the presidential campaign
of George Romney in 1968 and the role Mormonism played in the presidential
campaign of George Romney's son, Mitt, in 2008—and by asking what, why, and
how things had changed in the intervening four decades. This book ends with a
microcosmic epilogue of sorts that takes the same comparative approach—only
the two campaigns that become the bookends in this concluding comparison
are both Mitt Romney's, and the intervening time is only four years. Such is
the interpretive windfall provided by Romney's second run for the presidency
in 2012. And such is the accelerated pace of the age of new media—this era
of unfettered everyman-type journalism—that in four short years observable
changes and trends already hint at possible movements in Mormonism's public
standing.

Admittedly, with only a few months of historical hindsight, any talk of "peri-
odizing" the ebbs and flows of the Mormon image during the 2012 election cycle
might seem a little premature. Still, there is some use in doing just that, especially to reflect and collate what a number of observers have noted and proposed.
The timeline this chapter traces, therefore, begins with what might be called the
"inter-election Mormon milieu," when Proposition 8 and *The Book of Mormon*
musical headlined a string of Mormon-related stories that kept the religion and
its adherents in plain view, and presumptions about Mitt Romney's planned second campaign gave those stories continued national relevance. The next period
considered here, the season of the Republican primaries, roughly from late sum
mer 2011 until the spring of 2012, was a season that felt mostly familiar, as
conservative Christians wrestled again, privately *and* publicly, with the question
of supporting a Mormon candidate. Significantly, though, the end of the primaries seemed to be something of a pivot point on the Mormon image trend
line. There was a dramatic decrescendo in conversations about Mormonism from
Republican and evangelical quarters, and Mormons nervously tried to anticipate
how their faith would play in the media arena of a general, national election,
when opposition would come more from the political left rather than the usual
suspects on the right. Yet the late spring and summer of 2012 turned out to

be mostly noncontroversial on that front. So much so that by the time of the conventions of both parties and beyond, coverage of Mormonism remarkably, unexpectedly transcended coverage of Mitt Romney—and *Boston Globe* columnist Alex Beam proclaimed the election "a big win for the Mormon Church."[9] While there seems to be little question that the future will be as unpredictable as the past, this closing narrative might suggest some new points by which to plot the current latitude and longitude of the meaning of "Mormon."

The Inter-election Mormon Milieu: Proposition 8

The post-"Romney 2008" string began with perhaps the biggest surprise of Election Day 2008. It was a ballot initiative in California, not a presidential hopeful from Massachusetts, that proved to be the dominant Mormon-related hot topic as that campaign cycle came to a close.

Proposition 8 asked voters to consider whether the California constitution should be amended to define marriage as between one man and one woman and thus render same-sex marriages null and void in the state. The stakes were especially high since the state's Supreme Court had opened the way five months earlier for same-sex couples to wed in California. Despite consistent polling that gave the proposition's opponents a lead, as voting ended that day it became clear that the proposition's supporters had staged a stunning rally and the initiative passed, effectively ending same-sex marriage in California.[10]

Across the nation the proposition's passage made headlines. Advocates of same-sex marriage were devastated. Though other states had passed similar initiatives, Proposition 8 seemed different. California had often been at the vanguard of social issues, a bellwether state for societal change. Thus voter support for Proposition 8 in California was a major blow for gay rights activists. Their initial surprise at the defeat soon turned into anger directed toward the proposition's opponents. Singled out for specific attack was The Church of Jesus Christ of Latter-day Saints.

Earlier in 2008, LDS Church leaders accepted an invitation to join a coalition of other California religious groups to support Proposition 8. While the church directly donated less than $200,000 to the effort, its members were encouraged to consider the cause and then donate money and time according to their conscience. It was the organizational might of Mormonism that drew the ire of anti-Proposition 8 forces. They deemed the LDS Church as one of the proposition's major (if not *the* major) supporters and enablers. Some estimates put Mormons' individual donations at more than half of the $40 million raised by Proposition 8 backers and the number of Mormon volunteers at more than 25,000 a week.[11]

Not since the Equal Rights Amendment in the late 1970s had Mormons been so embroiled in national politics. There were good reasons to draw parallels between the two campaigns. In both cases, top LDS leaders stated their positions and provided the impetus but then allowed local officials to formulate specific tactics and plans. In both cases, a number of Mormons dissented vocally from the hierarchy's viewpoint. And in both cases, media representatives and political opponents raised questions about the appropriateness of a church exercising so much political influence, especially in their accusations that there had not been full disclosure of the amount of support the church rendered.[12]

What was strikingly different about the Proposition 8 campaign, though, was the lasting attention that Mormons received for being at the forefront of the drive to pass the initiative. While Mormon involvement was recognized by some as pivotal in the defeat of the ERA, the LDS Church generally remained in the background, as pundits focused most of the attention, and most of the credit, on the coalition of evangelical Christians and other conservative opponents of the amendment. Almost the reverse was true in the aftermath of Proposition 8. Mormons received alternately a significant share of the accolades and the blame for the success of the California measure. That alone underscored both the increased visibility of the church and the persistent suspicion of Mormon power and authoritarianism.[13]

This anti-Proposition 8, anti-Mormon impulse manifested itself in a number of arenas. The day before voting took place in California, opponents of the measure ran a commercial they called "Home Invasion." The sixty-second spot ran this way: two Mormon missionaries came to the door of a same-sex couple. With broad smiles the missionaries said, "Hi, we're from The Church of Jesus Christ of Latter-day Saints. We're here to take away your rights." They then forced their way into the home and demanded to see the women's marriage license and wedding rings, which they promptly (and proudly) confiscated and destroyed. When the women protested, one missionary said, "Who's going to stop us?" The message of the spot was clear: family-friendly Mormons were now destroying families. The narrator concluded, "Say NO to a church taking over your government."[14]

Within days of the proposition's passage, hundreds of protesters gathered on repeated occasions at a number of Mormon temples and chapels to express their displeasure at the church's involvement.[15] The controversy even prompted former Utah television reporter Reed Cowan to produce a full-length documentary for the Sundance Film Festival that decried Mormon participation in the campaign. When Cowan was asked why he chose to premiere his film *8: The Mormon Proposition* in Utah, he replied, "There was no other place on the planet where this could premiere. This is where the lies came from, this is where the money came from. The sharpest karma that could be leveled on the Mormon Church...has to be leveled in their own backyard."[16]

The uproar over Proposition 8 drew just as many supporters to the church, though, as it did protesters, and many of those supporters came from unexpected quarters. Catholic Bishops joined to express their appreciation for Mormons' energetic involvement in supporting the proposition and to offer solidarity with Mormons as they received the brunt of the backlash. So, too, did a number of prominent evangelical leaders who signed an "online petition thanking the LDS Church for its Proposition 8 efforts"; signatures came from "Charles Colson of Prison Fellowship, James Dobson of Focus on the Family, Tony Perkins of the Family Research Council, and Richard Land of the Southern Baptist Convention." The irony was that many of those Christians who rejected Mitt Romney because of his faith now felt indebted to that faith for its defense of marriage.[17]

That is what made Proposition 8, coming as it did on the heels of Mitt Romney's withdrawal from the election, such an interesting moment in the development of Mormonism's public image. The church's support for the initiative appealed to some communities that had been adversarial toward the church but then alienated other communities that had not actively opposed Mormonism. Kirk Jowers at the University of Utah noted that before Proposition 8, a "gay and lesbian leader...in D.C. called and volunteered to help [Jowers]...in any way that he could" in fighting the defamation of Mormonism that he saw during Mitt Romney's campaign. However, that offer of support changed with Proposition 8. A year after the proposition passed, Jowers's expectation was that Mormon advocacy of the initiative "[had] marginally helped Mitt [Romney] on the Republican side" with conservative Christians, "but it [had] more than marginally hurt him" with other voters who would participate "in the general election." Jowers then agreed that the same could be said generally of public opinion of the LDS Church. "Mormons will now have a far bigger stigma with moderates and liberals than [they] would have had before."[18]

The Inter-election Mormon Milieu: Stereotypes on Stage, Believers on Billboards

Proposition 8 thus complicated prognostications about the immediate future of Mormonism's wider reputation. When critics of the LDS Church's support of Proposition 8 raised specters about a church's meddling in politics—a church's use of its secret organizational might to unduly influence a public vote—they were tapping into a current of criticism that had run for more than a century and a half, flowing from fears of a Joseph Smith- or Brigham Young-led theocracy. But more recently, that current had also been fed by the exposés of the 1980s, the "Mormon Corporate Empire"-type conspiracy concerns. Gary Lawrence's

2008 national survey found that some degree of this suspicion of Mormons still prevailed in many American minds, even among those (unlike evangelical Christians) who were not motivated by a vested stake in the religious battle for souls.

Lawrence measured "trait perception" of Mormons through respondents' word associations. A significant number of respondents saw the LDS Church as "controlling" (57%); "powerful" (55%); "wealthy" (52%); and "secretive" (47%). Not surprising, only 46% of those surveyed said the church was "tolerant," and only 44% agreed that it was "open."[19]

When it came to opinions about Mormons as people, the word associations were a little kinder. Still, 38% of all respondents said Mormons were "brainwashed" and "fanatical." Even more (41%) called Mormons "narrow-minded" and "blind followers" (45%). Lawrence's analysis took the survey one step further. In presenting the data, he isolated the opinions of those respondents who, based on an earlier question, expressed "a somewhat or strongly unfavorable impression of" Mormons. Among that group, 57% agreed that Mormons were "brainwashed," 55% said they were "narrow-minded," and 62% said they were "blind followers." It seems worth repeating here Gary Lawrence's observation of his 2008 poll data: the Mormon "image," he concluded, "is being driven by both an ignorance factor and a fear factor."[20] The fallout over the Proposition 8 campaign observably stoked those fires.

Yet somewhat surprising, the visible flames and the vocalized fears surrounding Proposition 8 died down comparatively quickly. The church itself repaired some rifts with its official support in November 2009 of nondiscrimination statutes that gave rights to same-sex partners in Salt Lake City. Several outspoken antagonists softened after the church took this stand; Utah gay rights activists called the church's support "historic," and even afterward described the church as a "caring, loving, concerned institution." "The church supports these ordinances," LDS spokesman Michael Otterson said, "because they are fair and reasonable and they do not do violence to the institution of marriage." In this, Mormon leaders sought to distance themselves from anti-gay hardliners and strike the difficult balance between two essential tenets of the faith—the sanctity and eternal nature of marriage and the need for compassion and respect for the "human dignity" of every individual, as Otterson said, "even when we disagree."[21]

While the church's expressed support for civility and civil rights dampened the post–Proposition 8 outcries (as did, undoubtedly, the passage of time),[22] it was the next turn in the Mormon publicity saga—the next undisputed Mormon moment—that would prove to dominate the conversation and overshadow the recent controversy. That moment came in the form of a Broadway musical called, innocently enough, *The Book of Mormon*.

The irony of this moment was everywhere. Some of the voices that had reverberated the loudest in their protests against perceived Mormon intolerance came from the entertainment industry.[23] Yet it was an offering from two stars in that industry, Matt Stone and Trey Parker (of TV cartoon series *South Park* fame), that placed Mormons in a new and, to everyone's surprise, paradoxically positive spotlight. In a stage production that was by consensus judged to be as vulgar and irreverent as anything Broadway had ever seen, the "Mormon" characters came off by most accounts as likable, even sweet and redeeming. And in the end, it was attention to this play, a play that mercilessly exaggerated every Mormon stereotype, that perhaps gave Mormons themselves an unparalleled opportunity to address those stereotypes. A ground shift indeed.

The Book of Mormon musical was obviously not the first dramatic portrayal of Mormonism. Matt Stone and Trey Parker had themselves already dealt with Mormonism in their television and movie work. *The Book of Mormon* wasn't even the first award-winning play about Mormons to be staged on Broadway—Tony Kushner's *Angels in America* had won Tony Awards and the Pulitzer Prize in the early nineties. But *The of Mormon* seemed to resonate and buzz in an unprecedented way. Its impact represented the convergence of many forces, not the least of which was an increased national curiosity about Mormons because of Mitt Romney. *The Book of Mormon* also benefited from a catchy soundtrack that broke sales records, as well as the biting humor that has characterized all of Stone and Parker's work.[24]

On top of that, *The Book of Mormon* was instantly identifiable with the Latter-day Saints it parodied in a way that *Angels in America* was not. Apart from the title, advertisements and publicity for the musical utilized the recognizably iconic (even if caricatured) image of an exuberant Mormon missionary holding a copy of the Book of Mormon (Figure 10.1). There could be no mistaking how Mormons figured into this story.[25]

Figure 10.1. Billboards advertising the 2013 run of *The Book of Mormon* musical in Chicago—and trumpeting the show's critical acclaim. When the production hit Los Angeles, the LDS Church purchased advertising space in the playbill. One church ad's tagline: "The book is always better." Photograph by author.

Mormons' reaction to the musical also made this something new and different. Initial reports and preview-type press releases about the musical left many Latter-day Saints nervous. Not only was the musical to portray the incorrigible cluelessness of two American missionaries in war-torn, AIDS-ravaged Africa, it was to do so through songs and dialogue that reviewers admitted could not be played on broadcast airwaves because of the profanity involved. These were cringe-inducing reports—even "foreboding," in the words of one *outside* observer when he first considered the notion of a musical comedy about a church's sacred text.[26] Church spokesman Michael Otterson even blogged for the *Washington Post* why he would not be seeing the musical, since he worried that it could obscure the fact that the church took very seriously both the realities of life faced by the hundreds of thousands of its African members and the humanitarian needs of Africans in general. "I'm not buying what I'm reading in the reviews," Otterson wrote. "Specifically, I'm not willing to spend $200 for a ticket to be sold the idea that religion moves along oblivious to real-world problems in a kind of blissful naiveté."[27]

Yet in the wake of the musical's opening in March 2011, as reviewers heaped praise on the show (it would eventually sweep nine of the 2011 Tony Awards), many reviewers also noted that the show's writers (Parker, Stone, and Bobby Lopez) generally treated the Mormon characters as well-intentioned and sincere, even if they were hilariously naïve. Interestingly, some Mormon beliefs that had become *God Makers*–type fare were also peppered throughout the show—like references to unknown planets and the 1978 revelation opening the priesthood to men of all races (including, potentially, the African warlord in the musical). But what *The God Makers* had portrayed as sinister and ominous three decades earlier came across (like so many other religious beliefs over the years at the hands of Stone and Parker) as eccentric and laughable, but also, in this case, somehow innocent. While certainly softened by the comedy, the credulity of the characters in *The Book of Mormon* was not painted by reviewers as threatening or dangerous, even if it did imply a Pollyannaish sort of gullibility—and this because what was also inescapable was that the Mormon characters in *The Book of Mormon*, unlike the characters in so many other dramatic presentations of that faith, remained true to their beliefs in the face of increasing odds (in the song "I Believe," Elder Price sings, "A warlord who shoots people in the face—what's so scary about that?"). That persistence, even if ridiculously utopian (as in the song "Sal Tlay Ka Siti" [Salt Lake City]), came across as determinedly genuine and even admirable. "I'm a Mormon," Elder Price sings as he grabs the ruthless warlord by the hand, "and Mormons just believe."[28]

While audiences may not have agreed with the church's claims about the actual scripture called the Book of Mormon, even on stage the reality came through that the book *did* motivate millions of believers. National Public Radio's Robert

Smith said it this way: "But here's where the sweetness comes in. The Mormons in the musical embrace every quirk of their faith. It makes them stronger, and in the end the audience that laughed at them is won over."[29]

That sentiment was also the essence of the church's official one-sentence response to the musical, which many reviewers also included in their reports: "The production may attempt to entertain audiences for an evening, but the Book of Mormon as a volume of scripture will change people's lives forever by bringing them closer to Christ."[30] Observers noted that the church did not protest the play, and Parker and Stone found that response "just brilliant." The duo told NPR's Smith that "every time we do something on Mormons, their response makes us like them more."[31]

This one-sentence press release was the church's only explicit and direct reply to the musical, but the musical also gave an opening for an LDS media campaign that received nearly as much attention. The musical premiered in March 2011; by June 2011, signs on New York subways and taxis and even a billboard on Times Square appeared with the photos of a number of smiling faces around the caption, "I'm a Mormon."[32]

The billboards were a new platform for a media initiative that had its inception years earlier. Scott Swofford, who as director of media for the church's missionary department oversaw the campaign's development, described the years of research that led to the campaign as starting about the time of the Salt Lake Olympics. During a round of eleven different focus groups, Swofford remembered, "It was painful for [us] to sit behind that one-way glass and listen to people tell us what their perception was of Mormons." Researchers determined that stereotypes concerning Mormon clannishness and Mormon oddities were prevalent—as was sheer unfamiliarity; 58% of Americans, by one of the church's studies, said "they know little or nothing about [Mormons]." What also came out of the focus group research was the effectiveness of introducing to people individual Mormons who challenged those stereotypes. Thus was born the "I'm a Mormon" campaign.[33]

The "I'm a Mormon" video spots (shown on TV and online) featured Latter-day Saints who spoke about their lives, their diverse interests and occupations, their families. Then interested observers were directed to the church's Mormon.org website to view additional profiles. The campaign was already well underway in nine markets in the months before *The Book of Mormon* musical opened. However, what the publicity around *The Book of Mormon* musical prompted was the church's move to take the campaign from a handful of regional markets to the bright lights of Broadway. Swofford called the decision to procure the Times Square spot a "record" as "the quickest turnaround" in church administrative speed, a move that the decidedly careful hierarchy of the church considered and approved in less than twenty-four hours "because of the critical nature" of the publicity opportunity.[34]

Not all Latter-day Saints embraced the new campaign. There was some pub-licly expressed unease with profiles of individuals whose dress or grooming or habits did not seem to reflect the typical Mormon.[35] Yet designers countered that this was precisely the aim of the campaign—to challenge preconceptions about what was "Mormon." Kevin Kelly, advertising professor at BYU, noted that "this campaign breaks down all the stereotypes that people think about Mormons.... You can't define what a Mormon is just by looking at one profile"— and by 2011, Mormon.org had over 30,000 profiles that had been uploaded by Latter-day Saints.[36]

The prominence of "I'm a Mormon" signs plastered all over New York City gave the campaign a lot of traction, even if some of that attention was delivered tongue in cheek. Apart from the notice from news outlets, actor Zach Braff (of the TV show "Scrubs") tweeted to his followers, "The ad on this cab makes being a Mormon look super fun."[37] And actor Stephen Colbert gave the "I'm a Mormon" commercials perhaps the highest comedic compliment: a parody.

The background behind Colbert's piece was important. In late summer 2011, the news broke that a campaign staffer working for President Barack Obama had supposedly leaked the Democrats' potential strategy should Mitt Romney secure the 2012 Republican nomination. The plan was to attack Romney as "weird," which, David Brody told Chris Matthews on MSNBC's Hardball, was "pseudo to bring in to the whole Mormonism issue." While the Obama camp quickly disavowed any connection to the strategy, the moment was a reveal-ing one. Mitt Romney had left the 2008 race in the primary season; in many ways that meant that any quasi-official commentaries on Romney's faith from the Democratic Party—and from the part of the political establishment on the left more broadly—remained as untested waters. But with polling in 2011 con-sistently positioning Romney as the leading Republican contender, the antici-pation that criticism of this sort from the left would inevitably come seemed confirmed in these reports from Obama's staff. And considering the number of recent and repeated surveys that showed that a sizable percentage of Americans agreed that Mormons were "weird," it would be easy to see the practical appeal of such a strategy. All of these currents ran together in Stephen Colbert's memo-rable treatment of this "weird" issue.[38]

On his nightly Colbert Report program, Colbert said that just by looking at Romney anyone could tell that "in high school he was the weird kid who had lots of friends and led the football team to one of those weird state championships." Then Colbert brought up "that crazy religion of his," and his belief that "Joseph Smith received golden plates from an angel on a hill," even though, as Colbert reported, "everybody knows that Moses got stone tablets from a burning bush on a mountain." He then showed clips from some of the "I'm a Mormon" pro-files, and asked if Mormons are "normal." His answer was an enthusiastic yes. He admitted that the ad campaign made Mormons look "irresistibly cool." But then he asked himself, "What am I saying?! I'm a Catholic. Fight it!" He suggested that his own church needed an even better media campaign to top the Mormons. He offered for consideration a skateboarding, guitar-playing falconer who gave a tiger a high five—and who was, after all, a Catholic. "In your face, Mormons," was Colbert's closing tagline.[39]

The parody was telling. This significant tip of the hat from a popular cultural observer was, as Scott Swofford saw it, "a million dollars' worth of earned advertising." Layered in the piece was a thought-provoking "pot calling the kettle black"–type critique of religionists' dismissing another religion because of "weirdness." Not least of all, it was a sign of just how widely the "I'm a Mormon" ads had played. For that, ironically, Mormons could in part thank the caricatures and stereotypes on display in *The Book of Mormon* musical—a phenomenon that "put [Mormons] in the dialogue," in Swofford's view. Initial follow-up research indicated that "I'm a Mormon" was having the effect the church desired. As church spokesman Michael Otterson noted in an October 2011 *Washington Post* blog piece, "Since the series was launched last year, traffic to Mormon.org, the Internet site for visitors, has tripled." While the spots did not specifically address the negative "myths" associated with Mormons—and that was intentional, Swofford said—they were giving viewers new things to consider. What "that says," Swofford suggested, was that someone might think, "Stephen Colbert, who I think is cool, thinks the Mormons are cool. Does that mean I want to be a Mormon? No, but the next time somebody trashes Mormons, I'll be a little more careful about how I phrase that—they might be cool."[40]

Even The Killers lead singer Brandon Flowers showed up in an "I'm a Mormon" profile in the fall of 2011. Flowers introduced his wife and sons, and then reflected on his Mormon upbringing, a background that prompted him to consider carefully both his lyrics and the "fire" of faith that was "still burning" in him. The new faces of Mormonism were proliferating.

Adding to that variety and complexity, the *San Francisco Examiner* in the summer of 2011 told the story of Mitch Mayne, an openly gay man who had, a year before, ended a relationship with another man and recommitted to the LDS Church's standards of complete chastity outside of marriage. Mayne was called to a position of leadership in his local Mormon congregation (executive secretary to the bishop of the church's Bay Ward). He was also charged by local leaders to be a liaison to reach out to other gay Mormons in the area.[41]

In the wake of the bruising Proposition 8 battle, it was the increasing prominence of these types of profiles that complicated any easy stereotypes of Mormons. At the very least, this type of publicity coincided with a measurable change. Gary Lawrence's early 2008 poll showed that the Mormon image was, in his words, "upside down"—that is, more respondents rated the Mormons negatively than positively. Lawrence's firm found that same survey scenario reversed in their summer 2011 poll; a June 2011 Quinnipiac University poll showed the same change (45% positive to 32% negative). The change was noteworthy.[42] But what of the group that had consistently been most antipathetic to Mormons? Where did things stand in 2011 with evangelical Christians—and how would they respond to the same front-running Mormon presidential candidate many of them had rejected only a few years before?

Opening the Primary Race: A Cult, but a Theological Cult

By 2008, it had almost become a polling maxim that mainline and liberal Protestant respondents would rate Mormons more favorably than would the conservative Christian respondents in the same opinion surveys.[43] As noted above, though, Proposition 8 initially seemed to portend possible changes in those poll positions. Yet, at the same time that questions about Mormon intolerance and narrow-mindedness rose from quarters on the left, questions from the right about the durability of Mormon-evangelical alliances remained unsettled, even though evangelicals in large numbers aligned with Latter-day Saints over the California initiative. Midway between the 2008 and 2012 presidential elections, as Mitt Romney seemed poised to make another run, political observer Kirk Jowers reported that his conversations with a number of evangelicals led him to believe that many had adopted a "don't get too excited about it" attitude toward Mormon cooperation. "They are happy to use [the Mormons'] hose to put out the fire in their house but they are never going to invite us in for cookies." Utah pastor Bill Heersink also expressed doubt that Proposition 8 would "change the underlying prejudice" or fear of "doctrinal compromises" evangelicals might feel in voting for a Mormon. Robert Jeffress of the First Baptist Church of Dallas told *Christianity Today* after Proposition 8's passage that "the differences between Mormonism and Christianity aren't just minor theological differences that can be erased just because we agree on moral issues." A top evangelical leader who visited BYU disagreed with that sentiment, but he felt nevertheless that it would prevail even after Proposition 8: "Evangelicals in the future will do just what we did, because election of a Mormon president would be a signal of recognition and legitimization."[44]

That prickly, underlying question of legitimization stubbornly refused to stay submerged beneath the surface of public praise for Mormons' social morality. In late 2008, for example, James Dobson's Focus on the Family organization sheepishly removed an interview from its website that promoted well-known talk show host Glenn Beck's holiday book, *The Christmas Sweater*. The explanation the evangelical Christian organization gave for removing the promotional material was that it had not clearly identified Beck as a Mormon, and numerous patrons complained about this misleading endorsement that "[made] it look as if Beck is a Christian who believes in the essential doctrines of the faith." Only a year later, though, Beck was invited to deliver the May 2010 commencement address at Liberty University, the school founded by the late Jerry Falwell, one of fundamentalist Christianity's most recognizable leaders. Observers suggested that perhaps in an era of growing outrage against a perceived liberalizing of government institutions, this unexpected commencement address would prove emblematic of a new willingness on the part of evangelicals to accept allies wherever they could find them, even if that meant granting Mormonism a new degree of legitimacy.[45]

By the end of summer 2011, there was indeed a sense that Mitt Romney's Mormonism was not figuring as prominently and publicly into the 2012 campaign as it did in 2008. Kirk Jowers had noted in the spring of 2010 that "all of [Romney's] supporters hope that it [will be] like Massachusetts," when "everyone was kind of almost embarrassed of how they treated Mormons [when he ran] against Kennedy [in 1994], and by the time he ran for governor [in 2002] it was almost a nonissue."[46] There were some indications that this prediction was playing out. Several observers of Mormonism in the public arena noted both a "much more moderate" tone in Mormon-related reporting and an "old news" status for Mormon oddities.[47]

This is not to suggest that the religion issue simply went away, to be sure. Evangelical blogger Warren Cole Smith stirred the pot in May 2011 with his post that encouraged Christians to spurn Romney's candidacy because "a candidate who either by intent or effect promotes a false and dangerous religion is unfit to serve." In Smith's view, "a Romney presidency would have the effect of actively promoting a false religion in the world," and "a false religion should not prosper with the support of Christians"—hence the title of his post, "A Vote for Romney Is a Vote for the LDS Church." Smith's piece spread across the blogosphere and provoked divergent responses, even from evangelicals—some praised his honesty, and others worried about the implications of a tacit "religious test" for office.[48] There was also brief attention to the fact that presidential candidate Michele Bachmann changed churches—and that the pastor of her new church had delivered a 2007 sermon calling Mormonism "untrue" and "diluted." But the journalist who wrote the story on Bachmann's pastor admitted that the connection was not "widely reported."[49] Both episodes seemed in the end unremarkable.

More remarkable seemed to be a poll released in the summer of 2011 that suggested that only four out of ten Americans could even identify Mitt Romney's religion. What was less surprising was that at the same time, polling in the summer consistently showed that one situation had not changed: a significant segment of voters (36% in the Quinnipiac University poll) still felt "somewhat or entirely uncomfortable" with the faith of a Mormon presidential candidate. Taking the two numbers together suggested to pollster Gary Lawrence that religion in *general* was not a "tier-one" issue for most voters—yet Mormonism was the *specific* religion that gave the greatest number of voters (even though it was a minority of voters) pause.[50]

There was a sense in the summer of 2011 (as in the pre–Governor Huckabee days of 2007) that no candidate in the early, crowded Republican field had captured the full support and excitement of the conservative Christian bloc, those voters for whom religion *was* a tier-one issue. Fox News showed a poll in July that had only 13% of Republicans saying they supported Mitt Romney's candidacy. While Romney polled highest among the candidates in that survey, still 58% of Republicans at the time said they were "not sure" which candidate they favored.[51] But Texas Governor Rick Perry's entrance into the campaign changed things. He announced his candidacy in August 2011 and immediately created what the Associated Press's Thomas Beaumont called "rumblings" that "[threatened] to upend the race" and Romney's lead therein. Governor Perry had "sent a strong message to evangelicals [the previous] weekend by hosting a national prayer rally in Houston that drew roughly 30,000 Christians."[52] His potential impact had already been on the minds of commentators for weeks. In July *Fox & Friends'* Ainsley Earhardt framed Governor Perry's fundraising potential in that same way: "Well, the Christian Coalition, I think he can get a lot from that, [with] Romney obviously not being a Christian." Her use of the word "obviously" spoke volumes. [53]

In line with these predictions, Perry immediately shot to the top of the polls. While he slipped from the top spot after an initial round of Republican debates in the early fall of 2011, his evangelical Christian credentials were unimpeachable, which still made him a viable contender with the powerful Christian Right. In what looked like an unmistakable move to highlight those credentials, Governor Perry was introduced by Pastor Robert Jeffress of the First Baptist Church of Dallas at the October 2011 Values Voters Summit in Washington, D.C. In a matter of only a few words, that introduction catapulted Mormonism like a fiery projectile back into the camp of national controversy in a way that Warren Cole Smith, for example, or Ainsley Earhardt had not done.[54]

Reverend Jeffress's introductory comments were clear enough to define his views of Mitt Romney's religion: "Do we want a candidate who is a good moral person, or do we want a candidate who is a born-again follower of Jesus Christ? In Rick Perry, we have a candidate who is a committed follower of Christ." However, it was the pastor's post-introduction media interviews that made his remarks "breaking news"—his remarks "stole the Friday news cycle," as one commentator noted the next day. Reverend Jeffress told reporters that he believed Mormonism was a "cult," even though "it's not politically correct to say." He later told a CNN interviewer that "born-again followers of Jesus Christ should always prefer a competent Christian to a competent non-Christian."[55]

In one sense, this was hardly news. As Pastor Jeffress pointed out, the Southern Baptist Convention, what he called the "largest Protestant denomination in the world," had officially identified the LDS Church as a cult years earlier. Only days after the Values Voters Summit, headlines proclaimed that a new poll showed "75% of pastors say Mormons 'not Christians'"—or, as some outlets interpreted the data, "Mormons are a cult."[56] Jeffress was, as might be expected, only marching in step with his colleagues. What seemed, though, to be "breaking news" (as CNN's Anderson Cooper called it) in this instance was the degree to which it *became* "breaking news." For that reason, the sheer attention given to Jeffress's commentary added another snapshot to the Mormon image composite.[57]

It was a layered snapshot, full of shades and hues. One of those layers was the immediacy of the media's reaction to Jeffress's words. Before the night was out, CNN's Cooper had Jeffress on the air to discuss the introduction. Significantly, as Jeffress and Cooper spoke, a news banner running on-screen beneath them read this way: "Perry press secy.: Gov. doesn't have the same belief." Perry's quick distancing himself from the comment was telling; also telling was Anderson Cooper's related question to Jeffress: "Do you worry that you're harming your candidate?"

In the six-minute-plus segment, Cooper quoted from the LDS Church's website and restated the church's official belief in the divinity of Jesus Christ as Son of God and Savior of humanity. This led Jeffress to amend his earlier statement to say that Mormonism was a "*theological* cult" rather than a "*sociological* cult." It was the church's beliefs not the morality or behavior of its people that qualified it as a cult. When the pastor said, "I'm not labeling Mitt Romney as a bad person, or Mormons as bad people," Cooper quickly interrupted Jeffress and said, smiling, "But you're saying he's a member of a cult, I mean..." The pastor then tried to explain the distinction as something analogous to political affiliation: "You know, Anderson, you're not a Republican... I would say that, not because I think you're a bad person, but you don't hold to the basic tenets of the Republican party." The analogy did not fly with Cooper: "Saying someone is not a Republican is not a value judgment; saying someone's in a cult is a value judgment. I mean, it's an incendiary term."

As Anderson Cooper continued to push Jeffress to explain his position, the pastor muddied the theological waters somewhat he said he believed that Roman Catholics are Christians, but that the Catholic Church had nevertheless not been true to historic Christianity because of its emphasis on the salvific part played by participation in church sacraments, in contrast to the evangelical belief in being saved by faith/grace alone. According to Jeffress, this belied the Catholic Church's stated fidelity to the New Testament. Pastor Jeffress also explained that he accepted as authentic President Obama's profession of Christian faith, but that he would in fact vote for Mitt Romney over President Obama if forced into that choice because the non-Christian Romney, as opposed to the Christian Obama, favored political positions that were biblical.

As Cooper pressed Jeffress to say more on the beliefs which disqualified Mormons as Christians, the pastor demurred, since, he said, a heavy theological explanation would put viewers to sleep. Cooper quickly retorted, "I'm fine with putting people to sleep as long as we educate them." For Mormons, that one line was perhaps the most intriguing of the entire charged exchange. Something about this, Mormon observers agreed, felt different than 2007–2008.[58]

Pastor Jeffress made his comments on a Friday; before the weekend was out, CNN had a special op-ed piece on its website written by Richard Mouw, president of Fuller Theological Seminary. Mouw has been a leading evangelical participant in the semiannual evangelical/Mormon dialogue series. His piece was titled "My Take: This evangelical says Mormonism isn't a cult." Mouw wrote, "I know cults. I have studied them and taught about them for a long time." He also brought up accusations about evangelicalism: "It's worth noting that people have wondered whether I belong to a cult." But Mormonism was not a cult, in Mouw's mind, because "religious cults are very much us-versus-them.... They don't like to engage in serious, respectful give-and-take dialogue with people with whom they disagree." In contrast, the Mormons he associated with "talk admiringly of the evangelical Billy Graham and the Catholic Mother Teresa, and they enjoy reading the evangelical C. S. Lewis and Father Henri Nouwen, a Catholic. That is not the kind of thing you run into in anti-Christian cults." As to the "complicated question" of "are Mormons Christians?" Mouw answered, "While I am not prepared to reclassify Mormonism as possessing undeniably Christian theology, I do accept many of my Mormon friends as genuine followers of the Jesus whom I worship as the divine Savior."[59]

By the Monday after Jeffress's comments, the *Washington Post* ran a piece by John Mark Reynolds, a professor at the evangelical college Biola, titled "Why evangelicals must stand up to anti-Mormon bigotry." He called Pastor Jeffress a "bigot" since the cult label to "describe the Mormon faith is foolish and offensive in a political context.... Most of the public does not think doctrine, but danger when they hear the term cult. He imagines scary folk living in compounds drinking Kool-aid, not Harry Reid or Mitt Romney. In that popular sense, Mormonism is not a cult and should scare no American." After all, Reynolds reasoned, evidence for Mormon patriotism prompted an important question: "Can a Mormon die for the Republic in battle, but still not serve as commander in the White House?" Reynolds concluded on a personal note: "My Mormon friends do not complain or become defensive. Like the Christ, my experience has been resignation and love when my Mormon friends see slander"—and to Reynolds, that slander was "for mainstream evangelicals... an embarrassment."[60]

Other similarly strong reactions in the wake of the "cult" comments were noteworthy. *USA Today* reported that "Republican candidates distance[d] themselves from Mormon remark"—former Senator Rick Santorum was even quoted as saying that "he believes Romney, like every Mormon he knows, 'has great moral values,' and that Romney is a Christian if he says he is." The *Washington Post*'s Sally Quinn asked "megapastor" Joel Osteen about his views of the flare-up. She said, "I take it you don't subscribe to [Reverend Jeffress's] views?" Osteen answered, "No, I don't. I do not know Reverend Jeffress. I'm sure he's a good man, and he's passionate about what he believes. I'm not here to criticize him; I just see it a little differently than he does." What Pastor Osteen said next was significant: "He's not the only one. There are some very strong fundamentalists that believe that—and I don't fault them...I just see it differently."[61]

This act of separating themselves from the "Mormonism-as-cult" territory, on the part of politicians and professors and even pastors, reflected something critical about this ever-changing terrain—the rift in evangelicalism over the Mormon issue, at least in terms of politics, appeared to be widening. And in that gap, some saw an opening for a Mormon candidate just as 2012 dawned and the Republican primaries began in earnest.

The week after Pastor Jeffress's remarks, National Public Radio reported a poll that showed "nearly 60% of evangelicals could vote for a Mormon for president." Pollster Gary Lawrence noted that Romney's favorable/unfavorable rating as a candidate was even higher with evangelicals than with Republicans in general (63% versus 52%, respectively). Lawrence wondered if that represented in some cases a pastor/parishioner "disconnect" over the acceptability of voting for a Mormon.[62]

A survey released in September 2011 suggested that "a hardcore group of about 10% will never vote for a Mormon, but for the rest of the nation, a candidate's membership in this increasingly visible religion is not a salient factor in the vote decision." BYU professor Robert Millet, a leader in Mormon/evangelical dialogue, seemed right in calling that hardcore group "an eroding minority."[63] A CNN poll in mid-October 2011 appeared to bear that out: "Americans overwhelmingly (80%) say a presidential candidate being Mormon wouldn't affect their voting." The CNN poll also revealed that "fifty-one percent" agreed "Mormonism was a Christian religion."[64]

Millet then proposed that because of "tactics that are anything but Christian," the "influence" of this "strident" minority "is shrinking; they are gradually marginalizing themselves." Millet was not alone in his observations. Three days after Jeffress's comments, the Associated Press's Rachel Zoll quoted Fuller Seminary President Richard Mouw to illustrate what seemed to be the underlying motive of Mormonism's detractors during the campaign season: "It's no accident that this comes at a time when two of the candidates for president [Mitt Romney and former Utah Governor Jon Huntsman, Jr.] are Mormon....People who seem to have a vested interest in ensuring that others see Mormonism as a cult see this as an opportunity to make their case and stir up anti-Mormon sentiment." This was a key point. While Mormons themselves were in the limelight as never before, the attention surrounding the presidential campaigns gave Mormonism's *opponents* unprecedented national exposure as well, and a number of them capitalized on that chance to sound their warnings. Yet there was a growing sense, too, that many in the mainstream media were not content to let those detractors occupy that publicity platform unchallenged. Richard Bushman, who sat for interviews about Mormonism as often as anyone during the two campaign cycles, suggested that "we've got this peculiar situation where you have a liberal press corps that is actually more suspicious of the far Christian right than it is of Mormons." Bushman made those comments two months *before* the Values Voters Summit, but his words seemed especially prescient in the days after the summit. Another longtime Mormon observer, Jan Shipps, sensed the strong reaction to Jeffress's approach as a sign that "a lot of people [are] saying, 'He had no right to ask. He had no right to charge that'" (about Mormonism's cult status)—and this was, to Shipps, something different from the way things were in 2008 [65]

That change in tone would only accelerate as Romney's securing of the Republican nomination looked more and more likely. Initially, though, and for much of the winter and early spring of 2011–2012, there persisted an "anyone but Romney" sentiment among the conservative Christian wing of the Republican Party. The excitement over Rick Santorum, an almost-forgotten candidate by the time of his surprising first-place finish in the Iowa caucuses, left Romney supporters feeling like it was Mike Huckabee all over again.

As Santorum and Newt Gingrich battled over who could lay claim to the conservative banner, Gingrich won primary elections in South Carolina and Georgia, and Santorum in a handful of Midwestern and Southern states. Significantly, there seemed to be decidedly religious undertones in this palpable lack of enthusiasm for Romney, who was billed as almost the foregone favorite by everyone but the voters. (One hundred and fifty "high-powered" evangelical leaders had even endorsed Rick Santorum, a socially conservative Roman Catholic, in January after conferring at a Texas gathering.)[66] An Associated Press headline captured the feeling well in January 2012 in the days leading up to the South Carolina primary: "Concerns about Romney's faith quieter but not gone." Reverend Brad Atkins, president of the South Carolina General Baptist Convention, wrote to a reporter that "Romney's Mormonism will be more a cause of concern than Gingrich's infidelity." Forgiving sin, Atkins anticipated, would not be as big of an issue as the "struggle to understand how anyone could be a Mormon and call themselves Christian." Indeed, Romney struggled in a number of Southern contests where evangelical Christians dominated the Republican rolls—where news reports quoted people saying things like, "As a Christian, I can't vote for somebody who can't lead us in a Christian way."[67]

But by the end of March 2012, after winning six states on Super Tuesday and several more throughout the month, Romney's growing lead of delegates soon seemed insurmountable, and Republican voters—evangelical Republican voters—began to line up behind the party's candidate. As Reverend Atkins had accurately (if disappointedly) predicted, "The tragedy is that again this year the majority of committed Christians that will have registered and be able to vote, when push comes to shove, will cast their vote for a candidate on jobs—the economy."[68] Romney's credentials on that score delivered the 1,144 delegates he needed to shift his gaze to November.

The Post-Primaries Pivot: From Liability to Asset?

What happened from that point forward is perhaps best appreciated in retrospect. Only one week before the November election, San Diego State University Professor Joanna Brooks, who had become a prominent media voice after publishing her *Book of Mormon Girl* memoir, wrote for *Religion Dispatches* a piece that labeled the campaign season "a virtually religion-free ... contest."[69] For many, this was certainly the retrospective surprise of 2012, yet some saw it coming. In 2010, the University of Utah's Kirk Jowers had guessed that "if [Mitt Romney] doesn't win" in 2012, his religion this time "will not be the major cause" of his political demise.[70] What had been a well-considered forecast in 2010 was almost the consensus view in post–general–election 2012. As the dust settled after Romney's fairly narrow but clear loss to President Obama in November 2012, and as pundits analyzed the outcomes, there was a natural turn to consider the "Mormon effect." And commentator after commentator expressed some variation on this similar theme: at least from the days of the winding-down primaries, Mormonism had not been the hang-up for Mitt Romney's fortunes that some had expected it to be, especially given what had happened in 2008.

A Pew Research Center's Project for Excellence in Journalism study released one month after the November election confirmed that these consensus impressions matched some objective realities. "A striking feature of the 2012 race for the White House," the report began, "is how little the subject of religion came up in the media"—"just 1% of the campaign coverage by major news outlets (including broadcast and cable television, radio, newspaper front pages and the most popular news websites)" was "specifically about religion" or was "*focused* on the religion of the candidates or the role of religion in the presidential election." Even though "Romney received twice as much religion coverage as Obama," only "6% of the election-related stories in major news outlets contained any reference to religion."[71]

Part of that diminishing focus on religion was undoubtedly due to party solidarity. For many conservative Christians, defeating President Obama was the chief concern, and so they were willing to transcend the divisiveness of the primaries in favor of that larger goal. In early April, the Southern Baptist

Convention's Richard Land appeared on CBS's *Face the Nation* and essentially, as one reporter put it, "urged Santorum to abandon the race and throw his support to frontrunner Mitt Romney to increase Republicans' chances of defeating Barack Obama in November."[72] This conscientious turn to unity effectively dampened anti-Mormon rhetoric from quarters that had previously hosted the most vocal of its purveyors. A November 2011 Pew Research Center poll had prognosticated that very turn, noting that "Romney's Mormon faith [would] likely [be] a factor in primaries, [but] not in a general election," since evangelical Christians seemed "prepared to overwhelmingly back him in a run against Obama in the general election."[73]

Those encouraging numbers for Romney notwithstanding, as spring 2012 turned to summer, many Latter-day Saints felt proverbial pins and needles over the new level of attention that the *general* election phase of the campaign might bring, the mix of "pride" and "fear" that the *Boston Globe*'s Matt Viser detected when Mormons considered that one of their own would be a major party nominee. This "potentially volatile moment," Viser sensed, "comes with a nagging fear that their beliefs, often misunderstood, will again be subjected to scrutiny, even ridicule, on a national scale." In May 2012, LDS Church Public Affairs Director Michael Otterson described the mood as "cautious optimism" in the truest sense of that phrase; he gave an address to a panel of journalists assembled in June 2012 to consider the "promise and peril of the Mormon moment." And throughout the summer and fall, Otterson's team braced themselves for a Mormon-themed "October surprise."[74]

The biggest story in the end may be that the "October surprise" never came, especially since in the spring of 2012 many saw such a campaign scenario as possible—and even likely. In April 2012, for example, Utah Senator Orrin Hatch (a Mormon and a Republican) told supporters that "there is nothing [President Obama's advisers] won't do." "You watch," Hatch said, "they're going to throw the Mormon Church at [Romney] like you can't believe."[75] There were certainly enough rumblings along the lines of the "weirdness" strategy that Democratic tacticians floated (and Stephen Colbert skewered) to make Mormons uneasy. The *New York Times* posted on its "Room for Debate" pages in late January 2012 a roundtable discussion with five contributors who each considered the question "Why are so many Americans uncomfortable with Mormonism?" The five panelists did not bring up the typical evangelical Christian concerns about heretical beliefs, but instead focused on social and cultural issues like "male authoritarianism" and enforced conformity and LDS political opposition to the Equal Rights Amendment and gay marriage, issues that would jar many Democratic voters. One columnist in the roundtable charged that "the Mormon Church does not respect separation of church and state"—this was the so-called "dark side to Mormonism" that another columnist asserted "may look good on paper" but would "positively smother most Americans." Indeed, it seemed like the Mormon past could provide plenty of ammunition for Romney's Democratic opponents.[76]

But brief forays into this type of campaigning did not amount to much, and the real story of the summer of 2012 was that Mormon controversy did not hold center stage. True, as Brooks admitted a week before Election Day 2012, "hard-left bloggers, tweeters, and media figures [continue to] fixate on Romney's Mormonism as a secret and nefarious forces in his politics. But in the mainstream media, the candidate's religion has just not gotten much play." Her rearview-mirror assessment as of late October was that "there certainly has not been the kind of prying coverage many Mormons feared." [77]

Brooks's view was that "Obama campaign headquarters has shown little interest in making use of Romney's religion, and Democratic operatives have fallen in line as well"—perhaps because experience had taught savvy politicos that the stakes were too high.[78] When Democratic adviser Hilary Rosen said in April 2012 that Ann Romney, who had been a stay-at-home mom (like many of her female Mormon coreligionists), had "never worked a day in her life," the public backlash was so great that Rosen apologized on CNN and in writing. President Obama quickly stated that there is "no tougher job than being a mom." The exchange ignited the social media world and highlighted the incendiary potential of any comment that might inflame culture wars over traditional religious values. *USA Today* reminisced, almost reflexively, about President Obama's 2008 description of voters who "cling to guns or religion."[79]

The Obama camp's repeated official line was that "attacking a candidate's religion is out of bounds, and our campaign will not engage in it."[80] Yet other observers wondered if that hands-off approach would change as the campaign intensified. Romney's election hopes in his 1994 Massachusetts Senate race had been dashed in large part, at least as many saw it, by Ted Kennedy's turn to publicizing Mormon controversies. In what might have felt like political déjà vu, then, Edward Klein, writing for Fox News at the end of August, quoted unnamed "sources inside the [Obama] campaign" that suggested that David Axelrod, President Obama's chief campaign operative, had "discussed what might be called the nuclear option: unleashing an attack on Romney's Mormon faith via the mainstream media." The motivation for such an attack, according to Klein, was that "recent polls show[ed] Romney beginning to close the gap in seven key swing states." Klein concluded, "In case you haven't noticed, the media has recently declared open season on Mitt Romney's Mormon faith."[81]

While Klein did back up that statement with several "egregious examples" of mostly crude media characterizations of past Mormon leaders, in hindsight it seems clearer that any "nuclear option," if such ever was discussed, was never exercised—or at least never detonated. Elizabeth Flock, surveying Google search data for *U.S. News and World Report* in September 2012, referenced Klein's prediction, but noted that "there has been no indication of that kind of attack yet."[82] Klein's sources suggested "Axelrod recognized that playing the Mormon card contained several obvious dangers," like inviting "fresh charges of religious bigotry" that would come on the heels of the "bitter dispute with the Catholic Church over a health-insurance mandate for contraception," or "[encouraging] the Republicans to reciprocate by reopening the whole tangled issue of Obama and the Reverend Wright." After all, Joanna Brooks noted that at least as numerous as the vocal opponents of Romney's Mormonism were the "hard-right bloggers and tweeters [who] continue to use [Reverend Jeremiah] Wright (and charges that Obama is a Muslim)."[83] In late July 2012, the *Washington Post*'s Aaron Blake analyzed poll results that showed that "while there has been a lot of consternation about whether Americans will be hesitant to vote for a Mormon like Romney, misinformation about Obama's religion"—especially among the 17% of Americans who "think the president is a Muslim"—"may matter just as much come November."[84] These certainly must have been sobering (and, perhaps, restraining) variables in the political calculus.

That perilous risk-reward paradox may be why complaints and angst and even exposés about Mormon oddities never gained much national traction during the general election campaign season. Yet other impulses also seemed to be at work here. On the one hand, six intense years of coverage undoubtedly contributed to a saturation feeling for journalists who had repeatedly dealt with the same aspects of Mormon history and doctrine. On the other hand, the LDS Church public affairs team, capitalizing on this protracted attention to their faith, actively and repeatedly encouraged journalists to make new connections between Mormon faith and Mormon practice. And questions about Mitt Romney's service as a lay church minister (a "bishop" in Mormon parlance) provided the right launching point.[85]

What cannot be missed, and what is perhaps most interesting here, is the observable phenomenon of a growing chorus of voices throughout the summer of 2012 stating that Mormonism seemed to be tipping from liability to asset for Mitt Romney. *The Daily Beast*'s David Frum actually posted a piece in June 2012 suggesting the religion was Romney's "*greatest* asset."[86] The refrain that was most unexpected in the late summer of 2012 was that Mitt Romney needed to speak *more* of his Mormonism because his religion humanized him.[87]

Perhaps the clearest signal that the Romney campaign did not fear some Mormon-related "nuclear option" that would drive away voters was the Romney campaign's decision to bring up Mormonism at several points during the Republican National Convention. It was a decision based on several emerging realities.

First, it was Romney's wealth rather than his faith that Democratic strategists pounced on. The picture of Mitt Romney as an out-of-touch corporate raider dominated the political ads. *The New Yorker*'s Adam Gopnik suggested in mid-August that "class...more than creed" motivated Mitt Romney, who "is better understood as a late-twentieth-century American tycoon than as any kind of believer." Gopnik also painted modern Mormonism with the broad brush-strokes of a prototypical prosperity "Gospel of Wealth." But *New York Times* columnist Ross Douthat countered that claim with firsthand observation—Douthat had spent time in Salt Lake City accompanying lay Mormon ministers in their visits and their humanitarian welfare work. His conclusion was that "the level of commitment required of someone serving in those offices suggests a considerably higher level of religious devotion." It was this picture of Mormonism that Douthat felt should be included in the Republican Convention's "biographical movie that will play just before Mitt Romney accepts his party's nomination."[88]

This was a turn—what one reporter described as "interest in Mormonism shift[ing] away from beliefs that set Mormons apart to how Mormons worship and live"—that the LDS Public Affairs Department welcomed and cultivated.[89] The church's official and conscientious nonpartisanship (Michael Otterson even studiously avoided mentioning Mitt Romney's name when interacting with reporters) seemed to have the effect of pushing journalists to explore new angles of Mormonism.[90] Perhaps there was no clearer example of this than NBC's airing of a *Rock Center* special devoted wholly to Mormonism, one week before the Republican Convention in Tampa.

Originally, the NBC team contacted church press representatives and proposed something like a brief, eight-minute feature on the church consisting of a handful of interviews. Church Public Affairs representatives campaigned for something more extensive from the network and suggested that the timing was right to do something substantive. NBC producers eventually agreed.[91] The result was "Mormon in America," multifaceted, hour-long program that included a lengthy segment profiling a mixed-race Mormon family (the husband, black, an adult convert to the church; the wife, white, a lifelong member); and another long segment exploring the church's massive humanitarian relief complex in Salt Lake City—and reporter Harry Smith admitted that he was thoroughly taken aback by the extent of the welfare efforts.

The program also included a poignant conversation with several lapsed Mormons—including a man who spoke movingly about his own *real* missionary service for the church and then his *surreal* (for him) portrayal of a missionary as an actor in the *Book of Mormon* musical. The program also touched on polygamy and ceremonial temple undergarments. But, as a television critic for the *Salt Lake Tribune* noted, it was the way the program's time and tone were proportioned that had to hearten Mormons. [92] These proportions felt significantly different—and for Mormon viewers, more apt—than even PBS's 2007 *The Mormons*. After reviewing Joseph Smith's history of visions and miraculous discovery of gold plates, for example, *Rock Center* host Brian Williams quoted Yale University religion professor Jon Butler, who "gently reminds" that all religions have their "amazing stories." As Abby Huntsman (daughter of one-time presidential candidate Jon Huntsman)[93] fielded questions about Mormon undergarments, she said they were worn to remind Mormons of their commitment to Christ. And reporter Harry Smith opened his feature on Mormon welfare initiatives by explicitly connecting those initiatives to Jesus' New Testament admonitions to care for the poor and needy.

Church Public Affairs representatives had been urging that type of engagement with street-level Mormonism, the lived religion that obviously impressed Ross Douthat and Harry Smith. It was this practical side of the faith that prompted Republican Convention planners to bring in Romney's fellow parishioners.

First, Ann Romney mentioned their faith by name (something the campaign rarely did) in her opening-night convention speech. Two nights later, and in the hours immediately before Mitt Romney accepted the nomination, invited speakers included one of Mitt Romney's church assistants during the years that Romney led a Boston-area Mormon congregation. Then three members of that Boston congregation offered heartfelt testimonials about Romney's pastoral service at times when tragedy struck their families. This was the Mormon story line that was somehow overshadowing the controversial—and it was a story line that would begin to transcend party lines in new ways.

Observers agreed this move on the part of Republican planners was effective. A politically diverse panel of CNN commentators weighed in with their impressions of the Republican Convention, and even those who did not like Romney's speech or his policies sensed that the turn to his personal and religious biography would change some minds. Princeton Professor Julian Zelizer said, "Romney made progress" in his efforts "to introduce himself to the nation" by "sharing more about his religion as well as his family," and showing that "he was more than a ruthless capitalist." CNN's David Gergen offered that "for the convention as a whole, its biggest success may have been to warm up Mitt Romney"—and the "emotionally charged testimonials" of Romney's fellow Mormons "seemingly did well in erasing the impressions created by the barrage of negative advertising he's sustained." Even Hilary Rosen, who created the Ann Romney, stay-at-home mom dustup agreed that Romney "did . . . decently" in "[conveying] who he is as a person of empathy and good intent"; she said that if she were a Romney supporter, "all I would talk about" were the "personal stories of Romney's speech." Columnist Ruben Navarette asked, "Where have the Republicans been hiding this guy?" He liked "the kinder, gentler, more emotive Mitt Romney" so much that his conclusion was, "We got ourselves a ball game."[94]

There were moments over the course of the next two months when that "ball game" would feel incredibly tight. What was unlikely about the philosophical turn at the convention was that Mitt Romney's Mormonism actually seemed to improve his odds. Then Romney's commanding performance in the first debate in October vaulted him into a virtual dead heat with President Obama in a number of polls, and pundits predicted the race could end up being as close as any in a generation. Those predictions did not play out in quite that dramatic a fashion, and there is little question that the campaign will long be scrutinized for what it has to say in terms of partisan politics and electoral analysis and a host of other campaign subtexts. In terms of what the closing months of the campaign had to say about the public image of Mormonism, however, there appeared this memorable Associated Press headline in the weeks following the election: "And the Winner Is... the Mormon Church."[95]

This was a sentiment that had been growing since the late summer of 2012, as if the Republican Convention essentially confirmed that the public image of Mormonism became a separate story from the campaign fortunes of the nation's most famous Mormon. Such an observation is rife with the potential for overstatement. To be sure, national interest in Mormonism was fueled by Mitt Romney's prominence. Publicized Google search data in the week after the Republican Convention showed the potency of that connection.[96] But in retrospect, there was also a subtle shift that suggested that interest in Mormonism became an interest in its own right, and for its own sake. As Associated Press religion reporter Rachel Zoll put it, "The spotlight on Romney spread to a broad array of Latter-day Saints, including Harvard management gurus, authors, and bloggers"—even star Notre Dame linebacker Manti Te'o, "a Latter-day Saint who talks openly about how he prayed to choose among the dozens of college scholarships he was offered."[97] Author Stephen Mansfield spoke to that spreading spotlight in September 2012, for example, when he discussed his newly published book *The Mormonizing of America*. Whereas he had previously written *The Faith of George W. Bush* and *The Faith of Barack Obama*, he said he opted not to write *The Faith of Mitt Romney*, because "in this case I think that the story of the Mormon moment or this Mormon ascent is a bigger story than Mitt Romney." It was the story, Mansfield said, of an "unprecedented leap forward"—and in his view, "there is much more to come."[98]

And the Winner Is... the Mormon Church?

Semantically, it would seem that the story had now come full circle. *The Nation* called George Romney's Mormonism one of his political "assets" in 1962; in 2012, *The Daily Beast* called Mitt Romney's Mormonism "perhaps his greatest asset." This, of course, meant that 2012 felt like a far cry from 2008—and yet it was not 1962 or 1968 all over again, either. Fifty years of steadily intensifying interest in, and inquiry into, the LDS faith had added color and variety to the benign portrait that was midcentury Mormonism—and had also added, most importantly, an institutional overlay to that picture of Mormonism, and with that overlay came both light and shadow. With an eye on that complexity at the close of this narrative, the final questions to ask are these: in what ways did observers see the Mormon Church winning, and what might those "victories" mean in the long run?

The first victory that commentators proclaimed came in the form of the fifty million–plus ballots from Americans who were willing to vote for a Mormon to be president. On that basis alone, *Boston Globe* columnist Alex Beam proposed that November 6, 2012, "may qualify as the most important day—ever—in Mormons' history. What had long been America's most reviled, and openly rebellious, religious minority had become certifiably mainstream." A willingness to vote for a Mormon, of course, did not mean that voters were willing to accept— or even admit feeling comfortable with—Mormons' religious claims. Beam himself revealed his own discomfort with this development, given Mormonism's history of tension with American norms and American government. But this increasing willingness to consider a Mormon as a viable president did speak to some of the public perception "battles" that Mormon observers felt they had weathered successfully. Thus Mitt Romney may have "lost, but the Mormons won," Beam concluded.[99]

A year before the 2012 election, Mormon historians Terryl Givens and Richard Bushman independently articulated the feeling that, in Bushman's words, "at the beginning of the twentieth century, right after [Utah] statehood and the end of polygamy, we [Mormons] had two problems. One was, were we a dangerous, deluded people? Were we really a threat to American society? And two, how could anyone believe such a crazy theology as we have? And over the next fifty years,...Americans became convinced that Mormons were good people....So that battle, I think, we've won. The second battle, making our theology respectable, we haven't won." As Terryl Givens saw it, this "dichotomy...is still present. Mormons are perfectly welcomed to dance with the stars, to feed a continual stream of great quarterbacks into the NFL, they're good in a national disaster, the Mormon Tabernacle Choir continues to sing at the presidential inaugurals, but the theology continues to be completely marginalized as a system of thought, exploited only for sensationalistic reasons. This, even though as any well-informed theologian would tell you, many of the peculiarities of Mormon theology have moved more and more to the center of Christian theological thought (Figure 10.2)."[100]

That "dichotomy" assessment still seems accurate, but it is also worth asking, one year later, if the sharpness of that dichotomy has softened.

Insofar as discomfort with Mormon beliefs is a product of unfamiliarity, there seem to be good reasons for the widely reported Mormon optimism that their public standing is improving—that "Americans are growing more curious than fearful about the faith."[101] That optimism was captured in a landmark January 2012 Pew Forum survey of American Mormons. The survey found that while 68% of Mormons felt that "Americans as a whole do not see Mormonism as part of mainstream American society," and 62% of Mormons felt that most

Figure 10.2. Jimmermania—BYU's star point guard, Jimmer Fredette, became a
college basketball sensation in the 2010–2011 season. He won National Player of the
Year honors, and his name became part of the country's sports vocabulary. University
of Richmond Professor Terryl Givens saw Fredette as representative of the "clean-cut,
all-American" Mormon—one side of the Mormon image "dichotomy." Photograph by
Mark A. Philbrick/BYU.

Americans know "not too much" or "nothing" about Mormonism, 63% of
Mormons still felt that "acceptance of Mormonism is rising."[102]

Three professors at three universities teamed up on a study of attitudes
toward Mormonism during Mitt Romney's first campaign, and they released
their results in late 2009, through *USA Today*. Their conclusion was that
"Americans still have a [religious] bias against Republican Mitt Romney." While
that was certainly not a news flash in December 2009, it was their next conclusion that was especially interesting, especially for Mormon image watchers. They
wrote, "When people understood [Romney's] Mormon faith, the bias melted
away." Their methodology was inventive. They administered to respondents a
short quiz about Mormonism. "Those who scored 100% on [the] quiz...were
much less likely to be bothered by the claim that Mormons are not Christians.
In contrast, respondents who claimed they knew a lot about Mormons, *but who
actually did not* [as evidenced by their quiz results], were bothered most of all by
[controversial] claims about Mormonism."[103]

Given that analysis, Mormon observers might have been discouraged when, one month after the 2012 election, the Pew Forum sampled fifteen hundred Americans and then concluded that 82% "say that they learned little or nothing about the Mormon religion during the presidential campaign." Pew had found, in a November 2011 poll, that 49% of respondents said that they "know a great deal or some" about the Mormon religion; that figure was unchanged in the December 2012 Pew poll. But later results detailed in the December 2012 survey seemed to belie that flatline finding in favor of other revealing trends. In other words, Pew's headline might have missed the real story.[104]

Two outcomes were especially interesting. Pew reported that in December 2012, "more Americans mention positive terms such as 'good people,' 'dedicated' and 'honest'" when asked for "one-word impressions of" Mormonism "than did so [in 2011]"—a six-point percentage jump. More significant, while there was an overall four-point decrease in the number of Americans who saw Mormonism as "very different" from their own religious beliefs, the change among white, mainline Protestants on that front was surprisingly dramatic. In December 2012, 42% of respondents in that Protestant group said that Mormonism had "a lot in common" with their own religious beliefs, up from only 28% just one year earlier.[105]

Even among evangelical Protestants, a four-point boost on that same question was noteworthy for Mormons since it marked a measurable change in temperature.[106] For many evangelical Christians, of course, unfamiliarity with Mormon theology and practice is not the issue. They see Mormonism as distorted Christianity at best. But even there, where these two historically at-odds faith groups meet, observers are willing to concede that 2012 marked substantial "progress," and perhaps a real win for civility and understanding. Fuller Seminary's Richard Mouw suggested at the end of the election cycle that "evangelicals can be divided into thirds: one group that accepts Mormons, another that rejects it, and another group that is conflicted about the faith."[107] The change in tone in 2012 might have been most pronounced from voices in that undecided third.

To be sure, groups like that of Reverend Bill Keller berated fellow Christians for even participating in an election that had "Satan flipping a two-headed coin with his head on both sides."[108] Reverend Keller's crusade was to enlist voters to commit to write in "Jesus" on the presidential ballot, and reportedly 1.4 million had agreed to do so by late October 2012.[109] Yet despite these types of impassioned pleas against supporting a Mormon, more significant seemed to be what University of Virginia Professor Larry Sabato called the "shotgun marriage between two very different religions [that] are completely dependent upon one another for victory."[110]

Perhaps there was no better illustration of making the best of that "shotgun marriage" than Pastor Robert Jeffress's mid-September 2012 post on FoxNews.

com. The title of his piece alone was telling: "Romney and the disappearing evan-gelical dilemma." Jeffress acknowledged that one year earlier he had "ignited a national discussion about Mitt Romney's religious faith by labeling Mormonism as a 'cult'" and "[predicting] that if Romney became the Republican nominee, President Obama would win a second term." But now, a year later, Pastor Jeffress wrote that he was "willing to admit [his] prognostication may have been premature for several reasons"—mostly because President Obama's perceived attacks on Christian values and religious liberties had kindled an outrage that Jeffress expected would draw more evangelicals to the polls than the candidacy of Mormon Mitt Romney would have on its own. Plus Mitt Romney's choice of Paul Ryan as a running mate "sent a strong signal to evangelicals that they would have someone in the White House who represents their values." These factors "made Mitt Romney much more palatable to evangelical Christians—like me."[111]

While this endorsement came off as half-hearted at best, it neverthe-less reflected well the reasoning that had allowed many evangelical leaders to bury the theological hatchets that they had been less willing to relinquish for nearly three decades of political commingling with Mormons in the Republican Party.[112] Mitt Romney, like fellow Mormon Glenn Beck two years before, gave the commencement address at Liberty University in May 2012. He told the audi-ence, "People of different faiths, like yours and mine, sometimes wonder where we can meet in common purpose, when there are so many differences in creed and theology. Surely the answer is that we can meet in service, in shared moral convictions about our nation stemming from a common worldview. The best case for this is always the example of Christian men and women working and witnessing to carry God's love into every life"—and then, to illustrate that ideal, Romney invoked the memory of well-known evangelical Chuck Colson and told a story from Colson's prison ministry. Colson had died just the month before.[113]

Even the Billy Graham Evangelistic Association threw its weight behind Romney's campaign in only slightly veiled ways. In mid-October, Romney vis-ited the aging Billy Graham at his North Carolina home. Published photographs showed the two talking amiably. News reports mentioned that they had prayed together, and then Graham's organization took out full-page ads with a plea from the famous pastor to "vote biblical values Tuesday, November 6." While some expressed surprise at a partisan turn that seemed more Franklin Graham the son than Billy Graham the father, the episode nevertheless provided a strik-ing image of just how far the evangelical community was going to accept Mitt Romney's candidacy.[114]

The Election Day ticker told a story that confirmed Pastor Jeffress's grudging support rather than Pastor Keller's persistent antipathy. When the polls closed, and despite anecdotal evidence that suggested many evangelicals were simply going to sit out the election, a greater percentage of evangelicals had voted for

Mitt Romney than had voted for John McCain (79% to 73%), and this in an election when "the evangelical vote was 27% of the overall electorate—the highest it's ever been for an election."[115]

This was big news on at least two fronts. Even with the support of the overwhelming majority of evangelicals who voted, Mitt Romney still lost. The 2012 election might thus be remembered as the moment when the powerful Christian Right lost its "kingmaking" status in the Republican Party.[116] Only weeks before the election, news outlets across the country noted that for the first time in history Protestants made up less than half of the nation's population.[117]

And then, almost in tandem with that announced demographic reality of a growing religious pluralism, many evangelicals implicitly assented to a new acceptance of Mormons as political partners. As the Associated Press's Rachel Zoll suggested as early as January 2012, "the second time around, the shock [at the prospect of a Mormon president] has worn off."[118] The durability of those partnerships is not a done deal, of course—and there were reminders of that tenuousness throughout the campaign. As noteworthy as anything that the Billy Graham Evangelistic Association did in October may have been the report, subsequent to Mitt Romney's visit with Reverend Graham, that the association had also removed from its website explicit references to Mormonism as a "cult." The publicity surrounding that quiet removal made for some awkward backtracking, as a Billy Graham spokesman explained that the association did not want to be party to a theological debate that had become overtly politicized. What really made headlines instead was the evangelical outcry that the Billy Graham Evangelistic Association had gone too far. A number of Christian voices suggested that this move was going to backfire against the Romney campaign, since some who had been willing to stomach a vote for a Mormon could not, in good conscience, accept this sort of implied change in Mormonism's *religious* status. This to them was selling out on a scale of eternal magnitude. Once again, the depth of these undercurrents was on display.[119]

However, more representative of the new evangelical-Mormon reality might have been a roundtable hosted at the Southern Baptist Theological Seminary in September 2012 that tackled the question, "Can Christians vote for a Mormon?" The panel's response was affirmative, since evangelicals were "going to have to give up—on both sides—the idea of a president as religious mascot" and instead vote for a candidate with "the kind of wisdom to bear the sword on behalf of God's authority that He has granted to the state." The question to be asked was, "Can I trust that person to protect society?"—and the panelists implied that Mitt Romney fit that bill. At the same time, they anticipated that "if President Romney is elected, we're the people who ought to be able to say, 'We respect and honor this man as president. We're able to ... serve with this man as president, and we're the people who are willing to—if we're invited into the Oval Office— say, 'President Romney, here's where we agree with you; here's what we like about what you're doing. And we sincerely want to plead with you to believe the Gospel of Jesus Christ.'" While these panelists underscored again that voting for a Mormon did not preclude a desire to witness to that same Mormon about his/her misguided religious beliefs, the panelists nevertheless hoped the 2012 election would be "an education moment for evangelicals," a moment when they could "learn to think more carefully about how to agree with a person's policies while disagreeing with his theological beliefs."[120]

Vanderbilt historian Kathleen Flake, one week before the November election, took a utilitarian view of the situation: "Romney's nomination necessitated the silencing of evangelical anti-Mormons. Other explanations, it seems to me, underestimate their antipathy...of the present administration and their fear of a second term [for President Obama]."[121] Only time will tell how enduring the civility and the partnerships and the conversations prove to be, in terms of Mormon interaction with evangelicals and other Christians. Still, Richard Mouw cast the Romney campaign in a hopeful light about future trends, in that "Romney's candidacy didn't cause the shift, but was a sign of changes already under way."[122] In some ways, *any* level of agreement and agreeableness—like Franklin Graham's open letter in October 2012 ("while there are major differences in the theology of evangelical Christians and that of Mormons, as well as those who practice the Catholic faith or the Jewish faith, we do share common values that are *biblically based*")—seemed like a step forward.[123]

A number of commentators (including the Southern Baptist Seminary panelists) made the almost-inevitable comparison between Mitt Romney's two campaigns and John F. Kennedy's in 1960—or, perhaps more appropriately, Al Smith's in 1928 (or even Joseph Lieberman's in 2000 [Figure 10.3]). Those comparisons implied that Mormons had gained new ground, that new doors had been opened to them—and even evangelical voters had been a part of that. Did that also mean that abruptly shutting the door on Mormons in the future could entail the uncomfortable public scrutiny and public explanations of the kind Robert Jeffress experienced with CNN's Anderson Cooper?[124] Joanna Brooks described the October 2011 Cooper-Jeffress exchange as the "moment" that epitomized, for her, the real "shift" in tone in the media coverage of Mormons during the 2008 campaign versus the 2012 campaign. Brooks sensed that after Pastor Jeffress's October 2011 "cult" comments, the "taste in the mouth of the media chang[ed]." Mainstream media outlets began to "frame" Jeffress's words in terms of "prejudice," something that had not happened widely with Mike Huckabee's 2008 comments about Mormon beliefs, for example.[125]

This is not to suggest that the media began treating Mormonism with kid gloves, or that all media outlets lined up to defend Mitt Romney. But what did seem to manifest itself was a measured respect (what Brooks called "deference") and consideration of the Mormon perspective—especially in terms of the sacred. A defining case in point, for Joanna Brooks, was that

Figure 10.3. U.S. Senator Joseph Lieberman and LDS apostle L. Tom Perry (who at the time chaired the LDS Church's Public Affairs Committee) visit before Senator Lieberman's address at a Brigham Young University forum, October 25, 2011. Lieberman, an observant Jew, spoke about the then-current political situation, which saw two Mormons running for president, in remarks he titled "Faith and the Public Square." He told the audience that during the 2000 presidential campaign, when he was Democratic candidate Al Gore's running mate, "In that year I personally experienced the American people's generosity of spirit, their fairness, and acceptance of religious diversity." He also quoted the Reverend Jesse Jackson: "In America, when a barrier is broken for one, the doors of opportunity open wider for every other American." Photograph by Mark A. Philbrick/BYU.

the mainstream media "did not want to touch" the covertly filmed Mormon temple ceremony that a purveyor tried to peddle for over a month in the fall of 2012.[126] Based on those indicators, there may be new resistance to any attempt to return things to the way they were, and some roads may not have to be retraveled.[127]

If there was a new effort among journalists to "get it right," the increasing airtime given to Mormon voices seemed in line with that.[128] Church leaders since the time of the first Mitt Romney campaign had been actively urging media outlets to let the church represent itself and its beliefs.[129] As Joanna Brooks put it bluntly, though, the media wants independent voices and not institutional voices." The fact, therefore, "that media coverage during Mitt Romney's 2012 campaign prominently featured *both* types of voices speaks volumes. In one sense, that speaks to the working relationships developed on the part of the institutional press representatives in the church's Public Affairs Department.

If the earliest mantra of the LDS Church's public relations efforts was to bring the church out of obscurity (and Michael Otterson noted wryly in 2011 that on some busy days he suspected his staffers at LDS Public Affairs still "wish we had a little bit of obscurity"), the 2012 version of that mantra was, in Otterson's words, "trust, respect, and mutual understanding," with—importantly—no "spin." As a former journalist himself, Otterson said, "I've always hated [that] word." Such an attitude, in Richard Bushman's view, paid dividends. His experience in talking with reporters who had worked with LDS Public Affairs was that reporters generally felt they were talking with "straight shooter[s]."[130]

At the same time, the press also turned, more and more, to authentic but independent *Mormon* voices—commentators like Richard Bushman, Terryl Givens, Matthew Bowman, Jana Riess, Joanna Brooks, Spencer Fluhman, Patrick Mason, and a host of others, because of their ability to "translate" Mormonism. Although Brooks conceded that some Mormons would prefer the "univocal" response that the institutional church can provide, the end result was something that even church apostle Quentin L. Cook celebrated: "We've also noticed a realization outside the Church that Latter-day Saints aren't all the same; our people are very different from one another in good and interesting ways."[131]

On that note, one final "win" deserves to be considered here, since this change might, in the long run, prove to have the greatest impact on Mormonism's public image. Matthew Bowman told National Public Radio that, in his view, Mitt Romney's run had "done a fair amount to refute the great myth of Mormonism: that it's a monolith." The irony, as Bowman noted, is that Mitt Romney seemed the very picture of what the public might imagine when they think of a Mormon.[132] (*Newsweek* only tapped into that when they put on the cover of their June 13, 2011, issue a picture of Mitt Romney's head superimposed on the iconic photo of the leaping missionary from the *Book of Mormon* musical promo.) Yet broader exposure to the Mormon community over the course of two campaigns revealed a political and racial diversity that may not have been expected.

An unmistakable sign, for example, that the "Mormon moment" was larger than the Mitt Romney campaign alone—or that Mormonism was larger than conservative politics alone—popped up at the *Democratic* National Convention. One week after the Republicans convened in Tampa, National Public Radio reported on a meeting room in Charlotte, North Carolina, "packed with the curious, the media and a cadre of members of the Church of Jesus Christ of Latter-day Saints" who held "the first national meeting of Mormon Democrats" in conjunction with their party's national convention.[133] Senate Majority Leader Harry Reid (Figure 10.4) addressed his fellow Mormon Democrats. (It is worth noting that Reid's prominence in the Democratic Party and his increased visibility as a Mormon surely must have complicated any discussion in the Obama camp about launching the Mormon "nuclear option" that David Axelrod purportedly

Figure 10.4. U.S. Senator Harry Reid and BYU President (and LDS Church General Authority) Cecil O. Samuelson share a light moment before Senator Reid's address at a BYU forum on October 9, 2007. At the time, no Latter-day Saint had achieved an elected office higher than had Reid, the Senate's Majority Leader. Surveys in 2011 showed, however, that only 6% of Americans identified Reid as a Mormon. Some Latter-day Saints wish that identification rate was higher in order to dispel notions of a Mormon-Republican monolith. In his address at BYU, Reid said, "It is not uncommon for members of the Church to ask how I can be a Mormon and a Democrat ... I say that my faith and political beliefs are deeply intertwined. I am a Democrat because I am a Mormon, not in spite of it." Photograph by Mark A. Philbrick/BYU.

contemplated, especially considering the potential for collateral damage that an all-out attack could have had on one of the party's own—or on the image of the party itself, just as the caucus of "Mormon Democrats" was garnering attention.) And as a reflection of the sense that association with Mormonism was not a liability—at least in the closing months of the 2012 campaign—Harry Reid very publicly seconded a *Washington Post* op-ed written by fellow Mormon Gregory Prince: "Mitt Romney is *not* the face of Mormonism."[134]

Some charged Senator Reid with using the moment for political gain, yet the piece also said something larger. Both Prince and Reid gave voice to a prominent undercurrent among American Mormons who have felt that the ethics of their faith and its deeply rooted compassion for the poor align better with the Democratic Party—and these Mormons did not want the nation to miss that. NBC's *Rock Center* noted, significantly, that the fact that a feminist like Joanna Brooks or an openly gay (but celibate) man like Mitch Mayne (both of whom were featured in the program) could find a place today in the fold of practicing Mormons suggested something surprising about the church's growing diversity.

Another facet of that increasing diversity of Mormonism also was on display in 2012. At one point in the early spring, racial controversies from Mormonism's past threatened to flare up, just as Mitt Romney's primary successes fueled speculation that his nomination would surely portend an unprecedented intersection of questions about Mormonism *and* questions about race. The *Washington Post* ran a lengthy feature about the place of black Mormons in the church, both in historical and contemporary contexts. In an unfortunate attempt to put a rationale on the pre-1978 LDS policy restricting the priesthood ordination of black men (or perhaps in an attempt to merely articulate a rationale that others had used), a BYU professor implied in the *Post* article an underlying belief that blacks were not ready for the responsibility of the priesthood before 1978. A maelstrom of comments hit media outlets nationwide, many of them from Mormons themselves.[135]

There was almost a collective groan from the Mormon community over the possibility that historic racism would become, for the duration of the campaign, the primary focus of the media spotlight on Mitt Romney's religion. There was a palpable worry that this would lead to the public rehashing of an issue that had not plagued Mormons nearly as doggedly as had polygamy. What irked many of these Mormon commentators was that church leaders had disavowed the very types of rationales quoted in the *Post*. Other Mormons took this as evidence that the church's hierarchy had not gone far enough to put to rest the persistent, racially charged beliefs and explanations of an earlier generation that still lingered.[136] In response to the *Washington Post* piece, however, the church wasted no time in issuing what was its strongest statement yet in terms of distancing itself from those explanations: "The Church's position is clear—we believe all people are God's children and are equal in His eyes and in the Church. We do not tolerate racism in any form. For a time in the Church there was a restriction on the priesthood for male members of African descent. It is not known precisely why, how, or when this restriction began in the Church but what is clear is that it ended decades ago. Some have attempted to explain the reason for this restriction but these attempts should be viewed as speculation and opinion, not doctrine. The Church is not bound by speculation or opinions given with limited understanding. We condemn racism, including any and all past racism by individuals both inside and outside the Church."[137]

While this statement seemed to carry echoes of the position the church officially had taken in 1978 to "let the revelation speak for itself," the line that seemed most significant for observers was that "it is not known precisely why, how, or when this restriction began." While this did not satisfy those who wanted a clearer repudiation of past positions, it did admit to historical uncertainty—and that was meaningful in the eyes of Mormons who were willing to admit the cultural forces that might have come to bear on past leaders' views.[138] (In 2013, the LDS Church announced the release of a new edition of its scriptural canon. A new introduction to "Official Declaration 2"—the announcement of the 1978 priesthood policy change—put that historical uncertainty in even stronger terms than the spring 2012 press release: "The Book of Mormon teaches that 'all are alike unto God,' including 'black and white, bond and free, male and female' (2 Nephi 26:33). Throughout the history of the Church, people of every race and ethnicity in many countries have been baptized and have lived as faithful members of the Church. During Joseph Smith's lifetime, a few black male members of the Church were ordained to the priesthood. Early in its history, Church leaders stopped conferring the priesthood on black males of African descent. Church records offer no clear insights into the origins of this practice. Church leaders believed that a revelation from God was needed to alter this practice and prayerfully sought guidance. The revelation came to Church President Spencer W. Kimball and was affirmed to other Church leaders in the Salt Lake Temple on June 1, 1978. The revelation removed all restrictions with regard to race that once applied to the priesthood.")[139]

After this tempest, and as with so many other issues, the fact that Mormonism's history of race relations did *not* become the ever-present talking point that it threatened to become in March speaks to the complexity of the Mormon public image that emerged from the 2012 presidential campaign.[140] Only two months after the *Washington Post* article made such a resounding splash, *Sports Illustrated* featured on its cover the nation's top high school basketball player, Chicago's Jabari Parker. Here was a black young man who was quickly becoming a national phenom, and the *Sports Illustrated* cover story (as did a later Katie Couric feature on *Good Morning America*) made obvious that Jabari Parker was a devout Mormon. The cover proclaimed, "The best high school basketball player since LeBron James is Jabari Parker, but there's something more important to him than NBA stardom: his faith."[141] Coinciding with that story, Utah congressional candidate Mia Love drew national notice by winning her primary race. She was poised to become, if elected in November (she lost narrowly to incumbent Jim Matheson), the first black Republican woman elected to Congress—and she was a Mormon. Mia Love was also a featured speaker at the Republican National Convention.

Of course, complaints about Mormonism's past racial policies reappeared throughout the campaign, and some columnists vehemently questioned Mitt Romney's fitness to serve on that score because of his loyalty to the LDS Church.[142] Yet there also appeared stories like one in the *Los Angeles Times* that showed a picture of George Romney marching in a civil rights demonstration and wondered about the extent of Mitt Romney's inherited legacy of civil rights activism.[143] When NBC's *Rock Center* profiled the Jackson family in October 2012, the interviewer asked the African-American father of that family, Al Jackson, if he had ever felt discrimination in church. His immediate reply: "Never." These competing pictures seemed to defy any easy assumptions about who Mormons are—and these new faces of Mormonism seemed to lend credence to the idealized "I'm a Mormon" ads popping up across the nation.

"Invasion of the Body Snatchers Syndrome"— The Future of the Mormon Identity

After all of this talk of the Mormon Church winning, however, and if too many commentators sounded too triumphalist, coverage of the campaign also provided plenty of down-to-earth sobriety about the public's perception of Mormonism. While headlines about a Mormon "win" capture well the generally (and unexpectedly) positive press that, all things considered, Mormons enjoyed in the fall of 2012, those headlines should not obscure the reality that the immediate future of Mormonism's public image in America is not a settled question. Victory in this sense might feel for Mormons more like surviving some reality TV challenge only to face something new the next day.[144]

Some voices complained, for example, that the media gave Mormonism an undeserved pass. Sharon Toomer in the *Huffington Post* wondered in late October 2012 "why the press corps has gone lightweight on Governor Romney.... Religious affiliation mattered to the press corps in 2008. I don't understand why it does not matter in 2012." *The Daily Beast*'s Andrew Sullivan was as vocal on this as anyone, complaining that "once upon a time, when journalists were actually asking politicians tough questions, rather than begging for ... ratings," reporters did push Mitt Romney to talk more about his affiliation with Mormons—specifically his feelings about the church's past racial and priesthood-related policies. So "why," Sullivan asked Bill Maher a few days after the 2012 election, "was Mormonism off limits?" A week before the election, Sullivan posted the clandestinely filmed LDS temple rites mentioned earlier, and then reasoned, "If you are running for president, transparency is essential," even if other Christians were "willing to overlook the bizarre theology of Mormonism (and, of course, all theology is in some respects bizarre) in order to promote the policies most fundamentalists of all types favor."[145]

Yet it seems apparent that those who felt like the media gave Mormons the benefit of a "double standard" need not fear just yet that Americans have given the stamp of acceptability to Mormonism's "bizarre theology." While the Pew Forum's post-election December 2012 poll did find that attitudes toward Mormons and Mormon beliefs showed a positive turn since 2011, just over 60% of Americans still said that Mormonism was "very different" from their own beliefs. And only a quarter of those surveyed chose a "positive" term when asked for a "one-word descriptor" of Mormons.[146]

Limited play and broadcast reach notwithstanding, a number of media voices during the campaign both shaped and reflected persistent public uncertainty about Mormons. Even though overall attention to religion during the 2012 campaign on the part of "major news outlets" was minimal, the Pew Research Center's media survey of the 2012 campaign also analyzed "hundreds of thousands of messages about the candidates' faith on Twitter and Facebook" and determined that, for Romney's faith, "negative assertions" on social media "outnumbered positive ones by more than 3-to-1."[147] Historian Craig Foster, in chronicling media mentions of Mormonism, has argued that a media bias (and he argued that this grew out of the media's *political* bias) against Mormonism was less overt in 2012 but still influential. In his estimation, "while most stories have been professional and as neutral as possible, many have used stereotypical imagery to explain The Church of Jesus Christ of Latter-day Saints and its members."[148] Likewise, Lane Williams, in his "Mormon Media Observer" column for the *Deseret News* in October 2012, judged press references to Mormonism-as-cult this way: "Now, to be sure, most of these references to 'cult' were comprised of something like 'some evangelicals consider Mormonism a cult.' The reporters, if you will, aren't saying directly that Mormons are cult members. Nevertheless, framing theory suggests that merely bringing up a concept activates knowledge pathways much as it is essentially impossible to not think of an octopus when someone says 'don't think of an octopus.'"[149] While only seventy of the fifteen hundred–plus respondents to the Pew Forum's December 2012 poll mentioned the word "cult," that word was still the most common one-word descriptor offered in the survey.[150]

If some voices were happy to reinforce those types of insinuations (this was comedian Bill Maher saying that President Obama was going to beat Mitt Romney "like a runaway sister wife"),[151] some stereotypical images in the public mind are simply difficult to dislodge, a reality that LDS Church Public Affairs director Michael Otterson recognizes comes with the territory of public opinion. Church representatives like Otterson see a "win" in the degree to which the American press corps is "more informed about the basics of Mormonism than they were when Romney ran in 2008."[152] "Exhibit A" of those types of gains has come in the long effort to distinguish the church from fundamentalist polygamists. Otterson noted that in the years between Mitt Romney's campaigns, a number of media outlets responded positively to the church's requests to avoid the use of the phrase "fundamentalist Mormon" to describe polygamists who were not affiliated with the LDS Church. (Importantly, NBC's *Rock Center* program in August 2012 did not even mention contemporary fundamentalist polygamy, but instead featured LDS Church Historian—and General Authority—Steven Snow's explanation that the church discontinued polygamy because of a revelation to its prophet a century earlier.) Still, Otterson concedes at the same time that it is hard to tell how those efforts succeed when television shows like *Big Love* or *Sister Wives* draw millions of viewers—and imply a Mormon connection.[153]

This picture of polygamy might be one of those stubborn visuals that will persist with Mormonism indefinitely. After all, Jon Krakauer's *Under the Banner of Heaven*, with its premise that Mormonism (and religion in general) carries within it the seeds for irrationality and horrific violence, still landed squarely in December 2012 in the top ten in Amazon's list of best-selling Mormon-related books, ahead of all other books on Mormon history—and this at the same time that Warner Bros. and director Ron Howard's film adaptation of the book was reportedly moving forward. This worries Mormons who complain that Krakauer's book makes little distinction between polygamy past and polygamy present.[154]

Other, similarly troubling Mormon motifs also made repeated appearances during the campaign. A number of commentators stated flatly that they saw in Mitt Romney the very things that worried them about Mormonism: secrecy, intolerance, a driving ambition for economic and political power, and an all-too-ready willingness to jettison past positions in favor of expedience. If Mitt Romney, they said, saw his political positions as changeable as the now-famous "Etch-a-Sketch," he was only adopting an ethos he had learned from his church.[155]

It is not surprising, therefore, that the research trio of professors Campbell, Green, and Monson, in a follow-up to their 2008 polling, saw evidence in late 2012 of a persistent, underlying reluctance to vote for a Mormon. Ironically, their national survey found that Mormonism had essentially disappeared in terms of its measurable effect on Americans' willingness to vote for Mitt Romney *specifically*. But when the researchers proposed to respondents scenarios with hypothetical Mormon candidates for governor or mayor, Mormonism proved to have a measurable negative effect. While their research is still preliminary, one conclusion seems inescapable: "Mormon" still is "other."[156]

It seems telling that Brian Williams opened the August 2012 *Rock Center* "Mormon in America" program *not* by noting that some Americans were unwilling to vote for a Mormon—that issue was never raised during the hour—but that the majority of Americans still say they know little or nothing about Mormonism, six-plus years of twenty-four-hour news cycles notwithstanding. This sentiment of "knowing little or nothing" seems to reflect a nagging worry for Americans, in that the Mormons and Mormonism they *have* encountered do not make them feel any more certain they really understand the religion. This seems to say that Mormonism is confusing because it is so close to traditional Christianity in terms of worship practice and moral standards—yet different enough that the public does not feel comfortable with the differences (or knowing where the differences arise). On top of that, this seems to say that Americans are still suspicious that there is more to Mormonism than meets the eye—more than any number of stories in *The Atlantic* or *Time* or *BusinessWeek* or on *The Daily Show* or *The Colbert Report* or *Rock Center* can properly explain. Hence the sentiment that what has been shown still represents "little or nothing" about Mormons. This is the "otherness" of Mormons.

University of North Carolina Professor Laurie Maffly-Kipp put this public perception paradox in memorable terms in the January 2012 *New York Times* roundtable when she called it the "invasion of the body snatchers syndrome": "But just as Mormons seem to be ideal Americans, they also provoke typically American fears. While Mormons embody the economic and moral success endorsed by the American Dream, they also subscribe to beliefs that, to many, seem peculiar—even bizarre. Mormon beliefs, understandings of history, and practices such as temple rituals or a legacy of polygamy (which many—despite endless clarification—mistakenly believe the Church of Jesus Christ of Latter-day Saints still sanctions), not to mention their preference to keep some practices out of the public eye, all provoke unease and distrust. How can these people, so *like* many other Americans, be so *different*? I call this double legacy the 'invasion of the body snatchers' syndrome: no matter how much Mormon behavior conforms to what most consider admirable (and maybe *especially* because they look so wholesome), some Americans are convinced Mormons secretly await an opportunity to take over the world. Nothing Mitt Romney or others might say can assuage that deep-seated anxiety. And insisting it has no basis in fact only raises some people's fears further. Indeed, once those suspicions ignite, all otherwise admirable qualities of hard work and dedication become further cause for alarm. What if they are turned to the wrong causes, transforming the worker bees into deadly hornets?"[157]

With all of these competing depictions of the LDS Church and its members, Terryl Givens's recent history of Mormon culture seems aptly named—this indeed is a story about "a people of paradox."[158] There is a tension inherent in the public's views of this body of religious people—mostly positive—and the public's views of the religion that inspires that body—often negative, or at least conflicted. This paradox has meant that the evolution of Mormonism's public image has been fraught with surprises, contrasts, and irony.

Obviously any talk of the election-day "wins" of Mormonism must be tempered with these kinds of realities, meaning that a "win" in this case implies progress and possibility more than once-and-for-all finality. Yet in an October 2012 *Time* magazine cover story, Jon Meacham tapped into a vein of Mormon cultural thinking that he also saw in Mitt Romney: "Mormons are accustomed to conflict and expect persecution," but the religion's "can-do spirit" gave Romney the "instinct to survive and thrive in even the worst of storms."[159] While some journalists panned this kind of cultural and religious generalizing when it came to Mormonism, it is worth mentioning again that the extensive Pew study of Mormon attitudes found an undeniable strain of optimism about the faith's future place in American society.[160] That optimism seems to derive, at least in part, from the hope that some hurdles have been cleared, and maybe for good.

Mormons see reasons to be optimistic in the growing academic (and religious) interest in unique aspects of Mormon thought. Yale University's Harold Bloom characterized that doctrinal uniqueness this way, on Helen Whitney's documentary *The Mormons*:: "Of all the religions that I know, the one that most vehemently and persuasively defies and denies the reality of death is the original Mormonism of the prophet, seer, and revelator, Joseph Smith."[161] Five years later, Wabash College (Indiana) Professor Stephen Webb made significant waves when he wrote a provocatively titled piece ("Mormonism Obsessed with Christ") for the February 2012 issue of *First Things*. Webb is a convert to Roman Catholicism from evangelical Christianity, but he called on evangelicals and other Christians to reconsider their assessments that Mormons are not Christians, since Mormon theology (and scripture), Webb argued, was overwhelmingly "Christ-centered."[162] As might be imagined, comment boards and blogs lit up with those who charged Webb with something of a heretical and foolhardy turn. Yet Webb has persisted as a prominent voice in his advocacy of more scholarly (and religious) attention to Mormon theology. He gave an address in November 2012 to an understandably appreciative Brigham Young University audience where he proposed that a fascination with Mormon cosmology would grow in the academy and in the religious world, precisely because of what Mormonism has to offer in terms of a new philosophical conception of a material, yet infinite God. He speculated that anti-Mormonism would "dissipate" like anti-Catholicism in the 1960s, since Mormonism is "too true to Christ, too generous, . . . too interesting . . . to be dismissed like that."[163]

Webb's predictions about the sticking power of academic interest in Mormonism coincided with the October 2012 announcement of the new Richard Lyman Bushman Chair of Mormon Studies at the University of Virginia. Virginia thus joined the growing ranks of schools with specific emphases on the study of Mormonism, and this in a year that saw a spate of serious examinations of Mormon history and doctrine roll off of a number of university presses. Bushman himself saw the "academic community's interest in the Mormon experience and perspective" as having "grown exponentially" over the course of only a few years.[164]

The prospects for continued interest on that front seem bright. (So much so that Princeton historian Neil Young blogged for the *Huffington Post* that "as Mormonism continues to gain in cultural, political and religious relevance, historians may one day be describing a Mormon millennium rather than a moment.")[165] As never before, the LDS Church has placed an institutional push on promoting Mormon Studies. Reid Neilson, managing director of the church's History Department, said his "goal for the Church History Department is to help it become the epicenter of the entire Mormon Studies universe." With over two hundred employees in his department, Neilson said, "We want to be a resource. We want to be an advocate. We want to help facilitate all things Mormon Studies/ historical-related."[166] That spirit of openness and advocacy is generating notice, and this may be the type of attention that grows out of—and then outlasts—the current Mormon moment.[167]

Because of this type of institutional trajectory, it is hard to imagine the LDS Church authorities drawing back from public engagement, especially since the engagement impulse has been top-down—a direction that the church's apostles energetically endorsed. Otterson said "church leaders" have "strongly encouraged" a feeling of "transparency," to be "open and engaging." For those outside observers who might surmise that the public relations campaigns are the independent initiatives of the church's professionals, or that press statements do not reflect the thinking at the highest levels of the church's priesthood leadership, Otterson called such assumptions "nonsense." Because of the centralized nature of LDS Church governance and hierarchy, Otterson said, "No one in my position, or in any senior position of the public affairs department, would ever dream of taking any sort of major initiative, without making sure that it was reflective of the wishes of the [church's] leadership." This is a point that is worth emphasizing, since, as Otterson described it, the public outreach, the "I'm a Mormon" campaign, all "[represent] the thinking and the decisions" of the church's top leaders (Figure 10.5).[168]

As all of these forces have converged, what no one disagrees upon is that Mormons are now "in the conversation" in a way never before seen. That is why Michael Otterson has said, "I don't think this is really a 'moment.'"[169] And

Figure 10.5. In April and October of every year, Latter-day Saints gather at the church's 20,000-plus–seat Conference Center for the church's General Conference, which is simultaneously broadcast in eighty-plus languages. Copyright Intellectual Reserve, Inc. Reprinted with the permission of The Church of Jesus Christ of Latter-day Saints.

this fires Mormon optimism perhaps as much as any other reality. As Richard Bushman saw it, one lesson of Mormon history was that there was no bad publicity. He noted that he often gets some form of the question, "Are Mormons happy to be in the spotlight?...Is this good or bad for the church?...I've just come around to the position that every kind of publicity is good, that you almost never lose." [170] Pollster Gary Lawrence saw something similar in the attention paid to Pastor Jeffress: "If [Mormons] had initiated the discussion [with], 'No, we're not a cult,' we would have been ignored. But now that [Reverend Jeffress] has done it for us," the response should be, "bring on the media."[171]

Given that the Mormon story has always been a polarizing story, increased prominence has gone hand in hand with increased probing—and this since the late 1970s.[172] Richard Bushman sees a growing public sentiment of "Look, you're playing a big boy's game now, you've got to be willing to take it." But in his view, Mormons should be willing to take it: "We don't want to win everybody over, but we want to see [Mormonism represented as] a viable alternative to conventional Christian theology. And we're not going to do it by saying, 'We're just like you,' or by sort of diluting our theology....It's going to be those [unique Mormon] doctrines that are going to make a difference. If we're just another Christian sect, we won't get anywhere. So I'm hoping that that is being accomplished little by little."[173] Terryl Givens said it succinctly: "You want to be mainstream enough that people will give your message a fair hearing."[174]

There is something in Givens's choice of words—"mainstream *enough*"— that should not escape notice. For Latter-day Saints, their aspirations for an improved public standing are tempered by a desire to preserve their uniqueness. The *Boston Globe*'s Michael Paulson saw this as "the otherness of Mormons, which Mormons seem simultaneously to cherish and resent."[175] "Brigham Young once said that he feared the day," Givens told filmmaker Helen Whitney, "[when] Mormons would no longer be the object of the pointing finger of scorn. So again, it's one of these paradoxes that you want to have acceptability...[so] that you can fraternize with [others] as fellow Christians, but at the same time you don't want to feel so comfortable that there's nothing to mark you as a people who are distinct, who have a special body of teachings, a special [body of] responsibilities."[176] In contemplating Mitt Romney's attempts to win over evangelical voters, a Mormon law professor at William and Mary said, "I don't want us to fall in the trap of trying to present Mormonism as some sort of idiosyncratic brand of Protestantism."[177] Likewise, BYU Professor Daniel Peterson told Helen Whitney, "I worry that we may become too assimilated. We are different—we need to remember that, that we were in tension with the surrounding society and that there always ought to be some. We ought to be bothered if everybody always thinks we're just peachy keen."[178]

After all of Mormonism's struggles to shed its exoticness, this resistance to blurring the lines of Mormon distinctiveness might come across as somewhat unexpected—a "people of paradox" indeed. However, sociologist Armand Mauss, observing what he called "the Mormon struggle with assimilation" in mid-1990s America, suggested that "religious movements are considered successful to the extent that they avoid the assimilative embrace of the surrounding society and maintain a degree of tension with it." This "maintenance... of a separate identity," Mauss wrote, is crucial to a religion's survival—and to its very raison d'être. A viable religion must have something unique to offer. At the same time, though, if a religious group is so far removed from societal norms that it is viewed as a dangerous pariah, that group will struggle to survive if the host society sees it as so deviant and threatening that it needs to be eliminated. As Mormons have considered both ends of this spectrum, the trick, Mauss suggested, is to find "optimum tension."[179]

No Mormon could have been under the illusion that everybody thought Latter-day Saints were "just peachy keen" after Mitt Romney's first campaign, and yet somehow for Mormons that tension did not feel optimal either. What seemed to be missing, from the Latter-day Saints point of view, was the "mainstream enough" status to get a "fair hearing" for their theology. After 2012, that possibility felt somehow closer—as the *New York Times* put it, "a cautious step toward mainstream acceptance."[180]

At the end of Richard Bushman's conversation with CNN about the *Book of Mormon* musical, he told his interviewer why he did not mind all of the attention to his faith, even if some of it was painfully pointed: "If we came away knowing each other better, wouldn't that be wonderful?"[181] That is what seemed to fuel the optimism of Mormon image watchers during Romney's second campaign, the possibility for new conversations. Scott Swofford, who in 2010 left the LDS Church's missionary department to become director of content at BYUtv (a multinetwork broadcasting venture at church-owned Brigham Young University), noted that the mission for that network's programming was to draw viewers into a figurative funnel, and "the bottom of my funnel says *converse*" rather than "*convert*"—"I just want to get in the dialogue."[182]

In 2012, Mormons got that wish, for better or for worse, in a big way. And "dialogue" seems to strike just the right note as this chapter of the story closes. Whatever moment sparks the next national conversation about Mormonism, and whatever direction that conversation takes, the *Boston Globe*'s Alex Beam's prediction seems to be the safest bet about who at least will be at the table, even if those sitting next to them are not completely comfortable with it: "the outsiders," Beam wrote of the Mormons in November 2012, "are on the inside, to stay."[183]

Notes

Chapter 1

1. See Clark R. Mollenhoff, *George Romney: Mormon in Politics* (New York: Meredith Press, 1968), 22–24. For concise information on the details of the Reed Smoot hearings, see the Senate Historical Office, "The Expulsion Case of Reed Smoot of Utah (1907)," http://www.senate.gov/artandhistory/history/common/expulsion_cases/091ReedSmoot_expulsion.htm. For the Smoot hearings' impact on Mormonism's American standing, see Kathleen Flake, The Politics of American Religious Identity: The Seating of Senator Reed Smoot, Mormon Apostle (Chapel Hill: University of North Carolina Press, 2004); also Jonathan H. Moyer, "Dancing with the Devil: The Making of the Mormon-Republican Pact" (Ph.D. dissertation, The University of Utah, 2009). In 1904, the LDS Church issued a so-called "second manifesto" which took a decisive against continuing the practice of polygamy.

2. B. J. Widick, "Romney: New Hope for the G.O.P.?" *The Nation*, 3 February 3 1962, 96–97.

3. "Holy George," *The New Republic*, 3 December 3 1966, 4.

4. "Rove: 'I'd Pick Romney' As McCain's Running Mate," FOXNews.com, June 15, 2008, accessed 16 June 2008, http://elections.foxnews.com/2008/06/15/rove-id-pick-romney-as-mccains-running-mate/.

5. Bill Keller, "Daily Devotional," 11 May 2007, http://liveprayer.com/ddarchive3.cfm?id=2931/.

6. See The Gallup Poll #744, question qn15g, April 19–24, 1967, *Gallup Brain* database, http://brain.gallup.com/documents/questionnaire.aspx?STUDY=AIPO0744&p=4.

7. *Los Angeles Times/Bloomberg* poll, 13 December 2006; Gallup Poll, 29 March 1999; Polling the Nations database.

8. ABC News/*Washington Times* poll, 13 December 2006, Polling the Nations; NBC News/*Wall Street Journal* poll, December 2006, cited in Howard Berkes, "Faith Could Be Hurdle in Romney's White House Bid," *National Public Radio (NPR), Morning Edition*, 8 February 2007, transcript, http://www.npr.org/templates/story/story.php?storyId=7245768/.

9. Noah Feldman, "What is it about Mormonism?" *New York Times Magazine*, 6 January 2008, http://www.nytimes.com/2008/01/06/magazine/06mormonism-t.html?scp=1&sq=What%20 is%20it%20about %20Mormonism%20Noah%20Feldman&st=cse. Feldman also reports the results of the Harris poll; italics added.

10. J. Spencer Fluhman, *"A Peculiar People": Anti-Mormonism and the Making of Religion in Nineteenth-Century America* (Chapel Hill: The University of North Carolina Press, 2012), 1.

11. George M. Fredrickson, *The Black Image in the White Mind: The Debate on Afro-American Character and Destiny, 1817–1914* (New York: Harper & Row Publishers, 1971), xii, 321. There is also a more recent study with the same title: Robert M. Entman and Andrew Rojecki, *The Black Image in the White Mind: Media and Race in America* (Chicago: University

of Chicago Press, 2000). Other important books that deal with the shaping of group image include Matthew Frye Jacobson, *Whiteness of a Different Color: European Immigrants and the Alchemy of Race* (Cambridge, Massachusetts: Harvard University Press, 1998); Eric L. Goldstein, *The Price of Whiteness: Jews, Race, and American Identity* (Princeton, New Jersey: Princeton University Press, 2006); and Robert Alan Goldberg, *Grassroots Resistance: Social Movements in Twentieth Century America* (Prospect Heights, Illinois: Waveland Press, 1996; originally published by Wadsworth Publishing Company, 1991).

12. On the media's role as a filter, and the common biases and entrenched religious values in news reporting on religion, see Mark Silk, *Unsecular Media: Making News of Religion in America* (Urbana and Chicago: University of Illinois Press, 1995).

13. See E. D. Howe, *Mormonism Unvailed: Or, a Faithful Account of that Singular Imposition and Delusion, from its Rise to the Present Time...* (Painesville, Ohio, 1834; photomechanical reproduction, Salt Lake City: Utah Lighthouse Ministry). For a thorough description of the circumstances surrounding the publication of *Mormonism Unvailed*, see Richard L. Bushman, *Joseph Smith: Rough Stone Rolling* (New York: Alfred A. Knopf, 2005), 231–235. Bushman's biography has been hailed by Mormons and non-Mormons alike as the new standard biography of Joseph Smith, and Bushman's work informs much of the discussion here on Joseph Smith in the arena of American public opinion. For *Mormonism Unvailed*'s place in the history of anti-Mormon publications, see the survey by William O. Nelson, "Anti-Mormon Publications," in Daniel H. Ludlow, ed., *Encyclopedia of Mormonism* (New York: Macmillan, 1992), 45–52. On Hurlbut's selectivity of witnesses, see Dan Vogel, ed., Early Mormon Documents, vol. 2 (Salt Lake City: Signature Books, 1998), 13–14. See also Fluhman, *A Peculiar People*, for an important analysis of the role that anti-Mormonism played in the "negotiations of religion's conceptual boundaries" and in demarcating "just what American religion could be" (9, 127).

14. The catalog of Brigham Young University's Harold B. Lee Library is searchable at http://catalog.lib.byu.edu. The subject terms searched (with some overlap) on 15 July 2013 were "Mormon Church Controversial Literature," "Book of Mormon Controversial Literature," and "Church of Jesus Christ of Latter-day Saints Apologetic Works."

15. See Jan Shipps, *Sojourner in the Promised Land: Forty Years among the Mormons* (Urbana and Chicago: University of Illinois Press, 2000); Richard O. Cowan, "Mormonism in National Periodicals" (Ph.D. dissertation, Stanford University, 1961); Dale Pelo, "Mormonism in National Periodicals, 1961–1970" (master's thesis, (per CMS16), Brigham Young University, 1973); Adam H. Nielson, "Latter-day Saints in Popular National Periodicals, 1970–1981," (master's thesis, Brigham Young University, 2003); Matthew E. Morrison, "The Church of Jesus Christ of Latter-day Saints in National Periodicals 1982–1990" (master's thesis, Brigham Young University, 2005); Casey W. Olson, "The Church of Jesus Christ of Latter-day Saints in National Periodicals: 1991–2000" (Master's Thesis, Brigham Young University, 2007); Kevan L. Gurr, "An analysis of the newspaper coverage of Latter-day Saint temples announced or built within the United States from October 1997 through December 2004" (Master's Thesis, Brigham Young University, 2005). Published essays and theses by Dennis Lythgoe, Chiung Hwang Chen, and Ethan Yorgason overlap and augment Shipps's and Cowan's efforts, often providing nuanced readings of media trends. Taken together, these projects fix the media treatment of Mormons as the most studied component of this complex Mormon image-making process. See Dennis Leo Lythgoe, "The Changing Image of Mormonism in Periodical Literature" (Ph.D. dissertation, University of Utah, 1969); Chiung Hwang Chen and Ethan Yorgason, " 'Those Amazing Mormons': The Media's Construction of Latter-day Saints as a Model Minority," *Dialogue* 32, no. 2 (summer 1999): 107–128; Chiung Hwang Chen, *Mormon and Asian American Model Minority Discourses in News and Popular Magazines* (Lewiston, New York: The Edwin Mellen Press, 2004), especially chapters 2 and 3. See also Sherry Baker and Daniel A. Stout's helpful and exhaustive bibliography, "Mormons and the Media, 1898–2003: A Selected, Annotated, and Indexed Bibliography (with Suggestions for Future Research)," *BYU Studies* 42, nos. 3 and 4 (2003): 124–181.

16. For recent examples of this treatment of the question of the Mormon image in the nineteenth century, see Terryl L. Givens: *The Viper on the Hearth: Mormons, Myths, and the Construction of Heresy* (Oxford and New York: Oxford University Press, 1997)—an updated version with the same title was published by Oxford in 2013 ; Reid L. Neilson, *Exhibiting Mormonism: The Latter-day Saints and the 1893 Chicago World's Fair* (Oxford and New York: Oxford University Press, 2011); and Fluhman, *A Peculiar People: Anti-Mormonism and the Making of Religion in Nineteenth-Century America*. For representations of Mormons in twentieth-century American popular culture, see Cristine Hutchison-Jones, "Reviling and Revering the Mormons: Defining American Values, 1890–2008" (Ph.D. dissertation, Boston University, 2011). Hutchison-Jones argues that "stereotypes of Mormons persisted in American culture into the twenty-first century," and that "praise for Mormons has remained limited to those events and areas in which they have separated their peculiar religious beliefs from their day-to-day actions" (3).

17. See the "Epilogue" to Thomas G. Alexander, *Mormonism in Transition: A History of the Latter-day Saints, 1890–1930* (Urbana and Chicago: University of Illinois Press, 1986; Illini Books edition, 1996).

18. See, for example, Jan Shipps's essay "From Satyr to Saint: American Perceptions of the Mormons, 1860–1960," chapter 2 of *Sojourner in the Promised Land*, 51–97; also Klaus Hansen, *Quest for Empire: The Political Kingdom of God and the Council of Fifty in Mormon History* (East Lansing, Michigan: Michigan State University, 1967), 190, where he wrote of Mormonism's "present stature and prestige within the framework of *accepted* American religious values and persuasions " (emphasis added). Martin Marty, in the foreword to Hansen's book, summarized the work as demonstrating that "by 1980 the Mormons had grown to be so much like everyone else in America or, perhaps, had so successfully gotten other Americans to be like them, that they no longer inspired curiosity for wayward ways" (Marty, "Foreword," in Hansen, *Mormonism and the American Experience*, ix). The central thesis of Armand L. Mauss's Angel...*and the Beehive* is that by the 1960s, the Mormons had become so thoroughly Americanized that an alarmed LDS leadership enacted a series of retrenchment measures to resist the assimilationist trend that they observed among the Saints. See, for example, Mauss's preface to *The Angel and the Beehive: The Mormon Struggle with Assimilation* (Urbana and Chicago: University of Illinois Press, 1994), ix–xiii.

19. See Thomas F. O'Dea, *The Mormons* (Chicago and London: The University of Chicago Press, 1957), 259: "Now, say these critics, Mormonism has defeated its foes .... In short, it is their contention that the Mormon church is obsolete, that it has been the strategic weapon for conquering the wilderness, but that the measure of the its success is at the same time the index of its obsolescence.... Mormonism, they assert, still offers a meaningful way of life to many, but its sands are running out. Its fundamental *raison d'être* is gone, and the consequent absence of function will soon permeate into Mormon consciousness everywhere."

20. Ferenc Morton Szasz, *Religion in the Modern American West* (Tucson: The University of Arizona Press, 2000), 156: "In the eyes of most of the nation, the Saints had become simply another denomination, wrestling among themselves as to the proper degree of assimilation with mainstream American life.".

21. Compare O'Dea, *The Mormons*, "Sources of Strains and Conflict," chapter 9, 222–257, with this follow-up essay: Thomas F. O'Dea, "Sources of Strain in Mormon History Reconsidered," in Marvin S. Hill and James B. Allen, ed., *Mormonism and American Culture* (New York: Harper & (as on p. 283) Row Publishers, 1972): 147–167.

22. Gregory A. Prince and Wm. Robert Wright, *David O. McKay and the Rise of Modern Mormonism* (Salt Lake City: The University of Utah Press, 2005), 236, 404.

Chapter 2

1. "George W. Romney is ready and has the faith": William V. Shannon, "George Romney: Holy and Hopeful," *Harper's*, February 1967, 55, as quoted in Dennis L. Lythgoe, "The 1968 Presidential Decline of George Romney: Mormonism or Politics?" *BYU Studies* 11, no. 3 (Spring 1971): 231: "if America is yearning once again for that old-time religion,

George W. Romney is ready and has the faith." Portions of chapter 2 appeared in J. B. Haws, "When Mormonism Mattered Less in Presidential Politics: George Romney's 1968 Window of Possibilities," *Journal of Mormon History* 39, no. 3 (Summer 2013): 96–130.

2. "Text of Romney's Statement," *The New York Times*, 19 November 1967, 62.

3. Joseph Smith, the church's founding prophet, had announced his candidacy for the presidency in 1844, but was killed in late June of the same year, months before voting took place. Advocates of a third-party campaign courted church apostle Ezra Taft Benson, who had served as President Eisenhower's Secretary of Agriculture, to enter the 1968 election as a presidential or vice-presidential candidate, but no serious consideration was given that proposal. See Gregory A. Prince and Wm. Robert Wright, *David O. McKay and the Rise of Modern Mormonism* (Salt Lake City: The University of Utah Press, 2005), 304, 315, 318–319. See also Lythgoe, "The 1968 Presidential Decline of George Romney," 219–220, especially note 3, for a list of Romney's prominent Mormon political predecessors, as well as Lythgoe's view that "with his avowed candidacy in 1968, Romney became indisputably the most prominent Mormon in public life." For a recent study of ten Mormon candidates for presidents, see Newell G. Bringhurst and Craig L. Foster. *The Mormon Quest for the Presidency* (Independence, Missouri: John Whitmer Books, 2008). Bringhurst and Foster published an expanded version of their book in 2011 as *The Mormon Quest for the Presidency: From Joseph Smith to Mitt Romney and Jon Huntsman* (Independence, Missouri: John Whitmer Books, 2011).

4. See *The Gallup Poll* #744, question qn15g, April 19–24, 1967, April 19–24, 1967, *Gallup Brain* database, http://brain.gallup.com/documents/questionnaire.aspx?STUDY=AIPO0744&p=4: Two more recent examples: an ABC News/*Washington Post* poll in December 2006 found that 35% of those surveyed would be "less likely" to vote for a Mormon, and an NBC News/*Wall Street Journal* survey that same month was even bleaker, with 53 percent of the respondents saying "they were very uncomfortable or have some reservations about voting for a presidential candidate who is Mormon"; cited in Howard Berkes, "Faith Could Be Hurdle in Romney's White House Bid," *National Public Radio, Morning Edition*, 8 February 2007, transcript, http://www.npr.org/templates/story/story.php?storyId=7245768.

5. An October 2011 Google search showed that, during Mitt Romney's two campaigns, this very question appeared on the website pages of CNN, msnbc.com, *The Boston Globe*, *The Daily Show* and BBC News, among a number of others.

6. This point was made by filmmaker Adam Christing in an interview with a reporter for the website The Blaze. See Billy Hallowell, "Controversial New Documentary Asks: Is America Ready for a Mormon President?" 16 July 2011, http://www.theblaze.com/stories/controversial-new-documentary-asks-is-america-ready-for-a-mormon-president/. Christing's documentary, *A Mormon President: The True Story of Joseph Smith and the Mormon Quest for the White House*, was released in 2011. It is interesting to note that a webpage maintained on the University of Houston site, "Political Assassination: The Violent Side of American Political Life," includes this statement: "Attempts have also been made on the lives of one President-elect (Franklin D. Roosevelt in 1933) and three Presidential candidates (Theodore Roosevelt in 1912, Robert F. Kennedy in 1968, and George Wallace in 1972)," http://www.digitalhistory.uh.edu/topic_display.cfm?tcid=98. Wikipedia's "List of assassinated American politicians" does include Joseph Smith, http://en.wikipedia.org/wiki/List_of_assassinated_American_politicians.

7. Martin E. Marty, *The Irony of It All: 1893–1919, vol. 1, Modern American Religion* (Chicago and London: The University of Chicago Press, 1986), 301.

8. Bruce L. Olsen, interview with Jonice Hubbard, September 8, 2006, transcript in Hubbard, "Pioneers in Twentieth Century Mormon Media: Oral Histories of Latter-day Saint Electronic and Public Relations Professionals" (M.A. thesis, Brigham Young University, 2007), 121, http://contentdm.lib.byu.edu/cdm/ref/collection/ETD/id/1260 (accessed November 2, 2012). Olsen retired in 2008 as the managing director of the Church's Public Affairs Department.

9. John F. Kennedy, speech at the Rice Hotel, Houston, Texas, 12 September 1960, reprinted as Appendix 1 in Randall Balmer, *God in the White House: A History: How Faith Shaped the Presidency from John F. Kennedy to George W. Bush* (New York: HarperOne, 2008), 176.
10. For a transcript and a video recording of John F. Kennedy's speech to the Greater Houston Ministerial Association, see http://www.americanrhetoric.com/speeches/jfkhoustonministers.html.
11. For a discussion of the persistence of anti-Catholic sentiments in the United States, together with factors contributing to a mid-twentieth-century decline of those sentiments (including migration of Catholics from urban ethnic enclaves and into suburban neighborhoods, interaction between Catholic and Protestant soldiers during World War I and World War II, etc.), see Patrick Allitt, *Religion in America Since 1945: A History* (New York: Columbia University Press, 2003), 8–10, 65–57. For broader context, see Sydney E. Ahlstrom, *A Religious History of the American People* (New Haven and London: Yale University Press, 1972), 566–568, 900–901, 1006–1013.
12. On Reverend W. A. Criswell's anti-Catholic and anti-Kennedy pamphlet, see Sidney Blumenthal, "The Religious Right and Republicans," chapter 18 of Richard John Neuhaus and Michael Cromartie, eds., *Piety and Politics: Evangelicals and Fundamentalists Confront the World* (Washington, D.C.: Ethics and Public Policy Center, 1987), 271. A historical side note for modern readers is that one of Reverend Criswell's successors to the leadership of the First Baptist Church of Dallas was Robert Jeffress, who would gain widespread notoriety for his comments about Mitt Romney and the "cult" status of Mormonism in October 2011; see chapter 10 herein. On Paul Blanshard's 1949 book *American Freedom and Catholic Power*, see Balmer, *God in the White House*, 10–12, where Balmer notes that Blanshard's work "became a best-selling book; Beacon Press ordered eleven printings in as many months" (12); see also Allitt, *Religion in America Since 1945*, 65. On Carl McIntire's position, see Blumenthal, "The Religious Right and Republicanism," 277. On Norman Vincent Peale, see Balmer, *God in the White House*, 25–32; see also Allitt, *Religion in America Since 1945*, 65–66. Allitt there notes that "anti-Catholicism was widespread in America during the 1940s and 1950s, and socially respectable too" (65).
13. See Allitt, *Religion in America Since 1945*, 65: "[John F. Kennedy's] election marked an important moment in the history of American religious tolerance." See also Michael Cromartie, *Religion and Politics in America: A Conversation* (Lanham, Maryland: Rowman & Littlefield Publishers, Inc., 2005), 90: "The 'Judeo-Christian' civil religion of the fifties and the assassination of the first Catholic president permanently changed the boundaries of religious debate in the public square. No longer could anyone run for national office and say, 'My religion is better than yours.' They were all equal in the political marketplace."
14. Balmer, *God in the White House*, 14. For a good summary of the ecumenical spirit in post–World War II American Christianity, see Edwin Gaustad and Leigh Schmidt, *The Religious History of America: The Heart of the American Story from Colonial Times to Today*, rev. ed. (New York and San Francisco: HarperSanFrancisco, 2002), 393–397. Gaustad and Schmidt document the number of American Protestant denominations that put aside differences and joined together in new church organizations in the 1960s, as well as the simultaneous and ground-breaking Vatican II conference convened by Pope John XXIII.
15. See John Thomas, "George Romney," in Arnold K. Garr, Donald Q. Cannon, and Richard O. Cowan, eds., *Encyclopedia of Latter-day Saint History* (Salt Lake City: Deseret Book, 2000), 1041–1042. See also Clark R. Mollenhoff, *George Romney: Mormon in Politics* (New York: Meredith Press, 1968), 47–50, 171.
16. Balmer, *God in the White House*, 14–15.
17. "Michigan: The Mormon Issue," *Time*, 2 March 1962, 21.
18. Balmer, *God in the White House*, 156.
19. See *Meet the Press*, October 15, 1967, transcript, L. Tom Perry Special Collections, Harold B. Lee Library, Brigham Young University, Provo, Utah.
20. The fact that in April 1967 a national Catholic newspaper "called on all religious publications" to reject bias in their reporting on Romney speaks to the virtual impossibility of Governor Swainson's request five years earlier that religion be eliminated from campaign

288   NOTES

coverage. Yet significantly, the specific issue in April 1967 was the Mormon policy of not ordaining black men to the priesthood. The weekly *Ave Maria* (printed at Notre Dame University) asked "the religious press" to reject the association of Mormonism's black policy with Romney's politics as religious "prejudice" and praised how it had "overwhelmingly rejected" anti-Catholic bias directed toward Kennedy. See "Catholic Paper Decries Bias in Weighing Romney '68 Bid," *New York Times*, April 4, 1967, 48.

21. "Mormons Visibly Staking a Witness," *Christianity Today*, May 9, 1969, 48.
22. Balmer, *God in the White House*, 156.
23. An editorial writer for the *Christian Century* tended to agree, in calling for attention to candidates' stated positions, whether that candidate was Mormon George Romney, Catholic John F. Kennedy, or Quaker Richard Nixon. See "The Book of Mormon Enters Politics," *Christian Century*, 28 March 1962, 382: "Must candidates for high office in the U.S. either be secularists or deny some of their church's ultimate teachings? Would this whole matter go unnoticed except for the potential for exploitation from both sides when religion is mentioned?"
24. For a discussion and analysis of this genre of anti-Mormon literature, see "Mormonism and Fiction," part II of Terryl L. Givens, *The Viper on the Hearth: Mormons, Myths, and the Construction of Heresy* (New York and Oxford: Oxford University Press, 1997); an updated edition of the book was published with the same title in 2013 by Oxford.
25. Richard L. Bushman, *Joseph Smith: Rough Stone Rolling* (New York: Alfred A.Knopf, 2005), 396; Michael K. Winder, *Presidents and Prophets: The Story of America's Presidents and the LDS Church* (American Fork, Utah: Covenant Communications, 2007), 50–51.
26. See Winder, "Lyndon B. Johnson," chapter 36 of *Presidents and Prophets*, 301–309. Winder writes, "Without question, the friendship between Lyndon B. Johnson and David O. McKay was the strongest bond between a Church president and U.S. President in history" (301). Winder's remarkable book chronicles points of contact between Mormonism and every president of the United States through President George W. Bush. For President Eisenhower's esteem for Latter-day Saints, including his Secretary of Agriculture, Ezra Taft Benson, and for President McKay specifically, see Winder, *Presidents and Prophets*, 273–283. Ezra Taft Benson reported that President Eisenhower said to him that "he considered David O. McKay the greatest spiritual leader in the world" (281).
27. Winder, *Presidents and Prophets*, 305.
28. Winder, *Presidents and Prophets*, 303–304, 307–308. New regulations about formal clerical training threatened to exclude Latter-day Saints, who, because of their system of lay leadership, received no professional ministerial instruction. Elder Boyd K. Packer, a church general authority who represented the church in meeting with President Johnson on this issue, reported the president's comments to Deputy Secretary of Defense Cyrus Vance this way: "Listen here, these Mormons, from the minute they are out of their mothers' womb, have been praying and teaching and leading one another, and then they go out on missions....I cannot have Dr. McKay out in Salt Lake City sitting there thinking I am not doing the thing he has asked me to do, so you do it." President Johnson remarked to Elder Packer: "I don't know what it is about President McKay....[S]omehow it seems as though President McKay is something like a father to me" (307–308).
29. These membership statistics are drawn from Deseret Morning News, *2008 Church Almanac: The Church of Jesus Christ of Latter-day Saints* (Salt Lake City: Deseret Morning News, 2008), 654.
30. These statistics are based on percentages in James B. Allen and Glen M. Leonard, *The Story of the Latter-day Saints*, 2nd ed., rev. and enl. (Salt Lake City: Deseret Book, 1992), 565, and membership numbers in Deseret Morning News, *2008 Church Almanac*, 654. The 1996 announcement can be found in Jay M. Todd, "More Members Now outside U.S. Than in U.S.," *Ensign*, March 1996, https://www.lds.org/ensign/1996/03/news-of-the-church?lang=eng.
31. See Deseret Morning News, *2008 Church Almanac*, 653–655.
32. See Richard O. Cowan, *The Latter-day Saint Century* (Salt Lake City: Bookcraft, 1999), 162–163.

33. See Kathleen Flake, "The Mormon Corridor: Utah and Idaho," chapter 4 of Jan Shipps and Mark Silk, eds., *Religion and Public Life in the Mountain West: Sacred Landscapes in Transition* (Walnut Creek, CA: AltaMira Press, 2004), 91–114. Flake reviews the distinctive characteristics of the region that geographer Donald Meinig first called the "Mormon Corridor."

34. Two important passages from the Latter-day Saints canon that give this more symbolic sense of Zion are Doctrine and Covenants 97:21 ("for this is Zion—THE PURE IN HEART") and Moses 7:18 ("And the Lord called his people ZION, because they were of one heart and one mind, and dwelt in righteousness; and there was no poor among them").

35. One representative passage that Latter-day Saints interpret in this symbolic way is Isaiah 54:2: "Enlarge the place of thy tent, and let them stretch forth the curtains of thine habitations: spare not, lengthen all thy cords, and strengthen thy stakes."

36. See Cowan, *The Latter-day Saint Century*, 72; also Jan Shipps, *Sojourner in the Promised Land: Forty Years among the Mormons* (Urbana and Chicago: University of Illinois Press, 2000), 262.

37. Quoted in Prince and Wright, *David O. McKay and the Rise of Modern Mormonism*, 366.

38. Shipps, *Sojourner in the Promised Land*, 262–263.

39. Quoted in Prince and Wright, *David O. McKay and the Rise of Modern Mormonism*, 208.

40. Prince and Wright, *David O. McKay and the Rise of Modern Mormonism*, 205. The rate of membership increase is based on numbers reported in Deseret Morning News, *2008 Church Almanac*, 654.

41. Prince and Wright, *David O. McKay and the Rise of Modern Mormonism*, 208–209.

42. Gary James Bergera, "Tensions in David O. McKay's First Presidencies," *The Journal of Mormon History* 33, no. 1 (spring 2007): 189. For a brief overview of the deficit spending this building program occasioned, and First Presidency member N. Eldon Tanner's role in reversing it, see D. Michael Quinn, *The Mormon Hierarchy: Extensions of Power* (Salt Lake City: Signature Books, 1997), 219–220. See Prince and Wright, *David O. McKay and the Rise of Modern Mormonism*, 211–225, for a thorough discussion of the change in financial policies following the church's cash crisis of the 1960s. They quote Alan Blodgett, "who became the church's chief financial officer in 1969": "Deficit spending continued for about five years, and by 1962 a real liquidity crunch presented itself. Some writers claim the church was approaching bankruptcy, which is ridiculous. The church had vast holding of real estate and other assets and virtually no debt. It had merely run out of cash" (210).

43. Prince and Wright, *David O. McKay and the Rise of Modern Mormonism*, 209.

44. See Prince and Wright, *David O. McKay and the Rise of Modern Mormonism*.

45. Quoted in Winder, *Presidents and Prophets*, 307.

46. See Lloyd Newell, "Tabernacle Choir," in Garr, Cannon, and Cowan, eds., *Encyclopedia of LDS History*, 1213.

47. Shipps, *Sojourner in the Promised Land*, 351.

48. "Singing Saints," *Time*, 26 July 1963, 66; quoted in Dale Pelo, "Mormonism in National Periodicals, 1961–1970" (master's thesis, Brigham Young University, 1973), 62–63.

49. Newell, "Tabernacle Choir," 213. For the Cold-War implications of the 1962 broadcast, see Kirk Johnson, "Mormons on a Mission," New York Times, 20 August 2010, http://www.nytimes.com/2010/08/22/arts/music/22choir.html?pagewanted=all. See also Terryl L. Givens, "No Tabernacle Choir on Broadway: Music and Dance," chapter 13 of *People of Paradox: A History of Mormon Culture* (New York and Oxford: Oxford University Press, 2007), 253–263. He calls the choir the "most beloved public face of Mormonism" (254), and suggests that the fact that "CBS could call upon the choir to conduct a commemorative program upon the death of Franklin Roosevelt was a sign of how deeply secure its position had become as the musical voice of not just a church but a nation" (256).

50. Martin E. Marty, "Foreword," in Klaus J. Hansen, *Mormonism and the American Experience* (Chicago and London: The University of Chicago Press, 1981), xiii.

51. See Davis Bitton, "B. H. Roberts at the World Parliament of Religion[s]," *Sunstone* 31 (Jan.–Feb. 1982): 46–52. The importance of that 1893 moment is also underscored in Reid L. Neilson, *Exhibiting Mormonism: The Latter-day Saints and the 1893 Chicago World's Fair*

(Oxford and New York: Oxford Univeristy Press, 2011). For the 1911 tour and President Roosevelt's comments, see Cowan, *The Latter-day Saint Century*, 29.

52. Jan Shipps has noted that "distinctive LDS doctrinal tenets [have been] either blunted or altogether missing" in the "inspirational, but generically so" sermons included in the "Music and the Spoken Word" programs. Significantly, since such sermons "[reveal] little or nothing about the idiosyncratic LDS doctrines that separate Mormonism from the historic forms of Christianity—Catholic, Protestant, and Orthodox," in Shipps's opinion they contribute to a feeling of common religious ground. See Shipps, *Sojourner in the Promised Land*, 102.

53. "Died: Richard L. Evans," *Time*, 15 November 1971, 53. A church general authority colleague eulogized Elder Evans this way: "To millions he was the image of the Church. To multitudes of persons who were not well acquainted with the theology of The Church of Jesus Christ of Latter-day Saints, he was the only church they knew and the only religion they formally experienced. Countless others arranged their worship around his broadcasts" (Marion D. Hanks, "Elder Richard L. Evans: Apostle of the Lord [1906–1971]," *Ensign*, December 1971, 2).

54. Shipps, *Sojourner in the Promised Land*, 102.

55. See Lorry E. Rytting, interview by James B. Allen, 4 December 1979, transcript, Archives, The Church of Jesus Christ of Latter-day Saints, 4.

56. Lorry Rytting interview, 2.

57. The D. W. Evans and Associates advertising agency in Salt Lake City always provided critical support as needed, however. In fact, the initial arrangement was that the Evans agency "paid the bills," and then the salaries of those employees working in the Church Information Service "were billed back to the Church" (Lorry Rytting interview, 4–5). "In August 1966, Elder Mark E. Petersen arranged the transfer of Evans agency Church Information Service employees to the Church's payroll" (Public Affairs Department History, The Church of Jesus Christ of Latter-day Saints, unpublished, copy in possession of the author, 2).

58. For the church's less public efforts to build relationships and shape perceptions in the nineteenth century, see W. Paul Reeve, "Reconstructing the West: James M. Ashley's Answer to the Mormon Question," paper delivered at the Western History Association Conference, Oklahoma City, Oklahoma, October 2007.

59. Lorry Rytting interview, 4.

60. Lorry Rytting interview, 5. See Frank John Taylor, "Saints Roll up their Sleeves," *Saturday Evening Post*, 11 October 1958, 34–35.

61. See Hartzell Spence, "Mormons," *Look*, 21 January 1958, 56–64.

62. Lorry Rytting interview, 4–5. One telling example of the growing mutual trust between the Church Information Service and media personnel came in the preparation of Seymour Freedgood's article, "Mormonism: Rich, Vital, and Unique," *Fortune*, April 1964, 136–139. Lorry Rytting described the exchanges this way: "We entertained Seymour Freedgood and a researcher, who were assigned to do the piece on the Church. We worked very closely with them, and, recognizing the very distinctive and selective audience that Fortune magazine readers are, we secured tremendous cooperation from the Church's business affiliates in providing what was, up to then, the most complete report of the church's financial holdings. Naturally, they got into some sensitive areas as well, including the priesthood problem and even references to temple [rites]. We were able to review the early draft of the manuscript for the article. . . . Because we were able to respond with full, detailed, factual information, the article was revised to be more accurate, and the sensitive areas were treated in a much more discreet and satisfactory way" (Lorry Rytting interview, 7–8).

63. The best review of President McKay's interdenominational activities is Prince and Wright, "Ecumenical Outreach," chapter 5 of *David O. McKay and the Rise of Modern Mormonism*, 106–123. The chapter is subdivided into sections on relationships with Protestants, Jews, and Roman Catholics. One representative example deserves mention: President McKay took a significant symbolic stand in his response to Catholic protests surrounding the publication of *Mormon Doctrine*, a 1958 book written by LDS General Authority (?) Bruce

R. McConkie. Several entries in this encyclopedia-style doctrinal treatise linked the Roman Catholic Church with the scriptural "great and abominable church." President McKay and his associates—who had not seen the manuscript beforehand—responded quickly to requests for clarification from their injured Catholic friends, and Elder McConkie's book was reprinted only after related entries were amended or dropped. This incident seemed to signal a rapprochement from what had become an increasingly testy Catholic/Mormon relationship in mid-twentieth-century Utah. Many Mormon leaders at the time understood Catholic initiatives that sought to raise funds for Utah parishes as veiled attempts to bolster missionary resources and win converts away from Mormonism. On the other hand, Latter-day Saints had begun new missionary thrusts in predominantly Catholic nations. The two groups' historically harmonious interaction was thus threatened for a time, but the friendship of President McKay and Catholic Bishop Duane Hunt did much to repair the breach, paving the way for future Mormon/Catholic cooperation in humanitarian work. See Joseph Fielding McConkie, "The *Mormon Doctrine* Saga, 1958 and 1966," chapter 11 of *The Bruce R. McConkie Story* (Salt Lake City: Deseret Book, 2003), 182–193, especially page 186 for a partial list of related entries dropped in the second printing. See also Prince and Wright, *David O. McKay and the Rise of Modern Mormonism*, 112–123, for a discussion of Mormon-Catholic relations at the time of the publication of *Mormon Doctrine*, as well as this telling statement about President McKay's personal reaction to the *Mormon Doctrine* episode: "In the aftermath of the enormous embarrassment caused to the church and to himself by McConkie's book, McKay quietly abandoned his private criticism of Roman Catholicism for the remaining decade of his life" (122).

64. See David Lawrence McKay, *My Father, David O. McKay*, ed. by Lavina Fielding Anderson (Salt Lake City: Deseret Book, 1989), 206–207, for the story of Bishop Moulton's visit on President McKay's birthday that resulted in the exchange of blessings. For the account of the blessing, see Prince and Wright, *David O. McKay and the Rise of Modern Mormonism*, 108–109.

65. Quoted in Prince and Wright, *David O. McKay and the Rise of Modern Mormonism*, 111.

66. Ibid.

67. Jeanette McKay Morrell, *Highlights in the Life of President David O. McKay* (Salt Lake City: Deseret Book, 1966), 220.

68. See Morrell, *Highlights in the Life of President David O. McKay*, 229, and 249, for copies of both the evening's program, and for transcriptions of the evening's tributes. *Time* magazine covered the event, noting that "last week in Salt Lake City, nearly 500 business and civic leaders, representing Judaism and a dozen Christian churches, gathered at a testimonial banquet honoring the ninth man in Mormon history to be in direct communication with God.... There could be no questioning the sincerity of the praise for 'David O.' " See Hayes Gory, "The Ninth Prophet," *Time*, 21 December 1962, 37, quoted in Prince and Wright, *David O. McKay and the Rise of Modern Mormonism*, 112.

69. *Time*, 2 February 1970, 50; cited in Prince and Wright, *David O. McKay and the Rise of Modern Mormonism*, 107.

70. President McKay was also a well-traveled and recognized representative of the church internationally. As president of the church, he "accepted an invitation to a garden party at Buckingham Palace given by Queen Elizabeth" in 1952; he also met with "Holland's Queen, Juliana, the King of Sweden, the President of Finland, the President of Argentina [Juan Peron], and ... leading figures in every country which he has visited" (Llewelyn R. McKay, *Home Memories of President David O. McKay* [Salt Lake City: Deseret Book, 1956], 261). See also Prince and Wright, *David O. McKay and the Rise of Modern Mormonism*, 368. For evaluations by observers outside of Mormonism on the effectiveness of President McKay as an ambassador of American and Christian goodwill, see McKay, *Home Memories*, 261–263.

71. See Mary Jane Woodger, *David O. McKay: Beloved Prophet* (American Fork, Utah: Covenant, 2004), 228–232, for quoted tributes from Peale and DeMille, including these comments made by Cecil DeMille during a commencement address at Brigham Young University: "David McKay, almost thou persuadest me to be a Mormon!" (231). See Prince

and Wright, *David O. McKay and the Rise of Modern Mormonism*, 259, for an account of President McKay giving Cecil DeMille a private tour of the soon-to-be-dedicated Los Angeles Temple of the LDS Church. In a telling gesture, DeMille donated his papers to the Harold B. Lee Library at Brigham Young University.

72. Public Affairs Department History, 5.

73. See Brent L. Top, "The Miracle of the Mormon Pavilion: The Church at the 1964–65 New York World's Fair," in Larry C. Porter, Milton V. Backman Jr., and Susan Easton Black, eds., *New York*, Regional Studies in the Latter-day Saint Church History series (Provo, Utah: Brigham Young University, 1992), 235–256; and Nathaniel Smith Kogan's detailed overview, "The Mormon Pavilion: Mainstreaming the Saints at the New York World's Fair, 1964–65," *Journal of Mormon History* 35, no.4 (Fall 2009): 1–52. Kogan's discussion of David O. McKay's personal approval is on page 15. See also Lorry E. Rytting, interview by James B. Allen, 4 December 1979, transcript, Archives, The Church of Jesus Christ of Latter-day Saints, 6, where Rytting, an early Church Information Service employee, gives much of the credit to Salt Lake City advertiser David W. Evans for "generating ideas" for the church's new public relations department. "Perhaps the best example of this is the New York World's Fair project in 1964–65. A recommendation that the Church participate in the Fair had been submitted by Church leaders in the New York area. But no action was taken. When David Evans learned from Stanley McAllister [church stake president in New York] that a deadline for decisions was nearing, he telephoned Elder [Mark] Petersen [of the church's twelve apostles] and urged him to present the idea directly to the First Presidency. Approval was obtained within a day or two."

74. The church had previously hosted a well-received World's Fair exhibit at San Francisco's Treasure Island in 1939–1940 (the Golden Gate International Exposition), but on a smaller scale. The church's booth was a miniature replica of the Salt Lake City Tabernacle, with seating for fifty, housed within the Homes and Garden Building. The effort was spearheaded by Gordon B. Hinckley, who would become president of the church in the 1990s. For information on the planning of the exhibit, as well as public reaction to it, see Sheri L. Dew, *Go Forward with Faith: The Biography of Gordon B. Hinckley* (Salt Lake City: Deseret Book, 1996), 95–97.

75. For these statistics on visitors and follow-up requests, see Kogan, "The Mormon Pavilion," 45.

76. Top, "The Miracle of the Mormon Pavilion," 245. On the choir's performances, see Kogan, "The Mormon Pavilion," 19–25.

77. See Top, "The Miracle of the Mormon Pavilion," 253. Also Kogan, "The Mormon Pavilion," 36–44, for a detailed discussion of the layout of the pavilion's exhibits and the way those exhibits—and the film—were used to illustrate Mormon beliefs.

78. For a brief recounting of discussions behind early "visitor's centers" or "bureaus of information," see Alexander, *Mormonism in Transition*, 240; Cowan, *The Latter-day Saint Century*, 27–29, 35–37; and Allen and Leonard, *The Story of the Latter-day Saints*, 451. Some 150,000 people passed through the Temple Square Bureau's doors in its first year of operation (1902). By 1906, a similar information outpost had been established at the popular Saltair resort on the Great Salt Lake, and Temple Square tours included daily organ recitals in the Tabernacle.

79. On the reuse of the pavilion's building materials, see Kogan, "The Mormon Pavilion," 46–47. The church participated in subsequent World's Fairs in San Antonio, Texas; Osaka, Japan; and Spokane, Washington. Significantly, a new visitors' center opened on Temple Square in Salt Lake City in 1966, the year after the New York World's Fair. See Brent L. Top, "World's Fairs," in Garr, Cannon, and Cowan, eds., *Encyclopedia of Latter-day Saint History*, 1366–1367; W. Jeffrey Marsh, "Visitors' Centers," in Garr, Cannon, and Cowan, eds., *Encyclopedia of Latter-day Saint History*, 1300–1301; Deseret Morning News, *2008 Church Almanac*, 603.

80. Lorry Rytting interview, 6. See also Kogan, "The Mormon Pavilion," 46, where he notes the popularity of the Mormon Pavilion in that it outdrew Billy Graham's pavilion by

600,000 visitors, and the Protestant Center by nearly 3 million visitors. The Mormon Pavilion, among religion-themed exhibits, was second only in attendance to the Roman Catholic exhibit, which drew 26 million visitors, many of whom no doubt came to see "Michelangelo's *Pieta* making its first ever appearance outside of Italy."

81. See Kogan, "The Mormon Pavilion," 45.

82. Elder L. Tom Perry, later a member of the church's Quorum of the Twelve Apostles, estimated from his experience that "the Rego Park Branch [New York Stake] was maybe 75% converts resulting from the World's Fair" (in Top, "The Miracle of the Mormon Pavilion," 251). See also the state-by-state historical summaries in Deseret Morning News, *2008 Church Almanac*. For New Jersey, the almanac reported that "the following decade [the 1960s] saw another doubling of the state's LDS population, thanks in part to the 1964–1965 New York World's Fair...The New Jersey Stake was divided in 1967..." (249). For New York, the almanac reported that "further growth was spurred by the LDS pavilion at the 1964–1965 New York World's Fair....When the fair ended the pavilion was dismantled and used to construct a meetinghouse at nearby Plainview. As a result of the fair, there were thousands of baptisms in the area, making possible the creation of the Long Island Stake" (253–254).

83. See Conrad H. Thorne, "Research Study in Public Relations of the Mormon Church," 1966, unpublished manuscript, Archives, The Church of Jesus Christ of Latter-day Saints, 17: "Before the World's Fair opened the missionaries in the surrounding missions were having no success in converting people to the Mormon faith. For the first 10 months of 1965 New York State was number one in the Church and New Jersey number two for conversions, because of the interest people had after visiting the Mormon pavilion." See also Top, "The Miracle of the Mormon Pavilion," 251: "it is reported that during 1965, the New York, New Jersey, and Cumorah Stakes (those stakes encompassing and adjacent to the New York World's Fair) led the Church in convert baptisms."

84. Top, "The Miracle of the Mormon Pavilion," 253.

85. President Wilburn C. West, president of the church's Eastern States Mission, quoted in Top, "The Miracle of the Mormon Pavilion," 253.

86. Shipps, *Sojourner in the Promised Land*, 351: "Both because the church worked at its image so hard and because the media's purposes were served by pointing to real-life Leave-it-to-Beaver families (at least in the 1950s and 1960s), the LDS image was transformed during these middle decades from exotic outsider to inordinately wholesome, 'squeaky clean' insider."

87. "Broken nosed Mormon Elder" from "Clawed by a Tiger," *Time*, 2 November 1962, 74; "Doting father and regular church-goer" from "The Sporting Scene," *New Yorker*, 10 November 1962, 211; both articles quoted in Pelo, "Mormonism in National Periodicals," 28–29.

88. Al Silverman, "Boxing's Pious Battler," *Saturday Evening Post*, 27 April 1957, 37, 179.

89. "The Ten-Percent Tournament," *Time*, 1 July 1966, 58, quoted in Pelo, "Mormonism in National Periodicals," 26. It should be noted that there is, in the article's title, another reference to the Mormon practice of tithing.

90. "Crazy Fatso, the Putting Fool May Now Be the World's Best Golfer," *New York Times Magazine*, 6 April 1969, 33–42; "Has Anybody Here Seen Billy," *Sports Illustrated*, 10 July 1969, 24–29; both quoted in Pelo, "Mormonism in National Periodicals," 27–28. Pelo notes that Casper's religion may have made him a more interesting subject for feature stories: whereas Pelo counted only two articles in national periodicals on Casper between 1961 and 1966, "since his baptism in 1966, thirteen articles were written about the golfer. More than half of the articles mention the fact that he is a member of the [LDS] church, and many go into detail on his membership in the LDS faith" (Pelo, "Mormonism in National Periodicals," 26–27). That interest seems to speak to curiosity about Mormon beliefs and practices.

91. Shipps, *Sojourner in the Promised Land*, 100: "I am convinced that it was the dramatic discrepancy between clean-cut Mormons and scruffy hippies that completed the transformation of the Mormon image from the quasi-foreign, somewhat alien likeness that it had in the nineteenth century to the more than 100 percent super-American portrait of the late sixties and early seventies."

92. For thorough coverage of his February 1958 testimony before the Senate's Subcommittee on Antitrust and Monopoly, see chapter 10 of Mollenhoff, *George Romney*, 123–157.

93. See "The Dinosaur Hunter," *Time*, 6 April 1959, 84–89.

94. See Mollenhoff, *George Romney*, 160.

95. See Mollenhoff, *George Romney*, 167–171.

96. The fact that Clark Mollenhoff's 1968 biography of George Romney was subtitled "Mormon in Politics" seems to speak to this. Typical of much of the reporting on Romney is an early *Saturday Evening Post* article that quoted a Romney associate: "The more you see of George Romney, the more you realize his religion is the key to the man" (Stewart Alsop, "George Romney: The G.O.P.'s Fast Comer," *Saturday Evening Post*, 26 May 1962, 16).

97. Quoted in Balmer, *God in the White House*, 12.

98. See Deseret Morning News, *2008 Church Almanac: The Church of Jesus Christ of Latter-day Saints* (Salt Lake City: Deseret Morning News, 2008), 237, 654.

99. "Detroit 'Missionary' At Large...," *Newsweek*, 24 February 1958, 84–84, as quoted in Dennis Leo Lythgoe, "The Changing Image of Mormonism in Periodical Literature" (Ph.D. dissertation, University of Utah, 1969), 236.

100. "The Dinosaur Hunter," *Time*, 6 April 1959, 84.

101. See B. J. Widick, "Romney: New Hope for the G.O.P.?" *Nation*, 3 February 1962, 96.

102. In fact, this brand of golf became almost an iconic image of Romney in media profiles. See two nearly identical shots that appeared in two *Saturday Evening Post* articles separated by more than five years. See Alsop, "George Romney: The G.O.P.'s Fast Comer," 19, as well as Jules Witcover, "George Romney: Battered But Unbowed," *Saturday Evening Post*, 2 December 1967, 40.

103. See one example of this prominent attention to Sabbath observance: George Romney's appearance on "*Meet the Press*" in February 1964 was "prerecorded...in deference to his religion." The reporters noted that George Romney reserved Sundays for "church and family." See "*Meet the Press*," Sunday, 9 February 1964, transcript, L. Tom Perry Special Collections, Harold B. Lee Library, Brigham Young University.

104. Andrew Hamilton, "Those Amazing Mormons," *Coronet*, April 1952, 26–30.

105. Widick, "Romney: New Hope for the G.O.P.?",97.

106. See Lythgoe, "The 1968 Presidential Decline of George Romney," 240: "Romney's religion proved to be a handicap...George Romney's politics and his piety were inseparable, and the damage was more than his presidential aspiration could withstand." Lythgoe's piece is valuable for the way that it captures the contemporary political climate, but the perspective of additional hindsight and additional source evidence seem to recommend that his conclusions be qualified.

107. For "golden age" assessments, see Shipps, *Sojourner in the Promised Land*, 100, 110, where she brackets out the years "between, say, 1963–64 and 1975–56" (100); also Bruce L. Olsen, interview by Jonice Hubbard, 121; also Chiung Hwang Chen and Ethan Yorgason, "'Those Amazing Mormons': The Media's Construction of Latter-day Saints as a Model Minority," *Dialogue* 32, no. 2 (Summer 1999), 109. Those who saw in the second half of the sixties a return to the severe criticism of Mormons in the media include Dennis Lythgoe and, to a lesser extent, Dale Pelo. See Lythgoe, "The Changing Image of Mormonism in Periodical Literature," 267, where he wrote that "appraisal [of Mormons] became...very favorable in the 1950s and reverted to severe criticism in the 1960s." See also Pelo, "Mormonism in National Periodicals," 83: "The image of Mormonism in national periodicals during the period of 1961–1970 was of a slightly positive nature, but the last five years of the decade were negative." See the graphic representation of Pelo's assessment of this trend as "Direction of the Image of the Church," chart 1 on page 75 of his thesis.

108. Stewart Alsop in the *Saturday Evening Post* was suggesting this even in 1962. See his "George Romney: The G.O.P.'s Fast Comer," 15: "Courageous, right-thinking, true blue....Romney is all those things. There are times when Romney seems almost too good to be true."

109. See Lythgoe, "The 1968 Presidential Decline of George Romney," 240, for this telling summary of the place of religion, as Lythgoe read it, in the contemporary political climate: "The reaction of the public clearly suggested that any candidate relying heavily on

piety, *be it Mormon or any other faith*, could have serious credibility problems. Perhaps Romney's major liability was not necessarily Mormonism, but *rather religious dedication*. Conceivably, a candidate of another faith could be faced with a similar problem; or a Mormon better able to compartmentalize his faith and his politics might erase that problem" (italics added). Lythgoe seemed prescient in this closing paragraph of his article, in wondering whether a candidate who made overt references to personal religion could ever win over the public. He would only have to wait five years to find an appropriate test case: Jimmy Carter in 1976.

110. See Stewart Alsop, "It's Like Running Against God," *Saturday Evening Post*, 22 October, 1966, 20; the comment came from Zoltan Ferency, Romney's opponent in the 1966 Michigan gubernatorial race.

111. See Lythgoe, "The Changing Image of Mormonism," 241–247. This sentiment is clearly expressed in the title and text of a 1966 commentary in the *New Republic*: "Piety is often associated, alas, with inflexibility" ("Holy George," *New Republic*, 3 December 1966, 4).

112. This complaint was registered by AFL-CIO leader Gus Scholle in "Michigan: The Mormon Issue," *Time*, March 2, 1962, 21:"This business of trying to put on an act of having a pipeline to God in order to become Governor of Michigan is about the greatest anticlimax to a phony stunt I've ever seen."

113. See two examples of this type of coverage: Neil Morgan, "Utah: How Much Money Hath the Mormon Church?," *Esquire*, August 1962, 86–91; and Freedgood, "Mormonism: Rich, Vital, and Unique," 136–139, 166–171.

114. Alsop, "George Romney: The G.O.P.'s Fast Comer," 16. See also a report on a February 1966 Gallup poll that indicated "forty-three percent" of Americans surveyed were "able to identify Gov. Romney," and "seven persons in ten of those who identify Romney have a favorable impression of the man. Only seven percent of this group say they hold an unfavorable impression" (George Gallup, "43% in U.S. Can Identify Gov. Romney," *Washington Post*, 26 February 1966, photocopy included in "George Romney—Correspondence, 1965–1966," box 167, folder 3, J. Willard Marriott Papers, Special Collections, Marriott Library, University of Utah).

115. Compare Lythgoe, "The Changing Image of Mormonism in National Periodicals," 128, and Pelo, "Mormonism in National Periodicals," 53–54, with Lorry Rytting interview, 7–8, and Thorne, "Research Study on Public Relations in the Mormon Church," 20.

116. Lorry Rytting interview, 7–8; Grant Heath, quoted in Thorne, "Research Study on Public Relations in the Mormon Church," 20.

117. Morgan, "Utah: How Much Money Hath the Mormon Church?,"90.

118. Besides those articles already mentioned, see Donald L. Foster, "Unique Gospel in Utah," *Christian Century*, 14 July 1965, 890–892. Mr. Foster was pastor of the Orem, Utah, Community Congregational Church. With a touch of obvious disdain, he noted that "if, as is frequently said, this is the wealthiest church relative to size in the nation, it has reached that status by methods any church could duplicate in a few years' time if it believed that commercial operation was part of its mission" (890). One thrust of his article was to express the dissatisfaction of Utahans who felt that the church should be taxed more completely, although it is difficult to assess what level of public sympathy he would have garnered for the proposal to tax church enterprises which were, he admitted, directed toward welfare efforts and carried out through volunteer labor.

119. Dan L. Thrapp, "Mormons See Romney in Race on His Own, But Full Church Backing Is Assured," *Los Angeles Times*, 15 November 1966, as quoted in Prince and Wright, *David O. McKay and the Rise of Modern Mormonism*, 340.

120. For a thorough recounting of the episode, together with the references to the *Time* article, see Prince and Wright, *David O. McKay and the Rise of Modern Mormonism*, 325–330.

121. Comparing Richard Cowan's rating of articles (from 1851–1960) that dealt with Mormonism's origins with Dale Pelo's rating of similarly themed articles from the 1960s shows a marked change in tone toward favorability. See Pelo, "Mormonism in National Periodicals," 82. Pelo's opinion was that "in some respects the origins of the Church were handled in a fairer, more accurate way during this decade than during any previous period

since the organization of The Church of Jesus Christ of Latter-day Saints." Importantly, and in a noticeable change in tone from much of the reporting of an earlier generation, "none of the articles" which Pelo surveyed "called [Joseph] Smith an imposter or a deluded person" (Pelo, "Mormonism in National Periodicals," 55).

122. "Book of Mormon Enters Politics," *Christian Century*, 28 March 1962, 382.
123. Morgan, "Utah: How Much Money Hath the Mormon Church?,"86.
124. See Table 4 of Pelo, "Mormonism in National Periodicals," 82.
125. Warren Boroson, "George Romney: Man and Mormon," *Fact*, May-June 1967, 13. A copy of this article is included in the George Romney Resource Files, 1967–1971, Archives, The Church of Jesus Christ of Latter-day Saints. It is difficult, however, to judge the extent of *Fact*'s influence, since this was the same periodical that lost a libel suit brought against it by Barry Goldwater for "fabricating and doctoring quotations" and psychiatric evaluations to insinuate that Goldwater's psyche matched that of Adolf Hitler (Robert Alan Goldberg, *Barry Goldwater* [New Haven and London: Yale University Press, 1995], 223, 390, note 69).
126. Anthony A. Hoekema, "Ten Questions to Ask the Mormons," *Christianity Today*, 19 January 1968, 10, 14. Hoekema's questions presaged many of the issues which would define the "Are Mormons Christian?" debate, which would really heat up a decade later. Professor Hoekema had published in 1963 *The Four Major Cults: Christian Science, Jehovah's Witnesses, Mormonism, Seventh-Day Adventism.*
127. James M. Perry, "Discrimination in the Priesthood?: Mr. Romney's Latter-day Problem," *The National Observer*, 10 April 1967, 1. No source citation for the polls was given in the article, and the polls Perry mentioned do not seem to be cited by any other source and have not turned up in searches of opinion survey records.
128. Hoekema, "Ten Questions," 14; Perry, "Discrimination in the Priesthood?,"1; Foster, "Unique Gospel in Utah," 890.
129. Kogan, "The Mormon Pavilion," 36.
130. Gaustad and Schmidt, *The Religious History of America*, 395.
131. Walter Martin, for example, first published *The Maze of Mormonism* in 1962, and *The Kingdom of the Cults* in 1965.
132. Roy A. Cheville, "Mormonism on the Move," *Christian Century*, 30 October 1963, 1328–1330. See also "Pigskin Justice and Mormon Theology," *Christian Century*, January 21, 1970, 67, refers to the LDS Church as a "Christian body" by the magazine's editorial board. As further evidence of the willingness of other denominational voices to tolerate Mormon doctrinal positions, see "President Debases Chaplaincy Standards," *Christian Century*, 30 November 1966, 1465. The *Christian Century* protested President Johnson's order to allow for the commissioning of Mormon chaplains that had not met the requirement of three years of graduate seminary training. President Johnson allowed the exception because Latter-day Saint congregations were staffed wholly by lay members, such that Mormons engaged in no professional clerical training. Significantly, the *Christian Century* editorial never mentioned theology as a reason for opposing Mormon chaplains. Instead, the article expressed a full willingness to accept Mormon chaplains, provided they met the education requirement through university training, as Christian Science chaplains had done.
133. Perry, "Discrimination in the Priesthood?," 1.
134. "Two Romneys," *Time*, 3 March 1967, 25.
135. See this assessment by Cowan, *The Latter-day Saint Century*, 192–193: "During the 1930s, two new features were seen in the popular image [of Mormons] which have been characteristic since. First, the Church's image became predominantly positive. Second, *there was more media interest in Church social programs than in its theology*....During the second half of the twentieth century, more and more Latter-day Saints were achieving prominence in government service, in professional circles, and in a variety of other fields. These individuals had a very positive influence on the public's attitude. While praising them for their achievements, *the press almost always explicitly indentified them as Mormons*. The virtues of their religion were often described as contributing to their personal success" (italics added). Cowan's view is borne out by Dale Pelo's statistical analysis of periodical

features on Mormons in the 1960s. When grouped by theme, Pelo found that eighty-seven articles had Mormon "people" as a central theme, compared with only eleven that dealt with "theology," fifteen with "origins," and eight with "rites." See Pelo, "Mormonism in National Periodicals," 82. In Pelo's scoring system, the cumulative rating of the articles classed under "people" was favorable.

136. Carl Carmer, "The 'Peculiar People' Prosper," *New York Times Magazine*, 15 April 1962, 64, as quoted in Pelo, "Mormonism in National Periodicals," 66. Compare also "Church in the News: Story of Mormon Success: Hard Work and Sharing," *U.S. News and World Report*, 26 September 1966, 90; also "Mormon Church Flourishes," *Christian Century*, 23 January 1963, 103, which quoted Frank S. Mead's *Handbook of Denominations in the United States*: "Mormons' 'missionary experience' strengthens both them and their church, and offers a model of church service and zeal equaled in very few of the other larger churches in America."

137. Thorne, "Research Study on Public Relations in the Mormon Church," 21. The employee Thorne interviewed was Grant Heath.

138. The Tabernacle Choir was not the only Mormon musical group to appear regularly on national television during the 1960s and reinforce the church's family-friendly image. The clean-cut Osmond Brothers first appeared on *The Andy Williams Show* in 1962, and continued as regular guests throughout the decade. The popularity of the group (which would see dramatic recording success in the 1970s) was reflected in its inclusion as a headliner in newspaper advertisements for Williams's upcoming programs. See, for example, ads in *New York Times*, 1 October 1963, 60; *New York Times*, 24 January 1964, 57 (an ad for a Bob Hope special); *New York Times*, 4 August 1968, D4; *New York Times*, 22 November 1969, 75.

139. Shipps, *Sojourner in the Promised Land*, 100. Her evaluation of print *and* electronic media of the period led her "to advance the following argument: if you take the electronic media into account, the decade or so between, say, 1963–64 and 1975–76 forms a unique period in the history of perceptions of the Saints. During this time, the LDS Church had what Americans who embraced the civil rights movement regarded as a retrograde position on race, one noted and commented on in the print media, especially *Time*, *Newsweek*, the *Christian Century*, and elite newspapers on the East Coast and West Coast. But that encumbrance was *usually overlooked* in radio and television broadcasts" (100); italics added.

140. Compare, for example, Dale Pelo's comparison of Richard Cowan's study of national periodical coverage of Mormonism from 1851 to 1960 with Pelo's own parallel study of articles from the 1960s. Race was not even a category of analysis in Cowan's work, whereas it became a dominant theme in the articles on Mormonism in the 1960s. See table 4 in Pelo, "Mormonism in National Periodicals," 82.

141. The First Presidency to General Authorities, Regional Representatives of the Twelve, Stake Presidents, Mission Presidents, and Bishops, 15 December 1969, 2; a copy of the letter is included in "Compiled Information Concerning African Americans, BYU, and the Church," MSS SC 2969, L. Tom Perry Special Collections, Harold B. Lee Library, Brigham Young University. The document carried the signature of two of President McKay's counselors in the First Presidency. President McKay was very ill at the time, and would die only a month later, on January 18, 1970. Pressure from "*New York Times* reporter Wallace Turner," who "had obtained a copy [of the letter] and planned to print it," led the church to reprint the letter in the Church News section of the *Deseret News* in early January 1970 (Prince and Wright, *David O. McKay*, 101–102). Both Sheri Dew and the biographers of David O. McKay felt that senior apostle Harold B. Lee was the driving force behind the composition of the 1969 statement, although Dew noted that apostle Gordon B. Hinckley was the statement's principal author, with input from "prominent educators Neal A. Maxwell and G. Homer Durham" (Sheri L. Dew, *Go Forward with Faith: The Biography of Gordon B. Hinckley* [Salt Lake City: Deseret Book, 1996], 295). Extensive portions of the 1969 letter are reprinted in Prince and Wright, *David O. McKay*, 100–101. For two important and early overviews of the history of the priesthood restriction, see Armand L. Mauss, "Mormonism and the Negro: Faith, Folklore, and Civil Rights," *Dialogue* 2, no. 4 (Winter 1967):19–40; and Lester E. Bush, Jr., "Mormonism's Negro

Doctrine: An Historical Overview," *Dialogue* 8, no. 1 (Spring 1973): 11–68. More recently, see Newell G. Bringhurst, "The 'Missouri Thesis' Revisited: Early Mormonism, Slavery, and the Status of Black People," in *Black and Mormon*, ed. Newell G. Bringhurst and Darron T. Smith (Urbana and Chicago: University of Illinois Press, 2004), 13–33. For a discussion of various reasons for the restrictions propounded by past LDS thinkers and leaders, see Alma Allred, "The Traditions of Their Fathers: Myth Versus Reality in LDS Scriptural Writings," in *Black and Mormon*, 34–49. Bringhurst and Smith's entire collection is worthy of attention for its treatment of a wide variety of historical and contemporary questions about Mormonism's relationship with its black adherents. An important new study of the intersection of race and religion in Mormonism's history, W. Paul Reeve's *Religion of a Different Color: Race and the Mormon Struggle for Whiteness*, is forthcoming from Oxford University.

142. See, for example, statements by a variety of LDS Church presidents cited in Bringhurst and Smith, eds., *Black and Mormon*, 47, 53–54. See also a 1952 letter to the editor of *The Nation* written by Brigham Young University professor Roy W. Doxey, who strongly disputed Lowry Nelson's earlier article, "Mormons and the Negro," that appeared in the 24 May 1952 edition of *The Nation*. Doxey's opening point was that Nelson "grossly misrepresented the doctrine of the Church of Jesus Christ of Latter-day Saints" since "the Negro, contrary to Dr. Nelson's misrepresentation, was not neutral" in the pre-earth war in Heaven between Jesus and Lucifer. Doxey also stated that "in the ultimate and final purpose of God . . . in the future life the Negro will 'possess the priesthood, and receive all the blessings which we are now entitled to.' . . . Because we are all children of God, including the Negro, we should be interested in the social and economic welfare of the Negro" (Roy W. Doxey, "The Mormons and the Negro," *The Nation*, 16 August 1952, inside front cover). See also this retrospective statement by historian Richard Bushman: "The Church always believed blacks would receive the priesthood some day. It was only a question of when. The Church is conservative in the classic sense of changing slowly, but it does change deliberately in its own good time" (Jay Kernis, "Richard Bushman: The Book of Mormon is like looking into a fun-house mirror; the reflection is hilarious but not really you," a CNN blog posted on June 6, 2011; accessible at http://inthearena.blogs.cnn.com/2011/06/27/richard-bushman-the-book-of-mormon-is-like-looking-into-a-fun-house-mirror-the-reflection-is-hilarious-but-not-really-you/).

143. The First Presidency to General Authorities, Regional Representatives of the Twelve, Stake Presidents, Mission Presidents, and Bishops, 15 December 1969, 2.

144. The First Presidency to General Authorities, Regional Representatives of the Twelve, Stake Presidents, Mission Presidents, and Bishops, 15 December 1969, 2. For the LDS Church's more recent expressions about historical uncertainty in connection with the origins of the restriction, see the introduction to "Official Declaration 2" in the 2013 edition of the Doctrine and Covenants (one of the church's four canonical books, along with the Bible, the Book of Mormon, and the Pearl of Great Price). See http://www.lds.org/scriptures/dc-testament/od?lang=eng.

145. George Romney knew this would be the case. See Prince and Wright, *David O. McKay and the Rise of Modern Mormonism*, 339–340, for their account of a 1962 conversation between the church's First Presidency and George Romney, who was then contemplating running for governor in Michigan.

146. Susan Friend Harding, *The Book of Jerry Falwell: Fundamentalist Language and Politics* (Princeton, New Jersey: Princeton University Press, 2000), 26. Harding quotes one of Falwell's later sermons (from 1986): "In my adolescence and young adult years I don't remember hearing one person speak of the injustices of segregation. To the contrary, all my role models, including powerful church leaders, supported segregation. I have never once considered myself a racist. Yet, looking back, I have to admit that I was one. Unfortunately, I was not quick enough or Christian enough or insightful enough to realize my condition until those days of tumult in the 1960s" (25–26).

147. See "Mormon Church Flourishes," and "Meredith Requests Changes," *Christian Century*, 23 January 1963, 102–103. *Christian Century* went so far as to suggest that the University

of Mississippi should lose its accreditation if that institution did not remedy the plight of enrolled black student James Meredith. See also "Is Mormonism Reformable on Race?," and "Mississippians Pay Dear Price for Bigotry," *Christian Century*, 4 May 1966, 576–577. The colleges listed that refused to comply with the 1964 Civil Rights Act, and thus lost federal funding for student loans, included Bob Jones University in South Carolina, Freewill Baptist Bible College in Tennessee, and Mississippi College, "the oldest and largest Mississippi Baptist institution" (577)

148. Armand Mauss, *The Angel and the Beehive: The Mormon Struggle with Assimilation* (Urbana and Chicago: University of Illinois Press, 1994), 52.

149. Mauss, *The Angel and the Beehive*, 53.

150. The First Presidency to General Authorities, Regional Representatives of the Twelve, Stake Presidents, Mission Presidents, and Bishops, 15 December 1969, 1.

151. It is also difficult to know even how widespread public knowledge of the Mormon priesthood policy was in the mid-1960s. The *Christian Century* reported that in 1965, singer Joan Baez was not aware of the policy until only a few hours before her concert in the Salt Lake Tabernacle was scheduled to begin. She decided to play the concert, but announced that she would not return to that venue until the church reversed its policy toward blacks— and, incidentally, toward those who smoked and drank alcohol. See Wendell Peabody, "The Saints and Race," *Christian Century*, 9 June 1965, 756.

152. "Two Romneys," *Time*, 3 March 1967, 25

153. "Two Romneys," 25.

154. Transcript, *Meet the Press*, February 9, 1964, Perry Special Collections.

155. Warren Weaver, Jr., "Virginia Republicans Term Visit by Romney a Major Success," *New York Times*, 17 April 1967, 18; emphasis added. There was in this article no mention of Mormonism.

156. See "Is Mormonism Reformable on Race?" *Christian Century*, 4 May 1966, 576; "Mrs. Romney's Quandary," *Christian Century*, 8 February 1967, 165; Perry, "Discrimination in the Priesthood?" 11. Apparently Romney continued his activism even after receiving a letter from a church apostle, Delbert Stapley, privately concerned over that activism. See Edward J. Blum and Paul Harvey, "How (George) Romney Championed Civil Rights and Challenged His Church," *The Atlantic*, 13 August 2012, http://www.theatlantic.com/national/archive/2012/08/how-george-romney-championed-civil-rights-and-challenged-his-church/261073/.

157. See Glen W. Davidson, "Mormon Missionaries and the Race Question," *Christian Century*, 29 September 1965, 1183–1186, where he asserted, based on unnamed sources and hearsay evidence, that Mormon leaders dismayed that the priesthood policy might attract hard-core segregationists into the church's ranks.

158. See "Political Records: George Romney—Poll Data," box 167, folders 11–13, Marriott Papers, Special Collections, Marriott Library, University of Utah, for reports on Alabama, Arkansas, California, Colorado, Georgia, Florida, Kansas, Louisiana, Maine, Massachusetts, Mississippi, Missouri, Nebraska, New Hampshire, New Jersey, New Mexico, New York, North Carolina, Ohio, Oregon, Pennsylvania, South Carolina, Texas, Utah, Virginia, and Washington.

159. "Oregon," box 167, folder 12, Marriott Papers, 3: "The Mormon influence here is considerable."

160. Willard (Lefty) Hawkins, in "Arkansas," box 167, folder 11, Marriott Papers, 2.

161. Comments of Wes Powell, in "New Hampshire," box 167, folder 12, Marriott Papers, 4.

162. Comments of William Treat, in "New Hampshire," box 167, folder 12, Marriott Papers, 3.

163. In "New Jersey," box 167, folder 12, Marriott Papers, 3–4.

164. For the conservative-moderate divide in the party surrounding Barry Goldwater's nomination, as well as George Romney's position, see Goldberg, *Barry Goldwater*, 194–197, 202–206, 220–221, 232–237. See also David W. Reinhard, *The Republican Right since 1945* (Lexington: University Press of Kentucky, 1983), esp. 216–18, for the 1966 election victories of conservative, Goldwater-type Republicans.

165. Michael Kranish and Scott Helman, *The Real Romney* (New York: HarperCollins, 2012), 23.

166. These are the comments of former state chairman Wirt A. Yerger, Jr., in "Mississippi," box 167, folder 12, Marriott Papers, 1.

167. See the comments of Mrs. Charles Brooks, vice-chairwoman of the Party, and State Senator Oliver Bateman, in "Georgia," box 167, folder 11, Marriott Papers, 3.
168. See, for example, Perry, "Discrimination in the Priesthood?" 11: "Mr. Romney went on that year to win the governorship of Michigan. He was reelected in 1964 and again in 1966. Each time, he won more and more Negro votes, as the church issue became less and less controversial." See also Clayton Fritchey, "Romney's Record on Race," *Deseret News*, 7 March 1967: "Republicans used to get only 8 per cent of the Negro vote in that state [Michigan], but Romney got 11 per cent in 1962, 19 per cent in 1964 (compared with 4 for Goldwater) and over 35 per cent in 1966."
169. This feeling was expressed in interviews in Kansas, Missouri, Maine, Massachusetts, Nebraska, New Jersey, Oregon, New York, Colorado, and Utah. See subsections for each state in box 167, folders 11–13, Marriott Papers.
170. "Holy George," 4.
171. See, for example, the comments of Kansas Governor Bill Avery: "As far as I can see, the last Gallup poll showing Romney ahead of everybody, pretty well reflects the feelings of Republicans in Kansas" ("Kansas," box 167, folder 12, Marriott Papers, 1).
172. This sampling of Gallup polls, accessed from the Gallup Brain database, http://brain. gallup.com/home.aspx, demonstrates Romney's consistent prominence in the Republican race: The Gallup Poll #740, 1/26/67–1/31/1967, question qn3c: "Suppose the choice for President in the Republican convention in 1968 narrows down to Richard Nixon and George Romney. Which ONE would you prefer to have the Republican convention select? (3491 answered question): Nixon (40.50%), Romney (44.37%), No opinion (15.12%)"; question qn5a-b: "Suppose the Presidential election were being held TODAY. If George Romney were the Republican candidate and Lyndon Johnson were the Democratic candidate, which would you like to see win?: Romney (45.69%), Johnson (41.56%), Other (0.26%)." See also The Gallup Poll #741, 2/16/1967–2/21/1967, question qn5a: "Here is a list of men who have been mentioned as possible Presidential candidates for the Republican party in 1968. Which ONE would you like to see nominated as the Republican candidate for President in 1968? Just read off the number of the man you pick. [LIST INCLUDES: Mark Hatfield, John Lindsay, Richard Nixon, Charles Percy, Ronald Reagan, Nelson Rockefeller, George Romney.] (3509 answered question): Mark Hatfield (7.21%), John Lindsay (11.17%), Richard Nixon (45.17%), Charles Percy (11.91%), Ronald Reagan (16.56%), Nelson Rockefeller (32.15%), George Romney (51.33%), Don't know, no answer (24.45%)." See also these August 1967 polls, compiled only weeks before Romney's "brainwashing in Vietnam" comment: The Gallup Poll #749, 8/3/1967–8/8/1967, question qn7a: "Here is a list of men who have been mentioned as possible Presidential candidates for the Republican party in 1968. Which ONE would you like to see nominated as the Republican candidate for President in 1968? Just read off the number of the man you pick. [LIST INCLUDES: MARK HATFIELD, JOHN LINDSAY, RICHARD NIXON, CHARLES PERCY, RONALD REAGAN, NELSON ROCKEFELLER, GEORGE ROMNEY] (9506 answered question): Mark Hatfield (2.26%), John Lindsay (6.01%), Richard Nixon (22.72%), Charles Percy (7.05%), Ronald Reagan (12.52%), Nelson Rockefeller (18.36%), George Romney (20.58%), Don't know, no answer (10.51%); question qn7b: And who would be your second choice?: Mark Hatfield (3.00%), John Lindsay (8.69%), Richard Nixon (13.68%), Charles Percy (9.84%), Ronald Reagan (11.48%), Nelson Rockefeller (16.52%), George Romney (19.20%), Don't know, no answer (17.61%); question qn9a-b: Suppose the Presidential election were being held TODAY. If George Romney were the Republican candidate and Lyndon Johnson were the Democratic candidate, which would you like to see win? (9506 answered question): Romney (43.89%), Johnson (35.77%), Other (0.11%), Undecided (0.05%), Leans toward Romney (4.21%), Leans toward Johnson (3.84%), Leans toward Undecided (12.14%)."
173. For *Newsweek*'s analysis of the poll data in the spring of 1967, see "Romney's Week," *Newsweek*, 1 May 1967, 20–21: "Does Michigan's evangelistic Gov. George Romney have the staying power to capture the 1968 Republican Presidential nomination? Right now, Romney is the clear leader in the polls, the professed choice of most influential party

moderates and the most active non-candidate on the political landscape. Yet deep doubts about his White House mettle still nag the pros. . . . And the result of the week's developments seemed to shrink Romney's plausibility gap. . . . A new Gallup poll found *Republican county chairmen* around the nation convinced that the nomination would finally go to Nixon . . . Gallup's breakdown showed *Romney doing significantly better among rank-and-file voters.* The latest Louis Harris poll drew the line more clearly. Harris's figures showed Romney leading Lyndon Johnson 53 to 47 per cent while Nixon was trailing the President, 54 to 46 per cent. Romney rated better than Nixon in every part of the country (including, surprisingly, the South), among Republicans, Democrats and independents, and by every significant *ethnic* and age index" (italics added). This seems to reflect Romney's widespread appeal to a variety of voters, even though, as many observers noted, he was not a party favorite, a reflection at least in part of the conservative-moderate rift.

174. For the immediate context of the "brainwashed" comment, together with extensive excerpts from the television interview, see Mollenhoff, *George Romney*, 290–294.

175. This was certainly the angle taken by numerous commentators. See, for example, *Congressional Quarterly*, 15 September 1967, 1823–1824: Former Governor Henry Bellmon (Oklahoma) "said Romney's statement had shown a 'weakness'"; Barry Goldwater said, "Romney's statement was an insult to the other Governors traveling with him"; Governor Philip H. Hoff (D-Vt.) "said Romney was either a 'most naïve man or he lacks judgment.'"

176. See, for example, "How Republican Race Shapes Up Now," *U.S. News and World Report*, 25 September 1967, 55–56: "Suddenly, fortunes are shifting in the Republican Party, after Governor Romney's charge of being 'brainwashed' in Vietnam. . . . Another national leader observed: 'Romney is through. He won't be a factor at the Convention. . . . After George Romney's "brainwashing" remark, doubts rose about his chances." See also "The Bell Tolls for a Galloping Ghost," *Newsweek*, September 25, 1967, 27: "The funeral arrangements were made, the dirges were sung. In the wake of the great 'brainwashing' fiasco, George Romney resembled nothing so much as a case of inadvertent political suicide. His friends despaired, his enemies rejoiced, and the pollsters grimly catalogued his fall. Could it be that the leading Republican Presidential candidate had killed himself off even before he had made his campaign official? That was the message everyone seemed to be getting last week—everyone, that is, except the corpse." Romney, *Newsweek* noted, still felt that "brainwashed" sent the right message, but others apparently did not agree: "I'm glad I used that word. It woke up the country. Nobody was paying attention, when I only used words like 'snow job.'" *Newsweek*'s conclusion was that "after leading all the other Republican contenders against President Johnson for almost a year, Romney plummeted overnight to fourth place in the latest Harris survey" (28).

177. See J. Willard Marriott to Governor George Romney, 3 October 1967, box 167, folder 4, Marriott Papers, 1–2.

178. Though Dennis Lythgoe argued for the role religion played in Romney's sinking fortunes, he nevertheless noted that "many analysts, including Romney himself, have blamed his political decline on his famous 'brainwashing' statement made after a tour of Viet Nam" (Lythgoe, "The 1968 Presidential Decline of George Romney," 220). Two other researchers writing at nearly the same time as Lythgoe concluded that the Vietnam issue trumped any religious controversy. See the important thesis by a former worker on the Romney campaign, Richard Melvin Eyre, "George Romney in 1968: From Front-Runner to Drop-Out: An Analysis of Cause" (master's thesis, Brigham Young University, 1969), especially pages 66–73. Eyre's opinion was that the press was eager to show that Romney did not have a grasp on the issues confronting the nation, and that eagerness fueled coverage of the "brainwashing" comment. See also Pelo, "Mormonism in National Periodicals," 42–43.

179. Tom Wicker, "Impact of Romney Move: His Withdrawal Could Prove to Be One of Decisive Actions of Election," *New York Times*, 29 February 1968, 22.

180. These comments of Oklahoma Governor Dewey Bartlett were reported by Missouri State Senator Clifford Jones, who was Bartlett's college roommate at Princeton. See "Missouri," box 167, folder 12, Marriott Papers, 4.

181. See Richard Eyre's insightful and detailed list of reasons for Romney's failure to secure the Republican nomination. Mormonism did not figure into Eyre's list, although he did list it as a principal factor in Romney's initial popularity, since Romney's image of honesty and morality stood as the "antithesis" to Lyndon Johnson that many Republicans sought. See Eyre, "George Romney in 1968," 4, 66–69.

182. See C. Robert Yeager to David B. Goldberg, January 8, 1968, box 167, folder 4, Marriott Papers, 2: "It would be my judgment that we have to capitalize on Governor Romney's weaknesses," (which Yeager earlier described as being "too frank for his own good and too honest answering obviously controversial questions,") "and project him into an image of exactly what he is, a dedicated, honest, and deeply religious man who is not a politician. . . . In line with this, if you don't think it is too corny, I would suggest that he ask people, because people know that he is dedicated and religious, to pray for him in the things he is trying to do as a candidate. If he is not the man, in their opinion who can do the job, they should figure out who would be the best man and elect him."

183. The fact that during George Romney's October 1967 appearance on *Meet the Press* Mormonism never apparently was mentioned—even though his civil rights advocacy *was* mentioned—seems yet another confirmation that Romney's religion did not inspire widespread concern. See *Meet the Press*, October 15, 1967, transcript, Perry Special Collections. The New York Times's Wallace Turner, in his 1966 book The Mormon Establishment (Boston: Houghton Mifflin Company), was highly critical of what he called the LDS Church's "anti-Negro doctrine," yet he still closed his book with lines like these: "The Mormons are a fine people. Their contribution to American life has been considerable. With a few exceptions, which are very plainly set out in these covers, I find their doctrine to be humane, productive of progress, patriotic, wholesome and praiseworthy" (331).

184. See the opinion of Clark Mollenhoff, in his *George Romney*, 327, on the Mormon priesthood issue: "Although an opposing presidential candidate *would not dare* raise such a religious issue, there would be little difficulty in finding some civil-rights leaders or partisan political opportunists to ask the questions and touch off the debate" (italics added).

185. See two more examples of the complexity and conflicting pictures at work here: Wallace Turner, "Mormon Stand on Negroes Poses Problem for Romney if He Runs for Presidency," *New York Times*, December 28, 1965, 15, where that headline is followed by two subheadings: "Church Prejudice Would Be an Issue," and "Governor, a Mormon, Has Won Increased Support of Michigan Negroes"; also Turner's *The Mormon Establishment* (Boston: Houghton Mifflin Company, 1966), especially chapters 11 and 12. I am indebted to Cristine Hutchison-Jones for bringing these references to my attention.

Chapter 3

1. See Paul James, *Cougar Tales* (Sandy, Utah: Randall Books, 1984), 47–52, for a description of the halftime protest at Colorado State.

2. See Anthony Ripley, "Irate Black Students Stir Campus Tension," *New York Times*, 16 November 1969, 1.

3. James, *Cougar Tales*, 52. Edwards made this remark to Paul James "during a seminar at the University of Utah." See also a July 16, 1968, report by Art Rosenbaum in the *San Francisco Chronicle*: "The Black Amateur Athletic Union proposes to deal first with Mormon colleges, which, it is claimed, adhere to the theory that a black person is some kind of demon. 'We're going after them,' said (Harry) Edwards, 'and if they don't change their ways, we'll close them up'" (quoted in "Memo to Board of Trustees, Re: Charges of 'Racism' and 'Bigotry' Against BYU and the LDS Church," 29 October 1969, included in "Compiled Information Concerning African Americans, BYU, and the Church," MSS SC 2969, L. Tom Perry Special Collections, Harold B. Lee Library, Brigham Young University, Provo, Utah, 9).

4. See Gregory A. Prince and Wm. Robert Wright, *David O. McKay and the Rise of Modern Mormonism* (Salt Lake City: The University of Utah Press, 2005), 159–198, for a detailed examination of Ernest L. Wilkinson's relationship with David O. McKay, and for a

discussion of other church leaders' appraisal—and resentment—of Wilkinson's energetic campaigning for funding for BYU.

5. Ernest L. Wilkinson and W. Cleon Skousen, *Brigham Young University: A School of Destiny* (Provo, Utah: Brigham Young University Press, 1976), 744.

6. Wilkinson and Skousen, *Brigham Young University: A School of Destiny*, 752. Though this official centennial history of BYU was cowritten (per Web.11) by Ernest Wilkinson, chapter 35, which surveys Wilkinson's presidency, has a surprisingly candid appraisal of the difficulties in his relationships with BYU colleagues. See especially pages 751–754. (There is an editor's note at the beginning of chapter 35 that the chapter was written by W. Cleon Skousen, Wilkinson's coauthor (per Web.11), and Roy K. Bird.) See Prince and Wright, *David O. McKay and the Rise of Modern Mormonism*, 165: "David O. McKay made clear his dream for BYU before either he or Wilkinson became presidents. Speaking to the student body in 1948, he defined the reason for BYU's stature: 'Its paramount purpose is character,...to make great men, great scientists, great leaders....I look upon Brigham Young University as having resting upon it the greatest responsibility of any university in the world.'"

7. Gary James Bergera and Ronald Priddis, *Brigham Young University: A House of Faith* (Salt Lake City: Signature Books, 1985), 26. For a more detailed summary of the statistics related to BYU's growth during Ernest Wilkinson's presidency, see Wilkinson and Skousen, *Brigham Young University: A School of Destiny*, 745–749.

8. Wilkinson and Skousen, *Brigham Young University: A School of Destiny*, 746. Wilkinson was an Ogden, Utah, native with degrees from George Washington and Harvard universities. He left a successful Washington, D.C., law practice when he was named president of BYU in 1951. While the school was then seventy-five years old (Wilkinson himself was a graduate from the class of 1921), students and faculty in 1950 still complained that much of the campus consisted of "the architecture of Siberia, the desert of Arabia, and the wreckage of Korea," because of the school's assortment of used military and government buildings and the "piecemeal, half-hearted manner" of its "haphazard landscaping" (Bergera and Priddis, *Brigham Young University: A House of Faith*, 21). Wilkinson's short-lived predecessor (Howard McDonald was president of the university from 1945–1949) had only recently convinced the board of trustees to "[reaffirm] its commitment to Brigham Young University" after the board's executive committee had initially sent signals that "BYU was on the road out." See Bergera and Priddis, *Brigham Young University: A House of Faith*, 20; Howard S. McDonald Oral History, 7 August 1972, Special Collections, Harold B. Lee Library, Brigham Young University, 1, as cited in Wilkinson and Skousen, *Brigham Young University: A School of Destiny*, 350. Note that Wilkinson and Skousen cite the oral history interview as *1973*, but it is catalogued at BYU Special Collections as taking place in *1972*. In summarizing the tenuous start to McDonald's tenure, Wilkinson and Skousen wrote that "the First Presidency was apparently still considering whether or not Brigham Young University ought to continue as a university,...To one who was about to become president of BYU, this was most disheartening. It looked like he had been hired to work himself out of a job" (350). It therefore seems unlikely that anyone in 1951 would have envisioned the type of "phenomenally expansionistic" plans that Ernest Wilkinson brought to Provo (Bergera and Priddis, *Brigham Young University: A House of Faith*, 25–26).

9. Prince and Wright, *David O. McKay and the Rise of Modern Mormonism*, 165. Proposals were in the works—and some lands even purchased—to build colleges in Portland, Phoenix, Anaheim, the San Francisco Bay area, and to move Ricks College from Rexburg, Idaho, to Idaho Falls. Strong local opposition to the Ricks College move, along with budget shortfalls occasioned by building program deficits, caused the junior college plan to lose support among church officials who instead favored the expansion of LDS Institutes of Religion adjacent to existing colleges. See Prince and Wright, *David O. McKay*, 193–198.

10. See "Memorandum from Dr. Earl Crockett," 11 December 1965, in Wilkinson Papers, UA 1000, box 273, folder 4, Special Collections, Brigham Young University: "[President McKay] stated in no uncertain terms that no good purpose would be accomplished by bringing speakers to the campus to discuss" the "position of the Negro in the Church...nor for the faculty or students to debate the subjects, nor for articles to be written," since

"General Authorities [were] often being quoted and misquoted," and this brought "considerable concern and embarrassment to the Church because of unfounded statements."

11. Armand L. Mauss, *The Angel and the Beehive: The Mormon Struggle with Assimilation* (Urbana and Chicago: University of Illinois Press, 1994), 52–53.

12. While there was some question as to whether this was an official statement of the First Presidency or only part of President Brown's prepared remarks, it is important to note that in 1965 the church-owned *Deseret News* "reprinted it as a 'statement given officially' at the 1963 conference" (Prince and Wright, *David O. McKay and the Rise of Modern Mormonism*, 70). The 1963 statement is reprinted on pages 69–70 of *David O. McKay and the Rise of Modern Mormonism*, and can also be found in "Compiled Information Concerning African Americans, BYU, and the Church," Special Collections, Brigham Young University. As with so many issues during LDS Church President David O. McKay's administration, Prince and Wright's discussion of racial controversies related to the priesthood policy deserves high marks for being comprehensive and insightful. See their chapter 4, "Blacks, Civil Rights, and the Priesthood," pages 60–105. For an expanded discussion of the history of the priesthood prohibition, as well as a century of Mormon reaction to it, see Edward L. Kimball, "The Question of Priesthood Denial," chapter 20 of *Lengthen Your Stride: The Presidency of Spencer W. Kimball*, working draft (Salt Lake City: Deseret Book and *BYU Studies*, 2005). The "working draft" edition of Kimball's biography includes notes and text that were omitted in the published version, but were included on a CD-ROM (a joint project of Deseret Book and *BYU Studies*) that came with the book. Pertinent chapters of the "working draft" were also reprinted as Edward L. Kimball, "Spencer W. Kimball and the Revelation on the Priesthood," *BYU Studies* 47, no. 2 (2008): 4–78. For a recent and comprehensive overview of the complex relationship between blacks and The Church of Jesus Christ of Latter-day Saints, see a 2009 documentary film, *Nobody Knows: The Untold Story of Black Mormons*, written and directed by Darius Aidan Gray and Margaret Blair Young; the film's script was published in *Dialogue* 42, no. 3 (Fall 2009): 100–128.

13. Albert B. Fritz, in the *Salt Lake Tribune*, 7 October 1963; a copy of Fritz's statement can also be found in "Compiled Information Concerning African Americans, BYU, and the Church," Special Collections, Brigham Young University.

14. In 1968, Sterling McMurrin, a nationally prominent Mormon educator, revealed details of a decade-old conversation he had with President David O. McKay—and McMurrin later allowed another Mormon author to make those details public. McMurrin reported that President McKay told him in 1954 that the priesthood restriction was not a church doctrine but a *policy*, and thus subject to change. McMurrin's account of the conversation was corroborated by President McKay's son, who asked his father to confirm McMurrin's report. The whole episode was featured in a work in progress by Stephen Taggart, a Ph.D. student in sociology at Cornell. He asked McMurrin for permission to publish the conversation, and McMurrin agreed on the condition that Taggart check with President McKay's son Llewelyn. Taggart's manuscript reached Mormon authorities and figured into the discussions preceding the December 1969 letter from the church's First Presidency that reiterated the church's position that the priesthood prohibition could only be changed by a revelation to the church's prophet. A copy of the First Presidency's letter is included in "Compiled Information Concerning African Americans, BYU, and the Church," Special Collections, Brigham Young University. Stephen Taggart died before his research was published in 1970 as Stephen G. Taggart, *Mormonism's Negro Policy: Social and Historical Origins*. See Prince and Wright, *David O. McKay*, 96–100, 423, note 167.While for years numerous media outlets had quoted various Mormons restating essentially the same thing, this new report generated more speculation, and coincided with other Latter-day Saints voices that clamored for change. As significant as any was an open letter to the First Presidency from Stewart Udall, then U.S. Secretary of the Interior. The Arizona politician had served as a church missionary when he was younger, but he became less active in church participation over the years. He published the letter in *Dialogue*, an independent Mormon journal that was only in its second year of publication. See this representative passage in *Dialogue* 2, no. 2 (Summer 1967): 6: "Every Mormon knows that his Church

teaches that the day will come when the Negro will be given full fellowship. Surely that day has come." Udall also sent copies of his letter to the *New York Times* and the Associated Press. See F. Ross Peterson, "'Do Not Lecture the Brethren': Stewart L. Udall's Pro-Civil Rights Stance, 1967," *Journal of Mormon History* 25, no. 1 (Spring 1999): 272–287.

15. See, for example, the oft-quoted and influential "Memo from a Mormon," a 1963 article in *Look* magazine that concluded this way: "If we Mormons believe that God is directing our Church, we can hope that God is preparing a new revelation that will revise our present Negro doctrine. If we do not believe this, we can hope that *the more liberal element of the Mormon leadership* will produce a doctrinal change as the problem intensifies" (Jeff Nye, "Memo from a Mormon: In Which a Troubled Young Man Raises the Question of his Church's Attitude Toward Negroes," *Look*, 22 October 1963, 79; italics added). See also Wallace Turner, "Mormons Consider Ending Bar on Full Membership for Negro," special to the *New York Times*, 7 June 1963, 17, which quoted Hugh B. Brown of the church's First Presidency as saying, "We are in the midst of a survey looking toward the possibility of admitting Negroes.... Believing as we do in divine revelation through the President of the church, we all await his decision." "Negro Question," *Time*, 18 October 1963, 83, which quoted J. D. Williams, a professor at the University of Utah who had served as a Mormon bishop, saying, "the change will come, and within my lifetime"; and a *Detroit Free Press* article that quoted BYU professor Thomas Cheney under the headline, "End to Mormon Bias Against Negro, Seen by College Professor"—Cheney later complained that the intent of his presentation had been misrepresented, since he did not feel that "Mormons necessarily had a bias against Negroes" (quoted in Prince and Wright, *David O. McKay*, 89). This theme of an anticipated policy change continued in articles such as "Mormons and the Mark of Cain," *Time*, 19 January 1970, 46, and "Second-class Mormons," *Newsweek*, 19 January 1970, 84.

16. See "Black Saints of Nigeria," *Time*, 18 June 1965, 56. The whole episode is treated at length in Prince and Wright, *David O. McKay*, 81–94. The first such request for missionaries came from a Nigerian named O. J. Umordak in 1946. LaMar Williams from the church's Missionary Department was sent to Nigeria in the fall of 1961 after other requests came in the late fifties and early sixties. Williams found that there were "nearly one hundred congregations, totaling some 5,000 people, who wished to be admitted to the church," even after Williams explained that they could not at that time be ordained to the priesthood (81–83). The timing of the 1963 announcement about opening the Nigerian mission demonstrated that church officials were sensitive to public image issues, and suggested that this Nigerian initiative was not motivated by a desire to court the favor of the church's critics. President McKay consciously delayed the announcement until after the November 1962 election, "for the reason that if we were to baptize a considerable number of negro [*sic*] people at this time, certain politicians might take the view that it was done to influence the negro [*sic*] vote in favor of George Romney in his candidacy for Governor of Michigan" (84). Importantly, Lester Bush, who published a much-discussed article in 1973 on the history of the church's priesthood prohibition, attributed his interest in this topic to the "press attention to the subject during George Romney's 1962 gubernatorial candidacy and ... several major Church 'announcements' in 1963," the first of which was the "11 January"1963 announcement of "the first LDS mission to black Africa (Nigeria)." Also, in an interview in 1994, church general authority Marion D. Hanks acknowledged the "influence" of Bush's article on the mind-set (per Web. 11) of many church leaders by saying that it "started to foment the pot." In Lester Bush, "Writing 'Mormonism's Negro Doctrine: An Historical Overview' (1973): Context and Reflections, 1998," *Journal of Mormon History* 25, no. 1 (Spring 1999): 231, 266. Bush's award-winning original article appeared in *Dialogue* 8, no. 1 (Spring 1973): 11–68, and was reprinted in Lester E. Bush, Jr., and Armand Mauss, eds., *Neither White nor Black: Mormon Scholars Confront the Race Issue in a Universal Church* (Midvale, Utah: Signature Books, 1984), 53–129.

17. Jack Olsen, "In an Alien World," *Sports Illustrated*, 16 July 1968, 41. The quote also appeared in an Associated Press report. See, for example, "BYU Wins Triangular; Miners

Lag," *Austin American*, 14 April 1968; clipped article included in Presidential Papers of Ernest L. Wilkinson, UA 1086, box 443, folder 2, L. Tom Perry Special Collections, Harold B. Lee Library, Brigham Young University, Provo, Utah.

18. In Wilkinson Presidential Papers, UA 1086, box 443, folder 2.

19. Olsen, "In an Alien World," 30; see also Gary James Bergera and Ronald Priddis, *Brigham Young University: A House of Faith* (Salt Lake City: Signature Books, 1985), 299.

20. This quote from George McCarty came in the 1 July 1968 edition of *Sports Illustrated*, as reported in Ripley, "Irate Black Athletes," 35, and was still causing a stir a year and a half later. UTEP's President Ray defended the athletic director as being misrepresented, explaining that McCarty's southern accent accounted for the perception that he used the epithet.

21. Ernest L. Wilkinson Diary, 1 May 1968, in Ernest L. Wilkinson Personal Papers, UA 1000, box 102, folder 5, L. Tom Perry Special Collections, Harold B. Lee Library, Brigham Young University, Provo, Utah.

22. Joseph M. Ray to Ernest L. Wilkinson, 22 April 1968, in Presidential Papers, UA 1086, box 443, folder 2.

23. See "Memo to Board of Trustees, Re: Charges of 'Racism' and 'Bigotry' Against BYU and the LDS Church," 29 October 1969, 14.

24. See "Memo to Board of Trustees, Re: Charges of 'Racism' and 'Bigotry' Against BYU and the LDS Church," 29 October 1969, 4–6, for an explanation of BYU's recruiting practices before 1969.

25. See Ripley, "Irate Black Athletes," 35. This reasoning was the basis of most of President Wilkinson's early responses to protesters and reporters who questioned why there were so few black students in general at BYU. A restatement of that response was included in the pamphlet, "Minorities, Civil Rights, BYU, and You," 2: "There is not a large number of black students on the BYU campus, but that is a result of their decision and not our policy. Their decisions are undoubtedly influenced by the fact that there are no black families living in the county where BYU is located. Those who have come, and who are here now, have made no suggestion that racial discrimination is practiced against them. The exact number of black students attending now is unknown because the University does not ask for race on its admission forms." By this same reasoning, Wilkinson explained in statements that BYU enrolled "hundreds of American Indian students" and "a considerable number of Mexican-Americans" ("Statement made by President Ernest L. Wilkinson March 5, 1969, after a demonstration at University of New Mexico," included in "Memo to Board of Trustees, Re: Charges of 'Racism' and 'Bigotry' Against BYU and the LDS Church," 29 October 1969, 4).

26. See Wilkinson diary, 27 October 1969, UA 1000, box 103, folder 3; Prince and Wright, *David O. McKay and the Rise of Modern Mormonism*, 64–65; Bergera and Priddis, *Brigham Young University*, 298–299.

27. Gallup Poll, 01/28/1965–02/02/1965, Question qn9; accessed at Gallup Brain database, http://brain.gallup.com/home.aspx; italics added.

28. See Aaron Shill, "Football, Racial Issues—Then Understanding," *Mormon Times* (supplement to the *Deseret News*), 24 October 2009, 5: "[Hamilton] left school" after the coach's ultimatum "and joined the military.... Determined to earn his degree, Hamilton returned to school and the team in 1969 after receiving a letter from [Wyoming Coach] Eaton. 'I think it was eating on him as much as it was eating on me,' [Hamilton] said."

29. Wilkinson Diary, 1 May 1968, Wilkinson Personal Papers, UA 1000, box 102, folder 5. The letter from the Regional Office of the Department of Health, Education, and Welfare (Region VIII, headquartered in Denver) was dated April 11, 1968, the same day that the Associated Press called Wilkinson and informed him of the planned protest of the UTEP track athletes. The track meet was held on April 13, 1968. See Wilkinson Presidential Papers, UA 1086, box 443, folder 2, and box 463, folder 19.

30. The comments from the HEW representative came from Solomon Arbeiter, "higher education coordinator in the Office for Civil Rights and head of the review team which recently visited BYU" in a 3 July 1968 memo reporting on a meeting between Arbeiter's group and

a law firm representing the BYU administration. Robert Barker of the law firm offered his interpretation of the investigation in a letter to Wilkinson, 12 July 1968. Both documents in Wilkinson Presidential Papers, UA 1086, box 463, folder 19.

31. Copy of the minutes of approved items, as well as the April 30 statement on employment, are included in Wilkinson Presidential Papers, UA 1086, box 463, folder 19.

32. See the HEW team's official report and recommendations dated 24 May 1968, in Wilkinson Presidential Papers, UA 1086, box 463, folder 19.

33. Letter from Hollis B. Bach, Regional Civil Rights Director, Department of Health, Education, and Welfare, Regional Office, Office for Civil Rights-Region VIII, Denver, Colorado, to Ernest L. Wilkinson, 27 March 1969, included in "Compiled Information Concerning African Americans, BYU, and the Church," Special Collections, Brigham Young University.

34. Wilkinson diary, 1 May 1986, UA 1000, box 102, folder 5.

35. Wilkinson diary, 21 November 1968, UA 1000, box 103, folder 1, reporting on a conversation with the president of San Jose State. Wilkinson said that he told San Jose State's President Clark "that El Paso the year before had canceled the athletic grants-in-aid of their colored players who refused to play BYU. Later the President of El Paso had told me that was the best thing they had ever done because normalcy was again restored to the campus."

36. Wilkinson diary, 30 November 1968, UA 1000, box 103, folder 1. See also "Memo to Board of Trustees, Re: Charges of 'Racism' and 'Bigotry' Against BYU and the LDS Church," 29 October 1969, 9.

37. Wilkinson diary, 9 September 1968, UA 1000, box 103, folder 1.

38. Wilkinson diary, 13 December 1969, UA 1000, 103, folder 3.

39. Wilkinson diary, 28 November 1968, UA 1000, box 103, folder 1. The game took place two days later.

40. "Memo to Board of Trustees, Re: Charges of 'Racism' and 'Bigotry' Against BYU and the LDS Church," 29 October 1969, 10–11.

41. "Memo to Board of Trustees, Re: Charges of 'Racism' and 'Bigotry' Against BYU and the LDS Church," 29 October 1969, 11–12.

42. "Memo to Board of Trustees, Re: Charges of 'Racism' and 'Bigotry' Against BYU and the LDS Church," 29 October 1969, 12.

43. Ripley, "Irate Black Athletes," 35. The quote came from James Edwards, a student at San Jose State and Dr. Harry Edwards's brother.

44. See "Memo to Board of Trustees, Re: Charges of 'Racism' and 'Bigotry' Against BYU and the LDS Church," 29 October 1969, 6.

45. See Clifford A. Bullock, "Fired by Conscience: The Black 14 Incident at the University of Wyoming and Black Protest in the Western Athletic Conference, 1968–1970," *Wyoming History Journal* 68, no. 1 (Winter 1996): 6–13, for a thorough discussion of the weekend protest, as well as the reaction of those on the University of Wyoming campus and in the wider community. Bullock also notes that arguably the era's most prominent college football coach, Paul "Bear" Bryant at the University of Alabama, expressed support for Eaton's actions (see Bullock, "Fired by Conscience," 9). Yet Eaton's action seemed costly for his career. His team had been to the Sugar Bowl in 1967 and won the conference championship for three straight years before the protest incident; the year after, his team had only one win. Both Paul James and Clifford Bullock attribute most of the downturn to Eaton's inability to recruit black athletes after the "black 14" incident. See Bullock, "Fired by Conscience," 11, and James, *Cougar Tales*, 47. Sportscaster James remembered that "a Wyoming booster club offered to pay the...way out of town" for "seven faculty members" who "threatened to resign if the fourteen blacks were *not* reinstated" (James, *Cougar Tales*, 47). He also quotes James Michener's *Sports in America*: "Friends told me at the height of the trouble, bands of armed men drove around the streets of Laramie ready to shoot up the place if the blacks caused any trouble; word had been passed that two thousand Black Panthers armed to the teeth, were descending on Laramie from points like Chicago and San Francisco determined to

capture the town" (Michener, *Sports in America* [New York: Random House, 1976], 159, as cited in James, *Cougar Tales*, 47).

46. "Memo to Board of Trustees, Re: Charges of 'Racism' and 'Bigotry' Against BYU and the LDS Church," 29 October 1969, 7.

47. "Memo to Board of Trustees, Re: Charges of 'Racism' and 'Bigotry' Against BYU and the LDS Church," 29 October 1969, 17–18. Also included is the "Statement from the Black Student Alliance, University of Wyoming, Saturday, October 18, 1969."

48. "Memo to Board of Trustees, Re: Charges of 'Racism' and 'Bigotry' Against BYU and the LDS Church," 29 October 1969, 6; italics added. See, for example, Ripley, "Irate Black Athletes," 35, published in the *New York Times* less than a month after the Wyoming game: "The problem most recently drew public attention among the Western Athletic Conference, where Brigham Young University, a Mormon school, has come under attack from black athletes at other schools because of *the church's denial of full status to Negroes*"; italics added.

49. "Memo to Board of Trustees, Re: Charges of 'Racism' and 'Bigotry' Against BYU and the LDS Church," 29 October 1969, 23: "Paul James, who of course, mingles with all the athletic officials, newsmen, and television and radio broadcasters, predicted, if these protests continue to grow and if we do nothing to take some of the pressure off the opposing schools, that within six months we would be out of the 'athletic business.'" See also the October 23, 1969, comments of Jack Schroeder, "Tribune Executive Sports Editor," who "predicted the ultimate dissolution of the Western Athletic Conference" because "the arguments by the protestors is not so much what will happen at BYU and not so much what BYU does with its own cause, but rather, what will happen at their own schools and what their own schools represent in our social order"; quoted in "Memo to Board of Trustees, Re: Charges of 'Racism' and 'Bigotry' Against BYU and the LDS Church," 29 October 1969, 21–22.

50. Included in "Memo to Board of Trustees, Re: Charges of 'Racism' and 'Bigotry' Against BYU and the LDS Church," 29 October 1969, 25.

51. Wilkinson Diary, 23 October 1969, UA 1000 box 103, folder 3.

52. In "Memo to Board of Trustees, Re: Charges of 'Racism' and 'Bigotry' Against BYU and the LDS Church," 29 October 1969, 20–21. The commissioner's memo was sent in advance of an athletic directors' meeting held in Denver on November 3, 1969. See also Wilkinson diary, 22 October 1969, regarding "a very disturbing letter from Wiles Hallock, Commissioner of the WAC conference in which he would pit BYU against everyone in the Conference. This is most unfortunate."

53. In "Memo to Board of Trustees, Re: Charges of 'Racism' and 'Bigotry' Against BYU and the LDS Church," 29 October 1969, 21.

54. In "Memo to Board of Trustees, Re: Charges of 'Racism' and 'Bigotry' Against BYU and the LDS Church," 29 October 1969, 19.

55. See Bergera and Priddis, *Brigham Young University*, 300–301; James, *Cougar Tales*, 52–54.

56. Ripley, "Irate Black Athletes," 1, 35.

57. Louis Harris and Associates, Inc., *The Harris Survey Yearbook of Public Opinion: 1970* (New York: Louis Harris and Associates, Inc., 1971), 222.

58. *The Harris Survey Yearbook of Public Opinion: 1970*, 220.

59. See, for example, *The Harris Survey Yearbook of Public Opinion 1970*, for the following survey results: When asked, "Do you generally find yourself…in agreement with the aims and goals…[and] tactics of student protesters…?," 66 percent of women and 63 percent of men answered that they were either "somewhat opposed" or "strongly opposed" to the protesters' aims and goals; more than 80 percent of respondents opposed their tactics—24 percent of women and 19 percent of men said they were "somewhat opposed" to their tactics, while 61 percent of women and 64 percent of men said that they were "strongly opposed" to their tactics (274). When asked about student protests against the Vietnam War, 52 percent of respondents answered that they "condemn them" (275). Sixty percent of respondents felt that the Black Panthers were "a serious menace to this country," and 75 percent felt that the shooting deaths of Black Panthers by police officers were "the result of violence started by the Black Panthers themselves" (230–231).

60. Bullock sees the "law and order" philosophy of both university administrators and state government leaders as driving official support for Coach Eaton's decision; see "Fired by Conscience," 6. For a concise discussion of the context of Richard Nixon's political platform in the face of this widespread social unrest, see David Farber, *The Age of Great Dreams: America in the 1960s* (New York: Hill and Wang, 1994), 216–218. *The Harris Survey Yearbook of Public Opinion: 1970*, 48, reported that 82 percent of survey respondents agreed that the government should "[get] tougher on the subject of crime and law and order."

61. Farber, *The Age of Great Dreams*, 220.

62. Farber, *The Age of Great Dreams*, 224. See also Todd Gitlin, *The Sixties: Years of Hope, Days of Rage* (Toronto: Bantam Books, 1987), 335, for a similar conclusion. See *The Harris Survey Yearbook of Public Opinion: 1970*, 280–281, where 71 percent of survey respondents answered that they felt the "Chicago 7" (the convicted "leaders of the protests at the Democratic National Convention") "received a fair trial."

63. See also Bullock, "Fired By Conscience," 9, where he notes that, like officials at various universities, Commissioner Hallock "issued a statement raising the specter of a national Black conspiracy. Hallock, Coach Eaton, the NCAA, and administrators at Wyoming believed that Wyoming's nationally respected program, Eaton's policy of discipline, and the lack of previous racial disturbances had made Wyoming an obvious target." See Bergera and Priddis, *Brigham Young University*, 301, where they note that some university officials suggested the protests were only "part of a communist-inspired ploy to undermine the stability of the United States." For the persistence of that viewpoint, see also Wallace Turner, "Conservative and Liberal Mormons Advise Church on Negro Exclusion Policy," *New York Times*, 21 June 1970, 57.

64. John L. Lund, interview by the author, 4 August 2009, audio recording in possession of the author. In 1969–1970, Dr. Lund was an instructor at the LDS Institute of Religion adjacent to the campus of the University of Washington and a graduate student at the University of Washington.

65. See, for example, *The Harris Survey Yearbook of Public Opinion: 1971*, 56, where 73 percent of respondents favored increasing or at least maintaining federal spending toward "programs on racial equality," as opposed to only 16 percent who favored cutting back on that spending. Sixty-eight percent of respondents disagreed that "blacks are inferior to white people" (327). Compare also a Harris poll conducted in Utah in October 1971: When asked, "Should blacks be permitted to hold the priesthood in the Mormon Church?," 58 percent of non-Mormons answered "yes." Importantly, however, 38 percent of non-Mormons stated that they were "not sure." This sizable minority seemed to reflect the widespread uncertainty about the complexity of this and other race-related issues in that era. Cited in Wallace Turner, "Mormons Operating a Special Meeting Unit for Blacks," *New York Times*, 6 April 1972, 20.

66. "Memo to Board of Trustees, Re: Charges of 'Racism' and 'Bigotry' Against BYU and the LDS Church," 29 October 1969, 24.

67. See "Memo to Board of Trustees, Re: Charges of 'Racism' and 'Bigotry' Against BYU and the LDS Church," 29 October 1969, 2.

68. John L. Lund, interview by author. Word of the Black Panthers' planned vandalism got to the Institute before the Panthers did. As students left the Institute building out the back doors, Lund locked the front doors. He was standing in the entry when the Black Panthers arrived, and he overheard the confusion about the "Mormon Church." Other buildings on the University of Washington campus did not escape unscathed during racially related clashes. See "U. of Washington Students Raid 8 Buildings on Campus," *New York Times*, 12 March 1970, 63.

69. Mauss, *The Angel and the Beehive*, 53. Included on page 52 is a comparative table summarizing surveys from 1966–1969.

70. See Mauss, *The Angel and the Beehive*, 52, where only 12 percent of Utah Mormons agreed with the statement "it would be better for Negroes and whites to attend separate churches," as opposed to 28 percent of Presbyterians, 34 percent of Lutherans, and 67 percent of Southern Baptists.

71. Gary L. Bunker, Harry Coffey, and Martha A. Johnson, "Mormons and Social Distance: A Multidimensional Analysis," *Ethnicity* 4 (1977): 352, 356, 365–366. Their study implied that religious belief, not racism, drove most Mormons' opinions about the prospects of blacks being admitted to the priesthood. The study found that 93 percent of Mormons surveyed agreed that it was "absolutely true" that the head of the Church was a prophet—and another 6 percent said it was "probably true." Only slightly less unanimous was Mormon opinion about the "norm" against the priesthood ordination of black men: 83 percent felt it was "absolutely true"; 13 percent felt it was "probably true." Still, when asked about supporting a decision from the prophet to change that norm, a remarkable 98 percent said they would support such a change—and 93 percent opined that such a change would be a "function of revelation," while only 4 percent said it would come in "response to social pressure." This helps explain the disparity in a 1971 Harris survey in Utah: "Should blacks be permitted to hold the priesthood in the Mormon Church?"—58 percent of non-Mormons answered yes, 4 percent answered no, and 38 percent answered "not sure"; 16 percent of Mormons answered yes, 70 percent answered "no," and 14 percent answered "not sure." In Turner, "Mormons Operating a Special Meeting Unit for Blacks," 20.

72. Some discomfited Latter-day Saints even pled their case in national publications. Along with the aforementioned statements like those of George Romney, or Sterling McMurrin, or Stewart Udall, see June Adamson's essay "Mary," *Christian Century*, 11 February 1970, 175–176, in which she reminisces about her uneasiness with the restrictions in church participation placed on a childhood friend and her family—all of whom were black Mormons. See also Mormon sociologist Lowry Nelson's "Mormons and Blacks," *Christian Century*, 16 October 1974, 949–950. See also Stephen W. Stathis and Dennis L. Lythgoe, "Mormonism in the Nineteen-Seventies: The Popular Perception," *Dialogue* 10, no. 3 (Spring 1977): 107, where they cite Sandra Haggerty, "Blacks and the Mormon Church," *Los Angeles Times*, 5 July 1974, section 2 page 5: "Sandra Haggerty, a black columnist and a frequent contributor to the *Los Angeles Times* wrote on July 5, 1974, 'Although I have met a few Mormons who attempt to use their religious stance to justify outright racist attitudes and actions, others are somewhat embarrassed by that portion of the doctrine and feel it should be reversed.'"

73. William F. Reed, "The Other Side of 'The Y.'," *Sports Illustrated*, 26 January 1970, 38–39.

74. Reed, "The Other Side of 'The Y.'," 38.

75. Media outlets picked up on this. *Christian Century* deplored what it saw as the LDS Church's "incredibly primitive" and "obscurantist doctrine concerning race," but the same editorial nevertheless asserted that "Mormon liberals, including many educators and students, have been trying to rectify the matter" ("The Christian Century Editorial: Pigskin Justice and Mormon Theology," *Christian Century*, 21 January 1970, 67).

76. "Memo to Board of Trustees, Re: Charges of 'Racism' and 'Bigotry' Against BYU and the LDS Church," 29 October 1969, 29.

77. "Memo to Board of Trustees, Re: Charges of 'Racism' and 'Bigotry' Against BYU and the LDS Church," 29 October 1969, 27

78. See Bergera and Priddis, *Brigham Young University*, 300; see also Ernest L. Wilkinson and W. Cleon Skousen, *Brigham Young University: A School of Destiny* (Provo, Utah: Brigham Young University Press, 1976), 655. John L. Lund, interview by the author. Dr. Lund was a former BYU football player, and he was pursuing a graduate degree at the University of Washington at the time of this vote. He attended the meeting of the faculty senate. When he attempted to explain the Mormon priesthood policy and speak in favor of proceeding forward with the scheduled BYU game, he remembered that he was "shouted down" by protesters who filled the meeting room.

79. "Memo to Board of Trustees, Re: Charges of 'Racism' and 'Bigotry' Against BYU and the LDS Church," 29 October 1969, 25.

80. "Memo to Board of Trustees, Re: Charges of 'Racism' and 'Bigotry' Against BYU and the LDS Church," 29 October 1969, 27–32.

81. Ernest L. Wilkinson to N. Eldon Tanner, 3 January 1970, Wilkinson Papers, UA 1000, box 273, folder 21.

82. "Memo, Re: Minutes of Meeting Held Monday," December 29, 1969, included in "Correspondence, Heber G. Wolsey, 1969," Wilkinson Presidential Papers, UA 1086, box 489, folder 9.

83. The three-page statement released on 23 December 1969 is included in Wilkinson Papers, UA 1000, box 273, folder 21.

84. Ernest L. Wilkinson to N. Eldon Tanner, 3 January 1970, UA 1000, box 273, folder 21.

85. Wilkinson and Skousen, *Brigham Young University*, 656. They also suggest that "a number of Stanford alumni changed their yearly contributions from Stanford to BYU," such that "criticism of Pitzer by Stanford's alumni on this and other matters became so intense that he resigned on 25 June 1970."

86. Wilkinson diary, 24 January 1970.

87. Wilkinson diary, 19 November 1969. Because of the backlash Wilkinson observed, he wrote in his diary, "My prediction as of tonight is that within three months Pitzer will resign from Stanford. Time will tell whether I am correct." Pitzer did resign seven months later, citing a desire for "a more scholarly life at a less hectic pace" after dealing with the "destructive nature" of repeated protest activity. "Entirely too much of my time has been devoted to matters of an administrative or even of a police nature" (Wallace Turner, "President of Stanford Resigns after 2 Years of Disturbances," *New York Times*, 26 June 1970).

88. John Dart in the *Los Angeles Times* noted that "conservative columnists James J. Kilpatrick and Max Rafferty, California's superintendent of public instruction, . . . came to BYU's defense in December, 1969, after Stanford University said it would schedule no further intercollegiate competition with Mormon-sponsored schools" (John Dart, "BYU—A Campus of Peace and Patriotism," reprinted in Frederick Gentles and Melvin Steinfield, eds., *Dream on, America: A History of Faith and Practice* [San Francisco: Canfield Press, 1971], 68).

89. Both the telegram and the reply letter are included in the manuscript collection, "Compiled Information Concerning African Americans, BYU, and the Church," Special Collections, Brigham Young University.

90. "Excerpts from a Statement Dated August 6, 1970, Concerning Relationships between Blacks, Mormons, Brigham Young University and Seattle University, by Kenneth Baker, S. J., President, Seattle University," 3, in "Compiled Information Concerning African Americans, BYU, and the Church," Special Collections, Brigham Young University.

91. James Cleary, *The Creightonian*, 19 November 1971, included in "Compiled Information Concerning African Americans, BYU, and the Church," Special Collections, Brigham Young University.

92. Reed, "The Other Side of 'The Y.'," 39.

93. Heber G. Wolsey, "News Release," 12 November 1969, in Wilkinson and Skousen, *Brigham Young University*, 656.

94. Heber Wolsey, interview by Jonice Hubbard, in Hubbard, "Pioneers in Twentieth Century Mormon Media: Oral Histories of Latter-day Saint Electronic and Public Relations Professionals" (master's thesis, Brigham Young University, 2007), 198. Wolsey also recounted this experience in an address to the BYU student body given on 12 May 1970, "Minorities, Civil Rights, and BYU," *Speeches of the Year* (Provo, Utah: Brigham Young University Press, 1970), 7–8; a copy is included in the Wilkinson Papers, UA 1000, box 179, folder 15.

95. Heber Wolsey, interview by Jonice Hubbard, 202. Darius Gray verified Wolsey's recollections of the event in a conversation with the author, 7 June 2013. See also Bullock, "Fired By Conscience," 8, for background information on Willie Black. On the fortieth anniversary of the "black 14" incident, the LDS Church–owned *Deseret News* featured a story on Mel Hamilton, one of the Wyoming athletes involved in the armband protest, and his continued friendship with Darius Gray. One of Hamilton's sons later joined the LDS Church. In 2005, the director of the LDS Institute at the University of Wyoming invited Hamilton to address LDS students about the strides that had been made in healing the rifts between the two communities. See Shill, "Football, Racial Issues—Then Understanding," 1, 5.

96. Heber Wolsey, interview by J. Michael Allen, 19 July 1979, transcript, Archives, The Church of Jesus Christ of Latter-day Saints, 17.
97. Heber Wolsey, interview by Jonice Hubbard, 199–201.
98. Heber Wolsey, interview by Jonice Hubbard, 200.
99. Wilkinson and Skousen, *Brigham Young University*, 656–657. Their conclusion was that "these full-page advertisements won the support of many Mormon and non-Mormon citizens in the Northwest" (657).
100. Wolsey described the ad as a "position paper" in his address to the BYU student body, "Minorities, Civil Rights, and You," 7–8.
101. An expanded version of the ad was published by the university as a pamphlet for distribution, "Minorities, Civil Rights, BYU, and You," a copy of which is included in "Compiled Information Concerning African Americans, BYU, and the Church," Special Collections, Brigham Young University. The quoted minister was Reverend Blackman of the New Hope Baptist Church in Merced, California. His comments were also reported in "Toward Understanding," *Church News*, 7 February 1970; photocopy included in the collection "Compiled Information Concerning African Americans, BYU, and the Church," Special Collections, Brigham Young University.
102. Quoted in Heber Wolsey's address, "Minorities, Civil Rights, and BYU," 7–8.
103. See Dart, "BYU—A Campus of Peace and Patriotism," 68, for his observation that those who heaped "glowing praise" on BYU "view[ed] most other large campuses as havens for the immoral and politically radical." See also two telling survey responses in the *Harris Survey Yearbook of Public Opinion: 1970*, 272–273: 64 percent of respondents said "irresponsible students who just want to cause trouble" were a "major cause of campus unrest"; 55 percent of respondents agreed that "many young people who go to college get corrupted on drugs and pornography."
104. See Jan Shipps, *Sojourner in the Promised Land: Forty Years among the Mormons* (Urbana and Chicago: University of Illinois Press, 2000), 100–101, 110. See also "University without Trouble: No Flag-burning at Brigham Young," *U.S. News and World Report*, 20 January 1969, 58–59, for the account of a "Dr. and Mrs. Ray B. Reeves of Las Vegas, Nev., and Newport Beach, Calif., [who] donated 1,044 acres of California land worth several million dollars" to the school. "Before making the gift, Dr. and Mrs. Reeves came to Provo to take a look at BYU. They reported: 'The young people at BYU were all clean-cut, good-looking. There was no beatnik atmosphere. Those students had their feet on the ground. Instead of finding fault, they were accepting leadership. We like the way the university was being run. To show our support, we've given the university our ranch.'"
105. Hollis B. Bach to Ernest L. Wilkinson, 27 March 1969.
106. Dart, "BYU—A Campus of Peace and Patriotism," 68.
107. "The Conclusions and Recommendations Resulting from a Visit by an 'Interaction Team' of the Association of College Unions—International to The Church of Jesus Christ of Latter-day Saints and Brigham Young University," in "Compiled Information Concerning African Americans, BYU, and the Church," Special Collections, Brigham Young University, 1.
108. See the report issued October 3, 1970, by a fact-finding committee from the University of Arizona, included in "Compiled Information Concerning African Americans, BYU, and the Church," Special Collections, Brigham Young University, 2. Their opinion was that BYU students were "isolated" more than racist, and thus largely ignorant of black history and culture and mind-set (per Web. 11). They recommended campus exchanges with black students at other universities, as well as inviting prominent black Americans to speak to the BYU student body. Wilkinson had already sought (and received) approval from the Board of Trustees in May 1968 to invite black speakers to BYU's campus; see Wilkinson Presidential Papers, UA 1086, box 463, folder 19. Numerous black musicians had performed at the school over the years as well; see Deseret News, "Alpert Racial Charge Denied by Y. Chief," *Deseret News*, 13 June 1968, 12B. The conclusion that BYU students were largely isolated from national issues was also a principal assertion of Tammy Tanaka's master's thesis. See T. Tammy Tanaka, "Why No Revolts at BYU?: The Silent Language of

the Mormon World-view and Patriotism at Brigham Young University" (master's thesis, Brigham Young University, 1968).

109. "Mood Changes Toward BYU," *Tucson Daily Citizen*, 8 October 1970, 30 (editorial page), included in "Compiled Information Concerning African Americans, BYU, and the Church," Special Collections, Brigham Young University.

110. Report issued October 3, 1970, by a fact-finding committee from the University of Arizona, included in "Compiled Information Concerning African Americans, BYU, and the Church," Special Collections, Brigham Young University, 2.

111. It appears that Wilkinson first made that recommendation to the Executive Committee of the Board of Trustees in May 1968, proposing "that BYU be authorized to recruit Negro athletes who are members of the Church." The decision of the committee was to recommend the proposal to the full board. See Wilkinson Presidential Papers, UA 1086, box 463, folder 19. For his return to that recruiting issue, see "Memo to Board of Trustees, Re: Charges of 'Racism' and 'Bigotry' Against BYU and the LDS Church," 29 October 1969, 30–31, 34.

112. See Wilkinson diary, 19 December 1968, UA 1000, box 103, folder 1, for Wilkinson's report on the newspaper's "lead article today" that "indicated that Y students were in favor of recruiting Negroes." Wilkinson was not pleased with the article, since "this, of course, implies that the Negro has not been welcomed, which is, of course, untrue and is a very, very serious and misleading article."

113. Dart, "BYU—A Campus of Peace and Patriotism," 69.

114. See Bergera and Priddis, *Brigham Young University*, 301–302. One of the earliest black football players at BYU, Bennie Smith, eventually joined the LDS Church (see Bergera and Priddis, *Brigham Young University*, 477, note 58).

115. Quoted in the pamphlet "Minorities, Civil Rights, BYU, and You," 5. Report by a fact-finding committee from the University of Arizona, Special Collections, Brigham Young University, 2, 4.

116. See Bergera and Priddis, *Brigham Young University*, 302; Dart, "BYU—A Campus of Peace and Patriotism," 69.

117. See the letter from church apostle Mark E. Petersen to J. Willard Marriott, 1970, concerning a February 18 meeting in New York "to counsel with some of you brethren in the East concerning what steps we should take in the direction of public relations to help combat some of the unfavorable publicity that we have been having." Church apostle and (eventual church president in 1972) Harold B. Lee was also mentioned as a participant in the meeting. In J. Willard Marriott Papers, box 52, folder 14, Special Collections, Marriott Library, University of Utah, Salt Lake City, Utah.

118. "The Conclusions and Recommendations Resulting from a Visit by an 'Interaction Team' of the Association of College Unions—International to The Church of Jesus Christ of Latter-day Saints and Brigham Young University," in "Compiled Information Concerning African Americans, BYU, and the Church," 2.

119. There were several telltale signs that the controversy was already diminishing by the end of 1970. The protests against BYU dominated Ernest Wilkinson's diary in the months of October through December 1969. Yet in all of the daily entries for October 1970, he mentioned racial issues only once, in passing. See Wilkinson diary, UA 1000, box 103, folder 3, for the second half of 1969, and box 103, folder 5, for October 1970. Also, Brigham Young University filmmakers embarked on a project to interview several black Latter-day Saints for a documentary to explain that there were black Mormons who "like this church." By one account, the film was never released because church authorities worried that it would stir up tensions, since it also included interviews with blacks who were not Mormons and who opposed the church's policy. See Gregory A. Prince, " 'Let the Truth Heal': The Making of *Nobody Knows: The Untold Story of Black Mormons*: An Interview with Darius Aidan Gray and Margaret Blair Young," *Dialogue* 42, no. 3 (Fall 2009): 81–83. Gray and Young included footage from those original interviews in their 2009 documentary; Darius Gray was one of the interview subjects in the earlier project. However, another filmmaker who worked on the film in the late 1960s said that it was never released because the church felt that

the protests were subsiding, and church authorities worried that releasing the film would only stoke the embers. See Peter Czerny, interview by Jonice Hubbard, included in the appendix of Hubbard, "Pioneers in Twentieth Century Mormon Media: Oral Histories of Latter-day Saint Electronic and Public Relations Professionals" (M.A. thesis, Brigham Young University, 2007), 50: "We were so proud of [the film] and it never came out...by the time the film was done, things had kind of quieted down and so they decided not to release it after all."

120. "Editorial: Unity in Diversity," *Ensign*, August 1971, 89.

121. "Bonds of Brotherhood," *Church News*, 13 June 1970; photocopy included in the collection "Compiled Information Concerning African Americans, BYU, and the Church," Special Collections, Brigham Young University.

122. "Toward Understanding," Church News, 7 February 1970; photocopy included in the collection "Compiled Information Concerning African Americans, BYU, and the Church," Special Collections, Brigham Young University.

123. For Darius Gray's reminiscences of the origins of the Genesis Group, see *"Nobody Knows* Script," 116–117.

124. See Sheri L. Dew, *Go Forward with Faith: The Biography of Gordon B. Hinckley* (Salt Lake City: Deseret Book, 1996), 296, for this account of the group's inception: "At the First Presidency's request, he [Gordon B. Hinckley] and Elders Thomas S. Monson and Boyd K. Packer carefully studied the situation of blacks in the Church; their work led to the formation, on October 19, 1971, of the Genesis Group of the Liberty Stake. Under this program, black members of the Church remained members of their own wards but joined with other LDS blacks for auxiliary meetings and activities." See also Edward L. Kimball, *Lengthen Your Stride: The Presidency of Spencer W. Kimball* (Salt Lake City: Deseret Book, 2005), 205, note 17, for historical context about the group's organization. Kimball also notes that Spencer W. Kimball, at the time the senior apostle, "attended a Genesis picnic" and "personally took Christmas gifts to the homes of the Genesis presidency" (205).

125. Jessie L. Embry, "Separate but Equal? Black Branches, Genesis Groups, or Integrated Wards," *Dialogue* 23, no. 1 (Spring 1990): 14.

126. Turner, "Mormons Operating a Special Meeting Unit for Blacks," 20.

127. Heber Wolsey to Wendell Ashton, 18 Sept. 1972, in "Compiled Information Concerning African Americans, BYU, and the Church," Special Collections, Brigham Young University, 3.

128. Excerpts of interview between Robert L. Friedly, executive director of the Office of Communication of the Christian Church (Disciples of Christ), and Heber Wolsey and Darius Gray, transcript, in "Compiled Information Concerning African Americans, BYU, and the Church," Special Collections, Brigham Young University, 4–5. See also Darius Gray's description of his conversion to Mormonism in 1964 in *"Nobody Knows* Script," 112–115.

129. A. Dale Fiers, General Minister and President of Christian Church (Disciples of Christ) to Heber Wolsey, 13 September 1972, in "Compiled Information Concerning African Americans, BYU, and the Church," Special Collections, Brigham Young University. More recently, the LDS Church has officially expressed uncertainty about when the priesthood restriction began. See the introduction to "Official Declaration 2" in the 2013 edition of the Doctrine and Covenants, http://www.lds.org/scriptures/dc-testament/od?lang=eng: "During Joseph Smith's lifetime, a few black male members of the Church were ordained to the priesthood. Early in its history, Church leaders stopped conferring the priesthood on black males of African descent. Church records offer no clear insights into the origins of this practice. Church leaders believed that a revelation from God was needed to alter this practice and prayerfully sought guidance. The revelation came to Church President Spencer W. Kimball." Compare a church press release from 29 February 2012, http://www.mormonnewsroom.org/article/racial-remarks-in-washington-post-article: "It is not known precisely why, how, or when this restriction began in the Church but what is clear is that it ended decades ago." The complexity of this history will be explored

in W. Paul Reeve, *Religion of a Different Color: Race and the Mormon Struggle for Whiteness*, forthcoming from Oxford University Press.

130. Heber Wolsey to Wendell Ashton, 18 September 1972, 4–5.

131. See "Faith Always Helps," *Tempe Daily News*, 18 May 1972, in "Compiled Information Concerning African Americans, BYU, and the Church," Special Collections, Brigham Young University.

132. Larry R. Norris to Darl Andersen, 4 September 1972, in "Compiled Information Concerning African Americans, BYU, and the Church," Special Collections, Brigham Young University, 1–4.

133. Officials at Seattle University and the University of Arizona recommended that concerned citizens could better effect change at BYU through *increased* association with the Mormons, rather than disassociation and demonstration. See "Excerpts from a Statement Dated August 6, 1970, Concerning Relationships between Blacks, Mormons, Brigham Young University and Seattle University," by Kenneth Baker, S. J., President, Seattle University, Special Collections, Brigham Young University, 2: "If I may be so bold, I would like to offer a suggestion to those who would coerce the Mormon Church to change its belief by discriminating against BYU. . . . not by coercion, but by association, by discussion, by persuasion. Do not try to isolate BYU by breaking off all relations with her until she comes to her knees . . . increase your contacts with BYU." President Baker called BYU a "distinguished sister university"(4); see also the report by a fact-finding committee from the University of Arizona, in "Compiled Information Concerning African Americans, BYU, and the Church," Special Collections, Brigham Young University, 4.

134. See, for example, William K. Stevens, "Student Activists Turning from Campus to Society," *New York Times*, 9 March 1970, 1.

135. *The Harris Survey Yearbook of Public Opinion: 1970*, 341.

136. *The Harris Survey Yearbook of Public Opinion: 1970*, 253.

137. Louis Harris and Associates, Inc., *The Harris Survey Yearbook of Public Opinion: 1973* [New York: Louis Harris and Associates, Inc., 1974], 205. Compare the following survey results: in 1971, when asked about the "most important national problems," 20 percent of respondents answered that "programs on racial equality" were "important" (Louis Harris and Associates, Inc., *The Harris Survey Yearbook of Public Opinion: 1971* [New York: Louis Harris and Associates, Inc., 1972], 55). In 1972, 21 percent of respondents listed "racial problems" as a "volunteered response" when asked about the "biggest problems facing people . . . in this country today" (Louis Harris and Associates, Inc., *The Harris Survey Yearbook of Public Opinion: 1972* [New York: Louis Harris and Associates, Inc., 1973], 131. Significantly, in that same list of "biggest problems" in 1972, inflation and unemployment came in first at 58 percent; in 1973, the number who mentioned economy/inflation/unemployment had grown to 72 percent of the respondents. This trend seems to correspond with William Chafe's characterization of the 1970s as a time when the black community "bifurcated" into a growing middle class and a burgeoning underclass. Chafe's contention is that the civil rights movement of the 1960s had provided openings for black Americans who had access to education and opportunity. The gains made by many African Americans may have contributed to the sense that "equal opportunity" now meant that blacks had achieved equality. He also notes, however, that the "economic downturn" of the 1970s dominated public attention, such that "few talked about the problem" of those in the black community who descended into "an ever-deepening immersion in poverty"—and "an even smaller number attempted to do anything about it." He also quotes Daniel Yankelovich, who suggested that "our narrow self-concern threatens to get out of hand . . . [making us] . . . *bored . . . with the problems of race* and unemployment" (William H. Chafe, *The Unfinished Journey: America Since World War II* [New York: Oxford University Press, 1999], 442, 445, 446, 468, 469; italics added).

138. See, for example, this strongly worded essay that attacked the religious justification of the priesthood prohibition: Elmer E. Wells, "Unjustifiable Denial of Priesthood to Black Mormons," *Negro History Bulletin* 40, no. 4 (July-August 1977): 725–727.

139. See "N.A.A.C.P. Plans Suit Against Boy Scouts," *New York Times*, 28 July 1974, 44. See also James S. Tinney and Edward E. Plowman, "Message to Mormons: Open the Gates," *Christianity Today*, 22 November 1974, 58–59.

140. See "Boy Scouts Ask for Dismissal of N.A.A.C.P. Suit," *New York Times*, 29 August 1974, 17.

141. See "Behind Temple Walls," *Time*, 16 September 1974, 110–111; "A New Prophet," *Newsweek*, 14 January 1974, 84.

142. For the most detailed account of the deliberations leading up to the revelation and descriptions of the announcement and its aftermath, see Kimball, *Lengthen Your Stride*, chapters 20–24, pages 195–245. Because of space constraints, the full footnotes to Kimball's biography of his father are included on an accompanying CD-ROM. See also the reprint of this section of the book, with footnotes: Kimball, "Spencer W. Kimball and the Revelation on the Priesthood," 4–85.

143. Mauss, *The Angel and the Beehive*, 117. Compare also Jan Shipps's contemporary comments: "The timing and context, and even the wording of the revelation itself, indicate that the change has to do not with America so much as with the world. A revelation in Mormonism rarely comes as a bolt from the blue; the process involves asking questions and getting answers. The occasion of questioning has to be considered, and it must be recalled that while questions about priesthood and the black man may have been asked, an answer was not forthcoming in the '60s when the church was under pressure about the matter from without, nor in the early '70s when liberal Latter-day Saints agitated the issue from within" (Shipps, "The Mormons: Looking Forward and Outward," 761).

144. "*Nobody Knows* Script," 119.

145. "Smooth Succession?" *Time*, 14 January 1974, 41.

146. "Smooth Succession?" 41.

147. Kimball, *Lengthen Your Stride*, 8

148. Two other trends of President Kimball's leadership (discussed in the next chapter) also bucked the predictions of status quo: a higher profile in several matters of national politics and a comparative explosion of new temple construction.

149. For an extensive list of related news stories, see Linda Thatcher's compilation, "Selected Newspaper Articles on Mormons and Mormonism," *Dialogue* 12, no. 4 (Winter 1979): 116–117. She cites thirty-three articles from across the nation generated by the announced revelation. In addition, see this helpful contemporary media bibliography for a sense of the type of coverage the priesthood revelation generated in 1978: Stephen W. Stathis, "A Survey of Current Literature," *Dialogue* 12, no. 4 (Winter 1979): 113–117.

150. "Priesthood news spurs calls, stops the presses," *Deseret News*, 10 June 1978, in *Journal History of The Church of Jesus Christ of Latter-day Saints*, 10 June 1978, 15. The *Journal History* is a microfilmed collection of news clippings related to Mormonism that have been organized chronologically. The collection can be accessed both at the LDS Church Archives and at Special Collections, Marriott Library, University of Utah.

151. See "Carter Praises LDS Church Action," *Deseret News*, June 10, 1978, A-1; cited in Bringhurst and Smith, *Black and Mormon*, 10, note 5.

152. The statement, dated 8 June 1978, was officially accepted and canonized by the LDS Church as "Official Declaration 2" in the church's Doctrine and Covenants.

153. Dawn House, "A Heretic? U. Professor Distrusts LDS Orthodoxy, Pursues Reason," *Salt Lake Tribune*, November 20, 1988, B-1, as cited in Bringhurst and Smith, *Black and Mormon*, 2, 10, note 8.

154. See Twila Van Leer, "Black LDS Priesthood Holder Says, 'It's a Beautiful Day,' "*Deseret News*, June 12, 1978, A-1, as cited in Newell G. Bringhurst and Darron T. Smith, eds., *Black and Mormon* (Urbana and Chicago: University of Illinois Press, 2004), 3, 11, note 16.

155. See "LDS Decision Wins Praise," *Deseret News*, 27 June 1978, photocopy included in *Journal History of The Church of Jesus Christ of Latter-day Saints*,, 27 June 1978, for the comments of Billy James Hargis, "president and founder of the Christian Crusade": "I was very proud to see the president of the Mormon Church extend the priesthood to blacks.... This was the greatest limitation to the growth of the Mormon Church." He added that that he "[hoped] to see the LDS Church really extend its missionary program in Africa and other

areas." See also Robert Bryson, "Church Officials Applaud LDS Action on Blacks," *Salt Lake Tribune*, 10 June 1978; Marjorie Hyer, "Mormon Church Dissolves Black Bias," *Washington Post*, 10 June 1978; "Local Mormons 'Jubilant' Over Surprise Revelation to Prophet," *Port Arthur (Texas) News*, 17 June 1978; "Mormon Decision Aids Image," *Las Cruces (New Mexico) Sun-News*, 4 August 1978; and David E. Anderson, "Mormon Acceptance of Blacks Resolves Church Controversy," *Baltimore Record*, 11 August 1978.

156. See two representative examples: Kenneth Woodward, in "Race Revelations," *Newsweek*, 19 June 1978, 67, quoted "Salt Lake City businessman Lee Wheelock" as saying, "I'm not a bigot, but some people unfortunately think I am because I'm a Mormon." Woodward then concluded his article this way: "For Wheelock and Mormons like him, the revelation came as a blessing." See also Kenneth A. Briggs, "Mormon Church Strikes Down Ban Against Blacks in Priesthood," *New York Times*, 10 June 1978, 1, 24: "The rule change smoothes the way for better relations between the church and the nation's blacks and provides another example of adaptation of Mormon beliefs to American culture."

157. "Revelation," *Time*, 19 June 1978, 55. See Jan Shipps, "The Mormons: Looking Forward and Outward," *Christian Century*, 16–23 August 1978, 761: "A crucial obstacle which almost certainly would have prevented the LDS church from ever being a universal church was removed on June 9, 1978."

158. See Briggs, "Mormon Church Strikes Down Ban," 1, 24; Woodward, "Race Revelations," 67.

159. See "Marketing the Mormon Image: An Interview with Wendell J. Ashton," *Dialogue* 10, no. 3 (Spring 1977): 17.

Chapter 4

1. The heading "Obscurity, Not Opposition, Is the Problem" is paraphrased from the conclusion of LDS apostle Boyd K. Packer in summarizing the results of "Attitudes and Opinions Towards Religion: Religious attitudes of adults (over 18) who are residents of six major metropolitan areas in the United States: Seattle, Los Angeles, Kansas City, Dallas, Chicago, New York City—August 1973," L. Tom Perry Special Collections, Harold B. Lee Library, Brigham Young University, Provo, Utah, 33.

2. One important convert to the value of public relations expenditures was apparently Harold B. Lee. As a senior apostle, Lee initially balked at the proposed $3 million World's Fair pavilion. He told a subordinate that "if you feel that [the] estimate is anywhere near correct, cancel us out and we will not be in the World's Fair because I would not think of going to a three million dollar cost" (Brent L. Top, "The Miracle of the Mormon Pavilion: The Church at the 1964–1965 New York World's Fair," in *New York*, Regional Studies in the Latter-day Saint Church History series [Provo, Utah: Brigham Young University, 1992], 237–238). However, Elder Lee's superiors in the First Presidency opted to participate in the Fair, regardless of cost. The success of the pavilion impressed everyone involved, and, as noted here, when Harold B. Lee became church president a decade later, he actively supported the expansion of the new Public Communications Department.

3. The department was initially called "External Communications" in 1972. Originally, the title was meant to imply that the department was focused on people outside of the church, as opposed to "internal communications." In 1973, it was determined that "media people, with whom the new department primarily works, have been puzzled a bit with the 'External' title. 'Public Communications' is much easier for them to understand and to approach for assistance" ("Public Affairs Department," unpublished history, 6; copy in possession of author). It is significant that even this early name change reflected a new sensitivity to outside perception.

4. See Lorry Rytting, interview by James B. Allen, 4 December 1979, transcript, LDS Church Archives, 10–11. The comment about the "shift in emphasis" came from interviewer James Allen, who worked in the church's Historical Department.

5. For an excellent summary of the accelerating professionalization at church headquarters as membership expanded worldwide, see Leonard J. Arrington and Davis

Bitton, *The Mormon Experience: A History of the Latter-day Saints*, 2nd ed. (Urbana and Chicago: University of Illinois Press, 1992), 289–301. The completion in 1972 of the 28-story Church Office Building in Salt Lake City was a visible mark of what they describe as "expanding offices and departments, growing specialization, increased reliance of professionals" (290).

6. See Gregory A. Prince and Wm. Robert Wright, *David O. McKay and the Rise of Modern Mormonism* (Salt Lake City: University of Utah Press, 2005), 404, for their assessment that the correlation movement, which administratively moved most of the church's operations under the Quorum of the Twelve Apostles, "marked perhaps the most important administrative change in the church during the twentieth century."

7. On the tensions related to correlation and church education and intellectual freedom, together with the challenges in providing instruction for a church made up increasingly of converts, see Jan Shipps, *Sojourner in the Promised Land: Forty Years Among the Mormons* (Urbana and Chicago: University of Illinois Press), 374–381.

8. See the important chapter "A Uniform Look for the Church: Architecture," chapter 12 of Terryl L. Givens, *People of Paradox: A History of Mormon Culture*, (New York and Oxford: Oxford University Press, 2007), 241–252. See also Richard O. Cowan, *The Latter-day Saint Century* (Salt Lake City: Bookcraft, 1999), 180–181, for a discussion of the practical advantages of these new standardized building plans developed in the 1960s. See Shipps, *Sojourner in the Promised Land*, 352: "In what turned out to be a brilliant decision from the standpoint of the maintenance of LDS identity in an altered situation, leaders of the church decreed that the church's standard building plans would be used for all these LDS structures.... [T]he sagacity of the decision that led the Saints to build structures giving the appearance of a new 'religious' franchise is evident in retrospect."

9. See the important 1980 essay for the *Harvard Encyclopedia of American Ethnic Groups* by Dean L. May, "Mormons," reprinted in Eric Eliason, ed., *Mormons and Mormonism: An Introduction to an American World Religion* (Urbana and Chicago: University of Illinois Press, 2001), especially 61–63, 72–73.

10. See Jan Shipps, "Richard Lyman, the Story of Joseph Smith and Mormonism, and the New Mormon History," *The Journal of American History* 94, no. 2 (September 2007), 501, for this important insight about professionalization in the church's administration: "Until well past the mid-twentieth century, rather than having a true bureaucracy, the church had departments staffed by clerks and auxiliaries staffed primarily by volunteers." For worries about church leaders about overdependence on bureaucrats, see Quinn, *Extensions of Power*, 156.

11. See James B. Allen and Glen M. Leonard, *The Story of the Latter-day Saints*, 2nd ed., rev. and enl. (Salt Lake City: Deseret Book, 1992), 616.

12. Lorry Rytting interview, 11.

13. Wendell J. Ashton Oral History, 1984, LDS Church Archives, 173, as cited in Public Affairs Department, unpublished departmental history, copy in possession of the author, 5.

14. Ashton Oral History, 173, 175, in Public Affairs Department history, 5.

15. "Attitudes and Opinions Towards Religion," Special Collections, Brigham Young University, 33. While the summary of this study that is available in the Lee Library does not list the research firm that conducted the survey, Lorry Rytting stated that it was the Frank N. Magid company. See Lorry Rytting interview, 12. Heber Wolsey was apparently instrumental in pushing for the study. He consistently urged that "more attention and emphasis needed to be placed on hard objective analysis of the messages we're communicating." When Wolsey took over the Public Communications Department in 1978, he established a "Communications Analysis Division" (Lorry Rytting interview, 12; see also Heber Wolsey interview by Jonice Hubbard, 26 July 2006, included in the appendix of Hubbard, "Pioneers in Twentieth Century Mormon Media: Oral Histories of Latter-day Saint Electronic and Public Relations Professionals" [master's thesis, Brigham Young University, 2007], 213–214). See also "Public Affairs Department," unpublished history, 6, which reports that "Heber G. Wolsey . . . served as director of electronic media, promotions, and research" when he joined the department.

16. Chiung Hwang Chen and Ethan Yorgason, "'Those Amazing Mormons': The Media's Construction of Latter-day Saints as a Model Minority," *Dialogue* 32, no. 2 (Summer 1999), especially pages 107–110.

17. See Thomas F. O'Dea, "Sources of Strain in Mormon History Revisited," in Marvin S. Hill and James B. Allen, eds., *Mormonism and American Culture* (New York: Harper & Row, 1972), 154–155.

18. See Heber Wolsey, interview by Jonice Hubbard, 214: "One of the main things that we, as public communications people, tried to get over is to let people know really who we are, so we emphasized family."

19. Orson Scott Card, "Wendell Ashton Called to Publishing Post," *Ensign*, January 1978, 73–74.

20. Two succinct summaries of this can be found in Herbert F. Murray, "A Half Century of Broadcasting in the Church," *Ensign*, August 1972, 49; and Prince and Wright, chapter 6, "Radio and Television Broadcasting," in *David O. McKay and the Rise of Modern Mormonism*, 124–138. The church began broadcasting on its radio station in the 1920s. By the 1970s, the church owned radio and TV stations in Salt Lake, New York, Los Angeles, Seattle, Chicago, and Kansas City, with a "potential audience of over 40 million people—about one-fifth of the population of the United States" (Murray, "A Half Century of Broadcasting," 49).

21. Stephen B. Allen, interview by Jonice Hubbard, 6 November 2006, transcript included as an appendix in Hubbard, "Pioneers in Twentieth Century Mormon Media: Oral Histories of Latter-day Saint Electronic and Public Relations Professionals," 40. At the time of this interview, Allen was Managing Director of the church's Missionary Department. He began his employment with the church in the Public Communications Department.

22. Ibid.

23. Ibid. See also Heber Wolsey, interview by J. Michael Allen, 19 July 1979, transcript, Archives, The Church of Jesus Christ of Latter-day Saints, 12.

24. Quoted in "New Public Communications Director Called," *Ensign*, January 1978, 74.

25. See "If You Love 'Em, Let 'Em Know It Everyday," radio script, Archives, The Church of Jesus Christ of Latter-day Saints. Numerous *Homefront* commercials are available for viewing at the LDS Church Archives.

26. "Marketing the Mormon Image: An Interview with Wendell J. Ashton," *Dialogue* 10, no. 3 (Spring 1977): 15. Two other department officials estimated that by the late 1970s, that amount of air time had risen to eighteen million dollars worth per year. See Heber G. Wolsey, interview by J. Michael Allen, 9; Stephen B. Allen, interview by Jonice Hubbard, 41.

27. For statistics on *Homefront* viewership and awards, see the 1981 summary report, "Homefront Television and Radio Spots," Archives, The Church of Jesus Christ of Latter-day Saints. See also "Broadcasting Outlet Receives Radio Award," *Ensign*, June 1973, 71; "Freedoms Foundation Awards Presented," *Ensign*, April 1975, 80.

28. Richard L. Bushman, interview with author, August 12, 2011, transcript in author's possession, 3. Stephen B. Allen, interview by Jonice Hubbard, 41. See also "New Homefront Spot Released," *Ensign*, December 1993, 70–71, for a similar assessment by church employee Lynn Packham.

29. "Marketing the Mormon Image: An Interview with Wendell J. Ashton," 20.

30. "Marketing the Mormon Image: An Interview with Wendell J. Ashton" 20.

31. "Church Television Special Brings 90,000 Responses," *Ensign*, February 1977, 94.

32. "Church Television Special Brings 90,000 Responses," 94.

33. See "Marketing the Mormon Image: An Interview with Wendell J. Ashton," 15.

34. Compare "How to organize a public relations program in stakes and missions: The Church of Jesus Christ of Latter-day Saints," (Church Information Service: Salt Lake City, 1967), with "How to organize a public relations program in stakes and missions: The Church of Jesus Christ of Latter-day Saints (Revised June 1973)," (Public Communications Department, 1973). In L. Tom Perry Special Collections, Harold B. Lee Library, Brigham Young University, Provo, Utah.

35. See L. Tom Perry, "A Report on the Church's Participation in America's Bicentennial Celebration," *Ensign*, November 1976, 39; L. Tom Perry, "The Church and the U.S. Bicentennial: A Conversation with Elder L. Tom Perry of the Council of the Twelve," *Ensign*, June 1976, 7. L. Tom Perry, ordained an apostle in 1974, chaired the Church Bicentennial Committee. He had spent most of his business career living in cities in the eastern U.S., so his contacts there made him a natural choice for arranging for church participation in prominent bicentennial commemorations.

36. See "Ford Schedules Holiday Speeches," *New York Times*, 1 July 1976, 14; John Brannon Albright, "Notes: Out of Town It's Fourth of July, Too," *New York Times*, 27 June 1976, 262. See also "City Street Alive with Music," *New York Times*, 2 July 1976, 26. The newspaper ran a photo of the Mormon Tabernacle Choir singing before a large crowd that filled the streets at the corner of Wall and Nassau streets. The Choir sang at a ceremony on the steps of the Federal Hall Museum before traveling to Washington, D.C., for the weekend concerts.

37. Quoted in Stephen W. Stathis and Dennis L. Lythgoe, "Mormonism in the Nineteen-Seventies: The Popular Perception," *Dialogue* 10, no. 3 (Spring 1977): 99. Stathis and Lythgoe note that interviews and biographical sketches of Anderson appeared in *American Opinion, Life, New York Times, New York Times Magazine, Newsweek, Washingtonian, Washington Post,* and *Washington Star.*

38. Susan Sheehan, quoted in Stathis and Lythgoe, "Mormonism in the Nineteen-Seventies," 100.

39. Lester Kinsolving of the *Washington Star* and Susan Sheehan of the *New York Times Magazine*, quoted in Stathis and Lythgoe, "Mormonism in the Nineteen-Seventies," 100.

40. Pete Axthelm, "Miller—Golf's New Golden Boy," *Newsweek*, 3 February 1975, 44–48, as quoted in Stathis and Lythgoe, "Mormonism in the Nineteen-Seventies," 100. Stathis and Lythgoe also note that "feature stories on Miller and his family have appeared in *People Weekly, Reader's Digest,* the *Saturday Evening Post* and *Sports Illustrated*" and *Time.*

41. "The Marriott Story," with inset "Busy Like the Bees," *Forbes*, 1 February 1971, 24–25.

42. See Michael K. Winder, *Presidents and Prophets: The Story of America's Presidents and the LDS Church* (American Fork, Utah: Covenant Communications, 2007), 321, for a description of that memorial service in August 1985.

43. John Carmody, "Bill Marriott Jr., Looks Ahead to $1 Billion A Year," *Potomac*, 2 August 1970, as quoted in Stathis and Lythgoe, "Mormonism in the Nineteen-Seventies," 102.

44. See Heber Wolsey, interview with Jonice Hubbard, 212–213.

45. "Kings of Bubble Gum," *Newsweek*, 3 September 1973, 89.

46. "Kings of Bubble Gum," 89.

47. Sara Davidson, "Feeding on Dreams in a Bubble Gum Culture," *Atlantic Monthly*, October 1973, 72.

48. Davidson, "Feeding on Dreams in a Bubble Gum Culture," 66.

49. Quoted in Stathis and Lythgoe, "Mormonism in the Nineteen-Seventies," 101.

50. Heber Wolsey related that, in Australia, he "went to the head of a TV station and I said, 'I'd like you to consider putting some of these free public service announcements on your set, on your TV station.' And he says, 'What are they about?' I said, 'Well, they feature the Osmonds.' And he says, 'The Osmonds? Who are they?' And I said, 'Go out and ask your secretaries.' He walked out and came back and said, 'We'll take anything you've got, anything you've got we'll take, we'll be glad to take,' because his secretaries knew who the Osmonds were" (Heber Wolsey interview by Jonice Hubbard, 207).

51. Judy Klemesrud, "Strengthening Family Solidarity with a Home Evening Program," *New York Times*, 4 June 1973, 47. The opening lines of Klemesrud's piece are also quoted by Stathis and Lythgoe, "Mormonism in the Nineteen-Seventies," 104.

52. See James E. Enstrom, "Cancer Mortality Among Mormons," *Cancer* 36 (September 1975): 825–841, and Joseph L. Lyon, Melville R. Klauber, John W. Gardner, Charles R. Smart, "Cancer Incidence in Mormons and Non-Mormons in Utah, 1966–1970," *New England Journal of Medicine* 294 (15 January 1976): 129–133; as cited in Stathis and Lythgoe, "Mormonism in the Nineteen-Seventies," 104–105. Importantly, Dr. Enstrom

published several follow-up studies that allowed for a longer period of evaluation and bore out his original assertions. See James E. Enstrom, "Health Practices and Cancer Mortality among Active California Mormons," *Journal of the National Cancer Institute* 81 (1989): 1807–14, reprinted as chapter 15 in James T. Duke, ed., *Latter-day Saints Social Life: Social Research on the LDS Church and its Members* (Provo, Utah: Religious Studies Center, Brigham Young University, 1998), 441–460; and Enstrom, "Health Practices and Mortality among Active California Mormons, 1980–93," chapter 16 in Duke, ed., *Latter-day Saint Social Life*, 461–471. Both essays provide a helpful review of related studies and literature.

53. See Melvin Leavitt, "What Makes Mormons Run?" *New Era*, June 1976, 40. *New Era* is the LDS Church's magazine aimed at a teenaged audience.

54. "Marketing the Mormon Image: An Interview with Wendell J. Ashton," 15.

55. This is apparent in a survey of the *Reader's Guide Retrospective* database for periodical articles relating to Mormonism in the years 1969–1976. Controversy often breeds attention—as Mormon-related controversies (especially related to race relations) subsided, so did the level of overall national coverage devoted to the Saints in the 1970s. There were almost twice as many articles in 1970 on Mormonism (sixteen) as any other year in the period. The next closest was 1974, with ten—most of which were focused on the Washington, D.C., temple dedication.

56. "It's Now Do or Die for the ERA: Mormon Power Is the Key" was the headline to Judy Foreman's piece in the *Boston Globe*, 30 June 1981, 1.

57. See the section on this so-called "liquor-by-the-drink" legislation and the church's opposition to it—together with the Salt Lake Ministerial Association—in Prince and Wright, *David O. McKay*, 330–333. The bill to relax alcohol regulations in 1965 "died a quick death" after the "Church-owned *Deseret News* 'opened fire editorially'" (331). For another perspective on church involvement, see Dew, *Go Forward with Faith: The Biography of Gordon B. Hinckley*, 291–294. See, for example, Harry Waters, "Urban Shadows Fall on Sunny Salt Lake City," *Newsweek*, 15 March 1971, 102: "Certainly there is *nothing particularly ominous* about the dominion of a highly prosperous church, nor would anyone quibble with the notion that Salt Lake has benefited considerably from the traditional Mormon virtues of industry, resourcefulness and organization" (italics added). Even though Waters noted that the non-Mormon residents of Salt Lake City were essentially "disfranchised from both the sense and reality of participating in the decisions that shape their destinies," he found it "almost impossible to unearth an adult resident—either Mormon or gentile—who wants to live anywhere else" (104, 107). The sense of Latter-day Saints' provincial outlook was highlighted in Waters's observation that "the nation's only genuine theocracy . . . the Mormon burghers of Salt Lake City are so totally preoccupied with the affairs of Mormonism that the rest of the world is very much an intrusion" (102).

58. See the brief timeline of the ERA's up-and-down path toward ratification included with Foreman, "It's Now Do or Die for the ERA." See also Susan D. Becker, *The Origins of the Equal Rights Amendment: American Feminism Between the Wars* (Westport, Connecticut: Greenwood Press, 1981). For an overview of the career of the Equal Rights Amendment, see Kathryn Cullen-DuPont, "Equal Rights Amendment," in her *Encyclopedia of Women's History in America*, 2nd ed. (New York: Facts on File, Inc., 2000), 81, where she notes that "supporters . . . were successful in having the amendment introduced in Congress almost every year after 1923."

59. Kathryn Cullen-DuPont, in her *Encyclopedia of Women's History in America*, 229, called Phyllis Schlafly "the most visible female proponent of the defeat of the Equal Rights Amendment."

60. See Jane J. Mansbridge, *Why We Lost the ERA* (Chicago and London: University of Chicago Press, 1986), 13, 126–127, for her views about a correlation between the court decision and the subsequent drop-off in state ratifications of the ERA. After 1973, the ERA and abortion-on-demand became increasingly linked in the heated rhetoric over the amendment. Because of that link, opponents portrayed the ERA as an attack on traditional

families and morals. Opponents feared federal funding for abortions if the ERA passed, and again many ERA advocates readily agreed that these unpopular possibilities could be a part of the ERA package. See also Glenn H. Utter and John W. Storey, *The Religious Right*, 2nd ed. (Santa Barbara, California: ABC-CLIO, 2001), 8, 171–172.

61. See D. Michael Quinn, "A National Force, 1970s-1990s," chapter 10 of *Mormon Hierarchy: Extensions of Power* (Salt Lake City: Signature Books, 1997). For a history of the ERA from a Latter-day Saints standpoint, as well as an excellent commentary on the Mormon mind-set (per Web. 11) toward feminism in the early 1970s, see the first four chapters of Martha Sonntag Bradley, *Pedestals and Podiums: Utah Women, Religious Authority and Equal Rights* (Salt Lake City: Signature Books, 2005), 1–124; also the important survey of the history of Mormon women in Arrington and Bitton, "The Mormon Sisterhood: Charting the Changes," chapter 12 of *The Mormon Experience*, 220–240. See especially pages 227–229 for information related to educational opportunities for women and the suffrage movement among Mormons. In an ironic turn, the Edmunds-Tucker Act of 1887, which was meant to punish the LDS Church for its persistent practice of polygamy, also "abolished women's suffrage in the territory" (Dean L. May, *Utah: A People's History* [Salt Lake City: University of Utah, 1987], 127).

62. Mansbridge, *Why We Lost the ERA*, 5.

63. Quinn, *Mormon Hierarchy: Extensions of Power*, 373–376, where he traced early Mormon thought on women's rights, as well as the voting records of Mormon legislators on the ERA in the early 1970s.

64. These words are from Barbara Smith's address, quoted in Bradley, *Pedestals and Podiums*, 94–95. See Janet Peterson, "Spafford, Belle S.," in Garr, Cannon, and Cowan, eds., *Encyclopedia of Latter-day Saint History*, 1169–1168, for information about Spafford's long career. See Allen and Leonard, *The Story of the Latter-day Saints*, 659, and Quinn, *The Mormon Hierarchy: Extensions of Power*, 376–377, for a discussion of the Special Affairs Committee formed at church headquarters in 1974, consisting of general authorities who "gathered information on various questions that affected the Church and helped formulate a Church response" (Allen and Leonard, 659). It appears that it was with members of this committee, including elders Gordon B. Hinckley and James E. Faust, that Barbara Smith consulted before delivering her December 1974 speech.

65. The statement is reprinted in Edward L. Kimball, *Lengthen Your Stride: The Presidency of Spencer W. Kimball* (Salt Lake City: Deseret Book, 2005), 177–178. Church legal advisors counseled that the brevity of the amendment belied its conceivable breadth, since it had the potential to give judges the broad interpretative basis to strike down traditional protections for women and children. Would alimony be challenged? Would child support for divorced mothers be threatened? Mormon legal minds suggested that a combination of legislative actions could achieve the aims of equality in opportunity and salary—which the church supported—better than a sweeping but vague amendment. See, for example, Rex E. Lee, *A Lawyer Looks at the Equal Rights Amendment* (Provo, Utah: Brigham Young University Press, 1980). Lee was President Ronald Reagan's solicitor general from 1981 to 1985. He was named president of BYU in 1989, and held that position until the end of 1995, only three months before his cancer-related death. See Janet Lee, "Lee, Rex E.," in Garr, Cannon, and Cowan, *Encyclopedia of Latter-day Saint History*, 655. For an overview of LDS statements on this issue, together with a representation of the arguments against the ERA which church leaders employed, see the subsection "Nine Major Mormon Anti-ERA Documents," in chapter 4 of Bradley, *Pedestals and Podiums*, 93–111. The statements span the years 1974 to 1981.

66. D. Michael Quinn has argued that a primary reason Latter-day Saints only opposed the ERA beginning in 1974 was that President Harold B. Lee "was apparently unwilling to engage in a head-on confrontation about issues which many LDS women supported." Lee's death in late 1973 opened the way for his successor to speak more openly, since, as Quinn sees it, "Spencer W. Kimball had different perspectives." Quinn's assertion is based on a conversation with Harold B. Lee's grandson. See Quinn, *The Mormon Hierarchy: Extensions of Power*, 376, and 607, note 22. A recent biography of Kimball presents some difficulties

for that interpretation. Barbara Smith, the church's Relief Society president who first spoke out against the ERA in 1974, later sought out President Kimball to ascertain his feelings about her comments, suggesting that the church president had not communicated an opinion on the matter to general church officers. In fact, his biographer notes that Kimball's journals do not give any hint about his feelings regarding the ERA before 1975. See Kimball, *Lengthen Your Stride*, 176–177. Therefore, considering the similarities in Lee's and Kimball's teachings about womanhood and motherhood, just as persuasive, if not more so, is the argument that the ERA *as a movement* came to represent something different for Latter-day Saints over time. This seems to be the way historian Jan Shipps understood the development of Latter-day Saints' opposition to the ERA. She wrote, "When the ERA became a symbolic issue tied to women's liberation and a redefinition of appropriate female roles, LDS leaders concluded that it posed such a danger to family life that the church should place itself on record as standing against its passage" (Jan Shipps, "Sonia Johnson, Mormonism and the Media," *Christian Century*, 2–9 January 1980, 5).

67. This sense of a consistent message about traditional family roles is especially clear in Martha Bradley's survey in *Pedestals and Podiums*, 69–76. Bradley noted that "even before the Equal Rights Amendment was passed by Congress in May 1972, the LDS Church viewed the women's movement with suspicion and attacked the proposed changes feminists were advocating, calling Mormon women back to their home responsibilities" (93).

68. Clyde J. Williams, *The Teachings of Harold B. Lee* (Salt Lake City: Bookcraft, 1996), 195–197, for Lee's statements on abortion from 1955, 1971, 1972, and 1973. In 1955, Lee said, "there is another heinous practice, the sin of abortion, or the destruction of unborn children... Against this deplorable practice the leaders of the Church have declared from the beginning. This serious sin against the Lord's plan is committed by two groups of individuals: first, those who, having committed their first great error in yielding to sexual sin, seek to cover their sins after gratifying their lusts, by committing an even more heinous crime against the law of God; and, second, by those having entered into the sacred relationships of the married state but who, rather than accept the responsibilities of parenthood, yield to this awful practice by which they forfeit their rights to wonderful blessings which otherwise could have been theirs" (196). Then in 1972 he said, "We recognize that there are circumstances under which to save the life of the mother the doctors would find it necessary to have an abortion. But we are unalterably opposed to promiscuous abortion" (196). He had strong words for "those who project such measures to prevent life or to destroy life before or after birth," saying they "will reap the whirlwind of God's retribution, for God will not be mocked" (196).

69. Williams, *The Teachings of Harold B. Lee*, 197.

70. Williams, *The Teachings of Harold B. Lee*, 227.

71. Williams, *The Teachings of Harold B. Lee*, 227. President Lee made this statement to a group of college-aged young men; it was also reprinted in the *Church News*, 19 August 1972, 3, 5.

72. Williams, *The Teachings of Harold B. Lee*, 290.

73. Williams, *The Teachings of Harold B. Lee*, 285. See also Williams, *The Teachings of Harold B. Lee*, 288, for an excerpt from a February 1972 article in the church's *Ensign* magazine entitled "Maintain Your Place as a Woman," where he emphasized that women had traits and abilities that made them uniquely qualified for their "duties in the home, particularly in the education of the children.... It is in building their motherly intuition and that marvelous closeness with their children that they are enabled to tune in upon the wavelengths of their children and to pick up the first signs of difficulty, of danger and distress, which if caught in time would save them from disaster."

74. "Smooth Succession?" *Time*, 14 January 1974, 41, which quotes the new church president; see also a fuller report of this news conference statement in Edward L. Kimball, ed., *The Teachings of Spencer W. Kimball* (Salt Lake City: Bookcraft, 1982), 318.

75. Kimball, *The Teachings of Spencer W. Kimball*, 315. Compare an October 1973 statement from President Lee in Williams, *The Teachings of Harold B. Lee*, 252.

76. Arrington and Bitton mention the "Victorian role expectation" in terms of conflicts within Latter-day Saints feminism. See their *Mormon Experience*, 238. See also Bradley,

Pedestals and Podiums, xix, where she also associates many of these expectations related to traditional motherhood as a return in the 1950s to "the cult of true womanhood," referencing Barbara Welter, "The Cult of True Womanhood: 1820–1860," in *The American Family in Social-Historical Perspective*, Michael Gordon, ed. (New York: St. Martin's Press, 1983), 313–28. "According to Welter," Bradley writes, "ideal women of this period were characterized by piety, purity, submissiveness, and domesticity" (516, note 10). A 1971 edition of the independent Mormon journal *Dialogue* was devoted to women's issues and opened with this introduction: "Our group, largely made up of supportive wives and loving mothers who are also excellent homemakers and Church workers, has discussed the genesis of that model, how much of it is scriptural and how much traditional, and whether other models have met with acceptance in the Church" (Claudia Bushman, "Introduction," *Dialogue: A Journal of Mormon Thought* 6 [Summer 1971]: 7–8, quoted in Bradley, *Pedestals and Podiums*, 74–75).

77. Jan Shipps, "Sonia Johnson, Mormonism and the Media," *Christian Century*, 2–9 January 1980, 5: "In keeping with its generally conservative image, the Mormon Church is as committed to the traditional nuclear family as the foundation of stable society as are the members of Phyllis Schlafly's Eagle Forum. But since the nuclear family is the basic unit in Mormon culture, since the LDS church program is primarily designed with families rather than individuals in mind, and since LDS theology holds that temporally created family units will persist throughout eternity, the Mormon commitment to the family is more far-reaching than any form of political conservatism could possibly explain. It is such a vital part of the very fabric of Mormonism that any threat to the traditional structure of the family is also likely to be perceived as a threat to Mormonism itself...LDS leaders concluded that it posed such a danger to family life that the church should place itself on record as standing against its passage"" (Shipps, "Sonia Johnson, Mormonism and the Media," 5).

78. Quinn cites a survey published in the *Deseret News* in November 1974 that indicated that "63.1 percent of Utah Mormons favored ratification." However, in February 1975, after Barbara Smith's December 1974 speech, and the *Church News's* January 1975 editorial, Utah legislators voted against the amendment, 54–21. See Quinn, *The Mormon Hierarchy: Extensions of Power*, 376–377. Edward Kimball notes that "with a Church leader and a Church publication weighing in, popular opposition to the ERA among Utahns quickly rose by 20 percent" (Kimball, *Lengthen Your Stride*, 177).

79. The most comprehensive account of this IWY convention can be found in Bradley, *Pedestals and Podiums*, especially chapters 5, 6, and 7. For a more succinct summary, see Quinn, *The Mormon Hierarchy: Extensions of Power*, 378–384.

80. See Bradley, *Pedestals and Podiums*, 197.

81. Mormon women had a considerable impact on other IWY state conventions. See, for example, Cleo Fellers Kocol, "Civil Disobedience at the Mormon Temple," *The Humanist*, September/October 1981, 5–6, for Kocol's recounting of the Washington convention, where Kocol asserted that the events of this convention in Washington and the emergence of the "Mormon Menace" precipitated the protests at the church's Seattle Temple and the arrest of the "Bellevue 21" protesters.

82. Quinn, *The Mormon Hierarchy: Extensions of Power*, 377–378, and especially 608, notes 34 and 35, for the Utah- and Idaho-based media that covered the story. Elder Packer's speech did receive brief mention in a July 1977 feature in *Ms.* magazine as evidence that the LDS Church was making "defeat of the ERA a national cause" (Lisa Cronin Wahl, "A Mormon Connection: The Defeat of the ERA in Nevada," *Ms.*, July 1977, 68,80).

83. Lisa Cronin Wahl, "A Mormon Connection?: The Defeat of the ERA in Nevada," *Ms.*, July 1977, 68. Wahl called Gibson "probably the single most powerful legislator in Nevada" and implicitly accused him of stealing the vote away from the will of majority, which polls suggested lined up in support of ERA. Wahl noted that while "only about 10 percent of Nevadans are Mormons...the three most powerful Senate committees are led by Mormons" (70). She went on to report that "speculation" about behind-the-scenes

maneuvering led "proponents [to] ask, was there a special deal that killed the ERA? No one knows for sure what actually led to the defeat in the Assembly" (84).

84. See "Appeal to Supreme Court Vowed," *Boston Globe*, 24 December 1981, 1. In 1978, Congress voted to extend the deadline for ERA ratification by three years, giving the states until 1982 to consider the measure. At the same time, Congress invalidated the rescission votes in Idaho and four other states. The other states to rescind their votes were Nebraska, Tennessee, Kentucky (though the rescission was vetoed by the governor), and South Dakota. See the timeline in Foreman, "It's Now Do or Die for the ERA—Mormon Power Is the Key," 1. Idaho and Arizona challenged the constitutionality of those decisions. The case was assigned, by a lottery system, to one of three district judges; this appeal landed, ironically, in Judge Callister's courtroom. Callister refused to step aside on the grounds that such a precedent could impinge on the rights of scores of religiously-minded judges. The back-and-forth on the Judge Callister situation appeared in periodicals across the country. See Stephen W. Stathis, "Mormonism and the Periodical Press: A Change is Underway," *Dialogue* 14, no. 2 (Summer 1981): 52–54. The *New York Times* reported that Callister's Idaho associates, both Mormon and not, overwhelmingly trusted his judgment and supported his participation in this case. See Molly Ivins, "Idahoans Have Faith in Judge on Rights Amendment," *New York Times*, 26 December 1979, A20. In the end, Judge Callister did rule that the deadline extension and the disqualification of state rescissions were both unconstitutional congressional actions, but his verdict had little impact on the final fate of the ERA. The three-year extension expired six months after Callister's decision, and the extra time did not bring about the necessary number of ratifications, even when the states which voted to rescind their support were still included in the pro-ERA tally. See "Appeal to Supreme Court Vowed," 1. Judge Callister issued his opinion on December 23, 1981. The extension expired on June 30, 1982. See also Ellen Goodman, "No, the ERA Patient Is Not Dead—But Needs Some Intensive Care," *Boston Globe*, 29 December 1981, 1.

85. See several autobiographical-type contemporary features in which Sonia Johnson told her own story in media outlets: Sonia Johnson, "The Woman Who Talked Back to God and Didn't Get Zapped," *Ms.*, November 1981, 51, an excerpt from Johnson's book, *From Housewife to Heretic* (Doubleday, 1981); also Mary L. Bradford, "The Odyssey of Sonia Johnson," *Dialogue* 14, no. 2 (Summer 1981): 14–47. Bradford's article includes a timeline of Sonia Johnson's life, as well as a transcript of an interview with Johnson.

86. See Johnson, "The Woman Who Talked Back to God," 54, 89, 90, 92 for Sonia Johnson's account of the Washington march and the Senate hearing. She was invited to the "religious panel" for the "Senate Subcommittee on Constitutional Rights" by "someone on Senator [Birch] Bayh's staff" who "remembered [the Mormons for ERA] banner" (54).

87. See "A Savage Misogyny: Mormonism vs. Feminism and the ERA," *Time*, 17 December 1979, 80: "[Johnson] explains that the phrase was directed at Mormon culture in general."

88. Diane Weathers and Mary Lord, "Can A Mormon Support the ERA?" *Newsweek*, 3 December 1979, 88.

89. Church spokesman Don LeFevre later expressed the church's position this way: "It's all right to be pro-ERA; it's just not all right to be anti-Church." An important and conspicuous example of tolerance for dissent on this issue occurred in 1980. At the church's October General Conference, "three women rose at the back of the Tabernacle to vote in opposition" to the proposal to sustain the church's leadership, a vote that is always included as a component of the conference's administrative business. The women began to shout, "No—ERA policy—No." One of the church's apostles, Bruce R. McConkie, spoke from the rostrum and "invited the women to meet with [another apostle, Gordon B.] Hinckley, after the meeting. The women later reported that Elder Hinckley said they 'were entitled to [their] opinion' and that no action would be taken against them" (Kimball, *Lengthen Your Stride*, 179–180, 182).

90. Shipps, "Sonia Johnson, Mormonism and the Media," 6; Stathis, "Mormonism and the Periodical Press," 48–49. Savonarola was a fifteenth-century cleric who led the "Bonfire of the Vanities" in Florence and accused the papal court with corruption and immorality.

91. See Karen De Witt, "The Pain of Being a Mormon Feminist," *New York Times*, 27 November, 1979, B11; Ben A. Franklin, "Mormon Church Excommunicates a Supporter of Rights Amendment," *New York Times*, 6 December 1979, A26;

92. See Kimball, *Lengthen Your Stride*, 182.

93. Barbara Howard in *Christian Century* described the press coverage this way: "Reams of copy have been written about the recent decision by the Mormon Church to excommunicate Ms. Johnson" (Howard, "Sonia Johnson and Mormon Political Power," *Christian Century*, 6–13 February, 1980, 126). See also David Macfarlane, "Equal rights meets its martyr," *Maclean's*, 21 January 1980, 37–38.

94. See, for example, the full-page photo in *People* magazine of a weeping Sonia Johnson being comforted by a woman wearing a "Mormons for ERA" T-shirt (Michael J. Weiss, "Irked by Sonia Johnson's E.R.A. Crusade, Church Elders Throw the Book of Mormon at Her," *People Weekly*, 3 December 1979, 44). Her "formal excommunication trial" was described as "an 11-hour ordeal at which the witnesses who came forward to support her were not allowed to discuss the ERA and the reasons for Johnson's support of the Amendment," and "Johnson . . . grew exhausted with the arguments about what she did or didn't say" (Lisa Cronin Wahl, "A Feminist Latter-day Saint: Why Sonia Johnson Won't Give Up (?) on the ERA—or the Mormon Church," *Ms.*, March 1980, 42). A writer in *Christian Century* lamented that "another aspect of the trial profoundly affecting her situation is that no records are kept of the hearing; she therefore has no evidence with which to make an appeal" (Barbara Howard, "Sonia Johnson and Mormon Political Power," *Christian Century*, 6–13 February, 1980, 127). *People* magazine later featured a piece by Michael Weiss in which a weary Sonia Johnson is pictured sitting alone on the couch in her home. The half-page photo sat above this headline: "Sonia Johnson's Excommunication by the Mormons Cut the 'Big String' That Held Her Marriage Together" (*People Weekly*, 11 February 1980, 45–46).

95. See, for example, Molly Ivins, "Many Mormon Women Feel Torn Between Equal Rights Proposal and Church," *New York Times*, 26 November 1979, B9: The ERA "has become a source of fear, too, for those who support it." The article mentioned the LDS doctrine about "sons—and daughters—of perdition, including apostate Mormons, [who] will be cast out and sentenced to eternal punishment." Though the blanket inclusion of apostate Mormons in the group destined for eternal punishment does not, in reality, accord precisely with LDS doctrine, the message was clear: the threat of retribution was what led Jinnah Kelson, described in Ivins's article as a "gentle-spoken, middle-aged woman who describes herself as a 'non-active Mormon,'" to say that, "I am, for the first time, frightened." See also Wahl, "A Feminist Latter-day Saint," 39: "Today, Sonia Johnson stands excommunicated. . . . and according to Mormon doctrine, she will never in the afterlife join the family she worked so hard and lovingly to raise in this life."

96. See Foreman, "It's Now Do or Die for the ERA—Mormon Power is the Key," 1.

97. See Howard, "Sonia Johnson and Mormon Political Power," 127. Another common refrain was that national polls consistently favor the ERA, so "the success of the anti-ERA campaign depends on its ability to exaggerate the strength of a minority viewpoint" (Wahl, "A Feminist Latter-day Saint," 42). See also Foreman, "It's Now Do or Die for the ERA," 1: "Today, as its opponents crow and its proponents despair, the Equal Rights Amendment is nearly dead, despite this month's nation opinion polls that say Americans favor it two to one."

98. On tax-exempt status, see, for example, Ivins, "Many Mormon Women Feel Torn Between Equal Rights Proposal and Church," B9. See also the photo of "Mormons for ERA" demonstrators protesting at the Hill Cumorah, site of a famous Mormon pageant, with the banner "The Mormon Church Should Pay Taxes or Get Out of Politics," in Randall Balmer, *Religion in Twentieth Century America* (New York and Oxford: Oxford University Press, 2001), 91. On the undue influence of church leaders, see Wahl, "A Feminist Latter-day Saint," 42.

99. See Wahl, "A Feminist Latter-day Saint," 42, for this quote from Sonia Johnson: "When a state legislator gets a letter from a constituent on an issue, as a rule of thumb he estimates

that about 500 other private citizens feel the same way about the issue, but haven't bothered to write...The Mormon Church is hierarchical and tightly organized. An order from a [stake] president or a bishop to write legislators can pull hundreds of letters from obedient Mormons. When the Mormons don't identify themselves as Mormons, the legislator is likely to wildly exaggerate anti-ERA sentiment in his district." See Foreman, "It's Now Do or Die for the Mormons," 2: "In a 17-day period before a Nov. 7, 1978, election in Florida, for example, with the state senate two votes away from ratification, about $17,000 was reportedly raised by California Mormons alone and sent to a PAC in Florida called FACT (Families Are Concerned Today). Altogether, according to the *Miami Herald*, which confirmed church contributions and politicking with church leaders, about $60,000 was contributed to campaigns of four anti-ERA candidates in the immediate pre-election period. Two of them won, contributing to the defeat of the ERA in Florida." See Linda Cicero and Marcia Fram, "Mormon Money Worked Against Florida's ERA," *Miami Herald*, 22 April 1980, 1A; cited in Stathis, "Mormonism and the Periodical Press," 57–58. Importantly, "LDS headquarters officially maintained that chapels should not be used for overtly political activities connected with ERA." However, officials conceded that overzealous local church members may have crossed some lines. Still, Alan Blodgett, the church's chief financial officer at the time, told two different interviewers that "no church funds went directly to the campaign opposing the ERA." Alan Blodgett to Edward L. Kimball, *Lengthen Your Stride*, Working Draft, chapter 18, page 5, note 24; included in the Spencer W. Kimball CD Library, 2005. This "working draft" is an expanded version of Kimball's published *Lengthen Your Stride* biography. Deseret Book publishers included the CD Library with the published biography. Blodgett asserted the same to Michael Quinn; see Quinn, *Mormon Hierarchy: Extensions of Power*, 397.

100. One of the group's most recognizable trademarks was the plane hired to pull a pro-ERA banner and circle the church's Temple Square during semiannual General Conferences; one banner read "Mormons for ERA are everywhere." See Weiss, "Irked by Sonia Johnson's E.R.A. Crusade, Church Elders Throw the Book of Mormon at Her," 44–45. Members of the organization attempted to shout down church authorities in one such conference session, but their short-lived protest ended when church security personnel escorted the demonstrators out of the building.

101. Kocol, "Civil Disobedience at the Mormon Temple," 9. Kocol herself was one of the twenty-one protesters arrested.

102. This was a principal theme, especially in the introduction, of Mansbridge, *Why We Lost the ERA*. Also worth noting is the reality that women were the most visible opponents to the ERA. This apparent ambivalence on the part of women—the supposed beneficiaries of the ERA—weakened popular support. Andrew Hacker wrote in 1981 the "women opposed the ERA because it jeopardized a way of life that had entered in good faith...a critical reason for ERA's defeat was opposition from women" (Hacker, "ERA-RIP," *Harper's*, September 1980, 14, 10; cited in Quinn, *Mormon Hierarchy: Extensions of Power*, 391).

103. See this recognition in a contemporary (1981) article: Foreman, "It's Now Do or Die for the ERA," 1: "Though largely hidden from public view, except in the Western states, the Mormons' power to deliver—or more precisely, not deliver—the ERA is significant."

104. Michael Quinn, in his *Mormon Hierarchy: Extensions of Power*, 373, noted that while Mormon "sociologist O. Kendall White...concluded that Mormons had tipped the scales for the entire nation...two non-Mormon historians analyzing the ERA barely mentioned the LDS church." Those two historians and their works were Mansbridge, *Why We Lost the ERA*, and Mary Frances Berry, *Why ERA Failed: Politics, Women's Rights, and the Amending Process of the Constitution* (Bloomington: Indiana University Press, 1986). It is also telling that Kathryn Cullen-Dupont's extensive *Encyclopedia of Women's History in America*, 2nd ed., makes no mention, even in the index, of Sonia Johnson or The Church of Jesus Christ of Latter-day Saints. Cullen-Dupont does, however, include an entry for Phyllis Schlafly, calling her "the most visible female proponent of the defeat of the Equal Rights Amendment" (229).

105. Stathis, "Mormonism and the Periodical Press," 58.

106. See, for example, Shipps, "Sonia Johnson, Mormonism and the Media," 6: "More important, by their featuring all of the ins and outs of the Sonia Johnson story, the American
media have carried the message that Latter-day Saints really care about what happens
to the family into more homes than all the time and space the church has purchased to
get that message across put together." One example of this came to the fore when Phil
Donahue invited Sonia Johnson to be a guest on his talk show in 1980. The church's Public
Communications department requested equal time. When Sonia Johnson apparently
refused to discuss the issue on the air with Beverly Campbell, a spokeswoman designated
by the church, Donahue went forward with his interview of Johnson, inaccurately stating that Campbell refused to debate Johnson. However, Donahue later apologized for the
mistake and invited Beverly Campbell as well as Church Relief Society President Barbara
Smith to address the topic on a later installment of his show. The church's public relations
team judged the follow-up appearance to be effective in dispelling misinformation about
the church's ERA position. See Bradley, *Pedestals and Podiums*, 382–383, 584, note 47. For
the perspective of the director of church public affairs on this episode, see Heber Wolsey,
interview by Jonice Hubbard, 203–204. Significantly, Wolsey recounted how he called on
Jack Anderson for help in persuading the owners of the "Donahue Show" to reschedule
with Beverly Campbell and the president of the church's Relief Society, Barbara Smith.
107. Heber Wolsey, interview by J. Michael Allen, 3.
108. See Orson Scott Card, "Wendell Ashton Called to Publishing Post," *Ensign*, January
1978, 73–74.
109. Lorry Rytting told an interviewer in 1979 that "we can send a message to 50,000,000
prospective readers for less than a penny apiece in the Reader's Digest" (Rytting interview,
22). That would put the cost of one run of inserts at some figure below $500,000 dollars.
Considering the church ran 11 inserts from 1978 to 1980, the total cost of that run fell
somewhere in the neighborhood of five to six million dollars. Peggy Fletcher, the editor
of the independent Mormon periodical *Sunstone*, estimated that the *Reader's Digest* program cost, by 1982, twelve million dollars. See Fletcher, "A Light Unto the World: Image
Building Is Anathema to Christian Living," *Sunstone*, July-August 1982, 18. For information about the Daniel Starch Company survey, see Lorry Rytting interview, 19.
110. "Ad Industry's Highest Honor: Television Ad Takes 3 Top CLIO Awards," *Church News*, 23
June 1979, 8.
111. See an untitled transcript of a September 16, 1982, conversation between the pollster
George Gallup and church public communication officials and several of their general
authority advisers, in which Gallup discussed his organization's recent study of national
attitudes toward various religious denominations; copy in possession of the author.
Gallup reported that when considering Mormons, "on the positive side, people cite one,
strong families..." (page B-1; emphasis added).
112. See Howard, "Sonia Johnson and Mormon Political Power," 127, for this significant viewpoint: "Here, then, is the key issue. Churches are affected by political decisions and in turn
affect such decisions. But responsible institutions openly accept responsibility for their
actions....Are churches to be permitted to engage in political activity under banners other
than their own? If so, wealthy institutions such as the Mormon Church can be influencing
decisions affecting numbers of persons who are unaware that the opposition is not political but religious."
113. Two stark cases in point were a couple of book-length treatments on Mormonism that
came from respectable, national, secular presses in the mid-1980s. These books put apprehension about the growing Mormon influence on a new, highly documented footing. In
1984, Robert Gottlieb and Peter Wiley published *America's Saints: The Rise of Mormon
Power*, and in 1985, John Heinerman and Anson Shupe published *The Mormon Corporate
Empire*. Importantly, the anti-ERA campaign figured prominently in both books, showing
up first in the third paragraph of the first chapter of Heinerman and Shupe's *Mormon
Corporate Empire*, and the fourth paragraph of the first chapter of Gottlieb and Wiley's
America's Saints.

114. See Question qn19k, The Gallup Poll #978, 14 June 1977, Gallup Brain database, http://brain.gallup.com/home.aspx. The 1977 poll used a numerical scale to gauge opinion, from +5 (for a very favorable opinion) to –5 (for a very unfavorable opinion); 9.88% answered "+5," and 7.92% "+4," and 36% of respondents gave Mormons a "+1, +2, or +3" rating, meaning that 54 percent of those surveyed ranked Mormons on the positive side of the scale. George Gallup's comments are quoted in Gerry Avant, "Poll Reflects Views Toward LDS: Gallup Surveys Americans," *Church News*, 30 October 1983, 3–4; emphasis added. While the date of the specific Gallup poll discussed in the *Church News* article is not included in the article, it is likely, based on similar findings and discussions, that the meeting referenced is the same as recorded in an untitled transcript of a September 16, 1982, conversation between Gallup and church public communication officials and several of their general authority advisers; copy in possession of the author. Compare Barna Research Group, "Americans' Impressions of Various Church Denominations," 18 September 1991, copy in the author's possession, 1: "How favorably do you consider the Mormon denomination? Very favorably—6%"; only 21percent felt "somewhat favorable" about Latter-day Saints, meaning that 27% chose a "very" or "somewhat" favorable response in 1991. While the different metrics of the polls do not make for precise matches, for comparative purposes the decline is apparent. Also for comparison, see a Quinnipiac University poll from June 2011, when "only 45 percent of voters say they have a favorable opinion of the Mormon religion, while 32 percent have an unfavorable view of the faith" (Quinnipiac University poll, June 8, 2011, http://www.quinnipiac.edu/x1284.xml?ReleaseID=1608).

115. Importantly, William Chafe has noted that "depth of religious commitment constituted the only variable that correlated directly with opposition to the Equal Rights Amendment and abortion. Other indicators—social status, education, employment, region—proved secondary" (Chafe, *The Unfinished Journey: America Since World War II* [New York: Oxford University Press, 1999], 462).

Chapter 5

1. Kenneth L Woodward and Barbara Bugower, "Bible-Belt Confrontation," *Newsweek*, 4 March 1985, 65. Portions of chapter 5 appeared in J. B. Haws, "From *The God Makers* to the Myth Maker: Simultaneous—and Lasting—Challenges to Mormonism's Reputation in the 1980s," *Mormon Historical Studies* 12, no. 1 (Spring 2011): 31–51.

2. See "Attitudes and Opinions Toward Religion: Religious attitudes of adults (over 18) who are residents of six major metropolitan areas in the United States: Seattle, Los Angeles, Kansas City, Dallas, Chicago, New York City—August 1973," L. Tom Perry Special Collections, Harold B. Lee Library, Brigham Young University, Provo, Utah, page 17, point 43. This section of the study was labeled "image association series," and respondents were asked to rank various denominations based on given characterizations. For the characterization "has most influence on laws and government," respondents ranked Latter-day Saints eighth. While the summary of the study located at the Lee Library does not include the list of denominational options, there were at least fourteen choices, since the LDS Church ranked fourteenth for "most liberal." Other questions in the study include Presbyterian, Southern Baptist, Lutheran, Roman Catholic, Episcopalian, Unitarian, and Jewish options, so it seems reasonable that these same faith groups were included in the "image association" ranking section.

3. See an example of this emerging trend in Donald P. Shoemaker, "Why Your Neighbor Joined the Mormon Church," *Christianity Today*, 11 October 1974, 11–15. Shoemaker complimented Latter-day Saints for their admirable family focus, and even advocated that other Christians adopt similar programs, but asserted in no uncertain terms that Mormon theology was at least partly a result of diabolical influence, and thus "a concept Christians must reject." See also the intriguing essay by Richard Hofstadter, "The Paranoid Style in American Politics," in *The Paranoid Style in American Politics and Other*

Essays (New York: Alfred A. Knopf, 1966), 3–40. While Hofstadter wrote before the rise of the Religious Right movement (he mentioned specifically the conservative movement centered around Senator Barry Goldwater), his analysis has applicability here. He saw the "paranoid style" as a way in which "a small minority" could get "much political leverage" by "qualities of heated exaggeration, suspiciousness, and conspiratorial fantasy...[A] spokesman for the paranoid style finds [the hostile and conspiratorial world] directed against a nation, a culture, a way of life," which "goes far to intensify his feeling of righteousness and his moral indignation" (3–4). I am indebted to Professor Steven Harper at Brigham Young University for bringing this essay and its applicability to my attention. Significantly, Terryl Givens also quotes from this essay in the epigraph of chapter 6 of his *Viper on the Hearth: Mormons, Myths, and the Construction of Heresy* (New York and Oxford: Oxford University Press, 1997), 97.

4. Howe's book owns the distinction of being the first published anti-Mormon book, and it was largely based on affidavits gathered by a disgruntled former Mormon, Doctor Philastus Hurlbut. See E. D. Howe, *Mormonism Unvailed: Or, a Faithful Account of that Singular Imposition and Delusion, from its Rise to the Present Time...* (Painesville, Ohio, 1834; photomechanical reproduction, Salt Lake City: Utah Lighthouse Ministry).

5. This is the title of a 1979 collection of Jerry Falwell revival sermons, published by Sword of the Lord Publishers, Murfreesboro, Tennessee; cited in Susan Friend Harding, *The Book of Jerry Falwell: Fundamentalist Language and Politics* (Princeton, New Jersey: Princeton University Press, 2000), 282, 316.

6. Kenneth L. Woodward, John Barnes, and Laurie Lisle, "Born Again," *Newsweek*, 25 October 1976, 69. Their article was the issue's cover story.

7. See Randall Balmer, *Religion in Twentieth Century America* (New York and Oxford: Oxford University Press, 2001), 92, for a citation of a Gallup poll that "pegged the number at 50 million [evangelicals] in 1976." William Chafe reported that "the number of Americans who reported that they were 'born again' and had personally experienced salvation increased from 24 percent in 1963 to nearly 40 percent in 1978" (William H. Chafe, *The Unfinished Journey: America Since World War II* [New York and Oxford: Oxford University Press, 1999], 462).

8. See Randall Balmer's important full-length treatment of modern evangelicalism, *Blessed Assurance: A History of Evangelicalism in America* (Boston: Beacon Press, 1999), as well as George M. Marsden's helpful introduction, *Understanding Fundamentalism and Evangelicalism* (Grand Rapids, Michigan: Eerdmans Publishing Co., 1991). Also see Susan Friend Harding's well-written overview of fundamentalism in the twentieth century, "Fundamentalist Exile," chapter 2, *The Book of Jerry Falwell*, 61–82. For an encyclopedic approach to chronology, themes, and individuals, see Glenn H. Utter and John W. Storey, *The Religious Right*, 2nd ed. (Santa Barbara, California: ABC-CLIO, 2001). For a personal, participatory perspective on American fundamentalism, see Brett Grainger, *In the World But Not of It: One Family's Militant Faith and the History of Fundamentalism in America* (New York: Walker and Company, 2008).

9. See the helpful review essay by Max L. Stackhouse, "Religious Right: New? Right?—Understanding the Neo-Evangelicals," *Commonweal*, 29 January 1982, 52–56. Stackhouse noted that the ambiguity of the term "evangelical" partly stems from the reality that "in several languages, the word 'evangelical' is best translated 'Protestant.'" Yet importantly, in American popular discourse, not all Protestants are "evangelicals." Stackhouse then traced for his readers "three distinct branches" in "classical evangelicalism" in America: "puritan evangelicalism," which informed what he called "Protestant ecumenical, or 'mainline' churches"; "pietistic" evangelicalism, which was the tradition behind "counter-cultural" groups such as "the Mennonites, some Pentecostals," and "in large measure...the black churches"; and finally, "fundamentalistic" evangelicalism, "rooted in efforts to deal with problems of authority in the face of 'modernism.'" It was this third thrust of American Protestantism that essentially came to take the "evangelical" label in the American media and public mind. For a similar approach to the divisions within American Protestantism,

see Walter Russell Mead, "God's Country?" *Foreign Affairs*, September/October 2006, http://www.foreignaffairs.com/articles/61914/walter-russell-mead/gods-country.

10. "Foreword" of volume one of *The Fundamentals: A Testimony to the Truth* (Chicago: Testimony Publishing Company). A digitized reproduction of the twelve original volumes is available at http://www.archive.org/stream/MN40295ucmf_2#page/n5/mode/2up. Two brothers, "Lyman and Milton Stewart, founders of Union Oil Company in California, established a fund of a quarter-million dollars to publish and distribute" the "twelve booklets" that "appeared between 1910 and 1915" (Balmer, *Religion in Twentieth Century America*, 27).

11. For a thoughtful overview of the connection between the liberalizing thrusts of biblical criticism, scientific modernism, and the social gospel movement, as well as the fundamentalist reaction, see Martin Marty's chapter in John McManners, ed., *The Oxford History of Christianity* (New York and Oxford: Oxford University Press, 1993), 425–430. For the perspective of an evangelical Christian historian, see Bruce L. Shelley, *Church History in Plain Language*, updated 2nd ed. (Dallas, Texas: Word Publishing, 1995), 394–400, 412–414, 430–437. See also Allitt, *Religion in America Since 1945*, 7; also Balmer, *Blessed Assurance*, 101.

12. Balmer, *Religion in Twentieth Century America*, 23. See also his discussion of liberal theology and social gospel proponents and opponents on pages 21–28.

13. These five "essentials" of Christianity were enumerated in 1895 at the Niagara Bible Conference, and reiterated in the *Fundamentals* series (Utter and Storey, *The Religious Right*, 37–38; see also "fundamentalism" in their glossary, 350).

14. Marsden, *Understanding Fundamentalists and Evangelicals*, 1. Far from derogatory, this description, Marsden noted, was even "adopted" by "Jerry Falwell...as a quick definition of fundamentalism that reporters are likely to quote."

15. On the pivotal importance of the Scopes trial (over the teaching of evolution in schools) in the development of a "separated out" fundamentalist subculture, see Harding, *The Book of Jerry Falwell*, 61–78. See also Balmer, *Religion in Twentieth Century America*, 92: "The Scopes trial of 1925 had convinced American evangelicals that the larger world was corrupt and hostile to their interests, and they responded by retreating from that world into a subculture of churches, denominations, Bible institutes, and colleges of their own making."

16. See "premillennialism" in Utter and Storey, *The Religious Right*, 353: "the belief that steadily deteriorating world conditions (wars and rumors of wars) will precede the second coming, at which time Jesus will establish a thousand-year reign....This viewpoint is generally more harmonious with a conservative, pessimistic assessment of contemporary world conditions"; contrast "postmillennialism": "The belief that steadily improving world conditions will culminate in the second coming. By this interpretation, Jesus will return after a millennium of human progress. This optimistic viewpoint...reinforced the reform efforts of liberal social gospel ministers in the late nineteenth and early twentieth centuries" (353). See also Mead, "God's Country?" *Foreign Affairs*, for an overview of liberal, evangelical, and fundamentalist Protestantism, as well as the influence of pre- and postmillennial theology on each tradition's respective worldview.

17. An endnote citation is needed here: Quoted in Harding, *The Book of Jerry Falwell*, 22.

18. Jerry Falwell, quoted in Balmer, *Religion in Twentieth Century America*, 92. On voting, see A. James Reichly "The Evangelical and Fundamentalist Revolt," chapter 4 in Neuhaus and Cromartie, eds., *Piety and Politics*, 74: "Neither Graham nor the right-wing preachers had much success during the 1950s or 1960s in stirring the Evangelicals to political action. Several studies during the period showed 'without exception...that evangelicals were less inclined toward political participation than were their less evangelical counterparts.' One scholar concluded in 1971 that 'Evangelicals concentrate on conversion, and except for occasional efforts to outlaw what they deem to be personal vices, evangelical Protestant groups largely ignore social and political efforts for reform.' Yet studies in the late 1970s and early 1980s just as uniformly have shown Evangelicals to be the religious group most favorable to political action by the churches.

A Gallup survey in 1980 discovered that they were more likely to be registered to vote than nonevangelicals, despite being overrepresented in demographic groups that historically have been relatively low in political participation." Reichly quoted Robert Wuthnow, "Political Rebirth of American Evangelicalism," in Wuthnow and Robert C. Liebman, eds., *The New Christian Right* (Hawthorne, New York: Aldine Books, 1983), 168–169.

19. For the clearest exposition of the role that end-time prophecies played in offering a philosophical framework for conservative Christian politics and for the wide acceptance of John Nelson Darby's dispensationalism, see Robert Alan Goldberg, "The Rise of the Antichrist," chapter 3 of *Enemies Within: The Culture of Conspiracy in Modern America* (New Haven and London: Yale University Press, 2001), 66–104. See also "John Nelson Darby" and "Cyrus Ingerson Scofield," in Utter and Storey, *The Religious Right*, 81–82, 115–116, for biographical information on both writers. See also Brett Grainger, *In the World But Not of It*, 41–45, for his assessment of the "Scofield Reference Bible, which went on to sell more than 20 million copies and become the most influential work in the history of fundamentalism" (43). Grainger also asserted that "by the end of the twentieth century, Darby's disciples largely controlled fundamentalism" (44). For the influence of Darby's dispensationalism on two of fundamentalism's most visible political spokesmen, see Harding, "The Last Days," chapter 9 of *The Book of Jerry Falwell*, 228–246; and David Edwin Harrell, Jr., *Pat Robertson: A Personal, Religious, and Political Portrait* (San Francisco: Harper & Row, 1987), 143–155.

20. See Goldberg, *Enemies Within*, 74–78. See also Grace Halsell, *Prophecy and Politics: The Secret Alliance Between Israel and the U.S. Christian Right* (Chicago: Lawrence Hill Books, 1986), where Halsell detailed two visits to Israel with tour groups led by Jerry Falwell's associates, and their emphasis on the fulfillment of dispensationalist prophecies.

21. Quoted in Balmer, *Religion in Twentieth Century America*, 22.

22. For a summary of the three cases (*Engel v. Vitale* in 1962, *School District of Abingdon Township v. Schempp*, and *Murray v. Curlett* in 1963), see Allitt, *Religion in America*, 68–69. See also Reichly, "The Evangelical and Fundamentalist Revolt," chapter 4 of Neuhaus and Cromartie, eds., *Piety and Politics*, 76. See also Balmer, *God in the White House*, 95–96, for a discussion of a district court decision, *Green v. Connally*, that affected the tax-exempt status of Christian schools like Bob Jones University because of their segregationist admissions policy. Balmer argues that this court case prompted many Christians to political activism.

23. Allitt, *Religion in America*, 154. The militancy of this new brand of politically active Christians is evident in those "hard-line fundamentalists" who "[accused] even" such "nationally known figures...as Billy Graham and Carl Henry" of "'selling out' because of their interactions with ecumenically-oriented protestants and Catholics" (Stackhouse, "Religious Right: New? Right?" 54).

24. Several historians make persuasive arguments that it was the perceived loss of traditional, past hegemony that contributed to the forcefulness of the evangelical political resurgence. That interpretation is most clearly articulated by Randall Balmer. See his *Blessed Assurance*, 104–105: "Loss of hegemony can be frightening, and it can provoke a number of responses, from resignation to resentment and condemnation, from anger to action.... Having set the social and political agenda for much of the nineteenth century, evangelicals felt marginalized by cultural and intellectual currents of the late nineteenth and early twentieth centuries. Their initial response was withdrawal and even a sullenness, but a combativeness eventually reasserted itself." Balmer disputes recent fundamentalists' claims to historical hegemony in his *Thy Kingdom Come: How the Religious Right Distorts the Faith and Threatens America: An Evangelical's Lament* (New York: Basic Books, 2006). See also Harrell, *Pat Robertson*, 151–152: "In the 1960s and 1970s, for a variety of reasons, evangelicals began to reassert themselves politically. Partly, they were stunned by the secularization of American society...and finally by what they considered direct government assaults on them. But the political reawakening also had an intellectual basis. A new generation of evangelicals set out to reclaim their heritage, spurred by the notion

that the United States once had been an evangelical nation, that their ancestors had 'run the show.'"

25. "An Interview with the Lone Ranger of American Fundamentalism," *Christianity Today*, 4 September 1981, 24.

26. See, for example, Jerry Falwell's reasoning in 1981: "I support the Jews, first, for biblical reasons; I take the Abrahamic covenant literally. God has blessed America because we have blessed the Jews. God has also blessed America because we have done more for the cause of world evangelization than any other nation" ("An Interview with the Lone Ranger of American Fundamentalism," 25).

27. Quoted in Goldberg, *Enemies Within*, 74. See also Stephen Zunes, "Strange Bedfellows: The Curious Alliance between Menachem Begin and the Christian Right," *The Progressive*, November 1981, 29: "The theological explanation is straightforward enough: It rests on the fundamentalist belief that an ingathering of Jews to biblical Palestine and the establishment of a Jewish commonwealth must precede the second coming of Christ. In this view, the creation of modern Israel represents the fulfillment of biblical prophecy." Zunes also quoted evangelical Christians stating two related reasons for their strong support of Israel: "Israel's got to be strong for the final battle," organizer Elizabeth Smith said; High Adventure Ministries saw their "mission" as "[preparing] the Jewish soul for the coming of the Messiah."

28. William Chafe reported that "Reverend Jerry Falwell's 'Old Time Gospel Hour' was broadcast on 225 television stations and 300 radio stations. Fundamentalist talk shows like the '700 Club' or the PTL (Praise the Lord) hour reached millions more. All told, these broadcasts had an audience of almost 100 million Americans each week" (Chafe, *The Unfinished Journey*, 463). Pat Robertson, of the "700 Club" show, claimed "we have enough... votes to run the country, and when people say, 'we've had enough,' we're going to take over" (quote in Chafe, *The Unfinished Journey*, 463). See also Reichly, "The Evangelical and Fundamentalist Revolt," 74–75, for his discussion of "the electronic church" and the changes in religious broadcasting that resulted from modifications in FCC regulations in the 1970s. Before then, the FCC "required television stations to devote a fixed amount of their airtime to religious programming." But in the 1970s, the FCC allowed stations to begin "charging for the time they set aside for religion. Most mainline churches declined to enter this market. Religious time therefore became available, usually at bargain rates, to enterprising preachers—almost all of them Fundmentalists or Evangelicals—who financed their programs through fund-raising appeals made in the course of their broadcasts." For the story behind Jerry Falwell's entrance into this type of broadcasting, see Frances FitzGerald's biographical sketch of Falwell in "A Reporter At Large: A Disciplined, Charging Army," *The New Yorker*, 18 May 1981, 53. For the history of radio evangelists in the first half of the twentieth century, and those evangelists' role in the expansion of mass media in general, see Tona J. Hangen, *Redeeming the Dial: Radio, Religion, and Popular Culture in America* (Chapel Hill: The University of North Carolina Press, 2002). For a broad historical view of televangelism's relationship with other national broadcasters, see Jeffrey K Hadden and Anson Shupe, *Televangelism: Power and Politics on God's Frontier* (New York: Henry Holt and Company, 1988). See also Alec Foege's more recent *The Empire God Built: Inside Pat Robertson's Media Machine* (New York: John Wiley and Sons, Inc., 1996), especially page xiv for an instructive flow chart of Pat Robertson's media involvement, as well as page 10, for the stated official mission of Robertson's Christian Broadcasting Network: "to prepare the United States of America, the nations of the Middle East, the Far East, South America, and other nations of the world for the coming of Jesus Christ and the establishment of the kingdom of God on earth."

29. For an overview of President Carter's relationship with evangelical voters, see Balmer, "Born Again: Jimmy Carter, Redeemer President, and the Rise of the Religious Right," chapter 3 of *God in the White House*, 79–108. See Harrell, *Pat Robertson*, 183–184: "Jimmy Carter's election in 1976 greatly heightened evangelical expectation. Carter's presidency, typified by his support for ERA and gay rights, infuriated them. In 1981 fundamentalist Tim LaHaye wrote: 'Between 1976 and 1980 I watched a professing Christian become

president of the United States and then surround himself with a host of humanistic cabinet ministers.... These people nearly destroyed our nation.'"

30. See Nadine Brozan, "White House Conference on the Family: A Schism Develops," *New York Times*, 7 January 1980, D8. See also Balmer, *God in the White House*, 107.

31. The late 1970s saw the establishment of several notable evangelical-driven organizations. For example, California organizers rallied thousands of pastors to join "Christian Voice," with the prime directive of evaluating the "morality of politicians" (Utter and Storey, *The Religious Right*, 12, 46). Historian Bruce Shelley wrote that "in 1978 a ballot proposition in California tried to expand the legal protection of homosexuals. When a group of conservative pastors organized to defeat the measure, the Internal Revenue Service warned them that the tax-exempt status of their churches were endangered by their political activity. The pastors thought this was reason enough to form the Christian Voice" (*Church History in Plain Language*, 478). At the same time, Paul Weyrich, "a conservative political strategist," in dialogue with the Reverend Jerry Falwell, suggested organizing a religious coalition under the name "moral majority" (Utter and Storey, *The Religious Right*, 46). Moral Majority "[claimed] two million members" in 1980 ("A TV Preacher Sells America on Flag, Family, and Freedom, of Sorts," *People Weekly*, 29 December 1980–5 January 1971, 106).

32. See "Excerpts from Platform to Be Submitted to Republican Delegates," *New York Times*, 13 July 1980, 14: "We reaffirm our belief in the traditional role and values of the family in our society." See also "On Traditional Family Values," *Time*, 28 July 1980, 30, for reporting on moderate Republican "Senator Charles Percy's outrage over the Republican platform plank that encourages the appointment of judges 'who respect traditional family values and the sanctity of human life.'" A search of the *Reader's Guide Retrospective* database reveals that before 1980, the phrase "traditional family values" did not appear in the title of any article in the periodicals indexed by the *Guide*. The phrase "traditional values" only appeared one time (in 1977) before 1980, and the phrase "family values" only twice (in 1958 and 1974).

33. See Adam Clymer, "Bush Says No Single Group Gave Reagan His Victory," *New York Times*, 18 November 1980, B10.

34. *U.S. News and World Report* noted that "23 of 38 congressmen with low ratings on 2 million 'moral-issues report cards' distributed across the country by Christian Voice" lost in the 1980 election ("Religious Right Goes for Bigger Game," *U.S. News and World Report*, 17 November 1980, 42).

35. Balmer, *Thy Kingdom Come*, xvii: "Pollster Louis Fields determined that, without evangelical support in the 1980 presidential election, Reagan would have lost to Carter by 1 percent of the popular vote."

36. See Martin Tolchin, "Congress Democrats Running Scared," *New York Times*, 9 June 1980, B13; "Religious Right Goes for Bigger Game," *U.S. News and World Report*, 17 November 1980, 42; Tom Minnery, "The Religious Right: How Much Credit Can It Take for Electoral Landslide," *Christianity Today*, 12 December 1980, 52. See also Wallace Turner, "Group of Evangelical Protestants Take Over the G.O.P. in Alaska," *New York Times*, 9 June 1980, B12; and James Mann, "As Religious Right Flexes Its Muscles," *U.S. News and World Report*, 29 December 1980–5 January 1981, 69.

37. See Clymer, "Bush Says No Single Group Gave Reagan His Victory," B10. See also Balmer, *God in the White House*, 119–120, for a discussion of several high-level Reagan appointees with strong ties to the evangelical Christian political movement, including C. Everett Koop (Surgeon General), James G. Watt (Secretary of the Interior), and Gary L. Bauer as a "domestic policy adviser"; "A TV Preacher Sells America on Flag, Family, and Freedom, of Sorts," *People Weekly*, 29 December 1980–5 January 1971, 106: "If any citizen had greater cause for rejoicing on Election Day than Ronald Reagan, it was the Rev. Jerry Falwell."

38. For a list of Latter-day Saints appointees in President Reagan's administration, including Secretary of Education Bell, Treasurer Angela Buchanan, and Solicitor General Rex Lee, see Michael K. Winder, *Presidents and Prophets: The Story of America's Presidents and the LDS Church* (American Fork, Utah: Covenant Communications, 2007), 351–352. For President Reagan's comments about the Mormon welfare program at a Hooper, Utah, rally

on September 10, 1982, see "Reagan Declares He's 'Terribly Hurt' by Vote to Override," *Boston Globe*, September 11, 1982,?

39. Quoted in Randall Balmer, *God in the White House: A History: How Faith Shaped the Presidency from John F. Kennedy to George W. Bush* (New York: HarperOne, 2008), 94–95. In 1996, *Christianity Today* called Criswell one of "the 25 most influential pastors of the past 50 years"; http://www.christianitytoday.com/anniversary/features/top25preachers.html. In 1971, the Southern Baptist Convention "[called] upon Southern Baptists to work for legislation that will allow the possibility of abortion under such conditions as rape, incest, clear evidence of severe fetal deformity, and carefully ascertained evidence of the likelihood of damage to the emotional, mental, and physical health of the mother." The Convention "reaffirmed that position in 1974 and 1976" (Balmer, *God in the White House*, 94–95). See also Balmer, *Religion in Twentieth Century America*, 94.

40. See "Is Abortion a Catholic Issue?" *Christianity Today*, 16 January 1976, 29: "Mormons also oppose abortion, and in states where they exercise political clout the charge had often been made that abortion is a 'Mormon' issue." See also "Abortion and the Court," *Christianity Today*, 16 February 1973, 32–33; "Anti-abortion: Not Parochial," *Christianity Today*, 8 August 1975, 22. Clearly *Christianity Today* worried that the reluctance of some Protestants to join the anti-abortion cause stemmed from a persistent worry about the imposition of Catholic dogma on American politics. See also "What Price Abortion?" *Christianity Today*, 2 March 1973, 39: "Many arguments on abortion assume that the fetus is not a human being but give no grounds for this questionable assumption. Typical of these was the baffling analysis by W. Barry Garrett, Washington Bureau chief of Baptist Press. 'Religious liberty, human equality and justice are advanced by the Supreme Court abortion decision,' he wrote....Why the silence about liberty, equality, justice for the fetus? The fact that minority religious groups (e.g., Roman Catholics, Mormons) oppose abortion does not make easy abortion a triumph for 'religious liberty.'"

41. Balmer, *God in the White House*, 114. See, for example, Harrell, *Pat Robertson*, 184, where he argued that a grass-roots reaction to local issues, such as the tax status and perceived government-mandated integration of private religious schools, was what initially motivated political activism for many fundamentalist Christians, who then later included abortion rights and feminism as key issues in their new, national movement: "In the mid-1970s a few untrained lobbyists for the Christian schools began to appear in Washington. They, in turn, became educated on the other issues on the *emerging* conservative social agenda such as abortion"; italics added. Randall Balmer has argued even more strongly against narratives that give the 1973 *Roe v. Wade* verdict an early, formative role in the rise of the Christian Right. See Balmer, *God in the White House*, 99–100, for Paul Weyrich's account of a conference call in the late 1970s where several Religious Right leaders discussed issues to add to the movement's political agenda: "A voice at the end of one of the lines said, 'How about abortion?'" In another book, Balmer argued that "leaders of the Religious Right" have "shamelessly exploit[ed] the 'abortion myth,'" the fiction that the Religious Right mobilized in direct response to the 1973 Roe v. Wade decision" (*Thy Kingdom Come*, xvii).

42. See this example: "the editor of the Baptist *Biblical Recorder* acknowledged that 'there was a Mormon network at the core of the organization' of North Carolina anti-ERA forces" (Quinn, *Mormon Hierarchy: Extensions of Power*, 387).

43. See, for example, Michael S. Hamilton, "The Dissatisfaction of Francis Schaeffer," *Christianity Today*, 3 March 1997, 22–30, for a discussion of the influence prominent fundamentalist theologian Schaeffer exercised over Jerry Falwell in encouraging him to enlist non-Christian "cobelligerents" in the cause against abortion.

44. *The Fundamentals: A Testimony to the Truth*, vol. 8, http://www.archive.org/stream/MN40295ucmf_2#page/n1077/mode/2up/search/Mormonism, 110–111, 114. One website that hosts a digitized version of the *Fundamentals* reasoned for the contemporary relevance of the *Fundamentals* this way: "There is still a great need today to reaffirm the fundamental doctrines of Christianity, especially when we consider "The Jesus Seminar," "Evangelicals and Catholics Together," the current push by the Mormons to present themselves as just another Christian denomination, and a host of other groups claiming to

be Christian who deny these core truths" (http://www.xmission.com/~fidelis/; italics in original).

45. See, for example, "Pulpit Bullies: Goldwater Blasts New Right," *Time*, 28 September 1981, 27: "'I don't like what they're doing,' [Goldwater] said. 'I don't think what they're talking about is conservatism.... The religious issues of these groups [abortion, school prayer] have little to do with conservative or liberal politics,' he said." See also, "Censored!: Booksellers Speak Out on Recent Censorship Bills, The Moral Majority and Shifting Community Standards," a "Publishers Weekly Special Survey," *Publishers Weekly*, 11 September 1981, 53–58. See "Countering the Christian Right," *Christian Century*, 29 October 1980, 1031, for a report on groups such as Moral Alternatives in Politics [MAP] and the National Council of Churches protesting that "no group can legitimately claim to represent the 'Christian vote' to the exclusion of others." See also two pointed columns by Martin E. Marty: "Ganging Up on the Humanists," *Christian Century*, 15 October 1980, 991; and "The Gestalt Family," *Christian Century*, 1–8 July 1981, 719. Jan Shipps offered a personal perspective on this matter of "exclusive possession of the Christian label": "I am certain that the charge that Mormons are members of a non-Christian 'temple cult' must be as distressing to Latter-day Saints as the charge that liberal Protestants are secular humanists is disturbing to Methodists like me" (Shipps, *Sojourner in the Promised Land*, 349, 355).

46. Shelley, *Church History in Plain Language*, 472. Compare "Ups and Downs in Church Membership," where the National Council of Churches found that from 1971 to 1981, American membership in the United Presbyterian Church declined by 16.1 percent, in the Episcopal Church by 6.9 percent, in the United Church of Christ by 7.7 percent and in various Lutheran denominations by 3 to 5 percent. In contrast, as mentioned earlier, the Southern Baptist denomination *grew* by 12.4 percent, and Mormons *grew* by 25.9 percent.

47. Susan Friend Harding argued that the broadcast reach of fundamentalist preachers helped to bring evangelicalism back into the American cultural mainstream that had excluded them ("othered" them, in Harding's view, as "cultural outsiders") since the Scopes Trial (Harding, *The Book of Jerry Falwell*, 74). She observed that "during the 1980s, Bible-believing, white Protestant Christians in America broke through the array of cultural barriers that had quarantined them from other Americans for half a century. Suddenly, their old-fashioned kind of Christianity—Fundamentalism—seemed to be everywhere. A half-dozen national televangelists—Jerry Falwell, Pat Robertson, Jimmy Swaggart, Jim and Tammy Faye Bakker, James Robison—were the most visible leaders of this movement, this permeation, transporting images and voices of God-fearing Christians into living rooms all over the country.... [I]t seems clear that by the 1980s we were witnessing instead a major realignment of public religiosity in America. The realignment was not a changing of the guard—conservative Protestants did not come to dominate public life—but they reentered public life. They returned from exile. Marginalized groups were mainstreamed, but mainstream groups were not marginalized" (*The Book of Jerry Falwell*, 79–80).

48. See two articles under a banner that proclaimed "Slamming the Religious Right," *Christianity Today*, 23 October 1981, 60–61: Edward E. Plowman, "Charge: Manipulating Audiences," and "Charge: Others Are Born-Again, Too."

49. See Shipps, "Is Mormonism Christian?," chapter 16 of *Sojourner in the Promised Land*, especially pages 352–354. The study on fundamentalism that she cited was Martin Marty and Scott Appleby, *Fundamentalisms Observed* (Chicago: University of Chicago Press, 1991), 842.

50. Richard P. Lindsay, interview by author, 22 February 2007, transcript in possession of the author, 3.

51. See, for example, Jerry Falwell, "Maligned Moral Majority," as a "My Turn" feature in *Newsweek*, 21 September 1981, 17: "The Moral Majority is not a Christian or a religious organization (however, as a fundamentalist, I personally object to categorizing fundamentalists as bellicose and anti-intellectual). We are made up of fundamentalists, evangelicals, Roman Catholics, conservative Jews, Mormons and even persons of no religious belief

who share our concern about the issues we address." In reality, it appears that the small segment of Mormons who actively participated in Falwell's coalition represented what one set of researchers called "political fringe groups on the Mormon periphery" (Merlin B. Brinkerhoff, Jeffrey C. Jacob, and Marlene M. Mackie, "Mormonism and the Moral Majority Make Strange Bedfellows: An Exploratory Critique," *Review of Religious Research* 28, no. 3 [March 1987]: 236–251). Their article came in response to Anson Shupe and John Heinerman, "Mormonism and the New Christian Right: An Emerging Coalition?" *Review of Religious Research* 27, no. 2 (December 1985): 146–157. Shupe and Heinerman focus on the Freemen Institute and the John Birch Society, both of which were right-wing political organizations that only attracted a relatively small number of Mormon participants. To some national writers, the religious conservatism of Mormons made them identical to fundamentalist Christians. That was the implication of Peter Bart's piece, "The Mormon Nation," *New York Times*, 3 July 1981, A19, and his suggestion that "anyone interested in peeking into the new American Dream" of the "ubiquitous 'moral activists'" should "look no further than that part of the United States that Westerners call 'the Mormon Nation.'" Bart's essay and equation of Mormonism with the "moral activists" of the Christian Right drew a corrective letter to the editor from Kenneth L. Woodward, religion reporter for *Newsweek*. Woodward wrote that "the Mormon ethos is unique and not transferable to Americans who do not share the Mormons' singular mythos about the origin and destiny of man. Mr. Falwell, for example, regards Mormonism as a heretical cult and to date has neither solicited nor received support from the L.D.S. General Authorities" (Kenneth L. Woodward, "A Distorted View of Mormonism," *New York Times*, 23 July 1981, A22).

52. "An Interview with the Lone Ranger of American Fundamentalism," *Christianity Today*, 4 September 1981, 23–24.

53. Jan Shipps emphasizes the general effect the post–World War II LDS building boom—and especially the uniform look of LDS chapels—in the eastern United States as contributing to Mormon-Evangelical tensions, since "it challenged conservative Protestantism on its home turf" (Shipps, *Sojourner in the Promised Land*, 352). See a conversation between pollster George Gallup and LDS apostle Boyd K. Packer, 16 September 1982, B-12, transcript in possession of the author. Gallup met with leaders and staff of the church's public communications department to debrief recent poll results. Elder Packer asked Dr. Gallup specifically for a reaction to the surge in persecution surrounding construction of the Dallas Temple.

54. See "Pigskin Justice and Mormon Theology," *Christian Century*, 21 January 1970, 67, where the LDS Church is referred to as a "Christian body" by the magazine's editorial board. See also Lowry Nelson, "Mormons and Blacks," *Christian Century*, 16 October 1974, 949, where Nelson (a Mormon) wrote in an essay for the magazine that "Mormonism is a variety of fundamentalist Christianity."

55. See, for example, Leland Stowe, "When the Saints Come Singing In," *Reader's Digest*, April 1975, 45–50. The article was a condensed reprint from the April 1975 *Christian Herald*, and described the Choir's rendition of Handel's Messiah, "I Know that My Redeemer Lives," "Christ Went Into the Hills to Pray," and "Rock of Ages."

56. See "Ups and Downs in Church Membership," *U.S. News and World Report*, 4 October 1982, 7, where a graph on denominational growth showed that Mormon membership in the United States had grown 25.9 percent since 1971. The next closest denomination in terms of percentage growth was Southern Baptist, with a 12.4 percent growth.

57. See "Mormons and Christ," a sidebar to Rodney Clapp's article, "Fighting Mormonism in Utah: A Divorce, Death Threats, and Dogged Persistence," *Christianity Today*, 16 July 1982, 31–32, for a listing of Mormonism's departures from creedal Christology.

58. Anthony A. Hoekema, *The Four Major Cults: Christian Science, Jehovah's Witnesses, Mormonism, Seventh-Day Adventism* (Grand Rapids, Michigan: William B. Eerdmans Publishing Company, 1963).

59. See Walter Ralston Martin, *The Kingdom of the Cults: An Analysis of the Major Cult Systems in the Present Christian Era* (Grand Rapids, Michigan: Zondervan Publishing House, 1965), 325, 328–332, 335–336.

60. See "The Gallup Poll #120G," Gallup Brain database, 16 January 1979, question qn4f: "Please tell me whether you consider each of them to be a 'cult,' or whether you consider them to be a church or religion . . . Mormons? Cult: 11.23%; Church or Religion: 76:59%; Don't Know: 12.18%."

61. Walter Ralston Martin, *The Maze of Mormonism*, revised and enlarged (Santa Ana, California: Vision House Publishers, 1978), 9–10, 236; the "fastest-growing" description was included in promotional materials for *The God Makers* film; copy in possession of the author. On Martin's influence as "certainly the most prominent" of the "cult watchers," see Tim Stafford, "The Kingdom of the Cult Watchers," *Christianity Today*, 7 October 1991, 20–22. "Cult Patterns Similar: Jim Jones Ruse," *The Utah Evangel*, December 1978; reprinted in *Bible Believers Bulletin*, January 1979, 5; copy at Archives, The Church of Jesus Christ of Latter-day Saints. Ed Decker, "The Mormon Dilemma: Christian or Cult?" [sound recording] (Issaquah, Washington: Ex-Mormons for Jesus, 1979), and John Marler, "The Marks of a Cult" [sound recording] (Safety Harbor, Florida: EMFJ Ministries, 1982); copies at Archives, The Church of Jesus Christ of Latter-day Saints.

62. The quote comes from an endorsement of the book Decker wrote to accompany the film by best-selling evangelical author, Hal Lindsey. Included on the back cover of Ed Decker and Dave Hunt, *The God Makers: A Shocking Exposé of What the Mormon Church Really Believes*, updated and expanded edition (Eugene, Oregon: Harvest House Publishers, 1997).

63. This argument has been made by observers of anti-Mormon activity. See in particular Massimo Introvigne, "The Devil Makers: Contemporary Evangelical Fundamentalist Anti-Mormonism," *Dialogue* 27, no. 1 (Spring 1994): 153: "According to Ed Decker, an ex-Mormon who was the main producer of the film, its premiere marked the beginning of an epoch." Introvigne himself asserted, "I agree that the new wave of counter-Mormonism which emerged in the 1980s is different from both secular and sectarian anti-Mormonism which have existed since the birth of the Mormon church" (154). In this article and a later one, Introvigne asserted that *"The God Makers* marked the emergence of a new anti-Mormonism that I have called 'postrationalist.' . . . . [P]ostrationalist anti-Mormonism advances the theory 'that Joseph Smith was in touch with a superhuman source of revelation and power.' However, according to the postrationalist theory, the superhuman source was not God, but Satan" (Massimo Introvigne, "Old Wine in New Bottles: The Story Behind Fundamentalist Anti-Mormonism," *BYU Studies* 35, no. 3 [1995–1996]: 45). Introvigne also argued that this new brand of anti-Mormonism drew on an old tradition of "French nineteenth-century counter-subversion literature, which focused on Freemasonry and included tangential references to Mormonism." Daniel C. Peterson advanced a similar analysis. See his "A Modern 'Malleus maleficarum,'" in *Review of Books on the Book of Mormon 3* (Provo, Utah: FARMS, 1991): 231–260, cited by Introvigne, "The Devil Makers," 154.

64. See Nathaniel Smith Kogan, "The Mormon Pavilion: Mainstreaming the Saints at the New York World's Fair, 1964–65," *Journal of Mormon History* 35, no. 4 (Fall 2009): 36, for pavilion staffer Wilburn West's compilation of the five "most frequently asked questions at the pavilion." Number five on West's list was, "Why have we been led to believe that the Mormons are not Christians?"

65. See Heber Wolsey interview by Jonice Hubbard, 26 July 2006, transcript included as an appendix to Jonice Hubbard, "Pioneers in Twentieth Century Mormon Media: Oral Histories of Latter-day Saint Electronic and Public Relations Professionals" (master's thesis, Brigham Young University, 2007), 214, for a conversation between Wolsey (managing director of the church's Public Communications Department) and LDS Apostle Boyd K. Packer that precipitated the addition of the subtitle. Also see Woodward and Burgower, "Bible-Belt Confrontation," 65: "Privately Mormon officials have taken a number of steps to blunt [the] argument" that Latter-day Saints are not Christians. "They have added a subtitle, 'Another Testament of Jesus Christ,' to the church's basic scripture." See also a conversation between pollster George Gallup and LDS Apostle Boyd K. Packer, 16 September 1982, B-12, transcript in possession of the author. Dr. Gallup reacted this way to Elder Packer's question about evangelical Christian opposition to the LDS Church: "I would think

it would stem from one, intolerance to ignorance about your church.... I would think that the focal point of people's religious experience and I think it's increasingly so, is a personal encounter with Jesus Christ that's at the center of most faiths in the country and I think if that is constantly emphasized ... that theological differences are not that important to people, basically—on non-Mormons, at least. So, I think that if the focus is on a renewed encounter with Jesus Christ, that could take some of the animosity away, I think, possibly." The addition of the subtitle was announced by Elder Packer at the October 1982 General Conference of the church; see "Scriptures," *Ensign*, November 1982, 51.

66. Introvigne, "The Devil Makers," 154.

67. For an overview of the organization and evolving emphasis of Ex-Mormons for Jesus, see Sara M. Patterson, "'A P.O. Box and a Desire to Witness for Jesus': Identity and Mission in the Ex-Mormons for Jesus/Saints Alive in Jesus, 1975–1990," *Journal of Mormon History* 36, no. 3 (Summer 2010): 54–81.

68. *The God Makers*, Jeremiah Films, 1982. All quotations, unless otherwise noted, are from the author's transcription of the film.

69. Sandra Tanner, Utah Lighthouse Ministry, "Facts Misrepresented in 'Godmakers' Issue," letter to the editor, (*Boise*) *Idaho Statesman*, 3 March 1984; copy in possession of the author.

70. Bob Keeper, "Ex-Mormons' Film Sparks Controversy," *Eugene (Oregon) Register-Guard*, 14 January 1984; photocopy in possession of the author.

71. Bill Heersink, interview by the author, 15 February 2010. The newspaper ad quoted the movie's promotional cover and was reproduced nationwide; photocopies in possession of the author.

72. These endorsements were included in advertisements for the film (photocopy in possession of the author). These endorsers were household names in the evangelical community. Two historians called Hal Lindsey "the most successful spinner in recent years of apocalyptic scenarios," noting that his book met with "astonishing success" and "reportedly sold twenty million copies in fifty-two languages worldwide and was made into a movie in 1978" (Utter and Storey, *The Religious Right*, 98). The California pastor was John MacArthur of Grace Community Church in Panorama City, California. Thousands attended his church's weekly service. In 1996, *Christianity Today* called MacArthur one of "the 25 most influential pastors of the past 50 years," http://www.christianitytoday. com/anniversary/features/top25preachers.html. Hal Lindsey's and John MacArthur's comments also appeared on the back cover of the subsequent *God Makers* book.

73. See Donna Anderson, "Former Mormons Seek to Convert Mormons to Mainstream Christianity," *St. Petersburg (Florida) Times*, 10 December 1983, copy in possession of the author, where assistant director of Saints Alive Jim Witham said the primary thrust of his group's ministry was to "bring Mormons back to the Jesus of the Bible.... The secondary thrust is to acquaint Christianity with the true teachings of Mormonism," and *The God Makers* was "the group's most potent weapon." Anderson's piece traveled far on the Associated Press wire. News clipping services employed by the LDS Church sent in copies from papers in Washington, Louisiana, and California. For the persistence of Saints Alive's philosophy and activity, see also Scott Fagerstrom, "Ex-Mormons Warn Away Potential Church Converts," *Santa Ana (California) Orange County Register*, 27 February 1988, B10.

74. See, for example, this advertisement for a showing of the film, published in the *Hillsboro (Oregon) Argus*, 22 September 1983, copy in possession of the author: "This hard-hitting documentary peels back the lies to expose today's most respectable yet deceitful and fastest growing cult, who lure 75% of their converts from Christian Churches."

75. Diane Pettit, "Film Depicts Mormonism as 'Cult'," *Lewiston (Idaho) Morning Tribune*, 9 October 1983, 1A.

76. Greg Johnson, interview by author, 2 March 2010.

77. By early 1984, "filmmakers ... estimate[d] it is seen by up to 250,000 a month nationally" (Janet Barker, "Anti-Mormon Film Makes Impact on South Bay," *Torrance [California] South Bay Breeze*, 21 January 1984, B2).

78. Mark Davis, "Softball League Bounced," *The New Bern (North Carolina) Sun Journal*, 31 March 1983, section B. *The Charlotte Observer*'s editorial reaction was, "There is, of course, only one Jesus Christ, and the Christians involved in this particular episode paid shabby witness to Him" ("Editorials: On Softball, Bigotry and Jesus," *The Charlotte Observer*, 1 April 1983). See also "Sound Views: Religious Intolerance," *The Eastern Weekly*, 6 April 1983, 3-A.

79. The unwillingness to include Mormons was not universal, however. Significantly, mainline Protestant (United Methodist and Presbyterian) and Catholic officials offered to form a new league with the Mormons. "Mary Sue Noe, board chairman of First United Methodist Church in Morehead City" said, "It distresses me that in this day and age we've got that sort of thing" (Jerry Allegood, "Softball League with Mormons Sought," *Raleigh News and Observer*, 1 April 1983, 1D).

80. Dean Merrill, "Tuesday Is Our Family Night!" *Focus on the Family*, January 1984, 6. The venue for this article gave it clout. Dr. Dobson's organization reached millions of readers and listeners, eventually giving him a "larger reach than either Jerry Falwell or Pat Robertson at their height" (Utter and Storey, *The Religious Right*, 82).

81. Tom Minnery to Hugh McHarry, 28 February 1984; photocopy in possession of the author.

82. Pat Robertson to Hugh McHarry, 25 January 1984; copy in possession of the author: "When we were granted our first license [for the Christian Broadcasting Network], we were required by the government to represent that we would be fair in our treatment of other religions. . . . In the John Ankerberg Show that we refused to run, there was not only a discussion of Mormonism, but a film featuring animated characters engaging in a ritual, which Mormons consider to be as sacred as Protestants consider the communion, or Catholics the Mass. . . . I was told that no one objected to an analysis of Mormon beliefs in light of Scripture, or a contrast between Protestant beliefs and those held by Mormons."

83. See Anderson, "Former Mormons Seek to Convert Mormons to Mainstream Christianity": "the Rev. Anthony Auer of Mount Tabor Lutheran Church in Salt Lake City, said, 'I would not want it said that I endorse the film at all. I think it's very offensive.' Protestant churches don't need to rely on negative criticism to gain converts from Mormonism, Auer said. He said his congregation includes many who were born into Mormon families but turned elsewhere because they found Mormonism too authoritarian and restrictive." See also, Pettit, "Film Depicts Mormonism as 'Cult'," 1A: "The president of the Lewiston-Clarkston Ministerial Association [Rev. Larry Nicholson] said he wouldn't show the film in his church, or go to see it himself. He said such films 'generally are terrible distortions of what somebody else believes. I'm just not interested in it.' But Nicholson stopped short of criticizing churches that have shown the film." Nicholson also said that the movie had "not been discussed by the members of the ministerial association," and conceded that he thought "'what we would get would be a strong split' between the 'theological conservatives and liberals' in the group" (page 4A).

84. The analogy of a religious marketplace finds its clearest exposition in Roger Finke and Rodney Stark, *The Churching of America,1776–2005: Winners and Losers in Our Religious Economy* (New Brunswick, New Jersey: Rutgers University Press, 2006); chapter 7, "Why 'Mainline' Denominations Decline," is especially relevant to the discussion here.

85. Joseph Carey, "A time of turmoil for Mormons," *U.S. News and World Report*, 28 April 1986, 74.

86. Woodward and Burgower, "Bible-Belt Confrontation," 65. The actual rate, in those Texas figures, breaks down to over *six* convert baptisms a day, instead of sixty, but even that computational error highlights the impression that Mormon growth was prodigious.

87. Transcript for "Town Meeting," 19 February 1984, KOMO Channel 4 in Seattle; copy in possession of the author (the figure quoted in an independent LDS magazine was 30,000 converts credited to the Osmonds' influence—see *This People*, April/May 1983, 68); "'People Need to Know' About Mormons, Pastor Says," *Longview (Washington) News*, 21 November 1983; copy in possession of the author:

88. See L. Don LeFevre, manager of press relations in the LDS Church's Public Communications Department, to Tammy Tanaka (of Religious News Service), 6 February 1984, copy in possession of the author: "As I mentioned to you on the phone, we are aware of the film.... Meanwhile, there will be no debate by the Church with such antagonists. Such contention would be totally without merit. In fact, it would only be divisive and would tend to detract from the primary mission of The Church of Jesus Christ of Latter-day Saints, which is to help bad people become good and good people to become better. This can be done best by accentuating the positive and by concentrating on adherence to the beautiful and sacred teachings of the Savior Jesus Christ." See also Jerry Cahill/Phil Riesen Interview, 25 October 1983, transcript included in "Case Studies in Public Communications: Responding to Anti-LDS Messages," an internal document prepared by the "Domestic Section" of the LDS Church's Public Communications Department, 30; copy in possession of the author. Riesen reported for Salt Lake City television station KTVX. See United Press International's "Ex-Mormon Say Many Want Out," *Anchorage Daily News*, 3 December 1983; copy in possession of the author: "The leader of a group that hates Mormonism says he expects an exodus of Latter-day Saints from the church in 1984 because of his efforts to discredit the faith. But the LDS Church has decided to ignore the group—Saints Alive—and its 'lies and distortions' about Mormonism."

89. See Barker, "Anti-Mormon Film Makes Impact on South Bay," B2: "Although the church condemns the film for its inaccuracies, church leaders have refused to sue the producers of 'The God Makers.' [LDS spokesman Jerry] Cahill said such action would be counterproductive." See a report from a local LDS public communications representative: "I called Public Communications and talked with Kathleen Lubeck and asked her if she could get me a letter simply stating that the Church Film clip used in the "God Makers" is copyrighted and that no authorization has been given for its use commercially in any film. I had been told that although the Church could sue over its copyright, it had decided not to do so" (Mary Mostert to Elder George Merrill, Ken Woodward, Pres. Richard Montgomery, and Pres. John Porter, 31 October 1983; copy in possession of the author). See Keeper, "Ex-Mormons' Film Sparks Controversy," for Decker's statement, "Every doctrinal point we made in the film, we have talked to Mormon leaders about. I am willing to go to court on the merits of this movie." LDS educator Gilbert W. Scharffs did publish *The Truth About 'The God Makers'* (Salt Lake City, Utah: Publishers Press, 1986), but made it clear in an opening disclaimer that he did so independently of any official participation by the LDS Church.

90. "Leaders Urge Positive Reply to Critics," *Church News*, 18 December 1983, 2. Without mentioning Decker's group specifically, the First Presidency wrote to local church leaders about "films which pretend to represent the position of the Church on matters of doctrine and belittle the ordinances of the gospel, including the most sacred temple ordinances." The church's governing authorities counseled members to respond to negative church critics by looking for "opportunities...to present our message which do not involve contention or debate." An LDS stake president in Idaho sounded a similar theme: "'It actually seems to benefit our missionary work,' Young noted. He said membership in the Mormon Church has increased in the wake of anti-Mormon movements in the past. 'People can't believe what they are hearing,' he said, and so they find out more about the Mormon religion. 'It's not that we don't care' about the film, Young said. 'It's just that we're not that concerned. People come to their senses.'" In Pettit, "Film Depicts Mormonism as 'Cult'," 1A, 4A.

91. A search of several databases of national news organizations confirms this. For example, a search of "Godmakers" and "God Makers" in the LexisNexis Academic database for publications in 1982 through 1985 yields only four articles; a similar search of the ProQuest Newspapers database (including the Historical New York Times Database) yields only two articles. Accessed on December 31, 2009.

92. "Suggestions for developing a positive local perception of the Church," section III of "Case Studies in Public Communications," 79–80. It seems that there were at this time some in

Salt Lake who at least wondered if *the God Makers* phenomenon did not warrant a more vigorous, official response from church headquarters. See, for example, the report by Lorry Rytting to Richard P. Lindsay (managing director of the Church's Public Communications Department), 24 February 1984, copy in possession of the author. Rytting reported on a Boise, Idaho, area man who challenged proponents of *the God Makers* to an open debate on LDS doctrine. LDS public communications representatives determined that the man was an excommunicated Mormon who "just wants to stand up for the Prophet Joseph [Smith], in the absence of any action from the Church." Rytting closed his report this way: "It is a matter of speculation whether such a thing would have happened in Boise had there been a more direct response to the makers of 'The God Makers.'" This was the image conundrum facing public relations officials.

93. Memo from L. Gerald Pond to the Media Response Group of the Church's Public Communications Department, 21 March 1984; copy in possession of the author.

94. See, for example, the Public Communications Department memo "Mass Media Contents," 3 April 1984, copy in possession of the author, that lists seven pages' worth of notes on recent news reports under the heading "'The God Makers' (TGM) Items." See also Lynn J. Packham to Heber G. Wolsey, 17 June 1983, copy in possession of the author. Wolsey was at the time the director of the Public Communications Department. In this memo, Packham discusses Saints Alive's plans to build a visitors center close to LDS Temple Square to attract tourists to daily showings of *the God Makers*, as well as a recent conference where Christians "were urged to write and call *Eternity Magazine* to complain about the May '83 grouping of 'LDS' with other Christian groups.... In meeting with (LDS employee) Lorry E. Rytting yesterday, I recommended that lots of Mormons ought to commend *Eternity*'s editors for their accurate representation, and urge them not to bow to pressure."

95. See "Suggestions for developing a positive local perception of the Church," section III of "Case Studies in Public Communications: Responding to Anti-LDS Messages," an internal document prepared by the "Domestic Section" of the LDS Church's Public Communications Department, 79–80; copy in possession of the author. See Winston Caine, "Mormon Protest Halts Showing of Derogatory Film at School," 24 April 1983, A-1; also "Showing of Anti-Mormon Film Upsets LDS Members," *Lewiston Tribune*, 13 November 1983, copy in possession of the author, for Mormon complaints about plans to show *the God Makers* at an Issaquah, Washington, high school.

96. See Tammy Tanaka, "Ex-Church members employ Mormon techniques against the church," Religious News Service, 21 February 1984, 4: "However, [ads] have been accepted for publication by *The Denver Post* and other publications." See Charles Ashbaker, "Mormon Leader Defines Belief," *Hillsboro (Oregon) Argus*, 27 October 1983; copy in possession of the author. The op-ed piece contained this "editor's note": Controversy arose recently after the First Baptist Church of Hillsboro, in an advertisement for a film, implied Mormons are not Christians. Many letters to the editor subsequently were written on both sides of the issue. The Argus ceased publishing such letters last Thursday. However, Charles Ashbaker, president of the Hillsboro Stake that includes seven Mormon churches, had made arrangements prior to the moratorium to write the following statement." See also "Why Letters Weren't Run," *Wasilla (Arkansas) Valley Sun*, 6 December 1983, 4, where the paper's editors explained that, after an exchange of pro- and anti-Mormon letters to the editor regarding *the God Makers*, "the other three letters we received, which allege the Church of Jesus Christ of Latter-day Saints is a cult will not be published in this newspaper. While a newspaper may be the proper vehicle to debate political, moral and ethical issues, we do not believe it is the place to discuss which religion is 'true' and which is 'false.'" See Mary Mostert to Elder George Merrill, Ken Woodward, Pres. Richard Montgomery, and Pres. John Porter, 31 October 1983; copy in possession of the author. See Kathleen Lubeck to Gerry Pond, 24 April 1984, copy in possession of the author: "Mary Mostert of our Sacramento public communications council... indicated in a discussion with the head of Saints Alive in Sacramento (Jim Lindberg), with whom she has established a good rapport, he said that he had returned the 3 copies of the sequel

to 'The Godmakers' that he had ordered. Mary asked him why, and he hedged a little, so she asked him if it were because the film is inaccurate, and he said yes." See Keeper, "Ex-Mormons' Film Sparks Controversy": "Decker backed down when asked to substantiate his claim" about "teen-age suicide rate." "John Brockert, director of health statistics at the Utah Department of Health," said, "Statistics do not support the contention that teen-age suicide is a greater problem here that it is elsewhere...The statistics do not bear out what this group is trying to say." Sandra Tanner, one of the sources for information cited by Decker, told the Eugene newspaper that "she obtained her figures from news paper accounts, but could not provide further information about them." Decker later "insisted that despite whatever the statistics may show, suicide and child abuse are major problems in Utah because of the Mormon Church."

97. Roger R. Keller, interview by author, 24 February 2010. See also Tammy Tanaka, "Ex-Church members employ Mormon techniques against the church," 4: "The most articulate defense of the Mormons has come from a Presbyterian minister in Mesa [Arizona]. The Rev. Roger R. Keller, a former Mormon who has studied its theology, called the film 'religious pornography,' saying that it 'misrepresents and prostitutes what Mormons believe.' He added that while he disagrees with Mormon theology, he thinks Mormons are Christians." Several years later, Roger Keller rejoined the LDS Church. In 2009, he was teaching in the department of Religious Education at Brigham Young University. John Dart of the Los Angeles Times reported that although "the Mormon Church...has not sued the evangelical Christian film makers" of The God Makers the film makers sued the LDS Church, the NCCJ, and the B'nai B'rith Anti-Defamation League for $25 million dollars for "[making] false statements about the movie and thus [discouraging] rentals." An LDS Stake President, Robert D. Starling, who was also named in the suit, "said...that he believes the suit was filed to gain publicity. By charging that the film has caused them economic harm, he says, the film makers have demonstrated that they have 'turned religious persecution into a business'" (John Dart, "Mormon Church Sued for Criticism of Polemic Film," Los Angeles Times, 16 March 1985, 6).

98. "Fighting Mormonism in Utah," 31; Barker, "Anti-Mormon Film Makes Impact on South Bay."

99. See "Former Mormon Now One of Church's Most Vocal Critics," Associated Press wire service, 5 October 1985. The irony is that the report revealed that Ed Decker's son Jeff was serving as an LDS missionary in Chile at the same time that his father "was becoming one of the best-known opponents of Mormonism."

100. See LDS spokesman Don LeFevre's response in December 1983 in Anderson, "Former Mormons Seek to Convert Mormons to Mainstream Christianity." Another example of Decker's exaggerated claims: "In an interview, he claimed to have shattered the church's strength in the Pacific island nation of Tonga last summer. 'I think the work we did there in Tonga has totally put an end to Mormonism there,' he said. The church counters that it recorded 1,454 convert baptisms in Tonga in 1984 and 806 in the first six months of 1985" ("Former Mormon Now One of Church's Most Vocal Critics").

101. See Michael White, "Church Says Mounting Anti-Mormon Fervor Having Little Effect," Associated Press wire service, 5 October 1985: LDS Apostle Neal A. "Maxwell characterized recent anti-Mormon activities as the most intense in decades, though modest compared to the vilification and mob attacks that drove the polygamy-practicing Mormons of the 19th century to the sanctuary of Utah's desert wastes."

102. See Mary Curtius, "Mormon Plan for a Brigham Young University Site In Jerusalem Irks Some Israelis," Christian Science Monitor, 28 March 1985, 9; "B.Y.U. in Zion: Trouble for a Mormon Center," Time, 20 January 1986. The bomb threat was made against an LDS chapel in the Washington, D.C., area by "a person claiming to be a member of the Jewish Defense League" ("Bomb Threat at Church," The Washington Post, 29 July 1985, C5).

103. "Mormon Project Under Fire," Seattle Times, 9 August 1985, B4. See also Thomas A. Indinopulos, "Mormon-Jewish Turmoil in Zion," Christian Century, 4 December 1985, 1123: "Added voices of opposition come from Protestant, evangelical, Catholic and Eastern Orthodox officials who fear the proven success of Mormon missionaries will entice the

predominantly Arab laity of churches in the Holy Land into their fold. The battle line was drawn in early July when local Christian leaders challenged the Mormons' right to call themselves Christian." It took a May 1986 letter from 154 U.S. Congressmen in support of the completion of the BYU Jerusalem Center to finally secure government position for the lease. Students first occupied the unfinished center in 1987, which was ultimately dedicated in 1989 (James R. Kearl, "Jerusalem Center for Near Eastern Studies," in Garr, Cannon, and Cowan, eds., *Encyclopedia of Latter-day Saint History*, 570–571).

104. Val Edwards interview, 4.

105. Pettit, "Film Depicts Mormonism as 'Cult'," 1A, 4A.

106. Roger Keller, interview by author.

107. Professor Stark's research and essays on Mormonism have been compiled into one volume: Rodney Stark, *The Rise of Mormonism*, Reid L. Neilson, ed. (New York: Columbia University Press, 2005). The passages quoted comes from pages 139, 142. His original essay was published as "The Rise of a New World Faith," *Review of Religious Research* 26: 18–27.

108. See Jan Shipps, *Mormonism: The Story of a New Religious Tradition* (Urbana and Chicago: University of Illinois Press, 1985).

109. "In 1990, the Presbyterian Church (U.S.A.) produced a study paper that described the Mormon Church as 'a new religious tradition' that was 'not recognizably' Christian" (Sheler and Wagner, "Latter-day Struggles," *U.S. News and World Report*, 28 September 1992, 73).

110. In the "Introduction" of the 1984 internal document, "Case Studies in Public Communications," 2.

111. Even before the film was released, LDS authorities were mindful of the added impact of anti-Mormon activities organized by the clergy. See a conversation between pollster George Gallup and LDS Apostle Boyd K. Packer, 16 September 1982, B-12, transcript in possession of the author. Gallup met with leaders and staff of the church's public communications department to debrief recent poll results. Elder Packer asked Dr. Gallup, "Could I ask a question for your reaction? We're experiencing something that we've experienced over the history of the Church but it's been renewed and it's illustrated by two recent illustrations. We've started construction of a temple in Dallas. Now we always have some playback or reaction *but this is organized by the clergy....it's the clergy that are organizing*"; italics added.

112. See the Associated Press's "Opponents hit Mormon faith, draw return fire," *Longview (Washington) News*, 3 December 1983, copy in possession of the author: "Saints Alive has no quarrel with the fruits of Mormonism, [assistant director of Saints Alive Jim] Witham said. 'We don't deny the good work of the Mormon Church, (but) people who have eternal souls are being led off into eternal damnation.'"

113. See Pettit, "Film Depicts Mormonism as 'Cult'," 1A, for the reaction of First Christian Church Pastor Rev. Otto Schaufele to *The God Makers* film: "There are good Mormons...but this movie dispels the myth that the Mormon Church is a Christian church," and "presents information that Mormon leaders 'don't dare tell to their people.'" The head of Jeremiah Films, which presented *The God Makers*, said, "We feel sorry for anyone trapped by this religion. We would like to see the Mormons set free" (Pat Matrisciana, quoted in Barker, "Anti-Mormon Film Makes Impact on South Bay," B2).

114. See Val Edwards interview, 4, for reference to research about anti-Mormon curriculum.

115. Val Edwards interview, 1, 4.

116. The sales figure of 400,000 books comes from Ed Decker to Peggy Fletcher Stack, "'God makers II' to Recycle Anti-LDS Theme," *The Salt Lake Tribune*, 5 December 1992, C2. The 1997 reprint of the book included this banner on the front cover: "Over 300,000 copies sold." See Ed Decker and Dave Hunt, *The God Makers: A Shocking Expose of What the Mormon Church Really Believes*, updated and expanded (Eugene, Oregon: Harvest House Publishers, 1997).

117. Woodward and Burgower, "Bible-Belt Confrontation," 65.

118. "Interfaith Organization Denounces Anti-Mormon Movie," *Las Vegas Review-Journal*, 12 December 1992, 3C. The article was an Associated Press report.

119. "Cable Company Won't Air 'Godmakers II'," *The Salt Lake Tribune*, 9 January 1994, A13. The article was an Associated Press report. See also a memorandum from Stuart Reid to Val Edwards in the Church's Public Affairs Department, 28 March 1991, copy in possession of the author. Reid informed Edwards that *God Makers II* planned to take advantage of recent attention to the "Mormon cults in Mexico" in their upcoming film.

120. See Cindy Horswell, "Book Battle: Churches, Livingston council debate controversial writing," *Houston Chronicle*, 17 May 1986, 1. Horswell quoted the mayor of Livingston, Texas, who supported the librarian's decision to refuse the book because of problems with "bias and balance." The mayor, Ben Royden Ogletree, said, "Clearly, this book is a very controversial attack directed against the Mormon church and the Masonic lodge. In direct language, it accuses both of Satan worship and satanic rituals. I know people in both organizations and I don't see anything in the book that applies to the people I know." The two sides reached an eventual compromise: "the book is now on the library's shelves, next to a work rebutting its claims" (Cindy Horswell, "More books rejected as censorship effort grows," *Houston Chronicle*, 21 December 1986, 1).

121. Sandra Tanner, Utah Lighthouse Ministry, "Facts Misrepresented in 'Godmakers' Issue," letter to the editor, *(Boise) Idaho Statesman*, 3 March 1984; copy in possession of the author: "I felt the film...was an accurate portrayal of Mormon teachings, past and present. As to my reservations about the film, I feel it is an overstatement that Mormonism is one of the 'most dangerous groups in the entire world.'...The film's statement that Utah 'ranks among the highest in divorce' is an exaggeration...I felt the spooky background music was inappropriate."

122. Bill Heersink, interview by author.

123. Shipps, *Sojourner in the Promised Land*, 101.

124. Pat Matrisciana, head of Jeremiah Films that produced *The God Makers*, in Barker, "Anti-Mormon Film Makes Impact on South Bay."

Chapter 6

1. This excerpt from the Springfield, Massachusetts, *Union* is quoted in Dean L. May, *Utah: A People's History* (Salt Lake City: University of Utah, 1987), 127. Jon Krakauer also quotes it as "*Salt Lake Tribune*, February 15, 1885," in Krakauer, *Under the Banner of Heaven: The Story of a Violent Faith* (New York: Doubleday, 2003), 29. Portions of chapter 6 appeared in J. B. Haws, "From *The God Makers* to the Myth Maker: Simultaneous—and Lasting—Challenges to Mormonism's Reputation in the 1980s," *Mormon Historical Studies* 12, no. 1 (Spring 2011): 31–51.

2. "The Gallup Poll #120G," 16 January 1979, question qn3, Gallup Brain database, http://brain.gallup.com/home.aspx.

3. Rodney Clapp, "Fighting Mormonism in Utah," *Christianity Today*, 16 July 1982, 30–31.

4. Kenneth C. Danforth, "The Cult of Mormonism," *Harper's*, May 1980, 67, 68, 71.

5. James P. Mann, "Utah: 'Promised Land' Wrestles with its Future," *U.S. News and World Report*, 11 August 1980, 73.

6. Ken Wells, "The Mormon Church Is Rich, Rapidly Growing and Very Controversial," *Wall Street Journal*, 8 November 1983, 1, 20; Victor F. Zunana, "Leaders of Mormonism Double as Overseers of a Financial Empire," *Wall Street Journal*, 9 November 1983, 1. Wells also quoted J. D. Williams saying, "There is a disquieting statement in Mormonism: 'When the leaders have spoken, the thinking has been done.'...To me, democracy can't thrive in that climate" (20).

7. Danforth, "The Cult of Mormonism," 66; Zunana, "Leaders of Mormonism Double as Overseers of a Financial Empire," 1; Danforth, "The Cult of Mormonism," 68.

8. See Robert Gottlieb and Peter Wiley, *America's Saints: The Rise of Mormon Power* (New York: Harcourt, Brace, Jovanovich Publishers, 1986); these statements came

from the back cover of the paperback edition of the book—the original hardcover edition was published under the same title by G. P. Putnam's Sons in 1984; John Heineman and Anson Shupe, *The Mormon Corporate Empire* (Boston: Beacon Press, 1985); italics added. Jan Shipps also argued for the importance of "reputable and well-known presses" joining the field of publishers whose "books [were] designed to reveal Mormonism's underside" (*Sojourner in the Promised Land: Forty Years among the Mormons* [Urbana and Chicago: University of Illinois Press, 2000], 101).

9. For a good summary of the MX plan, as well as the LDS Church's position as "a powerful new foe" that will make it "much harder for President Reagan to adopt a plan that would implant missiles in the Mormon heartland," see "Nix to MX: Mormon Leaders Protest," *Time*, 18 May 1981, 28. See also Jacob W. Olmstead, "The Mormon Hierarchy and the MX," *Journal of Mormon History* 33, no. 3 (Fall 2007): 1–30, for a detailed discussion of the deliberations that preceded the First Presidency's decision to issue an anti-MX statement, as well as the influential role of Utah law professor Edwin Firmage in strongly advocating for such a statement. The full statement is included as an appendix to Olmstead's article (28–30).

10. "The Mormons and the MX," an editorial in the *New York Times*, 9 May 1981, 22, also bemoaned the church's "oddly selective summons to national morality" that was "disturbingly sanctimonious" as it "found its way to a sound conclusion for mostly wrong reasons." The *New York Times* also asked rhetorically, "What then of the 29 other states that house strategic missiles, bombers and submarines?"

11. See, for example, William E. Schmidt, "MX Opposition Gaining in Utah and Nevada," *New York Times*, 8 June 1981, B11. The thrust of Schmidt's piece was that "when the Carter administration proposed basing the MX missile system in the Great Basin of Utah and Nevada, most people here seemed prepared to agree with the plan or at least to give the Federal Government the benefit of the doubt....But the Mormon Church's decision last month to publicly oppose deployment of the missiles in the region has accelerated a dramatic shift in public opinion against the plan...[a] shift...so dramatic in Utah that some pro-MX people believe that it is now useless for the Air Force or others to attempt to turn public opinion in the other direction." Even "hawkish" Republican Senators Paul Laxalt (Nevada) and Jake Garn (Utah), with their "direct access to the White House," felt the "effect" of "public opinion" as they weighed their support of the MX plan and "said they favor some alternative basing system." *Science* noted that "the Mormon statement...expected to breathe new life into the anti-MX movement," since "many" in Utah's population, which was described, ironically, as "extremely conservative, patriotic, and defense-minded," had "come to regard [the MX] as inevitable" (Constance Holden, "Mormons Rebel on MX," *Science*, 22 May 1981, 904). Williams, "Regional Resistance: Backyard Autonomy," *The Nation*, 5 September 1981, 179; cited in Quinn, *Mormon Hierarchy: Extensions of Power*, 391.

12. See Michael K. Winder, *Presidents and Prophets: The Story of America's Presidents and the LDS Church* (American Fork, Utah: Covenant Communications, 2007), 357, where Senator Orrin Hatch from Utah is quoted as saying, "I have no doubt that when the LDS Church came out against the MX proposal, that that was the end of it. He [Reagan] respected the Church, and he respected the rights of the Church." See also Allen and Leonard, *The Story of the Latter-day Saints*, 660: "Ultimately the MX site was moved to Wyoming, partly, some observers believed, because of U.S. President Ronald Reagan's respect for the Church." See also Stephen W. Stathis, "Mormonism and the Periodical Press: A Change Is Underway," *Dialogue* 14, no. 2 (Summer 1981): 61–62, for selections from the *Washington Post*, *The Nation*, and the *St. Louis Post-Dispatch* that criticized the Mormons' "morality of convenience," or their "thoughtless intrusion into the logic of defense" which "weakens the defense of Western Europe."

13. Gottlieb and Wiley, *America's Saints*, 66, 93; Heinerman and Shupe, *The Mormon Corporate Empire*, 28, 176.

14. Heinerman and Shupe, *The Mormon Corporate Empire*, 2, 4.

15. Shipps, *Sojourner in the Promised Land*, 104, 119, note 25. Jan Shipps called *The Mormon Corporate Empire* a "neo-nineteenth-century expose, a kind of expose that deals almost entirely with the secular side of Mormonism." She also reported that Shupe used a "'higher law' argument to defend such misrepresentation."

16. Gottlieb and Wiley, *America's Saints*, 7. The *Church News* statement was published in its 2 September 1984 edition.

17. Gottlieb and Wiley, *America's Saints*, 8–9.

18. Peter McAlevey, "Bilking Utah's Faithful," *Newsweek*, 24 December 1984, 31, Gottlieb and Wiley, *America's Saints*, 121–122; "The 'Stock-Fraud Capital' Tries to Clean up its Act," *BusinessWeek*, 6 February 1984, 76; "Purity in Utah," *Forbes*, 11 March 1985, 12.

19. Richard E. Turley Jr., *Victims: The LDS Church and the Mark Hofmann Case* (Urbana and Chicago: University of Illinois Press, 1992), 316–317. Turley, at the time of writing, was the managing director of the LDS Church Historical Department. Because of his position, he had unprecedented access to church records, minutes, and leadership in the production of his book, making *Victims* the most detailed account of the church's side of the Mark Hofmann story. Two other important books about the Hofmann forgeries are Linda Sillitoe and Allen Roberts, *Salamander: The Story of the Mormon Forgery Murders*, 2nd ed. with a new afterword (Salt Lake City: Signature Books, 1989), and Steven Naifeh and Gregory White Smith, *The Mormon Murders: A True Story of Greed, Forgery, Deceit, and Death* (New York: Weidenfeld and Nicolson, 1988). Sillitoe and Roberts reported that, as a college student, Hofmann had told his one-time fiancée Kate Reid that "he did not believe in Mormonism and doubted the existence of God." After their engagement ended, Hofmann told Reid that he was dropping his plans for medical school to research Mormon historical documents full-time. When she countered, "I think that's dumb. You don't even believe in the church," he responded, "I have to remain a member of good standing so people will trust me and I can have access to what I need. But I can make good money at this, and eventually the documents I find are going to show people that they believe in a fairytale" (Sillitoe and Roberts, *Salamander*, 222–223, 231).

20. The databases searched in December 2009 were ProQuest Newspapers, LexisNexis Academic, and *The New York Times* Historical Database.

21. See, for example, Martin Marty's observation of this in the midst of Hofmann's discoveries. Marty gave the annual Tanner Lecture at the Mormon History Association meetings in 1983. He said, "Few others of the 20,870 separate denominations listed in the most recent encyclopedia of Christianity have as much at stake so far as 'historicness' is concerned as do Mormons.... If the beginning of the promenade of Mormon history, the First Vision and the Book of Mormon, can survive the crisis, then the rest of the promenade follows, and nothing that happens in it can really detract from the miracle of the whole. If the first steps do not survive, there can be only antiquarian—not fateful or faith-full—interest in the rest of the story" (Martin Marty, "Two Integrities: An Address to the Crisis in Mormon Historiography," in Dean L. May, Reid L. Neilson, Richard Lyman Bushman, Jan Shipps, and Thomas G. Alexander, eds., *The Mormon History Association's Tanner Lectures: The First Twenty Years* [Urbana and Chicago: University of Illinois Press, 2006], 359–360).

22. In 1981, Michael Quinn reported to BYU's history student association "a shift in anti-Mormon propaganda from doctrinal diatribe to the polemical use of elements from the Mormon past to discredit the LDS Church today." D. Michael Quinn, "On Being a Mormon Historian," a lecture given before the Student History Association, Brigham Young University, Fall 1981. http://www.mormonismi.net/kirjoitukset/quinn_mormonihistorioitsija.html, copy in the author's possession.

23. See this sentiment in Gottlieb and Wiley, "Preface to the Hardcover Edition," *America's Saints*, paperback edition, 16–19; in Heinerman and Shupe, *The Mormon Corporate Empire*, 209–215, where they quote George Orwell's *1984*: "Who controls the past controls the future; who controls the present controls the past" (214–215); in Danforth, "The Cult of Mormonism," 68–71; also see journalist Peter Bart's fictional novel, *Thy Kingdom Come* (New York: Linden, 1981). Jan Shipps noted that Bart's book "was reputed to be a roman a

clef, a novel in which real events and people were represented under the guise of fictions" (Shipps, *Sojourner in the Promised Land*, 104).

24. On the "climate" of believability, see this line from British philosopher Austin Farrer: "Rational argument does not create belief, but it maintains a climate in which belief may flourish." A number of Latter-day Saints authors have quoted Farrer; see, for example, Neal A. Maxwell (at the time Church Commissioner of Education; he would be a church apostle from 1981–2004), "Talk of the Month," *New Era*, May 1971, https://www.lds.org/new-era/1971/05/talk-of-the-month?lang=eng; also Terryl L. Givens, *By the Hand of Mormon: The American Scripture that Launched a New World Religion* (New York and Oxford: Oxford University Press, 2002), 118. Ezra Taft Benson, at the time the president of the church's Quorum of the Twelve Apostles (and the next in line to succeed church President Spencer W. Kimball), told instructors in the church's educational system in 1976, "We hope that if you feel you must write for the scholarly journals, you always defend the faith" (Ezra Taft Benson, "The Gospel Teacher and His Message," Address to Church Educational System Religious Educators, 17 September 1976, 6; copy in possession of the author). See also this perceptive line from church historical department administrator Glenn Rowe: "Helping people better understand the Church [and] accept it…is often closely connected to having a correct understanding of the history of the Church. Many of the questions that arise about the Church are historical in nature" (email correspondence with the author, 8 April 2010).

25. D. Michael Quinn and Leonard Arrington both give Howard Hunter much of the credit for initiating new policies at the church archives. D. Michael Quinn, interview by author, 20 March 2010; Leonard J. Arrington, *Adventures of a Church Historian* (Urbana and Chicago: University of Illinois Press, 1998), 69, 77–78.

26. For a brief and insightful review of post–World War II changes in Mormon historiography, see Jan Shipps's review essay, "Richard Lyman Bushman and the New Mormon History," *Journal of American History* 94, no. 2 (September 2007): 498–516. Importantly, Shipps was a charter member of the Mormon History Association, and Richard Bushman was one of the young Mormon graduate students making a name for himself in the 1960s. See also Ronald W. Walker, David J. Whittaker, and James B. Allen, *Mormon History* (Urbana and Chicago: University of Illinois Press, 2001). The three historians wrote their survey of Mormon historiography after producing a bibliography of some 16,000 works on Mormon history in 2000. Chapter 3 of *Mormon History*, "The New Mormon History: Historical Writing Since 1950," is especially pertinent here. For an important overview, see Davis Bitton and Leonard J. Arrington, *Mormons and their Historians*, vol. 2 of Publications in Mormon Studies (Salt Lake City: University of Utah, 1988). Chapter 9, "The Professionalization of Mormon History," is an especially helpful account of changes in the church's history department in the 1960s and 1970s, and guides much of the interpretation here.

27. See, for example, Davis Bitton, "Ten Years in Camelot: A Personal Memoir," *Dialogue* 16 (Fall 1983): 9–33; D. Michael Quinn, interview by author, 20 March 2010; Bitton and Arrington, *Mormons and Their Historians*, 137.

28. See this paraphrase of Leonard J. Arrington, "Scholarly Studies of Mormonism in Twentieth Century," *Dialogue* 1 (Spring 1966): 28, in Walker, Whittaker, and Allen, *Mormon History*, 60.

29. Bitton, "Ten Years in Camelot," 10.

30. Glen Leonard, interview by author, 3 March 2010; Arrington, *Adventures of a Church Historian*, 148. In this instance, Arrington quoted two unnamed members of the church's Quorum of the Twelve Apostles.

31. Edward Kimball noted that his father, Church President Spencer W. Kimball, "read and enjoyed…*The Story of the Latter-day Saints*" even though "other General Authorities found" this and similar publications "objectionable in certain respects" (Edward L. Kimball, *Lengthen Your Stride: The Presidency of Spencer W. Kimball* [Salt Lake City: Deseret Book, 2005], 187).

32. See Arrington, *Adventures of a Church Historian*, 143. The book went "essentially unadvertised and it was not used in the [church's] seminaries and institutes" as a textbook " as had been expected" (Kimball, *Lengthen Your Stride*, 188).

33. Curt Bench, interview by author, 10 February 2010.

34. D. Michael Quinn interview.

35. Apparently Spencer W. Kimball, church president at the time, was one of those in the church hierarchy who felt comfortable with this more open approach. His son and biographer reported: "When Spencer's own biography appeared in 1977, Spencer was surprised and pleased by how quickly it found a large and eager readership. He allowed the authors, son Ed and grandson Andrew Kimball Jr., freedom to tell his story candidly, including reference to his human foibles. Spencer presented a copy to each General Authority individually. Reactions varied. One reportedly said to a friend, 'I don't believe a book should portray an apostle as less perfect than the people expect him to be.' But other General Authorities and Church members appreciated the frankness. One reader wrote, 'As I read the biography I suddenly discovered a very important thing: the Prophet had once struggled with many of the same trials I was facing. He had triumphed—and so could I' " (Kimball, *Lengthen Your Stride*, 67). Compare also Arrington, *Adventures of a Church Historian*, 118–119, for a discussion about the church history division's first book, *Brigham Young's Letters to His Sons* (Salt Lake City: Deseret Book, 1974). One apostle disapproved of the inclusion of a letter in which Brigham Young counseled a missionary son to "omit the use of tobacco while on your mission, if you have not already done so."

36. Benson, "The Gospel Teacher and His Message," Address to Church Educational System Religious Educators, 17 September 1976, 5; copy in possession of the author. President Benson was quoting from another of his own speeches—"God's Hand in Our Nation's History," in *1976 Devotional Speeches of the Year* (Provo, Utah: Brigham Young University Press, 1977), 310.

37. Benson, "The Gospel Teacher and His Message," 6.

38. Boyd K. Packer, "The Mantle Is Far, Far Greater than the Intellect," Address to Church Educational System employees, 22 August 1981, 2, 3, 5; copy in possession of the author.

39. *Adventures of a Church Historian*, 111, 120. While Leonard Arrington was announced as Church Historian at the church's general conference in April 1972, there was no similar public announcement regarding the change in his position. There was, therefore, some persistent ambiguity, and Arrington reported that friends asked him if he was still church historian. He told them that the title "director of the History Division" better explained his responsibilities. When general authority Homer Durham was appointed managing director of the Church History Department in 1977, Arrington said that Durham essentially functioned as Church Historian. On the "correlation" question, see Arrington, *Adventures of a Church Historian*, 158–162,192; also Bitton, "Ten Years in Camelot," 12.

40. See Walker, Whittaker, and Allen, *Mormon History*, 67–68; also Arrington, *Adventures of a Church Historian*, 165–168, for a list of the volumes that did emerge.

41. Arrangements for moving the historians to BYU were initiated as early as 1978. In a July 2, 1980, press release to the *Deseret News*, Church President Spencer W. Kimball said, "The stature, objectivity, and effectiveness of our fine professional historians will be enhanced by association with the church's university"; quoted in Walker, Whittaker, and Allen, *Mormon History*, 68, and Arrington, *Adventures of a Church Historian*, 216–217.

42. Bitton, "Ten Years in Camelot," 18; Lawrence Foster, "A Personal Odyssey: My Encounter with Mormon History," *Dialogue* 16, no. 3 (Autumn 1983): 97. For an insightful and candid perspective on these tensions from a historian and LDS Church educator who was a firsthand (per Web. 11) participant, see Alexander L. Baugh's interview, "Mormonism's Remarkable History: A Conversation with Max Parkin," *Mormon Historical Studies* 12, no. 2 (Fall 2011): 95–140.

43. George Raine, "Historical Debate 'Formal'," *Salt Lake Tribune*, 28 February 1982, B–1, B–2.

44. Peggy Fletcher, "Going My Way: An Interview with *Newsweek*'s Kenneth Woodward," *Sunstone*, September-October 1980, 38.

45. Kenneth L. Woodward, "Apostles vs. Historians," *Newsweek*, 15 February 1982, 77. Woodward described how the speech by BYU professor D. Michael Quinn ("On Being a Mormon Historian") to the school's student history association "violated the Mormon taboo that proscribes the faithful from publicly criticizing" the church's apostles. Quinn specifically referred to Elder Ezra Taft Benson's 1976 speeches and Elder Boyd K. Packer's August 1981 address. *Newsweek* quoted Quinn's worry that biographical accounts of "benignly angelic Church leaders...would border on idolatry." Quinn said that he "had no anticipation" of the "national publicity" the talk would bring, since he had presented the address to a gathering of only thirty or so students. However, an independent student newspaper at BYU, the *Seventh East Press*, printed a transcript of Quinn's talk, and that article was subsequently picked up by local newspapers and then national media outlets (D. Michael Quinn, interview by author).

46. LaMar Petersen, "For the Letter Killeth: Mormon Justice," *The Humanist*, January/February 1978, 17, 19. See also Kenneth L. Woodward, "What Mormons Believe," *Newsweek*, 1 September 1980, 71, where he asserted that "what concerns [BYU historian Marvin] Hill and other Mormon intellectuals is their independence as scholars. They fear that the church does not respect the intellectual life and welcomes contact with Gentile theologians solely to score ideological points."

47. "Rewriting...Mormon history." In a prison interview, Mark Hofmann stated that this was one of his aims in forging the blessing Joseph Smith purportedly gave to his son, Joseph Smith III. See Turley, *Victims*, 317.

48. See "The Anthon Transcript," chapter 2, in Turley, *Victims*, 24–39. See also "The Treasure in a Bible," chapter 10, in Sillitoe and Roberts, *Salamander*, 235–253. While both books basically document the same chronology, the different scope of each book quickly becomes apparent. Sillitoe and Roberts conducted a vast number of interviews with Hofmann's friends and associates, thus emphasizing details about Hofmann's background and activities outside of his document dealings with the church. Turley concentrated on Hofmann's relationships and transactions with the LDS Church and its leaders, and the subsequent legal proceedings of his criminal trial.

49. See Mark William Hofmann, "Finding the Joseph Smith Document," *Ensign*, July 1980, 73; Danel W. Bachman, "A Look at the Newly Discovered Joseph Smith Manuscript," *Ensign*, July 1980, 69; as well as Bachman, "Sealed in a Book: Preliminary Observations on the Newly Found 'Anthon Transcript,'" *Brigham Young University Studies* 20 (Summer 1980): 325.

50. See Turley, *Victims*, 39.

51. See, for example, the photo of Hofmann examining the Anthon Transcript with the members of the church's First Presidency, included in Turley, *Victims*, 31.

52. Turley, *Victims*, 28.; see also pages 40–42 for the text and background of the "blessing."

53. See Mark A. Scherer, "Reorganized Church of Jesus Christ of Latter Day Saints (RLDS)," in Garr, Cannon, and Cowan, eds., *Encyclopedia of Latter-day Saint History*, 1000–1002, for an overview of RLDS history.

54. See "Church of Latter Day Splits: Scions of Smith and Young enjoy a schismatic Mormon birthday," *Time*, 21 April 1980, 83, for a contemporary look at the contrasts between the RLDS and LDS Churches. The *Time* article was prompted by the April 6, 1980, sesquicentennial anniversary of the church Joseph Smith organized.

55. See "And They Knew Not Joseph: An 1844 paper raises doubts about Mormon succession," *Time*, 30 March 1981, 77; also Kenneth L. Woodward, "A Mormon Revelation," *Newsweek*, 30 March 1981, 76.

56. Woodward, "A Mormon Revelation," 76; "And They Knew Not Joseph," 77.

57. "And They Knew Not Joseph," 77.

58. See John Dart, "Smith Wanted Son to Lead Mormons Document Says," *Los Angeles Times*, 20 March 1981, 1, as cited in Stephen W. Stathis, "Mormonism and the Periodical Press: A Change Is Underway," *Dialogue* 14, no. 2 (Summer 1981): 71; John M. Crewdson, "Succession Document Acclaimed by Mormon Branch," *New York Times*, 20 March 1981, A16.

59. Fred Esplin, "The Joseph Smith III Document: Juggling a Historical Hot Potato," *Utah Holiday*, April 1981, 11–12, as quoted in Stathis, "Mormonism and the Periodical Press: A Change Is Underway," 61.

60. Stathis, "Mormonism and the Periodical Press," 59.

61. "No family in America is immune....": John M. Crewdson, "Mormons of Missouri Humble, Happy, Documented," *New York Times*, 23 March 1981, A12.

62. "Founder Settles 137-Year-Old Latter Day Saints Dispute," *Christianity Today*, 24 April 1981, 42, as quoted in Stathis, "Mormonism and the Periodical Press," 61.

63. See "Fraudulent Documents from Forger Mark Hofmann Noted," *Ensign*, October 1987, 79, for a list of forged documents that the church obtained from Mark Hofmann, together with information about the public announcement about each item (before it was determined they were all forgeries).

64. Curt Bench interview.

65. The canonized account that was written by Joseph Smith is included in the LDS Church's Pearl of Great Price as "Joseph Smith—History."

66. See Turley, "The Salamander Letter," chapter 5 of *Victims*, 79–111, for a description of the letter, a transcription and photograph of it, as well as a discussion of the uproar the letter created. See also Sillitoe and Roberts, chapter 12, "The Birth of the Salamander Letter," chapter 12 of *Salamander*, 269–299.

67. See Turley, *Victims*, 83.

68. See John Dart, "Mormons Ponder 1830 Letter Altering Idealized Image of Joseph Smith," *Los Angeles Times*, 25 August 1984; and "Moroni or Salamander? Reported Find of Letter by Book of Mormon Witness," *Salt Lake City Messenger*, no. 53 (March 1984): 1, 4; as cited in Turley, *Victims*, 422.

69. See John L. Hart, "Letter Sheds Light on Religious Era," *Church News*, 28 April 1985, and "Presidency Comments on Letter's Authenticity," *Church News*, 28 April 1985, as cited in Turley, *Victims*, 100.

70. See Steve Eaton, "Mormon Research Beneficial to Church," *Salt Lake Tribune*, 6 May 1985, for coverage of the annual meeting of the Mormon History Association (MHA) at which historians "divulged details of their research on a document that has been dubbed 'the salamander letter' for the first time." The MHA's president, Maureen Ursenbach Beecher, said, "the document drew more attention by the press and the electronic media to the conference than that annual meeting has had in the past."

71. The Josiah Stowell letter was noted in Associated Press and United Press International wire stories in May 1985. See, for example, "Mormon Linked to Folk Magic," *Fort Lauderdale Sun Sentinel*, 11 May 1985, 5A. The article implied that the church had intended to keep the letter under wraps: "No explanation was given of how the church got the letter. But George Smith, president of Signatures Books of San Francisco, said it was his understanding that Gordon B. Hinckley, second counselor to Mormon Church President Spencer W. Kimball, purchased the letter in 1983 *in his own name* from collector Mark Hofmann. Hofmann declined comment"; italics added. Compare also Marjorie Hyer, "Mormon Church Stirred by Prophet's Letter; Document Suggests Element of Occult," *Washington Post*, 11 May 1985, A3; John Dart, "Letter Revealing Mormon Founder's Belief in Spirits, Occult Released," *Los Angeles Times*, 11 May 1985, page 4. The misunderstanding about the letter's path to church ownership was clarified in a press statement from President Hinckley and church spokesman Jerry Cahill, in which Cahill confirmed that President Hinckley had purchased the letter for the church. See Dawn Tracy, "Smith Letter Seems to Have Disappeared from View," *Salt Lake Tribune*, 29 April 1985, B-1; also "Church Has Letter," *Salt Lake Tribune*, 7 May 1985, a letter from Jerry Cahill confirming that he had misspoken when he originally told Tracy that the church did not have the letter. President Hinckley corrected Cahill, who was unaware of the acquisition, which had taken place in the office of the First Presidency.

72. See Joseph Smith's official account, included in the LDS canon as Joseph Smith—History 1:56: "In the month of October 1825, I hired with an old gentleman by the name of Josiah Stoal...He heard something of a silver mine having been opened by the Spaniards in

Harmony,... Pennsylvania... After I went to live with him, he took me, with the rest of his
hands, to dig for the silver mine, at which I continued to work for nearly a month, without
success in our undertaking, and finally I prevailed with the old gentleman to cease digging
after it. Hence arose the very prevalent story of my having been a money-digger."

73. Richard N. Ostling and Christine Arrington, "Challenging Mormonism's Roots," *Time*, 20
May 1985, 44.

74. Brent Metcalfe, quoted in Ostling and Arrington, "Challenging Mormonism's Roots," 44.

75. Peggy Fletcher Stack, interview by author, 12 December 2008, transcript in possession
of the author, 7: "These reporters would come and would want me to give them a primer
in Mormonism"; Shipps, *Sojourner in the Promised Land*, 105: "Peggy Stack... first put
into words for me the dilemma the Hofmann story presented to newspaper editors
and the supervisory staffs of other news organizations." Shipps had just published a
new book, *Mormonism: The Story of a New Religious Tradition*, in 1985, and she "started
getting requests from reporters for phone interviews only one day after Hofmann's
arrest."

76. William Plummer and Carl Arrington, "Mysterious Bombings Kill Two in Salt Lake City—
And Rock the Mormons," *People Weekly*, 4 November 1985, 121; Amy Wilentz and Michael
Riley, "Utah Docudrama: Murder Among the Mormons," *Time*, 28 October 1985, 48. See
also Jennet Conant and George Raine, "The Mormon Mystery," *Newsweek*, 28 October
1985, 44. Only three weeks after the bombing, Church President Spencer W. Kimball
died. News coverage of the appointment of his successor, Ezra Taft Benson, was filled
with references to the Hofmann scandal. See Richard N. Ostling and Christine Arrington,
"Awaiting the 13th Prophet," *Time*, 18 November 1985, 85: "But lately, [the church] has
been shaken by the mysterious bombing murders of two people connected with the sale of
historical documents that cast doubts on official teachings about the origins of the Book
of Mormon."

77. Robert Lindsey, "The Mormons: Growth, Prosperity, and Controversy," *New York Times*, 12
January 1986, section 6, page 19.

78. See Turley, "The McLellin Collection," chaptera 6 of *Victims*, 112–145; Sillitoe and Roberts,
"The McLellin Collection at All Costs," chapter 14 of *Salamander*, 319–357.

79. See Sillitoe and Roberts, *Salamander*, 324

80. Hugh Pinnock, quoted in Turley, *Victims*, 180; his full press release is included on pages
181–183. See Plummer and Arrington, "Mysterious Bombings Kill Two in Salt Lake City—
And Rock the Mormons," 122–123; Kenneth L. Woodward, "A Time of Testing for the
Mormons," Newsweek, 25 November 1985, 87.

81. Curt Bench interview. Bench revealed that even after the arrest, he hoped his friend was
innocent. See also Woodward, "A Time of Testing for the Mormons," 87: "It now turns out
that Hofmann hoped to sell the church a set of papers known as 'the M'Lellin Collection,'
which some scholars believe includes discussion of early Mormon scriptures that may
impeach the church's canonical history.... Before the papers could be acquired, however,
Hofmann himself was severely wounded when a bomb exploded in his car. The M'Lellin
papers—if they exist at all—have not been found." In an ironic twist, as part of its exhaustive archive search to look for documents that Hofmann had accused the church of hiding,
LDS employees in 1986 found that the church already *owned* some of McLellin's journals—and owned them since 1908 (although Hofmann admitted that he fabricated the
existence of the collection he described). The church subsequently published the journals,
which did not prove to contain the damaging material that Hofmann described. See Jan
Shipps and John W. Welch, eds., *The Journals of William E. McLellin, 1831–1836* (Provo,
Utah and Urbana: *BYU Studies* and University of Illinois Press, 1994). For the story behind
the journals' discovery and publication, see Shipps, *Sojourner in the Promised Land*, 211–
212, and 216, notes 22–24; also Turley, *Victims*, 248–251. For the subsequent publication of other McLellin papers, see Michael De Groote, "McLellin journal finally is located,"
Deseret News, 22 January 2009, http://www.deseretnews.com/article/705279446/
McLellin-journal-finally-is-located.html?pg=all.

82. See Dallin H. Oaks, "Speaking Today: Recent Events Involving Church History and Forged Documents," *Ensign*, October 1987, 63: "In a circumstance where The Church of Jesus Christ of Latter-day Saints could not say much without interfering with the pending criminal investigation and prosecution, the Church and its leaders have been easy marks for assertions and innuendo ranging from charges of complicity in murder to repeated recitals that the Church routinely acquires and suppresses Church history documents in order to deceive its members and the public."

83. Carey, "A Time of Turmoil for Mormons," *U.S. News and World Report*, 74. A paragraph later, the article revealed that "collector Mark Hofmann, charged in the deaths as well as *forgeries of some church-related documents*, is expected to go on trial this summer," yet there was no indication that Hofmann was the source of the Salamander Letter, or that one of the forgery charges related to the Salamander Letter.

84. Oaks, "Speaking Today," 64: In "January 1986, the Church turned all of its Hofmann-acquired documents over to the prosecutors, at their request. As a result, the Church could not make its Hofmann documents public to answer these innuendos of suppression without seeming to try to influence or impede the criminal investigation."

85. See Turley, *Victims*, 310–313, for a discussion of Hofmann's plea bargain and terms. See especially pages 479–480, note 27, for statements by the prosecution that the church was specifically not informed of the pending plea bargain to avoid the impression of church influence on the decision. Importantly, these statements contradicted one of the principal premises of Naifeh and Smith's *Mormon Murders*, since they repeatedly argued that church leaders pressured prosecutors to avoid a trial that could lead to potential embarrassment for the church. See *Mormon Murders*, 358, 407–408.

86. Oaks, "Speaking Today," 63. Jan Shipps, reviewing this episode over a decade later, agreed that "national coverage (in contrast to most of the local Utah coverage) of the story contained an astonishing amount of innuendo associating Hofmann's plagiarism with Mormon beginnings. Myriad reports alleged secrecy and cover-up on the part of LDS general authorities" (*Sojourner in the Promised Land*, 108). A database search of ProQuest Newspapers for "Mark Hofmann" results in eighty-three articles that appeared in major newspapers from October to December 1985. The story made the front pages of the *Houston Chronicle* and the *Orlando Sentinel*, page 2 of the *San Diego Union* and the *Seattle Times*, and page 3 of the *Boston Globe* and the *Chicago Tribune*. Only ten articles in the database were devoted to Hofmann's plea. While that plea was front page news in the *San Diego Union* (on January 23, 1987) and the *Los Angeles Times* (on January 24, 1987), the irony is that one month later, the *Los Angeles Times* carried the first of a two-part series on "The White Salamander Murders" (by Robert A. Jones, *Los Angeles Times*, 29 March 1987, 6). The announcement of Hofmann's plea and confession covered only 300 words; the "White Salamander Murders" piece, 6200 words. If readers did not see the second part of the series, published a week later (5 April 1984, page 14), they would have been left with this closing line: "Three bombs had exploded; two people were dead and one was in the hospital; the McLellin Collection had not been seen"—yet no mention that Hofmann had already confessed.

87. See Oaks, "Speaking Today," 67, for a transcript of an address at Brigham Young University on 6 August 1987. Oaks described how "concerned readers wrote letters to the editor of the *[Los Angeles] Times*. They appealed to fairness, journalistic ethics, and the need for assurance that the press was not being exploited for selfish purposes. They asked the *Los Angeles Times* to print the known truth so its readers could evaluate the credibility of the paper's articles about the Oliver Cowdery history and the Church's alleged suppression of it. None of these letters was printed."

88. See Dawn Tracy, "Hofmann Told Others He Was Shown Secret LDS History," *Salt Lake Tribune*, 17 October 1986, C13.

89. Jones, "The White Salamander Murders: The First of Two Parts," *Los Angeles Times*, 29 March 1987, 6; "The White Salamander Murders: The Second of Two Parts," *Los Angeles Times*, 5 April 1987, 14.

90. See "Tried to Kill Self, Mormon Artifacts Dealer Says," *Los Angeles Times*, 1 August 1987, 29: "Obviously like many others who had dealings with Hofmann, we were seriously misled...In retrospect, it's clear we erred in publishing it without verifying Hofmann's story with another source."

91. Oaks, "Speaking Today," 67.

92. Oaks, "Speaking Today," 64. The final chapter on Hofmann's forgeries has yet to be written, as researchers reported a newly discovered forged document in 2011—an affidavit related to the Mountain Meadows Massacre. See Richard E. Turley, Jr., and Brian D. Reeves, "Unmasking Another Hofmann Forgery," *Journal of Mormon History* 37, no. 1 (Winter 2011): x–xiv.

93. Robert D. McFadden, "Mormon Official Castigates Press," *New York Times*, 9 August 1987, A27.

94. Steven Naifeh and Gregory White Smith, *The Mormon Murders: A True Story of Greed, Forgery, Deceit, and Death* (New York: Weidenfeld & Nicolson, 1988); "LDS Official Denounces 'Scurrilous' Book: Says Misstatements in 'Mormon Murders' Leave Victims Defenseless," *Deseret News*, 16 October 1988, B2; Curt Bench interview; Jan Shipps, in surveying four books written about the Hofmann murders, said this about *Mormon Murders*: "From the standpoint of the Mormon image and most everything else, by far the worst of this quartet of books is the *Mormon Murders*" (Shipps, *Sojourner in the Promised Land*, 106). See also Jan Thompson, "Victims' Families Are Hurt, Appalled: Authors Deceived Us, They Charge," *Deseret News*, 16 October 1988, B1, B2.

95. Naifeh and Smith, *Mormon Murders*, 47.

96. "LDS Official Denounces 'Scurrilous' Book," 16 October 1988, B2.

97. Shipps, *Sojourner in the Promised Land*, 106.

98. Don Braunagel, "Story of Murders, Cover-up Implicates Mormon Church," *San Diego Tribune*, 30 September 1988, C3.

99. From the book's paperback cover; quoted in Shipps, *Sojourner in the Promised Land*, 106.

100. From the dustjacket of Turley, *Victims*.

101. Jan Shipps, "The Salamander and the Saints," *Christian Century*, 13 November 1985, 1020.

102. Richard D. Poll, "Review of Encyclopedia of Mormonism: The History, Scripture, Doctrine, and Procedure of the Church of Jesus Christ of Latter-day Saints, Daniel H. Ludlow, editor in chief, 5 vols. New York: Macmillan Publishing Company, 1992," *Journal of Mormon History* 18, no. 2 (Fall 1992): 205–213. The quoted portion comes from pages 205–206. I am indebted to Professor John Welch and his wife, Jeannie, for alerting me to this story. John Welch, email correspondence with the author, 29 June 2012.

103. See "The Whispered Faith," *Time*, 11 October 1971, 25: "They keep their private lives extremely private...There is more social than legal pressure on Utah's polygamists, since they have traditionally proved difficult to prosecute."

104. See "A Deadly 'Messenger of God': Cult Leader Ervil LeBaron Leaves a Trail of Death in the West," *Time*, 29 August 1977, 31; Catherine Fox, "The Gospel of Polygamy and Murder," *Maclean's*, 20 November 1978, 6.

105. Carolyn Banks, "Grisly Tale of Polygamist Cults and Killers," *Washington Post*, 12 January 1982; photocopy included in "Mormon—Aberrant Groups" folder, Cult Awareness Network files, MSS 3288, box 1, L. Tom Perry Special Collections, Harold B. Lee Library, Brigham Young University, Provo, Utah. A cover letter with this collection reveals that the Cult Awareness Network kept files on the Latter-day Saints through the 1980s and 1990s, even though the organization never designated the LDS Church a cult (although the files contain numerous letters urging CAN to make that designation). After the CAN came under new leadership, CAN officials sent their files on Mormons to Brigham Young University.

106. James Coates, "Murderous 'Revelations' Shake Mormon Followers," *Chicago Tribune*, 20 January 1985, 4. Perhaps the most chilling element in this story was the court testimony of the Laffertys' other brother, Alan, the husband and father of the victims. He testified that "Ronald showed him the revelation" before the killings, and that he told his brother

"he should be absolutely sure that was what God wanted." Alan did not "warn his wife because 'I did not want to worry her.'"

107. Coates, "Murderous 'Revelations' Shake Mormon Followers," 4.

108. "Mormon Sects' Feud Takes New Twist," *The Oregonian*, 29 May 1987, A20.

109. See James Coates, "Polygamy, Slayings Link Mormon Cults: Utah Shooting Latest in 15-year Feud," *Chicago Tribune*, 6 December 1987, 25.

110. See "Mormon Dissidents: Polygamy Under Siege," *The Economist*, 30 January 1988, 20. See also "Resurrection Dreams," *U.S. News and World Report*, 8 February 1988, 10, which described the "melodramatic end to the siege, Swapp was shot and wounded and an officer was killed." The Singer-Swapp standoff in tiny Marion drew an especially large number of reporters. James Coates in the *Chicago Tribune* described the Mormon church parking lot that served as the reporters' base as being "jammed [with] an array of semitractor trailers carrying satellite dishes, microwave antennae and high-powered telescopic television cameras" (Coates, "Small town shines during brief stay in the media spotlight," *Chicago Tribune*, 28 January 1988, 16).

111. Coates, "Polygamy, slayings link Mormon cults," 25.

112. Ellis E. Conklin, "'They had so many children...'," 19 May 1986; copy included in "Mormon Aberrant Groups" folder, box 1, Cult Awareness Network files, L. Tom Perry Special Collections, Harold B. Lee Library, Brigham Young University, Provo, Utah.

113. Mary Catherine Bateson, "The Uses of Polygamy: Review of *In My Father's House*, by Dorothy Allred Solomon," *New York Times*, 24 February 1985; copy included in "Mormon Aberrant Groups" folder, box 1, Cult Awareness Network files.

114. Deborah Laake, *Secret Ceremonies: A Mormon Woman's Intimate Diary of Marriage and Beyond* (New York: William Morrow and Company, Inc., 1993), 13.

115. Richard N. Ostling and Joan K. Ostling, *Mormon America:The Power and the Promise* (San Francisco: HarperSan Francisco, 1999), 357.

116. Laake, *Secret Ceremonies*, 11.

117. Laake, *Secret Ceremonies*, 11, 34, 234.

118. The *Phoenix New Times*, Laake's newspaper, reported Laake's experience with what she saw as "cadres of Mormon women, hand-picked by their male priesthood leaders, [who] appeared at book signings and on talk shows. On the Sonya Live TV show, Laake debated a former Miss America and a church authority named Beverly Campbell, whom Laake describes as a 'cross between Phyllis Schlafly and Dana Carvey's Church Lady.' 'They both just screamed at me for the entire hour and said I was a liar,' Laake says. At a local broadcast in Portland, Oregon, a packed gallery hooted and laughed at inappropriate moments, and—to Laake's mind—reacted out of proportion to what she had written. She challenged the audience, asking, 'How many of you actually read my book?' Two women raised their hands, so she snapped back, 'Oh, so you're angry on the basis of hearsay?'" (Michael Kiefer, "The Year of Living Literally: Best-Selling Author Deborah Laake Survives Success, Controversy, Malignancy," *Phoenix New Times*, 25 May 1994, http://www.phoenixnewtimes. com/1994-05-25/news/the-year-of-living-literallybest-selling-author-deborah-laake-survi ves-success-controversy-malignancy/.)

119. See, for example, Kenneth L. Woodward, "The Latter-day Secret Sharer: A Pray-and-Tell Book Mocks Mormon Rituals," *Newsweek*, 28 June 1993, 59, where Woodward reported that Laake held the church responsible "for her three failed marriages, for her attempted suicide and for the two months she spent in a psychiatric institution." Deborah Laake committed suicide in 2000. After Laake's death, one friend and colleague reminisced about the extent of the award-winning journalist's mental illness in poisoning her views of the church, and in contributing to her erratic behavior even before writing *Secret Ceremonies*. See Terry Green Sterling, "Secret Grief," *Salon* (an online magazine), 27 October 2000, http://archive.salon. com/people/feature/2000/10/27/laake/index.html?CP= YAH&DN=110. Sterling remembered that "after reading *Secret Ceremonies* for the third time, shortly after her suicide, I realized she had blamed Mormonism and the men in her life for her mental illness, for the terrible dark spells that followed the giddy manic highs. *Secret Ceremonies* is nevertheless a fascinating and compelling read about Laake's struggle to survive waves of self-destructive depression."

120. Approved statement in response to the book *Secret Ceremonies* by Deborah Laake, 19 April 1993; copy in possession of the author.
121. See Kiefer, "The Year of Living Literally."
122. See, for example, the work of former Brigham Young University professor D. Michael Quinn (who was excommunicated from the church in September 1993, several years after leaving BYU). The appearance of the Salamander Letter had prompted Quinn to work on a monograph that examined the influence of folk magic on early Mormonism. Despite Hofmann's admission of forgery, Quinn published *Early Mormonism and the Magic World View* in 1987, based on numerous bits of evidence that persuaded the historian that many of Joseph Smith's ideas were flavored by a family background in magic and the occult. Though the connections were often tenuous and relied on circumstantial evidence, Quinn raised questions about the origins of a number of unique Mormon tenets, and sparked an ongoing battle with other scholars who found fault with his work. For a sense of Quinn's battle with Mormon apologists, see the introduction to his *Early Mormonism and the Magic World View*, expanded 2nd edition (Salt Lake City: Signature Books, 1994).
123. Lavina Fielding Anderson, one of the scholars excommunicated in September 1993, published only a few months earlier an extensive timeline of episodes of conflict between various church intellectuals and church leaders. See "The LDS Intellectual Community and Church Leadership: A Contemporary Chronology," *Dialogue* 26, no. 1 (Spring 1993): 7–64.
124. See "Six Intellectuals Disciplined for Apostasy," *Sunstone*, November 1983, 65–75, for extensive coverage of the events surrounding the disciplinary councils for Lavina Fielding Anderson, Avraham Gileadi, Maxine Hanks, Lynne Kanavel Whitesides, Paul Toscano, and D. Michael Quinn.
125. See "Mormons Penalize Dissident Members," *New York Times*, 19 September 1993, section 1, page 31: "At least six Utah Mormons who have spoken out on church issues believe they are being stripped of certain church privileges this month in an effort by leaders to purge the faith of critics and dissidents." Also Dirk Johnson, "As Mormon Church Grows, So Does Dissent From Feminists and Scholars," *New York Times*, 2 October 1993, section 1, page 7; "Mormon Leaders Back Acts of Discipline," *Washington Times*, 23 October 1993, D4. Mark A. Kellner, "Latter-day Saints: Prophet's Grandson Quits Church in Public Protest," *Christianity Today*, 22 November 1993, 46. See "Mormon Leaders Back Acts of Discipline," D4; "Mormons Penalize Dissident Members," 31. Sandra Tanner to Mark Kellner, "Latter-day Saints: Prophet's Grandson Quits Church in Public Protest," 46.
126. Dallin H. Oaks's comments were published in the *Deseret News*, 2 October 1993; cited in "Six Intellectuals Disciplined for Apostasy," *Sunstone*, November 1993, 69, 73. D. Michael Quinn, interview by author.
127. See Ostling and Ostling, "Dissenters and Exiles," chapter 21, *Mormon America*, 351–371; Paul Toscano, interview by author, 15 February 2010.
128. See Ostling and Ostling, *Mormon America*, 357, and Newell G. Bringhurst and Craig L. Foster, *The Mormon Quest for the Presidency: From Joseph Smith to Mitt Romney and Jon Huntsman* (Independence, Missouri: John Whitmer Books, 2011), 223–225. Bringhurst and Foster summarize church and media attention to 1992 presidential candidate and "ultraconservative" James "Bo" Gritz and his "erstwhile Mormon followers." Local church authorities took action against Gritz after he openly refused to pay his income taxes, and then Gritz withdrew his LDS membership in 1994. Bringhurst and Foster also document the 1992 excommunication of James Harmston, who protested against "the church's support of the New World Order" and established "his own schismatic group" in Manti, Utah.
129. See Susanna McBee, "The Flowering of Religious Dissent," *U.S. News and World Report*, 8 September 1986, 63; Jeffery L. Sheler and Betsy Wagner, "Latter-day Struggles," *U.S. News and World Report*, 28 September 1992, 73.
130. Paul Toscano interview; Curt Bench interview; Ostling and Ostling, *Mormon America*, 363.
131. See T. R. Reid, "Thousands Mourn Leader of Mormons; Benson, Likely Successor, Presides Over Service," *Washington Post*, 10 November 1985, A3; "Man in the News: Ezra Taft Benson, New Chief of the Mormons," *New York Times*, 12 November 1985; A16; Kenneth L. Woodward and Jack Goodman, "Thus Saith Ezra Benson," *Newsweek*, 19 October 1981, 109;

132. Kellner, "Latter-day Saints: Prophet's Grandson Quits," 46.

133. See Kellner, "Latter-day Saints: Prophet's Grandson Quits Church," 46, for the statement by LDS spokesman Arnold Augustin that "church leadership is stable despite Ezra Taft Benson's advanced age." See also Peggy Fletcher Stack, interview by author, 5, where she talked about a story she wrote for the *Salt Lake Tribune* after Howard W. Hunter succeeded Ezra Taft Benson as church president. "I remember that lead as something like, 'We heard a prophet's voice for the first time,' because President Benson didn't speak at conference for like five years, and so I said that we had heard a prophet's voice for the first time in five years. People around here got really mad because they said there were other prophets."

134. See Peggy Fletcher Stack, interview by the author, 4, where she said that, in her experience reporting for the *Salt Lake Tribune*, LDS church public relations representatives "certainly did not want to talk about President Benson's health. Anyone who raised that issue was seen as suspect of somehow having a negative agenda."

135. See "Attitudes and Opinions Towards Religion: OK? or Religious attitudes of adults (over 18) who are residents of six major metropolitan areas in the United States: Seattle, Los Angeles, Kansas City, Dallas, Chicago, New York City—August 1973," L. Tom Perry Special Collections, Harold B. Lee Library, Brigham Young University, Provo, Utah, 17. Martin E. Marty, "Foreword," in Klaus J. Hansen, *Mormonism and the American Experience* (Chicago and London: The University of Chicago Press, 1981), ix; Oaks, "Speaking Today," 63; Barna Research Group, "Americans' Impressions of Various Church Denominations," 18 September 1991, copy in the author's possession, 1: "How favorably do you consider the Mormon denomination? Very favorably—6%"; Question qn19k, The Gallup Poll #978, 14 June 1977, accessed at Gallup Brain database, http://brain.gallup.com/home.aspx. The 1977 poll used a numerical scale to gauge opinion, from +5 (for a very favorable opinion) to -5 (for a very unfavorable opinion); 9.88% answered "+5," and 7.92% "+4," so that if "+5" and "+4" are taken together as "very favorable," 18% of respondents gave that rating. While the different metrics of the polls do not make for precise matches, for comparative purposes the decline is apparent. Also in 1977, 36% of respondents gave Mormons a "+1, +2, or +3" rating; in the 1991 Barna survey, only 21% felt "somewhat favorable" about Latter-day Saints. Therefore, in 1977, 54% of those surveyed ranked Mormons on the positive side of the scale, while in 1991, only 27 percent ranked Mormons favorably. Baptist churches ranked the highest in this 1991 favorability study at a 29 percent "very favorably" rating ("Americans' Impressions of Various Church Denominations," 2).

136. Val Edwards, interview by the author, 6, contrasting his experience in the church's public relations office, beginning in the early 1980s: "I think in the earlier days, the department was seen as just a channel by which the desires and kind of the messages of the Brethren were taken to the news media. Now [2008] obviously we still do that, but now we do so much more with that...we are talking to the journalist. That was just a huge difference than what it was, than what happened that I recall with the Hofmann issue."

137. See James L. Clayton, "On the Different World of Utah: The Mormon Church," *Vital Speeches of the Day*, January 1986, 186, http://brain.gallup.com/home.aspx, for an articulation of the individual versus institutional image situation in Mormonism.

138. John Ed Bradley, "BYU: Fourth-Ranked Cougars Are a Large Army of Do-rights Possessed with...Goodness," *Los Angeles Times*, 7 November 1984, B1 and B7; Peter Bart, "Prigging Out," *Rolling Stone*, 14 April 1983, 89; italics added. See also D. Donahue, "Miss America Explains How and Why She Says No to Sex," *People Weekly*, 26 November 1984, 109, 111; Tom Callahan, "Cougars: 'We Are Too 1!'" *Time*, 31 December 1984, 71.

139. Peggy Fletcher Stack, interview with the author, 3.

Chapter 7

1. The title of this chapter is taken from a book published by Gordon B. Hinckley, *Stand a Little Taller: Counsel and Inspiration for Each Day of the Year* (Salt Lake City: Eagle Gate, 2001).

2. Peggy Fletcher Stack, interview by author, 12 December 2008, transcript in possession of the author, 5–6. See also Sheri L. Dew, *Go Forward with Faith: The Biography of Gordon B. Hinckley* (Salt Lake City: Deseret Book, 1996), 510–511, for other reactions to the impromptu press conference. Bruce Olsen remembered that the press conference was not planned. Bruce Olsen, interview by author, 17 October 2008, transcript, 4. When Spencer W. Kimball was named church president in 1973, he also held a press conference. But reporters were caught off guard in 1995 because that had not happened in the cases of President Hinckley's two immediate predecessors. See Twila Van Leer, "Pres. Hinckley Ordained LDS Prophet," *Deseret News*, 13 March 1995, http://www.deseretnews.com/article/409421/PRES-HINCKLEY-ORDAINED-LDS-PROPHET.html?pg=all. Compare Edward L. Kimball, *Lengthen Your Stride: The Presidency of Spencer W. Kimball* (Salt Lake City: Deseret Book, 2005), 7–8. 145–146, for Spencer Kimball's experiences with press conferences.

3. Gordon B. Hinckley, "'Remember... Thy Church, O Lord'," *Ensign*, May 1996, 82.

4. Quoted in Dew, *Go Forward with Faith*, 543.

5. Dew, *Go Forward with Faith*, 511. See also the assessment of Associated Press writer Jennifer Dobner after the first ten years of Hinckley's presidency: "President Hinckley: 'A Man for His Time,'" *Salt Lake Tribune*, 2 April 2005.

6. Mark Tuttle, interview by author, 20 August 2008, transcript, 8–9; Bruce Olsen, interview by author, 12 August 2008, transcript, 2.

7. Dew, *Go Forward with Faith*, 537–538.

8. Out of the "defensive mode": Bruce Olsen, interview, 12 August 2008,, 1.

9. Stephen B. Allen, interview by Jonice Hubbard, 6 November 2006; transcript included in the appendix of Hubbard, "Pioneers in Twentieth Century Mormon Media: Oral Histories of Latter-day Saint Electronic and Public Relations Professionals" (master's thesis, Brigham Young University, 2007), 42.

10. Val Edwards, interview by author, 21 August 2008, transcript in possession of the author, 3–4.

11. Richard P. Lindsay, interview by Jonice Hubbard, 24 August 2006, transcript included in the appendix of Hubbard, "Pioneers in Twentieth Century Mormon Media," 98–99; "LDS Official Testifies on Families," *Deseret News*, 23 September 1983, B-1; "Religious Leaders Join Together, Pledge to Fight Drug-related Crime," *Church News*, 17 June 1989, 5; Richard P. Lindsay, interview by author, 2 February 2007, transcript in possession of the author, 3.

12. Peggy Fletcher Stack, interview by author, 3; Val Edwards, interview by author, 3, 6.

13. Barna Research Group, "Americans' Impressions of Various Church Denominations," 18 September 1991, copy in the author's possession, 3. Compare question qn19k, The Gallup Poll #978, 14 June 1977, accessed at Gallup Brain database, http://brain.gallup.com/home.aspx.

14. Bruce Olsen, interview by author, 12 August 2008, 1, 3–4.

15. Bruce Olsen, interview by author, 12 August 2008, 1.

16. Mark Tuttle, interview by author, 10.

17. M. Russell Ballard, "Sharing the Gospel Message through the Media," in *Out of Obscurity: Public Affairs and the Worldwide Church: The 8th Annual Conference of the International Society, 17–18 August 1997* (Provo, Utah: Brigham Young University, 1998), 3.

18. Mark Tuttle, interview by author, 20 August 2008, transcript in possession of the author, 2; Bruce Olsen, interview by author, 12 August 2008, 1; Bruce Olsen, interview by Jonice Hubbard, 107–108.

19. *How to organize a public relations program in stakes and missions: The Church of Jesus Christ of Latter-day Saints* (Salt Lake City: The Church of Jesus Christ of Latter-day Saints, 1967, 1973, and 1977), 1. Copies of all of the handbooks are available at L. Tom Perry Special Collections, Harold B. Lee Library, Brigham Young University, Provo, Utah.

20. *Public Affairs Handbook* (Salt Lake City: The Church of Jesus Christ of Latter-day Saints, 1992), 1, 7–8; compare *How to organize a public relations program in stakes and missions: The Church of Jesus Christ of Latter-day Saints* (1977), 4; Bruce Olsen, interview by author, 12 August 2008, 4.

21. *Public Affairs Handbook*, 2.

22. Report of the Communications Futures Committee, internal document, Public Affairs Department, The Church of Jesus Christ of Latter-day Saints, 4, 15, 46. The committee was chaired by Apostle David B. Haight, and included apostles James E. Faust and M. Russell Ballard, prominent political pollster Dr. Richard B. Wirthlin, and Bruce Olsen.

23. Report of the Communications Futures Committee, 24, 26–27.

24. Report of the Communications Futures Committee, 43–44; Bruce Olsen, interview by Jonice Hubbard, 108; *Deseret News, 1997–1998 Church Almanac* (Salt Lake City: Deseret News, 1996), 515. Compare also Ballard, "Sharing the Gospel Message through the Media," 3–4.

25. Dew, *Go Forward with Faith*, 539–540; Bruce Olsen, interview by Jonice Hubbard, 108.

26. Neal A. Maxwell quoted in Dew, *Go Forward with Faith*, 546; Ballard, "Sharing the Gospel Message through the Media," 3.

27. See Dew, *Go Forward with Faith*, 545; David van Biema, "Kingdom Come," *Time*, 4 August 1997, 56–57 (the interview was conducted by Richard Ostling); a copy of the September 1998 *Larry King Live* transcript, accessed 1 April 2010, http://www.lds-mormon.com/lkl_00.shtml. (See also W. Jeffrey Marsh, "When the Press Meets the Prophet," chapter 17 of *Out of Obscurity: The LDS Church in the Twentieth Century: The 29th Annual Sperry Symposium* (Salt Lake City: Deseret Book, 2000), 242–259. Marsh analyzed printed transcripts of twenty-five media interviews with President Hinckley and then tabulated the frequency with which various questions came up in the interviews. "The topics that were of significant interest to the media (averaging about one of every fifty questions) included Brigham Young University, the welfare program, excommunication from the Church, forgiveness, race relations, spouse or child abuse, revelation, temple and temple rites, and the health code in the Mormon faith (the Word of Wisdom)." Of "moderate interest" were "access to LDS historical documents" and "polygamy"; of "highest interest" were "the role of women in the Church, Mormon relations with people of other faiths," and "tithing and church finances" (248).

28. Transcript of *60 Minutes*, CBS, 7 April 1996, accessed 1 April 2010, http://www.lds-mormon.com/60min.shtml.

29. Bruce Olsen, interview by Jonice Hubbard, 110; Dew, *Go Forward With Faith*, 543; "Hinckley Takes LDS Case to the Nation," *Salt Lake Tribune*, 8 April 1996; Peggy Fletcher Stack, "Mike Wallace: CBS Icon Visits His Friend," *Salt Lake Tribune*, 23 July 2005. See Gordon B. Hinckley, *Standing for Something: 10 Neglected Virtues That Will Heal Our Hearts and Homes*, with a foreword by Mike Wallace (New York: Times Books, 2000).

30. David van Biema, "Kingdom Come," *Time*, 4 August 1997, 56; Kenneth L. Woodward, "A Mormon Moment," *Newsweek*, 10 September 2001, 48. BYU professor Robert Millet has made an important argument that the LDS Church's perceptible shift to more Christian or "evangelical" themes since the 1980s corresponded with Church President Ezra Taft Benson's call that Mormons study and teach from the Book of Mormon, a scripture replete with discourses on grace and the need for an atoning Savior. See, for example, Millet, "Joseph Smith and Modern Mormonism: Orthodoxy, Neoorthodoxy, Tension, and Tradition," *BYU Studies* 29, no. 3 (1989): 49–68. Renowned LDS historian Richard Bushman raised essentially the same point in a discussion with journalists and academics at the Pew Forum's biannual Faith Angle Conference, 14 May 2007. Bushman was the forum's guest speaker, and *Newsweek*'s Kenneth Woodward asked about the place of grace in Mormon theology. Bushman responded: "In dialogues with evangelical Christians, Mormons are recovering their own grace theology, which is plentifully presented in the Book of Mormon. And they are recovering it not just at the high level of discussion between BYU faculty and Baylor faculty, but right down in the congregation" ("Mormonism and Democratic Politics: Are They Compatible?" transcript, http://pewforum.org/Politics-and-Elections/Mormonism-and-Politics-Are-They-Compatible.aspx, 16).

31. David van Biema, "Kingdom Come," *Time*, 4 August 1997, 56–57; italics added.

32. Gordon B. Hinckley to Mike Wallace, transcript of *60 Minutes*, 7 April 1996.

33. Val Edwards, interview by author, 7; Ballard, "Sharing the Gospel Message through the Media," 5.

34. Ballard, "Sharing the Gospel Message through the Media," 5; Richard B. Wirthlin, "Public Affairs Challenges for the Growing, Global Church," in *Out of Obscurity: Public Affairs and the Worldwide Church*, 10

35. Val Edwards, interview by author, 7; Ballard, "Sharing the Gospel Message through the Media," 4.

36. Ballard, "Sharing the Gospel Message through the Media," 6; Doctrine and Covenants 1:30; Mark Tuttle, interview by author, 8; Casey W. Olson, *"The Church of Jesus Christ of Latter-day Saints in National Periodicals: 1991–2000"* (master's thesis, Brigham Young University, 2007), 129, 132.

37. Val Edwards, interview by author, 7; Mark Tuttle, interview by author, 8.

38. See, for example, Ana Figueroa, "Salt Lake's Big Jump," *Newsweek*, 10 September 2001, 52–53; William Booth, "An Olympic Challenge: Counter Mormon Image; Salt Lake City Says It's So Much More," *Washington Post*, 28 January 2002, A1.

39. "Focus for Public Affairs Work: First Presidency Presentation, 18 December 2002," copy in possession of the author, 5; "Public Affairs Department: Five-Year Plan, 2000–2004," copy in possession of the author, 13; " Public Affairs Department, 6.

40. An updated version (2007) of the "Myths and Reality" video is available at the LDS Church's Newsroom website: http://www.newsroom.lds.org/ldsnewsroom/eng/news-releases-stories/video-challenges-public-misperceptions-explains-myths-vs-reality.

41. "Public Affairs—Building on a New Foundation of Heightened Recognition for the Church—Resource Review, 25 June 2002," Public Affairs Department, internal document, copy in possession of the author, 3–6.

42. "Public Affairs—Building on a New Foundation of Heightened Recognition for the Church—Resource Review, 25 June 2002," Public Affairs Department, internal document, copy in possession of the author, 14, 17. "Core Purpose," Public Affairs Department, copy in possession of the author.

43. Tiffany E. Lewis, "Media Spotlight Shines on Church," *Ensign*, May 2002, 111; Hank Stuever, "Unmentionable No Longer: What Do Mormons Wear? A Polite Smile, if Asked about 'the Garment,'" *Washington Post*, 26 February 2002, C1. "U.S. Takes Gold as Perfect Host," *Chicago Sun-Times*, 26 February 2002, 23; Eric Fisher, "2002 Winter Olympics were as Good as Gold," *Washington Times*, 26 February 2002, A1; *Chicago Tribune*, 25 February 2002, as quoted in Lewis, "Media Spotlight Shines on Church," 110; C. G. Wallace, "Olympics Gave Mormonism Chance to Shine, Leader Says," *San Diego Union-Tribune*, 7 April 2002, A4; Stuever, "Unmentionable No Longer," C1. See also Felix Hoover, "Mormons Get the Word Out: Olympics Improved LDS Church's Image, Scholar Concludes," *Columbus (Ohio) Dispatch*, 8 March 2002, E1; Brandon Griggs, "Games Bright Spot in Otherwise Grim Year," *Salt Lake Tribune*, 1 January 2003, A1.

44. Amy Shebeck, "Colorblind Faith," *Chicago Reporter*, July/August 2006, http://www.chicagoreporter.com/news/2007/09/colorblind-faith.

45. Quoted in Armand L. Mauss, "Casting off the 'Curse of Cain': The Extent and Limits of Progress since 1978," in Newell G. Bringhurst and Darron T. Smith, eds., *Black and Mormon* (Urbana and Chicago: University of Illinois Press, 2004), 92–93. See also "Regional NAACP Meeting Begins Thursday in S.L.; LDS President Hinckley to speak at noon Friday," *Salt Lake Tribune*, 21 April 1998, B3; Peg McEntee, "Families Can Save Us, Hinckley Says; LDS leader addresses NAACP in S.L, a first for a Mormon Church president," *Salt Lake Tribune*, 25 April 1998, A1.

46. Bill Broadway, "Black Mormons Resist Apology Talk," *Washington Post*, 30 May 1998, B09; Richard N. Ostling and Joan K. Ostling, *Mormon America: The Power and the Promise* (San Francisco: HarperSan Francisco, 1999), 104–105; Mauss, "Casting off the 'Curse of Cain,'" 83, 92. See Mauss's summary of several studies that demonstrate that "Mormons had equaled or exceeded the national averages in their support of various civil rights for black citizens," and that "Mormons [are] among the more 'liberal' of the various denominations

in attitudes toward racial justice" (94–97); also Daniel K Judd, "Religiosity, Mental Heath, and the Latter-day Saints: A Preliminary Review of Literature (1923–1995)," in James T. Duke, ed., *Latter-day Saint Social Life: Social Research on the LDS Church and its Members* (Provo, Utah: Religious Studies Center, Brigham Young University, 1998), 485. See also Larry B. Stammer, "Mormon Leader Defends Race Relations; Interview: Gordon B. Hinckley says church does not need to further disavow its former teachings that blacks are cursed of God," *Los Angeles Times*, 12 September 1998, 4.

47. Bruce R. McConkie, "All Are Alike Unto God," address given to Church Educational System teachers, Brigham Young University, 18 August 1978, copy in the author's possession; "Apostles Talk About Reasons for Lifting Ban," *Provo Daily Herald*, 5 June 1988, 21; Mauss, "Casting off the 'Curse of Cain,'" 94. Compare also Juan Henderson, "A Time for Healing: Official Declaration 2," chapter 11 in *Out of Obscurity: The LDS Church in the Twentieth Century: The 29th Sperry Symposium* (Salt Lake City: Deseret Book, 2000), 151–160.

48. Mauss, "Casting off the 'Curse of Cain,'" 88–89.

49. See Henry B. Eyring, "Freedman's Bank Records Announcement," 26 February 2001, copy in possession of the author, 1–3. See also Mauss, "Casting off the 'Curse of Cain,'" 87–89.

50. Leonard Pitts, "Filling the Gap in Blacks' Lives," *Chicago Tribune*, 6 March 2001, 15; Marian Dozier, *(Fort Lauderdale) South Florida Sun-Sentinel*, 28 February 2001, 1B; "Mormon Church Releases Records of Former Slaves' Bank Accounts," *Los Angeles Sentinel*, 7 March 2001, A1; Vicki T. Lee, "New CD-Rom Makes Ancestor Search Easier: May Provide Clues to Millions of African-American Descendants," *Baltimore Afro-American*, 9 March 2001, A1; "Descendants of Slaves,...Know Thyself," *Chicago Defender*, 22 February 2001, 11. See also Linda Wheeler, "Ex-Slaves' Bank Data Compiled on CD-ROM; Searchable Disk Details Homeland, Kin of 480,000," *Washington Post*, 27 February 2001, B3; Jill Nelson, "Old Bank's Records Open View of Past," *USA Today*, 9 March 2001, A13.

51. Beverly Beyette, "Interest Grows in Freedman's Bank: The Mormon Church is behind a project that has put records from a bank for former slaves onto CD-ROM," *Los Angeles Time*, 4 April 2001, E1.

52. Shebeck, "Colorblind Faith"; Andy Newman, "For Mormons in Harlem, A Bigger Space Beckons," *New York Times*, 2 October 2005, http://www.nytimes.com/2005/10/02/nyregion/02mormon.html?_r=0 H. Allen Hurst, "Black Saints in a White Church; Mormon Church grows in urban areas despite racist reputation," *Baltimore Afro-American*, 23 December 2005, accessed 10 April 2010, HighBeam Research, http://www.highbeam.com/doc/1P1-117831794.html; Miriam Hill, "Mormons Gain in Inner Cities; Church is attracting more blacks and Hispanics," *Philadelphia Inquirer*, 10 December 2005, A1.

53. For example, beginning with the May 2000 General Conference edition of the *Ensign* magazine and counting through the November 2005 edition, 33 to 50 percent of all of the published photographs of Mormon conference-goers featured people of color. See J. B. Haws, "Behold, The Lord Esteemeth All Flesh In One," unpublished paper, 2005, 13–14. For earlier changes, see Newell G. Bringhurst, "The Image of Blacks within Mormonism as Presented in the *Church News* (1978–1988)," *American Periodicals* 2, (Fall 1992): 113–123. See also "Race Relations," Newsroom, The Church of Jesus Christ of Latter-day Saints, June 2008, http://www.mormonnewsroom.org/topic/race-relations. "President Hinckley Celebrates 90th Birthday," *Ensign*, Sept. 2000, 75; Bonnie Boyd, "New Museum Exhibit Highlights Relief Society," *Ensign*, Aug. 2007, 79–80.

54. "Outreach Efforts," Public Affairs Report to the First Presidency, 8 January 2003, copy in the author's possession, 1; Pastor Edward Lockett, Metropolitan Methodist Episcopal Church, Houston, quoted in "What Texans Are Saying About Members of the [LDS] Church," Newsroom, The Church of Jesus Christ of Latter-day Saints, 26 June 2008, http://www.mormonnewsroom.org/additional-resource/what-texans-are-saying-about-members-of-the-church.

55. President Hinckley's statement to the NAACP is quoted in Mauss, "Casting off the 'Curse of Cain,'" 92; Gordon B. Hinckley, "The Need for Greater Kindness," *Ensign*, May 2006,

58–59; Pastor Murray, in *"Nobody Knows: The Untold Story of Black Mormons*—Script," *Dialogue* 42, no. 3 (Fall 2009): 124–125.

56. "Dialogue Is the Christian Option": Craig Blomberg, interview by author, 12 September 2008, transcript in author's possession, 4.

57. John Hiscock, "Mormons Face Holy War," *(London) Daily Telegraph*, 11 June 1998, 23; Neil J. Young, "Southern Baptists vs. the Mormons: Mike Huckabee's and Mitt Romney's Faiths Have Tangled Before," *Slate*, 19 December 2007, http://www.slate.com/articles/ life/faithbased/2007/12/southern_baptists_vs_the_mormons.html; "Fundamental Differences," *New York Times*, 31 May 1998, SM19; Larry B. Stammer, "Evangelicals Crusading in Mormon Utah," *Los Angeles Times*, 8 June 1998, 1; "A Cordial Welcome to Baptists," *Deseret News*, 5 June 1998, A12; Peggy Fletcher Stack, "Dodge the Christianity Debate, Hinckley Says; Just Proclaim Faith in the Savior Without Acrimony Toward Other Churches, He Counsels; LDS Teachers Told They Have Sacred Obligation," *Salt Lake Tribune*, 5 April 1998, A1; Gustav Niebuhr, "In Face-Off of Faiths, Kindness Is Winner," *New York Times*, 14 June 1998, section 1, page 20. See also Linda Thomson, "LDS, Baptists Hold 'Gracious Talks,'" *Deseret News*, 6 June 1998, A1. See Jan Shipps's insightful survey of the episode: "Media Coverage of the Southern Baptist Convention in Salt Lake City," chapter 5 of *Sojourner in the Promised Land: Forty Years Among the Mormons* (Urbana and Chicago: University of Illinois Press, 2000), 143–154.

58. Gordon B. Hinckley, "This Is the Work of the Master," *Ensign*, May 1995, 71; the quote from Joseph Smith comes from *History of the Church*, 5: 498.

59. Gordon B. Hinckley, "Excerpts from Recent Addresses of President Gordon B. Hinckley," *Ensign*, August 1998, 72.

60. Stephen E. Robinson, *Are Mormons Christians?* (Salt Lake City: Bookcraft, 1991); Greg Johnson, interview by author, 2 March 2010; Robert L. Millet, interview by author, 16 March 2007, transcript in author's possession, 2; Craig Blomberg, interview by author, 2–3;

61. See Craig L. Blomberg and Stephen E. Robinson, *How Wide the Divide?: A Mormon and an Evangelical in Conversation* (Downers Grove, Illinois: InterVarsity Press, 1997), especially each author's introduction, 9–32. See also Craig Blomberg, interview by author, 2.

62. Craig Blomberg, interview by author, 3; Blomberg and Robinson, *How Wide the Divide?* 14.

63. Robert L. Millet, "What We Believe," Brigham Young University Devotional Address, 3 February 1998, accessed 17 April 2010, http://speeches.byu.edu/reader/reader.php?id= 2575&x=61&y=7.

64. "General Commentary—Year-end Closing 1998," Public Affairs Department internal document, copy in possession of the author, 3. See also Shipps, *Sojourner in the Promised Land*, 150: "The staff of the LDS Public Affairs Department was also satisfied, expressing no complaint about the media's characterization of Mormon theology and doctrine and the way they differ from Baptist belief." See "Carter Says Mormons Are Christians," *Sunstone*, November 1997, 79.

65. From a two-page, unpublished typescript of personal reminiscences by Truman G. Madsen, "The Richard L. Evans Chair," 1; copy in possession of the author. The background to the establishment of the chair is also explained, with additional details, in the pamphlet announcing the Chair's establishment. See "The Richard L. Evans Chair of Christian Understanding: A Special Heritage in Religion," Dean's Office, Religious Education, Brigham Young University; copy in possession of the author. Dillon K. Inouye, "Truman Madsen, Valued Teacher," in Donald W. Parry, Daniel C. Peterson, and Stephen D. Ricks, eds., *Revelation, Reason, and Faith: Essays in Honor of Truman G. Madsen* (Provo, Utah: Foundation for Ancient Research and Mormon Studies, 2002), xxx. Fifteen contributors to the four-volume encyclopedia were not Latter-day Saints. Lutheran official and former Harvard Dean Krister Stendahl even wrote an entry on baptism for the dead, commenting on the possibility of ancient Christian ties to Mormonism's unique concept of proxy ordinance work.

66. Robert L. Millet, interview by author, 16 March 2007, transcript in author's possession, 1–2.

67. See Robert L. Millet, "Richard L. Evans Professorship: Report of Activities for the Year 2001" and "Richard L. Evans Professorship: Report of Activities for the Year 2002," copies in author's possession; Roger R. Keller, "Synopsis of Evans Chair Activity: September through December 2001," and "Evans Chair Report: January 2003 to December 2003," copies in author's possession.

68. Carl Mosser and Paul Owen, "Mormon Scholarship, Apologetics, and Evangelical Neglect: Losing the Battle and Not Knowing It?" *Trinity Journal* 19 (Fall 1998): 179–205; Francis J. Beckwith, Carl Mosser, and Paul Owen, eds., *The New Mormon Challenge: Responding to the Latest Defenses of a Fast-Growing Movement* (Grand Rapids, Michigan: Zondervan, 2002), 9–10, 69.

69. Richard Mouw, "Foreword," in Beckwith, Mosser, and Owen, *The New Mormon Challenge*, 11; David L. Paulsen, "A General Response to *The New Mormon Challenge*," *FARMS Review* 14, no. 1 (2002); Craig Blomberg, interview by author, 4–5; Craig Blomberg, "Is Mormonism Christian?" in Beckwith, Mosser, and Owen, *The New Mormon Challenge*, 332.

70. Robert L. Millet, "Richard L. Evans Professorship: Report of Activities for the Year 2001," unpublished report, copy in author's possession, 2–3; Greg Johnson, interview by author; Craig Blomberg, interview by author, 5.

71. Greg Johnson, interview by author.

72. Greg Johnson, interview by author; Ravi Zacharias, "A Note from Ravi about the Mormon Tabernacle Event," accessed 13 February 2010, http://www.rzim.org/justthinkingfv/tabid/602/articleid/107/cbmoduleid/1047/default.aspx.

73. Standing Together ministries produced a DVD which included Richard Mouw's and Ravi Zacharias's addresses: *In Pursuit of Truth* (2004). Compare also the comments accessed 19 April 2010, http://www.standing together.org/itn_011505.html.

74. Greg Johnson, interview by author; Bill Heersink, interview by author, 15 February 2010. See also Keith Walker (Evidence Ministries), "A 'Mouwtainous' Mistake: An Open Letter to Richard Mouw and Other Academics Involved in Apologetics to Mormons," at the website "Apologetics Index," accessed 19 April 2010, http://www.apologeticsindex.org/cpoint13-1.html.

75. Robert L. Millet, *A Different Jesus?: The Christ of the Latter-day Saints* (Grand Rapids, Michigan: Wm. B. Eerdman's, 2005), 183. See this reaction from James White, whose apologetics ministry targets Mormonism: "Yes, friends and neighbors, not only has Richard Mouw apologized for all of us mean-spirited folks who have labored to witness the true God and the true Christ and the true Gospel to Mormons for decades, but now he has made sure to provide a 'Trojan Horse Apologetic,' a work that attacks the Trinity, deity of Christ, sola scriptura, justification by grace through faith alone, the sovereignty of God in salvation, the finished work of Christ on the cross—OK, like I said, it is an LDS work of apologetics, so it is pretty well opposed to sound theology at just about every point—and he has made sure that book will be right there in your local Christian bookstore (how many bookstore owners will recognize it for what it is? Then again, what section will they put it in anyway?). Cards, roses, and copies of the Book of Mormon can be sent to Fuller Seminary in thanks" (*Alpha and Omega Ministries Apologetics (Blog)*, accessed 19 April 2010, http://www.aomin.org/aoblog/index.php?itemid=398, on). See David L. Rowe, *I [Love] Mormons: A New Way to Share Christ with Latter-day Saints* (Grand Rapids, Michigan: Baker Books, 2005); "love" is bracketed because on the cover, the word is represented by a heart shape. The book has cover endorsements from Craig Blomberg and David Neff. See this telling passage: "I'm convinced there's another part of our fear that runs deeper: religions like Mormonism, rooted heavily (though only partially) in New England Protestant Christianity, may stand as an indictment to Protestants because they arose to compensate for some perceived failure in that Christian movement. The founder of Mormonism, Joseph Smith Jr., saw disunity among the Christian denominations and started a single 'true Church' that he believed would unify all members and spell an end to denominational schism; he saw traditional churches not always caring for the poor and needy, so he started a church with its own welfare system. I've often felt that part of

our own blindness amounts to fear of the reminder of our own failures, a reminder that stands up in front of us in the form of the other group's compensations. So rather than confess and fight the fear within us, we too often would rather go on the attack against their aberrant doctrines! We simply need to do what I was not ready to do back then. We need to confess, then overcome our fears and blindness by God's grace and find a better way to touch our LDS friends with the love of God out of our own security in that love." Compare Dave Hunt, *The Cult Explosion: An Expose of Today's Cults and Why They Prosper* (Irvine, California: Harvest House Publishers, 1980); Paul R. Martin, *Cult Proofing Your Kids* (Grand Rapids, Michigan: Zondervan, 1993).

76. "The truth...can't hurt us": Glen Leonard, interview with author, 3 March 2010.

77. Interview with Truman Madsen, 22 March 2007. See also the "Introduction" of Donald Parry and Dana M. Pike, eds., *LDS Perspectives on the Dead Sea Scrolls* (Provo, Utah: Foundation for Ancient Research and Mormon Studies, 1997), for a timeline of Latter-Saint involvement with Dead Sea Scroll scholarship. Beginning in 2006, ISPART was subsumed in a new umbrella institution at Brigham Young University, the Neal A. Maxwell Institute for Religious Scholarship. See "BYU renames ISPART to Neal A. Maxwell Institute for Religious Scholarship," 1 March 2006, http://news.byu.edu/archive06-Mar-maxwell.aspx. Now CPART (Center for the Preservation of Ancient Religious Texts) is one of several initiatives sponsored by the Maxwell Institute; see http://maxwellinstitute.byu.edu/.

78. Robert L. Millet, "Richard L. Evans Professorship: Report of Activities for the Year 2003," copy in author's possession, 3; David Paulsen, interview by author, 8 March 2007, transcript in author's possession, 1–2; Michael Paulson, "Colleges Scramble to Offer Curriculum on Mormon Religion," *Boston Globe*, 19 February 2008. See M. Gerald Bradford's thorough and informative essay, "The Study of Mormonism: A Growing Interest in Academia," *The FARMS Review* 19, no. 1 (2007): 119–174. For Utah Valley University, see http://religion.byu.edu/event/uvu-annual-mormon-studies-conference. For announcement of the first Tanner Center Mormon Studies fellowship, see http://www.unews.utah.edu/p/?r=042210-1, accessed 1 May 2010.

79. Douglas J. Davies, interview by author, 22 February 2007, transcript in possession of the author, 4, 6; Terryl Givens, interview by author, 15 August 2011, transcript in possession of the author, 3.

80. John L. Brooke, *The Refiner's Fire: The Making of Mormon Cosmology, 1644–1844* (Cambridge: Cambridge University Press, 1994), 304. See also Jan Shipps, *Sojourner in the Promised Land: Forty Years Among the Mormons* (Urbana and Chicago: University of Illinois Press, 2000), 205; compare also Richard Bushman, "The Mysteries of Mormonism," *Journal of the Early Republic* 15, no. 3 (1995): 501–505, and Philip Barlow, "Decoding Mormonism," *Christian Century*, 17 January 1996, 52–53.

81. On the staff consolidation, see "Joseph Smith Papers Project Moving Ahead," Newsroom, The Church of Jesus Christ of Latter-day Saints, 17 June 2005, accessed 19 April 2010, http://newsroom.lds.org/ldsnewsroom/eng/news-releases-stories/joseph-smith-papers-project-moving-ahead; "About the Project," accessed 19 April 2010, at josephsmithpapers.org.

82. Curt Bench, interview by the author, 10 February 2010; Glen Leonard, interview by author. Leonard was one of the three coauthors, along with Ronald Walker and Richard Turley. Their unflinching account was eventually published by Oxford University Press in 2008 as *Massacre at Mountain Meadows* (New York and London: Oxford University Press, 2008), and sold, by Curt Bench's estimate, 50,000 copies.

83. Richard Lyman Bushman, *Joseph Smith: Rough Stone Rolling* (New York: Alfred A. Knopf, 2005), xxii; Curt Bench, interview by author; Stout's appraisal comes from the dust jacket of *Rough Stone Rolling*.

84. Bushman, *Rough Stone Rolling*, xxiv; significantly, he was giving credit to Elizabeth Dulany and Richard Wentworth at the University of Illinois Press, longtime publishers of Mormon-related studies, as a "key factor" in the "fluorescence of Mormon studies." See "New Church History Library to Be Constructed," Newsroom, The Church of Jesus Christ

of Latter-day Saints, 20 April 2005, accessed April 19, 2010, http://newsroom.lds.org/ldsnewsroom/eng/news-releases-stories/new-church-history-library-to-be-constructed; Scott Christensen, comments to author, 5 March 2007.

85. Michael K. Winder, *Presidents and Prophets: The Story of America's Presidents and the LDS Church* (American Fork, Utah: Covenant Communications, 2007), 393–394.

86. See the report of the conference, published as "The Worlds of Joseph Smith: A Bicentennial Conference at the Library of Congress," *BYU Studies* 44, no. 4 (2005).

87. Winder, *Presidents and Prophets*, 50.

88. See the list at http://dsc.discovery.com/convergence/greatestamerican/top100/top100.html, accessed 19 April 2010. Compare Winder, *Presidents and Prophets*, 394–395; also the comments of Marlin K. Jensen, in Tom Christensen, "Historian from Huntsville," *Ogden Standard-Examiner*, 13 August 2005, 5E.

89. Dobner, "President Hinckley: 'A Man for His Time.'"

90. From the "Core Purpose" document, Public Affairs Department, copy in possession of the author; Truman Madsen, interview by author, 22 March 2007.

Chapter 8

1. See the important overview by Randy Astle, with Gideon O. Burton, "A History of Mormon Cinema," *BYU Studies* 46, no. 2 (2007): 13–163; pages 135–154 deal particularly with recent independent Mormon films. For insightful reviews of recent Mormon films, see Terryl L. Givens, "'There Is Room for Both': Mormon Cinema and the Paradoxes of Mormon Culture," *BYU Studies* 46, no. 2 (2007):189–208; adapted from Terryl L. Givens, "'Cinema as Sacrament': Theater and Film," chapter 14 of *People of Paradox: A History of Mormon Culture* (New York and Oxford: Oxford University Press, 2007), 265–284. See also Sean P. Means, "Four Days After First Screening, 'God's Army' Conquers Utah Movie Box Office," *Salt Lake Tribune*, 15 March 2000, D1. Also Mark T. Decker and Michael Austin, eds., Peculiar Portrayals: Mormons on the Page, Stage, and Screen (Logan, Utah: Utah State University Press, 2010).

2. "The Publicity Dilemma," Newsroom, The Church of Jesus Christ of Latter-day Saints, 9 March 2009, http://newsroom.lds.org/ldsnewsroom/eng/commentary/the-publicity-dilemma.

3. See Thomas F. O'Dea, *The Mormons* (Chicago and London: The University of Chicago Press, 1957), 1–2, 116–117; Dean L. May, "Mormons," in Eric Eliason, ed., *Mormons and Mormonism: An Introduction to an American World Religion* (Urbana and Chicago: University of Illinois Press, 2001), 47; May's essay originally appeared in Stephen Thernstrom, ed., *Harvard Encyclopedia of American Ethnic Groups* (Cambridge, Massachusetts: Harvard University Press, 1980), 720–731.

4. Jana Riess and Christopher Kimball Bigelow, *Mormonism for Dummies* (Hoboken, New Jersey: Wiley Publishing, Inc., 2005).

5. Riess and Bigelow, *Mormonism for Dummies*, 327–332.

6. See Peggy Fletcher, "A Light Unto the World," *Sunstone*, July/August 1982, 18: "Why are we as a people so taken with celebrity?"; Richard N. Ostling and Joan K. Ostling, *Mormon America: The Power and the Promise* (San Francisco: HarperSan Francisco, 1999), xx: "Mormons of every stripe are obsessive about their image." As evidence of that, Ostling and Ostling noted that the church's "biennial almanac...meticulously [lists] every LDS believer who ever participated in the Olympics" (xx).

7. See Joel Campbell, "Athletes' Missions Attract Attention," *Mormon Times*, 5 August 2008, http://www.mormontimes.com/mormon_voices/joel_campbell/?3200. Campbell, a BYU professor and former editor at the *Deseret News*, also wrote a "Mormon Media Observer" column for the *Mormon Times* subsection of the *Deseret News*. He observed, "When religious affiliation is known, journalists tend to mention that someone is Mormon in their reporting more than they label those of other faiths. For better or for worse, we as a 'peculiar people' have our faith amplified while the media barely mentions the faith of others in similar reports."

8. See "List of Latter Day Saints," accessed 24 April 2010, http://en.wikipedia.org/wiki/List_of_ Latter_Day_Saints; compare; also the extensive list in Ostling and Ostling, "Some Latter-day Stars," chapter 8 of *Mormon America: The Power and the Promise* (San Francisco: HarperSan Francisco, 1999), 130–146. Stephen Carter made the statement during his presentation on the "New Media and Pop Culture" panel, during the *Mormonism* in the Public Mind conference at Utah Valley University, 1 April 2009, http://www.uvu.edu/religiousstudies/ mormonstudies/conferences/publicmind/videos/index.html; author's transcript.

9. See "Worlds Without End," a website devoted to science fiction literature, for a listing of various prizes won by Orson Scott Card's books: http://www.worldswithoutend.com/ books_year_index.asp?year=1985; http://www.worldswithoutend.com/books_year_index. asp?year=1986; http://www.worldswithoutend.com/books_ year_ index. asp?year=1987. See Richard Paul Evans, *The Christmas Box Miracle* (New York: Simon & Schuster, 2001).

10. Carol Memmott and Mary Cadden, "Twilight Series Eclipses Potter Records on Best-Selling List," *USA Today*, 5 August 2009, http://www.usatoday.com/life/books/ news/2009-08-03-twilight-series_N.htm; compare also Tad Walch, "BYU Grad's Vampire Tale Eclipses Harry Potter on Book List," *Deseret News*, 11 August 2007, B01. For publishing numbers, see Diane Roback, "The Reign Continues: YA Queen Stephanie Meyer Holds on to Top Spots," *Publishers Weekly*, 22 March 2010, http://www.publishersweekly. com/pw/by-topic/childrens/childrens-book-news/article/42533-children-s-bestseller s-2009-the-reign-continues.html.

11. Lori Arnold, "Is Glenn Beck's Popularity Legitimizing Mormon Religion?" *Christian Examiner*, November 2010, http://www.christianexaminer.com/Articles/Articles%20 Nov10/Art_Nov10_05.html. See Peggy Fletcher Stack's biographical sketch, "Glenn Beck: Mormon Conservative Says He's on a Mission from God," *Salt Lake Tribune*, 11 May 2007, http://archive.sltrib.com/article.php?id=5872799&itype=NGPSID, for Beck's awareness of his effect on public perception of Mormonism, as well as the occasional discomfort his politics cause for some fellow Mormons. *Time* ranked Meyer seventeenth in the "Artists and Entertainers" category of its "100 Most Influential People" list in 2008, http://www.time.com/time/specials/2007/arti-cle/0,28804,1733748_1733752_1736282,00. html. Glenn Beck was listed twelfth in the "Leaders" category in *Time*'s 2010 edition http://www.time.com/time/specials/packages/ article/0,28804,1984685_1984864_1985415,00.html.

12. "About Ken" from Ken Jennings's official website, accessed 5 May 2010, http://www. ken-jennings.com/aboutken.html; Sally Atkinson, "America's Next Top Mormon," *Newsweek*, 6 May 2008, http://www.newsweek.com/id/135758. See also Sally Atkinson, "Latter-day Domination," *Newsweek*, 18 February 2008, http://www.newsweek.com/id/109605.

13. Kathryn H. Kidd, "Game Show Missionary," *Meridian Magazine*, 2004, http://www.lds-mag.com/lds-church-updates/1/7018/55/article/index.php?option=com_zine&view=art icle&ac=1&id=5332&Itemid=.

14. See Jana Riess's presentation during the "New Media and Pop Culture" panel, during the Mormonism in the Public Mind conference at Utah Valley University, 1 April 2009, for an insightful discussion of the way Mormonism informs Meyer's work and reputation, http://www.uvu.edu/religiousstudies/mormonstudies/conferences/publicmind/videos/ index.html. See, for example, Irene Sege, "Focus on the Family: Jane Clayson Johnson Left It All Behind to Have a Baby," *Boston Globe*, 12 October 2004, E1; Glen Warchol, "Clayson Happy with Decision to Leave TV," *Knight Ridder Tribune Business News*, 19 February 2005, 1; Barbara F. Meltz, "A Fresh Start," *Boston Globe*, 21 August 2006, E6; John Miller, "A New Calling for Harvard Dean: Head of Business School Is New President of Mormon College," *Washington Post*, 21 August 2005, A09. Miller's article for the Associated Press appeared in papers across the country.

15. Atkinson, "America's Next Top Mormon."

16. See Gene Wojciechowski, "Utah Owner Miller Won't Listen To Jazz on the Sabbath," *ESPN. com*, 11 May 2008, http://sports.espn.go.com/espn/print?id=3391439&type= Columnist &imagesPrint=off; Michael R. Walker, "The Many Names of Danny Ainge," *BYU Magazine*,

Winter 2009, 26–31; Linda East Brady, "Dose of Reality Hits Top of Utah," *Ogden Standard-Examiner*, 23 April 2010, GO! Section, 19.

17. Christian Smith, with Melinda Lundquist Denton, *Soul Searching: The Religious and Spiritual Lives of American Teenagers* (New York and Oxford: Oxford University Press, 2005), 38, 47; Elaine Jarvik, "LDS Teens Tops in Living Faith," *Deseret News*, 15 March 2005, accessible at http://www.deseretnews.com/article/1,5143,600118667,00.html; Bruce A. Chadwick and Richard J. McClendon, "Review of *Soul Searching: The Religious and Spiritual Lives of American Teenagers*," *BYU Studies* 45, no. 2 (2006): 168. Kenda Creasy Dean has a chapter entitled "Mormon Envy: Sociological Tools for Consequential Faith" in her *Almost Christian: What the Faith of Our Teenagers Is Telling the American Church* (New York and Oxford: Oxford University Press, 2010). For an important portrait of the religious make-up of the United States in the early 2000s, see Robert D. Putnam and David E. Campbell, with the assistance of Shaylyn Romney Garrett, American Grace: How Religion Divides and Unites Us (New York: Simon & Schuster, 2010). Putnam and Campbell's study suggested that "the three most religious groups in America are Mormons, Black Protestants, and evangelicals, in that order."

18. The scene came from "Treehouse of Horror IX," *The Simpsons*, season 10, episode 4. The missionary statistics are reported in Deseret Morning News, *2008 Church Almanac* (Salt Lake City: Deseret Morning News 2008), 612.

19. See "Probably," *South Park*, episode 411, 26 July 2000; "All About Mormons," *South Park* episode number 712, 19 November 2003; Peggy Fletcher Stack, "Radical Mormons Have Been Assimilated into American Culture," *Salt Lake Tribune*, 10 August 2006; Steve Evans, "South Park Mormonism," posting on the blog *By Common Consent*, 3 June 2006, http://bycommonconsent.com/2006/06/03/south-park-mormonism/; "All About the Mormons?" Wikipedia, accessed 12 May 2010, http://en.wikipedia.org/wiki/All_About_Mormons; "The Publicity Dilemma," Newsroom Press Release, Public Affairs Department, The Church of Jesus Christ of Latter-day Saints, 9 March 2009; accessed 24 April 2010, http://newsroom.lds.org/ldsnewsroom/eng/commentary/the-publicity-dilemma.

20. Astle, "A History of Mormon Cinema," 132. See Daniel A. Stout, Joseph D. Straubhaar, and Gayle Newbold, "Through a Glass Darkly: Mormons as Perceived by Critics' Reviews of Tony Kushner's *Angels in America*," *Dialogue* 32, no. 2 (Summer 1999): 140, 156. Reviewers more often focused on universal themes in the play rather than on Mormon-specific themes. See, for example, Jonathan Storm, "Touched by 'Angels': The Best Television in a Long, Long Time," *Philadelphia Inquirer*, 7 December 2003, H01: "Substitute any number of opposed words for Mormon and homosexual, and you synthesize the great hates that divide the country." See also Bernard Weinraub, "HBO Is Big Winner at Emmy Awards," *New York Times*, 20 September 2004, A22; Cynthia Greiner, "The Trouble with 'Angels': Love, AIDS, Hypocrisy on HBO Sunday Night," *Washington Times*, 5 December 2003, D04.

21. Tom Shales, "HBO's 'Angels': Glory Be!" *Washington Post*, 30 November 2003, N01; Robert Bianco, "Believe in HBO's 'Angels,'" *USA Today*, 5 December 2003, 13E; Vince Horiuchi, "Angels in America," *Salt Lake Tribune*, 5 December 2003, D1; Astle, "A History of Mormon Cinema," 132. See also Cristine Hutchison-Jones, "Center and Periphery: Mormons and American Culture in Tony Kushner's Angels in America," in Decker and Austin, eds., Peculiar Portrayals, 5–36, for her thoughtful assessment that "the entity that Kushner models as dangerous and subversive is not Mormon faith but the complex of conservative institutions and politics to which it is tied in the contemporary United States." Thus "Mormonism is not his primary target in the play" (25).

22. Astle, "A History of Mormon Cinema," 133; Brooke Adams, "Utahns React to HBO's 'Big Love,'" *Salt Lake Tribune*, 13 March 2006, C1. Another signal of the church's efforts to reach out to gay Mormons and their families was a website launched in late 2012, mormonsandgays.com, with statement from Mormon apostles: "There is no change in the Church's position of what is morally right. But what is changing — and what needs to change — is to help Church members respond sensitively and thoughtfully when they

encounter same-sex attraction in their own families, among other Church members, or elsewhere."

23. Vince Horiuchi, "LDS Leaders Aren't Big Fans of 'Big Love,'" *Salt Lake Tribune*, 25 March 2006, C3; "Church Responds to Questions on HBO's Big Love," Newsroom, The Church of Jesus Christ of Latter-day Saints, http://www.mormonnewsroom.org/article/church-responds-to-questions-on-hbos-big-love; Jennifer Dobner (of the Associated Press), "HBO, LDS Church at Odds on 'Big Love,'" *Deseret News*, 13 March 2009, B2; "The Publicity Dilemma," Newsroom, The Church of Jesus Christ of Latter-day Saints. Some observers saw the *Big Love* "temple episode" as retaliation for the LDS Church's support of California's Proposition 8 in 2008. See, for example, Orson Scott Card, "*Big Love?* Big Deal," *National Review Online*, 13 March 2009, http://www.nationalreview.com/node/227066/print. See also "comments" to Allyssa Lee, "HBO apologizes for, defends controversial 'Big Love' episode," *Show Tracker: What You're Watching (blog)*, 11 March 2009, http://latimesblogs.latimes.com/showtracker/2009/03/hbo-apologizes.html.

24. See Kimberly Nordyke, "'Big Love' Finale Most-Watched Episode of Season," *The Hollywood Reporter*, 22 March 2011, http://www.hollywoodreporter.com/live-feed/big-love-finale-watched-episode-170126.

25. *Saturday Night Live*, episode 517, 2 February 2002, viewed at salamandersociety.com. The sketch also revealed the difficulty the church had in emphasizing its official name and the centrality of Jesus Christ in its theology. The actors repeatedly referred to the church as the "Church of the Latter-day Saints," leaving out, significantly, "Jesus Christ."

26. Public Affairs Department, "Five-Year Plan, 2000–2004," copy in author's possession, 14.

27. Jon Krakauer, *Under the Banner of Heaven: A Story of Violent Faith* (New York: Doubleday, 2003), xxi.

28. "Church Response to Jon Krakauer's Under the Banner of Heaven," Newsroom, The Church of Jesus Christ of Latter-day Saints, 27 June 2003, http://www.mormonnewsroom.org/article/church-response-to-jon-krakauers-under-the-banner-of-heaven.

29. The quoted reviews are from *The New York Times Book Review* and *Newsweek*, and are included as endorsements on the back cover of the paperback editions of *Under the Banner of Heaven*; Maureen Dowd, "Mitt's No J.F.K.," *New York Times*, 9 December 2007, http://www.nytimes.com/2007/12/09/opinion/09dowd.html?scp=5&sq=jon%20krakauer%20under%20the%20banner%20of%20heaven&st=cse.

30. Krakauer, *Under the Banner of Heaven*, 4; see *The New York Times Book Review*'s "Paperback Non-Fiction Best Sellers List"; accessed 31 May 2010, http://www.dailypaul.com/files/nyt-bsl2.pdf. As of May 31, 2010, the book was number one on Amazon.com's "United States history, 1945-present" category, http://www.amazon.com/gp/bestsellers /books/4862/ref=pd_zg_hrsr_b_2_5_last. For a report on the movie plans, see Sean P. Means, "Report: Ron Howard to direct 'Under the Banner of Heaven'," *Salt Lake Tribune* blog posting, 20 July 2011, http://www.sltrib.com/sltrib/blogsmoviecricket/52226162-66/church-lds-book-krakauer.html.csp.

31. "Peoplehood": This is a term Martin Marty applied to Mormons, quoted in Givens, *People of Paradox*, 265.

32. Michael Alison Chandler, "Big-Screen Religion: Mormon Filmmakers Balance Faith with Their Hopes for Secular Appeal," *Washington Post*, 26 January 2006, C01. Chris Lee, "Out of the Picture: Richard Dutcher Was the King of Mormon Film—Then He Lost His Faith," *Los Angeles Times*, 19 August 2008, E1.

33. Some of these Mormon artists have pushed harder than others. The majority of these independent Mormon films still fit well with mainstream Mormon values, and most resolve themselves in a way that does not ultimately force viewers to explore the complexities of the Mormon worldview. This bothered Richard Dutcher, whose increasingly edgy productions impressed critics but made many Mormon viewers uncomfortable. In 2007, he publicly left the church, explaining in a published letter that he had progressed beyond the spiritual confines of the religion's organization. He also urged Mormon filmmakers to focus on more difficult themes that did not have easy resolutions. "Stop trying to make movies that you think the General Authorities would like," he wrote (Dutcher, "'Parting

Words' on Mormon Movies," *Provo Daily Herald*, 12 April 2007, A6, http://heraldextra. com/news/opinion/utah-valley/article_c07f4ae0-bbee-5265-89c1-bae7b12ce676.html). Dutcher then made *Falling* (2008), which was touted as the first R-rated Mormon movie, though most Mormon viewers would not consider the film "a Mormon movie" in the same way that these other films were Mormon movies, since it was not representative of the faith's mainstream membership. What made these independent Mormon films unique was that, ultimately, they provided an insiders' view of the faith since they were shot from the viewpoint of faithful Mormons. See also Lee, "Out of the Picture: Richard Dutcher was the King of Mormon Film—Then He Lost His Faith," E1.

34. Quoted in Givens, *People of Paradox*, 265. Along with Astle's important survey of these films in his "History of Mormon Cinema," see an insightful, comparative discussion about movie consumption by the Mormon niche audience, for Eric Samuelsen, "Finding An Audience, Paying the Bills: Competing Business Models in Mormon Cinema," *BYU Studies* 46, no. 2 (2007): 209–230.

35. Author's transcript of *American Prophet: The Story of Joseph Smith* (Groberg Communications, 1999), directed by Lee Groberg, written by Heidi Swinton. See also the PBS website for the documentary, http://www.pbs.org/americanprophet/index.html.

36. Astle, "A History of Mormon Cinema," 131.

37. "Public Affairs—Building on a New Foundation of Heightened Recognition for the Church—Resource Review, 25 June 2002," Public Affairs Department, internal document, copy in possession of the author, 3–6.

Chapter 9

1. Steve Marantz, "The Mormon Factor Looms Large for Romney," *Boston Herald*, 24 March 2002, 016.

2. See Kirk Jowers, Director of the Hinckley Institute of Politics, University of Utah, interview by author, 12 August 2008, 8–9; Greg Johnson, interview by author, 2 March 2010, where he discussed two meetings he and BYU professor Robert Millet had in Boston with Romney's "senior campaign staff."

3. Greg Johnson, interview by author. For polling that showed that a majority of Catholics and mainline Protestants viewed Mormons as Christians, see The Pew Research Center, "Public Expresses Mixed Views of Islam, Mormonism," 25 September 2007, http://www. pewforum.org/Public-Expresses-Mixed-Views-of-Islam-Mormonism.aspx.

4. Peggy Fletcher Stack, interview by author, 12 December 2008, transcript in author's possession, 9.

5. "Certain religious views should be deal breakers in and of themselves": Jacob Weisberg, "Romney's Religion: A Mormon President? No Way," *Slate*, 20 December 2006, http://www.slate.com/id/2155902.

6. Hugh Hewitt, *A Mormon in the White House?: 10 Things Every American Should Know About Mitt Romney* (Washington D.C. Regnery Publishing, Inc., 2007), 16–17.

7. Sara Rimer, "Religion Is Latest Volatile Issue to Ignite Kennedy Contest," *New York Times*, 29 September 1994, A22; "Kennedy Family Pit Bull?" *Boston Herald*, 20 September 1994, 22; Scott Lehigh, "Kennedy Believes Mormon-Racial Questions Proper," *Boston Globe*, 27 September 1994, 28. See also David Usborne, "Ted Kennedy in Fight for His Political Life," *Buffalo News*, 9 October 1994, F7. See also Newell G. Bringhurst and Craig L. Foster, *The Mormon Quest for the Presidency: From Joseph Smith to Mitt Romney and Jon Huntsman* (Independence, Missouri: John Whitmer Books, 2011), 235–239; Hewitt, *A Mormon in the White House?* 244. See also Frank Phillips, "Rep. Kennedy apologizes to Romney on Mormon issue," *Boston Globe*, 24 September 1994, 13. Not only did Representative Kennedy call Romney, he also issued a press release. However, Kennedy used the apology to remind readers of the issues that prompted his "comments that implied that I believe the Mormon Church continues to pursue intolerant policies." This approach left Romney's team less than satisfied about the sincerity of Kennedy's remorse. "Charles Manning, a

consultant to Romney's campaign, called back to condemn Kennedy. 'At first, we thought Kennedy's 20-minute call to apologize to Mitt was a private and apologetic matter. Now it's obvious it's just another sleazy campaign trick by the Kennedy people to try to attack Mitt's faith once again. I'd say Joe Kennedy was the sleaziest politician in Massachusetts but, if his uncle approved this stunt, then Joe is only second.'" See also Michael Harold Paulos, "Review of Craig L. Foster, *A Different God?* and Newell G. Bringhurst and Craig L. Foster, *The Mormon Quest for the Presidency*," *Journal of Mormon History* 36, no. 1 (Winter 2010): 246. Paulos's extensive review is a valuable essay in and of itself, because of the additional material that he presents to bolster Foster's case.

8. Rimer, "Religion Is Latest Volatile Issue to Ignite Kennedy Contest," A22; see also Kirk Jowers, interview by author, 12 August 2008, 8.

9. Terry Eastland, as quoted in Hewitt, *A Mormon in the White House?* 244.

10. Jowers interview, 12 August 2008, 8; see also Michael Paulson, "For Mormons, A Secular Victory: SJC Says Temple Can Have Its Steeple," *Boston Globe*, 17 May 2001, A1; Michael Poulson, "Religious Groups Back Legal Victory for Mormons," *Boston Globe*, 9 January 2001, A7; Brian MacQuarrie, "Old Rivals Tour Mormon Temple: Kennedy, Romney Offer Warm Praise," *Boston Globe*, 9 September 2000, B1.

11. Jowers interview, 12 August 2008, 8.

12. Kirk Jowers, interview by author, 12 August 2008, 8–9. See also Jonathan Darman and Lisa Miller, "Campaign '08: The Making of Mitt Romney," *Newsweek*, 8 October 2007, http://www.msnbc.msn.com/id/21049285/site/newsweek/: "Romney and his campaign wanted to deal with the Mormon question quickly and move on. The Massachusetts experience taught that Mitt the Mormon lost elections and Mitt the turnaround artist won them. In the first weeks of the campaign, Romney sat for lengthy interviews on his faith with *The New York Times* and *USA Today*; if the campaign could make the Mormon factor a tired story line, reporters would have no choice but to write about something else."

13. Noah Feldman, "What ok? or Is It About Mormonism?" *New York Times Magazine*, 6 January 2008, http://www.nytimes.com/2008/01/06/magazine/06mormonism-t.html?scp=1&sq=What%20is%20it%20about%20Mormonism%20Noah%20Feldman&st=cse.

14. Weisberg, "Romney's Religion."

15. Jowers interview, 12 August 2008, 5–6; Weisberg, "Romney's Religion"; Hewitt, *A Mormon in the White House?* 7. Father Neuhaus is quoted by Hewitt, *A Mormon in the White House?* 8.

16. Hewitt, *A Mormon in the White House?* 10.

17. *Los Angeles Times*/Bloomberg poll, 13 December 2006; Gallup Poll, 29 March 1999; Polling the Nations database.

18. ABC News/*Washington Times* poll, 13 December 2006, Polling the Nations database; NBC News/*Wall Street Journal* poll, December 2006, cited in Howard Berkes, "Faith Could Be Hurdle in Romney's White House Bid," *National Public Radio, Morning Edition*, 8 February 2007, transcript. http://www.npr.org/templates/story/story.php?storyId=7260620.

19. Feldman, "What Is It About(?) Mormonism?"; Kenneth Woodward, "The Presidency's Mormon Moment," *New York Times*, 9 April 2007, http://www.nytimes.com/2007/04/09/opinion/09woodward.html?emc=eta1; Richard Bushman is quoted in Howard Berkes, "Mormons Confront Negative Ideas About Their Faith," National Public Radio, 12 February 2008, http://www.npr.org/templates/story/story.php?storyId=18905399&sc=emaf.

20. "An issue [for] moderate and secular voters": Weisberg, "Romney's Religion."

21. Woodward, "The Presidency's Mormon Moment"; Joel Roberts, "Poll: Romney's Mormonism May Be an Issue," CBS News, 11 February 2009, http://www.cbsnews.com/2100-500160_162-2469572.html; Institute for Jewish and Community Research poll, May 2002, accessible at Polling the Nations database; Feldman, "What Is It About(?) Mormonism?" For similar survey results, compare The Pew Research Center, Public Expresses Mixed Views of Islam, Mormonism," 2: "51% have little or no awareness of the precepts and practices of Mormonism"; "Most Americans believe that their own religion has little in common with...the Church of Jesus Christ of Latter-day Saints....62% say"

that "their religion is very different" from "the Mormon religion." Still, "53% say they have a favorable opinion of Mormons."

22. Woodward, "The Presidency's Mormon Moment"; Institute for Jewish and Community Research poll, May 2002, Polling the Nations database; Feldman, "What Is It About (?) Mormonism?"; Darman and Miller, "Campaign '08: The Making of Mitt Romney"; see also Craig L. Foster, *A Different God?: Mitt Romney, the Religious Right, and the Mormon Question* (Salt Lake City: Greg Kofford Books, 2008), 101–102. See Greg Johnson, interview by author.

23. Feldman, "What Is It About (?) Mormonism?"; Darman and Miller, "The Making of Mitt Romney."

24. Andrew Sullivan, "Mormon Sacred Underwear," *The Atlantic*, 24 November 2006, in Foster, *A Different God?* 125. Chapter 5 of Foster's *A Different God?* is entitled "The Mormon Question: Left Hook." Foster's book gives remarkably thorough treatment to media coverage of Mitt Romney's campaign, and this present study is heavily indebted to his work for its survey of so many media voices, as well as its analysis and organizational framework.

25. Michael Graham, "In a Twist over Knickers: Morality Makes Mitt a Hit with Evangelicals," *Boston Herald*, 6 December 2006; in Foster, *A Different God?* 126; Darman and Miller, "The Making of Mitt Romney."

26. Laurie F. Maffly-Kipp, "A Mormon President?: The LDS Difference," *Christian Century*, 21 August 2007, http://www.christiancentury.org/article.lasso?id-3594.

27. Dave Wedge, "Does Mormon Mitt Have a Prayer?" *Boston Herald*, 3 December 2006, and John Dickerson, "Time to Talk Mormon, Mitt," *Slate*, 28 November 2006; in Foster, *A Different God?* 126.

28. A transcript of this installment of *The McLaughlin Group*, filmed on December 7, 2007, and aired December 8–9, 2007, http://www.mclaughlin.com/transcript.htm?id=629.

29. Lawrence O'Donnell, quoted in Paulos, "Review of *A Different God?*" 247.

30. Frank Rich, "Latter-day Republicans vs. The Church of Oprah," *New York Times*, 16 December 2007; http://www.nytimes.com/2007/12/16/opinion/16rich.html. See also Foster, *A Different God?* 132–134, for additional context to Lawrence O'Donnell's comments and reaction to them. For a brief but insightful discussion on Joseph Smith's abolitionist position, see Latter-day Saints historian Richard Bushman's presentation to the Pew Forum of Religion and Public Life's biannual Faith Angle Conference, 14 May 2007, "Mormonism and Democratic Politics: Are They Compatible?" transcript, http://pewforum.org/Politics-and-Elections/Mormonism-and-Politics-Are-They-Compatible.aspx, 5-6.

31. Scott D. Pierce, "Pundit Bashes Mitt, Mormons," *Deseret Morning News*, 14 December 2007, in Foster, *A Different God?* 133; Peggy Fletcher Stack, interview by author, 8;. Mike Allen's comments were made during a roundtable discussion session at the Pew Forum's Faith Angle Conference, "Mormonism and Democratic Politics: Are They Compatible?" 17.

32. Weisberg, "Romney's Religion"; Paulos, "Review of *A Different God?*" 249. E. J. Dionne's comments were made during a roundtable discussion session at the Pew Forum's Faith Angle Conference, "Mormonism and Democratic Politics: Are They Compatible?" 11. Transcripts of Bill Maher's comments made their way across the blogosphere; see, for example, the posting "Uh-oh" on the independent Mormon blog *By Common Consent*, 20 February 2007, http://bycommonconsent.com/2007/02/20/uh-oh/.

33. Jay Tolson, "QA: Elder M. Russell Ballard on the Mormon Way," *U.S. News and World Report*, 1 November 2007, http://www.usnews.com/articles/news/national/2007/11/01/qa-elder-m-russell-ballard-on-the-mormon-way.html; Darman and Miller, "The Making of Mitt Romney."

34. Jan Shipps in Berkes, "Mormons Confront Negative Ideas About Their Faith"; Senator Bennett is quoted in Foster, *A Different God?* 124.

35. "Perceptions of Mormons and the Church of Jesus Christ of Latter-day Saints," APCO Report, October 2007, 4, 7; in Report to the First Presidency, Public Affairs Committee, 11 November 2007, Public Affairs Department, The Church of Jesus Christ of Latter-day

Saints. Other commentators who have noted the impact of closed temple weddings include Kenneth Woodward, "The Presidency's Mormon Moment," and Jowers interview, 12 August 2008, 10–11. Jowers especially expressed the difficult irony Mormons face in knowing that temple ceremonies, which Mormons do not discuss because of their sacredness, are not bizarre or unnerving, despite the public's impression. Jowers said, "I don't think [temple ceremonies] would startle" outsiders (11).

36. "Perceptions of Mormons and the Church of Jesus Christ of Latter-day Saints," 4; italics added.

37. "Perceptions of Mormons and the Church of Jesus Christ of Latter-day Saints," 6.

38. Helen Whitney said that her "project began long before Romney announced his presidency,…but PBS officials urged her to add [Romney] to the film and she complied" (Peggy Fletcher Stack, "Filmmaker Gives Mormons National Exposure," Salt Lake Tribune, 28 April 2007). Whitney devoted several minutes to the significance and implications of Mitt Romney's prominence. See http://www.pbs.org/mormons/view/.

39. Stack, "Filmmaker Gives Mormons National Exposure"; D. Michael Quinn, interview by author, 20 March 2010.

40. Quoted in Stack, "Filmmaker Gives Mormons National Exposure."

41. Terryl Givens, interview by author, 15 August 2011, transcript in author's possession, 4.

42. Terryl Givens, quoted in Stack, "Filmmaker Gives Mormons National Exposure."

43. Marlin K. Jensen, interview by author, 24 March 2010, transcript in author's possession, 5–6. A Mormon professor who wrote a four-page open letter to PBS that was distributed widely on the Internet took much stronger exception to what he felt was Whitney's missing the essence of Mormonism: "You described a church that I do not recognize, which did not portray my beliefs, and almost wholly missed the mark for accurate journalism" (Thomas E. Sherry, "To: PBS—Frontline and American Experience," 8 May 2007; copy in possession of the author).

44. Marlin K. Jensen interview, 6.

45. Stack, "Filmmaker Gives Mormons National Exposure."

46. "Perceptions of Mormons and the Church of Jesus Christ of Latter-day Saints," APCO Report, October 2007, 17, 29. Terryl Givens remembered that this idea of a shared legacy of racial difficulties among American denominations was also the gist of historian Philip Jenkins's response to a question about the Mormon priesthood restriction during a question and answer session which followed Jenkins's keynote lecture at the Mormon History Association Conference in Sacramento in May 2008; Terryl Givens, interview by author.

47. For coverage of the Reverend Al Sharpton's criticism, see Foster, A Different God? 134–135. Ironically, Sharpton's comments about Mormonism's racial record came in response to criticisms leveled at Sharpton for his perceived bigotry against Mormons. He had said, during a May 2007 radio debate, "As for the one Mormon running for office, those who really believe in God will defeat him anyways, so don't worry about that; that's a temporary situation" (134). Gary C. Lawrence, Mormons Believe… What?! (Orange County, California: The Parameter Foundation, 2011), 134.

48. "Perceptions of Mormons and the Church of Jesus Christ of Latter-day Saints," APCO report, 17; Carrie A. Moore, "Media Gets a Big 'F' For Stories on FLDS," Deseret News, 12 May 2006; "Protecting the Church's Identity," Newsroom, The Church of Jesus Christ of Latter-day Saints, 26 June 2008, http://www.newsroom.lds.org/ldsnewsroom /eng/ commentary/protecting-the-church-s-identity; Thomas Burr, "Could Ancestors Haunt Romney?" Salt Lake Tribune, 21 August 2006. For commentary on Barack Obama's polygamous ancestry, see Foster, A Different God? 128; and Paulos, "Review of A Different God?" 246. The media's extensive interest in polygamy was evident during Richard Bushman's roundtable discussion with reporters at the Pew Forum's conference on "Mormonism and Democratic Politics: Are They Compatible?" 12–13.

49. In Part Two of The Mormons, "Reaching out to the Wider World"; at http://www.pbs.org/ mormons/view/.

50. "Perceptions of Mormons and the Church of Jesus Christ of Latter-day Saints," 16.

51. "The Mormon Moment," Newsroom, The Church of Jesus Christ of Latter-day Saints, 12 April 2007, http://www.newsroom.lds.org/ldsnewsroom/eng/commentary/the-mormon-moment; "Publicizing Good Works," 9 November 2007, http://www.newsroom.lds.org/ldsnewsroom / eng/commentary/publicizing-good-works.

52. Butler's comments came in "Act 3: Persecution" of *The Mormons*.

53. "Mormonism and Democratic Politics: Are They Compatible?" 18–19.

54. "Mormonism and Democratic Politics: Are They Compatible?" 19.

55. "Mormonism and Democratic Politics: Are They Compatible?" 19–20.

56. "Mormonism and Democratic Politics: Are They Compatible?" 20–21

57. "Mormonism and Democratic Politics: Are They Compatible?" 19. For the *On Faith* blog, see Michael Otterson, interview by author, 9 September 2011, transcript in author's possession, 8–9.

58. "There are some for whom these commitments are not enough": Mitt Romney, "Faith in America," an address at the George H. W. Bush Presidential Library, College Station, Texas, 6 December 2007, included as an appendix in Bringhurst and Foster, *The Mormon Quest for the Presidency* (2011), 353–359.

59. The Pew Research Center, "Religion in Campaign '08" 6 September 2007, 2, 4; "Mormonism and Democratic Politics: Are They Compatible?"13.

60. See Bringhurst and Foster, *The Mormon Quest for the Presidency* (2008), 266; Marlin K. Jensen, interview by author, 3–4; Greg Johnson, interview by author; Kirk Jowers, interview by author, 12 August 2008, 7–8.

61. Hewitt, *A Mormon in the White House?* 275–276; "Article VI Blog—About Us," http://www.article6blog.com/about/; Robert D. Novak, "Robert Novak: Romney's Candidacy May Face an Unfair Religious Test," *Union Leader*, 26 April 2006, in Foster, *A Different God?* 151.

62. Quoted in Foster, *A Different God?* 155. Compare also National Association of Evangelicals' Richard Cizik's comments to *The Washington Monthly*: "Most Evangelicals still regard Mormons as a cult" (in Ted Olsen, "Latter-day Complaints," *Christianity Today*, July 2006, 50).

63. Ted Olsen, "Latter-day Complaints," *Christianity Today*, July 2006, 50. Interestingly, Olsen began his article by noting the protests that arose in California when Richard Dutcher's *God's Army* sequel *States of Grace* (a Mormon-themed film) was advertised as "Christian cinema"; Berkes, "Faith Could Be Hurdle in Romney's White House Bid," *National Public Radio, Morning Edition*, 8 February 2007, transcript (including comments by Richard Land), http://www.npr.org/templates/story/story.php?storyId=7260620; Richard Land, in "Baptists Cool to Mitt Because Mormons Keep Luring Away Their Congregations?" *Hot Air* (blog), 20 November 2007, in Foster, *A Different God?* 158. Craig Foster's chapter 6, "Right Cross," provides numerous additional examples of similar expressions of evangelical reticence toward a Mormon candidate.

64. Robert Millet and Gerald McDermott, "Mitt's Mormonism and the 'Evangelical Vote'," *Christianity Today*, May 2007; see article and reader comments, http://www.christianitytoday.com/ct/2007/mayweb-only/122-42.0.html. The article's header mentioned that Millet and McDermott were coauthors on an upcoming book project, *Claiming Christ: A Mormon-Evangelical Debate* (Grand Rapids, Michigan: Brazos Press, 2007).

65. Both Dan Bartlett and the January 2008 Vanderbilt study are quoted in Foster, *A Different God?* 188, 206; Craig Blomberg, interview by author, 12 September 2008, transcript in author's possession, 5; Greg Johnson, interview by author. Compare also the results of pollster Gary Lawrence's February 2008 survey, where he found that 27 percent of respondents felt that "people who disapproved of Romney" did so "mainly because of his religion, but may have used another reason as their excuse" (Gary C. Lawrence, *How Americans View Mormonism: Seven Steps to Improve Our Image* [Orange, California: The Parameter Foundation, 2008], 59).

66. Hewitt, *A Mormon in the White House?* 10.

67. Ron Barnett, "Bob Jones III Endorses (?) Romney for President," *USA Today*, 17 October 2007, http://www.usatoday.com/news/politics/election2008/2007-10-16-jones-romney_N.htm.

68. Craig Blomberg, interview by author, 6.

69. Darman and Miller, "Campaign '08 The Making of Mitt Romney"; Barnett, "Bob Jones III Endorses (?) Romney for President."

70. Bringhurst and Foster, *The Mormon Quest for the Presidency* (2011), 245–246. See also Jowers interview, 12 August 2008, 5.

71. Bringhurst and Foster, *The Mormon Quest for the Presidency* (2011), 252–253.

72. Bringhurst and Foster, *The Mormon Quest for the Presidency* (2011), 253–254; the "brothers" question appeared in Zev Chafets, "The Huckabee Factor," *New York Times*, 12 December 2007, http://www.nytimes.com/2007/12/12/magazine/16huckabee.html?_r=1&hp=&pagewanted=print&oref=slogin. Chafets wrote that Huckabee asked the question "in an innocent voice"; Doug Wright's comments are quoted in Paulos, "Review of *A Different God?*" 252.

73. "Huckabee Apologizes for Mormon Remark," CBS News/Associated Press, 12 December 2007, http://www.cbsnews.com/stories/2007/12/12/politics/main3612914.shtml. For a discussion of the 1998 Southern Baptist Convention and Mike Huckabee's speech, see Linda Caillouet, "Huckabee: U.S. gave up on religion, school shootings were wake-up call, he says," *Arkansas Online* (of the *Arkansas Democrat Gazette*), 8 June 1998, http://www.arkansasonline.com/news/1998/jun/08/huckabee-us-gave-religion/; on Mormon suspicions that Huckabee was being disingenuous, see "Utah's Mormons Loathe Huckabee," CBS News, 4 February 2008, http://www.cbsnews.com/stories/2008/02/04/politics/politico/main3789419.shtml; see also "Mike Huckabee, Mormons, and Bigotry," at http://www.thereisaway.us/2007/12/mike_huckabee_mormons_and_bigo.html.

74. Laurie Goodstein, "Huckabee Is Not Alone in Ignorance on Mormonism," *New York Times*, 14 December 2007, http://www.nytimes.com/2007/12/14/us/politics/14mormon.html; Kirk Jowers, interview by author, 12 August 2008, 9.

75. Romney's comments on the *Today Show* were reported in Glen Johnson, "Romney: Attacks on Religion Go Too Far," *USA Today*, 12 December 2007, http://www.usatoday.com/news/politics/2007-12-12-3420073481_x.htm.

76. For the suggestion of a "coded" language, see "Huckabee Apologizes for Mormon Remark," http://www.nbcnews.com/id/22239946/ns/politics-decision_08/t/huckabee-apologizes-mormon-remark/#.4o, 13 December 2007.

77. Thomas Burr, "Romney's Big Investment in Iowa Turns Bitter," *Salt Lake Tribune*, 3 January 2008; Joseph Curl, "Once-dead Bid Bests Romney," *Washington Times*, 9 January 2008, A1.

78. Stack, "Filmmaker Gives *Mormons* National Exposure." See Bringhurst and Foster's excellent summary of the primary results in their *Mormon Quest for the Presidency* (2011), 257–260. See also "Low Blow," chapter 7 of Foster, *A Different God?* 173–210, for a more detailed narrative.

79. Quoted in W. H. Lawrence, "Kennedy Assures Texas Ministers of Independence: Says He'd Quit Presidency if Unable to Withstand Any Church Pressure," *New York Times*, 13 September 1960, 1. The entire speech was reprinted on page 22 of that same edition.

80. Mitt Romney, "Faith in America," in Bringhurst and Foster, *The Mormon Quest for the Presidency*, 353–359. See the insightful analysis of Mitt Romney's speech in Jan Shipps, "What Made Romney's Big Speech So Mormon: His Tent Vision Fits His Church's Bid to Enter the Religious Mainstream," *Christian Science Monitor*, 11 December 2007, http://www.csmonitor.com/2007/1211/p09s01-coop.html.

81. Romney's "comma problem" remark is quoted in Bringhurst and Foster, *The Mormon Quest for the Presidency* (2011), 255; Michael Steele made these comments in May 2009 on *Bill Bennett's Morning in America* radio program, quoted in Paulos, "Review of *A Different God?*" 249.

82. Peggy Fletcher Stack, interview by author, 8; Maffly-Kipp, "A Mormon President?"; Howard Berkes, "Romney Seeks to Put the Mormon Question to Rest," *National Public Radio, Morning Edition*, 7 December 2007; http://www.npr.org/templates/story/story/php?storyId=16996368&ps=rs.

83. Butler's comments came in "Act 3: Persecution" of Helen Whitney's *Mormons*.

84. Darman and Miller, "Campaign '08 The Making of Mitt Romney."

85. Jowers interview, 12 August 2008, 6. Jowers pointed out that election season polls suggested that evangelicals, ironically, had image problems of their own, and even "have more people disliking them that are not of their faith than [Mormons] do." See, for example, the December 2006*NBC News/Wall Street Journal* poll, cited in Howard Berkes, "Faith Could Be Hurdle in Romney's White House Bid." This poll had 53 percent of Americans expressing hesitation about voting for a Mormon presidential candidate; fifty-*four* percent of respondents in that poll said they would likewise hesitate to vote for an *evangelical* candidate. For information on the number of Americans who consider themselves "evangelical," as well as their opinions about Mormons' "Christian" status, see The Pew Research Center, "Public Expresses Mixed Views of Islam, Mormonism," 9–11, 19. For the complexity in pinning down the number of evangelicals because of variable of self-identification and other metrics in various polls, see Jay Tolson, "The Evangelical Vote: How Big Is It Really?" *U.S. News and World Report*, 24 September 2008, http://www.usnews.com/news/campaign-2008/articles/2008/09/24/the-evangelical-vote-how-big-is-it-really, where he notes that the range is as wide as from 41percent in some polls (like Gallup) to 7percent in a Barna poll (which measured specific beliefs.)

86. Tolson, "QA: Elder M. Russell Ballard on the Mormon Way."

87. Joel J. Campbell, "The Perfect Storm? LDS Media Events and the Foreign Press," transcript of a speech given at Meet the Mormons: Public Perception and the Global Church, the 19th Annual Conference of the International Society, 7 April 2008, copy in author's possession, 5; Howard Berkes, "Gordon Hinckley, LDS President, Dies at Age 97," National Public Radio, 28 January 2008, http://www.npr.org/templates/story/story.php?storyId=18482802&ps=rs.

88. Jan Shipps, in Berkes, "Mormons Confront Negative Ideas About Their Faith."

89. Tolson, "QA: Elder M. Russell Ballard on the Mormon Way"; Berkes, "Mormons Confront Negative Ideas About Their Faith"; Thomas Burr, "Romney's Run Good for LDS Church," *Salt Lake Tribune*, 23 April 2008.

90. Jan Shipps, in Berkes, "Mormons Confront Negative Ideas About Their Faith"; Bushman and Woodward's exchange is in "Mormonism and Democratic Politics: Are They Compatible?" 17; Bushman's description of Romney as a "thoroughgoing Mormon" is on page 20.

Chapter 10

1. "I don't think this is really 'a moment'": Michael Otterson, Managing Director of LDS Public Affairs, interview by author, 9 September 2011, transcript in author's possession, 4.

2. Jane Barnes, "There Is a Dark Side to Mormonism," *New York Times*, February 1, 2012, accessed 12 December 2012, http://www.nytimes.com/roomfordebate/2012/01/30/what-is-it-about-mormons/there-is-a-dark-side-to-mormonism. Barnes's piece was part of a five-author roundtable on the *Time*'s "Room for Debate "page. The topic for the roundtable was "What is it about Mormons?"

3. Marlin K. Jensen, interview by author, 24 March 2010, transcript in author's possession, 1.

4. Jensen interview, 1.

5. In June of 1977, 28.34 percent of the 2,700 people surveyed chose "don't know the name" when asked an opinion about "Mormons/Latter-day Saints" (Question qn19k, The Gallup Poll #978 Gallup Brain database, http://brain.gallup.com/home.aspx); Gary C. Lawrence, *How Americans View Mormonism: Seven Steps to Improve Our Image* (Orange, California: The Parameter Foundation, 2008), 16.

6. Author's notes; the game was played on October 27, 2007. Thomas L. Friedman, *The World Is Flat: A Brief History of the Twenty-First Century* (New York: Farrar, Strauss and Giroux, 2005), 36–38, 446, where Friedman notes that Neelemna's charitable giving is motivated by his Mormon beliefs.

7. The Pew Forum on Religion and Public Life study, "Benedict XVI Viewed Favorably but Faulted on Religious Outreach: Public Expresses Mixed Views of Islam, Mormonism," 25 September 2007, http://pewforum.org/Public-Expresses-Mixed-Views-of-Islam-Mormonism.aspx, 1.

For complete lyrics of the song, see Scott D. Pierce, "Conan O'Brien mocks Orrin Hatch, Mormons," *Mormon Times*, 17 December 2009, http://www.mormontimes.com/article/6898/ Conan-OBrien-mocks-Orrin-Hatch-Mormons.

8. Lawrence, *How Americans View Mormonism*, 41.

9. Alex Beam, "A big win for the Mormon church," *Boston Globe*, November 14, 2012, accessed 14 November 2012, http://www.bostonglobe.com/opinion/2012/11/14/the-gr eat-mormon-etch-sketch/0pFVAp7Reis7fQyoM2QIlK/story.html.

10. See John Cloud, "Why Gay Marriage Was Defeated in California," *Time*, 5 November 2008, http://www.time.com/time/nation/article/0,8599,1856872-2,00.html.

11. See Sarah Pulliam, "A Latter-day Alliance," *Christianity Today*, December 2008 (web-only edition), http://www.christianitytoday.com; Jennifer Dobner, "Film Blasts LDS Role in Prop 8," *Salt Lake Tribune*, 24 January 2010, B7. For the church's response to claims that it did not report its donations to the cause, see "Media Reports on Proposition 8 Filing Uninformed," Newsroom, The Church of Jesus Christ of Latter-day Saints, http://newsroom.lds.org/ ldsnewsroom/eng/commentary/media-reports-on-proposition-8-filing-uninformed.

12. For the letter that the church's First Presidency sent to California members in June 2008, see www.newsroom.lds.org/ldsnewsroom/eng/commentary/california -and-same-sex-marriage. One of the most prominent voices against Mormon involvement in the Proposition 8 debate was that of Tom Hanks, who called the church "un-American" for its position to "[codify] discrimination." A week after he made the comment, he apologized. See "Tom Hanks: Mormon Supporters of Prop 8 'Un-American,'" *The Huffington Post*, 16 January 2009, http://www.huffingtonpost.com/2009/   01/16/tom-hanks-mormon-supporte_n_158467. html; "Tom Hanks Apologizes for Calling Mormon Support of Prop 8 'Un-American," *The Huffington Post*, 23 January 2009, http://www.huffingtonpost.com/2009/01/23/tom-hanks-apologizes-for-_n_160424.html.

13. See the *New York Times* editorial, "Equality's Winding Path," *New York Times*, 5 November 2008, http://www.nytimes.com/2008/11/06/opinion/06thu1.html?emc=eta1: "The most notable defeat for fairness was in California, where right-wing forces led by the Mormon Church poured tens of millions of dollars into the campaign for Proposition 8—a measure to enshrine bigotry in the state's Constitution by preventing people of the same sex from marrying." See also Cloud, "Why Gay Marriage Was Defeated in California."

14. The commercial was accessed 2 June 2010, http://www.youtube.com/watch?v =q28UwAyzUkE.

15. See Nicholas Riccardi, "Mormons feel the backlash over their support of Prop. 8," *Los Angeles Times*, 17 November 2008, http://articles.latimes.com/2008/nov/17/nation/ na-mormons17.

16. Dobner, "Film Blasts LDS Role in Prop 8," B7.

17. Pulliam, "A Latter-day Alliance." For the statements released by the Catholic bishops of Sacramento and Salt Lake City, see http://newsroom.lds.org/ldsnewsroom/eng/ news-releases-stories/catholic-bishop-decries-religious-bigotry-against-mormons.

18. Kirk Jowers, interview by author, 26 April 2010, transcript in author's possession, 1–2.

19. Lawrence, *How Americans View Mormonism*, 32.

20. Lawrence, *How Americans View Mormonism*, 34, 36.

21. Matt Canham, Derek P. Jensen, and Rosemary Winters, "Salt Lake City Adopts Pro-Gay Statutes—With LDS Church Support," *Salt Lake Tribune*, 11 November 2009.

22. In the fall of 2011, "Equality California, the state's largest LGBT group," announced that it "would not lead any efforts to repeal Proposition 8 on the 2012 ballot." The group cited "public opinion" as well as the "significant challenges of the current political and economic climate" (Andrew Harmon, "Equality California: No Return to Ballot Over Prop. 8," *The Advocate.com*, 6 October 2011, http://www.advocate.com/News/ Daily_News/2011/10/06/No_Prop_8_Recall_in_2012/). However, in June 2013, the U.S. Supreme Court effectively reopened the way for same-sex marriages in California by ruling that Proposition 8 supporters did not have the "standing" to challenge a lower court's nullification of the proposition. See "Supreme Court Rules on Prop 8, Lets Gay Marriage Resume in California," Huffington Post, 26 June 2013, http://www.huffingtonpost.

com/2013/06/26/supreme-court-prop-8_n_3434854.html. The LDS Church released a brief, three-paragraph statement in response that ended with this line: "Notably, the court decision does not change the definition of marriage in nearly three-fourths of the states" ("Church Responds to Supreme Court Marriage Rulings," 26 June 2013, http:// www.mormonnewsroom.org/article/church-responds-supreme-court-marriage-rulings). Another significant trend that is still being played out is the LDS Church's position that activists who try to silence religiously minded opponents of same-sex marriage are threatening constitutional freedoms. Apostle Dallin H. Oaks has been a prominent spokesman for this position; see a report of an address he gave at the church's BYU-Idaho, in Eric Gorski (Associated Press Religion Writer), "Leader Likens anti-Mormonism to racism in '60s," *USA Today*, 15 October 2009, http://www.usatoday.com/news/religion/2009-10-15-mormon-gay_N.htm. See a number of related talks by church general authorities (and one by Roman Catholic Cardinal Francis George given at BYU in February 2010 called "Catholics and Latter-day Saints: Partners in the Defense of Religious Freedom") linked under the topic of "Religious Freedom" in the Newsroom section of the LDS Church's website, lds.org, http://newsroom.lds.org/official-statement/religious-freedom. Richard Bushman noted that he was "not sure how many non-Mormons are conscious of it as sort of a movement," and that he was "not sure exactly where it will go." He "had heard some responses to Elder Oaks saying, 'Look, you're playing a big boy's game now; you've got to be willing to take it,'" but he also thought that others who worried about the effort "to exclude religious discourse from public events" would "be very sympathetic" to this Mormon line of reasoning. Richard Bushman, interview by author, 12 August 2011, transcript in author's possession, 9.

23. See "Tom Hanks: Mormon Supporters of Prop 8 'Un-American,'" *The Huffington Post*, 16 January 2009.
24. See Kathleen Perricone, "'Book of Mormon' soundtrack goes to No. 3 on Billboard chart: Musical won nine Tony awards," *NY Daily News.com*, 15 June 2011, where Perricone notes that "the impressive feat makes the soundtrack the highest-charting Broadway cast album (and the first to crack the top ten) since 'Hair' spent 13 weeks at No. 1 in 1969"; http://articles.nydailynews.com/2011-06-15/entertainment/29681638_1_mormon-t ony-awards-billboard-chart.
25. For an insightful analysis of what both plays said about the place of Mormons in American popular opinion, see the conclusion to Matthew Bowman, *The Mormon People: The Making of an American Faith* (New York: Random House, 2012), 249–253.
26. This comment came in the review of the musical by Robert Smith, "On Broadway, A 'Mormon' Swipe At . . . Everything," National Public Radio, 24 March 2011, audio version and transcript, http://www.npr.org/2011/03/24/134803453/on-broadway-a-mormon-s wipe-at-everything. The audio and the transcript are slightly different; the "foreboding" comment came in the audio broadcast.
27. Michael Otterson, "A Latter-day Saint view of Book of Mormon musical," *Washington Post* blog *On Faith*, 14 April 2011, http://www.washingtonpost.com/blogs/on-faith/post/ why-i-wont-be-seeing-the-book-of-mormon-musical/2011/04/14/AFiEn1fD_blog.html.
28. Actor Andrew Rannells (who played Elder Price in the musical) performed the song "I Believe" during the broadcast of the 2011 Tony Awards, http://www.youtube.com/ watch?v=tggtPHDmrR8. See Ben Brantley, who invited readers to "feast upon ['The Book of Mormon's'] sweetness," for its portrayal of "naïve but plucky educators set down in an unfamiliar world, who find their feet, affirm their values and learn as much as they teach" (Brantley, "Missionary Men With Confidence in Sunshine," *New York Times*, 24 March 2011, http://theater.nytimes.com/2011/03/25/theater/reviews/the-book-of-mormon-at-eugene -oneill-theater-review.html?pagewanted=all). See also Peter Marks, "Review of Broadway's 'The Book of Mormon'," *Washington Post*, 24 March 2011, http://www.washingtonpost.com/ lifestyle/style/review-of-broadways-the-book-of-mormon/2011/03/24/ABguJSRB_story. html: "The marvel of the 'Book of Mormon' is that even as it profanes some serious articles of faith, its spirit is anything but mean. . . . It's easier, of course, not to feel stung by comedy when your background is not the one being gored. But even with the wallop of derision

that Mormonism comes in for on this evening, the wider subject for ribbing is that almost unbearable brand of optimism Americans tend to want to impose on the rest of the world. 'A Mormon just believes,' [actor Andrew] Rannells's Price sings at one point, a lyric that also seems to hold true for a national mind-set, one that clings to a faith that American hearts always remain in the right place." For a collection of Mormon bloggers' review of the musical—with the same general sense that the Mormons came off favorably and this "tipped [Mormon bloggers'] reviews towards the positive"—see Emily Jensen, "Book of Mormon Musical blog reactions," paper presented at the Mormon Media Studies Symposium, Brigham Young University, 9 November 2011, copy in author's possession.

29. Smith, "On Broadway, A 'Mormon' Swipe at . . . Everything." Compare also the positive reactions catalogued in Cathy Lynn Grossman, "Mormons may have last laugh at 'South Park'-like Broadway show," *USA Today*, 21 February 2011, accessed 16 May 2012, http://content. usatoday.com/communities/Religion/post/2011/02/mormons-broadway-south-park-/1#. UM9TYXfC0yJ.

30. "Church Statement Regarding the Book of Mormon Broadway Musical," LDS Church Newsroom, accessed 18 October 2011, http://newsroom.lds.org/article/ church-statement-regarding-the-book-of-mormon-broadway-musical.

31. Smith, "On Broadway, A 'Mormon' Swipe at . . . Everything," audio version of the story.

32. See Laura Ripabelli, "Mormon NYC Ad Campaign 'Very Savvy Branding,'" ABC News, 21 June 2011, http://abcnews.go.com/Business/mormon-nyc-ad-campaign-savvy-branding/ story?id=13888304#.TrZFY9S2WmA.

33. Scott Swofford, interview by author, 18 October 2011, transcript in author's possession, 2, 9.

34. Scott Swofford interview, 7; See also the comments of an LDS Church spokesman, Dale Jones, who said that "we've added New York to the cities we're going into this year [with the campaign] because of the conversations that are happening there" (in Katie Barlow, "N.Y. 'I'm a Mormon' ads creating missionary opportunities," *LDS Living*, 29 June 2011, http://www.ldsliving.com/story/65043-ny-im-a-mormon-ads-creating-missionary-opportunities).

35. See, for example, Doree Ashcraft, "Life portrayed in Mormon ads not consistent with reality," *Salt Lake Tribune* opinion blog, 9 and 11 April 2011, http://www.sltrib.com/sltrib/ opinion/51357520-82/mormon-ads-hair-less.html.csp, as well as the flurry of comments for and against her position.

36. Benjamin Tateoka, "LDS Church launches new advertising campaign in New York City," *(BYU) Universe*, 12 July 2011, http://universe.byu.edu/index.php/2011/07/12/ lds-church-launches-new-advertising-campaign-in-new-york-city/.

37. Braff's June 30 tweet is quoted in Tateoka, "LDS Church launches new advertising campaign in New York City."

38. For a transcript of the 9 August 2011 edition of *Hardball*, see http://www.msnbc. msn.com/id/44111513/ns/msnbc_tv-hardball_with_chris_matthews/t/hardball-ch ris-matthews-tuesday-august/#.TrZOzdS2WmA. For the denial of the original *Politico* report about the "weird" strategy from the Obama campaign, see Jamshid Ghazi Askar, "Obama adviser David Axelrod debunks Mitt Romney report," *Deseret News*, 13 August 2011, http://www.deseretnews.com/article/700170374/Obama-adviser-David-Axelrod-debu nks-Mitt-Romney-report.html?s_cid=rss-30.

39. The clip aired 10 August 2011, http://www.colbertnation.com/the-colbert-report-videos/ 394360/august-10-2011/yaweh-or-no-way—mormons—god-s-poll-numbers.

40. Scott Swofford interview, 3, 4; Michael Otterson, "Why 'I'm a Mormon'?" *Washington Post* blog *On Faith*, 30 October 2011, http://www.washingtonpost.com/blogs/guest-voices/ post/why-im-a-mormon/2011/10/30/gIQAVJCXXM_blog.html.

41. Brandon Flower's "I'm a Mormon" profile, accessed 20 October 2011, http://mormon. org/me/5233/. The instant popularity of Flower's profile in the U.S. and internationally is documented in Hillary Bowler, "More reaction to rock star Brandon Flowers' 'I'm a Mormon' video," *Deseret News*, 21 October 2011, http://www.deseretnews.com/ article/705392866/More-reaction-to-rock-star-Brandon-Flowers-Im-a-Mormon-video.

html. Bowler's piece provides links to other media outlets. For Mitch Mayne's story, see Mike Aldax, "Mormon church's new San Francisco liaison Mitch Mayne is openly gay," *San Francisco Examiner*, 5 September 2011, http://www.sfexaminer.com/local/2011/09/ mormon-church-s-new-liaison-mitch-mayne-openly-gay; for Mayne's story, as well as that of other self-identified gay Mormons who were active in the church (and active in abiding by its standards), see also Peggy Fletcher Stack, "Gay Mormon named to key local LDS leadership post in San Francisco," *Salt Lake Tribune*, 30 and 31 August 2011, http://www.sltrib.com/sltrib/news/52486958-78/mayne-gay-lds-ward.html.csp.

42. Gary Lawrence, interview by the author, 11 October 2011, transcript in author's possession, 2; Quinnipiac University poll, 8 June 2011, http://www.quinnipiac.edu/x1284. xml?ReleaseID=1608.

43. For one recent example, see a LifeWay Research poll released in October 2011 that showed that "pastors' self-identification as either Mainline or Evangelical was a predictor of their opinions regarding Mormons. While two-thirds (67 percent) of Evangelicals strongly disagree that Mormons are Christians, just 48 percent of Mainline pastors feel the same way." In Rob Kerby, "Pollsters: 75 percent of pastors say Mormons 'not Christians,'" *Beliefnet.com*, 11 October 2011, http://blog.beliefnet.com/news/2011/10/ pollsters-75-percent-of-pastors-say-mormons-not-christians.php.

44. Kirk Jowers, interview by author, 24 April 2010, 2; Bill Heersink, interview by author, 15 February 2010; Pulliam, "Latter-day Alliance." The pastor visiting BYU made the comment to Robert Millet; Robert Millet, phone conversation with author, 22 February 2010.

45. Joel Campbell, "Focus on Family Pulls Glenn Beck Article," *Mormon Times*, 27 December 2008, http://www.mormontimes.com/article/11725/Focus-on-Family-pulls-Glenn-B eck-article; Jason Arvak, "The Real Shocker about Beck at Liberty U," *The Moderate Voice*, 16 May 2010, http://themoderatevoice.com/72799/the-real-shocker-about-b eck-at-liberty-u/; David Gibson, "Glenn Beck to Address Baptist Grads, but His Mormonism Sparks Debate," *Politics Daily*, 14 May 2010, http://www.politicsdaily.com/2010/5/14/ glenn-beck-to-address-baptist-grads-but-his-mormonism-sparks-de/.

46. Jowers interview, 26 April 2010, 4.

47. Richard Bushman interview, 2; Gary Lawrence interview, 5.

48. For Warren Cole Smith's article, as well as the comments it generated, see http://www. patheos.com/Resources/Additional-Resources/Vote-for-Romney-Is-a-Vote-for-the-LDS-C hurch-Warren-Cole-Smith-05-24-2011.html. See LDS spokesman Michael Otterson's strong response to Smith's points: "To your third point, there's your assertion that the election of Mormons to high office would be a tacit endorsement of The Church of Jesus Christ of Latter-day Saints. This argument, while not new, is frightening in its implications. Substitute the word 'Jew' for 'Mormon' and see how comfortable that feels" (Otterson, "Evangelicals and the Beliefs of the President," *Washington Post* blog *On Faith*, 7 June 2011, http://www. washingtonpost.com/blogs/on-faith/post/evangelicals-mormons-and-the-beliefs-of- the-president/2011/06/07/AGnGX8KH_blog.html?referrer=emaillink).

49. Jamshid Ghazi Askar, "Michele Bachmann's Pastor on Mormonism," *Deseret News*, 6 September 2011, http://www.deseretnews.com/article/700176783/Michele- Bachmanns-pastor-on-Mormonism.html?s_cid=e_share.

50. Public Religion Research Institute poll, 25 July 2011, http://www.publicreligion.org/ research/?id=654; Quinnipiac University poll, 8 June 2011; Gary Lawrence, interview with author, 4. See also Gary Lawrence's analysis in a press release, "Lawrence Research Poll: Mormon Presidential Candidates Face Bias," 6 September 2011, http://www.market- watch.com/story/lawrence-research-poll-mormon-presidential-ok? or candidates?-face-b ias-2011-09-06.

51. That poll was announced on *Fox & Friends* in July 2011; accessible at http://www.mediaite. com/tv/fox-friends-romney-obviously-not-being-a-christian-helps-perry-run/.

52. Thomas Beaumont, "Analysis: Perry may pose biggest threat to Romney," Associated Press wire, 12 August 2011, http://news.yahoo.com/analysis-perry-may-pose-biggest-threat-r omney-071137116.html.

53. For the clip from *Fox & Friends* and additional commentary, see Frances Martel, "Fox & Friends: Romney 'Obviously Not Being a Christian' Helps Perry Run," 17 July 2011, http://www.mediaite.com/tv/fox-friends-romney-obviously-not-being-a-christian-helps-perry-run/. For one blogger's response that since "rather than being on opposite poles of a distinct debate, Mormons and Evangelicals are merely two points along a long, dynamic, and diverse spectrum, . . . the label of Christian serves less as a devotional identifier and more as a polemical tool," see Benjamin E. Park, "Obviously Christian," *Patheos.com*, 21 July 2011, http://www.patheos.com/Resources/Additional-Resources/Obviously-Christian-Benjamin-Park-07-21-2011.html.

54. Perry's spokesman, Robert Black, later told reporters that "it was the conference organizers, not the Perry campaign, who chose Jeffress to introduce Perry." See Rachel Weiner, "Mormonism Takes Center Stage at Conservative Event," *Washington Post*, 7 October 2011, http://www.washingtonpost.com/politics/mormonism-takes-center-stage-at-conservative-event/2011/10/07/gIQA9rX0TL_story.html.

55. For Jeffress's comments, see Weiner, "Mormonism takes center stage at conservative event" and the CNN clip with Anderson Cooper at Frances Martel, "Anti-Mormon Pastor to Anderson Cooper: Romney May Belong to a 'Cult,' But He Is Better Than Obama," *Mediaite.com,* 8 October 2011, http://www.mediaite.com/tv/anti-mormon-pastor-to-anderson-cooper-romney-may-belong-to-a-cult-but-he-is-better-than-obama/. Martel said Jeffress "stole the Friday news cycle."

56. Compare the reporting of the poll results from LifeWay Research, "a body affiliated to the Southern Baptist Church," as reported in "Mormons are a cult says 75% of American Protestant pastors," *Digital Journal*, 11 October 2011, http://digitaljournal.com/article/312648, and Kerby, "Pollsters: 75 percent of pastors say Mormons 'not Christians," *Beliefnet.com,* 11 October 2011. See also Napp Nazworth, "Mormonism Debate: What Is a Cult?" *Christian Post,* 12 October 2011, for a consideration of the poll numbers as well as the Southern Baptist Convention's Richard Land's explanation of the meaning of cult: "When we use the word 'cult,' that's a theological definition of a movement that claims to be within the confines of the Christian faith and clearly is not within the confines of the Christian faith. It is a new religion," http://www.christianpost.com/news/mormonism-debate-what-is-a-cult-57979/.

57. All of the quotes from Pastor Jeffress's exchange with CNN's Anderson Cooper come from the author's transcription of the clip, http://www.mediaite.com/tv/anti-mormon-pastor-to-anderson-cooper-romney-may-belong-to-a-cult-but-he-is-better-than-obama/.

58. See, for example, Joanna Brooks, interview by author, 9 November 2012 transcript in author's possession, 4; also Robert L. Millet, correspondence with the author, 1 November 2011.

59. Richard J. Mouw, "My Take: This evangelical says Mormonism isn't a cult," special to CNN, 9 October 2011, http://religion.blogs.cnn.com/2011/10/09/my-take-this-evangelical-says-mormonism-isnt-a-cult/.

60. John Mark Reynolds, "Why evangelicals must stand up to anti-Mormon bigotry," *Washington Post* blog *On Faith*, 10 October 2011, http://www.washingtonpost.com/blogs/on-faith/post/why-evangelicals-must-stand-up-to-anti-mormon-bigotry/2011/10/10/gIQA06PqZL_blog.html.

61. Cathy Lynn Grossman, "Republican candidates distance themselves from Mormon remark," *USA Today*, 10 October 2011, http://www.usatoday.com/news/religion/story/2011-10-09/ney-perry-mormon/50713614/1; Sally Quinn's interview with Joel Osteen is accessible at http://www.washingtonpost.com/local/joel-osteen-on-pastor-robert-jeffress-and-mormonism/2011/10/26/gIQAx3WuJM_video.html.

62. Barbara Bradley Hagerty, "Despite Divide, Evangelicals Could Support a Mormon," National Public Radio, 12 October 2011, http://www.npr.org/2011/10/12/141269923/despite-divide-evangelicals-could-support-a-mormon; Gary Lawrence interview, 4–5.

63. On the "hardcore group of about 10%," see "Lawrence Research Poll: Mormon Presidential Candidates Face Bias," 6 September 2011; Robert L. Millet, correspondence with the author, 1 November 2011.

64. Kevin Liptak, "CNN Poll: Mormon candidate not a problem for most Americans," CNN, 19 October 2011, http://politicalticker.blogs.cnn.com/2011/10/19/cnn-poll-mormon-candidate-not-a-problem-for-most-americans/; "Lawrence Research Poll: Mormon Presidential Candidates Face Bias," 6 September 2011; Robert L. Millet, correspondence with the author.

65. Robert L. Millet, correspondence with author; Rachel Zoll, "Mormon beliefs once again under attack," Forbes.com and Associated Press, 10 October 2011, http://www.forbes.com/feeds/ap/2011/10/10/general-us-rel-mormons-questioned_8726953.html; Richard Bushman, interview by author, 1; Jan Shipps, interview by author, 12 October 2011, transcript in author's possession, 3.

66. Jonathan Merritt, "Election 2012 Marks the End of Evangelical Dominance in Politics," The Atlantic, 13 November 2012, http://www.theatlantic.com/politics/archive/2012/11/election-2012-marks-the-end-of-evangelical-dominance-in-politics/265139/. For Roman Catholic Rick Santorum's political alignment with conservative evangelicals, see David Gibson, "Is Rick Santorum a Catholic or an Evangelical? Yes," Huffington Post, 11 January 2012, http://www.huffingtonpost.com/2012/01/11/rick-santorum-catholic-evangelical_n_1200219.html: at a South Carolina campaign gathering, one Santorum supporter, Deal Hudson, said, "There were a number of knowledgeable people who were very enthusiastic about Rick but didn't know he was Catholic," Hudson said with a quiet laugh. "I was really surprised." See also Stephanie Griffith, "Cracks emerge in Santorum's evangelical support," AFP News, April 8, 2012, accessed 14 December 2012, http://www.google.com/hostednews/afp/article/ALeqM5juYGF5fhMQ_xiK_-_ZFSdE1PXjxA?docId=CNG.9b85ddfd992bc880ec93ea69da75b738.541.

67. Rachel Zoll (Associated Press), "Concerns about Romney's faith quieter but not 18 January 2012 accessed 18 January 2012, http://www.foxnews.com/us/2012/01/16/concerns-about-romneys-faith-quieter-but-not-gone/?cmpid=cmty_email_Gigya_Concerns_about_Romney%27s_faith_quieter_but_not_gone; Atkins's comments originally appeared in Andrew Moore and Reilly Moore, "SCBC President: Forgiven Gingrich Tops Mormon Romney," Easley (South Carolina) Patch, 19 December 2012, accessed 11 December 2012 at http://easley.patch.com/articles/lesser-of-two-evils-south-carolinians-grappling-with-issues-of-faith-fidelity.

68. Moore and Moore, "SCBC President: Forgiven Gingrich Tops Mormon Romney."

69. Joanna Brooks, " 'Mitt Romney Style'—A Virtually Religion Free 2012 Contest?" Religion Dispatches, October 29, 2012, accessed 5 November 2012 http://www.religiondispatches.org/dispatches/joannabrooks/6552/%E2%80%9Cmitt_romney_style%E2%80%9D%E2%80%94a_virtually_religion_free_2012_contest/. Brooks's memoir is The Book of Mormon Girl: A Memoir of an American Faith (New York: Free Press, 2012).

70. Kirk Jowers interview, 26 April 2010, 4.

71. "The Media, Religion and the 2012 Campaign for President," Pew Research Center's Project for Excellence in Journalism, 14 December 2012, accessed 17 December 2012 http://www.journalism.org/analysis_report/media_religion_and_2012_campaign_president; italics added.

72. Griffith, "Cracks emerge in Santorum's evangelical support."

73. "Romney's Mormon Faith Likely a Factor in Primaries, Not in a General Election," Pew Research Center, 23 November 2011, accessed 5 November 2012, http://pewresearch.org/pubs/2136/mormon-mormonism-evangelical-christian-catholic-protestant-religion-politics-presidential-primaries-race.

74. Matt Viser, "Romney's run evokes pride, fear in Mormons," Boston Globe, 29 May 2012, accessed 30 May 2012, http://www.boston.com/news/politics/articles/2012/05/29/gop_nominee_mitt_romney_poses_fears_of_backlash_among_utahs_mormons/?camp=pm.

For Michael Otterson's address (as well as that of Mormon Harvard Professor Clayton Christensen) to journalists at the Ethics and Public Policy Center's Faith Angle Forum in June 2012, see http://www.eppc.org/news/newsID.4783/news_detail.asp. The "October surprise" comment came from Michael Otterson, interview by author, 21 September 2012 transcript in author's possession, 8.

75. David Catanese, "Hatch: Obama camp will 'throw Mormon church' at Romney," *Politico.com*, 4 April 2012, accessed 11 December 2012, http://www.politico.com/blogs/david-catanese/2012/04/hatch-obama-camp-will-throw-mormon-church-at-romney-119564.html.

76. For the entire panel, "What Is It About Mormon?" *New York Times*, January 30, 2012, see http:// //www.nytimes.com/roomfordebate/2012/01/30/what-is-it-about-mormons. The "separation of church and state" comment came from Jane Barnes's piece in the roundtable "There Is a Dark Side to Mormonism." The "smother" comment came from Ian Williams, "It May Look Good on Paper."

77. Brooks, "'Mitt Romney Style'—A Virtually Religion Free 2012 Contest?"

78. Brooks, "'Mitt Romney Style'—A Virtually Religion Free 2012 Contest?"

79. Jackie Kucinich and Martha T. Moore, "Hilary Rosen says Ann Romney never worked 'day in her life'," *USA Today*, April 12, 2012, accessed 12 December 2012, http://usatoday30.usatoday.com/news/politics/story/2012-04-12/ann-romney-hilary-rosen-work/54235706/1. See also Michelle Boorstein, "Ann Romney 'stay-at-home mom' debate: Mormons react," *Washington Post*, 13 April 2012, accessed 17 April 2012, http://www.washingtonpost.com/blogs/under-god/post/ann-romney-stay-at-home-mom-debate-mormons-react/2012/04/13/gIQAJIBmFT_blog.html, for recognition that Mormons of differing political persuasions "wondered if the controversy was a sign that Mormon culture or doctrine would be coming up more, now that the presidential field appeared to be effectively down to two."

80. Quoted in Catanese, "Hatch: Obama camp will 'throw Mormon church' at Romney."

81. Edward Klein, "Media declares open season on Mitt Romney's Mormon faith," *FoxNews.com*, 30 August 2012, accessed 12 December 2012, http://www.foxnews.com/opinion/2012/08/30/media-declares-open-season-on-mitt-romney-mormon-faith/.

82. Elizabeth Flock, "Google Data: Interest in Mitt Romney's Mormon Faith Higher Than Ever Before," *U.S. News and World Report*, 7 September 2012, accessed 12 December 2012, http//www.usnews.com/news/blogs/washington-whispers/2012/09/07/google-data-interest-in-mitt-romneys-mormon-faith-higher-than-ever-before.

83. Brooks, "'Mitt Romney Style'—A Virtually Religion Free 2012 Contest?"

84. Aaron Blake, "Obama's Muslim Problem=Romney's Mormon Problem," *Washington Post*, 27 July 2012, accessed 30 July 2012, http://www.washingtonpost.com/blogs/the-fix/post/obamas-muslim-problem—romneys-mormon-problem/2012/07/26/gJQAu2vcCX_blog.html?wpisrc=emailtoafriend.

85. See Michael Otterson interview, 21 September 2012.

86. David Frum, "It's Mormon in America: Romney's religion just might be his greatest asset," *The Daily Beast*, 11 June 2012, accessed 14 June 2012, http://www.thedailybeast.com/newsweek/2012/06/10/david-frum-on-how-romney-s-religion-is-his-greatest-asset.html; italics added.

87. See also Chelynne Headman, "Mitt Romney opens up about LDS faith to public; NBC's 'Rock Center' takes a look at Mormonism Thursday," *Deseret News*, 20 August 2012, accessed 14 December 2012 http://www.deseretnews.com/article/765598136/Mitt-Romney-opens-up-about-LDS-faith-to-public-NBCs-Rock-Center-takes-a-look-at-Mormonism.html?pg=all; also Michael Barbaro and Ashley Parker, "Scripture, Song and Six Grandchildren: Romneys Open Church Doors to Press," *New York Times*, 19 August 2012, accessed 17 December 2012, http://www.nytimes.com/2012/08/20/us/politics/romneys-at-church-scripture-songs-and-six-grandchildren.html?_r=0.

88. Adam Gopnik, "I, Nephi: Mormonism and its meanings," *The New Yorker*, 13 August 2012, accessed 13 December 2012, http://www.newyorker.com/arts/critics/atlarge/2012/08/13/120813crat_atlarge_gopnik; Ross Douthat, "Romney, Mormonism and Money," *New York Times*, 13 August 2012, accessed 13 December 2012, http://douthat.blogs.

nytimes.com/2012/08/13/romney-mormonism-and-money/; Ross Douthat, "Romney's Mormon Story," *New York Times*, 11 August 2012, accessed 13 December 2012, http://www.nytimes.com/2012/08/12/opinion/sunday/douthat-romneys-mormon-story.html?pagewanted=print&_r=0.

89. Rachel Zoll, "And the winner is . . . the Mormon church," Associated Press, 15 November 2012, accessed 17 December 2012, http://bigstory.ap.org/article/and-winner-mormon-church.

90. See Michelle Cottle, "Mormon Church Scrambles in Romney Spotlight," *The Daily Beast*, 18 June 2012, accessed 20 June 2012, http://www.thedailybeast.com/newsweek/2012/06/17/mormon-church-scrambles-in-romney-spotlight.html.

91. Michael Otterson interview, 21 September 2012 9–10.

92. Scott D. Pierce, "Mormons came out looking very good in 'Rock Center' report," *Salt Lake Tribune*, 24 August 2012, accessed 14 December 2012, http://www.sltrib.com/sltrib/blogstv/54758500-63/church-center-mormons-rock.html.csp.

93. While early in the 2012 campaign season there seemed to be considerable attention to the fact that *two* Mormons were presidential candidates in the same Republican field, the "Jon Huntsman, Jr.-as-Mormon" story played much differently than did stories about Mitt Romney. Part of this was likely due to the reality that Huntsman was a long-shot to secure the Republican nomination, such that he did not draw as much press coverage. But undoubtedly part of it was Huntsman's own characterization of his faith. He said in 2010, "I can't say that I'm overly religious," and "I get satisfaction from many different types of religions and philosophies"—and this sense of his tenuous ties to Mormonism seemed to mean that religion was muted as a biographical feature (Thomas Burr, "Is Huntsman distancing himself from LDS faith?" *Salt Lake Tribune*, 27 June 2011, http://www.sltrib.com/sltrib/huntsman/51779611–188/church-faith-former-governor.html.csp). Brian Williams, on *Rock Center*, noted that Abby Huntsman had disassociated herself from her family's faith.

94. "Did Mitt Romney gain ground?" *CNN.com*, 31 August 2012, accessed 12 December 2012, http://www.cnn.com/2012/08/31/opinion/opinion-roundup-romney/index.html.

95. Zoll, "And the winner is . . . the Mormon church."

96. Flock, "Google Data: Interest in Mitt Romney's Mormon Faith Higher Than Ever Before."

97. Zoll, "And the winner is . . . the Mormon church."

98. Stephen Mansfield, quoted in Joseph Walker, "Books on Mormons: LDS, non-LDS authors try to explain the faith," *Deseret News*, 16 September 2012, accessed 19 September 2012, http://www.deseretnews.com/article/765604658/Books-on-Mormons-LDS-non-LDS-authors-try-to-explain-the-faith.html; Stephen Mansfield, "The Mormonizing of America," *Huffington Post*, 6 November 2012, accessed 14 November 2012, http://www.huffingtonpost.com/stephen-mansfield/the-mormonizing-of-americ_b_2083125.html.

99. Beam, "A big win for the Mormon church."

100. Richard Bushman interview, 2; Terryl Givens interview, 1.

101. Zoll, "And the winner is . . . the Mormon church."

102. "Mormons in America: Certain in Their Beliefs, Uncertain of Their Place in Society," Pew Forum on Religion and Public Life, 12 January 2012, accessed 14 December 2012, http://www.pewforum.org/christian/mormon/mormons-in-america-executive-summary.aspx#moment.

103. David E. Campbell, John C. Green, and J. Quin Monson, "Tolerance? We Have a Ways to Go," *USA Today*, 30 November 2009; accessed 11 December 2009, http://blogs.usatoday.com/oped/2009/ 11/column-tolerance-we-have-a-ways-to-go-.html; italics added.

104. "Americans Learned Little About the Mormon Faith, But Some Attitudes Have Softened," Pew Forum on Religion and Public Life, 14 December 2012, accessed 17 December 2012, http://www.pewforum.org/Christian/Mormon/attitudes-toward-mormon-faith.aspx.

105. "Americans Learned Little About the Mormon Faith, But Some Attitudes Have Softened," Pew Forum on Religion and Public Life.

106. "Americans Learned Little About the Mormon Faith, But Some Attitudes Have Softened," Pew Forum on Religion and Public Life.

107. Quoted in Zoll, "And the winner is . . . the Mormon church."

108. See http://www.votingforjesus.com/; accessed 11 December 2012.

109. See Bruce Wilson, "Almost 1.4 Million Pledge for Jesus as Write-in Candidate in 2012, as Disgruntled Evangelicals Vent Their Anti-Mormon, Anti-Obama Ire," talk2action.org, 25 October 2012, accessed 11 December 2012, http://www.alternet.org/election-2012/almost-14-million-pledge-jesus-write-candidate-2012-disgruntled-evangelicals-vent.

110. Michael Kranish, "In twist, evangelicals now backing Mitt Romney," *Boston Globe*, 14 October 2012, accessed 11 December 2012, http://bostonglobe.com/news/nation/2012/10/13/campaign-twist-mitt-romney-now-relying-evangelicals-who-ove rcome-doubts-about-mormonism/R2gAmXFLHia7rgrwneHrZM/story.html.

111. Robert Jeffress, "Romney and the disappearing evangelical dilemma," *FoxNews.com*, 19 September 2012, accessed 11 December 2012, http://www.foxnews.com/opinion/2012/09/19/mitt-romney-and-disappearing-evangelical-dilemma/.

112. See John-Charles Duffy, "Conservative Pluralists: The Cultural Politics of Mormon-Evangelical Dialogue in the United States at the Turn of the Twenty-first Century" (Ph.D. dissertation: University of North Carolina at Chapel Hill, 2011), for Duffy's argument that evangelicals found a rhetorical place for dialogue and interaction with Mormons by avoiding doctrinal compromise—and this essentially allowed support for Mitt Romney, as long as that political cooperation did not require tacit acceptance of Mormons as Christians.

113. "Text of Mitt Romney's commencement address at Liberty University," *CNN.com*, 12 May 2012, accessed 15 May 2012, http://religion.blogs.cnn.com/2012/05/12/text-of-mitt-ro mneys-commencement-address-at-liberty-university/.

114. See Sally Quinn, "Sins of the son: Sad treatment for Billy Graham," *Washington Post* blog *On Faith*, 8 November 2012, accessed 11 December 2012, http://www.washingtonpost.com/national/on-faith/sins-of-the-son-sad-treatment-for-billy-graham/2012/11/08/a31f5de2-29f4-11e2-96b6-8e6a7524553f_story.html.

115. Merritt, "Election 2012 Marks the End of Evangelical Dominance in Politics." See also "The Media, Religion and the 2012 Campaign for President," Pew Research Center's Project for Excellence in Journalism, 14 December 2012, which calculated 79 percent of white evangelicals voted for George W. Bush in 2004 and Mitt Romney in 2012, while 73 percent of evangelicals voted for John McCain in 2008, based on exit polling; accessed 17 December 2012, http://www.journalism.org/analysis_report/media_religion_and_2012_campaign_president.

116. Wesley Theological Seminary professor Shaun Casey, quoted in Merritt, "Election 2012 Marks the End of Evangelical Dominance in Politics."

117. See, for example, Michael Gordon, "Pew Study: Protestants in U.S. a minority for the first time," *Charlotte Observer*, 10 October 2012, accessed 17 December 2012, http://www.charlotteobserver.com/2012/10/10/3587547/protestants-in-us-a-minority-for.html. The full study can be found at "'Nones' on the Rise," Pew Forum on Religion and Public Life, 9 October 2012, http://www.pewforum.org/Unaffiliated/nones-on-the-rise.aspx.

118. Zoll, "Concern about Romney's faith quieter but not gone."

119. Daniel Burke, "Billy Graham faces backlash over Mormon 'cult' removal," *Washington Post*, 24 October 2012, accessed 30 October 2012, http://articles.washingtonpost.com/2012-10-24/national/35501066_1_mormonism-evangelicals-christians.

120. "Panel asks: Can Christians vote for a ?" *Baptist Press News*, 11 September 2012, accessed 13 September 2012, http://www.bpnews.net/bpnews.asp?ID=38688.

121. Quoted in Liz Halloran, "What Romney's Run Means for Mormonism," National Public Radio, 1 November 2012, accessed 14 December 2012, http://www.npr.org/blogs/itsallpolitics/2012/11/01/164101548/what-romneys-run-means-for-mormonism.

122. Zoll, "And the winner is...the Mormon church." For additional evidence of those changes "already under way," see Richard J. Mouw, *Talking with Mormons: An Invitation to Evangelical* (Grand Rapids, Michigan: Wm. B. Eerdmans Co., 2012), where Mouw discusses his motivation for interfaith dialogue with Mormons, even in the face of stiff criticism from some Christian quarters. For an overview of the dynamics in the decade-long evangelical-Mormon dialogue headed by Richard Mouw and Robert Millet, see the fall 2012 edition of *Evangelical Interfaith Dialogue* 3, no. 2—the entire issue is devoted to the Mormon-evangelical interaction. The journal is published by Fuller Theological Seminary, and the journal's editor, Cory Willson, is himself a participant in the dialogue.

123. Franklin Graham, "Can an Evangelical Christian Vote for a Mormon?" *Decision Magazine*, 22 October 2012, accessed 11 December 2012, www.billygraham.org/articlepage.asp?articleid=8998; italics added.

124. University of Utah history professor Colleen McDannell made the Al Smith comparison during the question and answer period of a "Mormon and Politics" session at the annual meetings of the American Academy of Religion, 19 November 2012. Mormon historian Matthew Bowman told National Public Radio that "Romney is far different than Kennedy. Kennedy's election marked the culmination of a long process of Catholic integration in the U.S. Romney's run is still early in Mormonism' integration." In Liz Halloran, "What Romney's Run Means for Mormonism."

125. Joanna Brooks, interview by author, 9 November 2012, 1.

126. Joanna Brooks, interview by author. Andrew Sullivan eventually posted the video in a column he wrote for *the Daily Beast* in late October 2012, 1.

127. One important thread of discussion throughout the campaign was challenging the assumptions of, and philosophy behind, anti-Mormonism. See BYU history professor J. Spencer Fluhman's 3 June 2012 essay in the *New York Times*, "Why We Fear Mormons," for the pointed assertion that "making Mormons look bad helps others feel good. By imagining Mormons as intolerant rubes, or as heretical deviants, Americans from left and right can imagine they are, by contrast, tolerant, rational and truly Christian." Accessed 28 August 2012, http://www.nytimes.com/2012/06/04/opinion/anti-mormonism-past-and-present.html?emc=eta1&_r=0.

128. Historian Matthew Bowman characterized his interactions with, and observations of, the media this way: "I saw two waves of media coverage this time around; in 2008, I think we only got the first. The first wave came early on, and was, more or less, about fascination with the oddities of Mormonism: think Huckabee's offhand comment about Jesus and Satan, the fascination with proxy baptism, and so on. It's my impression that this dropped off around the end of primary season, and we started to see much more interesting and substantive coverage about what it's like to be a Mormon, Romney's experience as a bishop and stake president, the internationalization and Americanization of the church, and so on. The articles about church finance I'd put in this category. I think toward the end of this season the press really started to get it right." Matthew Bowman, correspondence with the author, 4 November 2012.

129. See Quentin L. Cook, "Sunbeams, Public Affairs, and Gospel Joy," *Ensign*, December 2012, 80, where he describes visits he and fellow apostle M. Russell Ballard made to "the editorial boards of major newspapers" in the hope of rectifying what they saw as a deficiency during coverage surrounding the first Mitt Romney campaign: "media outlets often contacted people who weren't members of the Church to find out about the Church." The apostles' message: "We want you to come and talk to us if you're going to discuss what we believe." Cook's assessment in 2012 was that "those visits were well received, and we found that our request resonated."

130. Joanna Brook, interview with author, 3; Michael Otterson interview, 9 September 2011 3, 6; Richard Bushman interview, 3.

131. Joanna Brooks, interview by author (the "translate" analogy is hers), 2, 3; Cook, "Sunbeams, Public Affairs, and Gospel Joy."

132. Quoted in Halloran, "What Romney's Run Means for Mormonism."

133. Liz Halloram, "Mormon Democrats Battling Romney—and What Would Be Church History," 4 September 2012, accessed blogs/itsallpolitics/2012/09/04/160570257/mormon-democrats-battling-romney-and-what-would-be-church-history.

134. See Gregory A. Prince, "Mitt Romney Is Not the Face of Mormonism," *Huffington Post*, 19 September 2012, accessed 27 September 2012, http://www.huffingtonpost.com/gregory-a-prince-phd/mitt-romney-is-not-the-face-of-mormonism_b_1897404.html?utm_hp_ref=email_share; see also Thomas Burr, "Harry Reid: Mitt Romney is not the face of Mormonism," *Salt Lake Tribune*, 24 September 2012, accessed 26 September 2012, http://www.sltrib.com/sltrib/politics/54958981-90/romney-reid-prince-mormonism.html.csp. For the view of a European Mormon academic about the more negative play of the "Mormon moment" in Europe, and his opinion that the attention to Mormon

democrats (while limited) created favorable impressions about Mormon diversity, see Wilfried Decoo, "The Mormon moment abroad: thank you, Jim Dabakis," Times and Seasons (blog), 13 December 2012, http://timesandseasons.org/index.php/2012/12/the-mormon-moment-abroad-thank-you-jim-dabakis/.

135. Jason Horowitz, "The Genesis of a church's stand on race," *Washington Post*, 28 February 2012, accessed on 1 March 2012, http://articles.washingtonpost.com/2012-02-28/politics/35443157_1_george-romney-first-mormon-presidential-nominee-michigan-governor/2. For immediate reaction and strong rejection of the professor's position, as well as the historical context of the priesthood restriction in the nineteenth century, see the blog post by University of Utah Paul Reeve: "Professor Bott, Elijah Abel, and a Plea from the Past," *Juvenile Instructor.org*, 1 March 2012, http://www.juvenileinstructor.org/guest-post-professor-bott-elijah-abel-and-a-plea-from-the-past/. One of Reeve's earlier blogs also was reposted in the wake of the *Washington Post* article: "Mitt Romney, Blackness, and the Book of Mormon, Part I," *keepapitchinin.org*, 14 February 14, 2012, http://www.keepapitchinin.org/2012/02/14/guest-post-mitt-romney-blackness-and-the-book-of-mormon-part-i/. Reeve is currently writing *Religion of a Different Color: Race and the Mormon Struggle for Whiteness*, forthcoming from Oxford University Press.

136. See, for example, Peggy Fletcher Stack, "Mormon church disputes BYU prof's remarks about blacks," *Salt Lake Tribune*, 29 February 2012, accessed 18 December 2012, http://www.sltrib.com/sltrib/mobile/53617297-68/church-bott-mormon-priesthood.html.csp; also see Mormon author Samuel Brown's comments on a *Huffington Post* blog: "Even as many, hopefully most, Latter-day Saints have moved beyond a racist past they unfortunately shared with most of white America, some holdouts will continue to cause difficulty for the Church and its members...We who value the church can earnestly hope that this debacle will persuade those Latter-day Saints who hold such moth-eaten, malignant beliefs that it is time to abandon them." Samuel Brown, "The End in Sight? The Waning of a Racist Mormon Fringe," *Huffington Post*, 29 February 2012, accessed 18 December 2012, http://www.huffingtonpost.com/samuel-brown/end-in-sight-of-racist-mormon-fringe_b_1309885.html; compare also Daniel C. Peterson, "An Unfortunate Attempt to Explain the Pre-1978 Priesthood Ban," *Patheos.com*, 28 February 2012, accessed 18 December 2012, http://www.patheos.com/blogs/danpeterson/2012/02/an-unfortunate-attempt-to-explain-the-pre-1978-priesthood-ban.html.

137. For the 29 February 2012 church statement (which also took the rare step of referring to the professor by name), see http://www.mormonnewsroom.org/article/racial-remarks-in-washington-post-article.

138. See, for example, Joanna Brooks, "LDS Church Ac 1 March 2012, accessed 18 December 2012, http://www.religiondispatches.org/dispatches/joannabrooks/5752/lds_church_acknowledges_past_racism,_repudiates_racist_remarks.

139. See http://www.lds.org/scriptures/dc-testament/od?lang=eng.

140. Matthew Bowman, in a 5 November 2012 email to the author, noted: "Mostly, I'm a bit surprised at two things: what became an issue, and what didn't. Mormons tend to talk about Mormonism mostly with other Mormons, which can mean the things which seize the attention of the national media may surprise them. I am surprised that the issue of the priesthood ban did not gain more traction."

141. Jeff Benedict, "Jabari Parker Is...," *Sports Illustrated*, 21 May 2012, http://sportsillustrated.cnn.com/vault/article/magazine/MAG1198498/index.htm; Jabari Parker's conversation with Katie Couric was aired on ABC's *Good Morning America*, 14 June 2012.

142. See, for example, Edward Wyckoff Williams, "Race Matters: Mormonism, Rev. Jeremiah Wright and the 2012 Presidential Race," *Huffington Post*, 10 February 2012, accessed 12 March 2012, http://www.huffingtonpost.com/edward-wyckoff-williams/mit-romney-mormon-race_b_1269016.html?ref=email_share; Sharon Toomer, "Probe Mitt Romney's Affiliation with the Mormon Church—It's Not Too Late and It's Required," *Huffington Post*, 29 October 2012, accessed 5 November 2012, http://www.huffingtonpost.com/blackandbrownnews/prob-mitt-romney-affiliation_b_2025327.html; Andrew

Sullivan, "Religion, Race and Double Standards," *The Daily Beast*, 23 October 2012, accessed 5 November 2012, http://andrewsullivan.thedailybeast.com/2012/10/religion-r ace-and-double-standards.html. One telling aspect of Toomer's and Sullivan's articles was their similar complaints that *not enough* attention had been devoted to the place of race in Mormon discourse and history.

143. See Maeve Reston, "Mitt Romney low-key on civil rights, in contrast to his father," *Los Angeles Times*, 8 July 2012, accessed 29 October 2012, http://articles.latimes.com/2012/jul/08/nation/la-na-adv-romney-civil-rights-20120708; John Randolph Wood, Jr., "The Civil Rights Legacy of George Romney," accessed 29 October 2012, http://www.blackison-line.com/2012/07/the-civil-rights-legacy-of-george-/. Compare also Susan Saulny, "Black Mormons and the Politics of Identity," *New York Times*, 22 May 2012, accessed 25 May 2012, http://www.nytimes.com/2012/05/23/us/for-black-mormons-a-political-choice-like-no-other.html?pagewanted=all&_r=0, where a number of black Mormons professed their faith.

144. "Invasion of the body snatchers syndrome": This memorable line comes from Laurie F. Maffly-Kipp, "Mormons' Double Legacy," *New York Times*, 30 January 2012, accessed 11 December 2012, http://www.nytimes.com/roomfordebate/2012/01/30/what-is-it-about-mormons/the-double-legacy-of-mormons.

145. Toomer, "Probe Mitt Romney's Affiliation with the Mormon Church—It's Not Too Late and It's Required"; Sullivan, "Religion, Race and Double Standards"; Sullivan's conversation with HBO's Maher is documented in "Andrew Sullivan: Romney's Mormonism Was Relevant During Campaign," *Real Clear Politics*, 10 November 2012, accessed 18 December 2012, http://www.realclearpolitics.com/video/2012/11/10/andrew_sullivan_romneys_mormonism_was_relevant_during_campaign.html; Andrew Sullivan, "When Christianism Bites Back," *The Daily Beast*, 29 October 2012, accessed 18 December 2012 http://andrewsullivan.thedailybeast.com/2012/10/when-christianism-bites-back.html.

146. "Americans Learned Little About the Mormon Faith, But Some Attitudes Have Softened," Pew Forum on Religion and Public Life, December 14, 2012.

147. "The Media, Religion and the 2012 Campaign for President," Pew Research Center's Project for Excellence in Journalism, December 14, 2012

148. Craig L. Foster, "Mitt Romney and the Media's Shaping of the Mormon Question," unpublished paper presented at the Mormon Media Studies Symposium, Brigham Young University, November 9, 2012, copy in author's possession, 1. Foster is also the author of *A Different God?: Mitt Romney, the Religious Right, and the Mormon question* (Salt Lake City: Greg Kofford Books, 2008), and, with Newell G. Bringhurst, *The Mormon Quest for the Presidency: From Joseph Smith to Mitt Romney and Jon Huntsman* (Independence, Missouri: John Whitmer Books, 20011).

149. Lane Williams, "Mormon Media Observer: A look at the media's use of 'cult' in LDS coverage," *Deseret News*, 22 October 2012, accessed 22 October 2012, http://www.deseretnews.com/article/865565011/A-look-at-the-medias-use-of-cult-in-LDS-coverage.html?pg=all, quoted in Foster, "Mitt Romney and the Media's Shaping of the Mormon Question," 4.

150. "Americans Learned Little About the Mormon Faith, But Some Attitudes Have Softened," Pew Forum on Religion and Public Life, December 14, 2012.

151. "Bill Maher Says President Obama Will Beat Romney 'Like a Runaway Sister Wife,'" *Mediate*, 26 January 2012, accessed 27 January 2012, http://www.mediate.com/tv/bill-maher-says-president-obama-will-beat-romney-like-a-runaway-sister-/, quoted in Foster, "Mitt Romney and the Media's Shaping of the Mormon Question," 5.

152. Cottle, "Mormon Church Scrambles in Spotlight."

153. Michael Otterson interview, 9 September 2011 8.

154. Terryl Givens locates the book's popularity in the way that "Krakauer repeats the winning formula of the nineteenth-century sensation novel, with only slightly more historical accuracy than his early counterparts." Terryl L. Givens, *The Viper on the Hearth: Mormons, Myths, and the Construction of Heresy*, updated edition (New York and Oxford: Oxford University Press, 2013), 186. The best-sellers list was accessed 18 December 2012, http://www.amazon.com/Best-Sellers-Books-Mormonism/zgbs/books/12430/ref=zg_bs_nav_b_2_12290#1. Ironically, the *Becoming Sister Wives* story in book form was number

three on the list, and *Under the Banner of Heaven* (Kindle edition) was sixth. On the movie, see Hal Boyd, "Ron Howard to direct 'Under the Banner of Heaven' film," *Deseret News*, 20 July 2011, accessed 18 December 2012, http://www.deseretnews.com/article/700164651/Ron-Howard-to-direct-Under-the-Banner-of-Heaven-film.html?pg=all. A blogger wrote in March 2012 that he had contacts in the Utah State Prison that told him that writers had been to the prison to interview Dan Lafferty about the movie. See "Update on 'Under the Banner of Heaven' movie," posted "Prison insider" on 13 March 2012, at exmormon.org, accessed 18 December 2012,http://exmormon.org/phorum/read.php?2,442537,442713.

155. See for example, Adam Gopnik, "I, Nephi": "The most striking feature of Mitt Romney as a politician is an absence of any responsibility to his own past—the consuming sense that his life and opinions can be remade at a moment's need"; David Axelrod told ABC News in July 2012 that Mitt Romney was the "most secretive candidate" since Richard Nixon, accessed 6 July 2012, http://abcnews.go.com/Politics/video/david-axelrod-abc-romney-secretive-candidate-nixon-16719855; Alex Beam's Boston *Globe* editorial in November 2012—"A big win for the Mormon church"—came under the heading "The Great Mormon Etch-a-Sketch," and traced what Beam described as changes to Mormon beliefs and practices based on "a revelation, if you will: If you can't beat 'em, join 'em."

156. David Campbell presented these initial findings in a keynote address at the Mormon Media Studies Symposium, Brigham Young University, November 8, 2012, and expanded on those comments in an interview with the author, 9 November 2012. The findings will be published in David E. Campbell, John C. Green, and J. Quin Monson, *Seeking the Promised Land: Mormons and American Politics* (Cambridge University Press, forthcoming).

157. Maffly-Kipp, "Mormons' Double Legacy."

158. Terryl L. Givens, *People of Paradox: A History of Mormon Culture* (Oxford and New York: Oxford University Press, 2007).

159. Jon Meacham's story "The Mormon in Mitt," *Time*, 8 October 2012, was reviewed by Joseph Walker, "Time magazine explores 'The Mormon in Mitt,'" *Deseret News*, 1 October 2012, http://http://www.deseretnews.com/article/865563544/Time-magazine-explores-The-Mormon-in-Mitt.html?pg=2.

160. See, for example, Jennifer Rubin, "The Mormon Obsession," *Washington Post*, 20 May 2012, accessed 20 May 2012, http://www.washingtonpost.com/blogs/right-turn/post/the-mormon-obsession/2012/05/20/gIQATyBPdU_blog.html, for complaints about projecting supposed "Mormon" values onto Mitt Romney to paint him as "*the* Mormon candidate."

161. Harold Bloom, in Part Two of *The Mormons*, http://www.pbs.org/mormons/view/. In that same vein, the work of British anthropologist and Anglican priest Douglas J. Davies has focused on what he calls Mormonism's "death conquest." See, for example, Davies, *The Mormon Culture of Salvation: Force, Grace, Glory* (Burlington, Vermont: Ashgate, 2000).

162. Stephen H. Webb, "Mormonism Obsessed with Christ," *First Things*, February 2012, accessed7March2012,http://www.firstthings.com/article/2012/01/mormonism-obsessed-with-christ.

163. Stephen H. Webb, "The Mormon Ecumenical Moment," Fifth Annual Truman G. Madsen Lecture, The Wheatley Institution, BYU, 15 November 2012, transcript, 10. Webb also explores themes about materiality and divinity—and Mormonism—in his *Jesus Christ, Eternal God: Heavenly Flesh and the Metaphysics of Matter* (New York and Oxford: Oxford University Press, 2012). His 2013 release, also from Oxford, was Mormon Christianity: What Other Christians Can Learn from the Latter-day Saints.

164. For the university's news release, see H. Brevy Cannon, "U.Va. Creates Richard Lyman Bushman Chair of Mormon Studies," *UVAToday*, accessed 17 December 2012, http://news.virginia.edu/content/uva-creates-richard-lyman-bushman-chair-mormon-studies; Richard Bushman is quoted in Joseph Walker, "University of Virginia Chair in Mormon Studies named for Richard L. Bushman," *Deseret News*, 12 October 2012, accessed 17 December 2012, http://www.deseretnews.com/article/865564373/

University-of-Virginia-Chair-in-Mormon-studies-named-for-Richard-L-Bushman. html?pg=all. By 2012, Utah State University and the University of Utah had (as might be expected) established recent professorships and fellowships in Mormon Studies, but so had the University of Wyoming and Claremont Graduate University. Along with Matthew Bowman's *Mormon People* mentioned earlier, other notable Mormon-related books that hit shelves during Mitt Romney's second presidential run include Terryl L. Givens and Matthew J. Grow, *Parley P. Pratt: The Apostle Paul of Mormonism* (New York and Oxford: Oxford University Press, 2011); Reid L. Neilson, *Exhibiting Mormonism: The Latter-day Saints and the 1893 Chicago World's Fair* (New York and Oxford: Oxford University Press, 2011); Patrick Q. Mason, *The Mormon Menace: Violence and Anti-Mormonism in the Postbellum South* (New York and Oxford: Oxford University Press, 2011); Samuel Morris Brown, *In Heaven as It Is on Earth: Joseph Smith and the Early Mormon Conquest of Death* (New York and Oxford: Oxford University Press, 2012); John G. Turner, *Brigham Young: Pioneer Prophet* (Cambridge and London: The Belknap Press of Harvard University Press, 2012); Paul C. Gutjahr, *The Book of Mormon: A Biography* (Princeton and Oxford: Princeton University Press, 2012); and J. Spencer Fluhman, *"A Peculiar People": Anti-Mormonism and the Making of Religion in Nineteenth-Century America* (Chapel Hill: The University of North Carolina Press, 2012).

165. Neil J. Young, "Is the Mormon Moment Over?" *Huffington Post*, 20 November 2012, accessed 18 December 2012, http://www.huffingtonpost.com/neil-j-young/is-the-mormon-moment-over_b_2160270.html.

166. Reid L. Neilson, interview with author, 14 December 2012, transcript in author's possession, 1.

167. See, for example, John Turner's gratitude, in the "acknowledgements" of his *Brigham Young: Pioneer Prophet*, for the LDS Church History Department's making available to him "the entirety of the massive Brigham Young Papers and several other key collections" (487)—a type of access that researchers complained they could not get less than two decades earlier. See, for example, John L. Brooke, *The Refiner's Fire: The Making of Mormon Cosmology, 1644–1844* (Cambridge and New York: Cambridge University Press, 1994), 304: "the church hierarchy has staunchly opposed the course" of "[embracing] the past with all its shadows" by "closing its archives..."

168. Michael Otterson interview, 9 September 2011 5.

169. Michael Otterson interview, 9 September 2011 4.

170. Richard Bushman interview, 1.

171. Gary Lawrence interview, 4.

172. Kathleen Flake told National Public Radio in November 2012, "Certainly, more people will have heard of [Mormonism]" after coverage of Mitt Romney's campaign, "but with few exceptions, what they have heard pro and con seems remarkably similar to what was being said in the 1970s." Liz Halloran, "What Romney's Run Means for Mormonism."

173. Richard Bushman interview, 7–9.

174. Terryl Givens on Part Two of *The Mormons*, transcript, http://www.pbs.org/ mormons/interviews/givens.html.

175. Paulson's comments came in a speech he gave at Utah Valley University; see his account at Michael Paulson, "Reflecting on Mormonism and the media," 4 April 2009, http://www.boston.com/news/local/articles_of_faith/mormonism/.

176. Givens's comments came in Part Two of Helen Whitney's 2007 documentary, *The Mormons*, http://www.pbs.org/mormons/view/; for a transcript, see http://www.pbs.org/mormons/interviews/givens.html.

177. Sally Atkinson, "Mormons and Mitt Romney," *Newsweek*, 8 February 2008, http://www.newsweek.com/id/109478.

178. Daniel Peterson, in Part Two of *The Mormons*;, transcript, http://www.pbs.org/mormons/interviews/peterson.html.

179. Armand L. Mauss, *The Angel and the Beehive: The Mormon Struggle with Assimilation* (Urbana and Chicago: University of Illinois Press, 1994), 8–9.

180. Sheryl Gay Stolberg, "For Mormons, a Cautious Step Toward Mainstream Acceptance," *New York Times*, 7 November 2012, accessed 17 December 2012, http://www.nytimes.com/2012/11/08/us/politics/at-least-a-degree-of-validation-for-mormons.html?pagewanted=all&_r=0.

181. Kernis, "Richard Bushman: The Book of Mormon is like looking into a fun-house mirror."

182. Scott Swofford interview, 3, 4.

183. Beam, "A big win for the Mormon Church." Long-time scholar of Mormonism Jan Shipps agreed, saying in November 2012, "After this, it's hard to say the Mormons are really out-siders" (Zoll, "And the winner is...the Mormon church").

Bibliography

Manuscript Collections

"Compiled Information Concerning African Americans, BYU, and the Church." L. Tom Perry Special Collections, Harold B. Lee Library, Brigham Young University, Provo, Utah.

Cult Awareness Network Files. L. Tom Perry Special Collections, Harold B. Lee Library, Brigham Young University, Provo, Utah.

George Romney Resource Files, 1967-1971. Church History Library and Archives, The Church of Jesus Christ of Latter-day Saints, Salt Lake City, Utah.

Journal History of The Church of Jesus Christ of Latter-day Saints. Church History Library and Archives, The Church of Jesus Christ of Latter-day Saints, Salt Lake City, Utah.

Marriott, J. Willard. Papers. Special Collections, Marriott Library, University of Utah, Salt Lake City, Utah.

Public Affairs Department Papers. The Church of Jesus Christ of Latter-day Saints. Salt Lake City, Utah.

Public Communications Department Papers. The Church of Jesus Christ of Latter-day Saints. Salt Lake City, Utah.

Wilkinson, Ernest L. Diary. In Ernest L. Wilkinson Personal Papers. L. Tom Perry Special Collections, Harold B. Lee Library, Brigham Young University, Provo, Utah.

——. Presidential Papers. L. Tom Perry Special Collections, Harold B. Lee Library, Brigham Young University, Provo, Utah.

Interviews and Correspondence

Bench, Curt. 10 February 2010.

Blomberg, Craig. 12 September 2008.

Bowman, Matthew. 4 November 2012.

Brooks, Joanna. 9 November 2012.

Bushman, Richard. 12 August 2011.

Campbell, David. 9 November 2012, 6 June 2013.

Davies, Douglas. 22 February 2007.

Edwards, Val. 21 August 2008.

Givens, Terryl. 15 August 2011.

Heersink, Bill. 15 February 2010.

Jensen, Marlin K. 24 March 2010.

Johnson, Greg. 2 March 2010.

Jowers, Kirk. 12 August 2008, 24 April 2010.
Keller, Roger. 24 February 2010.
Lawrence, Gary. 11 October 2011.
Leonard, Glen. 3 March 2010.
Lindsay, Richard P. 22 February 2007.
Lund, John L. 4 August 2009.
Madsen, Truman G. 22 February 2007.
Millet, Robert. 16 March 2007, 22 February 2010, 1 November 2011.
Neilson, Reid. 14 December 2012.
Olsen, Bruce. 12 August 2008, 17 October 2008.
Otterson, Michael. 9 September 2011, 21 September 2012.
Paulsen, David. 8 March 2007.
Quinn, D. Michael. 20 March 2010.
Rowe, Glenn. 8 April 2010.
Shipps, Jan. 12 October 2011.
Stack, Peggy Fletcher. 12 December 2008.
Swofford, Scott. 18 October 2011.
Toscano, Paul. 15 February 2010.
Tuttle, Mark. 20 August 2008.

Books and Selected Articles

Ahlstrom, Sydney E. *A Religious History of the American People*. New Haven and London: Yale University Press, 1972.
Alexander, Thomas G. *Mormonism in Transition: A History of the Latter-day Saints, 1890–1930*. Urbana and Chicago: University of Illinois Press, Illini Books edition, 1996.
Allen, James B., and Glen M. Leonard. *The Story of the Latter-day Saints*, revised and enlarged edition. Salt Lake City: Deseret Book, 1992.
Allitt, Patrick. *Religion in America Since 1945: A History*. New York: Columbia University Press, 2003.
Anderson, Lavina Fielding. "The LDS Intellectual Community and Church Leadership: A Contemporary Chronology." *Dialogue* 26, no. 1 (Spring 1993): 7–64.
Arrington, Leonard. *Adventures of a Church Historian*. Urbana and Chicago: University of Illinois Press, 1998.
Arrington, Leonard J., and Davis Bitton. *The Mormon Experience: A History of the Latter-day Saints*, 2nd ed. Urbana and Chicago: University of Illinois Press, 1992.
Astle, Randy, with Gideon O. Burton. "A History of Mormon Cinema." *BYU Studies* 46, no. 2 (2007): 13–163.
Bachman, Danel W. "Sealed in a Book: Preliminary Observations on the Newly Found 'Anthon Transcript.'" *Brigham Young University Studies* 20 (Summer 1980): 321–345.
Baker, Sherry, and Daniel A. Stout. "Mormons and the Media, 1898-2003: A Selected, Annotated, and Indexed Bibliography (with Suggestions for Future Research)." *BYU Studies* 42, nos. 3 and 4 (2003): 124–181.
Balmer, Randall. *Blessed Assurance: A History of Evangelicalism in America*. Boston: Beacon Press, 1999.
———. *Religion in Twentieth Century America*. New York and Oxford: Oxford University Press, 2001. *Thy Kingdom Come: How the Religious Right Distorts the Faith and Threatens America: An Evangelical's Lament*. New York: Basic Books, 2006.
———. *God in the White House: A History: How Faith Shaped the Presidency from John F. Kennedy to George W. Bush*. New York: HarperOne, 2008.
Baugh, Alexander L. "Mormonism's Remarkable History: A Conversation with Max Parkin." *Mormon Historical Studies* 12, no. 2 (Fall 2011): 95–140.
Becker, Susan D. *The Origins of the Equal Rights Amendment: American Feminism Between the Wars*. Westport, Connecticut: Geenwood Press, 1981.

Beckwith, Francis J., Carl Mosser, and Paul Owen, eds. *The New Mormon Challenge: Responding to the Latest Defenses of a Fast-Growing Movement*. Grand Rapids, Michigan: Zondervan, 2002.

Bergera, Gary James. "Tensions in David O. McKay's First Presidencies." *Journal of Mormon History* 33, no. 1 (Spring 2007): 179–246.

Bergera, Gary James, and Ronald Priddis. *Brigham Young University: A House of Faith*. Salt Lake City: Signature Books, 1985.

Berry, Mary Frances. *Why ERA Failed: Politics, Women's Rights, and the Amending Process of the Constitution*. Bloomington: Indiana University Press, 1986.

Bishop, Daniel E. "Runaway Officials," In *Encyclopedia of Latter-day Saint History*, ed. Arnold K. Garr, Donald Q. Cannon, and Richard O. Cowan. Salt Lake City: Deseret Book, 2000, 1045.

Bitton, Davis. "Ten Years in Camelot: A Personal Memoir." *Dialogue* 16, no. 3 (Autumn 1983): 9–33.

Bitton, Davis, and Leonard J. Arrington. *Mormons and Their Historians*. Vol. 2 of Publications in Mormon Studies. Salt Lake City: University of Utah, 1988.

Blomberg, Craig L., and Stephen E. Robinson. *How Wide the Divide?: A Mormon and an Evangelical in Conversation*. Downers Grove, Illinois: InterVarsity Press, 1997.

Blumenthal, Sidney. "The Religious Right and Republicans." Chapter 18 in *Piety and Politics: Evangelicals and Fundamentalists Confront the World*, ed. Richard John Neuhaus and Michael Cromartie. Washington, D.C.: Ethics and Public Policy Center, 1987, 269–286.

Bowman, Matthew. *The Mormon People: The Making of an American Faith*. New York: Random House, 2012.

Bradford, M. Gerald. "The Study of Mormonism: A Growing Interest in Academia," *The FARMS Review* 19, no. 1 (2007): 119–174.

Bradford, Mary "The Odyssey of Sonia Johnson." *Dialogue* 14, no. 2 (Summer 1981): 14–47.

Bradley, Martha Sonntag. *Pedestals and Podiums: Utah Women, Religious Authority and Equal Rights*. Salt Lake City: Signature Books, 2005.

Bringhurst, Newell G. "The Image of Blacks within Mormonism as Presented in the *Church News* (1978-1988)." *American Periodicals* 2 (Fall 1992): 113–123.

——. "Fawn McKay Brodie: Dissident Historian and Quintessential Critic of Mormondom." In *Differing Visions: Dissenters in Mormon History*, ed. Roger D. Launius and Linda Thatcher. Urbana and Chicago: University of Illinois Press, 1994.

Bringhurst, Newell G., and Craig L. Foster. *The Mormon Quest for the Presidency*. Independence, Missouri: John Whitmer Books, 2008.

——. *The Mormon Quest for the Presidency: From Joseph Smith to Mitt Romney and Jon Huntsman*. Independence, Missouri: John Whitmer Books, 2011.

Bringhurst, Newell G., and Darron T. Smith, eds. *Black and Mormon*. Urbana and Chicago: University of Illinois Press, 2004.

Brinkerhoff, Merlin B., Jeffrey C. Jacob, and Marlene M. Mackie. "Mormonism and the Moral Majority Make Strange Bedfellows?: An Exploratory Critique." *Review of Religious Research* 28, no. 3 (March 1987): 236–251.

Brooke, John L. *The Refiner's Fire: The Making of Mormon Cosmology, 1644–1844*. Cambridge: Cambridge University Press, 1994.

Brooks, Joanna. *The Book of Mormon Girl: A Memoir of an American Faith*. New York: Free Press, 2012.

Bullock, Clifford A. "Fired by Conscience: The Black 14 Incident at the University of Wyoming and Black Protest in the Western Athletic Conference, 1968–-1970." *Wyoming History Journal* 68, no. 1 (Winter 1996): 4–13.

Bunker, Gary L., Harry Coffey, and Martha A. Johnson. "Mormons and Social Distance: A Multidimensional Analysis." *Ethnicity* 4 (1977): 352–369.

Bush, Lester E., Jr. "Mormonism's Negro Doctrine: An Historical Overview." *Dialogue* 8, no. 1 (Spring 1973): 11–68.

——. "Writing 'Mormonism's Negro Doctrine: An Historical Overview' (1973): Context and Reflections, 1998." *Journal of Mormon History* 25, no. 1 (Spring 1999): 229–271.

Bush, Lester E., Jr., and Armand Mauss, eds. *Neither White nor Black: Mormon Scholars Confront the Race Issue in a Universal Church*. Midvale, Utah: Signature Books, 1984.

Bushman, Claudia L. *Contemporary Mormonism: Latter-day Saints in Modern America*. Westport, Connecticut. Praeger Publishers, 2006.

Bushman, Richard L. "The Mysteries of Mormonism." *Journal of the Early Republic* 15, no. 3 (1995): 501–505.

——. *Believing History: Latter-day Saint Essays*. Edited by Reid L. Neilson and Jed Woodworth. New York: Columbia University Press, 2004.

——. *Joseph Smith: Rough Stone Rolling*. New York: Alfred A. Knopf, 2005. On the Road with Joseph Smith: *Joseph Smith: An Author's Diary*. Salt Lake City: Greg Kofford Books, 2007.

——. *Mormonism: A Very Short Introduction*. New York and Oxford: Oxford University Press, 2008.

Campbell, Joel J. "The Perfect Storm? LDS Media Events and the Foreign Press." A speech given at "Meet the Mormons: Public Perception and the Global Church," the 19th Annual Conference of the International Society, 7 April 2008. Copy in author's possession.

"Carter Says Mormons Are Christians," *Sunstone*, November 1997, 79.

Chafe, William H. *The Unfinished Journey: America Since World War II*. New York: Oxford University Press, 1999.

Chen, Chiung Hwang. *Mormon and Asian American Model Minority Discourses in News and Popular Magazines*. Lewiston, New York: The Edwin Mellen Press, 2004.

Chen, Chiung Hwang, and Ethan Yorgason."'Those Amazing Mormons': The Media's Construction of Latter-day Saints as a Model Minority." *Dialogue* 32, no. 2 (Summer 1999): 107–128.

Christensen, Bruce L. "A Light Unto the World: Public Relations Is Necessary and Legitimate for the Church." *Sunstone*, July-August 1982, 24–26.

Cowan, Richard O. "Mormonism in National Periodicals." Ph.D. dissertation, Stanford University, 1961.

——. *Temples to Dot the Earth*. Springville, Utah: Cedar Fort, Inc., 1997.

——. *The Latter-day Saint Century*. Salt Lake City: Bookcraft, 1999.

Cromartie, Michael. *Religion and Politics in America: A Conversation*. Lanham, Maryland: Rowman & Littlefield Publishers, Inc., 2005.

Cross, Whitney R. *The Burned-Over District: The Social and Intellectual History of Enthusiastic Religion in Western New York, 1800-1850*. Ithaca, New York: Cornell University Press, 1950.

Cullen-DuPont, Kathryn. *Encyclopedia of Women's History in America*, 2nd ed. New York: Facts on File, Inc., 2000.

Dart, John. "BYU—A Campus of Peace and Patriotism." In *Dream on, America: A History of Faith and Practice*, ed. Frederick Gentles and Melvin Steinfield. San Francisco: Canfield Press, 1971: 67–73.

Davies, Douglas J. *The Mormon Culture of Salvation: Force, Grace, Glory*. Burlington, Vermont: Ashgate, 2000.

Dean, Kenda Creasy. *Almost Christian: What the Faith of Our Teenagers Is Telling the American Church*. New York and Oxford: Oxford University Press, 2010.

Decker, Ed, and Dave Hunt. *The God Makers: A Shocking Exposé of What the Mormon Church Really Believes*, updated and expanded edition. Eugene, Oregon: Harvest House Publishers, 1997.

Decker, Mark T., and Michael Austin, eds. Peculiar Portrayals: Mormons on the Page, Stage, and Screen. Logan, Utah: Utah State University Press, 2010.

Deseret Morning News. *2008 Church Almanac: The Church of Jesus Christ of Latter-day Saints*. Salt Lake City: Deseret Morning News, 2008.

Deseret News. *1997–1998 Church Almanac*. Salt Lake City: Deseret News, 1996.

Dew, Sheri L. *Ezra Taft Benson: A Biography*. Salt Lake City: Deseret Book, 1987.

——.*Go Forward with Faith: The Biography of Gordon B. Hinckley*. Salt Lake City: Deseret Book, 1996.

Duffy, John-Charles. "Conservative Pluralists: The Cultural Politics of Mormon-Evangelical Dialogue in the United States at the Turn of the Twenty-first Century." Ph.D. dissertation, University of North Carolina at Chapel Hill, 2011.

Duke, James T., ed. *Latter-day Saint Social Life: Social Research on the LDS Church and its Members*. Provo, Utah: Religious Studies Center, Brigham Young University, 1998.

Eliason, Eric, ed. *Mormons and Mormonism: An Introduction to an American World Religion*. Urbana and Chicago: University of Illinois Press, 2001.

Embry, Jessie L. "Separate but Equal? Black Branches, Genesis Groups, or Integrated Wards." *Dialogue* 23, no. 1 (Spring 1990): 11–36.

Enstrom, James E. "Health Practices and Cancer Mortality among Active California Mormons." *Journal of the National Cancer Institute* 81 (1989): 1807–1814. Reprinted as chapter 15 in *Latter-day Saint Social Life: Social Research on the LDS Church and its Members*, ed. James T. Duke. Provo, Utah: Religious Studies Center, Brigham Young University, 1998, 441–460.

———. "Health Practices and Mortality among Active California Mormons, 1980–93." Chapter 16 in in *Latter-day Saint Social Life: Social Research on the LDS Church and its Members*, ed. James T. Duke. Provo, Utah: Religious Studies Center, Brigham Young University, 1998, 461–471.

Entman, Robert M., and Andrew Rojecki. *The Black Image in the White Mind: Media and Race in America*. Chicago: University of Chicago Press, 2000.

Epperson, Steven. *Mormon and Jews: Early Mormon Theologies of Israel*. Salt Lake City: Signature Books, 1992.

Evans, Richard Paul. *The Christmas Box Miracle*. New York: Simon & Schuster, 2001.

Eyre, Richard Melvin. "George Romney in 1968: From Front-Runner to Drop-Out: An Analysis of Cause." Master's thesis, Brigham Young University, 1969.

Farber, David. *The Age of Great Dreams: America in the 1960s*. New York: Hill and Wang, 1994.

Finke, Roger, and Rodney Stark. *The Churching of America, 1776–2005: Winners and Losers in Our Religious Economy*. New Brunswick, New Jersey: Rutgers University Press, 2006.

Flake, Kathleen. "The Mormon Corridor: Utah and Idaho." Chapter 4 in Jan Shipps and Mark Silk, eds., *Religion and Public Life in the Mountain West: Sacred Landscapes in Transition*. Walnut Creek, CA: AltaMira Press, 2004.

———. *The Politics of Religious Identity: The Seating of Senator Reed Smoot, Mormon Apostle*. Chapel Hill: University of North Carolina Press, 2004.

Fletcher, Peggy. "Going My Way: An Interview with *Newsweek*'s Kenneth Woodward." *Sunstone* 5, no. 5 (September-1980): 32–39.

———. "A Light Unto the World: Image Building Is Anathema to Christian Living." *Sunstone*, 7, no. 4 (July-August 1982): 16–23.

Fluhman, J. Spencer. *A Peculiar People: Anti-Mormonism and the Making of Religion in Nineteenth-Century America*. Chapel Hill: The University of North Carolina Press, 2012.

Flynt, Wayne. "Religion for the Blues: Evangelicalism, Poor Whites, and the Great Depression." *Journal of Southern History* 71, no. 1 (February 2005): 3–38.

Foege, Alec. *The Empire God Built: Inside Pat Robertson's Media Machine*. New York: John Wiley and Sons, Inc., 1996.

Foster, Craig L. *A Different God?: Mitt Romney, the Religious Right, and the Mormon Question*. Salt Lake City: Greg Kofford Books, 2008.

Foster, Lawrence. "A Personal Odyssey: My Encounter with Mormon History." *Dialogue* 16, no. 3 (Autumn 1983): 87–98.

Fredrickson, George M. *The Black Image in the White Mind: The Debate on Afro-American Character and Destiny, 1817–1914*. New York: Harper & Row Publishers, 1971.

Friedman, Thomas L. *The World Is Flat: A Brief History of the Twenty-First Century*. New York: Farrar, Strauss and Giroux, 2005.

Garr, Arnold K., Donald Q. Cannon, and Richard O. Cowan, eds. *Encyclopedia of Latter-day Saint History*. Salt Lake City, Utah: Deseret Book, 2000.

Gaustad, Edwin. "Historical Theology and Theological History: Mormon Possibilities." Chapter 21 in *The Mormon History Association's Tanner Lectures: The First Twenty Years*, ed. Dean L. May, Reid L. Neilson, Richard Lyman Bushman, Jan Shipps, and Thomas G. Alexander. Urbana and Chicago: University of Illinois Press, 2006.

Gaustad, Edwin Scott, and Philip L. Barlow. New Historical Atlas of Religion in America. New York and Oxford: Oxford University Press, 2000.

Gaustad, Edwin, and Leigh Schmidt. *The Religious History of America: The Heart of the American Story from Colonial Times to Today*, rev. ed. New York and San Francisco: HarperSanFrancisco, 2002.

Gitlin, Todd. *The Sixties: Years of Hope, Days of Rage*. Toronto: Bantam Books, 1987.

Givens, Terryl L. *By the Hand of Mormon: The American Scripture that Launched a New World Religion*. New York and Oxford: Oxford University Press, 2002.

——. *People of Paradox: A History of Mormon Culture*. New York and Oxford: Oxford University Press, 2007.

——. *The Latter-day Experience in America*. Westport, Connecticut: Greenwood Press, 2004.

——. " 'There Is Room for Both': Mormon Cinema and the Paradoxes of Mormon Culture." *BYU Studies* 46, no. 2 (2007): 189–208.

——. *The Viper on the Hearth: Mormons, Myths, and the Construction of Heresy*. New York and Oxford: Oxford University Press, 1997.

——. *The Viper on the Hearth: Mormons, Myths, and the Construction of Heresy*. Updated edition. New York and Oxford: Oxford University Press, 2013.

Glanz, Rudolf. *Jew and Mormon: Historic Group Relations and Religious Outlook*. New York: Waldon Press and Lucius N. Littauer Foundation, 1963.

Godfrey, Kenneth W. "Nauvoo Charter." In *Encyclopedia of Latter-day Saint History*, ed. Arnold K. Garr, Donald Q. Cannon, and Richard O. Cowan. Salt Lake City: Deseret Book, 2000.

Goldberg, Robert Alan. *Barry Goldwater*. New Haven and London: Yale University Press, 1995.

——. *Grassroots Resistance: Social Movements in Twentieth Century America*. Prospect Heights, Illinois: Waveland Press, 1996; originally published by Wadsworth Publishing Company, 1991.

——. *Enemies Within: The Culture of Conspiracy in Modern America*. New Haven and London: Yale University Press, 2001.

Goldstein, Eric L. *The Price of Whiteness: Jews, Race, and American Identity*. Princeton, New Jersey: Princeton University Press, 2006.

Gottlieb, Robert, and Peter Wiley. America's *America's Saints: The Rise of Mormon Power*. New York: Harcourt, Brace, Jovanovich Publishers, 1986.

Grainger, Brett. *In the World But Not of It: One Family's Militant Faith and the History of Fundamentalism in America*. New York: Walker and Company, 2008.

Gurgel, Klaus D. "The 1974 Washington Temple Survey: A Socio-spatial Analysis." Ph.D. dissertation, Syracuse University, 1975.

Gurr, Kevan L. "An Analysis of the Newspaper Coverage of Latter-day Saint Temples Announced or Built Within the United States from October 1997 through December 2004." Master's thesis, Brigham Young University, 2005.

Hadden, Jeffrey K., and Anson Shupe. *Televangelism: Power and Politics on God's Frontier*. New York: Henry Holt and Company, 1988.

Halsell, Grace. *Prophecy and Politics: The Secret Alliance Between Israel and the U.S. Christian Right*. Chicago: Lawrence Hill Books, 1986.

Handy, Robert T. "The American Religious Depression, 1925–1935." *Church History* 29, no. 1 (March 1960): 3–16.

Hangen, Tona J. *Redeeming the Dial: Radio, Religion, and Popular Culture in America*. Chapel Hill: The University of North Carolina Press, 2002.

Hansen, Klaus J. *Quest for Empire: The Political Kingdom of God and the Council of Fifty in Mormon History*. East Lansing, Michigan: Michigan State University, 1967.

——. *Mormonism and the American Experience*. With a Foreword by Martin E. Marty. Chicago and London: The University of Chicago Press, 1981.

Harding, Susan Friend. *The Book of Jerry Falwell: Fundamentalist Language and Politics*. Princeton, New Jersey: Princeton University Press, 2000.

Harrell, David Edwin, Jr. *Pat Robertson: A Personal, Religious, and Political Portrait*. San Francisco: Harper & Row, 1987.

Haws, J. B. "Mormonism and Other Faiths." In *Mormonism: A Historical Encyclopedia*, ed. W. Paul Reeve and Ardis E. Parshall. Santa Barbara, California: ABC-Clio, 2010, 312–319.

Heineman, John, and Anson Shupe. *The Mormon Corporate Empire*. Boston: Beacon Press, 1985.

Henderson, Juan. "A Time for Healing: Official Declaration 2." Chapter 11 in *Out of Obscurity: The LDS Church in the Twentieth Century: The 29th Sperry Symposium*. Salt Lake City: Deseret Book, 2000, 151–160.

Hewitt, Hugh. *A Mormon in the White House?: 10 Things Every American Should Know About Mitt* Washington, D.C.: Regnery Publishing, Inc., 2007.

Hinckley, Gordon B. *Standing for Something: 10 Neglected Virtues that will Heal Our Hearts and Homes*. With a foreword by Mike Wallace. New York: Times Books, 2000.

——. *Stand a Little Taller: Counsel and Inspiration for Each Day of the Year*. Salt Lake City: Eagle Gate, 2001.

Hoekema, Anthony A. *The Four Major Cults: Christian Science, Jehovah's Witnesses, Mormonism, Seventh-Day Adventism*. Grand Rapids, Michigan: William B. Eerdmans Publishing Company, 1963.

Hofstadter, Richard."The Paranoid Style in American Politics." In *The Paranoid Style in American Politics and Other Essays*. New York: Alfred A. Knopf, 1966, 3–40.

Howe, E. D. *Mormonism Unvailed: Or, a Faithful Account of that Singular Imposition and Delusion, from Its Rise to the Present Time*... Painesville, Ohio, 1834; photomechanical reproduction, Salt Lake City: Utah Lighthouse Ministry.

Hubbard, Jonice. "Pioneers in Twentieth Century Mormon Media: Oral Histories of Latter-day Saint Electronic and Public Relations Professionals." Master's thesis, Brigham Young University, 2007.

Hutchison-Jones, Cristine. "Center and Periphery: Mormons and American Culture in Tony Kushner's Angels in America." In Mark T. Decker and Michael Austin, eds. Peculiar Portrayals: Mormons on the Page, Stage, and Screen. Logan, Utah: Utah State University Press, 2010, 5–36.

——. "Reviling and Revering the Mormons: Defining American Values, 1890-2008." Ph.D. Dissertation, Boston University, 2011.

Inouye, Dillon K. "Truman Madsen, Valued Teacher." In *Revelation, Reason, and Faith: Essays in Honor of Truman G. Madsen*, ed. Donald W. Parry, Daniel C. Peterson, and Stephen D. Ricks. Provo, Utah: Foundation for Ancient Research and Mormon Studies, 2002, 33–53.

Introvigne, Massimo. "The Devil Makers: Contemporary Evangelical Fundamentalist Anti-Mormonism." *Dialogue* 27, no. 1 (Spring 1994): 153–169.

——. "Old Wine in New Bottles: The Story Behind Fundamentalist Anti-Mormonism." *BYU Studies* 35, no. 3 (1995–1996): 45–73.

Jackson, Kent P., ed. *Manuscript Found: The Complete Original "Spaulding Manuscript."* Provo, Utah: Religious Studies Center, Brigham Young University, 1996.

Jacobson, Matthew Frye. *Whiteness of a Different Color: European Immigrants and the Alchemy of Race*. Cambridge, Massachusetts: Harvard University Press, 1998.

James, Paul. *Cougar Tales*. Sandy, Utah: Randall Books, 1984.

Johnson, G. Wesley, and Marian Ashby Johnson. "On the Trail of the Twentieth Century Mormon Outmigration." *BYU Studies* 46, no. 1 (2007): 41–83.

Kimball, Edward L. ed. *The Teachings of Spencer W. Kimball*. Salt Lake City: Bookcraft, 1982.

——. *Lengthen Your Stride: The Presidency of Spencer W. Kimball*. Salt Lake City: Deseret Book, 2005.

——. *Lengthen Your Stride: The Presidency of Spencer W. Kimball*, working draft. Salt Lake City: Deseret Book and *BYU Studies*, 2005. The "working draft" edition of Kimball's biography includes notes and text that were omitted in the published version, but were included on a CD-ROM (a joint project of Deseret Book and *BYU Studies*).

——. "Spencer W. Kimball and the Revelation on the Priesthood." *BYU Studies* 47, no. 2 (2008): 4–78.

Kimball, Edward L., and Andrew E. Kimball, Jr. *Spencer W. Kimball: Twelfth President of The Church of Jesus Christ of Latter-day Saints*. Salt Lake City: Bookcraft, 1977.

Kearl, James R. "Jerusalem Center for Near Eastern Studies." In *Encyclopedia of Latter-day Saint History*, ed. Arnold K. Garr, Donald Q. Cannon, and Richard O. Cowan. Salt Lake City: Deseret Book, 2000, 570–571.

Kogan, Nathaniel Smith. "The Mormon Pavilion: Mainstreaming the Saints at the New York World's Fair, 1964–65." *Journal of Mormon History* 35, no. 4 (Fall 2009): 1–52.

Krakauer, Jon. *Under the Banner of Heaven: A Story of Violent Faith*. New York: Doubleday, 2003.

Kranish, Michael, and Scott Helman. *The Real Romney*. New York: HarperCollins, 2012.

Laake, Deborah. *Secret Ceremonies: A Mormon Woman's Intimate Diary of Marriage and Beyond*. New York: William Morrow and Company, Inc., 1993.

Lankford, John. "The Impact of the Religious Depression Upon Protestant Benevolence, 1925–1935." *Journal of Presbyterian History* 42, no. 2 (June 1964): 104–123.

Lawrence, Gary C. *How Americans View Mormonism: Seven Steps to Improve Our Image*. Orange, California: The Parameter Foundation, 2008.

———. *Mormons Believe . . . What?!* Orange, California: The Parameter Foundation, 2011.

Lee, Rex E. *A Lawyer Looks at the Equal Rights Amendment*. Provo, Utah: Brigham Young University Press, 1980.

Louis Harris and Associates, Inc. *The Harris Survey Yearbook of Public Opinion: 1970, 1971, 1972, 1973*. New York: Louis Harris and Associates, Inc., 1971–1974.

Lund, John Lewis. *The Church and the Negro: A Discussion of Mormons, Negroes and the Priesthood*. Salt Lake City: Paramount Publishers, 1967.

Lythgoe, Dennis Leo. "The Changing Image of Mormonism in Periodical Literature." Ph.D. dissertation, University of Utah, 1969.

———. "The 1968 Presidential Decline of George Romney: Mormonism or Politics?" *BYU Studies* 11, no. 3 (Spring 1971): 219–240.

MacKinnon, William P. " 'Lonely Bones': Leadership and Utah War Violence." *Journal of Mormon History* 33, no. 1 (Spring 2007): 121–178.

Mansbridge, Jane J. *Why We Lost the ERA*. Chicago and London: The University of Chicago Press, 1986.

Marsden, George M. *Understanding Fundamentalism and Evangelicalism*. Grand Rapids, Michigan: Eerdmans Publishing Co., 1991.

"Marketing the Mormon Image: An Interview with Wendell J. Ashton." *Dialogue* 10, no. 3 (Spring 1977): 15–21.

Marsh, W. Jeffrey. "Visitors' Centers." In *Encyclopedia of Latter-day Saint History*, ed. Arnold K. Garr, Donald Q. Cannon, and Richard O. Cowan. Salt Lake City: Deseret Book, 2000, 1300–1301.

———. "When the Press Meets the Prophet." Chapter 17 of *Out of Obscurity: The LDS Church in the Twentieth Century: The 29th Annual Sperry Symposium*. Salt Lake City: Deseret Book, 2000, 242–259.

Martin, Paul R. *Cult Proofing Your Kids*. Grand Rapids, Michigan: Zondervan, 1993.

Martin, Walter Ralston. *The Kingdom of the Cults: An Analysis of the Major Cult Systems in the Present Christian Era*. Grand Rapids, Michigan: Zondervan Publishing House, 1965.

———. *The Maze of Mormonism*, revised and enlarged edition. Santa Ana, Califronia: Vision House Publishers, 1978.

Marty, Martin E. *The Irony of It All: 1893-1919*. Vol. 1, *Modern American Religion*. Chicago and London: The University of Chicago Press, 1986.

———. "Two Integrities: An Address to the Crisis in Mormon Historiography." Chapter 20 in *The Mormon History Association's Tanner Lectures: The First Twenty Years*, ed. Dean L. May, Reid L. Neilson, Richard Lyman Bushman, Jan Shipps, and Thomas G. Alexander. Urbana and Chicago: University of Illinois Press, 2006, 354–372.

Mason, Patrick Q. *The Mormon Menace: Violence and Anti-Mormonism in the Postbellum South*. New York and Oxford: Oxford University Press, 2011.

Mauss, Armand L. "Mormonism and the Negro: Faith, Folklore, and Civil Rights." *Dialogue* 2, no. 4 (Winter 1967): 19–40.

May, Dean L. *Utah: A People's History*. Salt Lake City: University of Utah, 1987.

———. "Mormons." In *Mormons and Mormonism: An Introduction to an American World Religion*, ed. Eric Eliason. Urbana and Chicago: University of Illinois Press, 2001, 47–75.

May, Dean L., Reid L. Neilson, Richard Lyman Bushman, Jan Shipps, and Thomas G. Alexander, eds. *The Mormon History Association's Tanner Lectures: The First Twenty Years*. Urbana and Chicago: University of Illinois Press, 2006.

McConkie, Joseph Fielding. *The Bruce R. McConkie Story*. Salt Lake City: Deseret Book, 2003.

McKay, David Lawrence. *My Father, David O. McKay*, ed. by Lavina Fielding Anderson. Salt Lake City: Deseret Book, 1989.

McKay, Llewelyn R. *Home Memories of President David O. McKay*. Salt Lake City: Deseret Book, 1956.

McManners, John, ed. *The Oxford History of Christianity*. New York and Oxford: Oxford University Press, 1993.

Millet, Robert L. "Joseph Smith and Modern Mormonism: Orthodoxy, Neoorthodoxy, Tension, and Tradition." *BYU Studies* 29, no. 3 (1989): 49–68.

——. *A Different Jesus?: The Christ of the Latter-day Saints*. Grand Rapids, Michigan: Wm. B. Eerdmans, 2005.

Millet, Robert L., and Gerald R. McDermott. *Claiming Christ: A Mormon-Evangelical Debate*. Grand Rapids, Michigan: Brazos Press, 2007.

Mollenhoff, Clark R. *George Romney: Mormon in Politics*. New York: Meredith Press, 1968.

Morrell, Jeanette McKay. *Highlights in the Life of President David O. McKay*. Salt Lake City: Deseret Book, 1966.

Morrison, Matthew E. "The Church of Jesus Christ of Latter-day Saints in National Periodicals 1982-1990." Master's thesis, Brigham Young University, 2005.

Mosser, Carl, and Paul Owen. "Mormon Scholarship, Apologetics, and Evangelical Neglect: Losing the Battle and Not Knowing It?" *Trinity Journal* 19 (Fall 1998): 179–205.

Mouw, Richard J. *Talking with Mormons: An Invitation to Evangelicals*. Grand Rapids, Michigan: Wm. B. Eerdmans Publishing Co. 2012.

Moyer, Jonathan H. "Dancing with the Devil: The Making of the Mormon-Republican Pact." Ph.D. dissertation, University of Utah, 2009.

Naifeh, Steven, and Gregory White Smith. *The Mormon Murders: A True Story of Greed, Forgery, Deceit, and Death*. New York: Weidenfeld and Nicolson, 1988.

Neilson, Reid L. *Exhibiting Mormonism: The Latter-day Saints and the 1893 Chicago World's Fair*. New York and Oxford: Oxford Univeristy Press, 2011.

Nelson, William O. "Anti-Mormon Publications." In *Encyclopedia of Mormonism*, ed. Daniel H. Ludlow. New York: Macmillan, 1992, 45–52.

Neuhaus, Richard John, and Michael Cromartie, eds. *Piety and Politics: Evangelicals and Fundamentalists Confront the World*. Washington, D.C.: Ethics and Public Policy Center, 1987.

Newell, Lloyd. "Tabernacle Choir." In *Encyclopedia of Latter-day Saint History*, ed. Arnold K. Garr, Donald Q. Cannon, and Richard O. Cowan. Salt Lake City: Deseret Book, 2000, 1212–1213.

Nielson, Adam H. "Latter-day Saints in Popular National Periodicals, 1970-1981." Master's thesis, Brigham Young University, 2003.

"*Nobody Knows: The Untold Story of Black Mormons—Script*." *Dialogue* 42, no. 3 (Fall 2009): 100–128.

Novick, Peter. *That Noble Dream: The "Objectivity Question" and the American Historical Profession*. Cambridge and New York: Cambridge University Press, 1988.

Oaks, Dallin H., and Marvin S. Hill. *Carthage Conspiracy: The Trial of the Accused Assassins of Joseph Smith*. Urbana and Chicago: University of Illinois Press, 1975.

O'Dea, Thomas F. *The Mormons*. Chicago and London: The University of Chicago Press, 1957.

——. "Sources of Strain in Mormon History Reconsidered." In *Mormonism and American Culture*, ed. Marvin S. Hill and James B. Allen. New York: Harper and Row Publishers, 1972, 147–167.

Olmstead, Jacob W. "The Mormon Hierarchy and the MX." *Journal of Mormon History* 33, no. 3 (Fall 2007): 1–30.

Olson, Casey W. "The Church of Jesus Christ of Latter-day Saints in National Periodicals: 1991–2000." Master's thesis, Brigham Young University, 2007.

Ostling, Richard N., and Joan K. Ostling. *Mormon America: The Power and the Promise*. San Francisco: HarperSan Francisco, 1999. Revised edition, New York: HarperOne, 2007.

Out of Obscurity: Public Affairs and the Worldwide Church: The 8th Annual Conference of the International Society, 17–18 August 1997. Provo, Utah: Brigham Young University, 1998.

Parry, Donald, and Dana M. Pike, eds. *LDS Perspectives on the Dead Sea Scrolls*. Provo, Utah: Foundation for Ancient Research and Mormon Studies, 1997.

Patterson, Sara M. "'A P.O. Box and a Desire to Witness for Jesus': Identity and Mission in the Ex-Mormons for Jesus/Saints Alive in Jesus, 1975–1990." *Journal of Mormon History* 36, no. 3 (Summer 2010): 54–81.

Paulos, Michael Harold. "Review of Craig L. Foster, *A Different God?* and Newell G. Bringhurst and Craig L. Foster, *The Mormon Quest for the Presidency*." *Journal of Mormon History* 36, no. 1 (Winter 2010): 241–256.

Paulsen, David L. "A General Response to *The New Mormon Challenge*." *FARMS Review* 14, no. 1 (2002): 99–111.

Pelo, Dale. "Mormonism in National Periodicals, 1961–1970." Master's thesis Brigham Young University, 1973.

Peterson, Daniel C. "A Modern 'Malleus maleficarum.'" *Review of Books on the Book of Mormon* 3. Provo, Utah: FARMS, 1991, 231–260.

Peterson, F. Ross. "'Do Not Lecture the Brethren': Stewart L. Udall's Pro-Civil Rights Stance, 1967." *Journal of Mormon History* 25, no. 1 (Spring 1999): 272–287.

The Pew Forum on Religion and Public Life. "Mormonism and Democratic Politics: Are They Compatible?," 14 May 2007. Transcript accessible at http://pewforum.org/Politics-and-Elections/Mormonism-and-Politics-Are-They-Compatible.aspx.

The Pew Research Center. "Public Expresses Mixed Views of Islam, Mormonism," 25 September 2007. Accessible at http://pewforum.org/Public-Expresses-Mixed-Views-of-Islam-Mormonism.aspx.

Prince, Gregory A. "'Let the Truth Heal': The Making of Nobody Knows: *The Untold Story of Black Mormons*: An Interview with Darius Aidan Gray and Margaret Blair Young." *Dialogue* 42, no. 3 (Fall 2009): 74–99.

Prince, Gregory A., and Wm. Robert Wright, *David O. McKay and the Rise of Modern Mormonism*. Salt Lake City: The University of Utah Press, 2005.

Putnam, Robert D., and David E. Campbell, with the assistance of Shaylyn Romney Garrett. *American Grace: How Religion Divides and Unites Us*. New York: Simon & Schuster, 2010.

Quinn, D. Michael. *Early Mormonism and the Magic World View*, expanded 2nd ed. Salt Lake City: Signature Books, 1994.

———. *The Mormon Hierarchy: Extensions of Power*. Salt Lake City: Signature Books, 1997.

———. "On Being a Mormon Historian." Lecture given before the Student History Association, Brigham Young University, Fall, 1981. Accessed 2 February 2005 at http://www.xmission.com/~country/reason/mormonhist.htm. Copy in author's possession.

Reinshard, David W. *The Republican Right since 1945*. Lexington: University Press of Kentucky, 1983.

Reeve, W. Paul. "Reconstructing the West: James M. Ashley's Answer to the Mormon Question." Paper Delivered at the Western History Association Conference, Oklahoma City, Oklahoma, October 2007.

Riess, Jana, and Christopher Kimball Bigelow. *Mormonism for Dummies*. Hoboken, New Jersey: Wiley Publishing, Inc., 2005.

Robinson, Stephen E. *Are Mormons Christians?* Salt Lake City: Bookcraft, 1991.

Rosenblatt, Joseph. "Interfaith Relationships: Jewish." In *Encyclopedia of Mormonism*, ed. Daniel H. Ludlow. New York: Macmillan, 1992.

Rowe, David L. *I [Love] Mormons: A New Way to Share Christ with Latter-day Saints*. Baker Books, Grand Rapids, Michigan: Baker Books, 2005.

Rudd, Glen L. *Pure Religion*. Salt Lake City: The Church of Jesus Christ of Latter-day Saints, 1995.

Samuelsen, Eric. "Finding an Audience, Paying the Bills: Competing Business Models in Mormon Cinema." *BYU Studies* 46, no. 2 (2007): 209–230.

Scharffs, Gilbert W. *The Truth About "The God Makers*." Salt Lake City, Utah: Publishers Press, 1986.

Shelley, Bruce L. *Church History in Plain Language*, updated 2nd ed. Dallas, Texas: Word Publishing, 1995.

Shipps, Jan. *Mormonism: The Story of a New Religious Tradition*. Urbana and Chicago: University of Illinois Press, 1985.

———. *Sojourner in the Promised Land: Forty Years among the Mormons*. Urbana and Chicago: University of Illinois Press, 2000.

———. "Richard Lyman Bushman, the Story of Joseph Smith and Mormonism, and the New Mormon History." *The Journal of American History* 94, no. 2 (September 2007): 498–516.

Shipps, Jan, and Mark Silk, eds., *Religion and Public Life in the Mountain West: Sacred Landscapes in Transition*. Walnut Creek, California : AltaMira Press, 2004.

Shupe, Anson, and John Heinerman. "Mormonism and the New Christian Right: An Emerging Coalition?" *Review of Religious Research* 27, no. 2 (December 1985): 146–157.

Silk, Mark. *Unsecular Media: Making News of Religion in America*. Urbana and Chicago: University of Illinois Press, 1995.

Sillitoe, Linda, and Allen Roberts. *Salamander: The Story of the Mormon Forgery Murders*, 2nd ed. with a new afterword. Salt Lake City: Signature Books, 1989.

"Six Intellectuals Disciplined for Apostasy." *Sunstone*, November 1983, 65–75.

Smith, Christian, with Melinda Lundquist Denton. *Soul Searching: The Religious and Spiritual Lives of American Teenagers*. New York and Oxford: Oxford University Press, 2005.

Stark, Rodney. *The Rise of Mormonism*, ed. Reid L. Neilson. New York: Columbia University Press, 2005.

Stathis, Stephen W. "A Survey of Current Literature." *Dialogue* 12, no. 4 (Winter 1979): 113–117.

———. "Mormonism and the Periodical Press: A Change Is Underway." *Dialogue* 14, no. 2 (Summer 1981): 48–73.

Stathis, Stephen W., and Dennis L. Lythgoe. "Mormonism in the Nineteen-Seventies: The Popular Perception." *Dialogue* 10, no. 3 (Spring 1977): 95–113.

Stout, Daniel A., Joseph D. Straubhaar, and Gayle Newbold. "Through a Glass Darkly: Mormons as Perceived by Critics' Reviews of Tony Kushner's *Angels in America*." *Dialogue* 32, no. 2 (Summer 1999): 133–157.

Szasz, Ferenc Morton. *Religion in the Modern American West*. Tucson, Arizona: The University of Arizona Press, 2000.

Taggart, Stephen G. *Mormonism's Negro Policy: Social and Historical Origin*. Salt Lake City: University of Utah Press, 1970.

Tanaka, T. Tammy. "Why No Revolts at BYU?: The Silent Language of the Mormon World-view and Patriotism at Brigham Young University." Master's thesis, Brigham Young University, 1968.

Thatcher, Linda. "Selected Newspaper Articles on Mormons and Mormonism." *Dialogue* 12, no. 4 (1979): 116–117.

Thomas, John. "George Romney." In *Encyclopedia of Latter-day Saint History*, ed. Arnold K. Garr, Donald Q. Cannon, and Richard O. Cowan. Salt Lake City: Deseret Book, 2000, 1041–1042.

Thorne, Conrad H. "Research Study in Public Relations of the Mormon Church," 18 April 1966, unpublished manuscript. Church History Library and Archives, The Church of Jesus Christ of Latter-day Saints, Salt Lake City, Utah.

Top, Brent L. "The Miracle of the Mormon Pavilion: The Church at the 1964–65 New York World's Fair." In *New York. Regional Studies in the Latter-day Saint Church History*, eds. Larry C. Porter, Milton V. Backman Jr., and Susan Easton Black. Provo, Utah: Brigham Young University, 1992, 235–256.

———. "World's Fairs." In *Encyclopedia of Latter-day Saint History*, ed. Arnold K. Garr, Donald Q. Cannon, and Richard O. Cowan. Salt Lake City: Deseret Book, 2000, 1366–1367.

Turley, Richard E., Jr. *Victims: The LDS Church and the Mark Hofmann Case*. Urbana and Chicago: University of Illinois Press, 1992.

———. "The Mountain Meadows Massacre." *Ensign*, September 2007, 14–21.

Turley, Richard E., Jr., and Brian D. Reeves, "Unmasking Another Hofmann Forgery." *Journal of Mormon History* 37, no. 1 (Winter 2011): x–xiv.

Turner, Wallace. *The Mormon Establishment*. Boston: Houghton Mifflin Company, 1966.

Utter, Glenn H., and John W. Storey. *The Religious Right*, 2nd ed. Santa Barbara, California: ABC-CLIO, 2001.

Vogel, Dan, ed. Early Mormon Documents, Vol. 2. Salt Lake City: Signature Books, 1998.

Walker, Ronald W., Richard E. Turley Jr., and Glen M. Leonard. *Massacre at Mountain Meadows*. New York and London: Oxford University Press, 2008.

Walker, Ronald W., David J. Whittaker, and James B. Allen. *Mormon History*. Urbana and Chicago: University of Illinois Press, 2001.

Webb, Stephen H. *Jesus Christ, Eternal God: Heavenly Flesh and the Metaphysics of Matter*. New York and Oxford: Oxford University Press, 2012.

Wells, Elmer E. "Unjustifiable Denial of Priesthood to Black Mormons." *Negro History Bulletin* 40, no. 4 (July-August 1977): 725–727.

Woodger, Mary Jane. *David O. McKay: Beloved Prophet*. American Fork, Utah: Covenant, 2004.

Wilkinson, Ernest L., and W. Cleon Skousen. *Brigham Young University: A School of Destiny*. Provo, Utah: Brigham Young University Press, 1976.

William, Clyde J., ed. *The Teachings of Harold B. Lee*. Salt Lake City: Bookcraft, 1996.

Winder, Michael K. *Presidents and Prophets: The Story of America's Presidents and the LDS Church*. American Fork, Utah: Covenant Communications, 2007.

"The Worlds of Joseph Smith: A Bicentennial Conference at the Library of Congress." *BYU Studies* 44, no. 4 (2005): 1–325.

Wuthnow, Robert. "Political Rebirth of American Evangelicalism." In *The New Christian Right*, ed. Robert Wuthnow and Robert C. Liebman. Hawthorne, New York: Aldine Books, 1983, 168–169.

Index

Note: Italic entries refer to figures.